# Yellow Garden

## by J.J. Van Gasse

Proctor Publications

LCCN: 97–68870

Publisher's Cataloging-in-Publication
*(Prepared by Quality Books, Inc.)*

Van Gasse, J.J.
      Yellow garden / by J.J. Van Gasse. -- 1st ed.
      p.cm.
      ISBN: 1–882792–50–5

      1. Prisoners of war--Laos--Fiction. 2. Prisoners of war--Vietnam--
Fiction.      I. Title.

PS3572.A45Y45 1997                    813'.54
                                      QBI97–40940

Dedicated to Kathryn.
She knows why.

# Prologue

The building was long and narrow, a squat second story pressing down upon the lower level, the roof drooping wearily at both ends, the center slightly higher, and when seen dimly outlined against the night sky, the structure had an odd appearance. It resembled a dromedary, the one humped camel, a miniature Camelback hiding in the jungle instead of proudly flaunting its famous profile in the Arizona desert.

But in the dark, a darkness broken only by the faint light escaping through an open front door and two small dirt stained front windows, it was difficult to see much more than that. The light illuminated, barely, a narrow wooden porch with a lopsided overhang of rotting wooden shingles, no longer protecting the soft wooden planks below from the frequent rains. They were curling, rotting, decaying, sagging in the middle, and a single broken step led from the porch to a muddy path ending at the river's bank fifty feet away.

Down there, sluggishly making its way towards the Mekong river and the ocean beyond, providing passage for an endless stream of garbage, broken tree limbs, and the occasional bloated bodies of dead animals or unknown humans, the unnamed river struggled to carry its odoriferous cargo away – to somewhere else. The river had a name, of course. Everything does, at least on maps, but maps of this area were wildly inaccurate, so few knew what the name was, even fewer cared, and when someone said the "river," when someone said "they went up the river" or "it came by the river," everyone knew exactly what they were talking about. The river was simply the "river."

It was navigable from the Mekong to this place, to this landing, and possibly even beyond if one was willing to accept the risk. Not many made the trip. What was the point? To drink foul tasting native beer? Or Mekong whiskey? Or to eat almost raw, always greasy fish, chicken or pork, thrown onto a filthy plate, covered with sodden tasteless noodles or sticky rice? To sit amidst filth, rot, mildew, and swarms of ravenous biting insects, a thousand blue bottle flies waiting to pounce upon any food or exposed skin they might find, inside the building as well as outside as there were no screens to keep them at bay?

And yet this place, it was difficult to know what it should be called – a tavern, a bar, a den, dive or house of ill repute, take your pick, had customers. Some walked through the surrounding jungle, a few came from the nearby

1

villages, on muddy trails, through brush that clawed and tore at the skin, and occasional passengers stepped off a boat onto the rickety dock, all of them to spend a few minutes, an hour, seldom much more, on the few pleasures to be had – food, provisions, fuel, drink, and it was rumored, drugs and women. Food, drugs, and women can be found almost everywhere. Prices and quality, not always in direct relationship, vary widely. Fuel and provisions are somewhat different. They were unobtainable, except here, for miles in any direction. Naturally, they were expensive – sold for cash or for items that could be readily converted to cash.

Impassively, the river, not caring what man did in this decaying hulk of a building, maundered along, following its twisting, tortured course through the tangled jungle more than fifty miles to finally disgorge its putrid debris into the Mekong, one day at a time, through centuries.

Strangely enough, even by day, the building seemed to cloak itself in darkness, hiding under enormous trees, shrouded by thick underbrush that had grown up on both sides and in back, leaving only the front open to a few hours of sunlight that played upon the river's edge at midday. Someone, several years earlier, had managed to splash on an ochre color, painted part of the front wall, tired quickly, had gone back inside out of the heat, and the fading yellow brown remnant of this mark of civilization had all but disappeared into the gloom of its surroundings.

The river, too, for almost all of its entire course, was in shadows, as dark as night along most of its route, giant trees blocking out sunlight even at midday. And now it was dark, thick clouds hanging low in the sky, almost touching the treetops, still heavy with moisture after dumping inches of rain over the northern half of Thailand, the storm now ponderously working its way across Laos on its way to Vietnam and the south China sea.

It had rained earlier, but it had stopped, although water still dripped noisily, rhythmically, from the trees, from the soggy brush, from the edges of the rotting roof, through the shingles onto the porch below. The wind had been surging with 40 mile per hour gusts, but it had eased, although thick boughs still waved crazily back and forth as if an unseen force was in control of the mindless forest. Out on the river, the surface of the water was still choppy but no longer throwing forth the white froth as it sometimes did when the real storms roared down from the Laotian highlands, like the one that had come through an hour earlier.

It was a night when few would be about. Or so it seemed. Yet, suddenly, there was a pounding from the side of the building, a harsh cry, what sounded like a curse, a jostling as if someone had been forcibly thrown against a hard surface, and then with a brightness seldom seen along the river bank, an unexpected light came on from an overhead fixture hanging above a door that few even realized was there. In that instant, as if frozen on stage as the curtain was raised for the first act of tonight's play, four men were clearly visible in front of that closed door. The door flew or was kicked open, bounced, and almost closed again, but then two of the men, acting as if on cue, pushed, perhaps even picked up and tried to carry a struggling figure inside. There were cries of anger, or pain, or a plea for help, it was hard to determine what it was, and the struggling intensified. As they dragged or carried their burden across the threshold, a fourth man, much taller, suddenly leaped forward and struck once, twice, three times, and the struggling and shouting ceased. This fourth man issued an order, there was an answer from inside, everyone disappeared from view, and the door was slammed once again. The light was extinguished. A moment later, the front door snapped shut and the dim yellow light from inside faded even more and blackness seemed to close around the building as if it had become a darkened cave. One small light suddenly appeared on the second story, just to the left of the camel's hump.

But even the darkest night has eyes. In that brief instant, when the light first flashed on and the door was opened, a fisherman who had waited for the wind and rain to abate and was now out on the river in his silent paddle craft, had seen the struggling figures. A mother carrying a month old baby, on her way to retrieve laundry forgotten along the river bank earlier in the day, saw the commotion and heard the curses. A boy of eleven, squatting uncomfortably in the wet bushes to relieve himself, had an excellent view of both the side and front doors. Two others were even closer, not more than 20 feet from the side door itself. Although the ground was wet and clammy, they had again chosen the same grassy knoll, surrounded by tangled underbrush protecting it from casual passersby, that had served them so well two nights earlier. The girl, lying on her back, had been shocked by the sudden light, certain that her father had discovered their secret place, and for a moment feared for her life. The boy, too, right at the moment he was expecting to feel something far more satisfying, was momentarily dazed instead by the brilliance and the noise, but both, to their credit, had remained absolutely quiet, and most surprising of all, motionless, during the disturbance. They had the best view of all, especially the girl who was looking directly at the light; she clearly saw all four men. She was surprised that it took three of them to drag the fourth, who appeared to be thin, frail, and older than the others, and that one of the men, the taller one, was actually striking him, possibly beating him into insensibility. She knew that she had never seen any of the men before and was certain of one thing, and for days afterward she wondered about it. The tall man, the one who was hitting the older one, was white. A Westerner.

Her lover agreed.

They decided to speak to no one about what they had seen. The fisherman, the mother, and the boy in the bushes, none of whom knew about the others, made the same decision. The dark building squatting in the steamy jungle alongside the fetid river, and the people in it, were best left alone.

# 1

I took the call from Marge just before I left the Willard. "It sounded important," she told me. "He said he had to talk to you right away."

"Who was 'he'?" I wanted to know

"Mr. Towel. I had him spell it." And she spelled it for me. "He said you knew him, or had met him, or something like that, and when I said you were in Washington, he said he knew that, that he hadn't been able to reach you and if you called I was to be sure to tell you. To see him right away, like I said. He made it sound important."

"Did he give you a clue about what the problem was? I was just walking out the door when the phone rang and I have a plane to catch. I really don't have time."

"I know, Doctor, but this Mr. Towel said it was important. He used the word urgent, as a matter of fact, several times to impress me how important this really was. He insisted that I talk to you, tell you to see him before you left town. Right away, is how he put it."

Marge has been with me for twelve or thirteen years, possibly fourteen. Who counts? She still calls me Doctor, and that's all right as I am one, but several years ago, about the time she joined the office, I stopped seeing patients and became an administrator, some said a businessman, but since when weren't physicians businessmen anyway? Now I was a consultant and a corporate officer, spending my time looking for, and helping others look for, new drugs. New drugs could be found anywhere: synthesized in the laboratory, extracted from a mold, fungus, plant, bacteria or rock, just as likely to be found in the backyard or basement as in the hitherto unexplored nooks and crannies of the world. Of course, it was a lot more fun and adventure looking in those remote, out of the way places, even if it was more expensive.

Right now, because of an intense personal commitment, I had an interest in finding weapons to use against cancers, ovarian and breast cancers in particular. It was more than an interest. It had become something of an obsession.

We had fired up our computer models, turned batteries of horn rimmed Ph.D.'s loose upon the project, formed alliances with other firms and academic centers working on the same project, and if hard work and dollars were a guarantee of success, we should have been close to our goal. We weren't. Not yet. What we needed was luck, and strangely enough, maybe we had suddenly gotten some. That's why getting up to New York was so important, and continuing on to Malaysia was even more important. Anything a Mr. Towel might have to say was of secondary interest. Or was it? Who was Mr. Towel and what did he know that was so important to him, even if I doubted that it could have the same significance to me? Unless, if, as Marge had indicated, he really did know me, or if I knew him. In that case, I suspected who he might be, or at least who he might represent, and I was thinking about what to do when Marge clinched it for me.

"He said to tell you, if you were wondering what this was all about, that it was something you owe Mr. Green. I think he said Mr. Green, although I've been thinking about it since and he may have called him something else. Some other title. But it was something or other Green. I'm sure of that."

"Oh, I see," I told her, pausing while I digested the news. "OK, give me the phone number so I can call him."

"He doesn't want you to call. He wants to see you, as soon as possible. He gave me his address and said he'd wait there until you arrived."

I knew now that the name didn't really matter because I knew who would be there. Let me qualify that. I didn't know *who* would be there but I could guess what he would represent. That wasn't important. The name Green was and I made my decision. "OK, Marge, give me the address. Then call New York and reschedule everything for tomorrow. Make it lunch time. That should work out. Any other messages?"

There weren't and when she read the address to me, I recognized it at once. In Georgetown. I'd been there before.

The cabbie didn't seem to know his way around town, but at least he spoke English, grunting in response when I told him "turn left" and then "at the next corner, make a right." He handled both turns smoothly, although the second was a trifle wide and we grazed a fire hydrant, but he straightened out and seemed to have things under control once again when I realized we had just passed the building we were looking for. The nondescript brownstone looked much as it had six or seven years earlier, two enormous blocks quarried in New Hampshire anchoring each front corner, called upon to distinguish it from its undistinguished neighbors. Someone had chiseled a three foot high 'X' into the right cornerstone while the one on the left, although stained by decades of water overflowing from a rusted eaves trough was unblemished by the workings of an eccentric stone mason.

"We just passed it," I shouted. "Back there, with the 'X' in the stone."

The brakes worked and the driver's prompt reaction almost vaulted me from the rear to the front seat as he stopped with squealing tires and the smell of burning rubber, then reversed, all in one continuous motion. Fortunately, an elongated black Mercedes with diplomatic plates was able to swerve and continue without making contact, although I heard its horn blaring as it disappeared down the street.

"Here?" the driver asked, peering doubtfully at the building but brightening when he noticed the stone with its distinctive marking. The first two times I'd been here I asked about the 'X.' From the alphabet or a Roman numeral, I wondered? I found that no one knew and no one cared, and I hadn't asked since. So much for the history of our nation's capital.

The meter read a reasonable $3.65; I paid with a ten spot which the driver pocketed without offering to make change, and asked, "want me ta wait?" Apparently the tip had been adequate.

"No, I'll find a way back."

"Hey, it better be in a cab. You don' wanna be walkin' in this town. Not at night. Sure ya don't want me ta wait?"

I thought about it, decided I didn't know if I could afford the waiting time, and assured him I would be fine. I closed the door, started up the walk, and the cab pulled away, almost sideswiping another in the process, this time both horns blaring noisily as they disappeared into the early December darkness.

The sign was made of polished stainless steel mounted on two solid black poles set in concrete just to the left of the staircase. "PAN UNION TRADE ASSOCIATION" it declared. I was quite certain that the last time I had come calling it had proclaimed "PAN UNION ARTS FOUNDATION" and had been mounted on white poles. Many of the letters appeared to have been recycled.

The building was typical of the others nearby, half the lower level below ground, the main entrance reached by climbing nine steps of crumbling concrete up to the small flat porch without railings, a faded plastic mudcatcher almost worn through in the center, and a small silver button in the center of a well worn black ring. I kicked a baseball sized piece of loose concrete aside, pushed the button and listened to the sudden whirring of the hidden television monitor strategically mounted high above as it moved into position, looking for me, finally focusing directly on my face, and settled in to watch. I smiled for the person on the other side. Might as well look happy if they were going to all of this trouble. Nothing happened for thirty seconds or so and by then it was too much of an effort to keep smiling so I reverted to my usual grim face and just stood there. When the door clicked, I pushed on it and went inside.

Same hallway, same carpeting, even the same musty smell, the nose tickling kind that warns of an impending sneeze. And behind the same wooden desk of chipped white oak was the same white haired little Miss Corby, or Canby, I'd forgotten the name again, but not the insipid face. She simply stared at me, saying nothing, so I stared back and handed her my card, a legitimate one, which read 'Osten-Burrows Inc., Pharmaceutical Consultants.' Down in the right hand corner, it had my name, A. Mikhail Osten, M.D., Ph.D., President.

The name? That's what they gave me, my parents. I never held it against them. Other than that, they were good parents. The A. was for Alfons and in my town where I grew up, there were five or six other kids in school with the same name, and they were all called Fons. So I was happy when people started calling me Mike and in college it seemed fashionable to be A.M., but then word got out what the A. stood for and I became Al. That was all right for a while but then, naturally, someone changed it to Big Al, which was a misnomer because I wasn't big at all, and tiring of that, I managed to get it back to Mike, or just Osten, and quit worrying about it. It was never a problem for patients of course, after I got out of school. They called me Doctor, and like I said, so did Marge and just about everyone in the office. Burrows usually used Mike and I called him Everett, and we all got along just fine that way. The point being whatever name I used was my own, unlike some of the people I was likely to meet here in Building X, as we had taken to calling this PAN UNION outpost. They didn't always do that.

Burrows, by the way, was still around, which surprised many who had assumed he had retired to play golf. He did that, a lot, but was still instrumental in putting our budgets together, keeping a wary eye on finance, kept the banks and brokers happy, and ran the office in my absence. He was invaluable to the company and almost as important to the many charitable groups who counted upon him to participate in the summer-long celebrity golf outings where sometimes we were a sponsor and, incredibly, sometimes the program listed him as a celebrity. His card, identical to mine except for the lower right hand corner that read 'Chairman.'

I had decided her name was Canby and she was still looking at my card as if uncertain what to do with it. The television monitor to her immediate left showed an elderly man wandering past on the sidewalk, the camera aimlessly panning around without a specific target. She was ignoring it and that explained the thirty seconds. Finally, she looked up and asked, "Mr. Osten?"

I reached across the desk and took the card from her, peered at it, asking, "Did I give you the wrong card? No, it's the right one. See, right here, this is my name on it. But notice, right there, it's not Mr. Osten, but Doctor Osten. See that?" I didn't want to be hard on her, but we had met before.

When I handed the card back she looked at it carefully to confirm what I had just told her. "Possibly you may have heard that I was coming," I continued. "At least, your Mr. Towel knows as he's the one who called and asked me to come. He should be expecting me." I spelled the name for her, which was the ritual in Building X, only I spelled it T-O-W-E-L, which if things hadn't changed, was the way it should be.

"Yes, of course, but you spelled it incorrectly," she told me. "It should be T-O-W-L-E."

It was refreshing to know that some things never changed; that the codes and games were as silly and useless as ever, but we still had to play by the rules. In this building that meant by Pan Union rules.

Having completed this bit of business for the moment, either not trusting an intercom or simply not having one, she pushed her chair back, stood up, and said, "If you'll wait here for a moment, I'll see if Mr. Bath is free."

Bath! Bath towel! Good God. I could have been halfway to New York by now.

She left me standing in the hallway and disappeared. That gave me time to observe that the same paintings I had seen on my previous visits were still hanging in their accustomed places. Early 1960's discount store art. Dreary, cheap prints of unattractive gardens, landscapes of uncertain origin, seascapes dark and foreboding. Who had picked this junk out and why? To hide cracks in the wall or to cover hidden cameras, secret microphones, embarrassing graffiti? But a flash of color further down the hallway caught my eye and when I wandered down to see what it was, I was rewarded by the fascinating sight of an Apache shaman plying his trade, dancing and singing over a fallen warrior lying on a bed of hides, smoke from his small sacred fire drifting lazily towards the rim of the canyon, anxious women standing by ready to help, fearful of losing a son, brother, husband. Down in the corner was the artist's name. Howard Terpning. A renowned world class painter of western scenes. Someone, and I wondered who, had added a touch of class to the old house after all.

Canby came back from wherever she had been and with her came the mixture of floral fragrance and dust that so often made me sneeze, which I proceeded to do. Twice. She stepped back quickly as if afraid of being contaminated and I didn't blame her.

I apologized and she said, "Bless you," as if she didn't mean it. That out of the way, she added, "He's in the second room on the left, around the corner, and he said to come right on down."

"Fine. Thank you," I told her and started in that direction.

I was three or four steps down the hallway when she called out, "Mr. Osten, you forgot your card." When I turned she was holding it up, waving it back and forth as if beckoning me to return.

"That's all right. I have others," I assured her and waved back. When I reached the corner, she was still holding the card in front of her, looking at it, apparently still not certain what to do with it.

The second door on the left was closed, so I tapped on it. No response, so I tapped again and then knocked, forcefully enough to rattle the wooden panels and shake the glass transom overhead. This time a voice called, "come," so I went, opening the door and looking inside.

The man behind the desk lived up to his name, if it was Mr. Bath. He was clean, cleanly shaven, and immaculately dressed in a dark blue suit, dazzlingly white cotton shirt, red and gray striped tie, wire rimmed reading glasses perched on his nose. The only jarring note was his hair; black, too black, dyed black, slicked straight back with something greasy and then sprayed on so that it wouldn't move, not even in gale force winds. That and his face. No expression. None.

The only thing on his highly polished rosewood desk were his firmly clasped hands, fingers entwined with one another, extending from below his French cuffs, a substantial gold ring grasping a massive ruby on the pinkie of his right hand, nothing at all on the left. The fingernails were polished and trimmed to perfection and I could see no wrist watch, but if there was one up there under the white cuffs, it would be an expensive one. The slight bulge just below the left lapel of the well fitted jacket suggested that he was wearing a gun. Aside from that discordant note, he looked like a mannequin in the men's department of your favorite clothier. I disliked him at once.

I disliked him even more when he became the gracious host. "Osten, so good of you to drop by like this. On short notice." Unclasping his hands for a moment, he motioned limply towards the three chairs arranged around his desk, one on each side with the third arranged precisely in front, facing him. It was clear he expected me to sit there, across the desk, so I moved to one side, pulled back the chair on the left, and sat down. He frowned, but to his credit, he hid disappointment well. "Ah, yes, are you comfortable there? Sure the light from the window isn't in your eyes?" I didn't point out that the blinds had been drawn and that the sun had already set.

I indicated that I was fine, comfortable, yes, just fine right where I was, and folded my hands.

He hesitated, then deciding that if I wasn't planning on moving, he might as well get on with the agenda, went back to the basics. "Ah, Osten, we'll be joined by some people you know, but before they get here, would you be so kind as to give me your mother's maiden name, you know, her name before she was married? And the year and month of her birth? Just for the record, that sort of thing."

Like I said. Just the basics, and all the while I was revealing my mother's secrets, even she didn't tell anyone her age, I knew there was someone on the other side of a monitor comparing my photo image to a master file, comparing voice prints to earlier recordings, and by now even looking at the fingerprints from the card Canby had been holding gingerly when last seen. Like I said, Pan Union rules.

But I played along, wanting to see where all of this would lead. "Percette. March 23." I left off the year. Some things just shouldn't be revealed to strangers. It didn't seem to matter.

"Ah, yes. French, isn't it? I love French names."

Regretfully, I told him, "No, not French. Swiss. My mother is Swiss. But the name does roll off the tongue smoothly doesn't it?" So did JoElle's, and she *was* French. It had been much too long since I'd seen her.

He peered at me over his glasses and I had the feeling that he couldn't speak French, didn't understand French, and was puzzled because the sheet of paper he was glancing at inside his open top desk drawer read Antoinette Percette, born in Lisle, France, March 23, 1905. All correct, but what it didn't tell him was that mother was Swiss, had been born in France only because that was where grandmother had gone into labor while on a visit to her aged grandmother. The baby had spent eight days in France before returning to Neuchatel, where she grew up and started to travel. She was still living and still traveling, now residing in Brussels, tending to her colorful flower garden in the summer while others tended to her productive vineyards back home. She spent the winter gossiping and playing cards with widowed friends high in the mountains of her native land, the broad windows of her chalet filled with a panorama of the snowy Alps, her cellars stocked with each year's harvest of fine whites and reds, her bank account swelling from worldwide sales of the choice vintages. "The most beautiful sight in the world," she assured me, alluding to the view. "Come visit me. Even better, come live with me." Visits were made and enjoyed. Wine was tasted and appreciated. It was tempting to consider making it home. But not yet.

Apparently convinced, despite the gaffe about mother's birthplace, that I was who I said I was, Bath was saying, "I hope you haven't been inconvenienced by my request for this sudden meeting, but when we found that you were in Washington and headed for a trip to the Far East, I knew we had to meet before you left. The timing couldn't have been better."

I was curious. "How did you learn that I was in Washington?"

Smugly, as if he had successfully completed a major espionage coup, he replied, "From your office. Your associate Mr. Burrows was most cooperative when I called him this morning. When he learned that we could be of help to you during your trip to the Far East, he was most eager to have me get in touch with you."

That was nice. Not Burrows helping find me. Not that. I could have done without that. But hearing that 'they,' whoever 'they' were, were going to help me; that was nice. As for Burrows, well, he was always putting people in touch with me, figuring that sooner or later someone would arrange to do something nice for the business. Maybe this was the time. But I was sure that he had been scheduled for an early morning tee time despite the threat of snow. Had he taken the cellular with him again?

Bath had unclasped his hands as he was talking and while the right remained in sight on the desktop, the left slowly dropped out of sight. He was pushing a button and didn't want to be obvious about it.

He leaned forward as his left hand found its way back to its mate and asked, "You don't mind if a couple of old friends join us, do you Osten? Men you've worked with in the past. Acquaintances from the old days." I knew he didn't expect, or want, an answer.

As if on cue, but more likely it was a response to the button, the door opened and my old acquaintances were standing there, coming inside as Bath beckoned. I knew them. Bath was right about that, but it was something I would never have bragged about. There was Fred Magellan, he'd picked up the name "the Explorer" long before I met him and still had it, but ever since high school, instead of seeking a new world, he had spent his time seeking to avoid blame when anything went wrong. And if Fred was involved in an operation, any operation, no matter how simple, things always went wrong. When I'd last heard of him, what had it been, two or three years ago?, he had been assigned to some remote outpost. Where was it? Ulan Bator in Outer Mongolia? Or some place in Siberia? Neither, it turned out. He had just been recalled from Uzbekistan instead. Not that there's much difference.

The man with him, Alex Fantus, had a nickname, too. The Phantom. It was appropriate as whenever the going got tough, Alex didn't get tougher. He simply disappeared.

As Bath had said, I had worked with both of them in the past – one at a time, never both of them together. I didn't relish the thought of even being in the same room with them and knew that working with either one was something to be avoided at all costs, if possible.

We didn't shake hands, only nodded coolly to one another and I watched in amusement as they tried to find a place to sit. Fantus looked around, immediately went to the right side of the desk, pulled out a chair identical to mine and sat down. That forced Magellan to sit in the chair directly opposite Bath, and he squirmed uncomfortably in his seat as if this wasn't the way it had been diagrammed in pregame planning. We made a cozy little group clustered around the gleaming desk, all dressed up and posed, waiting for the photographer to arrive for the picture session. Then, a little late, I realized no one would have to come in to take the picture as three small cameras mounted high in the walls, just below the ceiling, were already moving back and forth, busily snapping away, making a record for the archives. Maybe. Sometimes, when the budget was tight, it was rumored that film was omitted.

No one spoke for a moment as we all settled back in our chairs, Fantus and Magellan shuffling their feet to get comfortable. Bath clasped and unclasped his hands several times and I thought it might have been a signal to his two associates, but finally decided he was only trying to get a look at his wristwatch, as if he too had somewhere he wanted to go.

I took the occasion to break the ice by pushing back my chair, starting to rise, and saying, "Well, it was certainly nice of you to invite me in like this and I wouldn't mind staying but I really have to get up to New York on business, so if we have nothing further to discuss, I'll be on my way."

Magellan and Fantus almost came out of their chairs, while Bath seemed to slide lower in his. All three started to talk at once, with the Phantom and the Explorer both glared accusingly at Bath, wondering if the two of us had concluded whatever business we had come for before they had even entered the room. Bath recognized the danger, held up both hands placatingly, and hurriedly told them, "Osten and I haven't talked about anything yet. Nothing at all. Like I told him, or like I was about to tell him, the two of you want to talk to him. Not me. I'll just listen, for now."

Fantus looked at me, and when I sat down, he said, "OK" and did the same. Magellan remained on his feet a moment longer and then sat on the edge of his chair as if he would just as soon be elsewhere. I ignored the Explorer. He wasn't in charge here. It had to be Bath or Fantus, and if Bath was going to remain silent, I was going to have to get my information from Alex.

I looked at him and asked, "What is this all about? Why was it so important to see me this afternoon?"

Fantus had aged since we'd last seen one another. So had I, I suppose, but when he had first walked into the room I had been surprised by the lines in his face, the bags under both eyes, the gray in the hair. The pot belly. Then I thought back to what I had seen in the mirror that morning while shaving and realized he could be sitting over there saying the same thing about me. Except for the pot belly. Not yet. I had wondered at first if it really was Alex.

"Mike," he began.

Had he ever called me Mike before? Maybe. Maybe long ago, because we went back a long way, the two of us. A long way back, all the way to a cool day in Korea, a steaming morning in the Congo, and a blazing hot day in Vietnam, as well as sitting together in a number of air conditioned offices listening to speakers and planners talking at great length about not so great problems, and the plans, which seldom were needed, to solve them. All of this over a span of twenty five, twenty six years, and nothing now for almost a decade, only to meet here. And now he called me Mike. Hadn't it always been Osten before, if he had used a name at all? I think so.

Sure, this was the Phantom, despite the obvious changes, because there are some faces you don't forget, some men you never forget. And I hadn't. Why? That's easy. On two occasions that I had seen him in action, and on several others that I had heard of and had no reason to doubt, he had left men behind to die when he could have helped save them. Survivors had vowed to kill him, but obviously it hadn't happened and here he was. Oh, yes, this was Alex Fantus. You don't forget what a man looks like when you recall the one occasion when you agreed with the survivors; when you found yourself thinking that they were right, he needed killing. Or worse.

My mind had been wandering and I realized that he was still talking. "Do you remember a Vietnamese student by the name of Lee Duc Than?" he was asking. When I didn't respond immediately, he added, "at the University. Was in a class you taught, stayed in it for two years, and then went back to Saigon."

At the University? That would have been almost twenty years ago, back before we had even started Osten-Burrows, back when I was teaching, practicing medicine, and was still married. I'd taught epidemiology, which I likened to medical detective work, and had foreign students around all of the time. Vietnam, the southern half at any rate, was friendly, so sure, I had Vietnamese students in the room. I could see the faces, some of them, all looking so much alike with dusky skin, jet black hair, brown eyes, scuffed shoes, and casual dress. But names? I couldn't recall a single one.

So I told him, "Lee Duc Than? I don't remember. Maybe he was in a class. Maybe he wasn't."

Fantus interrupted impatiently, "You don't understand. Lee Duc Than *was* in your class. We've already confirmed that with the school. What I was asking was whether you remembered him, what he looked like, who he was. Could you, in other words, identify him?" He fumbled around for a moment in a plain unmarked manila folder, pulled out a glossy 3 x 5 inch photograph, and slid it across the desk. "Does this help? It was taken when he was enrolled at the school."

I looked at the face staring back from the black print. A man, about 25 years old, thin features with deep set eyes, hair combed straight back, and not a single distinguishing mark about him that I could see. Aside from a small blemish just lateral to the left eyebrow. Another small imperfection on his left earlobe or was it my imagination? Perhaps someone had retouched the negative, changed it slightly, and what I was seeing was really nothing at all. I shouldn't say that. I *was* looking at the picture of what appeared to be a male Vietnamese, but then we already knew that, didn't we?

I shook my head. No, I did not remember any such student. He may have been there, but I couldn't swear to it.

Fantus had another picture, much larger, a group shot of thirty or forty men and women, three rows of a dozen or so each, shorter men and women in front, medium sized in the middle, tall ones, mostly men, in the back. And cars around the edge, just visible, indicating that it had been taken in a parking lot. I recognized it, remembered when it had been, and saw myself in the center of the middle row, smiling, looking happy and contented, her blonde head resting lightly against my upper arm, and although I couldn't see it, her hand tightly clasping mine down at our side. Abby. For a moment I didn't see anyone else, didn't care about anyone else, but then I realized I was looking at a picture taken at a party I had given for my final class, just before graduation, when I recklessly invited all of my students to "join us for dinner Friday, about six or so, at the house."

It wasn't the smartest thing to do, as Abby and I had a very small house, and she pointed that out to me when I came home and told her of the invitation. "Don't worry," I assured her, "not many will come. They'll be too busy getting ready to leave town after the ceremonies tomorrow and we'll be lucky if a half dozen show up."

We laid in the beverages, a little of this and a little of that, and Abby put together a medium sized bowl of greens. I purchased an extra bottle of blue cheese dressing and the ribeye steaks, a dozen of them properly marbled, we borrowed an extra set of stainless steel silverware and dishes, just in case, figured where to seat the ten guests, which I estimated to be the number nodding affirmatively when I issued the invitation, and cleaned the house. By 6:15, there were thirty people crowded inside the small living room, another dozen milling in the kitchen where ice cubes had became a scarce item and there wasn't a glass to be found, and cars were still pulling up outside. Abby looked up despairingly from the empty salad bowl, held up an empty container of onion dip, and I realized I had made a mistake.

Andy Whitaker bailed me out. A good friend, Andy owned the Iroquois, a moderately priced restaurant a mile away, one with a reputation for good steaks, cold beer, and congenial atmosphere.

"How many people you got in your house?" he wanted to know and was incredulous when I told him. "By God, I bet Abby isn't happy with that."

I didn't bother to answer. I just pleaded for help. And found it.

"Bring everyone over. I can put you in the banquet room. That is, if you don't mind being in there with red and yellow balloons, baby booties and other things we put up for a baby shower tomorrow. You promised steaks. I'll give them steaks. You wanted salad, we'll fix them salad. And beer. We've got plenty."

And he delivered. Everyone had a fine time, thought it was great of us to have first invited them to the house just to say hello and then adjourn to a restaurant for the real food, even though that wasn't what I had planned.

And this photo brought it all back. A picture taken that night by someone who had brought a camera and gotten us to stand in one place for a moment to record it all for posterity. Interestingly, Fantus had gotten his hands on it, and was pointing now, indicating a face in the front row, tapping it with a pencil, saying, "This is him. Lee Duc Than. Right here in front of you. Recognize him?"

I looked at the face, the same one I had seen in the previous photograph, and still didn't remember. What I remembered was Abby warning me that we might have to declare bankruptcy after she saw the bill from the Iroquois, but I knew deep down she was delighted that I had issued an invitation that so many had chosen to accept and that had turned out to be the best party of our lives. We had escaped bankruptcy, she hadn't been serious about that, but were forced onto a strict budget for several months and didn't mind at all.

Fantus was still pointing to a face, asking, "What about it? Do you recognize him? This one, right here."

I shook my head. "It was too long ago to be sure. Why is this one man so important? Why not this one," and I pointed to another face in the front row, "or this one?"

And found myself looking at Abby's face again, thinking of her lilting walk, her sparkling smile, her unselfish love, all of it gone.

I realized that Magellan was talking for the first time. "Osten, did you know who Lee Duc Than was? Or what became of him?"

I didn't know then and I didn't know now. Students came and students went, passing without leaving much of a trace behind, occasionally surfacing down the road years later when appointed to a new position, accepting an honor for some good deed or a jail sentence for some bad deed. Or making a contribution to the school, most likely that, when a brief mention would be served up in the alumni bulletin.

Magellan was quick to enlighten me. "He was sent here by the South Vietnamese government to study health administration. After his second year on campus, he returned to Saigon and was sent up to Hue, running a provincial hospital. He seemed to be doing well from everything we can find and then one day, without a word, he disappeared and showed up Hanoi working for the other side. Just like that. A traitor, a defector or a double agent. Take your pick. After the south collapsed, barely a year later, he came right back to Saigon, didn't seem to mind at all that they renamed the city after Ho Chi Minh, and continued working. He was still a young man and, in time, he was apparently placed in charge of all medical care being provided to our former South Vietnamese allies while they languished in reeducation centers. Probably an easy job because medical care for those unfortunates was a low priority item and after a time they gave him another assignment as well – maintaining the records on the medical status of captured POW's – meaning Americans for the most part. We haven't been able to prove that, but at least that's what he claims."

My ears perked up at that. "That's what he claims? How do we know what he claims?"

Magellan suddenly went silent, as if he had lost his voice which had been working well just a moment earlier. Bath was staring at his hands as if they had suddenly done something he hadn't expected them to do, although they were still sitting there, obediently, one holding the other as if afraid it might wander off and become lost. Fantus broke the silence, speaking softly, as if he wanted no one else to hear what he was about to tell me, although I doubt that it was any secret to his companions.

"We have him, Mike. He's in our hands and he's been talking."

He should have been happy, smiling, up on his feet and dancing in celebration. He wasn't. Instead he was sitting warily, watching me for a reaction, waiting to hear what I might have to say. And Bath? Bath was looking nervously up at the cameras, avoiding my eyes, and why were beads of perspiration forming on his forehead? Magellan seemed to have fallen into a coma.

A word about Pan Union and its many reincarnations. Whatever name was out front on the sign, no matter how hard they worked to disguise it, Pan Union was government, something or other. I'd worked for it, like I said, on several occasions and that's a long story, and they'd told me, "What we do, Osten, is collect information. All kinds of information. About the economy of a country, about its leaders and their habits, especially bad habits, which can always be useful, things like that." I found out what they really did was collect junk intelligence, information that could often be found with no greater effort than reading daily newspapers or magazines available on almost any newsstand, and when too lazy to read, I suspected that they often just faked it. Made it up. What they had asked me to do was talk to people. About drugs, illness, who was sick and who wasn't, what was a problem and what wasn't, in countries all around the world, with special attention to those places behind iron and bamboo curtains. I did that and more on a few occasions, and reported what I had found. What they did with it I never knew, didn't much care, and doubted that I had ever learned much that could have helped us in a global struggle with the bad guys.

Once I'd asked about danger. After all, working for an intelligence agency had to be dangerous, didn't it? The former director drummed his fingertips on a desk remarkably like the one Bath now occupied, thought for a long while, and then replied, "Dangerous? Occasionally it can be dangerous, I suppose. We have had a few injuries, narrow escapes, that sort of thing, but no, all in all, I wouldn't call it dangerous."

He had been lying, I found out later, having neglected to mention the several fatalities that sprinkled the roster of former Pan Union employees, and I should have been suspicious when I saw the sudden appearance of perspiration on his forehead. That's why I was interested just now to see the same thing happen to Bath. That's why I said to myself, "They're lying!"

If they had the man called Lee Duc Than, if they had their hands on him, a man with information about American POW's, a treasure trove of facts, they would be wherever he was, talking to him, pumping him for whatever he knew of the fate of the 2,800 still unaccounted for servicemen missing in Vietnam. But they weren't. They were here. Tight lipped and sweating, talking to me instead.

So I stared at Bath and told him, "That's good news, I'm sure. But what does this have to do with me? Why does it matter if I can identify this man or not?"

"Because," he explained, looking at Fantus while he clarified what I had been told, "what Alex meant to say, right Alex, is that we almost have him."

I recognized the difference immediately. Almost having someone is not quite the same as having him.

Bath was still not through clarifying. "While Fred was in Uzbekistan, he picked up rumors that Lee Duc Than was willing to talk to us, to give us information, to come over to our camp, you might say, and we decided that we should have someone fly over to Bangkok and see what was going on."

"Wait a minute. Why Bangkok? I thought Lee Duc Than was in Ho Chi Minh City or at least somewhere in Vietnam."

Looking mildly irritated by the question, Bath continued, "The rumors were originating from Bangkok, so naturally that's where we sent Fred."

Fred? They'd sent Fred? Fred, on a mission that even Pan Union intelligence must have recognized as a delicate, hot button issue, a sensitive issue, an important issue? The Explorer, a man who could get lost on the way to his own bathroom and blame someone else for the mishap! Incredible.

"What were the rumors and how reliable did you think they were?"

"We had every reason to think they were very reliable. Almost certainly reliable, in fact, isn't that true, Fred?"

Magellan nodded vigorously. "I would risk my reputation on it."

I wondered if anyone, besides me, had considered how little he had risked. I turned my attention to him. "Then, in fact, you don't actually have your hands on Lee Duc Than? Do you have any physical evidence that he exists and has made contact with you? For instance, have you seen him or talked to him? Or is all you have nothing more than, what did you call it, a rumor?"

Bath slowly stood up and walked around to the front of the desk, standing directly behind Magellan, who visibly paled, and unsuccessfully tried to see where his leader had gone. He tensed when Bath placed his hands on the Explorer's shoulders, squeezed as if to massage strength into the man from Uzbekistan, and then looked directly into the camera on the back wall, and uttered these memorable words, "Tell him, Fred, why we must have help in this matter."

Magellan, too, suddenly seemed conscious of the unblinking lenses overhead, looked straight ahead and mumbled, "Well, when I talked to his agent. . ."

"You talked to what," I blurted, wondering what bizarre turn we were taking now. "What agent? What were you negotiating? A professional sports contract? Who the hell was his agent?"

"Mike, let him explain, for God's sake," said Fantus. "I know this sounds unusual, but this man is important to us."

Magellan continued, as if he hadn't heard. "I met with a Thai lawyer. He was the agent."

Fantus interrupted this time, and I wondered why he didn't just tell the story if he knew it. Certainly he had superior linguistic skills. "The lawyer, he's legitimate. Chamburon Primavitavit. Decent enough reputation in Bangkok. Get on with it, Fred," he ordered.

"Well, I met with this lawyer, Cham–"

Fantus cut him short. "Fred, forget the damned name. It's too long. Just get on with it."

Bath agreed. "Yes, Fred. Get on with it."

"Well, I met with this Thai lawyer, the one with the long name, and he told me that Lee Duc Than was out of Vietnam, wanted to talk to us, and had a lot to say. Especially about missing Americans, POW's, that sort of thing and I knew we would be interested. So I told Cham–, I mean the Thai lawyer, that we wanted to meet." Apparently worried that he may have overstepped his authority, he tried to make eye contact with Bath who was still out of sight behind him, pressing down on his shoulders and holding the Explorer tightly in his chair. Unable to find reassurance in that direction, he decided to plunge ahead with his story. "And the lawyer said 'fine,' he could produce his client, that's what he calls him, his client, once we met a few conditions."

Just to be helpful, I offered, "And one of the conditions is money?"

Magellan seemed relieved at how well I was following his story. "Right. Yes. One of the conditions was money. Not a lot of money, really, we often encounter people asking for more when they don't have nearly as much to offer, but one of the conditions was money. But that wasn't the only condition."

Bath, possibly impatient at how slowly the conversation was moving, pressed harder with both hands, then kneaded the muscles, as if trying to squeeze more life from a dying battery. The Explorer flushed, but sat still as Bath told him, "Fred, will you tell Osten what the other conditions were to satisfy his curiosity. To move this along." I couldn't help but wonder if the two of them didn't have some relationship of their own that needed exploration.

But Fred did move it along. "Yes, sure, I'll do that. But don't blame me if anything goes wrong. I was doing the best I could without any clear instructions or backup." Vintage Magellan.

The implied criticism didn't go unnoticed by Bath who released his grip, went back to his chair, took his seat, folded his hands once again and nodded to Fantus who took over the story. As I suspected, he did know it.

"Mike, here's the situation. This lawyer, this agent, whatever you want to call him, tells us that Lee Duc Than is sick. He wants you to treat him."

"What are you talking about? Me treat him! For what? Why should he want me to treat him? I don't even remember who he was."

"Maybe not," Fantus said smoothly, "but he apparently remembers you. More than that. He says you treated him when he was a student, and he wants you to treat him again."

It was possible that I had. I did occasionally see students back then, having still not terminated my active medical practice while I taught part time. "What's the problem," I asked. "Don't they have doctors in Bangkok?" I knew that they did. Some very good ones.

Fantus was undeterred. "I suppose they do, although we aren't absolutely certain that he's in Bangkok, are we Fred?"

Fred had started to wheeze. I remembered that he had always started to wheeze when under stress and the three of us watched in fascination as he slowly removed a bright yellow canister from his suit pocket, shook it, removed a cap, and triggered the device with a well practiced move, inhaling two puffs, about thirty seconds apart. He returned the device to his pocket and seemed to be breathing better. The wheezing was less noticeable when he answered, "Right, we're not sure where he is."

While Magellan had medicated himself, everything had been on hold, but with his recovery and reply, Fantus went on, "Maybe he trusts you and doesn't trust any doctors he might find in his part of the world. Maybe he's afraid that his former employers will get to him through a doctor, something like that. Whatever it is, I don't know, but he did ask for you. By name Fred tells me."

Fred nodded. The wheezing was definitely better.

I still was willing to bet that the money was more important than seeing me for medical treatment. "Let me get this straight. You're telling me that someone I haven't seen for two decades and someone I may or may not have treated for something or other back then wants me to make a house call halfway around the world. That's going to cost someone a hell of a lot of money. Does he have health insurance?" I was joking. They, not surprisingly, took it seriously.

Not blinking at all, Bath reached into a desk drawer and removed a bright blue plastic file folder. I was impressed. Bright blue meant top priority, operational and contingency, already reviewed and approved by everyone who was important enough to add his (no women, so far as I knew, had yet reached that level) initials to the small boxes in the lower right hand corner of each sheet. Crisp white sheets, bright blue folders, the plastic so slippery that I had never been able to handle one without everything sliding out onto the floor. After a few accidents such as that, I was never entrusted with priority files again.

Bath was methodical; I can't fault him for that. He leafed through the entire folder, page by page, and it didn't take more than a minute or two before he looked up to announce, "It doesn't say, but I doubt if he has any coverage," implying by his tone that someone in top management was certain to hear of this oversight.

I wondered what he had expected to find. That Lee Duc Than was covered by the national health insurance plan of Vietnam or a jungle HMO. The man was a defector, if I could believe what this triumvirate was telling me, and the only thing the North Vietnamese were likely to cover him with was six feet of dirt. If they could find him. Not being thrilled by the direction this project seemed to be going, I played my trump card. "Anyway, I don't have a license to practice medicine in Thailand." That should do it, I thought.

They were way ahead of me. "That's not a problem, Mike," Fantus assured me. "We've talked to some people over there, people who owe us, and that's not a problem. They understand the situation and technically you'll be working under the direction of our embassy. Whatever you have to do will be perfectly legal."

Bath seemed far more worried about financing than the license. "Osten, we know that getting you over there will cost some money and we're more than willing to pay your expenses, as long as they're reasonable. And they should be reasonable as you were planning on going to South East Asia anyway, right?"

I was thinking how Burrows would handle this, and then decided, why not let Burrows handle this? "I'll let my associate handle that end of it," I told him, wondering if he and Burrows would be able to agree on a definition of reasonable. As soon as the words were out of my mouth, I realized I had just agreed to go. Well, why not. It sounded interesting, and besides, a side trip to Bangkok was never a hardship. JoElle was there. Did they know that? I'd wanted to see her. Now I could.

But something was still bothering me and I finally decided what it was. "Alex, where is this sick former University student right now? Fred says you have him, then you say we don't have him but we have been in touch with his lawyer who can give him to us if we meet his conditions, but no one has said where this man actually is. What about it? Do you know or don't you know?"

No one seemed in any hurry to answer, the question hanging there in midair. Magellan was looking anxiously at Bath who was staring at Fantus who seemed to have found something interesting in the closed window blinds. Bath finally solved the problem by directing Magellan to reply, saying, "Fred, you have been the closest to the situation. Tell Osten what he wants to know."

Which prompted the Explorer to suddenly remove a wrinkled white handkerchief from his back trouser pocket which he used to wipe his sweating brow. I was cool, the air conditioner didn't seem to have failed, yet everyone but me, make that everyone but me and Fantus who also seemed comfortable, had become warm and overly flushed. Stress, I decided, too much of it. And lies. Lies and stress, a combination that often made people sweat. Magellan succeeded in wiping his brow, returned the handkerchief to his pocket, turned to Fantus rather than Bath who had given him his orders, and said, "Look, Alex, it's not my fault. . ."

He found no sympathy in that quarter. "Damnit, Fred, nobody is talking about fault. Just tell Mike what you know about Lee Duc Than's whereabouts."

It didn't take him long.

"I don't know where he is," is what he said.

Which wasn't surprising considering the hints that he had dropped earlier. But I couldn't just let it rest there. "What do you mean you don't know?" I prodded. "You must know something if you were talking to his lawyer." I didn't feel comfortable using the word agent. "Didn't he tell you or give you a clue of some kind where in Bangkok he had hidden his client?"

This time I had the feeling he was telling the truth. "No, not really. He might not be in Bangkok at all because Cham–, the Thai lawyer referred to going 'up north' a couple of times, wherever that might be. That's about all he said, though, just that and the fact that he was sick. Very sick."

"And wanted to see me?"

"Yes. Wanted to see you. He kept on saying that over and over. That seemed awfully important."

Usually when a patient wanted to see their doctor, they came to the office. This one was playing hide and seek. "Let's say I fly to Thailand. How will I find him? Can you reach the lawyer and set that much up?"

Magellan looked hopeful, sensing that he might yet escape being blamed for anything going wrong, if he could connect on one more phone call. "I think so. I can try."

"All right, so let's try. And while we're at it, do you know why he wants to see me? You said he's sick. With what? Why does he need to see a doctor? Just knowing that much might help. Him and me."

Bath unclasped his hands, closed the blue folder, lifted it and carefully, making sure nothing slid out, tucked it safely into a desk drawer, locked it with a small key, and then softly said, "About that, Osten, we were hoping you might be able to help us."

"Why were you hoping that? How would I know what his problem is?"

Bath glanced at his wrist again. He was definitely wearing a watch. "His agent was quite clear on that point, Osten. He tells us that you have treated Lee Duc Than before and that he has the same thing again. From what he told Fred, it is the same illness, only worse."

Well, that didn't narrow it down much. There are a lot of things you can be treated for twenty years earlier and get again. Influenza, a cold, sinusitis, headaches, even gonorrhea and herpes, but somehow none of that seemed to make sense. Those were the kinds of things students usually complained of when I saw them. Throw in infectious mono and hepatitis, some minor trauma, hives and hay fever – that was about it. No one would need the same doctor to take care of something like that. All they would need is any doctor. So why this obsession with me? That's what I told Bath.

"Possibly your old records may contain a clue as to what was wrong," he observed.

And that was a possibility, although just where all the old records might be was another problem. I started thinking about it when Magellan broke in once more, first wiping his forehead and then leaving me with this to ponder, "Mike, let me level with you." Which made it sound as if he hadn't been telling the truth until now. "This is more complicated than it seems."

What I had learned already sounded complicated so about all I could say was, "Oh?"

"Yes, you see, there's another Lee Duc Than. At least there's another man claiming to be him. This one may be in Laos. Says the same thing. He's sick and needs your attention. We don't know which one is the real one and we were kind of hoping you could clear this up for us."

My practice was booming. When I entered the building I had been a retired physician with a nice administrative position, planning a business trip to Malaysia. Forty-five minutes later, I had two patients by the name of Lee Duc Than, both claiming to have the same illness, and both wanting me to make a house call to cure something I had treated before. Both lived some 12,000 miles away but were reluctant to give out their address. Problem was, I didn't know anyone by that name, and to get in touch with either, or both, I was going to have to deal with Fred Magellan, the Explorer. Wasn't that nice?

"OK, Fred, where did this second Lee Duc Than come from? Does he have an agent and what does he want, in the way of money, I mean?"

"Someone passed a handwritten note to our commercial attaché in

Vientiane. We have it. The note. It says Lee Duc Than is in Laos, that he's sick, wants to come over to our side, and needs medical care."

I hated to sound like a broken record, but I asked, "From me?"

"That's what he said. Or the note said, I should say. From you. Naturally, at first we thought it might be the same man with two different people speaking for him, one in Thailand and one in Laos. They aren't that far apart, you know, just a river between them. But now we don't think so. We think they're two different men who just happened to pop into view at the same time."

I liked his view of Thailand and Laos as being the same except for a river between. There were other differences as well, things like ideology, concepts such as freedom and civilization on one side of the river, and chaos, terror, and barbarism on the other, and we had one Lee Duc Than to the south and another to the north, allegedly, of that river. I might need more than a stethoscope on this trip.

I knew from past experience that Pan Union people tended to make things complicated. It made them feel important. Helped justify budget requests that were submitted in disguise to legislative bodies that rarely asked the right questions. I knew all that, but even for Pan Union this whole story seemed needlessly complex. But I hadn't heard everything yet. They had saved that for dessert.

"So we've got another Lee Duc Than up in Laos. Who's talking for him? A Laotian lawyer?"

Fantus started to reply but got only as far as "No, Mike, that's the strange part. . ." before Bath abruptly cut him off.

He finished the sentence. "It's Ken Green, Osten. You know him, or at least you knew him."

I felt the goose bumps develop, first on the back of my neck, then the arms, neck, even the scalp tingling in surprise. It wasn't the air conditioning; the room was no cooler than it had been a minute before and Magellan was still sweating. It was shock because Ken Green was dead. Had been for fifteen years. Dead after a helicopter crash in Vietnam.

These men knew that. They all knew his father, General Jordan Green. Knew him well. Worked with him here at Pan Union until he retired, or had he retired? I had never been sure. The three of them just sat there and looked at me as I bristled and said, "Green? Kenny Green? He's dead. What gives you the crazy idea that he is speaking for a Vietnamese defector or anyone else? Dead men can't speak from the grave." As I said it, I knew that no one, at least no one on this side of the Pacific, had ever seen that grave.

Bath didn't argue. "Our records show that he's dead. His father confirmed that he's dead. So does the Army. A dozen witnesses saw his helicopter crash and burn and there were no known survivors. So all of us had accepted the fact that he was dead. Until now."

"Why now? What makes you think this note was from Ken Green? Anyone could put his name on a piece of paper and pass it off as coming from the son of an American general. It could be a fake. A scam. After all, the General is a famous man. And he has money."

None of this was news to Bath. "Yes, we thought of that. Right off. So we checked it carefully. Our investigation indicated that the message was written on a piece of cheap lined stationery, probably purchased in Hong Kong at a Spencer and Marks outlet in Kowloon. This type of paper, a special blend of cotton fibers, new wood pulp, and recycled post-consumer waste has only been in production for approximately five years. The writing was done with a ball point pen, most likely a Bic, which could have been purchased just about anywhere. Our own ink experts used spectrophotometry and were able to determine that it had not been exposed to air for more than thirty days. We immediately showed a copy of the note to the General and he was able to find old letters and diaries from his son. Military graphologists compared them to the Vientiane note and declared them a match. In other words, Ken Green had written the note, within the past month."

Investigators in a variety store in Hong Kong. Paper experts, ink experts, spectrophotometry, graphologists! Maybe Pan Union had become more efficient than in the old days when we clipped articles out of the newspaper or went to cocktail parties to pick up the latest gossip.

Obviously, if what I had just heard was true, then Ken Green was not lying in an unmarked grave in the jungles of South East Asia. My decision to go to Bangkok, and from there to wherever the trail might lead, made reluctantly a few minutes earlier, had just been finalized. If the General's son was alive, even if there was just the remotest possibility that he was alive, I had to help look for him. For the General. For Jordan Green. I owed him that much, and more.

I didn't need my ticket on the shuttle to New York, which was fortunate because by now I would probably have missed it. Bath took care of that when, after sneaking another look at his wrist, he announced, "We should get going if we want to meet with the General tonight. He's expecting us. Alex, call Washington National and tell them we'll be there in thirty minutes. The three of us."

Fantus looked at him questioningly and Bath repeated it, "The three of us. Me, you, and Osten. Tell them to have the plane ready."

"The plane?" I asked.

"Our plane," he explained. "It will be waiting when we get there."

When you travel with Pan Union, you travel first class. Or better, in this case. On our own plane.

Magellan was still sitting in his chair, uninvited, with nothing to do. But not forgotten. Pausing on his way out of the room, Bath gave him his orders. "Fred, I want you to go down to communications and wait for anything coming in from Bangkok. I want to know at once if you hear anything, anything at all, from our people over there. From Green, or the Lee Duc Than situation – what should I call it?"

His dilemma was real. Everything at Pan Union was given a name. It was Operation This or Operation That, never just a 'situation.' Helpfully, I suggested, "How about calling this Operation Patient? That's what we have here, one or two patients." I left Ken Green out of it. I didn't know how to classify him. Missing in action? POW? Former dead helicopter pilot? That was going to take more time to resolve.

Surprisingly, Bath, a man I had figured to reject most ideas not his own, seemed eager if not pleased by the idea. "Operation Patient? Not a bad name and we need a name, so let's use it. Fred, enter that into the log and start a new file. Operation Patient. Brief and descriptive. Good suggestion, Osten."

Always willing to improve upon perfection, I offered another suggestion. "Maybe it would be more descriptive if we used another name. Something like Operation Sick?"

His eyes narrowed, his face turned hard, his lips a bloodless mask across the lower part of his face, as he considered: was I joking, was I ridiculing him or putting him down? Or was I serious? He decided to treat it as the latter, while I decided that if properly provoked, Bath could be a dangerous man.

Magellan was standing by, waiting for his final instructions, obviously not wanting to get it wrong. "What should I enter into the log – Operation Patient or Operation Sick?" Of course, simply by asking the question, he got it wrong and he realized that when Bath turned glacial gray eyes in his direction, pressed his lips together ever more tightly, and hissed, "As I said, Fred, I shouldn't have to repeat it, Operation Patient is the name. Can you remember that and spell it correctly?"

"Sure, Mr. Bath, I've got it. I'll get right on it." Clearly chastened, he turned to leave, but stopped to ask, "How long do you want me to wait in the communications room?"

Bath fixed him with another icy stare. "Until someone communicates with you, Fred. There's a twelve hour time difference over there so right now it's early morning in Bangkok. The people you need to talk to are probably still in bed. Sooner or later, they'll get up," he said it in a way that implied that they'd better or else. "Start moving around, do some work, and then, if they learn anything of interest or have anything to say, they'll communicate with you. That's how it works. Remember?"

Any plans Magellan might have had for the evening had just been blown away.

Bath snapped another quick look at his wrist and this time I saw it. The watch. A Patek Phillipe. Swiss. Advertised in appropriately understated fashion in rather exclusive publications as the finest watch in the world. Expensive, of course. I found myself wondering how a middle level civil servant, working in an obscure agency off the beaten track, could afford such a prize. Not on his government salary, certainly. Independent means? Inheritance? A rich wife? Wise investments? Outside income? Probably that, I decided, but what kind?

I looked at my Benrus, which I made little effort to hide under long cuffs, and saw that it was 6:40 P.M. Well, I consoled myself, if it was ever lost or stolen, I wouldn't feel nearly as badly about it as Bath would about losing his.

# 2

A black stretch limousine had been waiting for us at the curb when we came outside, Bath and Fantus clutching identical black leather briefcases as if the nation's secrets were locked inside. For all I knew, they were. Fantus walked around to the far side and reappeared on an already pulled down jump seat. Bath started to enter ahead of me, thought better of it, and pulled back, saying "Thoughtless of me, Osten. After you, please," and promptly dropped his briefcase on his foot, leaving me standing by the open car door with no place to go. I watched as he fumbled around in the dark, for a moment thought about going around to the other side, but changed my mind when he finally found the handle, picked up the briefcase, which seemed unusually heavy, and backed away, muttering, "Sorry. Clumsy of me."

The trip to Washington National went smoothly after that. Gates opened promptly on the far side of the field, allowing us to pull alongside an unmarked Gulfstream, and we went aboard. The customized interior was luxurious with four tilt back seats, each accompanied by its own four-slotted beverage table and magazine rack. Two full sized couches, one fore and the other aft, with telephones and power outlets for electronic equipment, a full galley, and a unisex restroom completed the furnishings.

Bath hurried to the front couch, opened his briefcase, removed a laptop, plugged it in, sorted through files, some blue, some gold, and others red, and went to work. His laptop didn't appear to have been damaged when he dropped it. Fantus went to the second couch, opened his briefcase, took out a laptop, shuffled a pile of green and gold files, finally set half of them to one side, laying the rest on the floor in a neat pile. They both started tapping away on their computers without a word. The hotel had sent my luggage off to the shuttle so it should be on its way to New York by now. All I had with me was a copy of USA Today that I had found in the limousine. I started to read it, catching up on all the news that was fit to print – or was that some other newspaper? Probably as interesting as anything was the handwritten Post-It note attached to the top page of the sports section. I always read the sports page first. Force of habit. The note, printed in ball point pen, said, "Be careful. VERY careful." No signature.

Neither Bath nor Fantus were paying the slightest attention to me, both obviously busy with file folders. Blue I knew all about. Top priority plans. Red – red meant problems. Green and gold, I had no idea. I was pretty sure neither of my traveling companions had left me a note. They would be more likely to send it by e-mail. Once again, that narrowed things down quite a bit. I decided to eliminate the limousine driver as a possibility as well. That narrowed it even further. I decided I needed a laptop. I could probably use it to solve mysteries such as this or to work while on airplanes and stop wasting so much time.

The tapping of two keyboards, combined with the muted sounds of two powerful Allison engines, was soothing. As carefully as I could, I tilted the seat to a comfortable angle and closed my eyes. Thinking of the General, and Korea. Yes, Korea, not Vietnam. The General and Ken had both served in Vietnam. That was their war. But the General, he was a captain then, and I had been together in Korea, long before, when Ken was still a baby. That was our war. That was 1950 when the North Koreans had sent tanks and men crashing into the South, and now 35 years later, I was on a plane with men using code names, one of them at least, wearing a gun, both of them almost certainly, and tapping on computers. Why?

I could see lights far below as we cleared brilliantly lit Washington, D.C. I'm not sure if I fell asleep and took a nap or if I was hypnotized by the sounds and sights after a busy day, but it all seemed to come back once again – those years so long ago, which I had almost, but never quite entirely, forgotten.

It began in college, when money was short and bills just kept coming. Even students on scholarship have unexpected expenses and, despite part-time jobs, several of them at once during one semester, I was falling ever deeper into debt. So I joined the Army Reserves. The recruiting posters made it sound exciting, complete with adventure, and I was healthy, young, and needed money, so why not? It worked out reasonably well. Six weeks of intensive summer training for two straight years was no real hardship. In fact, it was fun, spending one of them in San Antonio, Texas and the second in swamps around Camp Polk, Louisiana. Hot, sure it was hot, and humid and I never realized it was possible to sweat that much or to need so many uniform changes each day. And showers never felt so refreshing or beer so cold at the end of training in the field. And one day, they called me a second lieutenant, put shiny gold bars on my collar, started paying me forty dollars a month, and asked only that I continue attending classes during the school year and be present each summer for two weeks of additional training. Not a bad deal.

You may not recall those times, that was a long while back, like I said, but they were relatively carefree days for America. The Germans and Japanese had surrendered five years earlier, ending World War II. The Russians were an annoyance, having developed nuclear weapons, but ours seemed more advanced and we were still king of the hill. Over on the other side of the world, the Chinese Communists were chasing the Nationalist Chinese off the mainland, distressing many Americans, especially Senator Joseph McCarthy who kept asking, "Who lost China?" but no one had an answer, and he finally went away in disgrace.

Congress and our President seemed convinced that we would never need to use force again, we were that powerful, and acted, or perhaps it was because they failed to act, as if the military budget could be reduced to the bone. Cut this and that, eliminate money for new weapons, scrap warplanes and ships, reduce inventories of ammunition, that sort of thing. It didn't bother me too much as I had my gold bars, monthly paycheck, clean uniforms, and could look forward to the two weeks off in some nice hot part of the country to continue my abbreviated career. Life was great and about to get better as in two more years, I would graduate as a physician and go out into the world as a doctor, making a lot of money serving mankind. I was young, optimistic, enthusiastic, and happy. What could be better?

In February, Major Kaehl, our campus military advisor, called three of his newly minted officers into the ROTC office. He seemed cheerful, which should have put us on alert. We hadn't been in the Army long but we had been warned, especially in Camp Polk. When officers, especially majors, look cheerful, be careful of volunteering, we had been told. Actually, a senior noncom went even further. Don't ever volunteer for anything, was his advice. Never, ever.

The major began, "I have an opportunity to make this an interesting summer for you. Something has just come up that I think you'll like. Want to hear about it?"

No one said a word, which didn't seem to faze Major Kaehl a bit. He went on, "Instead of wasting your two weeks in some God-awful camp, I can arrange to have you go to Korea for something truly worthwhile. To work with our military advisory group over there, helping the South Korean Army become the finest fighting force in the world."

Personally, I thought his description of the South Koreans as the 'finest fighting force in the world' was a little strong. Wasn't that supposed to be us?

He had barely warmed up and continued, "Their men are great, but look, their support services are woeful. Medical services in particular. They're terrible. They have no experience in setting up front line aid stations, little concept of how to evacuate casualties, how to handle triage, that sort of thing. Everything is still pretty primitive and KMAG has asked the Army for help. We'll send medical officers, of course. Doctors. But they need more than that. They need men like you. Men I've helped train, here at school or at summer camps. Men who've read the manuals I've put together."

It was odd. I still considered myself marginally trained, not familiar with the things he said the South Koreans needed so badly, while the major seemed to regard us, me, Lew Garvey, and Sid Bloomstein, as secret weapons in the American arsenal.

By the way, I had no idea what the initials KMAG stood for and neither did Lew, which was why he asked. The major was quick to respond. "Good question, Lew. Should have explained that. KMAG stands for Korean Military Advisory Group. Americans helping Koreans, that's what it is. About 500 Americans over there standing shoulder to shoulder with our allies, helping turn this rabble into the fighting force I was telling you about."

Rabble? We were dealing with rabble? I didn't have the dictionary handy but it seemed to me that a rabble was a disorganized mob of people or something like that. A mob wasn't an army, but maybe we could make it into one. Or was that overreaching?

"So we'd be in the Army," I observed, incorrectly, as the Major made clear, more or less.

"Not exactly. Everyone in KMAG is military, I think. But KMAG itself is not a part of the occupation force, which is being pulled out anyway. KMAG is a part of the State Department, under civilian control, of course, as it's primarily a people to people thing and we don't want the Communists up north to get the wrong idea."

What wrong idea? If our people were helping the South Koreans become a better fighting force, the best in the world, as the Major said, wouldn't the men from up north understand what that meant? It seemed clear to me they might view our presence as a hostile act and wouldn't care whether KMAG was a nice civilian agency or a warlike military cadre. It was still trouble for them. But we were king of the hill, remember, so we could do anything we wanted.

Major Kaehl was a helluva salesman. I had some misgivings, sure; a number of questions, sure. But eight weeks? What could happen in eight weeks and it was the first real adventure I would have in my Army career, if you didn't count the time in Camp Polk when Lew and I gave our seats on the bus to a black woman and a bunch of regular army toughs didn't think that was the right thing to do. Plus they would pay me for eight weeks. More money than I had expected to earn in the summer.

The Major finished on an enthusiastic note, upbeat all the way. "I know that you would enjoy this and it would be a tremendous experience for the three of you. Maybe even help your careers." That shouldn't have had any effect. I didn't plan on making the Army my career.

The Major was often that way. He seemed to really like the Army. Maybe his assignment, teaching a few hours a week on a picturesque college campus while dating a cheerleader, had something to do with it.

But the Major was so upbeat about this upcoming summer assignment that I was surprised at his answer when Lew asked him, "Major, will you be coming with us?"

"No, Garvey, unfortunately, I can't. They've assigned me to a new class and I'll be stuck teaching a group of nurses this summer. I just won't be able to get away."

There was a touch of sadness in his voice. He was crestfallen. Dejected. In his spare time, Major Kaehl performed with the University Repertory Players at the Arts Center. He was considered to be a very good actor. This was one of his better performances.

He sensed our hesitation, was aware that none of the three of us had leaped with joy and volunteered by this time, and wisely concluded, "I don't need a decision right now. We need three officers from this campus but I have until March tenth to send in the names. Think about it and let me know."

We thought about it, talked about it, and finally Lew and I signed on. The third original invitee, Sid Bloomstein, also thought about it, must have talked to better advisers, and then exercised what turned out to be better judgment by coming up with what sounded like a plausible excuse (I don't recall what it was, possibly a sister getting married, something like that) and stayed home. Art Waines took his place.

Surprisingly, the expedition started out as high adventure. Classes ended the last week of May and, with a good feeling about final exams, a relaxing two weeks at home with the family, listening to Dad warn me about 'being careful' one more time, I shook his hand, embraced mother, and boarded a lumbering old C-54 military transport with hard wooden racks substituting for seats.

Grinning even now at the remembrance, I snuggled deeper into the comfort of the Gulfstream's recliner, marveling again at how the young adapt to life's discomforts. Hard wooden benches or not, despite the cold of the unheated rattling fuselage or the unmuffled roar of four engines that seemed to need lubricants, I slept all the way to Hawaii, apparently not even waking during a refueling stop in San Francisco. That confirmed what I had long suspected – during the entire time I spent in college, I had been a sleep-deprived individual.

We had a one day stopover in Hawaii, and as far as I was concerned, we could have stayed there for the summer. I made the obligatory trip out to Pearl Harbor, to the Arizona Memorial, and then spent the next six hours on the beach at Waikiki. The girls were fantastic: tanned, thin, friendly, and I almost forgot about cheerleaders. I guess I haven't mentioned that I'd broken up with the one I'd been dating, a friend of the Major's. She'd begun dating a football player, apparently deciding that an athlete in hand was a better prospect than a doctor down the road. At least that's how I saw it.

Lew seemed to have enjoyed himself every bit as much and as we banked over Diamond Head the next morning, heading west away from the rising sun, he said, "You know, this may turn out to be a good summer after all."

I refrained from pointing out that Hawaii and Korea were two separate and distinct places, and that so far, we had been on active duty for exactly one day, hadn't even put on uniforms, but I didn't want to spoil his mood, or mine, so I kept silent and went back to sleep.

We flew all day and then into the night, with a single stop at Guam where we didn't even deplane, before landing in Japan. And the next morning, still groggy from the time change and long cramped flight, we were herded into our first official, big-time military briefing. I fought hard to concentrate on what a hyperthyroid light-colonel was saying, but I fell asleep. An hour or so later, hoping I hadn't missed anything important, I managed to gather my wits and keep my eyes open, only to find that just about everyone else was asleep. It seemed that when I fell asleep, the colonel was telling us that the South Korean Army was a mess, which was not quite what Major Kaehl had told us, and when I woke up, the briefing officer was still talking about what a mess we would find. Poor equipment, he was saying, junk, or near junk, in the hands of men who didn't know how to maintain it, which probably wasn't too bad as they also didn't know how to use it. And, instead of preparing to fight the North, where a much larger army was being capably trained by "those Russian Commies," the South Koreans were chasing bandits up and down the peninsula and seldom catching them.

Wonderful. The colonel, really warming to his task now, went on to assert, "Despite all of the problems, though, bad equipment, poor training, terrible leadership, we've started to make progress. We've gone back to basics. Started with squad drills, then to platoons, soon we'll work with entire companies, and then later, we'll get to battalion and regimental operations. We'll get them organized yet. Another six months, maybe a year, and we'll have a real army here."

Obviously we weren't going to get it all done in our eight weeks. So where would we fit in?

The colonel was way ahead of me. "Now, you men in support services, especially you people in transport and medical stuff, listen up. These Koreans don't do a good job of feeding people, moving 'em from one place to another, putting clothes on 'em or getting 'em guns and ammunition. And what's more, they're absolutely terrible when it comes to taking care of anyone who gets shot or sick. They don't know how to do anything at all. Maybe it's not part of their culture or something, but that's what you're here for. Get 'em organized. Show 'em how to do it." Unfortunately, he didn't explain how we were to do that. At that point, he just walked out of the room.

After a hurried lunch of cheese sandwiches, dill pickles, and succotash, not bad for the Army as I was to find out, we reconvened, just eight of us this time, in another room, with a captain, wearing perfectly tailored khakis, in charge. He got our attention immediately by slapping a four foot wooden pointer against a huge wall map with a smack that resounded across the room and out the door. The message was clear: there was to be no sleeping in this room. When he slapped the pointer a second time, every eye was riveted on a foot high red Roman numeral VIII that seemed to be his target. "Look at this map," he ordered. We did. It was a map of Korea, the entire peninsula, all the way from the Chinese border to the tip, just opposite Japan.

"This is our destination. The ROK 8th infantry division." And he whacked the big red VIII one more time for emphasis. At least I was following the briefing so far. ROK stood for Republic of Korea. We were going to join one of its divisions, the 8th apparently, no not apparently, certainly, as this officer seemed to know what he was talking about. It was encouraging to know that the ROK army had at least eight divisions.

"It's here on the east coast, in rough terrain, and scattered in the mountains. That's going to make our job much harder. One regiment is up along the border with North Korea. Another is along the coast." His pointer flicked back and forth, from place to place. "The third regiment is supposed to be here, in reserve," and the pointer wandered around aimlessly to the south, "but it really doesn't exist, except on paper."

Maybe they didn't have eight divisions after all.

"We're going up to the border first to work with the frontline troops and then move back to the coast. OK?"

My nose had started to run and when I wiped it with the back of my hand, my GI handkerchiefs being stowed inconveniently in my duffel bag, I found it to be wet and sticky. Blood. That had happened once in a while when I was a kid and the doctor back home had looked at it and said, "Allergies. You have allergies." I wasn't sure why that made my nose bleed, it was one of the things I was going to medical school to find out, but now I started to wonder if I was allergic to Japan. Maybe, though, I decided, it was the dry air in the plane, and I took my forefinger and thumb, squeezed tightly and the flow stopped. It usually did, but the squeezing had made my eyes start to water. Maybe I was allergic to something after all.

The captain was still talking. "The rough terrain may be a blessing. These mountains are the least likely place for an attack to occur. If that ever happens, this is the place where it will happen," and he carefully placed the tip of the pointer to a spot just north of Seoul. "Right here and they'll come through Uijongbu or Munsan. Makes more sense. Better roads, shorter distance to the capital, no mountains to worry about. But we're not to worry about that," he cautioned. Why not? "The official line is that they won't attack. The South Koreans are too tough. That's the official line." He didn't sound convinced. Neither was I because if what I had heard in the other room was fact, then the official line was fiction.

The bleeding had stopped but my eyes were still itching. My shirt was spotted with blood, blood that had splashed off my chin before I had been able to cut off the flow.

"We'll leave in the morning," the captain continued. Obviously we weren't to have time for a sightseeing tour of Japan. "We'll fly to Kimpo airfield, close to Seoul," using his pointer once again. "We'll be joined there by a South Korean military escort, driven in trucks to here." Squinting, I could make out the name Chungchon about in the center of the peninsula. "The roads are adequate to this point but then we move into the mountains and it will be slower. Plus the risk of guerrillas. They operate in the mountains. But don't worry about it. We'll have an armed escort and you'll probably find this part of Korea to be interesting. It should take us three or four days to cross to our operational area. Then we'll get to work. Any questions?" There had to be a lot of them but after a long mind-numbing day, to say nothing of the part of our anatomy we sat on, no one dared ask.

It didn't seem to bother the captain. This time he thrust the pointer straight out in front as if parrying a fencing move by an opponent, frightening a partially hypnotized sergeant who thought he was under attack, and said, "See those binders over there, on the table by the door? I want each of you to take one and study it from cover to cover. That's our Bible. That's what we'll use to teach our South Korean counterparts. It covers everything we want them to know. Keep it with you on the plane, on the truck, when you eat, and even when you sleep. When you have nothing else to do, study it, even if for only a minute or two at a time. I don't want to sound melodramatic, but every second counts as we don't know how much time we have." Like the colonel, when he was done, he was done. He headed for the door and we all pushed back our chairs to stand up.

As he passed me at a brisk pace, he suddenly stopped and turned, looking me up and down and then asking, "You OK? Looks like you're getting a cold."

"Nose bleed, sir," I told him. "Happens every once in a while for no apparent reason. My doctor says it's probably allergies."

"Maybe not Oster," he was looking at my name tag, "maybe it's the low humidity from the long airplane ride. Planes are notorious for that."

A kindred spirit and wise man, I decided, and then hastened to correct his mispronunciation of my name. "It's Osten sir, not Oster."

"Oh, sorry. I didn't see the rest of the N. That spot of blood makes it look more like an R. Covers it up and makes it hard to read. Before you go into the mess hall you probably should get a clean shirt and have that one laundered so it's ready to go when you are." With that, he disappeared, carrying his pointer, occasionally thrusting and parrying imaginary swords as he strode briskly down the hall. He had fenced at the military academy. Epee.

That was my first contact with Jordan Green. That's who it was, according to his name tag. Captain Jordan Green. Later while eating, another lieutenant that knew Green told me that I was a lucky man. "He cares about his men," he said. Several others within hearing nodded in agreement.

We tossed our gear, including my newly laundered shirt free of blood stains, on board a plane the next morning at 10 AM, three hours later than scheduled. I had taken advantage of the time to purchase three boxes of tissues, in case my nose sprung another leak, and two 24 count cartons of milk chocolate bars, one with almonds, one without. Then I read the manual until we lifted off while Lew talked about the Red Cross girl who had served him coffee and doughnuts. He thought she was a beauty and he was right, but I doubted we'd ever see her again, so what did it matter?

The flight itself, in a rattling, shaking C-47 transport that had seen better days, was uneventful unless you consider the smoking left engine an event. The pilot didn't seem bothered by it, the copilot hardly seemed to know where he was, and Captain Green reassured us by saying, "These old planes are tough. This one probably flew the hump in the war so it's seen a lot of rough use, but I'm sure the crew can handle it. These crates can fly on one engine if they have to."

Minutes later, we had to. Frighteningly, it was the right propeller, which had been spinning smoothly, that sputtered, then stopped, leaving us with the left engine, which continued to smoke, as our sole source of power. We flew over a choppy ocean with six foot swells, barely crested several jagged mountains, wobbled from side to side over rice paddies and finally found a runway devoid of traffic and came in for a landing. As we lumbered along a pitted concrete path, the left engine decided enough was enough, and with one last puff of black smoke and a bright flash of orange, it shut down. We rolled another two hundred feet, lost forward momentum, and came to rest just short of a clump of sturdy trees, the front wheels mired in soft grass. We collected our duffel bags and clambered down the rear ramp to find a mechanic standing by with a hand held fire extinguisher. As he watched the smoke slowly dissipate, another mechanic strolled over carrying a toolbox. Neither said a word or did a thing and, after a minute or two, they shrugged and walked away.

Amazingly, we had landed at Kimpo, only to find that the trucks had never arrived. An American officer in a Jeep directed us to a cluster of tents pitched perilously close to the runway and told us we were welcome to move in. We stayed there three days and found that no trucks meant no food as well. I shared my chocolate bars with my tent mates and by the end of the first day, I was down to two – one plain, one almond. Luckily, someone rounded up a case of K rations and, shortly thereafter, two trucks and a squad of South Korean marines showed up.

They were accompanied by another KMAG captain and it was obvious that he and Green were old acquaintances. What made him popular, however, was the fact that he had brought along beer, cases of Japanese beer. It was warm, but what difference did that make? It was the first drinkable fluid we had tasted since our arrival in Korea.

The new captain, I never did get his name, and lowly second lieutenants knew better than to ask too many questions in the presence of superiors, joined us around an open fire later that evening, sharing beer – and a warning, "They're coming. The North Koreans. I've been up at the border near Kaesong for the past two months and they've been probing, raiding, patrolling every single night. Looking for soft spots and I think they've found what they wanted to know because in the last week or so, they've been quiet. Lulled us to sleep, too, I'm afraid. I'm on the border with the ROK 1$^{st}$ Division and I've never seen a bunch less ready to fight than them."

"How bad is it?" Green wanted to know, waiting for an answer while the visitor finished one can of beer and opened another.

"Bad. It's worse than bad. I've got a single ROK infantry company on the line. One company, maybe 200 men although I doubt it because just about every unit is under strength. In addition, they're outgunned, outnumbered, and out-motivated. There are at least a dozen tanks just across the border; we see them and hear them moving about day after day. I don't have a single antitank gun, not even a bazooka. But there's nothing to worry about, according to the ROK division commander. He insists we're in great shape and that his men would tear any invaders to pieces. My American superiors, who must know better, tell me the same thing. They're all crazy. They're like little kids whistling as they pass the cemetery at night. Unfortunately, I'm the guy inside the cemetery and I'm finding the place is real spooky."

The captain from Kaesong left a little later but his words continued to haunt me. "They're coming," he had said. But he hadn't said when and he hadn't said where, although when I looked at my map, I saw Kaesong was located just north of the spot where Green's pointer had come to rest during our briefing back in Japan. North of Seoul. We should be OK, headed as we were for the other side of the peninsula.

Getting to Chungchon wasn't easy. The trucks were old, hadn't the colonel said everything the South Koreans had was old?, and one of them broke down almost before we were out of sight of Kimpo. Naturally, we had no mechanic with us, and the ones back at the airfield hadn't inspired much confidence.

It took a conference between Green and a South Korean officer to decide what to do, which was for all of us to get off the trucks and send the operational vehicle back for help. There would be a lot of these conference decisions in the next few days. Americans conferring with Koreans, language always a barrier and hampering decisive action. That's why they called the Koreans our counterparts; we weren't supposed to do it for them, but it was instead a case of being assigned to help them decide how to do it, after first teaching them what it was we thought they should do. Cumbersome. Also dangerous.

I spent the eight hours it took the truck to return reading my manual, staying out of the direct sunlight, and then, at Green's order, supervising the digging of our first foxholes in Korea. This was going to be a realistic exercise. We moved back into the trees, away from the road, started fires and heated tinned meat and beans as well as brewed coffee. A picnic.

Our truck brought two more with it, an additional twenty South Korean infantrymen crowded about, looking for something to eat, turned up their noses at the meat, and whipped up their own sticky rice. They did drink our coffee, however, and then dug their own foxholes. The coffee surprised me. I had always expected them to drink tea.

Our Sergeant Broward and several Koreans spread a large map across the hood of one truck and were in deep conversation, aided by arm waving and pointing until they finally seemed to have settled on where we would go next. There didn't seem to be much choice as there was but one road. We could either go east or west. It appeared that east had won out.

The captain joined us as we sat with empty mess kits, wishing we had more beans, but having to settle for soggy crackers. "Good news," he told us. "Someone decided to send along additional security because there are reports of bandits or guerrillas operating ahead. So now we have three trucks, an improved radio, and new instructions. First of all, everyone is to remove his name tag, right now. Second, you are to be issued a helmet, not just a helmet liner, but the real thing. Steel. Wear it from now on, except when sleeping. In a few minutes, Sergeant Broward will also be issuing weapons and ammunition. The officers," he indicated me and Lew, "will have a sidearm and carbine. The rest of the men will each have an M1 rifle."

Like he said, this was the good news. He had more. "We'll post sentries tonight and every night from now on. Because it's almost dark, we'll stay here tonight, although we should have occupied the higher ground over there," pointing to the north. "Remember that in the future. Dig in where the enemy has to come to you and where you have a good field of fire. Tonight, we'll put men up there to cover us. Osten, you take the first tour with another American and two Koreans. Garvey will bring three new men up at 2 A.M. Broward will clear it with the ROK major who came with the second contingent. Any questions?"

"Captain," I asked, "what about interpreters? We need some if we're going to talk to the Koreans."

"That's a good point." He looked around in the gathering darkness and asked, "Do any of you speak Korean?" Eight American heads were shaking no. "I was afraid not. You'll pick up some words pretty quickly so work on it. I know that Broward speaks it well enough to make himself understood and so do I. I know that the Koreans have one interpreter with them and I'll check to see if anyone else knows our language. That's the best we can do. Later, when we reach the 8th Division area, we should be better off. They're supposed to have plenty of English speaking counterparts waiting for us."

We made it to the top of the knoll just after dark, but not without some difficulty. Not from the climb, that was easy enough. It was the ROK major. He didn't want to release men for the project, saving face because he hadn't thought of the idea, and after a fifteen minute discussion, in which Broward must have used all of his Korean and a few choice American cuss words, he seemed to have convinced the South Koreans that it *had* been their idea and an American kid from Kentucky, name of Starks, and two Korean marines, followed me noisily up the rocky incline. A South Korean infantryman followed reluctantly. "That one," Broward indicated the straggler as we prepared to push off for our four hour tour, "is supposed to be able to speak English. You may need him."

I never found out if he could speak English or not. At the summit, he sat huddled under a tarp some fifty feet away from the rest of us and never said a word all night. In any language.

Starks and a Korean guarded the reverse slope of the ridge. I sat with another Korean looking down at the campsite, fires slowly dying. It was far enough away so that sound was unable to reach us as the remainder of the contingent turned in for the night.

An hour later, it started to rain and we couldn't see a thing. My Korean counterpart had produced a poncho and draped it over his head. He didn't offer to share. The rain pelted off my steel helmet and sounded exactly the same as the rain hitting the tin roof of a tree house I had built back home when I was nine or ten years old. As long as I was wet, I decided to check on Starks and his counterpart, tapped my companion to let him know I was leaving for a moment, and was rewarded by one eye peering from under of the raised edge of his cover. I don't know if he understood what I was up to or not, the interpreter was too far away to be of any help, so I motioned towards the back of the slope and scuttled that way. Starks was as wet as I was and I couldn't see his counterpart at all. He saw my questioning look and pointed down slope where I saw a figure, I took it to be the Korean, sheltered against a rock which seemed to be keeping him relatively dry. The problem was, from where he was, he couldn't see a thing. The whole North Korean army could be coming up the hill and he wouldn't know it until too late. I slapped Starks on the back in what I hoped was a reassuring manner and scuttled back from where I had come. As I picked my way through jagged rocks that littered the hill, there was a brief flash of light off to the northwest. Lightning, I guessed, and heard the accompanying growl of thunder. My Korean companion, huddled under his rubberized protection, clutching his unprotected M1 rifle and muttered something I didn't understand. Two weeks later, I had learned enough Korean to realize what he had said was "artillery."

Lew and our replacements came up as scheduled but almost missed us in the dark. They stumbled across our interpreter who didn't say anything but just pointed in our direction. I collected Starks and we went back down to the campsite where Broward was anxiously waiting, reminding me of my father when I had been out on a high school date with the car. "Everything all right, Lieutenant?" he asked.

I assured him it was and looked for a place to sleep. Two empty foxholes, probably vacated by Lew and his men, were partially filled with water. I looked under the nearest truck. A sea of mud. I did the next best thing and started to climb into the uncovered flat bed of the vehicle. "You should have taken a poncho with you, Lieutenant," Broward said, as he handed me one. "You never know when it might rain." I grudgingly said, "Thanks" and climbed up pushing a half dozen other bodies aside to make room. The Sergeant was maybe two years older than I was, but he was regular army. Made me feel like a little kid.

Morning was little better. The rain had ceased but the road was a torrent of mud. The trucks slipped and slid, the wheels often spinning uselessly on easy grades and several times trucks slid off the road, the whole column stopping to push them back again. We passed no other traffic, which the major seemed to find strange. Even stranger, abandoned carts were everywhere. No animals to pull them. No people. Just empty carts. The few dwellings we passed were empty. No one could be seen working in the fields.

Even the South Korean soldiers and marines seemed uneasy. It was as if everyone had left; as if the whole world had heard something, knew something, that we didn't know. Yet our radio was silent. Our regular three hour transmissions were received and acknowledged and a cryptic KMAG voice continued to advise, "Report in three hours. Out." And when we did, everything was still fine. But it wasn't. You could sense that it wasn't.

And yet, two days later, with the sun out once again, we reached Chungchon where there were people, fuel, and supplies to replace our dwindling stocks. Things looked almost normal, despite a hard to define undercurrent of tension on the faces of people in the streets watching us as we passed by. There had been no bandits, no guerrillas, no shooting and that was just fine with us.

One truck and a squad of South Korean soldiers turned around and started back, an obvious indication that we had passed the point of greatest danger. We were left with two trucks, twelve South Korean marines and their officer, a dozen more South Korean infantrymen, three noncoms, a lieutenant, and the ROK major. The American complement was made up of Captain Green, Lew and me, six enlisted reservists, two truck drivers, an interpreter, and Sergeant Broward. Forty two of us in all. Art Waines had never been with us. He had been sent to another ROK division and was off rattling around in some truck with another group. After we had loaded our supplies, the extra fuel and water, adequate rations and ammunition, there was hardly room enough for everyone. We needed the now departed third truck. The two that we had were badly overloaded.

We dined well that night in Chungchon, after our Marines 'requisitioned' several small pigs from neighboring farms and cooked them over open fires. We slept well, sentries posted properly even though we were within the confines of town, and perhaps were a bit sluggish and slow to react the next morning when we were surprised by the high pitched whine of an aircraft engine coming directly at us out of the rising sun. I heard it but couldn't see it, even with my hand shielding both eyes as I searched the eastern sky looking for the source of the noise. Then I saw a dark shadow flash by and something started to claw for altitude as it circled for another pass. I could see red stars on its wings. Didn't we use white? I was sure we used white! But maybe the ROK's used red. If they had any planes.

While I was trying to sort out the ownership of colored stars, Broward and Green were more businesslike. More professional. They were screaming, "Out of the trucks. Everyone out of the trucks, now." Their voices were joined by shouts from Koreans, officers and enlisted men alike, most of whom were leaping from the trucks and running for cover in the nearby ditches. By then, having decided we used white stars to identify our aircraft, I did the same. But some, as if spectators at an air show, were still standing in the stalled trucks or on the road watching as the red-starred machine turned and came back. This time there was a new sound, a staccato burst of fire-crackers audible above the wicked snarl of the engine. Then a huge fireball, screams, and bodies hurled high into the air changed the scene from chaos to pandemonium. The ground trembled, then erupted with small puffs of dirt and dust as machine gun fire reached out, sweeping the road, searching the ditch, probing into the trees, seeking contact with fragile, unprotected flesh. Then with a flash, the aerial intruder pulled up, was past us, continued to climb and disappeared to the north.

One truck was afire and we had suffered casualties. The driver of the undamaged vehicle gunned his engine and careened precariously through the roadside ditch, narrowly missing several huddled South Koreans, and sought safety under the nearby trees.

Broward dusted himself off, watched the disappearing dot in the sky, and snorted, "Yak. A dammed Yak. North Korean, but probably some Russian flying it. What the hell is going on?"

A quick headcount revealed the extent of our casualties: six dead, ten wounded. One of the dead was Starks, the kid from Kentucky, who had sat with me in the rain a few nights earlier. Starks, Army Reserve. Mission: help the South Koreans. Result: this. Death on a dusty road. Another American Reservist, Fred Slocumb from Ohio, had taken shrapnel from the explosion and was bleeding profusely from a wound in his right shoulder.

The South Koreans had a medical aid man with them, at least he had some kind of a kit to work with, and Lew and I joined him to see what we could do for the wounded. We bandaged Slocumb and stopped the bleeding. Meanwhile, Green was on the radio while Broward was trying to restore some semblance of order to the confused and milling mass of men on the road.

Broward was doing better than the Captain. Helped by the Korean officers, he established a defensive perimeter, even setting up a light machine gun in case our airborne intruder returned. He checked on the remaining truck and found it roadworthy. He ordered an inventory of our stock of supplies.

The airways, however, had gone berserk. No more calm, measured words from an unseen KMAG operator, no more reassuring platitudes, in fact, no more English at all. Nothing but Korean, shrieking, shouting, frenzied Korean. Our calls went unanswered. He switched to the backup emergency frequency and found nothing but continuous static.

Green gestured to the map as Broward and I joined him. "We are at least 20 miles from the border so this was no accidental incident, no case of mistaken identity. We were deliberately attacked by hostile aircraft. What did you say it was, Sergeant?"

"Yak, sir. Russian built fighter-bomber that the Commies used in World War II. The North Koreans have them but rumor is that Russians still fly most of them."

And this was our introduction to what became known in diplomatic parlance as a 'police action,' which in actuality was the invasion of South Korea by the North Korean People's Army. The main thrust had come, as the captain from Kaesong had correctly predicted, right through his position and on towards Seoul. Before it ended three years later, more than 50,000 Americans and several hundred thousand Koreans from both sides of the shattered border would die.

That was all in the future. The present was bad enough as we found hours later when radio communications were partially restored to normalcy. Attacks had commenced all along the line, with tanks rolling virtually unopposed into the south, and Yaks roaming the skies without hindrance. Infantry was across in waves, some on foot, others packed into trucks spouting clouds of black diesel fumes, and even a few riding trains. Most ominous of all, we finally heard from the sputtering radio, was that a large column of NKPA with numerous tanks had entered Chungchon, the town just behind us, the one we had just left.

We couldn't stay where we were. The truck was still smoldering, the wounded had been attended to, but there wasn't much we could do aside from bandaging and administering pain medication. And we didn't have much of that, having planned on receiving all of our medical supplies when we reached the 8th Division. Earlier in Chungchon, our roster had included forty-two men. Now we were down to twenty-six fit for duty, six Americans and twenty South Koreans. Minutes later, it was twenty-one as a three man South Korean infantry patrol we had sent out was joined by two marines who had taken up position on a ridge line, and all five literally 'went over the hill' and never came back.

We had the one truck, its fuel tank almost full, but the reserve petrol had been lost in the explosion.

The wounded were the problem. Stung by the desertion of his men, the South Korean major angrily upbraided his lieutenant, turned his wrath upon the marine officer, and ordered a wounded noncom to remain alongside the road with the injured men. Through the interpreter, he and Green had a furious argument; Green insisting we take them along hoping to find a medical facility somewhere down the road, the major rejecting that out of hand. I thought Green would win the argument but in the end, rank won out. Military custom. Majors outrank captains. Especially when the captain is simply an advisor.

As we pulled away, I looked back at the pathetic little band we were leaving behind. One South Korean noncom, arm in a sling, in charge of his last command, eight burned or wounded soldiers. The only injured American, Slocumb, was with us in the truck. Green had flatly told the major that we took our casualties with us, dead and wounded. Starks was there, too, wrapped in a tarp. The major had shrugged and walked away.

It was late when we started to move again and darkness overtook us before we had gone far, probably four or five miles. The truck decided to die at the same time. First it shuddered, the engine coughed, and it stopped. Silence, almost total, aside from the gentle hissing of steam from the front end of the truck. Far off, I heard that sound again, the one from the ridge. Thunder? Or artillery?

The driver was crawling under the hood with a flashlight, pointing to something at the end of a beam of light, and the interpreter told us, "He thinks that's it. Needs another to fix."

Green surveyed the anxious Americans crowded around and asked, "Any of you men know what he needs?"

A stocky young man, hell, we were all young men or had been that morning, by the name of McLemore, said, "Yeah. What he's looking at is the water pump."

"Could you get the one off the other truck?"

"If it didn't burn in the fire, I suppose I could. Seems like the fire was mostly in the rear where the gasoline was so maybe the engine ain't damaged too bad. If we got tools, I can get it."

We had tools, a whole toolbox full, and while McLemore was rummaging through it to see what he should take with him, Green assessed the situation. "We need this truck. I don't want to abandon it yet as we don't know how far we have to go before finding help. So Osten, take McLemore and another of our men with you and I'll see if the major will send along some of his people as backup. Get the pump if you can. Stay on the edge of the road, maintain silence, and be careful when you come up to the men we left behind. They still have weapons and one of them might start shooting at noises in the dark. Drop off two men about a mile down the road from here. They can cover you as you return, serve as our rear guard while you're gone. Meanwhile, we'll dig in. Got it?"

I had it, didn't like it, but had it. As a matter of fact, by the time Green had gotten to the "Osten, take McLemore," I knew what he had in mind. And I knew he had the wrong man. This was a job for the regular army. For Broward. An infantryman, one with training. When he had finished with his instructions, my silence still resounding in my ears, I said, "Yes, sir" and wondered what to do next.

What I did was choose Tommie Glick, a New Yorker with an accent as thick as the onions he professed to love on his deli sandwiches, and when the South Korean major, no argument this time, pointed to three marines and a pair of infantrymen, we started off down the road with McLemore carrying a bundle of tools and a flashlight, extra dry cell batteries, just in case. Following instructions, I dropped off the two infantrymen, watched them disappear into the weeds along the roadside ditch, and we trudged on. I hoped they wouldn't open fire on us as we returned, especially since I remembered that we hadn't arranged for a password, something suggested on page 14 of the manual.

I was no stranger to the woods, hunting, carrying a weapon, even the darkness. I hunted many times with a rifle, shotgun, and handguns. My father often gave me instructions remarkably similar to those issued by Green, things like go down this logging trail a mile or two, then follow the fire break back to the road where we'll meet. Or, go to the top of that hill, down the other side and cross the swamp to the creek, then ford it on the rocks and meet me in the little clearing where I shot that twelve-point buck four years ago, remember? I could do that. Never got lost. But, and this was the difference, at home I knew the terrain. I knew the little clearing. It was like an old friend. Been there many times. I understood the swamp. Wet and mucky, but nice. The roads were familiar ones, places I walked on and drove on. And we hunted in the daytime, not on almost moonless nights like this one. This one reminded me of pre-Halloween night, only darker, when we had been out trying to soap windows as a kid. Strangely enough, that memory made me feel better, because then, wax or soap in hand, unsuspecting neighbors reading the paper in living rooms, we were the predators, the aggressors, and we had the advantage. So stop worrying, I urged myself, and think like a predator once again.

I still worried a little, though, as we made our way back along the edge of the road, cautiously as the captain had instructed. Never while hunting, absolutely never on Halloween, had I encountered anything like this. Planes shooting at us, people hurt, tanks in our rear, things like that. Then I felt better again. Planes weren't likely to be up in the dark. Tanks we could hear. Things weren't so bad after all and, about then, we saw the dim outline of the abandoned truck ahead.

It wasn't as dark as I had thought. A decent moon was overhead, the cicadas were shrilly accompanying the crisp sound of our booted feet on the roadside gravel, and the final flickering remains of the fire that had been burning earlier had disappeared. The engine should be cool enough for McLemore to do his thing and get us out of here.

No one challenged us as we approached. They hadn't posted a sentry, all of them having fallen asleep while awaiting the arrival of an enemy that was to provide medical care for them. I guessed that was the idea, as I hadn't been in on the decision to leave them behind.

I motioned for McLemore to get started and then proceeded into the trees to seek out the noncom. I didn't know why, but I felt I should ask if there was anything we could do to help while we were there. A South Korean marine accompanied me while the rest of my little band deployed on the road. I hoped they wouldn't vanish like some of the others.

One man lay on a blanket over there, another partially under a blanket close by, and although the night was seasonably warm, it had turned cool enough so that the wounded should be covered. I bent to replace the blanket nearest me and then stepped back in shock. The eyes were open, staring at me as if pleading for help, questioning, accusing, then accepting. Accepting that the gaping neck wound, all but separating his head from the rest of his body, was beyond fixing. Beyond repair.

They were all dead, every last one. The noncom was slumped against a tree, his rifle lying uselessly across his knees, a grimace on his face and a mass of congealed blood covering the front of his light jacket. His arm had fallen from his sling as if at the last moment he had tried to protect himself from the blow that killed him.

The marine saw me looking at the wounds and explained it as best he could by drawing his bayonet and making a cutting motion, vividly demonstrating, 'here's how'. Like the killing of the helpless in a slaughterhouse.

I no longer felt like a predator of the night. The North Koreans had reclaimed the title, for I had little doubt that they had been here.

Cautiously backing away from the scene, escaping the metallic odor of spilled fresh blood, I retreated to where McLemore was busily engaged in trying to remove an object that seemed to be giving him trouble. Without elaborating, I simply said, "We've got to get out of here. Right now. Can you get the pump?"

"I can get it if this dammed guy holds the light steady. I can get it if I can see it."

"Understood." I seized the light, planted both elbows firmly on the charred fender, aimed the beam directly onto the water pump and indicated that was the way it was to be done. That way. No movement. Hold it steady. In pantomime, of course. He got the message, took the light, and did it right.

McLemore apparently knew his business. Once he could see, it took him less than ten minutes to remove the pump, pack up his tools, and we were ready to leave. Both of them still unaware of the death all around us, he handed the pump to Glick who held it high in the air for me to see, as if it were a bowling trophy. Our South Korean marines had stayed, heads swiveling back and forth as if at a tennis match, looking for trouble first one way, then the other. They knew what had happened and didn't want it to happen to them.

We started back using basic tactics I thought I remembered from a course at Camp Polk. Three of us on each side of the road, spaced twenty yards apart, me at the head of one column, McLemore in the rear and a marine in the middle. A South Korean marine headed the other column, Glick in the rear. No talking, I warned, and don't shuffle. Lift your feet. It worked reasonably well until the shots came out of the darkness, from a small hill on our left. At first I cursed myself for having forgotten to arrange the password, then I realized that the shooting wasn't coming from our men in the ditch, it was from higher up. Next I threw myself into the ditch on the right where I was joined by Glick and a couple of marines. Next I did what seemed like a sensible thing to do, a way of venting frustration and anger, to say nothing of overcoming the fear that had been building up for almost 24 hours. I raised my carbine and started firing back at the hill. I couldn't see anything else. I was suddenly aware of a clatter alongside me, a roar in my ears, and realized that firing back is contagious. The Korean marine alongside me was doing the same thing. Another rifle joined in. The racket had awakened our pickets, they had been unaware of our approach, and now one of them, startled by the firefight in his neighborhood, was infected and started discharging his weapon as well.

As suddenly as it had started, the shooting stopped. The hillside was quiet.

We waited another five minutes, nothing happened and we slipped out of the ditches and hurried back to camp to find Green and everyone else anxiously waiting, weapons loaded, expecting trouble. While McLemore was replacing the pump, I made my report and watched the captain's face become grim when I described what had happened to the wounded men. Although his distress was evident, he said nothing other than, "You did a good job, Osten. Especially on the way back when you came under fire. You handled that well." I wasn't aware that I had handled it at all. The only thing I knew was that none of us had been hit and I doubted very much that we had hit anyone else.

Fitted with a new pump, the radiator filled with foul smelling turgid water from the roadside ditch, the truck seemed eager to go once again, and it took on a personality of its own. Twenty five of us piled aboard and we were on the road once more. "Did you count the men," Green asked Broward. "We seem to have more than we had before."

"Yes, sir. We do. A couple drifted in out of the dark while we were waiting. They looked like they were on our side and the South Koreans haven't said anything so I guess they're all right."

"Strange sense of discipline," Green observed.

"Yes, sir, different from what I'm used to," was Broward's reply.

As to that personality, the truck looked us over, took note of the disparate uniforms, assorted faces, and jumble of equipment, and said, "Let's go," then proceeded to shimmy, shake, snort, and rattle down the dark road. It was overloaded, overworked, overheated, and kept going. At times, the engine roared like an enraged animal, then softened and snuffled, and we feared that it would die, but after a restorative shudder, it always recovered and plunged on, mile after mile, headed south along a maniacally twisted road, climbing ridges and rocky hills, diving into deep valleys, fording a half dozen small streams that loomed up like shining ribbons of steel as the moon struck glass smooth surfaces. Headed to safety.

The radio was working again and the news was depressing. North Koreans seemed to be everywhere. They were already in Seoul, the capital of South Korea. They were in Chungchon, they were here, there, and everywhere. Green, Broward and the major reviewed the maps and decided that the nearest NKPA were at least ten miles behind us. I wasn't so sure. Someone had killed our wounded last night and fired at us from the hillside.

"What about last night?" I asked. "Who killed the wounded?"

Marauding North Korean irregulars, Broward suggested. They didn't take prisoners. Just killed them. As to the ambush on the road? Probably the same people, he thought, figuring to take a crack at us and then when we bit back, even if our teeth weren't very sharp, they backed off and disappeared over the nearest hill, looking for softer targets.

"We're here," Green observed, pointing at the map. A finger this time, his pointer far behind in Japan. "Almost due east of Seoul, some 70-75 miles I take it. According to the reports, there are hordes of North Koreans over there. Wonju is south of us, sixty air miles below Chongchun, which has already fallen. There must be ROK units at Wonju. The major says it's a place they'll try to make a stand. If anything happens to separate us, you must keep heading south. There's an airfield there and sooner or later we should run into South Korean reserves moving up, possibly even some Americans. I'm surprised we haven't heard of American troops coming into this already. What about it, Broward, where are our men?"

"They may be a long time coming, Captain. What we have in Japan, well, it isn't much. Not trained, not combat ready, not well armed. Not much better than the South Korean army and they don't seem to be doing too well."

Broward's assessment was far from reassuring. The Captain's statement about getting separated was frightening. All along, I had been confident that we would keep going, on this truck, together, to somewhere up ahead, when we would all be hauled out of this nonsense and go home. Becoming separated would change all of that, so I made eye contact with Lew and we made a silent vow to stay together, with Broward and Green, at all costs.

The truck finally failed us. Or maybe I should say we failed it. We starved it to death. No fuel. It went as far as it could and five miles north of where the maps said Wonju should be, it coughed several times, sighed, and died. The villages we had passed had been entirely deserted. It struck me as odd that aside from the cold stares of passersby in Chungchon and the few uniformed Koreans in our party, I had hardly seen a Korean since I had been in Korea. Where were they all?

We tipped the ancient Studebaker onto its side and set it on fire, but with no fuel in the tank it didn't seem inclined to burn very vigorously. "It will delay pursuit," Green told us. I didn't think so as a tank would brush it aside as nothing more than a flake of dandruff on the collar of a dark dress suit. Infantry would walk around it as if it weren't there at all.

If their aim had been a little better, the ROK's at the roadblock three miles down the road could easily have killed us all. Once again, I found myself sprawling in the roadside ditch as bullets sailed ominously over our heads. I had been spending a lot of time in Korean ditches, much more than I had ever spent in roadside ditches back home, and had just come to realize that ditches were among the few safe places to be in Korea at that time. Our South Korean Marine lieutenant found a white handkerchief from some-where, tied it to a dried twig he found nearby and stood up waving it slowly back and forth. A bullet struck the white cloth, passed through, and then the shooting stopped. The lieutenant slowly walked up to the roadblock and five minutes later, we were all waved through the not so impressive barrier of logs, railroad ties, and a score of empty oil drums. More dandruff.

"Well," Broward mused as we walked past the staring front line infan-trymen, "Our Marine officer must have had military experience with the Japanese army. He knows how to surrender." Green had no comment, being too busy asking the interpreter to see if we could get a vehicle, any vehicle, to go back to where we had left Starks' body, alongside the burning truck. The captain was still trying to bring all of his men back home.

This is where I first met Alex Fantus. The Phantom. Not at the road-block. I doubt that Fantus has ever been at a roadblock in his life. He was at the airfield. I was to have an opportunity to see how he had earned his nick-name. It was a sobriquet no one ever used as a compliment.

He was dressed in a suit, which, under the circumstances, I thought rather odd. We were filthy, blood stained, oil encrusted, unshaven, and smelly, which he seemed to find even worse. Three civilian Koreans stalked angrily away as we approached, whatever they had been discussing had seemingly not gone well, at least from their standpoint, and Fantus stepped back when Green approached him and extended his hand. Apparently contact with an unwashed American officer was dangerous, although we had seen things much more dangerous than that in the past 72 hours. Maybe it didn't help that we had removed our insignia. Maybe he thought Green was asking for a handout on the streets of New York.

"KMAG people, you say." He said it like he didn't believe it. "Shouldn't you be at the front somewhere with your ROK unit?"

He seemed unaware that there was no front; unconcerned that we had no way of finding our unit and were lucky to have gotten this far. What he could do, he told Green with a dismissive wave of his hand as he turned to leave, was, "let the folks back in Pusan know where you are. They'll be in touch and tell you where to go."

Where he was going, it was now obvious, was to board a small blue and white Cessna sitting on the runway not more than a hundred yards away, propeller ticking over indicating it was ready for flight. He barely paused as he looked at Green and said, "I'm sorry to hear you have a casualty, but I'm not authorized to carry casualties." Green had described Slocumb's wound, now suppurating, draining pus, looked like hell. "I'm State Department, not a military ambulance. I couldn't take the responsibility if anything went wrong."

Green persisted. Fantus demurred. "No. No. Even if you sent a medic along I couldn't take the responsibility. My people would come down hard on me. After all, I came up here to arrange for provincial elections next month and now the whole thing will probably have to be delayed. I have to get back and notify my superiors of the problem."

He was worried about a postponed election when the whole country was being overrun! I was astounded. I was also disappointed because when I heard Green talk of sending a medic along, he had to have meant Lew or me. I was hoping it was me. Now it would be neither. Unless. . .unless. . .

All the while, Fantus had been edging towards the plane with Green following him, making his case. I was alongside and when Fantus turned to unlatch the aircraft door, made ready to climb aboard, Broward suddenly brushed past me and said, low enough to be inaudible to the Phantom but easily understandable for the captain and me, "Let me take the plane, sir. This guy can walk back with the rest of us while we fly Slocumb out of here." He was unbuttoning the holster of his Colt .45.

Green looked at him, then fixed Fantus in an icy stare, and shook his head, slowly, no. The Phantom climbed aboard, closed the door, the pilot revved the engine, and the plane moved out onto the field for takeoff. There were two empty seats. Not a very charitable act, I was thinking. No one waved good-bye.

"Who the hell was that guy?" growled Broward.

"Says his name is Fantus. Alex Fantus. State Department," Green responded absently, watching the white stars fading away into the distance.

"Figures," said Broward. "Most of them I've met are pricks, like this one. You should have let me take that plane, Captain. For Slocumb."

"Maybe I should have, Sergeant. Maybe I should have," answered Green walking back to where the rest of our men were waiting.

It should have taken the Cessna three hours to reach Pusan. We waited three days for instructions and heard nothing. No message, no plane, no relief. Nothing. Slocumb grew weaker, became delirious, and then a dozen North Korean tanks brushed aside the pitiful roadblock north of Wonju and shot their way into the city. We had obtained, borrowed or stolen, I never asked, two old Jeeps from the South Koreans, filled them with fuel and headed south once again, one jump ahead of the pursuing armor. Now we were down to seven Americans, one of them wounded seriously and deteriorating at an alarming rate, Broward, Green, a South Korean marine lieutenant, one noncom, and four South Korean soldiers, plus the interpreter who was still hanging in there. The South Korean soldiers apparently had decided to stick with us as no one had told them where else to go, although many others all over the country just went home, deciding that for them, the war was over, but of course, as events proved, they were wrong. It had barely begun.

Starks stayed behind, the Captain, giving up for the moment, his mission and bowing to reality. We had buried him with a Bible reading and prayers at twilight, and carefully marked the location on our maps so that we could go back some day and bring him home.

Now, suddenly, we saw Koreans. No more empty roads and vacant fields. They were everywhere. I thought they looked surly and suspicious, glaring at us with a distinct lack of courtesy my manual said we were likely to find, and were as often openly hostile as they were friendly. "Quit worrying about friendly, courtesy, respect, any of that stuff," Broward advised. "Just keep your eyes open and finger near the trigger. I suspect many of these people are infiltrators headed south to raise hell. They are as likely to shoot you as smile at you."

Our new goal was to reach Chonju, forty miles south along winding roads where rumor had it that a ROK regiment was digging in at a major road junction. Another wild rumor being circulated, one we greeted with unbridled enthusiasm, was that American troops had landed and were about to engage the enemy. This thing was about to turn around, even if we were still headed the wrong way, and we felt better that night when we stopped for a rest. We didn't know that the first American unit had already been defeated and scattered with heavy casualties and the North Korean march southward continued. The invasion rolled on. Ironically, it was July 5th and the fireworks we had been watching night after night were real, nothing like what the folks at home had been watching to celebrate Independence Day.

A day later, we encountered trouble, recognizing it from where we sat high atop a ridge looking down at a bridge below. A tangle of carts piled high with household possessions, burned vehicles, bleating oxen and sullen water buffalo all intermingled with a desperate mob of hundreds of men, women, and children formed a solid wall across the road. Everything was at a standstill. Green observed the antlike throng carefully through a pair of field glasses. "We've got to clear the bridge," he commented, more to himself than anyone in particular.

"What do you think, Sergeant?" he asked Broward.

"It's a mess, sir. A real mess. A show of force might get some of them to move but the problem is, we don't have any force," Broward told him realistically.

And he was right. Fifteen men was hardly a force adequate to do the job that had to be done down there. Yet Green did the best he could. He sent Broward to the left to set up the light machine gun which was still with us. The marine noncom went with him. "If things go wrong, fire high at first to avoid civilian casualties. Maybe just the gun itself will scare them off the bridge." He sent Lew to the right with two South Korean marines. "Same thing Garvey, fire high unless you have no choice."

Looking around, I knew who that left and my orders weren't long in coming. "Osten, take the marine officer and a couple of men and go down there and try to move those people off the bridge. Use the interpreter. He can explain we have to cross and that we want to get the children and women off while we do it so no one gets hurt. If you have to, point up here so they can see the machine gun. That might convince them." I still remember his parting words. "Don't get hurt. I don't want anyone to get hurt."

Yet someone did. Me. Others, too.

It was a hand grenade and I saw it coming. Saw what appeared to be a youth of 13 or 14 suddenly stand up from alongside an abandoned cart in the midst of several small children and a half dozen men that appeared to be far too healthy, far too smart to be hanging around a bridge with nothing to do, and detected the movement of his arm. Turning, I watched an object hurtling through the air, dimly recognized the sudden appearance of rifles from under the loose fitted shirts of several men as my brain screamed, "Grenade!" This time I wasn't quick enough to find a ditch. There wasn't any as

I was standing on the stone bridge itself and I could only watch as something flew past me, struck the ground beyond, and exploded. I was thrown forward, face down onto solid stone, and the last thing I remembered was the rapid fire of an automatic rifle just to my left where the marine lieutenant had been. That and what may have been the chatter of a machine gun.

Up on the hill, closely watching everything below, Green never hesitated. With a lone marine hanging on to the back, he gunned the engine, drove the Jeep straight down the hill at breakneck speed, roared onto the bridge, steered directly at and struck another 'civilian' who was rushing over to where I lay, his bayonet drawn, to finish what a comrade had started. Then he opened fire on several more men who had suddenly begun brandishing weapons. Broward's machine gun swept the edges of the crowd, fired high, then fired for effect, and the bridge was cleared in a matter of seconds, save for the bodies that would not be getting up.

"Had he hesitated for an instant, you were a dead man," Broward explained later. Much later. "He reacted as if someone had pushed the right button, like he'd done it before. But I know for a fact he hadn't. It was instinct. Either you've got it or you don't. The Captain, well, he has it.

"By the way," he added, "I wouldn't be surprised if some of these weren't the same men that killed our wounded back up the road. At least the same kind of men. They had bayonets on them and looked like the kind that work best with knives in the dark. But there's a lot less of them now. At least a dozen less."

I wasn't seriously injured, although I was unconscious for more than an hour. I did have a three inch gash in my left leg, probably shrapnel from the grenade, and a contusion on the back of my head where something had struck me below the steel helmet. A small cut on the left upper arm completed the damages, and bandages, aspirin, and rest seemed to be what I needed most. Which was fortunate as that was about all we could provide.

The South Korean lieutenant hadn't been as lucky. He opened fire when he saw the grenade, survived the blast, and then died when several shots hit him before Green arrived. But by drawing attention to himself and momentarily diverting the bayonets from me, he had given Green time to make his wild dash onto the bridge and save me. To save my life, to be blunt about it.

Broward apologized for his earlier remark about the white flag. "Maybe he knew how to surrender," he admitted ruefully," but somebody sure as hell taught him how to fight. Maybe he had that instinct, too. Like Green."

And although I wasn't hurt badly, the blow to the head made me dizzy, made me lose track of what was going on, and I felt like I was driving along a country road in thick fog, Dad telling me to look out for the deer. "They jump out in front of you," he warned, "before you know it. They can wreck the car." I always thought it would be worse for the deer. And with fog on my mind, I wasn't sure that what I saw one day was a high flying F-84, identified, I think, by Broward. American, he said. Then later I think I heard him say, "The radio is dead." Then, was it him or was it the Captain?, said "We're almost out of fuel. Another ten miles and we've had it." It must have been the Captain because Broward said, "There isn't any to be found, so we'll walk when that happens."

And then the cut on my leg started to hurt, the bandage turned green, and I couldn't understand why no one changed it. Or how about the one on Slocumb? My God, his whole body looked green and he smelled something awful. Infection. Or was that me? Or both of us? And then I vomited several times and felt better. The fog lifted although I still felt hot.

And then the next morning, our Jeep motionless while Green and a marine reconnoitered the road ahead, Tommie Glick was there and I didn't want Tommie. I could smell the onions although he had no onions. There weren't any onions here. I wanted Lew. I missed Lew. Missed hearing about his Red Cross girl, how he would date her when we got back to Japan, and what we would do when we got back to school. And cursed Tommie when he lied to me, when he told me that Lew was dead, that Lew had taken a bullet in the chest back at the bridge, had hung on for two days and then died. Body buried back down the road because we had no room in the Jeep. Marked on the map. And that I had been "out of it for three days" and never knew that Lew was gone. He kept on lying and I cursed him again and again and then Broward came back and told me Lew was gone and I knew that was the truth. If Lew was still here, he would be with me and he wasn't. Poor Tommie. Poor Lew. Poor dead Lew. It shouldn't have been this way. That wasn't the way this was supposed to end. But then it never is supposed to be that way, is it?

My fever broke and I knew that I wanted to go home.

I got there. On July 22nd, we saw a vehicle pulled across the road ahead of us. Guns bristled from both sides of the road. Looking through his binoculars, Green said, "Damn. Americans." There was a white star on the door, another on the hood.

It was an advance party from the 25th Infantry Division, redeployed from Japan, taking up positions in what was to be known as the Pusan perimeter. The beachhead. They looked at us in wonderment, found it hard to believe that we had traveled so far, so few with so little, almost a Churchillian journey. They traversed, they whispered, the Korean peninsula from the 38th parallel to the tip, almost the whole length north to south. They passed us through speedily to the nearest medical facility, an army hospital, where Slocumb received prompt treatment, much belated, but prompt in the proper hands, and made it. Both he and I were sent on to Japan for further care, but I didn't need much. Mainly something to eat, a change of dressings, and some new kind of drug called penicillin. A South Korean marine, wounded at the same bridge as Lew and I, died minutes after he reached safety. Perhaps this was his home.

Oh, yes, Fantus. Officially, we were told that he had been so busy that it had been impossible for him to pass on messages from troops in need. There simply had been so many messages. One couldn't handle them all.

Green protested, vigorously and repeatedly, that the least we could have expected from a fellow State Department representative, as that's what he was, and that's what KMAG was, was that he pass on our location to the proper authorities. And that he not take off with empty seats when we could have used them to evacuate our wounded man. What was the problem, we were told, your man didn't die, did he? And of course, Slocumb hadn't died. But Lew had. What if Green had selected Lew to go back with Slocumb? You see, that could have made a difference. It didn't matter. They told Green to forget it, that he had earned considerable recognition in accomplishing what he had done, in bringing as many men back as possible from trying circumstances. Good things were added to his file. He would go far in the army, because now he was back in the army. He did, of course, go far. All the way to four stars. He got the first of numerous medals, and both Green and Fantus went on with their careers.

I recovered fully and went home. Green visited me several times in the hospital, never talked about what we had been through, just talked about my future: medicine, marriage, kids, all that sort of stuff, keeping the conversation away from the hurtful loss of a good friend. Steering it away from his own disappointment, for no matter what the War Department may have thought, he considered the failure to bring all of his men home a personal defeat.

It was more than that, though, as Broward told me as we waited at Haneda for the flight to take me out of Japan. "He wants to go home, too. Misses his kids. He could have rotated out of here earlier in the year but the

Captain stayed on, hoping to help the South Korean Army become better before he left. He did, believe it or not. He did help. It wasn't good enough, but it was better. Then he stayed on a little longer to work with the reservists this summer. He'll stay longer, until they tell him they don't need him anymore."

I was interested. "I didn't know the Captain had children."

"Yeah, twins. A boy and a girl. Cute as all get out. He carries pictures with him wherever he goes."

"What about you, Sergeant?"

"No, no kids, none I can speak of."

"What about the Army?"

"You mean am I staying in? Hell, yes. This is my home, my life. It's what I do. I'm a soldier. I'll stay here as long as they need me and then go somewhere else."

True to his word, he stayed, earning his lieutenant's bars after a battlefield promotion while helping take Pork Chop Hill for the third, or was it the fourth, time, three years later.

I learned a lot of things in Korea. About myself, about Green, about the nature of man. About villainy. One thing I had promised never to forget was that Alex Fantus could not be trusted. Not then. Not now.

When I opened my eyes, he was standing there, looking down at me. I must have dozed off and I came awake as the wheels of the Gulfstream touched down smoothly, with just enough of a thump to waken me. He said nothing, waited for the plane to stop rolling, and then moved on to the door, obviously expecting to be the first off when the ramp was lowered.

Bath was next. "A nap, Osten. That's good. I often wish I could sleep on a plane, but I don't have the luxury. I always need the time to catch up on my work. There's always so much to do." Poor overworked public servant.

The door opened and cold air rushed in. Fantus was already out of sight as Bath stepped to the top of the ramp and pulled his overcoat tightly around him. I buttoned mine.

He turned slightly as we went down the steps. "You and I will take a limousine over to the General's place. As I said, Alex has other matters to attend to and will try to meet us at the hotel later."

It seemed as if the General and Fantus had not yet fully made their peace.

# 3

The doorman, wearing a uniform as resplendent as those seen for a short time at the Nixon White House, looked us over, picked up his phone, dialed a number, gave our names and listened for a moment, and then led us to the elevator, even pushing the button for us and stepping aside as we entered. He acted as if he expected a tip. He didn't get one. Fifteen floors and ten seconds later, ears popping along the way, we stepped off into the ornate hallway, a score of blue and white plaster cherubs greeting us from up where the ceiling met the walls, a permanent smile fixed on their faces. Carefully wood-framed paintings, of much better quality than anything found at the Pan Union offices, dotted the short hallway leading to the solid white French doors where the General's aide, Montgomery, was waiting. I glanced again at the six foot tall bronze statue of the flag raising on Mt. Suribachi guarding the General's door. Montgomery glanced at the slight bulge in Bath's jacket, taking note of a possible threat to his employer. Montgomery had been with the General since Vietnam, apparently intending to stay.

The apartment looked the same. Lavish and comfortable, two walls in the study were filled floor to ceiling with books, mostly history and classics, some novels, and all had been read, but some hadn't been opened for years. At one end was the same familiar mahogany desk, like Bath's, gleaming with a high gloss and the top devoid of any object, a high backed leather executive chair, and incongruously, to one side, a computer, the monitor calling attention to itself by continuing to scroll through a colorful pattern of dancing dots. Technology had invaded the inner sanctum.

Green had been standing with his back to us, hands clasped behind him, looking out a window that I knew presented a stunning view of Central Park. When he turned to face us, I was shocked by how he had aged. He was still the tall, erect, well dressed man that he had always been, cleanly shaved, hair carefully cut and styled, casually but expensively dressed, but it was his face, the lines in his face and his eyes, that shocked me. In the two years since I had last seen him, he must have aged no less than twenty.

That last time, at a publisher's reception to introduce his ghost written memoirs, his eyes were flashing with laughter, his face glowing with good health, his arm around Kendra, his beautiful daughter, Ken's twin, and I thought at the time, the best looking couple in the room. I envied him. I wanted Kendra to be with me.

Don't laugh. It can happen. Man 54, all right, almost 55, falls in love with a woman, 38. It can happen. Should have happened earlier, years earlier, but there was always something, some kind of complication. The underlying problem was that she was the General's daughter. I was worried that he wouldn't approve. Like I said, don't laugh, but that's the kind of a person I am. Or was, because I'm still evolving. At any rate, Kendra was still unmarried, had survived a couple of romances that went awry, and was as smart and beautiful today as she had been back in college when I first realized how smart and beautiful she had become. I had hoped she would have found an excuse to be here tonight, she lived less than a mile away, but there was no sign of her.

That night, after seeing them together in the same room, I thought, "Lord, she's gorgeous. My God, he looks better than I do." Not now. Looking at him as he extended his hand in greeting, I realized that he looked terrible. Was he ill? And what about that tear in his eye? I'd never seen him cry, but what else could it be? And why?

His grip, however, was as firm as ever, and when I glanced out of the window to see what he had been looking at, I saw nothing except the street lights, traffic lights, and headlights down on Central Park South.

When I said, "Jordan, it's good to see you again. It's been far too long," he nodded in agreement and then suddenly became aware that Bath was standing across the room. Green didn't acknowledge his presence but simply said, "Let's sit, shall we?"

I settled into a comfortable fabric chair while the General sat opposite me on a matching couch, across from a coffee table. Bath perched himself self-consciously on a straight backed hardwood chair that I recognized as an old trophy from the General's first duty assignment at Ft. Hood many years before.

Tilting his head in Bath's direction, Green asked, "He tell you about Ken or at least what they think they know about Ken?"

"About the note? Yes, they've told me about the note. I'm hoping you can tell me more."

"I don't know much more than that either, Mike. Maybe Bath does by now. His people are supposed to be following the situation, hour by hour, isn't that right Bath?" Challenging. Hostile. Not at all like the friendly General I had usually found in this same room.

Bath didn't seem disturbed by the cool reception, but he didn't have much to add. "Nothing new, General. Magellan is monitoring all communications with Bangkok and if he hears anything, he'll be in touch with me at once. Meanwhile, I've had Fantus contact friends at the UN; he's there now, hoping to come up with new leads. A few things have come up in the last couple of days that need to be pursued."

The General caught Montgomery's eye with an unseen signal and the aide immediately moved to the wet bar where he poured several inches of bourbon into an empty glass, added two ice cubes, did the same with scotch, and brought the refreshments back on a small tray, placed the bourbon before the General, handed the scotch to Bath, and looked questioningly at me. "Diet something, I told him." Two reasons. Weight, number one, and two, I wanted a clear head in case Kendra showed up later.

The General sipped his drink with obvious relish and then peered over the rim of the glass, fixing his gaze on Bath. "I've never liked the Phantom, Bath. Never. Never trusted him!"

"I know, General, I know. But he's been a valuable resource to us over the years. Has a lot of contacts and I think he'll be able to help us on this project as well."

Green lowered the glass thoughtfully and stared at his bookcases. "Project. You called it a project. I suppose you've come up with a name by now. You always have a name for your projects."

Bath seemed pleased to be able to respond affirmatively. "Yes, we do have a name. We're calling it 'Operation Patient.' We've already opened the file."

The General opened his eyes in mock astonishment and asked, "Blue file? Or gold?"

"Gold, General. You know it can't go blue until after the committees have approved it. Until then, it stays gold, unless it has to be upgraded to red. So far, that hasn't been necessary. We hope it never becomes necessary."

I wasn't on any of the committees, although the General was. Had been for years. I didn't know which one or how many or just what he did there, but he hadn't fully retired, that much I did know.

"Operation Patient. Clever name, Bath. Must have taken quite a while to come up with it." The General took another small sip, watched as Bath took a substantial gulp, and then turned to me. "Mike, I'm glad you're going to Bangkok. If Ken is over there, bring him back."

I hadn't told him I was making the trip so I considered the possibilities. Bath had called him before we left Washington. I didn't think so. Fantus had called him once he got off the plane, when he disappeared while we drove over here in the limousine. But the General didn't like Fantus, did he? Or Magellan had called from the communications room. But why? Or Green had Bath's office bugged. I decided to toss that out and concentrate on the other three.

First though, I decided to play it straight. "Jordan, if I'm going to be of any help in clearing up this mystery, I need a lot more information than I have. Bath says you've seen the note from Ken. Was it his handwriting? Are you absolutely certain of that?"

"I identified it as his handwriting, if that's what you mean. So did the experts. I called in army experts immediately and gave them old documents to compare and they said, beyond any doubt, the note was in Ken's handwriting. Not only that, it was recent."

"Bath says it was given to someone in Vientiane. Does that indicate he's in Laos? Is he a prisoner? Are any American POW's held in Laos to the best of your knowledge?"

Strangely, the General was avoiding eye contact. Was it because there were tears again, tears that he didn't want me to see, or was there something else? "Mike, you know that his helicopter went down in Vietnam, so he couldn't have been held there initially. But there have been rumors for years that the Vietnamese moved prisoners around from one place to another, so I suppose it's possible that he could have been taken to Laos if he actually survived the crash. We have no hard evidence one way or the other. Just rumors, most of which have proved to be false."

"Most of which have been false?" I responded. "I was under the impression that all of the rumors had been false."

The General suddenly leaned forward, more animated than he had been since our arrival. "Let me tell you this, see what you think about it. Have you ever heard of Operation Pocket Change? Not one of Bath's operations, but screwed up as badly as some of his." Bath cringed but remained silent.

I shook my head. No, I hadn't heard the name.

Green continued. "It involved the caves and camp at Nhommarath." Another place I'd never heard of. "Well, back in 1980, the CIA had reports from an informer that Americans were being held there. Reports from what was considered to be a reliable source. They talked to people in the Pentagon and bumblers from the two organizations decided to check it out. After deciding that there was something to the story, they started to plan a rescue operation. You see, spy satellites had confirmed the presence of a camp right where the informant had told them it would be. Then they sent in a reconnaissance mission to look the place over and the idiots didn't include a single American in the party. Not a one. The hired hands they sent in came back and said, 'Yes, there's a camp there. With prisoners. Probably Americans among them.'" He paused and stared at Bath as if needing to compose himself.

"You want to tell him what happened next, Bath?" When Bath remained silent, the General went on. "So they knew there was a camp right where they had been told it was. They knew Americans might be in it. And you know what? Not a single solitary soul in our government, looking at all that information, had enough guts to make the hard decision to go in there with enough firepower to take it over. Instead, the usual intra-agency wrangling took over, everyone recalling the egg on our face when Carter's desert raid to free the hostages in Iran backfired, and no one willing to say 'Let's do it. Let's go look for our boys.' While they were all sitting there wringing their hands and agonizing over this terrible decision they were being asked to make, someone naturally leaked the information to the media, and that great American institution, the free press, jumped on it, printed the whole story, and that blew away any chance we had of rescuing our men. End of story. Or did I leave something out, Bath?"

Bath still didn't seem to have anything to add.

"No, I guess I didn't. That was about the whole story. Except for the broken hearts of families that may have lost a chance to see loved ones again instead of living in limbo, like they still are five years later. The experts screwed up. Too many people worried about their piss-ant careers and not enough concern for their countrymen." Green slumped on the couch and took another small sip of his drink. The glass was still more than half full. Bath's was empty and Montgomery attentively refilled it for him.

Interesting story. I'd lied when I said I'd never heard of Operation Pocket Change. I had heard some of it before, but I wanted to see what version the General would pass on. It sounded like the right one. And he'd added details I hadn't known.

There were still a few things I wanted to know, because they had never been clear to me before. "Where was this camp, General?"

"Not far from the Laotian-Thai border, maybe 40-50 miles across the Mekong. The camp's still there, but it's unlikely they've kept any Americans locked up in it after reading all about the place in the *New York Times*. That doesn't mean they didn't move our Americans to other camps, some of them near by. We don't know, have never gotten another good lead since, and probably won't. What bothers me is that my own son may have been in that camp or someplace like it. I never gave it a thought at the time because we thought Ken was dead. Now, I just sit here and wonder. While I've been wondering about it, I kept thinking, why in the hell doesn't someone go and take a look?"

"And you want that someone to be me? You flatter me, General. I'm not sure I'm capable of doing what the CIA and Pentagon couldn't do. I don't have their resources, for starters."

Green stood and quickly strode to the wet bar, that was more like the General I knew, poured his unfinished drink into the sink, filled his glass with water, added an ice cube, removed a pill from a small bottle standing on the shelf in front of him, swallowed it with a mouthful of water, and had an answer for me. "You're better than they are. You're smarter, tougher, and not afraid to make hard decisions. You can do what they couldn't do."

He was still flattering me. Excessively. It wasn't that I disagreed with the smarter, tougher, and able to make hard decisions part, but it was clear to me that I still didn't have their resources.

Bath took care of that. "And he'll have us," he added.

The General made a face and said, "Yeah, I almost forgot, he'll have you." To me he repeated, "You'll have them. Pan Union – what do you call it now, Bath? Pan Union what?"

"Pan Union Trade Association."

"Right. Mike, you'll have them working with you. With Fantus and Bath by your side, what could go wrong? You hardly need any other resources."

The idea of Fantus and Bath at my side was hardly reassuring. On the other hand, their resources could be of considerable help. Meanwhile, I continued to ask myself why the General wasn't as enthusiastic as I had expected him to be, as I would be if I had just learned that my long lost son was still alive. Was it because he didn't believe it, had suspected it all along or, and I could hardly forgive myself for even thinking it, was sorry that he was still among the living?

I asked, "Jordan, let's assume for a moment that the handwriting was Ken's."

"Is Ken's, not was. Is. Proven beyond any doubt," he interrupted, making the point vigorously.

"As you say, it's Ken's handwriting. But what about this other man or, for that matter, the two other men that seem to have come into view, both claiming to have some kind of an illness that only I can treat? Has Bath told you about them and the claim that I treated someone by the name of Lee Duc Than nearly twenty years ago? Now we have two Lee Duc Thans, which doubles the mystery as far as I'm concerned. All the more puzzling, frankly, because I can't recall the man or the incident."

Green was looking at a melting ice cube in the bottom of his glass, thought about drinking the small amount of water that had come free, and mused, "That is an odd thing, isn't it? Ken talking about a sick man, someone else claiming to be the same man, both wanting to talk to you. Only you. Why do you think that is, Mike?"

Why did I think that was? I had no idea why that was. "General, if this man is really Lee Duc Than, either one of them for that matter, then why are we sitting here talking about him? Why don't the real spooks go and get him, like the CIA, Army Intelligence, someone like that? After all, the guy is a gold mine if he is who he says he is. Look at what we know about his credentials. Defector to the north in the middle of the war. Why? He could tell us a lot about what was going on in the South Vietnamese government when he left. Then, working in the north, he had access to all of the data they collected on us. That could be interesting. Next, he was in reeducation camps for South Vietnamese prisoners, events that we still know too little about, and finally, in what could be the biggest coup of all, he could bring information about missing American prisoners back with him and set a lot of minds to rest. As I said, why are we sitting here talking about him fifteen floors above Central Park when we should just go and get him? Using everyone's resources, of course," I added to mollify Bath who appeared to be ready to argue my premise.

Mollified or not, he had an answer. "Deniability." He made it sound like a virtue. "They don't want to be seen thrashing about the jungle looking for a needle in a haystack, looking foolish if they don't find it, and looking worse if they, as the General put it earlier, screw it up."

"So it's OK if we look foolish or screw it up?"

Bath wasn't sure he had meant to imply that, and hastened to add, "No, of course not. But if Pan Union is looking, the administration can just say it's a private foundation poking around. They couldn't say that with the CIA. Besides, they don't know where to look."

For the first time he looked smug, as if he might really know something. "And you do?"

Still smug, grinning, he said, "We have some ideas, yes. Pretty good ideas."

"But why me? What do I bring to the table?"

The General broke in. "Mike, Lee Duc Than brought you to the table. Personally, I'm glad he did even if I don't know why. There must be something to what he claims: that you treated him medically once before. No one could make that up. Maybe you'll find an old record, old notes, something to help you remember, but over and above that, there's another thing that you've forgotten. You know Ken. You can identify him if he's alive. And, God forbid, if he's sick, and after fifteen long years in a prison camp, we have reason to fear that he may be, you could treat him in an emergency as well.

"Another thing, Bath's talk of deniability is real. Everyone knows that you travel a lot, have been in South East Asia a half dozen times in the past three years on legitimate business trips. In and out of Bangkok, Kuala Lumpur, Singapore, Hong Kong, all over, so another trip won't arouse any suspicions. They also know what you do. You look for plants and trees to use in making drugs, so if they see you poking around the countryside, even in the jungle, that wouldn't be out of character, would it?"

In other words, if I ran around looking for a needle in a haystack, they wouldn't think I was suspicious, just crazy.

"Instead of going to Malaysia this trip, you could change your itinerary and manage to show up in Thailand and Laos, whatever the case may be, and see what you find." The General decided to drink the last of his melted cube and leaned back as he did so. "You could do it, couldn't you?"

I could do it, but how had he learned of my trip in the first place?

As if reading my mind, Bath said, "I called the General and told him you might be going to Malaysia, as your associate told me."

Ah, yes, Burrows. Well, if Everett had gotten involved, I'd really give him something to do. It was clear that I was going to need transit permits for me, my equipment, and anyone I intended to take along. Someone else would have to go to Malaysia, we'd need clearance to remove soil and plant samples from the host country, and then to return them to the United States. We'd need new travel documents, tickets, and a budget. Everything worked on a budget. Sure, I could go to Thailand, Laos or any place on earth. It just took a little planning. Let Burrows do it while I did what the General had suggested – look through old records to see what I could find concerning the elusive Lee Duc Than.

But I still wasn't satisfied with the Ken Green story. I went back to it.

"General, have you ever had any reason, any information at all, that Ken might have survived the crash? Anything in the past fifteen years?"

There was just the slightest hesitation before he replied, but I knew him well enough to detect it, to know that it was there. "Mike, we've talked about the crash before, you and me. I didn't want to believe that he was dead and, at first, I was in denial. I read the reports from eyewitnesses, then talked to one of them myself, a fellow pilot who was within 100 yards of Ken's ship when he was hit. He saw the chopper go straight down in flames and saw the impact. Everyone agreed, 'No chance of survivors.' One Huey circled the site for at least ten minutes and the gunners hammered Cong troops trying to get at the wreck. All the while, the plane was burning black smoke over the site and then a huge explosion rocked the area, tossed the second chopper about and the pilot was forced to leave. There was no sign of any survivor and when the crew of the second ship looked back, they saw the Cong swarming over the area and dancing with glee. The second pilot was furious. He told me, 'If I'd of had another ounce of fuel, I would have gone back and they'd have danced in hell forever.' But that wouldn't have helped Ken.

"The next day, three gunships went back and one actually landed at the site. No bodies. None. No Ken, no sign of the five other men who had been on board. That's all we know." He had gone over to the window again and was once more looking at a darkened Central Park. I could see a few lights illuminating the deserted walkways; no one walked in Central Park at night and there were fewer headlights in view than before. It was getting late.

Interesting. He had told me what happened, again, exactly as I'd heard it before. But he hadn't answered my question.

Resuming his seat on the couch, he continued. "You know most of what happened after that. His mother cried for weeks. Kendra was inconsolable. You know how close she and Ken had always been. What I've never told you is how it was with Ken and me, with us as a family. Especially in those days leading up to his entry into the Army.

"You can remember the Sixties. Ken was up at Columbia where it had become fashionable to march in protest against the war in Vietnam. Not only to march but burn flags, throw bottles, scream, break windows, occupy buildings, all that sort of stuff. Smoke pot and drink. Ken was no exception. But he had his own peculiar problem. Me. I was in uniform. Worse, I was an officer. One of the mad dog killers his peers considered the worst of all. He began to tell his mother how ashamed he was to have me as a father, began to act as bad as the rest of the activists up on campus and got in trouble. First came the bad grades, then the warnings, then what his mother felt was excessive drinking, and finally, suspension.

"Kendra was at Brown then, out of town, but when she was home, the two of them argued, sometimes vehemently. Their mother became distraught, her jangled nerves sent her to a half dozen doctors looking for relief, and she didn't know what to do. Kendra pointed this out to Ken and, although he seemed concerned about the effect his actions were having on her, it didn't stop him. He seemed to have a mission, a one track mind. Stop the war!

"I had no idea how bad things were because I was in Europe. Oh, sure, I got letters from my wife and even more often from Kendra, but they were circumspect about Ken and his problems. I sensed that something was wrong but I didn't know what it was. Neither one wanted to worry me. They wanted to spare me needless anxiety and that was typical of my women. To protect me, no matter at what cost to themselves. Leah. . ."

The General had rarely referred to his wife by her name since her death so I considered it significant that he did now. Old memories. Difficult memories. After a long pause, he resumed his anguished story.

"Leah and I talked by phone from time to time and at first, what I thought she was telling me wasn't anything I hadn't heard from fellow officers or from enlisted men for that matter. A lot of these kids that were in the streets protesting the war were actually protesting against having to go to the war. They liked it in school, liked the soft life they had, someone else paying for an education that didn't seem to matter to them, and that they had grown so soft that they wouldn't trade it for the roughness of serving in the military. Yes, maybe even a touch of cowardice entered my mind. What I thought they wanted was a draft deferment, and if they got one because luckily drawing a high lottery number, figured out a way to get a 4F physical excuse, or were just able to extend college deferments, they would shut up and let us get on with a dirty war that none of us wanted either. Wishful thinking, Mike. Wishful thinking. The angry young men of that generation were just warming up. They wanted more, but most of all, I suspect that we had simply spoiled them. Given them everything. All of the material goods anyone could want, all of the comforts, the education and the toys and cars and hula hoops, anything they had their hearts set on. Except maybe the love, the time, that we should have spent with them. I know now, I knew then for God's sake, that I was gone too often. Too many assignments, too many places, too many days and nights away from home leaving my wife with two growing, smart little kids and not doing enough parenting of my own. But being gone, being in the army, serving my country, all of that was important to me, Mike. I think you know that. Don't you?"

Of course I knew that. That's why he had become a General. He didn't wait for an answer so none was needed.

"You know, the amazing thing is, Ken did well in college even though he missed so many classes. He apparently was interested in geology, took courses in oil exploration, mineralogy, physics and did well enough to make his mother proud. Me, too, naturally. Then on a Tuesday afternoon, with three years of college credits in the bank, less than a year to his degree, he walked in, an eye blackened as if someone had hit him, and told Leah he had enlisted in the Army. She was shocked beyond belief. She had been forced to watch him do crazy things for almost two years, but this was the craziest of all. At that time, we still didn't know he'd been booted out of Columbia.

"Naturally, I wasn't home. Still in Europe. I hadn't been in Vietnam at all up to that point but apparently Ken and the others didn't differentiate between one part of the world and another. To them, if you wore the uniform, you were the enemy. And that's why Leah was crying. She couldn't understand why Ken had suddenly decided to put on a uniform. It certainly wasn't because he wanted to be like me, she said, in a barely concealed rebuke. That hurt, because by then I had decided maybe she was right. Maybe I had neglected my responsibilities as a father, but the best I could do right then was to see if Kendra would talk to Ken and see what this was all about. She was the only one he had been willing to talk to all along anyhow. She tried, I guess, but it didn't do any good.

"But you know something, Mike? I wasn't sorry he had signed up. Might do him some good, I thought. Maybe some discipline might do him some good."

Apparently responding to another silent signal, Montgomery poured the General a small glass of Martel. I joined him. Bath, who had been silently listening all this time, offered his glass for a refill of scotch and got it.

"He was gone before I ever got home. Off to Ft. Rucker where he learned to fly helicopters after his basic. One advantage of being an Army officer is that you have friends everywhere and I relied on them to keep me posted on his progress. He learned to fly readily enough and, in fact, was very good in the air. But aloof, they all told me. Stayed by himself. Excellent ratings, graduated, received advanced training, spent a month or so in

Hawaii doing search and rescue flights up in the mountains, and was sent to Vietnam.

"Fate had it that I was sent to Vietnam no more than a month later. I'd been there earlier, years earlier, when the French were still trying to hold onto it as a possession, but that was as an observer. Now I went to Saigon as an intelligence officer," I noticed that Bath was listening even more intently at this point, "and decided that I should make every effort to get together with Ken. I knew Leah would feel better if I did. Hell, I would feel better if I did. After several tries, he was either on a flight, away from his post or I was tied up when he was free, we did arrange to meet and he showed up at a good restaurant in Saigon where we had dinner. There was tension in the air, and that first meeting was strained, but we made a second date, and he came again. Then a third time and that time, he started to laugh at a story I told and he told one that made me laugh and I thought, 'there's nothing wrong with this kid. He's going to be all right.' Until then, I hadn't asked him why he had suddenly decided to join the army and when I did, it was a mistake. His face turned red, he was clearly angry, got angrier, downed his drink, swore a couple of times, and suddenly leaped to his feet, knocked over a couple of chairs, and went running out of the place. I went after him, but how can a colonel go running down the street after a man half his age? With less than half the rank? He caught a taxi and was gone. I never saw him again and he wouldn't come to the phone when I called. What I heard next, a week later, was that he had gone down in flames. They told me, and I confirmed it as you know, that there were no survivors. That was, what?, fifteen years ago."

I had heard some of the story, Kendra's version. But there were things the general had just told me that even Kendra couldn't have known. Not surprisingly, what bothered Green most of all was the violent outburst his son had exhibited on the occasion of their last meeting.

"Mike, I've been haunted by his running out of the restaurant. Haunted for 15 years. It's a curse hanging over my head. Was it his hatred for me all coming to the surface at once, hatred because I left him alone so often when he was a child? Because I wasn't a good enough father, though God knows I tried to be one. When it was safe to do so, I always took the family along. Like to London, a year in Stockholm, even an assignment in Japan. And there were times I spent a year or more right here in the states, home almost every night like every other father. I played with the twins when I could, provided for them, gave them my love unconditionally, prayed for them, but even after all that, I must have failed. Failed my son at least. Because in the end, he just ran out on me and left me wondering what I had done wrong. I've never understood it and I've never gotten over it."

How many fathers, this very evening, were asking these same questions all over America? All over the world? That's the problem with being parents. All of them are amateurs with the first child or, in this case, the first two. The only training you get is on the job training. With twins, it may be even harder. One turned out angry and running. Running away to disappear. The other turned out loving and stayed. Continued loving. I wanted to say, "Hell, Jordan, one out of two isn't bad. That's a better batting average than most." But the General was a perfectionist so what I said was, "It's hard to figure, Jordan. One never knows." I could get away with a platitude because I knew he wouldn't be listening, absorbed as he was in his own thoughts.

He hadn't quite finished. "It killed his mother, you know." I knew that's what he had always believed. "They said she died of a leaking heart valve. Heart failure. Medical BS. She died of a broken heart. Torn in two when she lost her son." He'd said 'medical BS' as if he blamed all other doctors, not me.

He was having trouble sitting still now and was suddenly up once again, standing at the window. This was a far more agitated Jordan Green than I was used to. Maybe having a son return from the dead was unsettling. If true, I suppose it could be.

Suddenly he turned to Montgomery and said, "Monty, would you please show Mr. Bath into the next room? I must talk to Dr. Osten alone." He emphasized the 'alone.'

Startled, Bath rose to his feet, picking up his half empty glass of scotch. "We won't be long, Bath. Just some private business. Monty will make you comfortable. Monty, please see that Mr. Bath's glass is freshened. More scotch. More ice." I knew Bath could have all of the scotch that he wanted. The General never drank any, kept it around solely for the occasional 'barbarian,' his word, who came to visit.

There are people you think you know well and then suddenly they act in a way that makes you wonder if you had known them at all. That's what happened when the door closed behind Montgomery and Bath, leaving Green and me alone in his study. First, there was that suspicion of a tear in his eye once again. Then there was the sudden anger, the shock of having him slam a fist against the desktop, watching as he strode across the room to remove a book from a waist high shelf. Several small pieces of paper were inserted, as if he had marked pages he had been reading.

He stood there with the book in his hand, neither opening it nor looking at the notes that seemed to be crying for attention. "Mike, I want you to bring that dammed kid of mine home." He seemed to have forgotten that the 'kid' was now 38 years old. "Drag him back if you have to. I allowed him to play his crazy games 20 years ago but I don't have that luxury anymore. I had learned to accept his death. I did accept it. Accepted all that went with it. But not now. If he's alive, he must come home. Now. No delays. I won't accept anything less."

He was talking in riddles. "Accept what, Jordan? His death? You don't have to accept that if he's alive. But we still have to find him to prove it."

He looked at me as if I was the one talking in riddles. "No, Mike. You misunderstood." With both hands on my shoulders, he looked at me from inches away and I realized he was strong enough to shake me like a rag doll if that was his intent. "I don't care about Ken. He could stay dead for all I care. But we need him!"

Jordan Green had risen to four star rank in our Army, written, all right, with help, a moderately successful book, was writing another, served on numerous corporate boards, lived in a handsome Manhattan apartment, seemed to have more than enough income, some of which may originate from the Pan Union organization, and was in good health, so I couldn't understand what he meant by needing a son who had disappeared 15 years earlier. He might miss him, love him, want to see him, but I couldn't see the General needing him. Accordingly, I asked, "Jordan, who needs him? Who needs Ken?"

He released me and stepped back abruptly. "You don't know? She hasn't told you? I was certain she had. That's why you didn't ask about her. You didn't even know."

He had to be talking about Kendra. I hadn't talked to her for three weeks, maybe more. Busy, her office said, when I called. Out, another time. Not available, still again. And no letters, cards or notes even though I'd written a half dozen of my own and sent them from wherever I happened to be at the time.

"No, Jordan, no one has told me a thing. Why don't you tell me?"

Well, one thing about the General that hadn't changed over the years was his tendency to tell it like it was. He never pulled punches. He didn't now. "She's dying, Mike. Has less than a month to live, the doctors say, unless we find that damned brother of hers. He's her only real hope."

It was as if he had struck me in the stomach. Numbed, for a moment I wasn't certain that I had heard him correctly. A 'month to live'? Who had a month to live? He'd said 'she,' but did he mean Kendra or had his mind wandered and he was actually thinking of his wife, who had died years ago? It couldn't be Kendra, thirty-eight year old Kendra. Not her. And yet I'd been in medicine long enough to recognize that when people start talking about months to live, someone has made a mistake, is perpetrating a hoax or is critically ill. But not Kendra, not the girl with the golden hair and the bright smile, not the one I jokingly called from Dublin less than a month earlier and jokingly told, "I'll be in New York in less than four weeks and we'll go out to dinner. Maybe, if you're lucky, I'll try to make an honest woman out of you yet."

I was still wondering what I had committed myself to and whether I had the courage to find out. I still remembered her laughter, could see the corners of her eyes crinkle in delight, listened as she said, "Really. You'd be willing to do that? Do you think you know how?"

Did I? Did I know how? Did I even know what it was I had promised? At any rate, she made it easy by adding, "Dinner. It's a date," and not pursuing the honesty question any further, allowed me more time to find the answer. I had been working on it ever since, and now this.

Green saw my confusion, may have even understood my problem because I had never known what Kendra had told him of our relationship and said, "You're shocked. I can understand that. We all were. Everyone who knows Kendra is in shock."

"I'm more than in shock. I'm stunned, Jordan. What is this all about? What is this month to live? How can anyone come up with a figure like that? I talked to Kendra less than a month ago. We made a date for dinner for this weekend. She sounded fine, she laughed, joked, and was her usual self. Now you're telling me that she's ill? Worse than ill?"

He suddenly seemed aware of the book he was holding and carefully extracted one small slip of paper from it, glanced at it, and offered it to me. "This is the problem. I wrote it down because I knew you'd ask, but you can get all of the information you need from her doctor. I told him you'd be in town and he's expecting to hear from you. He's supposed to be good, they tell me he's the best in his business, and he's the one that started talking about a month to live. He's the one that told me that Ken is the one last hope that she has. That's why I want him back here. That's why I want you to find him. For Kendra. Not me."

Carefully printed in bold black capitals were two words:

MYELODYSPLASTIC SYNDROME. I stared at the ominous words he had written, understanding but not comprehending what they meant. Myelodysplastic syndrome! Hell, that was a disease of older men, men my age, older than that, men the General's age, not a woman of 38. If what I was reading was accurate, and I was sure the General couldn't have come up with these words without reliable medical help, then Ken may well be the only hope that Kendra had.

That explained why she hadn't been in her office, wasn't able to answer her phone, and wouldn't be able to keep a dinner date. She was ill. I wanted to, had to, see her.

"She's at Manhattan Central Hospital," Green said. "She's been there since shortly after she began feeling weak and dizzy. When they found the abnormal blood count, they admitted her at once. First they thought it might be the flu, a cold or anemia, but after more tests, they said, no, it's this myelo—thing, and she's been in the hospital ever since. All the while, they've been looking for a donor."

Of course, a donor. Needed for a bone marrow transplant. That's why they needed Ken. The best donor is a sibling. The very best is an identical twin, but obviously Ken and Kendra didn't qualify. But as a sibling, Ken could still be the match she needed. I could hear the experts discussing it with the General now. "We'll look through our donor registries for a possible match, but that won't be easy." And they would. They'd scroll through computer records of thousands of blood specimens already on file and they'd find nothing. Then they would tell him, "A sibling would be the best bet." Upon learning of Ken, they would smile, look at one another, and say, "That will help. What, he's a twin? Even better. Much better. Bring him in for testing. Oh, he's dead. That's too bad. But you're not certain that he's dead? He might be alive? Is there any way you can find out? Because we should see if his blood will match. He could be the donor."

And that was why the General wanted me to bring back his son. If he was alive. If I could find him. He had saved my life once, and although he had never once brought that up, I found it hard to forget. I'd paid part of the bill on earlier occasions and I had been thinking of marking it paid in full several times, but now, with Kendra on the balance sheet, I knew that at least one more installment had come due.

I was aware that Green was still talking. "Oddly enough, it was Kendra who insisted that Ken had never died. They were always exceptionally close to one another. Tuned in onto the same frequency was how Leah used to put it. They seemed to know what the other was doing before they did it. Seemed able to communicate without words, even after they had gone away to different colleges. Then, after we got the word that Ken had been shot down and was missing, she told me, "He's not dead. Not Ken. He's resourceful and smart, but even more than that, I know he's still alive. I can feel it, almost hear him out there, talking to me."

"I thought she was talking like that to keep my spirits up, to make Leah feel better, but even after her mother died, she still insisted that Ken was alive. She went to POW rallies, stayed in touch with the families of other POW's and MIA's, and visited everyone she knew in the State Department and Department of the Army. Because of me and because of her sheer determination to get help, she was seldom ignored."

I could attest to that. More than once, we had been at dinner or a theater or just relaxing in her apartment when the phone or beeper would sound and she would talk earnestly to someone in distress about a missing loved one. Or to a legislator, pressing him to intercede on behalf of a family, to introduce a bill. Or to a clergyman or lawyer – to anyone who might be able to help and she had never lost the enthusiasm that made her such a vibrant and compassionate human being. Now she needed Ken. To live.

Then there was that night a year ago, less than a year ago, when we had been at her place and she unexpectedly said, "Mike, I've got to stop." My heart skipped a beat or two. I was certain she meant us. Stop seeing each other. I was surprised but relieved when she told me, "I'm afraid you and Dad are right. We've lost him. There are still times when I'm sure he's alive out there, that he's calling to me, and my heart says Ken couldn't die. But my brain tells me he did. If he were alive, he would have contacted us in some way. And he hasn't." She meant Ken.

Later that same night, at dinner, she mentioned that she had been to Washington one last time, seeking information. She had met with a man who had numerous contacts throughout Southeast Asia, made frequent visits there, talked to officials of almost every country, and he had never picked up the slightest clue, not even the faintest rumor, of a surviving POW still alive in all of Vietnam. Not one. Which I thought was odd. Rumors like that abounded. I'd been hearing them for years, magazines and newspapers were full of them, and I had never gone anywhere in the area without someone whispering in my ear the latest scuttlebutt about who had seen this and who had heard that. Most of the whispering concerned Americans said to be still there.

"How did you meet this man?" I inquired, toying with a piece of limp lettuce and a fat-free dressing. I was watching my weight that far back, too.

"Dad told me to call on him. I'd heard his name off and on for years, and he turned out to be about as nice a man as I've met down there in a long while. Just wasn't able to help much."

The lettuce slid off my fork and fell back into the bowl. I didn't pursue it. "Do I know him?"

"You may," she smiled. "He's about your age. Alex Fantus. He's with some kind of a trade organization. Met him?"

"Fantus? Probably have. Maybe a long while back. Maybe the General introduced us."

I put the fork down, sparing the lettuce. I hadn't heard from the Phantom for several years. Obviously he was still around. And he hadn't heard any rumors of missing POW's and MIA's. Must have been the only man in Washington who hadn't.

So the General had sent Kendra to see Fantus? Interesting. And Fantus had known nothing. Even more interesting. Meanwhile, the General was telling me, here in his own study, "Kendra could tell when Ken had done well in a class. Knew when he scored a touchdown in football. Out of the blue she would say, Ken did this or he did that and when Ken came home, he would confirm it. She hadn't been there. She just knew. It was uncanny. It even made him mad on those occasions when he wanted to tell us the good news himself. Kendra would often have already divined it, told us and Ken would glare at her and tell her, "Stop doing that!" But she would just laugh and tousle his hair, saying, 'You're just jealous because I got it right again.' Within minutes, they were both laughing and all was forgotten as they went off to do something together. I realized that Leah was probably right. They were on the same wavelength. It was clear that she wasn't just guessing. She knew. It was eerie."

"But it worked both ways. He often knew what she was thinking. Kidded her about it. I remember one time when your name came up, Mike, and they had a real row. He'd come home that evening after having a great basketball game, scored 25 points or something like that, and she told him the score and how he'd done before he said a word. That day, for some reason, it irked him and it was the day after you had been here on a visit. Both of them were seniors in High School and you had taken them out to dinner. Ken told her, you're not the only one who can read minds. I can read yours like a book. You've got a crush on Mike Osten. Go ahead, deny that."

The way the General stopped and waited made me realize that he was expecting a reply. He wasn't recalling an incident in the lives of his twins as much as waiting for a response. He had asked a question, hadn't he? I chuckled, forced it, but made the effort. "Well, Jordan, you've got to admit, I was a bit old for her, wasn't I?"

"That's what Leah said. She told Ken, 'That's nonsense. Kendra's still in school.'"

The whole family must have been standing around discussing my age, which then, as now, was exactly sixteen and a half years older then Kendra's. That was a major impediment for a high school girl. Would it be to a career woman of 38? I wanted to know, "What did Kendra say to Ken? About the crush?"

"Oh, just about what you said just now. Something like, 'Why, Ken, isn't he a little old for me?' That's what she said, but it was funny, Mike, she never denied having a crush on you, even when Ken brought it up again and again over the next few months. Then Ken switched tactics. He said no matter how old you were, you were the perfect match for her. He said she needed someone who could teach her manners. Someone a bit older. Like you."

I didn't ask what Kendra might have said about that idea. I didn't ask what he thought about the idea of his daughter and me, well, going together, is that the right way to express it? And I didn't ask why he was dealing with Fantus and Bath on something as important as finding his son. Not the right time for any of those questions.

He finally got around to removing the second slip of paper he had been using as a book marker and handed it to me. Typed neatly were the words Ivo Bertinoldi MD and an address with the initials IHMD. "This is her doctor. He's at the Institute for Hematology and Myeloproliferative Disorders here in Manhattan." That explained the IHMD. "He'll be expecting you at 10 A.M."

To my surprise, he had a third fragment of paper tucked away inside the front cover. He held it out where I could see it but kept a firm grip on it as he said, "I'm not going to give you this. I want no one to see it, other than you. Memorize this name and number. This is the man to contact when you arrive in Bangkok. Don't believe that crap about Bath having resources that will be available to you. He has resources, I can vouch for that, but he has a peculiar habit of hiding them away just out of reach to the detriment of those most in need. Take what he gives, but this is where you get your primary resources. He can get you anything you need, no questions asked. Just tell him Broward, you remember Broward from Korea?, sure you do, just tell him Broward vouches for you, recommended him, told you to call. Don't worry about references. That's all you need. Everything else is taken care of."

Handwritten in large capital letters was the name AcChan and a telephone number, a Bangkok exchange.

"Got it memorized?" he asked. Not only memorized, but by then it was seared deeply into my brain where it could be recalled unless some major calamity shook it loose.

I nodded and true to his word, he walked over to the fireplace and tossed it in where the real wood fire greedily reached out to consume another choice morsel of pulp. We both stood by and watched it burn. AcChan, I repeated silently, phone number -------. I remember it. It was so secret then, and still is, that I won't even write it down now, many years later.

I had expected Bertinoldi to be tall, dark, thin, wearing horn-rimmed glasses, and speaking with a distinct Italian accent. I was right on the first three but he didn't wear glasses at all and the accent had to be back bay Boston. He was expecting me, as the General had promised, and after exchanging ritual doctor to doctor greetings, there was a momentary pause while we took measure of one another. He was wondering what I knew that he didn't know and I was wondering the same thing, in reverse.

He made the first move. "About Kendra Green, Doctor, her father has asked me to give you whatever information you might need. I should add that Ms. Green also has been asked for her consent and was willing to have me bring you up to date on her situation." He wasn't happy about my being there. Doctors seldom are. It's one thing if they ask for a consultation, then they need help and are willing to share confidences. But this, this was different. Bertinoldi hadn't asked for my medical opinion, probably doubted that I had any advice that he could use, and wasn't likely to use it if I offered any. He considered himself the expert. I'd checked the night before. He was. What I might be able to do, if he could unbend a little to consider it, was find the donor he had been unable to locate. So, sure, he was touchy about my being here. Hell, I would feel that way myself if the shoe was on the other foot.

I wanted him to understand that. "Doctor," I explained, "I'm no expert on myeloproliferative disorders. I did some reading last night to go with my general understanding of the subject but I'm still like a rookie playing in his first major league ball game. Tell me about her problem. Assume that I don't know a thing." Was that humble enough, I wondered? It should be. It was almost the truth.

He was immaculately turned out like television's perfect physician in a starched coat so white it glared and almost hurt the eyes when the light from the side window struck it, a stethoscope casually strung around the neck, and a small silver pocket flashlight peeking from a coat pocket, a prescription pad in a side one. He relaxed now, recognizing that I was not a threat to his position as lead doctor in a high profile case, and located a file amidst the clutter on a credenza behind him. Opening it, he told me, "this is her record. Let me tell you what we have. About six weeks ago," about the time, I realized, when she had suddenly become hard to reach, out of the office, away from the phone, "she became extremely fatigued. It crept up on her and got worse. She was tired all of the time. She noticed it first at work where she wasn't able to concentrate."

Kendra worked with manuscripts day in and day out. Concentration was an essential part of her work. She would sense that something was wrong.

"At the end of the day, she'd drag herself home, eat sparingly as her appetite had all but disappeared, and fall into bed. This was not normal as she had always been active, challenged each day eagerly, and now suddenly she didn't want to do a thing. She lost weight, stopped going over to visit with her father, missed her weekly dinner with him, looked pale, and in no time, her co-workers and General Green were concerned, especially by the weight loss, and urged her to see her internist. She finally did."

Bertinoldi was separating the file into several small piles, some of which I recognized as laboratory reports, others being handwritten notes and computer generated printouts. Willing to share now, apparently having decided I was a good listener, he offered, "If you need any of these reports, I'll have copies made."

I thanked him and asked, "What did her internist find?"

"Same things we found. She was anemic; had a low red cell count, hemoglobin was down, and at first, he suspected that was the problem. He was thinking inadequate diet, possibly not enough iron, but wondered about excessive blood loss, natural enough in a woman that age if she starts having a gyn problem, irregular periods, heavy menstrual flow. Things like that. But when the pathologist looked at the peripheral blood smear, he was puzzled by the presence of atypical hypogranulated neutrophils. He thought what he was looking at was a pseudo-Pelger-Huet anomaly, you know, the bilobed neutrophils resembling juvenile neutrophils."

Somewhere in his last sentence, he had lost me. None of this was in the books I'd been able to get my hands on the night before, but naturally, I couldn't admit that, so I kept silent and listened as he continued.

"There was another unusual finding that caught his attention. Large platelets, very large ones, and, surprisingly, they had decreased granulation. When he saw this, along with the other anomalies, he sent Ms. Green over to see me." What he meant was, to see the expert. That had been three weeks ago.

"The case is unusual," he continued, "because although the pathologist suspected a form of myeloproliferative disorder almost from the beginning, he was reluctant to diagnose the myelodysplastic syndrome, just as I was when I saw her, because we're dealing with a 38 year old woman. We see leukemia in patients this young, but the myelodysplastic syndrome, well, that's usually seen in older men, in their 60's and 70's, not in a healthy young woman like this. So naturally, we repeated the blood smears and other studies and when they turned out exactly the same the second time, we sought her permission to do a bone marrow aspirate and followed that with a bone marrow biopsy. When we had all of the data in hand, there was only one conclusion; she had a refractory anemia with excess blast cells and the only diagnosis we could make was the myelodysplastic syndrome. Some consider it a subacute form of myeloid leukemia, a chronic myelomonocytic leukemia, a smoldering myeloid leukemia or a preleukemia – but whatever you choose to call it, we're talking about a very serious disease."

I hadn't understood the pseudo-Pelger-Huet anomaly, but I could understand leukemia. Serious, he had called it. Yes, of course, very serious.

"What's likely to happen from this point on?" I asked, knowing that I had to get the books out and make more telephone calls, looking for as much information as I could find. It wasn't that I didn't trust Bertinoldi. He seemed to have command of the situation. What I needed to find out was if there was anyone, anyone at all, who was better.

Meanwhile, Bertinoldi was in his element now. This was what he knew best. "What we have to worry about are the risks of hemorrhage and infection. Because of poor white cell function, infections are an ever present risk, and because of the reduced platelet levels, the chance for sudden hemorrhage is much greater. To be frank about it, many of these patients die from one of these intercurrent problems before acute leukemia ever develops. But if not, well, you know how the process works. Myeloid cells, in this instance the white blood cells, normally follow a fixed pattern of development in the body. They divide in a fixed cycle, each cell developing up to a certain point in the life cycle, then enter the peripheral blood from the marrow, circulate through the body fighting off infections en route, then die off and are replaced by new ones. That's called apoptosis, a programmed cell death. But in some patients, this apoptosis goes awry and the myeloid cells, instead of dying off like they're supposed to, live on and continue to divide, and the mass of cells in the marrow builds up, becoming enormous. There are just too many cells in the marrow and some of the wild ones escape into the peripheral bloodstream. So many of them get out there that they begin to engorge other organs: the spleen, liver, lymph nodes, lining of the brain, places like that, and they impair the way those organs function. In time, there are so many myeloid cells in the body that they squeeze these vital organs to death. Meanwhile, there are so many useless white cells in the body and the marrow keeps on making more, that there are no effective disease fighting cells left to protect against infection. It has been estimated that as many as 1.7 liters of these cells are present in terminal cases. That's almost 2 quarts of leukemic cells; almost the total volume of the average adult marrow, between 2-4 pounds of wild, worthless cells in the body, enough to kill. That's why people die of leukemia."

I had to remind myself that he was talking of what could happen. It hadn't happened yet.

"What can we do for her now?"

"For now? Symptomatic treatment, that's about it. She was so anemic we gave her blood. Had to. That's risky, because she was already showing early signs of circulatory overload and, of course, we were worried about the possibility of the HIV virus being transmitted in the blood itself. But when she weighed the situation, she decided to allow us to proceed. Now we're considering the use of prednisone in an effort to compensate for the anemia, but we haven't done it yet because that might increase the risk of infection. Two other drugs, hydroxyurea and mercaptopurine sometimes bring down the white blood count and reduce the swelling we talked about in the liver and spleen, but neither alter the natural course of the disease although they might help for a time."

He spread his arms expressively, and continued, "What she needs, Doctor, is a bone marrow transplant. We've been looking for a suitable donor, as I'm sure General Green told you, but we've failed to find one. That's not unusual. Finding one in the general populace is a lot like looking for a needle in a haystack. The ideal donor, everybody agrees, is an identical twin. That enables us to do an isogeneic transplant and if it works, it is possible to restore bone marrow function with the damaged marrow often returning to normal. Then the patient has a fighting chance. But there is no possibility of an identical twin here. What we do have, more or less and I'm not entirely clear what the situation is, is a fraternal twin brother. That could be important, though, because in some 30-40% of the cases, a sibling will prove to be a histocompatible donor. Obviously, that's not ideal, because we don't have the perfect transplantation match, but even though many of the imperfect matches are rejected, there are a number of drugs to modify the rejection response, and the recipient has a chance. Not as good as with the perfect match is what I'm saying, but there is a chance. That's better than no chance at all. Without a donor, without the transplant, there's hardly any hope at all."

Bertinoldi now acknowledged that I could be of some help after all. "What about the brother?" he asked. "Does anyone know where he can be found?"

"We're working on it," was my response and it seemed inadequate, so I didn't blame him for looking at me quizzically, as in, "What do you mean you're working on it? Don't work on it. Do it."

Irritated, Bertinoldi said, "Well, where is he? No one has told me why we can't pick up the phone and tell him to come in for a blood test."

"Not that easy. He's in Southeast Asia and doesn't have a phone that we know of."

He looked at me curiously. "Southeast Asia? That doesn't narrow it down very much. You can't do better than that?"

"A little. I'm planning on going to Bangkok to start looking."

Surprisingly, he seemed pleased to hear that and brightened noticeably. "That's a break," he enthused. "You'll be right near Hong Kong."

I wasn't sure where he had studied geography but the two cities weren't exactly in the same neighborhood. I watched as he whipped a notepad from his top desk drawer and wrote on it. "Here, take this along with you. When you find the brother, get a blood sample from him and get it to her, to Loretta Diaz, at Marcum-Whangpo Institute in Hong Kong. One of my former students. She's got all of the facilities you'll need, she's top notch, and it'll save us a lot of time. If she says it's a match, it's a match. I'll send her everything she'll need to do the work. Believe me, you can trust her. One of the best people I've ever worked with." I wondered if he had a crush on her.

As we were saying good-bye, he told me again, "If Loretta says it's a match, bring the brother home. We'll do the transplant here and maybe we can lick this thing Ms. Green is up against. If his blood doesn't match," and his voice trailed off. He had nothing more to say, having said it all before.

I couldn't leave without knowing. "How much time do we have, Doctor?"

He suddenly seemed to find the calendar with the photo of a Canadian goose flying over Chesapeake Bay very interesting. Studied it for a full minute before saying, "Three, four weeks, I would say, but you know how wildly inaccurate we doctors are at predicting things like that."

Sure, I knew. On the other hand, if the wild cells had started to fill up the marrow and were poised to escape into the bloodstream, then three, maybe four weeks was a reasonable guess. Not much time to find a needle in a haystack, because that's what Ken had become, a very small needle in a very large haystack. If he was, in fact, alive at all.

Bertinoldi extended his hand and we shook. He wasn't a bad guy after all. "Say hello to Loretta Diaz for me. In Hong Kong."

I promised that I would.

# 4

Sixty year old Frederick Bernard pushed back his half eaten plate of red-skin potato crusted whitefish and asparagus tips, carefully wiped his lower lip with a white linen napkin, and sipped from his glass of chilled California Chardonnay. This was his turf, the executive dining room of Clozyme, our principal client. He was the original purpose of my trip to New York.

Ten years earlier, he had taken over a bankrupt drug distributor with a $20,000 investment, money borrowed from his brother-in-law. Now two divorces later, one ex-brother-in-law suing for millions allegedly due to the original investment, and two former wives suing for everything else, Bernard soldiered on, carrying the twin titles of Chairman and Chief Executive Officer, his company burdened by debt, but considered to be a major success story by investment bankers, brokers, and shareholders alike. That's what happens when sales move from a sleepy five million to five hundred million dollars in a decade. Most outsiders viewed Bernard as a happy and contented man, an image his publicists did nothing to dispel. In fact, he was miserable, discontented, and frustrated beyond words.

The reason was simple. He was thinking billions. Dollars. Not millions of dollars, but billions of dollars. He wanted to run with the elephants, not cavort among the javelinas.

To do it, he needed a blockbuster. That one big drug that would propel Clozyme into the top rank of the world's pharmaceutical giants. Those are hard to find and in time, with prompting from Burrows who had done a masterful job of selling our skills to the CEO/Chairman, Bernard had settled on anticancer drugs as his field, and Osten-Burrows as his consultant. And here I was, just three weeks away from his annual meeting, the shareholders showing incipient signs of revolt because Clozyme stock continued to languish in the low 20's in an otherwise soaring market.

"It was a master stroke," he told me. "The timing couldn't have been better. My shareholders are going to see this and it will take a lot of the fire out of them, have them salivating again. I wouldn't be surprised to see our shares bounce nicely on the markets worldwide before this day is over."

I had no idea what he was talking about, but decided to follow his lead and push my empty plate back and see where this was going. Actually, the whitefish had been quite tasty.

"You're referring to which of the many things that we have going?" I prompted, angling for any clue, any at all. The truth was, we did have a lot of things going and I wasn't sure if one of them had hit gold, and it was always possible that Clozyme's research laboratories had finally come up with something worthwhile, although that was, at best, a remote possibility.

The man responsible for my being able to make that statement was sitting across from me now, completely untouched fish still lying inert in the center of his plate. Carroll Bradley rarely touched his lunch when I was in town for a meeting, leaving unexplained his 260 pound frame. Bradley was a vice-president of Clozyme, vice-president of research, the third to hold that office over the past four years. Job tenure not being one of the perks of that job, he was understandably nervous. The problem was simple enough; despite lavish spending on research, more as a percent of sales than all but three other pharmaceutical houses in the United States, Clozyme kept coming up empty. There was nothing in the pipeline or there hadn't been anything in the pipeline until TA97-C. That was ours, a finding we had brought to Clozyme two years earlier, had been refining and improving, and were now moving rapidly, with them, to get into advanced human testing. It could be that one big one and from Bradley's point of view, it came as a mixed blessing. It was a drug his people could work with, but it was one they hadn't discovered, and so far, his people had managed to get nowhere with it while mine were moving ahead rapidly. He had to be thinking, 'Is there a new research director out there, just waiting?' That wasn't my problem. My problem was in finding out what Bernard was talking about.

And he wasn't being much help. At least not at first. "That story in this morning's *Times*. Magnificent. It was perfect."

I hadn't read the *Times* and had no idea what story he was referring to. The morning newspapers of our country tend to print a lot of junk science, half baked articles abut medicine, that are usually contradicted by another story a week later, but if this one was, as Bernard put it, "perfect," it had to relate to something he was interested in. That meant TA97-C, Clozyme or himself.

Shocked to find that I hadn't seen whatever it was, he sent a white jacketed waiter off to find a copy and he was back in Olympic record time, paper open to page two, ready for easy reading. I discovered that a famous American physician, a researcher with a reputation for discovering new antitumor compounds, known to have an uncanny knack for finding botanicals and fungal elements with pharmaceutical activity, had done it again. This time it was a potent anticancer drug with a mysterious symbol that was the object of his interest, and he was leaving within days to lead an expedition to an unknown destination in Southeast Asia to establish an assured source of supply for this wonderful new miracle. The drug would be marketed by Clozyme, an American pharmaceutical firm with exclusive rights worldwide according to Mr. Frederick Bernard, CEO, Chairman, and so on and so on. The symbol was revealed for the first time in print – TA97 something or other. My name was there, too. I was the famous researcher trekking off in search of this marvelous material.

Wonderful! There go the secrets, here comes the competition. But what if that was the idea? What if this was the red herring the General had hinted at last night when he mentioned deniability? What had he said, "You look for plants and trees used in making drugs so another trip into the jungle won't arouse any suspicions. Poking around in the countryside wouldn't be out of character for you, would it?" Maybe not. Then again, maybe we weren't giving whoever may not want me poking around in the countryside enough credit for intelligence.

There was another possibility, of course. Burrows may have planted the story. It was the kind of thing he did once in a while, considering public relations and the sensational story to be part of his job description, not that of the people we hired to do that sort of thing. Whoever had done it though, I had to admit, they had managed to make me come off as a pretty impressive kind of guy. I liked that part about famous American physician with a knack for and a talent for research. That sort of thing. I'd have to make sure that our clipping service added several extra copies of the issue to our files.

While I liked it, Bernard loved it. "Can you imagine anyone holding our stock seeing this? They'll be on the phone to the broker buying more. I had no idea you were planning a trip like this, Osten. No one told us. You've come up with new leads, have you?"

I could play the game, too, when necessary. If Bernard was happy, we were happy. He was the client. And if the General was the author, maybe it was the red herring we needed. So I said, "Yes, and they're so promising that I'm not the only one going. Actually, I'll be headed up into Thailand and Tony Howsam will follow up on our leads in Malaysia. Between the two of us, we should accomplish what we have to do in much less time than one of us alone." I was stretching things a little, but we *did* have some worthwhile leads in Malaysia and who knows what I would find in Thailand. Ken Green, of course, but who knows what else.

I hastened to get on to the business I had come for, directing my question to Carroll Bradley who was glumly using his fork to doodle on the soft white tablecloth. He was writing TA97-C. It could be his only hope and he knew it. "How is your lab progressing with the compound?"

He was not nearly as thrilled about the article as was his boss. He clearly was not happy to be in the company of a famous American researcher, a title he aspired to, but should have despaired of achieving before ever leaving his pharmacology teaching position at Hofstra. "It's active, but weaker than we had hoped for. We're trying to concentrate the extract further. It's an alkaloid, you know, and we think it's poisonous at stronger dilutions so there is a fine line here between therapeutic doses and toxic levels. But the antitumor activity is there. There's no doubt about that."

This, essentially, is exactly what we had told him in a detailed prospectus forwarded by my laboratory three months earlier. True to form, Clozyme's vaunted research facilities, already the subject of snickers whenever serious scientists convened, had accomplished nothing. I began to consider the possibility that it wasn't Carroll Bradley alone causing the problem; it might be the entire support staff he had accumulated, or inherited, and continued to tolerate. Regardless, watching Bernard's face darken as Bradley rambled on, I suspected there was indeed a new research director in the wings, awaiting a summons to center stage.

TA97-C was derived from the yew tree, the tree that had become our prime target. We know that Indian tribes living along our Pacific northwest coast had often chewed the bark of the yew when ill. They had made compresses of the leaves and applied the mixture to aching, swollen knees, and then taken the small red berries, squashed them, and spread the paste on skin rashes and boils. They hadn't done case studies, nor had they left a written record, but the oral history passed down from generation to generation was clear; they considered the yew to be a plant of magical properties.

The tree itself is a handsome evergreen, often growing more than sixty feet tall, with a short, thick trunk of extremely hard wood. The crown is usually broad and low, and the leaves, and they are leaves although many call them needles, are dark green, extending straight out from the twigs. The fruit, a scarlet globe like disk, caps many twig endings and contains an ellipsoidal brown seed, which looks good enough to eat, but isn't. To the dismay of those who have tried it, they are likely to be seized by violent cramps, become short of breath, find themselves with widely dilated pupils, develop huge purple lumps on their skin, and then go into sudden vascular collapse. Poisonous. Nothing to trifle with.

# Yellow Garden

I knew that's what was bothering Bradley. Toxicity. It's nothing new in botanicals; for that matter, it's nothing new in any drug where the possibility of side effects is ever present. It becomes a race, finding a way of retaining the good while eliminating the bad, at a cost that that doesn't break the bank. Research people do this type of work every day, and ours, back in our laboratory, understood that. Here in New York, Bradley's scientists didn't seem to have a good grasp of the situation at all. They had hit a stone wall and the head man, Bernard, couldn't tolerate that much longer. Not with the shareholders growing uneasy. An article in the *Times* might quiet them for a while, even make the stock go up, but what Clozyme needed, was a new drug that worked. They needed TA97-C and I suspected they were never going to get it unless we delivered the whole package to them. On a platter.

TA97-C was known as a taxine or taxol alkaloid separated from the yew tree, mainly the bark. Our computer models suggested that it would be active against two scourges of women, ovarian and breast cancers. When we had produced enough of the material to run preliminary tests, it was. The problems, aside from the toxicity? Mainly scarcity; there were too few yew trees to ensure an adequate supply of the drug if it proved to be the answer to the control of these cancers. Why? Well, to get the bark, the tree had to be stripped. That exposed delicate inner tissues to parasites, molds, fungi, bacteria, insect pests, and other organisms and the tree was likely to die. So? Grow more trees. Unfortunately, it isn't that simple. The tree is a slow growing specimen and it takes many years to reach the stage of development where there is another crop of inner bark where the alkaloid is found, ready for harvesting.

Medical people said, all right, so the tree dies, but people may live. So let's use the trees God put on earth and when they're gone, we'll think of something else. Maybe by then we'll be able to synthesize it, find another source of tree or another drug will have come along even better than this one. Wrong! God had also decided to place the spotted owl right where the yew was growing; in fact, the owls love the yew as nesting sites and now it wasn't a medical matter alone – it was an environmental one. The owls were winning.

We still had the other options. Synthesize it, which Clozyme had tried and spent a fortune on the process, only to find that what they had created was inactive. They hadn't attached the correct sidechain, had lopped off a nitrogen where they should have put a sulfate radical, one thing or another, and hadn't been able to figure it out yet. Bernard had thrown up his hands in despair and sent it to our laboratory where Tony Howsam was working on it. He was optimistic, but had no answer as yet.

Option two: find another source. Another yew tree, a similar tree, a different tree or bush with the same chemical and alkaloid components. One more abundant, faster growing, easily accessible – accessibility being a relative term in this instance as we could go anywhere in the world and bring it back quickly in the interests of science and business, but most important of all, one where the spotted owl wasn't in residence.

We scoured the literature, talked to botanists around the world, and hired our own. We sought out naturalists, taxonomists, earth scientists, medicine men, herbalists, world travelers, fakes, fakirs, and assorted holy men. Tracked down rumors, considered legends, analyzed myths, reread Homer's Odyssey looking for a clue we had heard was hidden in the text, and came up empty. That isn't to say we didn't find yew trees elsewhere. There were some in England, a few located in Montana, even scattered groves in India. Samples from each new source were obtained and found wanting; the alkaloid not as active as the Pacific yew, the trees too few to permit an adequate harvest and long term supply, and the ones in Montana came with their own environmental caveat. They were too close to the archaeological sites where diggers were unearthing the already extinct dinosaurs. That made it 2-0 in favor of the environment.

And then we got a break from an unlikely source: Burrow's favorite golfing partner. Tired of fall, apprehensive of the coming cold weather, he packed up his gear and left on a camera safari to Malaysia. From high atop a swaying elephant, trooping through the barely penetrable jungle foliage, he lost his pith helmet, knocked from his head by an unseen limb. The mishap jolted him from an alcohol induced haze, the direct result of a three martini lunch, no mean feat to accomplish from a picnic basket while perched on a pachyderm in 98 degree heat, but it hadn't rendered his sense of humor inoperable. While a guide scrambled to retrieve the undamaged helmet from the jungle floor, Old Jack, Jack Fleming, looked more closely at the offending limb that had all but unseated him and saw that it was a sturdy looking thing with green fuzz growing abundantly at the end of long limbs, a red fruit scattered here and there amongst the branches, and recalled vaguely something about an elusive tree that Burrows had mentioned over a drink after a particularly satisfying round of golf, a particularly satisfying round being one in which he had taken $20 out of Everett's wallet. As a joke, a lark, he picked some of the green fuzz, selected twenty or more red fruits, three or four of the larger brown globules, snapped off a half pound of twigs, and tossed them into a plastic bag, tucked it into the cooler, took another drink, clapped his helmet back onto his head, and continued on his way looking for the even more elusive tiger. Later that evening, back in civilization, he wrote a short note, put everything into a manila envelope, and mailed it to Burrows at our office. The note said, "This is the tree you're looking for. Try and find it. Ha ha. Jack."

It shouldn't have gotten to us, having to pass postal inspectors, agricultural inspectors, drug inspectors and all the rest on its journey across eleven or twelve thousand miles. He hadn't even put on the correct postage, but despite all that, it was delivered where Burrows opened it, read the note, laughed, passed it on to Marge who read the message, didn't understand it, and put it all on my desk. I saw it, looked it over, tossed it into Tony Howsam's basket, and forgot about it. Until three days later when he asked, "Where did that stuff you gave me come from?"

"What stuff?" I was always giving him stuff. That was the business we were in.

"The stuff that looked like a yew tree, but didn't look like a yew tree, if you know what I mean," was his reply.

"Oh, that stuff. That came from Marge who got it from Burrows who got it from his old friend, Jack, what is his name? Fleming, Jack Fleming."

"It's loaded with taxine. Just loaded. Highest levels we've ever seen. Where do you suppose Jack Fleming got it?"

Serendipity strikes again.

Burrows was at the club when I reached him and he started laughing again when I asked him where the stuff came from. "That stuff? You mean the stuff from old Jack? He's just having fun with us and I was just having fun with you. That was something he picked up on his trip. You know old Jack. Always the jokester. Don't waste any time on it Mike. I should have told you it was a joke."

I didn't know old Jack, hadn't ever seen him so far as I could recall, and Burrows stopped laughing as soon as I mentioned the taxine. He made the smooth transition from golfer to business executive in a matter of seconds. "No, I'm not sure where he was, Mike, but I'll call his office. I'm certain he left an itinerary with his secretary, or did she go with him, no that was his former secretary, so sure, I'll call over there right now and get back to you."

Hours later, he reached Jack on another golf course, one not far from

Penang. "Yeah," Jack told him, "sure I sent that little gift. Nice, wasn't it? Hoped it wasn't poison ivy or anything like that. What did you say, Everett? You want some more? That's what I thought you said. Yeah, well I got all of that stuff just ten miles from here so I can go back and get some more. No problem. I'll need a ladder and have to hire some guy to climb it for me because I don't intend to crawl back up anymore dammed elephant's back. Too old for that nonsense. Matter of fact, sounds like fun. Gives me something to do tomorrow and I wanted to go back there anyhow to get a shot of a tiger. No Everett, I'm not going to shoot a tiger. Get a shot of a tiger. With a camera. A picture. I don't even have a gun. But you want more of that stuff, especially the berries and the little brown things. OK, I'll go get some. And you want me to mark where I am on a map and send that too? Why, do you think I'm lost? OK, look for some berries and little brown things in the mail. Be seeing you when I get back. Have your wallet open."

Even before the next shipment arrived, I had decided to schedule a trip to Malaysia. Now I was changing plans. I didn't tell Bernard why, and really didn't have to. The article in the *Times* seemed to satisfy him and the knowledge that I was going one way and Tony Howsam another in a two pronged search for the most important drug since the advent of, what? – antibiotics, tranquilizers, cholesterol lowering agents, non-sedating antihistamines, gastric acid inhibitors or even genetically engineered marvels designed to treat heart attacks – met with his enthusiastic approval. "It could be expensive, this next phase," I warned him.

"The budget is flexible. Don't worry about it. Just go and do what has to be done. Burrows and I will take care of the budget," was his response. Fine, that was the way I liked it. I didn't mention Ken Green. There was a separate budget for him.

All Bernard wanted to know was when we would be leaving. "Two or three days," I promised and knew I was cutting it awfully close.

"Excellent," he said. "Keep in mind that the shareholders meet exactly five weeks from today and I need something to show them, some results to report by that time. Results, Osten, that's what I'm asking for."

He shot a meaningful glance at Bradley, who stopped doodling and seemed to shrink into his chair. For someone that large, it was an incredible feat of magic.

I picked up a small bouquet of flowers on the way to the hospital. Yellows, rusts, brilliant red, sprinkled with the greens and white of Angels' breath. Howsam could have identified them all but I was more into trees and weeds. The General said Kendra wanted to see me, Bertinoldi said to be prepared for a shock, and the hospital said to come by at two. I was a minute or two early and she was sitting in a recliner, asleep, her silken blond hair lying softly alongside her face. She was pale, much thinner than when I had last seen her, her lips brushed by the faint pink she used so sparingly, but never needed. A rich blue velvet robe, tied at the waist, with the gold and red insignia of the General's last command on the pocket, was open at the neck where I could see the matching delicate gold and ruby pendant I had given her for Christmas, two years ago, was it?

She was beautiful.

And she was faking. "Come in, Mike. Come in. You don't have to stand there staring at me."

"Caught at last. My secret is out. I enjoy staring. Some of the best times of my life have been spent in staring. It's a favorite pastime. And don't try to kid me – beautiful women like to be stared at. Everyone knows that. I read it in a book somewhere."

I kissed her, chastely, because of the surroundings, the hospital and all, hugged her, and asked, "Got a vase?" brandishing the flowers.

"Flowers for me?" eyebrows raised in mock surprise.

"Of course not. For your nurse. The cute one I met in the hall. I've fallen madly in love with her."

"You cad," she said, reaching up with both arms, pulling me close and kissing me, a satisfying, much needed kiss for both of us. I responded and when she released me, looked quickly to see if the flowers, still in my one hand, had wilted from the sudden heat. "Maybe," she purred, "that will keep your mind in the room and not in the hall, for a while at least. And yes, I do have a vase. Over in the drawer. We didn't squash the flowers, did we?"

"No, they're fine. I've already checked." And they were. Spread out in the vase with her help, absorbing fresh water, they looked even better than they had in my hand.

"They're fine," I repeated. "How about you? How are you doing?"

She shrugged, a who knows type of shrug, often more expressive than the spoken word. "What have they told you, Mike, about all of this?"

"Enough. I've talked to the General and to Dr. Bertinoldi. They've brought me up to date."

"They've told you about the donor situation? How we've screened thousands of possible donors and found none that could be used?"

"Yes," I admitted, "they've told me."

"They've told you about Ken? How he could be the one?"

"Yes, that, too." She was so thin. Her cheek bones so sharply outlined as if the weight loss had been sudden and was continuing. Were we losing her, already, before I had a chance to tell her, what? I had had chances for years and allowed them to pass by, unused. Even now, I wasn't sure what I wanted to tell her. "Bertinoldi will keep looking, though, he assured me of that."

"Oh, I know that Mike. He's almost a man possessed. But he's made it clear by the look in his eyes, the tone of his voice, that our best hope is Ken. Our last best hope. If he's alive."

Did she doubt it, while the General was certain? "About the note, Kendra, did you see it?"

She shook her head. "No, not really. It came at about the same time I started feeling so weak and I've been having blood tests and treatment ever since so they've never showed it to me. But they used some of Ken's letters to me, sent when he was in the army, to help verify the handwriting. Jordan tells me that it was Ken's handwriting. The handwriting experts, what are they, graphologists?, from the military, and he knows dozens of them, and from the University, even some man who does it commercially by advertising in the newspaper that he can predict the future from your handwriting, they all agree; Ken wrote it. So there's no doubt that Ken wrote it and that's weird."

"What's weird?" I asked.

"Coming after all this time. Coming just after I had given him up for dead after insisting for almost fifteen years that he was still alive."

And she had. Almost since that day when we first heard his helicopter had gone down, Kendra alone was convinced that he had survived. "I would know if he was dead," she told me, told anyone who would listen. "Ken and I were always close," and twins often are, "and we had this ability to communicate with one another. Something that we could never explain but which was real."

She'd told me of the game they played as children. Continued playing as adults, even in college. Much of this I already knew, knowing the family so well for so many years, but it was wonderful to listen to her. She spoke of how one of them would think of an object, color or idea and the other would try to guess what it was. At first they were no better than anyone else at coming up with a match. Then gradually, they improved, until by high school they were able to predict what the other had done, or would do, and they were sometimes pleased, or just as frequently annoyed, at what they discovered about one another. Surprisingly, they concluded that Kendra was better at receiving these paranormal messages, for that's what they were talking about, and Ken excelled at sending them, although either one could change roles from time to time.

And now she was telling me, "When Ken disappeared, when they said his plane had gone down, I didn't get that, what would you call it, that extrasensory out of body message, that told me he was dead. I never did get it. Even when the chaplain and condolence officers came, even when Jordan came back and told us he had talked to eye witnesses, even then I never had the feeling that Ken was dead. First they said he was missing, then presumed dead, then dead. I never believed it because I kept getting conflicting flickers, weak messages I suppose you could call them, as if he was trying to get through to me, that kept saying, 'I'm here. I'm still here.' I didn't tell anyone about them, not even you, because I was afraid that I was imagining things, knowing how badly I wanted Ken to be alive. Maybe, I worried, I was just unwilling to accept the inevitable."

She was right about one part of the story. She hadn't told me any of this. Oh, I knew about the message parts, what they had done before Ken disappeared. We all knew about that, had laughed about when they were kids, marveled at it as sort of a parlor trick when they were older. The part I hadn't known was that she was still, or had been until recently, receiving weak messages from her lost brother after all this time.

She was the one staring now, right past me, looking out through the window. "It was the second part of the message that I never understood."

Lightly touching her chin I refocused her eyes upon mine and asked, "What second part? You say you were convinced until recently that he was alive. That you were sure of that. What was the rest of the message?"

"I never mentioned it to anyone, Mike, because I just couldn't be sure what it was and what I was getting I didn't want to believe. What I think he was saying was that he never intended to come home, ever again. No matter what!"

I was startled, not as much by what she said as by the way she said it. She believed it. As a game, this paranormal message business was fun; in the present circumstances, it was disconcerting. I made a mental note to check with Bertinoldi to see what medication he had prescribed. Any hallucinogen, for instance?

She wasn't through. "Ken loved the General." She often referred to her father as the General, something we all did, even me, and I realized that I had started thinking of him as a general, even when he was still a captain, back in Korea. If he loved his father, I wanted to ask, why did he rebel against him, fight with him, and ultimately walk out of a restaurant on him in Saigon, cursing as he went? I didn't ask and she didn't say. Maybe she thought I knew.

"It was a tremendous shock when he was kicked out of college and joined the army. It was devastating to mother. She had always said that one military man in any family was enough. And we had one, so she never understood what Ken was doing. On the day he left, he just threw a few things into a suitcase and walked right past us. Mother and me. Jordan was in Germany. I cried out, my heart breaking, and he stopped, softened and hugged me. Then he did the same to mother, although I think he originally intended to walk out without saying a word to either of us. All he said now was, 'Don't save any of my things. I won't be back.' Mother took it to mean until he was discharged. I didn't. I knew he meant it to be good-bye forever. That's why, as over the years since he has been missing I kept getting messages that he's still alive, I knew he wouldn't come back anyway.

"That is, until now. Now I don't know anymore. Is he alive and does he really want to come home? Why? What's happened?"

"What about you? Have you been sending messages to Ken telling him that you're ill?" I was sure that she had.

"You forget," she said seriously, "I'm better at receiving than sending. Ken always had trouble receiving." She waited for a moment, then added, "Do you think he might have heard me?"

"If you sent a message, yes, he might have. Did you?"

"I've been praying a lot. To God. To my patron saint. To the Virgin Mary. But sometimes, when I had the time, I have tried to contact Ken. I've tried hard."

"Has he responded recently? Since you've been making a renewed effort, I mean."

She looked at me, afraid that I wouldn't believe her. "Once. He replied once, it was faint, but it was Ken."

She had me mesmerized. I didn't know if any of this was real, but it was eerie, just as the General had said. "What did he tell you?"

"It won't help much, I'm afraid. I wish he had been more clear."

"Let me judge how much help it'll be. What did he say?" I realized I was acting as if the two of them had been on the phone talking to one another.

"He said he was in the jungle, Mike. Jordan said he might be in Bangkok. He isn't. Look in the jungle. That's where he is."

"Any specific jungle, Kendra? Anything more than that?"

I was afraid she was going to cry. Her chin quivered, tears formed in both eyes, and I grasped her hand in reassurance. "I knew that wouldn't be of any help," she said, her voice breaking under the strain of disappointment.

"Wrong," I told her. "Knowing that he's not in Bangkok is of enormous help. It narrows things down quite a bit." Words spoken to make her feel better, I knew, as the jungle is a big place. There are lots of jungles, not only in Southeast Asia, but elsewhere. "But did he say anything else that might help?"

"Only about the garden. It's not so much what he said, as what I saw when he was talking. The garden. Yellow flowers everywhere. Like those in the vase, only larger. Like the ones you brought."

Her eyes were drooping in fatigue. She was medicated, something to make her sleep.

I kissed her again, drawing an icy stare from the nurse who had just entered to check on her patient. I'm not certain whether she was more worried that I was about to catch a disease or transmit one. I ignored her and whispered to Kendra, "I'll check out those jungles, Kendra. We'll find the garden with the yellow flowers. That shouldn't be all that hard." If I thought she was almost asleep, I was mistaken.

"So she's the one you brought the flowers for," she accused, rolling her eyes at the not too attractive woman hovering nearby.

"Yeah," I told her, "I just can't wait to get out of here. See how she's waiting for me? But before I go, I want to give you a message for Ken. Send it as soon as you can and keep repeating it. Tell him to stay in one place, to pack his suitcase, and be ready to leave. Tell him I'm coming to get him."

"I already have. I told him that as soon as the General said he had contacted you. But I'll keep on telling him, if you think it would help."

"Hey, it can't hurt. He is the donor you need, after all, so why not let him know that we want him?"

She surprised me, answering, "Even then, Mike, it's only a 30-40% chance that he's the right one. But even so, that's better than a needle in a haystack." Bertinoldi must have been reading the odds to her as well and he was certainly consistent in his choice of words.

I squeezed her hand again and prepared to leave. "If not Ken, then we'll find someone else. But 30-40% isn't bad. I know you understand that as the General always said you were a whiz at math."

"That's a generous compliment. Thank you. And him." She continued to hold my hand, gazed intently at my face, and finally said, "do you remember when we were talking about sending messages, reading minds? I have always been able to read other minds too, not everyone's, but some. Do you remember when we were talking about that?"

"Sure, I remember."

"Do you believe me?"

"Of course I believe you. You're much too pretty to lie."

"Then do I have permission to answer a message I've been receiving over and over, for years, and even today?"

I looked at her in wonderment, not knowing what she meant, and nodded.

"I love you, too, "she said. "Always have, since I was a little girl."

This time I kissed her even more convincingly, hearing the nurse harrumphing behind me in vigorous disapproval. As I walked out into the hallway, I thought I heard Kendra say something that sounded like 'be careful,' but when I turned to look I couldn't be sure. An Ivac temperature probe was between her lips and her eyes were closed.

Maybe I was going to have to take this business about messages from Ken more seriously than I had originally thought. She had been absolutely right about the message she had been getting from me.

I reached Burrows at home, telling him that I would be back on a nine o'clock flight that evening. I told him what I wanted Marge to do and that I needed Tony Howsam free at once, ready to travel. I told him what else had to be done and who I wanted to see, no later than 9:30.

"OK, I can have the people there tonight, but about all the rest of this list, when do you want that done?" he asked. He was incredulous when I told him. "Two days! That's it? Two days?"

I didn't explain. It was far too complicated for that. I simply said, "That's all the time we have Everett. Can you do it?"

"Mike," he was deeply wounded, "of course I can do it. That's my job. We're a team here, all of us. You need it, you've got it." Actually sounded excited. I found out why. We came to the part he liked best. "You want me to draw up a budget and submit it to who for all of this?"

"Two budgets, Everett. Not one. One for Clozyme to replace the one you already sent them. Add Tony Howsam to it and all of the additional things we need down there. Then another for Pan Union Trade Association. You remember talking to their Mr. Bath yesterday? We have an address in the files that Marge can give you. Label that one Operation Patient and fax it to them. We need it signed right away. I'll give you the rest when I get there."

"Mike, what kind of surgery are you planning on doing? You don't see patients anymore."

"No, Everett, I'm not doing surgery. That's military jargon, like saying Operation Overlord, things like that. Just label it Operation Patient and you'll be fine."

"OK. No problem. I'll get Craig in and have him help me on that." Craig was the company financial genius. "By the way, are you sure I talked to someone by the name of Bath at this Pan Union outfit, whatever they are? I thought I was talking to a Mr. Towel."

"Everett, it doesn't really matter. Send everything to Mr. Bath. No, I don't have a first name for either of them. But believe me, they'll get it. Send a copy for each if it makes you feel better."

He was agreeable but observed, "Incredible, Mike. Doesn't it seem odd to have men named Bath and Towel working for the same company?"

"Not only that, they work out of the same office," I told him. "If you ever meet them you'll understand just how incredible it really is."

"I hope to have the pleasure one of these days. They sound like interesting people. Well, I'll get right on this. It's late afternoon here now and I did have a tee time, despite the lousy weather, but I'll cancel it and go right back to the office." There was a note of sadness in his voice as he hung up. Well, I reflected, we all had to make sacrifices on occasion. Burrows would make up for his disappointment another day.

# 5

I flew into Detroit Metro Airport right on schedule and found Eddie Chun waiting for me, courtesy of Burrows. A nice touch. I'd always thought it vaguely romantic, if not glamorous, to descend from a crowded public conveyance, which is what our aircraft have become, to find a uniformed chauffeur holding aloft a stick and sign bearing your name. It indicated prestige, put the world on notice that someone cared enough to arrange for a greeting, to provide transportation, and to, in a sense, wrap you into a protective cocoon of safety. In this case, however, Eddie wasn't in uniform, he didn't have a stick and sign, he was just there, waiting. We knew one another. He was the night security guard in our parking lot.

Forty minutes of driving, easy at this time of night, brought us to our campus-like complex a short mile from the edge of the University. We were surrounded by towering old oaks, maples, and linden trees, enjoyed ample green spaces with luxuriant grass upon which rested a half dozen picnic tables where our employees could gather for lunch. In summer. At this time of the year, cold and gray most days, the tables sat empty, gathering dust and dead leaves. I should point out that I called them employees. To Burrows, they were associates, occasionally our staff, but never employees. He believed in participatory management as long as our associates believed in the way he wished to manage. The tables had been a relaxing place to enjoy lunch and watch the fox squirrels frolic and dig up or bury whatever it was they were constantly digging up and burying. Or had been that kind of place until a month earlier when someone had assaulted and beaten to death a housewife who lived a scant two blocks away as she returned from the grocery store. Not at night. In broad daylight. The perpetrator hadn't been caught and it was then that Burrows had doubled our nighttime security staff and hired, for the first time, a daytime man as well. He grumbled that it cut into the bottom line, which it did, but it was something that had to be done. Eddie was one of the night men, the original one.

On the way back from the airport, I had decided to take him to Southeast Asia with me. Not for his size, as he was about five-five and weighed something like 134 pounds, and it wasn't for language reasons as his only language was English. But Eddie, Korean background by the way, not Chinese, was loyal to a fault, all too rare a commodity these days, and he was tough as hell. Don't let the fact that he worked out with a church Tai Chi session weekly, or sang in the Episcopalian choir, and occasionally wore

**101**

horn rimmed glasses fool you. He had been a paratrooper, could handle weapons, carry a heavy pack, and had the endurance of a water buffalo, small sized. He'd been with us five years, according to our records, had been involved in several tavern brawls that we knew about, always started, according to the record, by someone else, and always finished, according to the record and popular legend, by Eddie. Other than that, the record said, he had been a model employee, sorry, associate, who was attending college classes by day, working for us at night.

Later when I told Burrows I wanted Eddie on the trip, he seemed surprised by the idea. "What do you want that violent little hoodlum for? He has a nasty temper, argues with everybody in sight, trusts no one, can't be trusted, fights at the drop of a hat, and is just, in general, an all around evil person." This confirmed a suspicion I had long harbored. Everett had never liked Eddie, even though he had been the one to hire him.

Nevertheless, I was able to calm him by pointing out, "Everett, you have just listed all of the qualities I need for this job. He's a perfect fit."

Burrows was adaptable. "OK, take him then, but you realize this means I'll have to get someone else for the parking lot."

Calming him even more, I reassured him, "You can do it. Remember, we're only talking a few weeks here. He'll be back." And so I had my first traveling companion.

As Burrows had promised, he did round up everyone I needed to see. Tony Howsam was there. Marge was there. Horace Carmichael was there. Even Clovis was there, although I didn't know why. She was Marge's backup, or assistant, usually sat right outside my office door, guarding it from intruders, reluctant to allow even the people I wanted to see past her desk. Eddie of course, was still there after driving me from the airport.

By far, the majority of our associates were scientists, many of them with a Ph.D. after their name, but we also had the usual assortment of clerks, technicians, secretaries, financial people, computer whizzes, and assorted maintenance and custodial people. Our growth had far exceeded our wildest dreams and we recognized that we had started the company just at the right time, catching the rising tide of outsourcing that pharmaceutical companies had decided to utilize as a cost cutting maneuver. We set up clinical evaluations and kept the data on our computer banks ready for FDA review; we evaluated compounds in our own laboratories, modified molecular structure, wrote the product literature, reviewed advertising to see that it complied with all appropriate regulations, and were prepared to do anything else that a client might need. That went so far as to train their salesmen or to provide our own as a supplemental staff for new product launches. And now, we were finding and developing drugs for them. As with Clozyme, the prime example.

What the two of us had begun ten years earlier, Burrows, me, Marge, and a handful of people in two small laboratories, was now a full fledged corporation, employing, as I said I use the word even if Burroughs doesn't, more than 500 people. Most of them were working right here on our own campus although we occasionally farmed out a few to work in the facilities of a client or two, when asked. Best of all, no shareholders. We had amassed plenty of debt, but it all belonged to Everett and me, plus the banks and private lenders that were as interested as we were in our success, only they didn't have a vote, unlike the situation over at Clozyme.

I met with Horace Carmichael next, a tall, six-seven, big, burly, gentle, power forward from Tennessee A&T. The gentle kept him from the NBA, which is what he had in mind while in high school, so he joined us right out of college once he realized he wasn't going to make it in the land of flashing elbows and three point shots. He adjusted, found that the clinical laboratory courses he had taken in college had value after all, and remained reasonably content as long as he was able to play three nights a week in local basketball leagues. The pay was less, but locally he was a star and because Everett was willing to sponsor a company team, we had accumulated a whole shelf full of trophies, presently adorning the wall right over the lobby reception desk.

I might need Horace and I might not, depending upon what I found when I got over to Thailand to see these sick people that were clamoring for my attention. He could also see that any specimen I was able to obtain from Ken Green was properly handled, sent either to Bertinoldi or to Loretta Diaz, who I still had to meet. So Horace was on the travel list. He seemed eager to go.

Howsam was there and when I explained that I needed him to go to Malaysia in my place, he just asked, "When?" There wasn't a better man in the company for that assignment and I knew it.

I told him, "Two days. At the most, three. Meanwhile, do some reading on what you're likely to find there. Look at old Jack's map and concentrate on that area initially." Before going home to pack, he went down to the extensive library and started pulling books to study.

With the travel roster completed, it was time to find out what Marge had been able to come up with. Plenty, it turned out. I found her in the conference room next to my office where she was busily sorting mounds of old records, separating patient files from the daily logs. Her arms piled high with still more file folders, Clovis stumbled through the door behind me and almost dropped the entire load before regaining her balance and greeting me with, "Hi, Doctor Osten. Back, huh?" She didn't seem bothered that my being back meant late night hours.

I idly opened one of the black covers of an annual log, dust flying as the long disused pages were awakened from a deep slumber. Each book, 365 pages long, an extra day every fourth one, a year of my life, details now forgotten, but here as a reminder of successes, failures, frustrations, and dreams. What would our life look like when all of this, instead of transcribed onto paper, was homogenized onto a hard drive and reproduced on the flickering blue white screen of the computer or whatever new marvel that replaced it?

As Clovis managed to unburden herself of her cargo, Marge greeted me. "You know what?" she asked.

"What?"

"Whoever was doing your billing way back was one of the sloppiest bookkeepers I've ever seen. Nothing seems to balance. She forgot to send statements, didn't record payments on the proper account cards or both. Records are incomplete and you just don't have an appropriate audit trail here. It's a mess. I should have looked at this long ago but seeing you're not in the doctor business anymore, I didn't do it."

Was this possible? Had my accounts been mismanaged? I not only had a bookkeeper in those day, back when, as Marge said, I was in the doctor business, but I had hired an accountant to balance the books, give me regular reports, and handle taxes. Nobody had ever found anything wrong at the time.

"Not she, Marge. He. It was a he. Clark, what was his name? Clark Wherrington. He came highly recommended from a large group across town. I thought he did a good job while he was here."

"He didn't and you should have been suspicious right away. Why would a man leave a big clinic group across town and come to work for you? Maybe to rip you off, that's why. Maybe he'd already ripped them off and they sent him packing. Did you take him in without checking? You did, didn't you?"

Now that she was asking, I was ashamed to admit I couldn't remember. As near as I could recall, the group's business manager said, "He's OK. Good man" or something like that, when I finally got him on the phone. But in truth, what did that mean? If they had told me he was a crook and I hadn't hired him, he would have sued the group for passing on the information and me for using it. Philosophically, I accepted Marge's news. So my records were a mess. I had been, probably, ripped off. That was then and this was now.

"Marge, we're not staying up late to do an audit on old records. I need information about patients. From way back. At least twenty years. Let's find it." That didn't mean I wasn't interested in having an audit done later. For information only, like maybe to find the answer to something that had nagged me for years. Specifically, how come Wherrington had always driven a Buick while I had been tooling around in an older Chevrolet?

"I know. Everett already told me what you're looking for. The answer is nine."

"Nine what?"

"You treated nine students that at one time or another took a class you were teaching."

Nine! I hadn't expected it to be that many. "How many were Vietnamese?"

"Vietnamese? There's nothing on the record about what country they came from but I suppose I can tell by the names. Let's see. One-two-three-five altogether. Two marked F, women I suppose, and three marked M. Must be men, although I can't tell a woman's name from a man's name, and I don't know which are which even when I know which ones are men and women – know what I mean? But based upon the F and the M, I would say you saw three men and two women. Vietnamese, that is. And four others, Americans, I suppose.

Marge often sounded like that and I didn't always know what she meant. But if her account was correct, she had narrowed it down for me. Three men. That wasn't too bad. "And is Lee Duc Than one of them?"

"You want the names? OK, here they are. You saw Co Phan, Ho Phan Van, and Truang Van Dang. And the two women. I can see you're frowning and you're ready to ask me if one of them is named Lee Duc Than. The answer is no. You didn't see anyone by that name. Man or woman."

I took the list and verified what she had just told me. No Lee Duc Than. A setback.

"What did I see these three for? What was their complaint? We should have that information."

"Maybe, if you can believe it. Like I told you, the records were a mess back then."

"Marge, we're talking about two different things. What I treated them for, that should be on my medical notes. I kept good records for that, didn't I? The billing and accounting, that we can get into some other time." Where had Wherrington gone after he left me? Why had he left?

"Well, all right then." Marge picked up one of the folders and reviewed the patient summary I had carefully made after each office visit. "Co Phan. You saw him once. Smashed his finger on something, can't read your writing here. There was blood under the fingernail."

I leaned over to see what she was reading. The handwriting wasn't that bad. "Caught his finger in a car door, Marge, is what it says."

"That's what that says? If you say so, I suppose, it's your handwriting. Anyhow, you drilled a hole in his nail and he must have gotten better because he never came back. That was an emergency surgical procedure and there's no record here you ever billed it. You could have, you know."

"Marge, forget the past due accounts. What about the other two? What did I see them for?"

"Ho Phan Van had a cough, a fever, a headache. Sounds like a cold. Clovis found something in the computer files and it looks like you made a tentative diagnosis of a viral infection, possibly flu. Gave him a cough syrup. He came back two more times, seemed better, and then you never saw him again." She was carefully checking the corresponding day sheet, probably to see if he had been billed.

"What about Truang Van Dang?"

"Him? He had a cold, too. According to your files, there seemed to be a lot of colds that year. Lots of people coming in with the same symptoms. You know how college campuses are. Everybody gets the same thing at the same time. An epidemic. You saw him at the beginning of the new quarter, just before Labor Day when everyone was coming back to campus. I always wondered why they brought students back before Labor Day, had two days of classes, and then everyone took a long holiday break before coming back again. Dumb, don't you think?"

I had always wondered why they did that, too. "Did I get lab work, x-rays, anything like that on these patients, especially the last two?"

"You did. You sent bloods over to the lab, got chest x-rays, even did a tuberculin test on Truang Van Dang. Make that on both of them. You did one on Ho Van Phan as well. Negative, according to the notes."

"What about the x-ray reports?"

106

"Nothing here, but Clovis can get that from central records in the morning. It's on the computer. Everything went to the computer a couple of years ago. Lab work, too. She'll pull it up and make copies."

"Did Truang Van Dang come back again? Make a second visit?"

"Three more times. Then never came back the rest of the year."

"And there's nothing at all on Lee Duc Than? No one by that name anywhere in the records? Not even on the computer?"

"Not according to the records, but like I told you. . ."

"I know, they're a mess. In the morning, though, check with the University. See if they had a student by that name and whether he was in any of my classes. As a matter of fact, do that for all of the others as well. See what the University has on them."

"You want me to check on the man with the fingernail, too?"

It didn't seem likely that a damaged fingernail twenty years earlier had become a medically relevant problem, but who knows? "Sure, verify his existence too. Find out what the alumni office has on them. Maybe they can tell us where they live now. Nobody keeps better track than they do. And God knows, if any of them made a contribution to the school, the alumni office will have a detailed dossier. Find out if there are any old professors around," the minute I said it, I knew it sounded bad. I had been one of the professors, one of the younger ones, I told myself, consolingly. "Maybe they'll be able to recall something we can use. Same for landlords, barbers, restaurant owners, people like that. Use your imagination but find out everything you can. One other thought, ask around and see if there is any chance they saw a dentist while here. Dental records could help, too. Show anyone who can remember those days this picture." I handed her the one Bath had given me. "This is Lee Duc Than. Ask if anyone recognizes him."

"How much time do we have to do all of this?" she asked, looking up from a yellow legal pad that contained the notes she had been making while I talked. She was on page three.

"Tomorrow. That's it. Not much time, I know, so you'll have to use Eddie, Clovis, and anyone else you can borrow to help."

"Eddie? Eddie Chun, the security guard?"

"Him. By the way, that reminds me. First thing in the morning, make reservations for four of us, me, Tony, Eddie, and Horace Carmichael, to Bangkok. Make that Howsam to Kuala Lumpur, but I want him traveling with us as far as Hong Kong. We have a meeting in Hong Kong. Reserve rooms for us at the Hong Kong Shangri La. In Bangkok, make it the Oriental."

She handed the patient files to me and I went over them again to see if there was anything else that she might have missed on the initial review. No doubt about it, from the notes I had made twenty years earlier, Ho Phan Van and Truang Van Dang had each come in, separately and on different days, with the symptoms of a cold. Fever, cough, headaches, nasal congestion, head feeling like a balloon, according to Ho Phan Van's own words. His cough was deeper and he was bringing up thick, yellow tinged mucus. Truang Van Dang was sneezing, had a watery nasal discharge, and complained of a cough that started almost as soon as he laid down in bed. Their fevers? Not unusually high. Just 99.5 degrees. About what you'd expect to see with a cold or what everyone called the flu.

Eddie was waiting to drive me home and as I was walking out of the door, Marge called after me, "Doctor, before I forget. Mr. Towel called from New York, before you got here. He said he would be in touch with you this morning. First thing." My Benrus confirmed that it was, indeed, already past midnight. Clovis, carrying another pile of records, stumbled again as she called, "Night, Doctor. See you then." Whenever that was.

He did call back and I wasn't there, having already left on another errand. Anticipating that possibility, I had instructed Marge to transfer the call to Burrows, which she did. From what Everett told me later, I suspect that Towle/Bath/Towel, I wasn't sure what name he was using at the moment, almost choked when Burrows gave him the figures. The budget figures for Operation Patient. With half of it up front, the rest payable within ten days, it came to $455,879. It even shocked me.

"That much?" I asked, incredulously.

"Could be more. He understands that. Depends on how long it takes. If the three of you stay over there more than two weeks or if you need more equipment than you had on your list or if that Loretta something or other costs more than you think, then it has to be more. And if you need a helicopter, then even more."

"Diaz. Loretta Diaz is her name. I wrote it down on the notes I gave you."

"Where? Right there? That says Loretta Diaz?" He peered at it a second time. Dubiously, he continued, "Well, if you say so."

From where I was standing, the handwriting didn't look that bad. "What's this about a helicopter?" I wanted to know.

"A helicopter. Thing that flies and no one understands why. You'll probably end up using one and that'll cost more."

"I did not write down a helicopter anywhere in my notes. I don't plan on using one. Where did you come up with that idea?"

"Algeria. Don't you remember when you were in the Atlas Mountains looking for that bush? The one with the oleaginous material, you called it, that was supposed to have some kind of effect on the lungs? You had to get out of there in a hurry and you called someone in Oran and they sent up a helicopter that we had to pay for? Recall that?"

I recalled it readily enough. The reason I had to leave was the little matter of a war, the civil kind, the Algerian Army shooting at what they called dissidents and our little bush was right in the middle of the turf they had decided to argue about. "I figure if you're going to Thailand, or Laos, like you said, then maybe you'll need a helicopter again."

Looking at it from that aspect, maybe Everett was right. "OK, as long as he understands that those are extras," I told him, conceding the point. "As for the basic budget, did he go for it?"

"Sure he went for it. Grumbled, but what the hell can he do? He wants you, that's obvious, so he pays. Besides, it's an honest budget. That's what it costs. Cost, plus markup, that's how we do business."

And that was why I left that end of the business to Burrows.

While talking, he had wandered over to the bookshelves along one wall where he picked up another trophy. I hadn't realized that he kept any in his office. "Taking Carmichael with you, that could be a problem, you know. Could cost us another one of these," he held up the two foot tall wood and metal trinket for my inspection, "if he misses too many games. Carmichael is why we win these, you know. That Bath, or whatever, he wanted to know, really that seemed to be all he really wanted to know, was when you would be leaving for Hong Kong. I told him tomorrow. Was I right?"

I confirmed that that was my intent. Then I left to review x-ray films with Dan Emmet.

He was my favorite radiologist. And being confined to a wheelchair was no barrier whatsoever in his efforts to master his field of expertise. Over the years, he and I had looked at a lot of films together in more dimly lit rooms than I could remember and he didn't miss much. His eyes often picked up things that other eyes might miss; it could be a fine shadow, a subtle shading of gray, a tiny imperfection in bone or soft tissue, things like that, which he would either explain at once or search until he found an answer. I was hoping he could do it again.

Marge had told him of my problem and he had already pulled the films and had them in a viewing box when I walked in.

"I have two sets of films here, Mike. Must be Vietnamese patients from the names on them. What's the problem?" I checked the names to make sure we had sets of x-rays for Ho Phan Van and Truang Van Dang. We did. I briefed him on the history.

"I saw these two men back twenty years ago while they were students at the University. Both had similar symptoms. Cold like, slight fever, cough, nasal congestion, nothing very dramatic and neither seemed very ill at the time. One of them came once, maybe twice. The other came three times for follow-up visits and then disappeared. Both apparently went back to Vietnam at the end of the year and I haven't seen either of them since."

"So what are you looking for? After twenty years, who wants to know?"

"Maybe no one, Dan, but what I was wondering was, did we miss anything back then? You weren't the radiologist on the case so having another pair of eyes looking at the same films might make a difference."

He peered at the view boxes, examined the sharply delineated ribs, finger touching the heart shadow on the left, following the midline esophagus to its penetration of the diaphragm, looking for a shadow, mass or abnormality in the soft tissues of the lung. Today, we have a different set of pictures to view in many cases, the almost 3D CT scans, MRI's, and PET's, cleaving the body segment by segment, baring our internal secrets in shocking detail, showing the devastating effects of disease or the reassuring normalcy of good health. X-rays are different. One shadow often overlies another, hides the problem from prying eyes, and it takes a skilled and determined medical tactician to find a way through the blind alleys, false avenues, and to work through the maze to find an answer. It's not a game and, in real life medicine, they call it diagnosis.

Ten minutes later, Emmet shook his head and confessed, "Not much here, Mike. Both appear essentially normal. What about lab work? And did you ever make a diagnosis on the clinical signs?"

I read from the reports I had picked up earlier. "Ho Phan Van had a slightly reduced white count with a slight lymphocytosis, but everything else was fine. Truang Van Dang had a normal white count, normal differential, well, almost normal aside from 5% eosinophilia. Hemoglobin and red cell counts were normal for both. Mono tests and tuberculin were negative for both patients."

"Do you remember why you did the mono and tuberculin tests?"

"Not really, but I suspect it was because both were college students where we encounter mono frequently even though they were a little older than our usual student population. That's often the case with foreign students, as you know. The tuberculins were done because the two men hailed from a country where the disease was endemic. Besides, both of them had been coughing."

Dan was still staring at the films, seemed interested in the one on the right much more than the one on the left. "What you're telling me is that you saw these two men briefly twenty years ago and one of them wants you to treat him now? For the same thing? That's what Marge said but maybe I didn't get the story right."

"Partly right or should I say yes and no. Here's the problem, Dan. Twenty years ago, I did see these two patients and treat them. Now a third Vietnamese student who was on campus at the same time says he wants me to treat him, like I did then. Problem is, my records don't show that I ever saw or treated anyone who calls himself Lee Duc Than. That's who he says he is."

Emmet's face was barely visible in the darkened room but I could sense his confusion. "If someone by the name of Lee Duc, whatever the rest of it was, says you treated him, then why are we looking at x-rays of two other guys? Unless one of them changed his name once he went back to Vietnam."

Unless one of them had changed his name. That was worth thinking about. I didn't bother to mention Co Phan. Why bother? We had no x-ray of his finger.

I wasn't quite ready to give up. "See anything that might help me?"

He pointed to the film on the right. "I don't want to start planting things in your fertile mind, but look here. Here, here, and here. Now compare this one with the same area on the other film. There's a difference. Not a great difference, but it's there. Now, I know no two patients are exactly alike, so this may be a stretch, but here," pushing vigorously with both heels he propelled his wheeled stool across the room like a sprinter coming out of the blocks and removed another chest film from an unlighted viewing box, shot back across the room, slapped it next to the anterior-posterior views we had been examining, and said, "Now, look at this film from a different patient altogether. Notice how this film looks a lot like this old one of yours. But see here, see the difference on the other one? Right there in the hilar area. What do you think?"

At first, all three looked alike, then suddenly I saw the area he had been talking about. It grew before my eyes, a hidden shadow suddenly transformed into a possibility, then a real possibility, and finally, almost a certainty. I pointed to it, in rising excitement, and said, "You mean here. Right here?"

"Exactly. That's the place. Looks like hilar adenopathy. Hard to see at first, not massive, not pronounced, but it's there. Probably the original radiologist was looking for pneumonitis, even TB, and didn't think this was significant. I'm not sure it is, even now, but it could be."

Despite his hedging, I was a convert. It looked as obvious to me as the Grand Canyon from five thousand feet in the air.

I was momentarily elated, until I realized that none of this had anything to do with Lee Duc Than. Unless someone had changed a name! But who, why, and when, if at all?

Back in my own office, Marge was able to report that the University could confirm that all four Vietnamese men, the three I had registered as patients plus Lee Duc Than, had been students and all of them had been in one or more of my classes. I had given passing grades to all four. Not great grades, just passing, not the A's the University would have preferred for these privileged foreign students, who were given just about everything else. I felt they should earn a grade, not be awarded it for showing up on a scholarship paid for by American taxpayers. "Out of step," grumbled one academic advisor trying to nursemaid his charges through with perfect 4.0's, something he was more concerned with than they were. My passing grades, C's, meant that one tenured adviser was doomed to fail in his quest for perfection and for a time, he suggested students in his care avoid my classes.

Where did the four go after leaving the University? The alumni office had those records, as I had suspected. All four had returned to South Vietnam. They were supposed to because they had all worked for the government of that half of the country. It appeared that Co Phan must have subsequently returned to the United States as he was last reported living in Washington state from where he had been sending annual contributions and belonged to the President's scholarship fund. As it took an annual check of $1,000 to join that select circle, Co Phan, bad finger and all, must have done well after leaving college. I should have billed him after all.

There wasn't much else available on the others. Went back to South Vietnam, said the record up at Alumni Circle, and haven't been heard from since. I didn't tell them but Bath and Magellan could help them there. Their records continued where the University's left off.

Marge had diligently tracked down a former teaching assistant from those days, he had become a full professor of econometrics, whatever that was, and when he looked at the class picture, he unhesitatingly picked out all four Vietnamese and claimed he had taught all of them. The problem was, he mixed up the names referring to Co Phan as Truang Van Dang, Ho Phan Van as Lee Duc Than and so on. In other words, he was in the same dilemma as I was. He couldn't keep them straight either.

Then amazingly, Clovis tracked down a former admissions clerk who was still employed as the director of housing and when Marge talked to her, she unerringly pointed to the four, rattled off their names, and got them right. She singled out Lee Duc Than, pointed to him, as Fantus had done two days earlier and said, "That's him. Lee Duc Than. I always remembered him. He was kinda cute and always so polite. In fact, he asked me out once but I didn't dare go. My mama would have killed me. She kept telling me that these Vietnamese were the enemy and besides, she said, he was too short. He was kinda short, like she said, I'm five six myself and he wasn't that tall, as I recall, but he was real polite. Whatever happened to him?"

"What'd you tell her?" I asked.

Marge shrugged. "I told her that her mama was right. That one turned out to be the enemy after all."

That's when Bath called. Magellan, he told me, had finally made contact with Bangkok. My God, had the poor man been sitting in the communications room for two days?

"Your associate said you would be ready to leave for Thailand tomorrow when I talked to him earlier. Is that correct?" he asked.

"As things stand right now, yes. Does that meet with your approval?" Not that it mattered, but seeing this was a joint operation, I felt that a veneer of manners was called for.

"The sooner the better. Magellan learned from his informant that the patient is sicker than originally reported so we had better get to him before it's too late. We may be running out of time."

"Which patient are you referring to? The one we presume to be in Thailand who has an agent or the one Ken Green says he has?"

"The one in Thailand. We haven't heard anything more from Green so far."

I was ready to hang up when he suddenly asked, "By the way, who are all of these people you're bringing along with you? Horace Cornpeeper, Edmund Chung, Anthony Howitzer, Benito Diaz – sounds like you're bringing the entire office with you."

Either his hearing had gone bad, he couldn't read a typewritten fax sent to him by Burrows or we were on the worst telephone connection in the history of electronics, so I patiently went through the roster of my fellow travelers for him one more time. "You have the names wrong. It's Horace Carmichael, a clinical laboratory assistant; Eddie, or if you prefer, Edmund, Chun, not Chung, my assistant; Anthony Howsam, not Howitzer, another assistant; and Loretta Diaz, not Benito, who isn't coming with me but is already in Hong Kong. She's a laboratory specialist. At any rate, it sounds as if you received the budget from our Mr. Burrows and find it acceptable."

He exploded. "Acceptable! Absolutely not. The man's a bandit. A bandit, do you hear? Not you, Osten. Not you. Him. An absolute bandit."

"Then you don't want us to make the trip?"

"Of course I want you to make the trip. That's been decided. And I'm wiring the money to your bank like he wanted. I just want you to know that he's a. . ."

"I know. A bandit."

"Exactly." Everett wasn't his favorite person and he had more questions before leaving the line. "Loretta Diaz? A woman? What do we need her for? You said she was what, a laboratory specialist?"

"Her and her firm, Marcum-Whangpo. They provide diagnostic help doing things such as photospectrometric analysis, blood typing, special immunologic studies, review of pathology specimens, and much more." As they always say in a commercial.

"We're going to need all of that? What for?"

"Bath, when you're flying 12,000 miles to see sick patients, you never know what you might need. I just want to be sure it's there. Loretta Diaz and the Institute are our insurance policy." Maybe he didn't know about Kendra.

"All right. It doesn't really matter. Let's just get going. Get the whole mob over there. What airline are you on?"

"I've asked for a flight to Hong Kong via Northwest in the morning. I'll need a day in Hong Kong with Diaz and then we'll be on to Bangkok."

I heard him talking to someone in the background and he came back on the line to say, "All right, we'll meet you in Hong Kong. We're leaving in three hours so we'll be there before you. Call and let us know what flight you'll be on."

It seemed fair to ask, "Who do you plan on taking along?"

As if expecting the question, he responded at once, "Magellan and Fantus, of course. They've been in on this from the start. And Avran

Naroogian from our security detail. Just a precaution."

"You're expecting trouble, then?"

"No. Not really. But the policy is to bring along security whenever we go to a less secure area of the world."

"You consider Hong Kong a less secure area of the world?"

"No, not Hong Kong. Hong Kong's fine. But Bangkok, well, Bangkok's different."

"Yes, I suppose it is. The traffic and smog are unbearable. Where in Hong Kong will you be staying?"

"Haven't I told you? The Regent. We always stay at the Regent. We'll reserve rooms for your party as well. I suppose I'll find that on the bill, too, right? The bill from the bandit?"

I didn't want to mislead him, so I answered, "You'll find that Burrows usually includes hotel accommodations in the budget. If he hasn't already." But I knew that there wouldn't be a bill from the Regent because I had already instructed Marge to get us rooms at the Shangri La.

I questioned Burrows about the inclusion of Howsam on the Pan Union budget. He waved me off. "Don't worry about it. Howsam's on there because he's going to Malaysia in your place. I'm only including his travel expenses, not his in-country expenses, and Clozyme pays the rest. It's OK with Clozyme and it had better be OK with this Bath/Towel fellow because that's the way it is. If he has any problem with it, have him talk to me." I didn't think that would ever happen.

I had waited long enough to make my phone call to Atlanta and was pleased to find that an old friend was available. He never hesitated when I asked and in five minutes, he confirmed that they could indeed arrange for the delivery of a special package directly to my hotel in Bangkok. Then I called downstairs to our own clinical and research laboratories and asked them to prepare a small packet of materials that I might need: syringes, scarifiers, needles, rubber gloves, selected test antigens, and a number of reagents and culture kits. Most of them probably were available in the South East Asia but why take a chance?

Marge had made the call to the travel agency. "They suggested the Regent," she informed me.

"Call them back. Make it the Shangri La. Like I said. The Shangri La. The Regent, rumor has it, caters to a lower class of customers."

The raised eyebrows indicated that the news came as a shock to her. It was news to the people at Vista Winds travel as well.

"They're changing it," she told me, as she hung up the phone. "But there weren't any business class seats left on the flight."

It was my turn for raised eyebrows as I discovered we would have to rough it in first class.

# 6

The lumbering Boeing 747 was bucking strong headwinds all the way. We crossed the Rockies in the clear and looked down upon an enormous snowpack. Even from 39,000 feet, it seemed possible to make out an interstate highway, trucks, buses, skiers or was I imagining things? Howsam was studying the in-flight map. "We're over Utah or is it Colorado?" A short time later, he changed his mind. "Maybe it's Montana," he decided. Wherever it was, it was a bleak, featureless landscape, occasionally interspersed with the faint green of pines repeatedly interrupted by the appearance of mountains marching in a long craggy row as far as the eye could see, some to the north, others to the south.

Satisfied as to our whereabouts, he reached into his carry-on and removed detailed topographical maps of Malaysia. He spread them on the drop down tray and studied them. Next, he took out computer generated lists of known Malaysia flora and fauna and began marking off those areas where each species was supposed to be found in abundance. Our search had found no mention of the species of the tree Old Jack had sent back to Burrows, but inasmuch as Jack was still in his hotel suite in Penang, Howsam was planning on taking him along as a guide. He was eager, Burrows told us, to point out the exact spot he had come upon those intriguing sprigs of green and the shiny brown globules that had so impressed us with their ability to produce such impressive quantities of taxol.

Tony would leave us in Hong Kong and go directly to Kuala Lumpur and then to Penang, but we had made arrangements to keep in touch through Carmichael who would be setting up his base of operations at Chulalongkorn University in Bangkok. "Get up-country as fast as you can," I suggested. "Collect and tag your specimens and send them back to Horace. Make sure to add soil samples as you go. That Malaysian highland area is one where we haven't collected many soil specimens to date."

Howsam was reliable, a veteran field trained researcher. I wasn't telling him anything he didn't know but I felt the need to talk, trying to avoid thoughts of Kendra's blonde hair arrayed on the pillow, her pale skin, her obvious weakness and fatigue. Most of all, I was thinking of wasted years, the lost opportunity, for me, for both of us. I cursed myself a fool for not acting. Possibly too late, I realized a simple truth. You act on love, not dream about it.

I might have dozed off again, only to come awake when Howsam suddenly asked, "Maybe you won't want to answer, but who are these people we're meeting in Hong Kong?"

"Who told you about meetings in Hong Kong?"

"Burrows."

I should have known. The Chairman was never one to keep secrets unless it involved his golf handicap or our budget.

"It's complicated Tony. We have two meetings, actually. One of them with a Loretta Diaz of the Marcum-Whangpo Institute. She'll be working with Horace on any laboratory work that I might need. She might also have facilities to do some preliminary work on your specimens as well. We'll have to see what kind of operation they have."

"I've heard of the Institute. They're supposed to be excellent. Do good work. I went to school with one of their biochemists, Martin Lee Ko."

"How about Loretta Diaz? Know her?" I asked.

"Not her. Just Martin. I wouldn't mind going along to see him again."

That was no problem. "Consider yourself invited," I offered. "I would appreciate your opinion of the physical facilities and personnel, so come along."

He didn't ask about the second meeting. Tony had been around long enough to know that once in a while, perhaps every 18 months or so, I disappeared for a week or two and came back with unusual specimens from a site not on my normal itinerary. And didn't file a formal report of the trip.

Once, he had laughingly made the comment, "It isn't everyone who has a spy for a boss," and I wondered what Burrows had told him about that trip, one on which I had actually done a little spying. Not the usual cloak and dagger stuff that movies are made of, just the more routine industrial stuff that government reports are made of.

I laughed, too, and said, "You should be so lucky. And so should I," and was happy when Tony didn't bring it up again.

But that couldn't stop me from thinking about it once more. And about Jordan Green. The General.

It was 1957 again and I had just finished my residency in internal medicine, my passport to a decent living. Jordan Green was on the other end of the phone. "Mike," he sounded pleased to be talking to me, "I hear you've finished the residency grind. Good for you."

We'd been in touch by letter or phone calls about every six months, so he had been aware of my progress. A year earlier, he had stopped by City Central where I was in training and took me to dinner. He was a trim, fit lieutenant colonel then, still very much in the army and looking much better than me. I'd been sleeping too little, always a problem, eating a lot of the wrong foods, and not getting nearly enough exercise. In other words, I'd been doing all of the things I was telling patients not to do. I had even taken up smoking but couldn't inhale because the smoke made me cough. By the time Green dropped by, I had at least given up that habit.

He started off by saying, "You look great, Mike. Just great." I should have been suspicious right then.

He was about to leave on a new assignment, he told me. To Vietnam. No, we weren't doing any fighting there at the time. The French were and our involvement came later, but in the 1950's, we were sending over a handful of advisers, technical experts, specialists, people like that to "help keep the peace." Sound familiar? Preparing the people of Southeast Asia for peace and tranquillity rather than the clash and clatter of war that was ultimately to cost 50,000 American and countless Vietnamese lives. Peace and preparing for it, as Green explained it, was a noble cause. I couldn't argue with that and didn't. Instead, I asked about the twins.

Growing like weeds, he told me, and produced photos to prove it; a sturdy serious faced little boy and a smiling, golden-haired little girl, already showing evidence of the beauty that was to blossom further down the road. Ken and Kendra. I'd met them and they were great kids, the kids I'd never had. Never would.

Now, a year later, he was on the phone making an offer. "You're still a reserve officer, Mike. I'm glad you stayed active."

I didn't point out that the reason I was still active in the reserve was because he had urged me to do so. Once promoted, I was now a first lieutenant, could expect to do better than that as a medical officer, and was thinking about what to do next.

"Mike, I need you. In Vietnam. I can pull a few strings and have you sent over there where you can do us some good. For the past year, we've been having all sorts of visitors come out from Washington, Congressmen, advisors, politicians, State Department experts, newsmen, others, visiting our training camps and resettlement areas up in the central highlands and they get sick. Not all of them, of course, but too many of them. We could make use of your training and put to you to work right away. Not to treat people, we have enough help to do that already, but maybe you can take a look around and tell us why they're getting sick in the first place so we can prevent it. What do you say?"

You know what I said. Yes. What clinched it, aside from it being Green making the call and he probably could have talked me into just about anything at that time in my life, was his off the cuff comment, "The pay is pretty good and it'll be like a vacation. Pretty country. Nice people."

Although I wanted to get on with making a life in medicine, taking him up on his offer did sound interesting. At least I asked, "How long would I be in Vietnam?"

He knew he had me. "Whatever you want to make it. A few weeks, a couple of months. You decide. We can leave it open ended. I want you to feel comfortable with whatever you decide and can make it for any length of time at all. I've a free hand to do that."

It was a decision like this, made at the behest of Major Kaehl back in college, that had brought Green and me together in the first place and to that fateful day at the bridge in Korea. I hadn't forgotten, I just didn't think it could happen again. Besides, I owed Green. More than that, I liked him. Or was it the other way around?

Green gave me a number in Georgetown. "Just call it and they'll make all of the arrangements." The name of the outfit making those arrangements turned out to be the Vietnam Foundation for Science, something I found out when I did call. That was a surprise. Why wasn't the Army handling the arrangements directly? I didn't worry about it, just wondered about it, because if Green said this was the way it should be, that was the way it was. After all, he was in the Army and must know what he was doing. Later I was to find that the Foundation was located in a brownstone in Georgetown, the same one where Pan Union signs later sprouted from the sparse front lawn. The one with X in the right corner of the New Hampshire brownstone.

Everyone at the Foundation seemed eager to please and was very helpful, waiting for my call. I identified myself, told the unidentified voice at the other end that I was calling as instructed by Colonel Green, then I heard, "Osten? Lieutenant Osten? Yes, we've been expecting your call. The paperwork is done and we'll be sending your travel papers by overnight delivery. If you have any questions after you receive them, just call me. Fantus. Alex Fantus. You may not remember, but we met once. Long ago."

It hadn't been that long. Seven years and I did remember. I should have called the whole thing off right there. But if I had, I probably wouldn't have been sitting here in a 747, flying the Pacific, right now.

I caught the flight attendant's eye and asked for something cold. My skin was dry and itching and I was afraid my nose was about to act up again.

Howsam had begun idly leafing through the in-flight magazine and, as I sat there with a cold soft drink, my thoughts drifted back once more to Fantus and the Vietnam Foundation for Science. The early signs were promising. Orders arrived as promised and ten days later, crouching low and holding onto my garrison cap, I stepped from a helicopter onto the landing pad at Pleiku to find Colonel Green, wearing an Australian bush hat, waiting for me.

The health problems he had described weren't all that bad. Engineers had sited several of the camps in poorly drained locations, two of the re-settlement camps for displaced Vietnamese and hill tribesmen were in in-sect ridden swamps, and the water supply was contaminated by raw sewage. Add to that nearby mosquitoes, the spread of enteric disease by hordes of flies, and the ravages of numerous tropical and subtropical parasites, you were bound to have health problems. It was easy to drain the worst areas, to spray for insects, to use mosquito netting and screens to seal tents and build-ings, and to bury garbage, keeping it away from food preparation areas. We moved toilets away from wells, paid better attention to food preparation and trained the people doing it, and then watched to see what would happen.

Predictably, we almost immediately saw a decline in cases of diarrhea, nausea, vomiting, and unexplained fever, and a Congressman from New York came to visit the advisers, (remember, no troops yet, although the ad-visers carried guns), and went back home raving about the wonderful food and accommodations he had received. I thought that was a bit too much but when Green heard about it back in Saigon, he called and had high praise for our cleanup efforts.

"Sounds like you've got things under control there, Mike. Come on down here as soon as you can get a ride. I've got someone I want you to meet."

I helicoptered down the next day and found that Fantus, wearing a loose fitting Hawaiian shirt outside his slacks, was the surprise. His casual garb in an area populated almost entirely by military uniforms was probably intended to disguise the fact that he had gained weight since Korea. As if he were introducing an old and dear friend, Green greeted me, nodded to the Phantom, and breezily said, "You know Alex, don't you, Mike? Met him in Korea, as I recall. He's with the State Department."

What kind of a game was this? Did I know Fantus, did I remember him from Korea? You bet I did and I knew more than that. Green wasn't likely to have forgotten, or forgiven, his abrupt departure from a runway in Korea.

But here he was almost embracing him with kindness, and the good feeling and hospitality extended through the lunch hour as, over sandwiches and cold beer, Green told me of a new project, one he wanted me to join.

"We're putting together a small strike force for special missions, Mike. Not combat stuff. Special things. Diplomatic things, medical things, something like you just did up in the highlands. Helping friends of our country when they can't help themselves. We're asking a few people from the Army and a few from the State Department to be a part of this and, because you're the kind of man we need, I want you to join us." Green was recruiting from the Army. Fantus, as you might expect, was seeking recruits from the State Department.

"I'm a doctor now," I pointed out. "I'm planning on going home to practice medicine. It's time I got started on building a practice."

"That's the beauty of this, Mike. We want you to practice medicine. Stay current with all of the latest techniques and use all of the available tools. That's perfect. It's the best cover of all. Because if anyone should ever check, they'll find that what you do is practice medicine."

Who would want to check?

Green was still talking. "Everyone will have a regular job. Some will be in government service, even active military duty or in private life. Doctors, dentists, mechanics, teachers, policemen, lawyers, we've enrolled them all. With more to come. We need specialists of all kinds and they'll stay in a regular job until we have a need for them. Then we'll call, they'll leave for a short time, do what has to be done and when finished, go right back to where they came from. Smarter, wiser, more experienced than before, having rendered a service to their country."

Major Kaehl had been a good salesman. Colonel Green was even better. I signed on. Didn't actually sign anything, just telling Green I was in was good enough and we sealed it with a handshake. Fantus looked on approvingly and suggested, "Stay in the reserves. That will make the processing much easier in case we ever have to call upon you."

Green agreed, and after thinking about it, I realized that it made sense.

The cabin intercom disturbed Howsam's nap and snapped me back to the present. "Because of headwinds," the voice intoned, "we will have to land at Anchorage for refueling before continuing the flight." An unscheduled stop, one hazard of late fall traffic across the Pacific. Most likely we would arrive late in Tokyo and miss the connecting flight to Hong Kong. The best laid plans. . .

Why was Green working with Fantus after what had happened in Korea? Why had they set up a joint strike force years later and then continued to work together, were still rumored to be working together, many years later? And what about me? Why had I joined them and why had I stayed?

Thinking about it made me uneasy. Thinking about what I was trying to do now made it worse. It seemed simple enough. I wanted to find Ken Green. But was he alive? Where did Lee Duc Than fit into the picture and how could there be two of him? Why was he saying that I had treated him when my records said I hadn't? Who was Bath and why was he using code names? Or was Bath a code name and Towel his real name? Why the smoke screens? Why wasn't anything as simple as it seemed? Why couldn't I just go and find Ken Green and help Kendra? Why couldn't I decide what to do?

Suddenly I felt chilled in the cool air of the cabin. The cabin attendant spread a rich burgundy red blanket over my shoulders, I murmured my thanks, and felt a chill along my spine as the color brought back memories that usually came in the dark of lonely nights. The rich burgundy was the color of the tough outer shell of the areca noir, a strange East Asian and African fruit I had encountered but once and hoped never to see again. When dried and chewed, this mind-altering alkaloid was capable of turning placid natives into maniacal killers, the eyes becoming hollow shells with the red rage of hate lighting the way to murder. Why did that remind me of Bath and Fantus, who would be waiting for us in Hong Kong? I stirred uneasily under the blanket and glanced behind me. Eddie Chun and Horace Carmichael had eaten and fallen asleep in their comfortable reclining chairs. The cabin attendant was removing the last tray and dropping an empty Budweiser can into her plastic trash container. Everyone else within sight was asleep or tethered to a head set, listening to music. It looked peaceful enough. But areca noir had reminded me of danger. Sudden, unimaginable danger.

I reached back and pulled on Eddie's ankle. He awoke with a start, his eyes wide.

"Stay awake," I told him.

He nodded, sat up, popped his seat into the erect position, stood up, and viewed the cabin, walking back several paces to peer into the coach section, as if in need of exercise. The attractive Chinese cabin attendant paused in her work to smile at him. Eddie smiled back. Then he returned to his seat, sat down, and said, "Right."

Areca noir again. It brought back a jumble of memories; none of them good, involving jungles and their dreadful secrets, the sense of terror that the word Congo brings to mind, the darkness, the smell of fear, and most of all, the sight of the dismembered bodies, all that remained of the patrol, lying where they had been slain, and Fantus. Fantus, once again never looking back as he ordered a half empty boat, the last boat, the only boat, to pull away in the sluggish current, leaving behind desperate men who had nowhere to go, and the dozen bodies for whom it was already too late for escape.

The Congo! Yes, the Congo. Jordan Green's special operations group in action. Its first action, if you don't count the mosquito and sanitation job in Vietnam. Like I said, I signed on, went back home from Vietnam, and went into a group practice to start seeing patients. Put some money into the bank, bought a new car, went to parties, and met a nurse. Sounds familiar, you say, doctor meets nurse, they marry and live happily ever after, raising little doctors and nurses or whatever. But it didn't work out that way as the nurse had a friend and I fell in love with her instead. She worked in the hospital clinical laboratory, worked evenings as did I, and soon we were dating. Soon decided we were in love and, over coffee in the hospital cafeteria, close to Christmas, we became engaged. Her name was Abby and her father was a professor at the University. That's the way it was done back then. All of this has become much more complicated now as men and women worry more about making 'commitment,' developing a relationship, and finding just the right time and place for the wedding, rather than just getting married. I should know as I was still having difficulty making a commitment, making a decision about what to do even now, and my hair was getting gray.

But back then, when my hair was still dark brown, thick, and wavy, our main problem was finding a hall big enough for the wedding. At least that's what we thought our problem was. That and a shortage of cash. That's almost always a problem, but God moves in strange ways and as if to prove it, help came from an unexpected source. Sure, from Jordan Green.

He was on the phone, asking something like, "What's new?" and I blurted out the hitherto unrevealed news that I was planning on being married.

He sounded disappointed, not because of the pending marriage, but because I hadn't told him sooner. "Why the secrecy? You weren't planning on telling me?"

We hadn't told anyone yet, other than her family, because of the money problems, although I knew that Abby expected her father to pick up the bills. That left me feeling guilty, though, because with both of us working, it seemed as if Abby and I should be able to pay for this important move by ourselves. "Tradition," she told me. "The father of the bride pays." Looking at the family home, the ivy covered brick walls and lush garden, and the cars, three of them, I suspected that her father might be able to do just that. I still felt guilty. That's what I told Green.

"You need a place for a reception and want to keep the costs down? Nothing wrong with that even if her father pays. That's just common sense, Mike. But let me help. I know people who can take care of everything with one phone call." The offer sounded too good to be true.

But there was a catch. There's always a catch. Having apparently solved one problem, he created several new ones. "Mike, listen, could you get married to Abby, that's her name?, before the end of May if I take care of those details we were talking about? I need you for a little project during the first week of June."

Abby was planning a September wedding, if the hall was available, later if it wasn't. The calendar on the wall by the phone read April 29th. The end of May was a month away. I had no problem with the new date. In fact, I was delighted. Made more sense instead of waiting, but I wasn't sure how this would be received in the McIntyre household, or more importantly, by Abby herself.

The little project Green had in mind? "I need someone for a nice soft job in Switzerland," that was his description and those were his exact words, "with the World Health organization. Calls for a medical background and you're perfect for the job. As soon as it came up, I said to myself, 'That's perfect for Mike Osten. Couldn't find a better man.' Problem is, I need someone free as soon as possible, need time to brief him, get him in place, have him settled into a nice apartment. In Geneva. Great place for a honeymoon. You and your Abby would love it."

He must have had a calendar by his phone, too, as he suddenly said, "Wedding four weeks from Saturday. That would be perfect. Plenty of time for your young lady to get ready, try on her wedding dress, line up attendants or whatever they call them, and for you to wrap up your practice for the time being. While you're doing all of that, I'll make arrangements for the reception, find you a place to live in Geneva, and we'll have everything done. What do you think?"

What did I think? It all seemed a little fast, almost too good to be true, and I couldn't help but feel that I was still going to feel guilty about something. But overall, why not? Living in Geneva sounded good. Honeymooning in Geneva sounded better. Being married, rather than waiting, sounded best of all. Maybe raging hormones were doing my thinking, and when I think back now it seems as if I should have just said no, but I didn't. Once again, I said yes. I had a habit of saying yes to Jordan Green.

Having said that, I added a qualifier, "I'll have to see what Abby says." I hung up with his words ringing in my ears.

"Talk it over with her, Mike, and get back to me right away. If you can't go, I'll have to come up with someone else."

Irrationally, I didn't want him to even ask anyone else. I wanted to go. With Abby, naturally.

She expected to be married in St. Octavius, the family church. Had been the church for three generations. The reception, she insisted, had to be at the Country Club, catered by the famous N. Caruso who was in constant demand and unlikely to be free for any date prior to September, if then. People waited a year or more just to have Caruso handle the wedding reception. He was likely to be a problem for a May date. This was the minimum, Abby told me. Her folks would rather die than do anything less, she assured me. She was wrong.

I discovered that a week later when we dined with the family, a dinner that had been called specifically to discuss this highly irregular proposition. Abby was skeptical that Green could deliver what he had promised. I told her never to bet against the man, even though I harbored some doubts of my own. One of Abby's sisters, the married one, (Abby had four, three unmarried with two engaged and one teetering on the brink), thought the idea was 'so romantic, a honeymoon in Geneva,' and seemed all for it. The others had no comment. They sat silently now, around the table with the intendeds, hoped-fors, and the one already married spouse, sharing roast beef, long grain wild rice, and petit pois, while the professor and his wife chatted amiably in soft tones at one end of the table. Abby and I held hands, hoping to reassure one another that all would be well, although fearing that it wouldn't, and waited. We were still waiting when after dinner, brandy snifter in hand, the professor, (an assistant department head in geology), motioned me into the garden to see "my fabulous tomatoes and tulips." It being early May, the tulips were in bloom while the tomatoes, being grown from seed, were barely out of the ground. The plants, both varieties, were healthy, but hardly fabulous. It was obvious that he had more on his mind than gardening.

We stood watching the new moon low in the southeast sky, just beyond a line of white pines outside the brick walled enclosure. The garden had the smell of new things growing, the damp odor of properly prepared soil, and a mist was forming just outside the wall as if waiting for permission to enter. I was worried about how the professor viewed me. What would he think of a prospective son-in-law who was giving up a reasonably successful new medical practice to take a salaried position in far-off Switzerland, albeit a position with a decent title and good fringe benefits, like housing, travel expenses, a car, medical care, things like that? I expected he would bring all of this up, as his wife had started to do inside before he abruptly cut her off. I wasn't sure how I would answer, as I wasn't even certain I should leave.

So I was surprised when his first words were, "Do you think he really means this about the reception? Could he do it?"

That was easy to answer. "Yes," I told him. "Colonel Green can do this, if he gets the go ahead. He's never promised anything he couldn't deliver." I really believed that, although I wasn't privy to all of the promises Green had made in his life. Any he had made to me, though, he had kept.

"So we have to assume the offer is genuine. Why? Why would anyone make such an offer?"

"Professor, I. . ."

He was holding up a hand in protest, saying, "Bob, Mike, please call me Bob. Everyone in the family calls me Bob and we consider you family now, so make it Bob."

He considered me family? So soon. So sudden.

I still considered him the Professor, but I can follow orders, so I explained as best I could, the name sticking slightly the first time I used it, "Bob, he's a friend from the Korean War days. My commanding officer in Korea, to be exact. He's the man making the job offer in Geneva and because time is so important, I have to be there before the middle of June, he wants to make it possible for Abby and me to be married by then. That's why he offered to help."

"Aren't these little rascals beautiful?" he asked, stooping to caress the top of a small tomato plant in the dark. "Started them in the sun room almost six weeks ago. Pried the seeds out of an old Italian across town. He grows the best plants in the county but keeps everything a secret."

I was still visualizing the Professor, Bob, prying seeds out of an old Italian, (what was he using, a chisel, screwdriver, back of a hammer?), as he continued, "I was a lucky man to get these, and following instructions to the letter, put them into clay pots, you can't use plastic, spoils everything, watered them and fertilized them every day. Talked to the agronomists at school and they gave me tips on the proper mix of soil and fertilizer. I'm doing it right. Everything by the book and do you know what my goal is for this year?" I had a hunch what it was. "To beat the old Italian at his own game. To grow better plants, get the first ripe tomatoes, harvest bigger tomatoes than he does. What do you think of that?"

I had heard others refer to the Professor as single-minded. Another term that could be used was competitive. I knew which old Italian he was talking about and was still willing to bet on him, but you can't be too careful about what you say to a member of the family, so I was essentially noncommittal, saying only, "I bet you can do it, too."

Still holding his glass of brandy in the moonlight, he nodded imperceptibly, appreciating my confidence in his horticultural ability, and at the same time, noticing that I hadn't brought along my after dinner drink, he managed to look disappointed. "Good stuff," he said, raising his glass in a single toast and downing it. "I have one glass of this every night, before going to bed. Habit, I suppose, but from what I hear, you doctors approve. A little drink is good for you, isn't it, Doctor?"

"Bob, call me Mike. Think of me as family. About the brandy, I think it's a splendid idea," although I had no idea whether it was or not.

For a moment, I thought he was considering throwing his empty glass against the brick wall in celebration over acquiring another family member, but instead he suddenly asked, "Mike, let me ask you. What did you see inside at the table tonight?"

It was a surprising question. "I don't understand, Bob. What do you mean what did I see?"

"Around the table. What did you see around the table? Sitting there."

I still didn't understand the question. "Around the table? Around the table, in this order, I saw you, Mrs. McIntyre, your married daughter Beth and her husband Tex, three other daughters and their boyfriends or betrothed, I'm not sure which or what their names are, and then Abby and me. I think that's everybody."

He threw both arms into the air as he said, "Tex! Isn't that a gaudy name for a man who comes from Vermont? He got it riding a mechanical bull in a Boston saloon."

I hadn't known that.

"No, Mike, that's not really what you saw around the dinner table tonight. Not if you looked hard enough and knew what to look for. What you saw when you looked around the table tonight, and I'll deny this to my grave if you ever mention this to a soul, was bankruptcy. Four unmarried daughters is a heavy burden, Mike. We've already paid for one marriage and here we are with four more staring us in the face. Mrs. McIntyre demands that we go for the whole shot. The country club, the fifteen piece orchestra, the drinks, the catered dinner, Caruso, just Caruso alone costs a fortune, the flowers, enough flowers to beautify the church and city hall for a year, the whole thing. Do you have any idea of the cost? Times four?"

I did have some idea because Abby and I had been pricing it out as we went. Bob didn't wait for my answer. He was on a roll.

"I was telling Marthe last night," so Mom's name was Marthe, I'd have to remember that although so far, she had not objected to being called Mrs. McIntyre, "we won't make it. Can't make it. Fact is, Bob, we're living over our heads. Have been for some time and it's all beginning to catch up with us." I began to doubt that Bob limited himself to a single glass of brandy just before going to bed. He seemed to have consumed more than that, at least for this dinner party.

"It's simple. Too much going out, not enough coming in. Money. Look at this house. Big, right? Garden. Big, right? Cars, three big ones, right? Look at the furniture, big right? And expensive. Look at Marthe's hair. Her hairdresser bills. Big, right? Look at the dance lessons for four girls, used to be five, and the golf lessons, tennis lessons, riding lessons, ballet, sports for all of the kids, best equipment, best coaches, best clothes, best everything. Big, big, big. Can't give one girl anything without giving the same to all five. Make that four now. Fact is, Mike, we're dammed near broke. Mike, we need you, and three more like you. Take the girls out of here, pay the bills for them, and get them off our backs. Maybe, just maybe, then we'll be able to stay out of bankruptcy."

I had been worried about whether Bob would find me acceptable for his daughter. Now I had a new problem. He was looking at me as a savior, a white knight who had come to rescue the family from the clutches of the bankruptcy lawyers.

"Mike, Abby will marry you no matter what. She's in love. I know that. So, let's take that friend of yours up on his offer. If he wants to provide the hall and pay for some of the expenses, hell, let's swallow our pride and do it." After a moment of reflection, he modified his stand. "I don't know if your pride is involved. I'll swallow mine. Is that better?"

What would Marthe think about all of this? "Don't worry about her.

She understands what we have to do and she's ready to compromise."

The rest was easy. Abby was ecstatic, the logjam was broken, things started to move, and the date was fixed. We were married early in June, it turned out that Green's date was flexible all along, and Abby didn't miss out on a St. Octavius wedding after all. Miraculously, another wedding was canceled and the church opened up on the chosen Saturday. We went down the aisle there, Abby radiant in a magnificent gown and Bob looking as happy as I have ever seen a father look as he escorted her down that carpet and turned her over to me.

The reception was in the officer's club of the nearby army base. Balloons were everywhere, crepe paper, satin ribbons and lace cutouts adorned every surface, and flowers of every color overloaded the senses with beauty. The band played on and everyone danced until midnight, and the sit-down dinner was worthy of royalty – or Army officers. There was no end to the refreshments and N. Caruso could have done no better than Master Sergeant Buck Hapthorn, of Big Bend, Texas, the club's manager. Unlike Tex from Vermont, Buck was a true Texan. In every sense of the word.

Jordan Green, in full dress uniform, was there and hardly a guest left without having a hand shaken and an ear bent by the Colonel. He was everywhere, smiling, meeting, socializing, a side of the man I had never seen until then. Late in the evening, my new father-in-law pulled me aside to whisper, "The Colonel thinks you have a great career ahead of you. This Geneva thing, it's a wonderful thing for someone so young, from what he says."

Green still hadn't briefed me on what the job would entail so I could make no comment other than to say, "That's nice to hear." Of course, it was nice to hear.

A week earlier on the phone, I had raised that very point. "Don't worry about it," he advised. "Just enjoy the wedding and later I'll tell you everything you need to know. It won't take long."

McIntyre was stunned when he saw the bill. Speechless, in fact. He was billed for the cake, ordered by his wife from Why Not Fresh?, a bakery better known as a maker of classic breads than for wedding cakes, but truly they outdid themselves. Four layers of golden batter, covered with thick cooked white frosting, and the usual colorful names and curls and dates, that sort of thing, enough to feed the multitudes, as Father O'Reilly pointed out, that bucolic man apparently sensing the similarity between feeding the throng of wedding guests and Jesus feeding so many with the limitless dozen fishes and loaves of bread in Biblical times. So McIntyre was billed for the cake, a substantial sum to be sure, and three phone calls that someone, unidentified, had made on the club manager's private telephone. That was it. Everything else had been billed to, and paid by, the UN Society for World Peace. They had an address in Georgetown.

Staring at the bill in disbelief, the Professor asked, "Who the heck are they?"

"A nice bunch of people who support the UN and believe in world peace," I guessed. McIntyre paid his part of the bill, willingly. The remainder, that part was actually billed to me, later, in several different installments. Not in money. In services.

As the reception was ending, Green pulled me aside and handed me an envelope with news of a surprising change of plans. "Here are plane tickets to Bermuda. A week at the Princess. It's all set up. Enjoy the honeymoon and then be in Geneva on the fifteenth. While Abby settles in the apartment, here's the address and keys, it's all furnished, rent a car and drive up to Lausanne. I'll meet you at the Beau Rivage and brief you on what we want you to do. Meanwhile, while in Bermuda, read this stuff. All of it. It's critical that you know it, understand it, and master all of it before we meet in Switzerland." The book he handed me was eight inches thick, three times as thick as the briefing manual he had issued in Korea. That, I understood, was the first installment on the bill.

The second installment was to come due in the Congo.

First though, we spent a summer of happy days in Geneva. The Colonel remained in Lausanne during most of that summer and I drove up on alternate weekends to report on what I had seen and learned. There were other members of an action group reporting to him at his hotel, but all of our visits were timed so that one man would be arriving as another was leaving and we never met together, never were introduced to one another, and had no official knowledge that anyone else was even there. In fact, buried in my briefing manual were the instructions that ordered me to ignore them, not make myself known to them, and to avoid speaking to them even if I knew who they were. I could do that easily enough, but I still could pick some of the frequent visitors to the Beau Rivage out of the crowd of bureaucrats and advisors down at World Health organization offices in Geneva. Never acknowledged them, of course, just marked them and wondered who they were.

That's where I was, of course. Working with the WHO along with thousands of others from every member country in the United Nations. Milling about, drafting proposals to improve health standards around the globe, to identify dangerous situations where epidemics might occur, and to eliminate disease, malnutrition and poverty from countries where most of their unfortunates were still struggling just to survive. And to listen, "especially listen to gossip, rumors, hints, anything at all like that coming from Soviet bloc country WHO personnel," said the Colonel. "Make casual contact with them, talk in coffee houses, at lunch, in hallways, after meetings, and talk shop to anyone who you can get to listen to you. But don't say much. Listen to them. Then report to me. Don't make notes. Just report to me. Verbally.

"We are especially interested," he continued, "in anything they may have to say about polio, typhus, smallpox, botulinus, any suggestions they are engaging in germ warfare or developing toxins to poison water supplies, foodstuffs, soil. Even an innocent comment from one of their scientists at a meeting could be of tremendous importance. Listen to all of it. Report to me." And then he warned again, "They'll be doing the same to you, so be careful of what you say."

Later, he added, "About their leadership. The top men in their government or even top scientists. Listen very carefully to any comment that might indicate a medical problem. Is someone ill? Does someone have a disease? Drink too much? Smoke too much? Have VD? Have they suffered a stroke or have chest pain? All of this could be important to our people in dealing with their people at some point in time."

And later, "Read. Read everything you can get your hands on from all Soviet bloc countries, but don't ignore our friendly allies. Sometimes there are interesting bits of information you can pick up from them or about them."

Easy job? Not really. The talking and listening part wasn't bad. Most of that was done during the day with some of it spilling over to evening conferences and social sessions. The reading part was another six hours a day, in the libraries, at home, Abby waiting for me to finish and come to bed or later, just going to bed while I read on.

It wasn't all work. My official assignment had me sitting on several WHO task force committees and on another UN committee loosely attached to WHO. We argued over financing of the many programs being considered, planned for contingencies if, for instance, smallpox should break out in remote areas of Gabon or the Ivory Coast or if polio should run amok in Baton Rouge, Louisiana. There were thousands of contingency plans, a million rumors, and no end of things to report to Green. And there was the activity of the other side, brought home forcefully one afternoon when Jared Chamblis, the deputy director of the American delegation to the WHO, warned, "Be careful of what you say to your committee chairman. Everything he learns is reported directly to his Moscow handlers."

The committee chairman, the mosquito eradication committee, was a Senegalese, who had shown an active interest in my insect control experience in Vietnam two years earlier. Problem was, along with mosquitoes and insecticides, he had shown an interest in how American gun emplacements were sited in relation to bunkers and barbed wire, all of which I had dutifully reported to Green. We were shortly to learn that our chairman had received his engineering degree from Moscow University on what we would call a full scholarship back in the States. "Moscow University," the Colonel somberly advised me, "is known to have turned out a substantial number of Third World spies working on the Soviet payroll."

Spies? I was surrounded by spies? In Moscow, was someone adding my name to a file of American spies? Was reading medical literature and listening to gossip spying? Depends, I suppose, on how one defines the art of spying.

But like I was saying, it wasn't all work. Most evenings and weekends were free and Abby and I had plenty of time to become better acquainted. We were fascinated by Geneva, enjoyed lazy hours walking the city, sitting along the waterfront watching the windblown spray from the fountain, dining in excellent restaurants or idling in one of many nearby coffee shops. Several times, she accompanied me to Lausanne and, after I made my report to Green, we drove on to Vevey or Montreux and twice joined him for dinner on the terrace of the Beau Rivage, watching the sun set against the snow cap on Mt. Blanc across the lake in France. We traveled to the snowy Alps, rode on the trams, and managed to spend one weekend in Bern and another in Zurich. And, of course, almost once a month during our stay, we drove or took one of the speedy interurban trains to Neuchatel to visit my mother, her home since my father died suddenly of a massive heart attack, and sample the fruit of her vineyard. Then finally, we made plans for an excursion to Lichtenstein, something Abby had talked about since our arrival in Europe.

"Why?" I asked teasingly.

"I want to see the Grand Duchy, whoever or whatever that is," she replied. The truth was, so did I, so we decided to go on the very next free weekend we could find.

And then the Belgians pulled out of the Congo, granting it independence. Only the Congo wasn't a country. In reality, it was nothing more than a collection of tribes held together by the presence of the Belgian Army and, when the disciplined military force fell back to the capital, the rest of the country splintered into a hundred pieces and the killing began. Tribes, loyal only to themselves, fell upon neighbors, hating, burning, destroying anyone different than themselves. The age of colonialism, according to the UN, had ended. The age of chaos had begun.

Having encouraged the Belgians to leave, the UN was horrified at what was happening and decided to intervene. Then, as now, the UN was an unsatisfactory policeman, usually sending far too few men and too little equipment to do an effective job. Nowhere was this more evident than in the Congo where the roads were mainly dirt trails, transport all but nonexistent, and mud was everywhere. Airfields, all too few to begin with, were primitive strips carved from the jungle without adequate beacons or communications facilities, most of them unlighted and unsuited for night operation. Railways were few and ran on fixed tracks through impenetrable jungle where ambush or sabotage was easy. And into this nightmare of killing and terror came a handful of UN soldiers, recruited from a dozen countries, given blue helmets and told to restore law and order. And, as usual, to keep the peace. It was a hopeless task.

As was bound to happen, it always does, one warring faction turned upon helpless outsiders, seized hostages, and threatened to kill them all unless, well, nobody really knew what the unless was. Maybe they just wanted hostages to kill. The outsiders were all white, most of them nuns and priests from several missions in the heart of the deepest jungle, all sworn to help God tame the raging passions of natives drunk now with visions of power and independence, and who were more interested in that than what God had to offer. Hostages usually capture the attention of the world, that's why hostages are taken, and the knowledge that three priests, eight nuns, five nurses, three technicians, and a doctor had been seized, beaten, and locked away led to agonizing meetings in UN offices along the East River in New York. Lights burned until late in the night and then the decision came down: rescue the hostages.

The Belgians, belatedly recognizing the quagmire they had left behind, were willing to assist in mounting a rescue mission and prepared to dispatch paratroops still based at Elizabethville. The UN sent in lightly armed infantrymen and the combined force, insufficient for the task, called upon the only other available disciplined military force in the Congo for help.

Semi-disciplined at least, and when the breakaway mineral rich province of Katanga answered the call, the operation began.

It was obvious that there would be shooting, or worse, and that casualties would ensue. Casualties meant doctors and as I was one of the closest doctors to the scene, already UN accredited, just a short flight away, someone pushed a button and said, "Send him."

Green called and issued the order, "Go," he said, and that was the second installment on the wedding reception bill.

In military terms, the plan was a double envelopment, the paratroopers arriving over the target just as the Katangese infantry arrived from the river side and the UN contingent checked in after a difficult truck ride through the jungle. The Katangese on the left, UN on the right, Belgians overhead, to put it another way. Maybe that made it a triple development. I joined the Katangese at a remote airstrip where an ancient DC-3 deposited me one afternoon, accompanied by an assorted collection of other Americans and Frenchmen, most of them journalists, hoping to win a Pulitzer prize with a quick visit to a war zone and then a quicker trip back to civilization to write and talk about it for a lifetime.

"You'll meet up with an Irish UN platoon just outside the city," my briefer told me as I boarded the plane in Elizabethville. "You'll be their medical officer and our observer. The Irish will brush aside any resistance on the way into town, there shouldn't be much to worry about, and once in town, head directly for the church where the hostages are held, free them, and start back. The paras will keep everyone tied down in the city center so it should be easy. A flotilla of boats will be waiting ten miles downstream to carry you and the hostages to safety. Any questions?"

The plan sounded perfect and probably looked that way, too, on paper. But with the rescuers speaking a half dozen different languages, wearing a half dozen different uniforms and with no means of effectively communicating with one another, it broke down. Not surprisingly. To start with, we were late, our trucks having bogged down in mud. The paratroopers were early and we could see them dangling, white and olive parachutes blossoming against a blue sky, while we were still three miles from our objective. Then the small arms fire began, black smoke arose from the city center as several loud explosions rocked the air, and the chatter of machine guns could be heard clearly on our immediate front. A dozen of our trucks managed to cross a small stone bridge and we were suddenly driving through a maze of rusted corrugated metal shacks, mud huts, and shanties of rotting wood from which men, women, and children could be seen scrambling to safety. Incredibly, several Jeeps appeared on our left flank and we could see the welcome blue berets of the UN Irish platoon we had been promised as support.

One hundred yards from the main gate of the church compound, easily identified by the towering spire topped by a cross, a half dozen figures ran away without a backward glance. They were all carrying weapons, but none of them fired a shot.

The gate was open, the top hinge shattered allowing the heavy wooden gate to dangle crazily, threatening to topple at any moment. Several Irish troops entered warily, crouched low, and advanced across the open courtyard, pausing to peer into the first open doorway they encountered. Then they stood erect and silently waved for others to follow.

We had arrived five minutes too late. All of the hostages had been brutally beaten, then slain, and bodies were lying where they had fallen, scattered about in the church itself. Priests, nuns, all of them, slashed, cut, and mutilated, several of them still impaled with six foot long metal tipped killing sticks. Most appeared to have been assaulted with whatever weapon was at hand – knives, spears, clubs, rifle butts, machetes, pangas, even several crucifixes seized from the altar and now smeared with blood. Fresh blood, in fact, was everywhere and the bodies were still warm. An Irish trooper suddenly called out that one of the nurses was still alive, still breathing, but as I urgently searched for a vein hoping to insert an intravenous line, the pulse faded and we lost her as well.

Aside from burying the dead, there was little else we could do here. And the Irish Captain wasn't even sure about the burying. "They'll likely just dig them up and commit even worse atrocities after we leave," he said. And he may have been right, but the looks of his men and his own decency prevailed and, working hurriedly, using whatever tools were at hand, shallow graves were prepared in the consecrated church cemetery behind the burned shell of what had been the center of hope and Western religion in this far off place. Had the priests and nuns who had come all this way to save souls expected this to be their own final resting place? Probably not.

The UN commander and his Katangese counterpart didn't want it to be ours either and as soon as he had recited a few words over the graves, he ordered a return to the trucks for an attempt to link up with the Belgians who, as we could hear, were still engaged in a vicious firefight north and west of our position.

By the time we reached them, in the center of a blazing downtown, we found that the paratroopers had been doing much better than it had sounded. Most of the armed looters and would-be revolutionaries had scattered before them, unwilling to face a force of professional soldiers. A few had holed up in nearby buildings and were firing sporadically, without effect. The paratroopers had suffered few casualties, a half dozen wounded at most, and had things well in hand, for the moment.

They were to pull back to the airfield and hold it, while in New York, diplomats, again arguing far into the night, decided what to do next. Our orders were unchanged, even if our circumstances were. We were to fall back down river, rendezvous with boats waiting to spirit rescued hostages to safety, and be withdrawn. The problem was, we had rescued no one. But orders are orders and assembling the convoy of three Jeeps, four old trucks, and a battered old Chevrolet pickup, leaving the rest behind, we departed. I was riding in the second Jeep in line and behind me came the trucks with thirty Irishmen, about the same number of Katangese infantrymen, a dozen Indonesians manning three light machine guns that had yet to be fired, an Englishman, whose mission was unknown, and a Bulgarian observer, who it was rumored, reported to the UN secretariat.

All went well until the ambush, the attack hitting us on a twisting stretch of road with thick underbrush coming within inches of each vehicle as it passed. One moment we were moving, the sides of our Jeep fighting off the clutching jungle grasses, mud slithering off tires sunk to the axles in the rutted trail, our view obscured by chaff flying free of the pollinating heads of massive weeds that almost totally hid the road in front, and in the next instant, we were under sudden, violent attack. The first Jeep, fifty feet ahead, disappeared around a curve and we followed. For just an instant, we both were out of sight of the following trucks, now some 200 feet to the rear. That's when I saw movement to my left, heard one or more shots ahead and started to rise from the seat to see what was happening to the lead Jeep. That action may have saved my life as a stabbing stick intended for my throat tore into my left thigh instead, the searing pain confirming that the weapon had struck home. Despite the pain, or maybe because of it, I turned and instinctively fired the heavy Colt .45 that I had started to draw when I heard the first shot. I fired once, then a second time, and had the impression of a figure falling back from the side of the Jeep just as I fell into the ditch, the Jeep toppling a moment later.

Lying there, once more in a roadside ditch, I became aware of the generalized firing that had broken out all along the column. I was more concerned with the red hot poker that had buried itself deep into my left thigh and the heavy weight lying across my right leg. I pulled my good leg free, checked to see if I was still holding my Colt .45, and rolled over, the stabbing stick falling out of my leg at the same time. The pain was excruciating. The firing had stopped. I heard shouting, then the murmur of voices. The smell of blood and cordite hung in the air.

As if in answer to a silent prayer, an Irish medic was there, tearing the blood stained trouser leg to inspect the wound, ripping open a packet I had brought with me from Geneva, applying antiseptics, taping a bandage in place, offering pain medication, and administering an antibiotic. In the minute or two that it took him to tend to my wound, I realized that I wasn't badly injured, concluded that I had survived, and began to feel better. With his help, I rose unsteadily and limped after him to see if we could be of help elsewhere.

One man had died, the driver of the lead Jeep having taken a bullet in the chest, and three others had been injured. Just a rogue group of bandits, of no particular political persuasion was the consensus, but even rogue groups can be fatal, as we had discovered.

We halted on a small rise just before dark, three or four miles from our intended rendezvous on the river. Our captain sent a twelve man patrol ahead to establish camp on the riverbank just in case the boats arrived before 7 A.M. The rest of us bivouacked for the night, posted sentries, did all of the things the book calls for when in hostile surroundings. We sited the machine guns to cover every approach, ate cold rations so as to not give away our position by lighting a fire, and tried to sleep. My leg started to throb and I used more of the pain killers and took another antibiotic tablet.

Shortly after five, as the first rays of sunlight thrust probing fingers through the misty dawn, we were back in our vehicles, headed for the river. Twenty minutes later, the reflection of sunlight from glass showed us the way to the patrol's truck, parked just off the trail, within sight of the placid river lying just beyond. It was quiet. Too quiet. Aside from the fact that this was in daylight, it was strangely reminiscent of a night in Korea when no sentries had been in evidence when they should have been there. Mist was clinging tenaciously to the river's edge, thinning as it moved ashore, and the Irish captain signaled for his men to dismount, three of them moving cautiously through the chest high saw grass.

A Katangese sergeant mumbled in his native tongue and several of his men slipped from the rear truck and deployed across the road behind us, others moved to the flanks. And it was then that we discovered another massacre, my third, I realized, and wondered how it was that I was keeping score. One on a dark night in Korea, another yesterday at the church, and now, number three, the Irish patrol at the river's edge. Here, along a muddy road in the jungles of the Congo, twelve Irish soldiers wearing the blue of the United Nations and the green shamrocks of their home island, had been slain. Not only killed, but their bodies had been stripped and then hacked to pieces.

The Katangese sergeant looked at the scene impassively, his expression suggesting that he had seen things like this before. The Irish looked on in horror. The sergeant pointed to dark dried splotches scattered here and there on the bodies of the dead men and the Katangese soldiers crowded about pointing, talking among themselves, and nodding. I had never seen anything like the strawberry colored adherent crusts that were everywhere on the dead men. It wasn't blood. In disgust, the only thing I could compare it to was what happened to your freshly washed automobile when you parked it under a tree chosen as a roost for a flock of itinerant starlings.

The Katangese were still murmuring among themselves and the Englishman had been listening attentively. "Do you know what they're saying?" I asked.

"I think so. From what I gather, they've decided that this was the work of Okmongos, a tribe that believes in the invincibility of areca noir. It's a bean or fruit, whatever you want to call it. When they chew it, they go berserk, their mind is obsessed with killing and sex, they go into a frenzy and are likely to do this sort of thing. What's more, they believe that when they chew areca noir, bullets can't touch them. They can act with impunity and they become, as I said, invincible. I suspect this was the same bunch that attacked us earlier. They came on and found these poor unfortunates here, and killed them all."

Invincible? Couldn't be touched by bullets? I pointed out that the one who had stabbed me had proven them wrong. He had been shot dead, on the spot. So had three others.

"They'll have an explanation for that. Possibly, they'll think, he hadn't chewed enough to be fully protected or he might have gotten a poor bean, something like that. In other words, he was killed by a bullet because of an aberration, not a failure of the belief system."

He sounded as if he believed the stuff about invincibility himself. "So they're invincible. But what is this reddish black stuff all over the bodies?"

"How can I put this delicately? It's spittle. They spit on the bodies. First they chew the black nut, then they kill and desecrate the body, that's important, the desecration thing, then they spit on the body to show utter contempt for an enemy. That black stuff, that's the dried areca noir from the spit."

While I was digesting this information, we heard the rumble of a diesel from downstream and suddenly there it was, one boat, not a flotilla as we had been led to expect, pulling into shore. And the first man to step off was Alex Fantus. Our rescuer! Behind him, there was a crew of four manning a spacious thirty foot boat that could carry us back to civilization in a matter of hours.

The Phantom looked the situation over, clearly in a hurry to be off, ordered the Indonesians and their machine guns aboard, took the Englishman and Bulgarian, explaining, "observers from the secretariat, you see," leaped aboard, and prepared to cast off. "Return to the city and link up with the paratroopers. They may need you," he told the Irish captain. He did recognize me, I wondered if he would, and glancing at my bloodied trousers with the stained bandage clearly visible, he suggested, "Osten, go back with them. In case you find a stray refugee or two. That's what you came for, wasn't it? To care for refugees?" He had a malevolent gleam in his eyes as he said it and it didn't soften a bit as he added, "Blood on your pants? Must have been bleeding. As soon as you get back, you should have that looked at."

The way he said it sounded more like "if you get back" rather than "when you get back."

Once again, with a machine of deliverance in his possession, Fantus took it away half empty and left others behind. What kind of man was this? The shaken Irish commander, stung by the loss of a dozen of his men still lying fifty feet away in the jungle camp, could only stand in helpless rage, his fists tightly closed as he restrained his grief and anger, as the boat disappeared downstream, as quickly as it had come. If I were Fantus, I decided, I would not want to meet this man again, day or night, anywhere on earth.

We were able to link up with the paratroopers later that same day. By the next morning, my leg was infected and I had developed a fever, but at least the stabbing stick hadn't been treated with a toxic poison, as some were rumored to be, death usually arriving suddenly and horribly when they were. What I had was bad enough, however, and proved to be totally unresponsive to our limited supply of medications. It got steadily worse and then a Katangese medicine man, not a doctor of medicine but the old fashioned kind of jungle witch doctor accompanying the soldiers of Moise Tshombe, packed it with a kind of green moss, leaves, and bark, and it got better. That piqued my curiosity and later I made a career out of looking for that kind of stuff.

We were flown out of the jungle ten days later as the Belgians were rotated home and replaced by fresh soldiers. In Elizabethville, just to be safe, I was given injections of a new antibiotic, administered several other shots, one of them a tetanus booster, and finished the healing. Despite the wonder drug, I was convinced that the moss had done the job. While lying in bed receiving medication, Fantus, incredibly, was being honored with a commendation. As the beautifully inscribed parchment touchingly put it, "At great personal risk, he was successful in removing from hostile hands two unarmed members of the United Nations staff, without injury or loss of life." The words impressed me, for a moment, until I remembered that I had been there and seen it. I didn't quite recall it that way.

I still have the ten inch scar on the front of my left thigh to remind me of that forlorn adventure. It almost matches the scar on the back of the same thigh, a memory of Korea. Abby and I went back to the states for a month, rested, visited, lived normally, and then came back to the shores of Lac Leman where I returned to the grind of daily committee meetings, coffee house sessions, arguing, debating, and writing reports. There were solitary picnics beside mountain streams of rushing water, nearby meadows framed by golden flowers and brilliant green hues, wintry hikes over fields of unbroken new snow, where, in our imagination, our footprint was the first to have ever walked the earth, and there were night after night before the crackling fireplace, holding hands, listening to soft music, and talking of how it would be, forever and ever. We were in love, but for one reason or another, we never made that trip to Lichtenstein.

Then it was time to return home to teach, to start seeing patients again, and to attend weddings, Sarah and Beth walking down the aisle one month apart. There were dark circles of worry under the professor's bloodshot eyes. This time there was no Friends of the UN offering to pick up the tab.

The huge 747 shrugged off sudden turbulence like a chunky Golden Lab shaking water from its coat after a refreshing swim, and Carmichael awakened with a start in the seat behind us. Eddie Chun had turned sideways in his seat, both feet hanging over the armrest into the aisle, and he was looking back toward the darkened coach section as if expecting a threat to materialize from that direction. Every time anyone went up or down the winding staircase leading to the upper level, his eyes narrowed as if registering the image on film.

"Everything all right?" I asked.

"Just staying awake," he explained, possibly chiding me for having awakened him earlier, but he hadn't gone back to sleep, which had been the idea. I suppose if you were the night watchman in a parking lot, and I wondered anew how he had wound up in that kind of a job with a framed college certificate hanging on the guardhouse wall, the darkened coach seats in the rear of the plane were as close to blacktop as you could find at 39,000 feet in the air.

Carmichael and Howsam switched seats and I took the opportunity to brief Horace on what he was to do in Hong Kong and, more importantly, in Bangkok once we reached our destination. It was easy. He was a quick study and competent. "You'll meet a woman by the name of Loretta Diaz in Hong Kong. Set up communications with her. Any specimens I send to you have to be rushed to her so make all the arrangements. If Tony sends anything in from Malaysia, see that it gets forwarded to our laboratory at once. Make sure we have everything we need to collect, package, and ship specimens, especially blood. You'll have laboratory space at Chulalongkorn University and any staff help you need will be provided. Both Tony and I have worked with them before and they'll go out of their way to make it easy for you.

"One more thing, read up on your blood typing protocols. This is the critical part of the mission. It's something Loretta Diaz does well and I know you've done a lot of it in our immunology laboratory. Talk to her about how to process each specimen and what to do to make sure we have backup samples in case anything goes wrong during shipment. Most important of all, I'm expecting a package to be delivered to me in Bangkok from Atlanta. The CDC, you know, the communicable disease center. If I'm not there when it arrives, sign for it and refrigerate it. Don't freeze it, just refrigerate it. Then take it along to the university with you. It's important. Very important. Any questions?"

I didn't expect there would be and when Horace remained silent, I continued. "About logistics. In Bangkok, we'll all stay at the Oriental. Eddie and I probably won't be in Bangkok long in the first place so I want you to remain at a permanent base. I want you to be either at the hotel or at the University so we can make contact in an emergency, regardless of where we are. Even if you don't hear from us, call the office daily and brief them. Even if there's nothing to report. OK?"

This time he had a question. "What about basketball?"

Basketball? I had forgotten. Horace played basketball every day and his muscles were probably already in withdrawal from inactivity.

Before I had a chance to work on that problem, I noticed that Eddie had suddenly straightened in his seat and was watching intently as a short swarthy man with slicked back black hair was making his way past the galley and climbing upwards to business class. He was looking back at Eddie, then quickly turned away. But not before managing to get a quick glimpse of me.

"Seen him before?" I asked.

Eddie shrugged. "Not before today. He goes to the bathroom a lot."

"Maybe he drinks too much coffee," I suggested.

"Maybe," he agreed, then called softly to the cabin attendant. "Got a cup of coffee?" he asked. He sat facing the stairway, sipping it cautiously. You could tell from the steam rising out of the cup that it was hot and fresh.

I turned my attention to Carmichael once more. "About basketball. You can play, but if you're out of the lab or hotel, make sure someone is answering the phone. Take a cellular phone with you and be available."

It was clear that we wouldn't make our connection in Tokyo. The stop at Anchorage had made us late and while my watch said we should be landing about now, there was nothing below us but the darkness of the Pacific. No lights, no sign of habitation, and it was another hour before the first reds and yellows appeared, twinkling below, and even later came the first faint glow of civilization, a village here and another there, and suddenly a massive orange-yellow emanation bouncing off low lying clouds meant only one thing. . .Tokyo underneath.

Narita's landing lights flashed by as we descended through wispy fog and rain, splashing onto a wet runway. Humpbacked shuttle buses took us from tarmac to terminal speedily enough and then on to an airline provided hotel just outside the gates of the heavily guarded airport. The rooms resembled modest sized cardboard boxes with one small window looking out at nothing, a slightly larger door just big enough to admit Carmichael after he bent sharply at the waist to avoid striking his head, and a compact fiberglass bathroom that appeared to have been designed to be lifted bodily from the building, removed and taken outside to be thoroughly hosed down and replaced. Even so, there weren't enough rooms to go around so Howsam and I shared one while Eddie and Horace occupied another.

It was just after midnight by the time we were settled and because of the time difference, I knew Marge would be at her desk. She always ate there when I was out of town, just in case, and she answered on the first ring.

"You're in Tokyo? I thought you'd be in Hong Kong by now," were her first words.

"Bad weather. Listen, Marge, let Burrows know we're running late. Then call Loretta Diaz in Hong Kong and tell her. They tell us we'll be on a Thai International flight in the morning and should arrive about noon. Also the hotel. Tell them. The Shangri La, right?"

"Right. Like you said. But your hotel reservations are guaranteed, so that's no problem."

"Guaranteed for what? For tonight and we're not there, so it is a problem. Guarantee them again for tomorrow night." I could see the small print on the reservation form now. 'Cancel by 6 P.M.,' so we'd owe a night's lodging even after she called, but at least we'd have rooms for the next day. Burrows would smile and tack the charge onto the Pan Union bill. No problem there.

Ivo Bertinoldi was in, also working through the noon hour. "I'm glad you called," he said unconvincingly, sounding as if he was on his way to an urgent meeting. He always sounded, I reflected, as if he was in a hurry. "Kendra has been having problems that we didn't anticipate this soon. She has become cytopenic and hasn't enough neutrophils to fight off a sudden infection. We've started antibiotics again, orally and intravenously, changed them twice so far, and she still hasn't responded so we decided to try doing something about the neutropenia itself."

"By doing what?"

"We're going to use something called G-CSF and try to raise the cell count."

"I didn't know G-CSF was approved. I didn't think any was available."

"It's not approved, but some is available for experimental use and we've gotten permission to add Kendra to a clinical trial we're running here at the Institute."

I'd been reading the literature, too. "From what I've heard, isn't there a risk of triggering uncontrolled cell mitosis and actually converting the myelodysplastic syndrome into acute leukemia?"

I sensed the hesitation before he responded. "I've discussed that with the patient," not Kendra anymore, but the patient, "and her father, pointing

out the possibility of that occurring, but when they understood the serious-
ness of the situation, how difficult it has become to control the infection in
any conventional way, they signed the consent forms and we've gone ahead.
I should stress once again, as I have to them repeatedly, that it is of the
utmost urgency that we find a donor. Before it's too late."

He made it sound as if the failure to come up with a donor was my fault
or theirs, not his.

What had been done, was done. I promised to continue the search,
which hadn't started yet, and to keep in touch. I broke the connection, next
rang the General, but he was out. At the hospital, a nurse informed me that
Kendra was asleep. "Sedated," she explained.

Before falling asleep myself, I pondered the problem. Cytopenia. Not
enough white blood cells to fight off life threatening infections; not enough
to transport life giving oxygen. And an experimental drug called in to fine
tune the blood making apparatus of the body, creating another dilemma.
Would the fine tuning result in just the right number of new cells to assist in
the fight or would it unbalance the entire situation, leaving her with an excess of new cells, not a deficiency, so that her bloodstream would become a
raging torrent of destruction, overwhelming every organ in her body? Too
little; too much. Which would it be?

I slept poorly but the next morning was alert enough to spot the short,
swarthy, coffee drinking fellow passenger as he boarded the shuttle bus ahead
of ours for the return to Narita.

I nudged Eddie, but needn't have bothered. "I see him," he said without turning.

"I didn't see him on our bus or at the hotel last night," I commented.

"He stopped to go to the bathroom in the terminal," Eddie explained.
"I saw him get on the bus right behind ours."

The flight to Hong Kong was smooth and mercifully short, allowing
me just enough time to review the medical records Marge had packed for
me. I reviewed several chapters on blood diseases from Scientific American
Medicine which I had crammed into a bulging carry-on bag. As I put the
records aside, I found myself idly fingering an earlobe, my brow furrowed,
trying to remember. Something from my notes reminded me of – what?
About old patients with Vietnamese names? Or was it something else? Unable to come up with anything definitive once again, I stopped pulling on
my earlobe and started to review what I knew or had read about cytopenia,
the myelodysplastic syndrome, and anemia. Also, about blood typing. Things

of practical importance under the circumstances.

The plane banked sharply and I could see heavily wooded Lantau Island ahead. Mountainous Victoria hove into view, the mountain tops partly blasted away, the rock turned into landfill for hungry developers creating a monument to capitalism, all of which was scheduled to revert to Chinese control in the not too distant future. Skyscrapers of brick, aluminum, stainless steel, and glass gleaming in the sunlight, marched resolutely higher and higher, an irresistible tide of commercial infantry assaulting the last line of Wellington's defenses on the heights above. Straight ahead, a narrow finger of reclaimed rock and concrete reached out in welcome, saying come land on me if you dare. And our pilot, accepting the challenge, picked his way between towering apartment houses, balconies all but touching wingtips, glided smoothly over smokestacks and warehouses, past monstrous oil tanks and water reservoirs, turning and twisting precisely in response to unseen voices intently watching flashing green radar screens, and guided his Airbus to touch down precisely in the center of the all too narrow and much too short runway, immediately reversed his thrusters, and brought the plane to a stop directly in front of the man with the yellow paddles, who pointed to an empty gate. We had arrived at Kai Tak, the air hub of the city that never sleeps: Hong Kong. A shopper's paradise. Only we hadn't come to shop. We had come on business.

# 7

Security is usually tight at Kai Tak and it was now. Armed constables, radios attached to the epaulets of starched khaki uniforms, patrolled two by two, inside and outside the terminal. Aside from the usual surging crowds thronging the arrival and departure areas, nothing seemed unusual as we cleared customs and immigration. There was the usual ritual scanning of computer printouts by an unobtrusive functionary who searched for our names on his list of undesirables. Had we been on that, we wouldn't have been allowed past his lowered barrier, but we did pass and headed for the exit leading to ground transportation where a car would be waiting.

What happened next was a complete surprise. As the automatic door slid back into place behind us, there was a sharp crack and at the same instant, I was struck from behind and knocked forward, falling to the ground and avoiding serious injury by being fortunate enough to land on hastily extended forearms. My palms were bruised, but I was lucky. It could have been my face. Startled, unable to understand what had happened, I rolled to one side and found Eddie Chun lying directly behind me. It was clear that his head and shoulder had struck me in the small of the back in a perfectly executed football tackle. As I started to rise, he hissed, "Stay down" just as something pinged off the fender of a Rolls Royce parked just to our left and went whining off into space. Then the glass in the doorway just over our heads was split by a mysterious object and I finally recognized the sound of gunfire. Someone was shooting a small weapon, probably a revolver, and had so far managed to hit a car, a glass door, and, what about the first shot? Then I saw where it had made contact; buried into the soft side of a stylish Gucci bag, in the hands of a turbaned traveler who had been rushing to catch a taxi. The bag had intercepted a bullet that had been on a direct collision course with me. Strangely, the bag seemed to be bleeding, a stain slowly spreading across its side, beginning right at the center of the wound, finally dripping onto the concrete roadway just beyond my nose. I smelled musk and it turned out the bullet had struck dead center into an expensive bottle of cologne.

By now, Eddie was up and running, pursuing a figure darting between the limousines and taxicabs waiting for startled, open-mouthed passengers who had not been expecting this kind of reception. To be honest, neither had I.

Horace and Howsam were uninjured and after I had dusted myself off, the three of us waited, wondering whether to proceed to the hotel or wait for

Eddie to return. We didn't have to make the decision, however. A police inspector made it for us.

Inasmuch as all three bullets had passed reasonably close to me, he seemed to have concluded that either I, or possibly the unfortunate Bengali with the strong odor of cologne, had been the intended victim. He took charge of my interrogation while another officer took aside the man still holding his stained suitcase.

"Fong," he said by way of identification. "Inspector Fong."

Before Fong was able to say another word, there was a commotion along the walkway and the crowd parted as three constables, one pulling and two pushing, hustled two men, hands secured behind their backs, into a waiting van with flashing lights. With no further ceremony, the vehicle pulled away, klaxon blaring and lights flashing even more rapidly. I had no trouble recognizing one of the two. He was dark and swarthy, had weak kidneys, and had been on the plane with us all the way. The second man was completely unknown to me. In the space left vacant as the van departed, I could see Eddie standing with two constables, one of whom patted him reassuringly on the back in a gesture of 'good job, old boy' and they all laughed as Eddie started back towards us. Had he run down and captured two men? On foot? This might qualify him for a bonus when we got back.

One of the constables walked up to Inspector Fong and handed him a piece of paper, perhaps I was imagining things but it looked like a photograph of some sort, and spoke for a moment in Chinese. That placed me at a considerable disadvantage as I didn't speak the language. After he walked away and began dispersing the crowd that had gathered, Fong turned to me and asked in English, "Doctor Osten, you say you know of no one in Hong Kong who might wish you harm?"

I hadn't said that. I hadn't said anything at all yet. How did he know my name?

"No, Inspector, I don't recall saying that, but if you are asking, I would have to say that is correct. I certainly don't know anyone at all in Hong Kong who could possibly wish me harm. Or for that matter, to harm any member of our party." Spread the blame around. "We just now arrived from Tokyo."

"Yes, on a Thai flight, I believe."

"That's correct."

"You stayed last night in Tokyo?"

"Yes, we did. Our flight from the United States was late and we missed our connection so we flew on down this morning."

Several more constables had appeared and were scurrying about the area, stretching yellow tape to block access to the scene, sweeping up glass fragments and putting them into small plastic bags, vacuuming a much broader area of walkway, probably searching for shell casings or other evidence. Fong watched the activity for a moment, spoke into his radio, and motioned for us to follow him into an office inside the terminal. He left Eddie, whom I had not yet had a chance to talk to, Horace and Howsam in the hallway, closed the door, indicated I should take a chair, and then said, "Based upon many years of experience, I have to conclude that someone just tried to shoot you. Now, I've been wondering these past few minutes why anyone would want to do that. To a stranger in our midst. That's something I do whenever anyone gets shot at on my shift. Can you help me understand, or even better, help me solve this problem that I have?"

His request was reasonable enough. He knew that I wasn't about to help him, but had to ask just the same. "Inspector, as you can imagine, I've been wondering the same thing. I really have no idea who might have done this." Which wasn't quite true. I had several ideas, but I didn't think the inspector was the right man to talk to about any of them.

"I see," he said. "Tell me Doctor, what kind of business are you in and why did you come to Hong Kong?"

"Research. Clinical investigations, pharmaceuticals, development of new medicines, that sort of thing." I handed him one of my cards.

He read it, carefully wrote everything into his notebook, put the card in his pocket, and wanted to know, "While here, who will you be seeing?"

I told him. The people at Marcum-Whangpo, principally Loretta Diaz, a researcher at that firm. He wrote that down as well. Extending his hand, he asked for my passport, collected the others from the hallway, and studied all four. Finally, holding mine, he observed, "You travel a lot."

"Business," I explained, truthfully. "It's important for the kind of work we do."

He repeated the process with Tony's passport, comparing dates and destinations with mine. "Mr. Howsam travels a lot also, but the two of you seldom travel together."

"Yes, that's the way it is. We rarely go to the same places."

"Except this trip?"

"No, not even on this trip. We've come this far together but my destination is Thailand and his is Malaysia."

Of course the inspector was thinking drugs. Not pharmaceuticals, but drugs. Illegal drugs. Frequent travelers to Southeast Asia sometimes dealt in drugs and people dealing in drugs are likely to get shot at, which local police know only too well. Yet, as I was certain the Inspector knew, not many people get shot at in Hong Kong because, after all, it is much easier, if you want to shoot someone, to do it in places like Chiang Mai, Chiang Rai, Manila or even Bangkok, where the police forces weren't as well trained or as incorruptible. And there was that other problem about committing a crime in Hong Kong. It was an island and it wouldn't be that easy to shoot someone and escape – would it? So someone, if I was the target, was in a hurry. In a hurry for what?

"You're not with the government, then. So many Americans who come to Hong Kong seem to be with the government. You're with a private company. Your own company, from the name on the card. And the men out in the hall work for you?"

"Correct."

"And you're a doctor? Of medicine?" he said, handing all four passports to me.

"Yes, I am."

He was still making notes in his black book. "Are you in any way associated with the organization known as the Pan Union Trade Association?" he asked unexpectedly.

What did he know? This was potentially dangerous ground and I was trying to be careful as I replied, "As I mentioned, we're here to meet with Marcum-Whangpo on a special project. Perhaps you've heard of them. I expect to be here for a day, possibly two, and then we'll be on our way."

"No, I'm not familiar with that company. What did you say the name was again?"

So I repeated the name for the third time, watched him write it down for the third time, and then he asked, for the second time, "So you've never had dealings with this other group, the Pan Union one?"

Still treading cautiously, I asked, "Do they have an office here in Hong Kong?"

"No, not an office. Rather I would guess that they might be having a convention or large meeting of some sort in our city. But you've never dealt with them in the past?" He was persistent, had his pen ready to record my answer, and didn't seem willing to accept what I had already told him.

I tried again. "Inspector, we may have dealt with them. We deal with so many clients that it is hard to keep them all straight. That's our business, as you know." I was sure he did know. "We're a consulting firm. We consult for anyone who needs our help and it's possible Pan Union has been a client in the past. For all I know, the Hong Kong police may have been our client in the past. But I can assure you, we are not here to attend a Pan Union convention or whatever they may be having. We are here to meet with the scientists at Marcum-Whangpo as a phone call to Loretta Diaz at her office will confirm. I have the number here if you would like it." I thought the touch about having consulted with the Hong Kong police was a nice one. In fact, we may have done so and I would have to check with Burrows on that.

He moved on. "The Pan Union group has reserved rooms at the Regent. Quite a large number of rooms. By the way, where are you staying?" His face seemed to be saying, gotcha.

"The Shangri La, if they've held our rooms. We are a day late but my office assured me that they were guaranteed."

If he was disappointed, he hid it well. "The Shangri La. Yes, an excellent hotel. Prefer it to the Regent myself. If I were staying in a hotel, which I never do as I live so close to my work, I would choose the Peninsula. You might want to try it some time. Don't worry about them holding your rooms. I'll call and explain why you have been detained. They'll take good care of you."

He wasn't doing us a favor. He was checking to see if I had been telling the truth. "That isn't necessary, Inspector," I told him. "You needn't bother."

"No bother, Doctor. It's the least we can do to make up for your rude welcome to our city. We don't usually treat visitors this way."

I didn't want to leave without finding out what had happened. Or what would happen to the men in handcuffs. "I was wondering, Inspector. It seems your men caught the people doing the shooting. Who were they?"

"Yes, we did catch them thanks to some timely assistance from one of your traveling companions." He opened his notebook again and flipped back through several pages. "Your Mr. Chun. He's out in the hall right now, isn't he? The little one. He saw the shooter, actually saw him raise the gun and fire the first shot right at you. At least, that's what he thought was happening. Then after knocking you down out of harm's way, he leaped up and chased the man to a waiting car driven by an accomplice. The car sped away but Mr. Chun continued chasing it on foot to the street where he was joined by one of our officers who had heard the shots and decided to run along. The officer thought he knew which car they were chasing and radioed the make, model, and license number to patrolling units nearby but all of a sudden, a half block further, right where the exit from the terminal joins the main access road, they came upon the car where it had struck a passing bus. Both men were still sitting there, too dazed to run, too confused to object when they were handcuffed and brought back here.

"The shooter, let's call him that for the moment although the charge still must be proven in a court of law, carried a passport in the name of Mr. Ngoc. It was an Australian passport, by the way, almost certainly a forgery, and this Mr. Ngoc, according to Mr. Chun, had traveled with you on the plane all the way from the United States. Most unusual, don't you think? The second man had no identification on him. None at all. Not even a driver's license so we have him right there as he was driving the car involved in the accident." So they have one of them for a traffic violation. Great. Hardly a major crime, such as shooting someone.

"It's Mr. Ngoc who interests me, Doctor. What did you do to him on the plane or in the hotel in Tokyo that could have made him so angry that this stranger, someone who has never seen you before, arrives in Hong Kong, whips out a pistol, and starts shooting? You are going to have to be more careful in the future. Also, I wonder where he was able to obtain a gun so soon after arriving. Certainly he didn't carry that aboard an airplane, did he?"

Yes, I concluded, Mr. Ngoc was an interesting character. Once again, truthfully, I was able to say, "Inspector, aside from seeing him on the plane and on the airport bus, I've had no dealings with this man so I'm at a loss to understand what he was doing. It must have been an act of random violence."

I didn't think Fong would buy it. He didn't. "I might be able to accept that except for one thing."

"What one thing?"

"This," he said, handing me a photograph. "We found this in his inside coat pocket. You may find it interesting."

I did. It was a picture of me. Black and white and not particularly flattering. Taken at night as I was entering a black limousine, my face looking a little puffy, and I realized that the diet I had been considering was an idea whose time had come. Over my left shoulder, clearly outlined against the limestone foundation of the building, was a large 'X' carved into the cornerstone. The Pan Union sign was partially visible to the right. Obviously, the picture had been taken as I was departing Washington four days earlier, passed on to a dark, swarthy man with black hair and leaking kidneys, and he had used it to identify me, to track me, and finally, to shoot at me.

The Inspector could hardly have missed the Pan Union sign but he made no comment other than to say, "It appears to be a photograph of you."

There was no point in denying the obvious. "Yes. It certainly does."

"But you don't know Mr. Ngoc, the man who was carrying it?"

"No, Inspector, I don't."

"That's strange. Don't you consider it strange that he would be carrying your picture? And aren't you puzzled over how he could have obtained it?"

I was and I told him so.

He was still studying the picture, right now with his head tilted, he appeared to be peering directly at the Pan Union sign but seemed not to have taken note of it as he said, "We'll question him of course, to see what he has to say. We'll ask him those questions you would ask him yourself if you had the opportunity, such as where he got it and who gave it to him. And, of course, why. Why would he have your picture at all? If we learn anything or if we need to contact you, where did you say we could contact you? Oh, of course, I'm sorry, it was the Shangri La wasn't it?"

"Please do," I replied and went out into the hallway with a final word, "if they've held our rooms."

They had.

We rode in silence on the short drive from Kai Tak to the hotel until Eddie put things into perspective. "Man follows us on plane, keeps us in sight in Tokyo, reboards same aircraft, and follows us to Hong Kong. First chance he gets once back on the ground, he takes a shot at us. I should say you, boss, not us. He took a shot at you because he had your picture in his pocket and he aimed right at you. No doubt at all. You were the target. Not me or Tony or Horace; he didn't have our pictures. He had yours. But why didn't he do that earlier, in Tokyo for instance, or even back in the States?"

I had the same questions and had been working on the answer. "Probably because he had no gun. Too big a risk to try boarding a plane with one so he most likely was given a gun by someone as soon as he arrived in Hong Kong. Then he acted, hoping to get lost in the crowd and escape."

Later in my suite, where hot tea and almond cookies were promptly delivered within minutes after we reached the room, Eddie was still working on the problem. "OK, so someone gave him a gun here in Hong Kong. Who?"

"I can't see anyone from Clozyme doing it. Maybe Carroll Bradley would think of it, but I doubt that he has the connections," I observed wryly.

"What about our other client, the men from Washington?" Howsam was thinking of Pan Union and so was I. But to what purpose? They needed me, didn't they? Hadn't they made that clear?

"Doesn't make sense, Tony. They asked me to make the trip to help bring back a defector. It wasn't my idea." I didn't bring up Ken Green. Or Kendra's problem. Private matter, so far.

Carmichael finished his third or fourth cookie and paused in the process of selecting a fifth to suggest, "Maybe somebody doesn't want you to bring back a defector." It was a point worth considering.

I was enjoying a cookie and my cup of fragrant jasmine tea as we all fell silent again. There was much to do and little time to do it before we were to leave Hong Kong and Eddie interrupted my planning session by announcing, "Boss, I gotta get a gun."

It wasn't a bad idea, one that I had been considering myself. But it wasn't a good idea either. That's how I handled it. "We don't want to do anything stupid here in Hong Kong and having a gun is illegal. It's best to leave the matter up to the police. They seem to be quite competent."

Eddie persisted. "Where were they this morning when we needed them? Not there. So we were huddled on the ground trying to avoid bullets."

"Even if you had a gun, Eddie, that wouldn't have stopped anyone from firing at us. It wouldn't have been a deterrent."

"I'm not talking deterrent. I know I couldn't have stopped the first shot. That was sneaky and he got it off while I was knocking you down, but there wouldn't have been a second or third shot. I guarantee it. I saw him clear as a deer in poacher's spotlight when he fired shots two and three. And if I had a gun on me, he would have been downed in his tracks."

While knocking me down, yes, while doing that and making my neck sore and back ache and I wondered how a man so small could hit so hard. Had he ever played football? Not likely.

I wasn't in favor of a gun because had Eddie used one, we would have spent more time with Inspector Fong answering questions and had less time to do what we had come to do. "We'll be all right, Eddie," I decided. "The police have the man in custody, we'll be out of here in a day or so, and will leave this all behind. I doubt that we have to worry about this sort of thing happening again."

Carmichael had just found the last cookie in the basket and was examining it for flaws when he began to intone, "If at first you don't succeed. . ." and I cut him off immediately.

"Yes, Horace, I get it. I know the rest."

"See, even he thinks I should get a gun," Eddie implored.

"No, Eddie. No gun. Inspector Fong and his men have all the guns we need. Leave it at that."

Loretta Diaz had a soothing, melodic voice on the telephone and soothing was what I needed after the long flight and unexpected turmoil of the last two hours. I arranged to meet her at Marcum-Whangpo at 3 P.M., giving me time for a shower, a change of clothes, my suit having accumulated a considerable amount of pavement dirt during the knockdown at Kai Tak, and a cleansing of an abraded knee suffered at the same time.

On the way to the Star Ferry, Eddie at my side, I made a quick stop at Harry Kee's in Tsim-Sha-Tsui just off Nathan Road. Harry is a clothier, reputedly owning the fastest sewing machines in the Far East. He has my measurements on file but checked once again to make certain nothing had changed since my last visit. Nothing had. Maybe I didn't need to rush into that often delayed diet just yet. Two suits and three pair of slacks would be ready by morning. He guaranteed it. The fabrics? Are these suitable? A stripe, a solid worsted, the finest English weaves, all wool with just enough synthetic something or other to give it body.

I assured him that the fabrics and color were fine, and didn't question how something could be all wool and yet contain a touch of synthetic for added body. It didn't matter as I knew that Harry Kee produced a quality garment every time and, in all the years I had been wearing his suits (I'm wearing one now), no one had ever walked up to me and said, "I see you have an all wool suit with a touch of. . ." or "You have a synthetic suit with a touch of. . ." No. Not once. What they said was, "Nice looking suit. Where did you get it?"

Not only did Harry make good suits, his staff a group of artists, he was an astute businessman. Before I got out of the door, I had also purchased several shirts, Oxford cloth, French cuffs, one white, one light blue striped, and one with the collar a different color than the shirt itself. For me, revolutionary.

As I said, Harry Kee was a good businessman, although at first he wasn't sure what to make of an intense Eddie Chun who watched the entire transaction, hands in his pockets, saying nothing. But when Harry found that Eddie was in the market for a gun, he smiled, and proved to be very useful.

Loretta Diaz was waiting when we arrived at exactly 3 P.M. She sat behind a perfectly clean, glittering mahogany desk, offering an outstretched hand and a winning smile. Did everyone, aside from me, work at uncluttered polished wooden desks? She was wearing a long white laboratory coat so precisely starched that one fiber rubbing against another as she sat back down produced the oddly reassuring sound of crackling Christmas gift wrappings. A name badge was attached to the left lapel, she was wearing a lemon yellow blouse and light gray skirt, wore horn rimmed glasses which only made her olive skin look more alluring, and her overall appearance was, as Burrows would say, fetching. I would have described it as smashing, but you get the idea. Despite the name, she had the delicate body and coloring of a young Chinese woman with European features, the confident bearing of an educated scientist, and was the product of a Portuguese father from Macao and a Chinese mother from Guandong. She had trained in London, Switzerland, and the United States. On the wall behind her was an array of framed certificates. Not a Miss, Mrs. or Ms., this Loretta Diaz. A doctor. Ph.D.

I could understand why Bertinoldi might have remembered her. How could he forget?

She rang for tea and while waiting for it, she asked, "How was the trip?"

"Uneventful. Good weather and a smooth flight." I didn't mention the reception at Kai Tak.

The tea was hot and tasty and the ever present cookies reeked of calories. Not too many, I warned myself, or the new suits won't fit.

She had been well briefed by Bertinoldi, as I found out almost at once. "I understand you are faced with a bone marrow transplant situation and need to find a donor-patient match. Dr. Bertinoldi tells me you hope to find a sibling of the patient and obtain blood samples. He already has sent the patient's typing results here so all we need are the samples you send us, once you have them. We can get an answer to you very quickly after that. Is that the gist of it?"

"That's about it. I don't know where the brother is, by the way, and he's a twin who disappeared 15 years ago, so it isn't as easy as just tightening a tourniquet on the arm and drawing blood. But if we find him, we'll get a specimen back to you as soon as possible. I'll want you to meet with an associate of mine to set the whole process up."

She nodded. "Are you familiar with bone marrow transplants, Dr. Osten?"

"I know the basics, but this is not really my field."

If she was surprised by my candor, she didn't show it. "Do you mind if I go back and review the history of bone marrow transplants with you so that both of us are on the same page? Dr. Bertinoldi may have done this but sometimes he gets so technical that he overwhelms everyone else. Ivo is one of the best in the world at treating the myelodysplastic syndrome but sometimes he forgets that the rest of us see cases like that very rarely and do not have his expertise."

It was my turn to appreciate her frankness. "I don't mind at all. I'd appreciate a review course."

"All right. Stop me if you have any questions as we go along. Before 1957, patients who had been treated with irradiation and chemotherapy for leukemia and cancer were found to have lost almost all functioning bone marrow. They were vulnerable to massive and deadly infections and efforts were finally made to control this problem by way of human bone marrow transplantation. In theory, this should work. Most of the original studies were done at the University of Washington in your country and there were successes and failures, as in most things medical.

"Usually when we talk of human transplants, we think of removing a discrete organ, a kidney, a heart, lung or liver from one person and implanting it into another. Bone marrow is different. It's not an organ that can be lifted from one bone and put inside another person's bones. What really happens is that bone marrow cells are drained from the center of bones of the donor and then given by intravenous infusion to the recipient. The patient who donated the cells rapidly makes new ones and the recipient borrows the cells and hopefully recovers. That's the theory. It's a win-win situation, if it works. It's not necessary for one person to die before another can benefit.

"The process is relatively simple. The donor is anesthetized and marrow cells are drawn from several sites, strained to remove dangerous particles, tested for safety to exclude other diseases, and then given by way of intravenous drip to the patient.

"If the donor is a monozygous twin, identical that is, the results are sometimes spectacular. There is very little chance of rejection and no immunosuppressive drugs are needed so there is less chance of a secondary infection. But that's not the situation here. Obviously, the patient's brother is not an identical twin, so he is no different as a donor than any other sibling; he was, in fact, simply a second egg fertilized at the same time, or very nearly the same time, as his sister. But we know that siblings can be successful donors and this is where we can be of help.

"Genetics plays a major role in the acceptance or rejection of a graft. You're familiar with the blood types A, B, and O. They're critical in determining whether a graft will be accepted, but they're not the only immunologic markers involved. Not by a long shot. Equally important are immunologic markers on the membranes of every nucleated cell in our body. These have been named human leukocytic antigens, HLA's for short, and they appear to be a cluster of genes sitting on the short arms of chromosome 6, you remember the short arms and long arms of the chromosomes, don't you?"

I did, just barely.

"Somebody gave them the name of major histocompatibility complex or MHC. There's a HLA-A and HLA-B and other things – I'm not making this too complicated, am I?"

She wasn't *making* it complicated. It *was* complicated and I was still back struggling with the short and long arms of chromosomes, but I didn't want to stop her now. "No, I'm still with you. Go right ahead."

Dubiously, as if sensing that I might have been left behind, she waited a moment and then continued, "All of this sounds so mysterious when you try to explain it, but once you get into the laboratory and have a specimen to work with, it all just falls into place.

"So, as I was saying about the HLA's, if we find a graft from an ABO-compatible donor with at least one matching HLA antigen, there is a much better chance of success than without the HLA match. You see, the identical twin would have exactly the same HLA types and all of the other genes would match as well. Accordingly, the success rate would be higher. But even if you only match one HLA, there is still a chance of a successful take and that's why we try to do it. Match up the ABO type, add the HLA typing, try to identify the best histocompatibility you can get, and go for it. In order of priority, that usually is identical twin, best of all; a sibling, even a fraternal twin like this case, next best; parents, further down the list; and then, trying to find a donor from the general public is truly looking for a needle in a haystack."

I remembered Bertinoldi using the same term earlier.

She wasn't done. "Among siblings, by the way, only one in four is likely to possess two HLA types in common. When lucky, you find that half have one common HLA while one in four have no HLA types in common at all. Parents will never have more than one type in common so they are seldom of much help in this kind of problem. They want to be, but they just aren't genetically capable. The premise: the greater the commonality between prospective donor and needy recipient, the higher are the chances of success in doing a transplant. But remember, it all starts with having the same blood type and we go to the HLA testing to improve the odds."

I took out a small slip of paper and handed it to her. She read it and looked up. "This says type A positive."

"Yes. Ken Green's blood type. They did that when he went into the army."

She looked at the record she pulled from a drawer. "According to this, his sister, Kendra, has type A positive blood as well."

"That's correct," I said. "From what you've just said, that should be a help."

She grinned. "You have been following me. And yes, that does help. It's a starting point. Now find the brother and let's see where that takes us. But even then," she cautioned, "even if we find HLA that matches, there are still more studies to do and options to consider."

"Such as?"

"For instance, her physician, Bertinoldi let's say, may decide to use a drug called cyclophosphamide or try total lymph tissue irradiation to lessen the risk of rejection, even if we come up with a good match. Meanwhile, if the leukemia had become active while all this was being done, intensive chemotherapy would be needed before we could do anything else. So we are a long way from being able to fight this thing effectively at the moment." Her voice trailed off as if she had become weary of the prospect of a long arduous struggle.

"Let's say we do a transplant. What kind of complications are we likely to encounter?"

She immediately warmed to the subject once more, responding, "I've talked of the possibility of rejection, the body rejecting the transplanted organ. That's the complication everyone talks about but strangely enough, there's another one just as ominous. The graft, in this case the transplanted marrow, may reject the new body it finds itself occupying. This is called graft versus host disease or GVHD. It's as if the transplanted marrow takes a look at its new surroundings and says, 'I don't like it here' and withers away. Fails to take root, as it were, and abandons the patient to his or her fate.

"Then there are infections, opportunistic infections. Remember, these patients are immunocompromised and have little resistance to bacteria and viruses lurking in our environment. Pneumonia is a frequent problem, many of them developing about a month after the transplant. Herpes zoster is always a risk. The same diseases that attack AIDS patients are likely to show up in transplant cases also, and for essentially the same reasons; both lose their immunity, in AIDS because of the destructive effects of the virus on the T cells and other components of the immune response and the transplant patient because we are using immunosuppressive agents to avoid rejection. As you can see, it is always a battle, the good guys versus the bad. To win, we must be nimble and willing to gamble. But it is possible to win."

Which was the good news. As she had been talking, I recognized that there was an awful lot of the bad mixed in there along the way. But Loretta Diaz knew her field and she hadn't pulled any punches.

She had one more to throw before we were done. "You're wondering about what the odds are, aren't you?" she asked, proving that she was also adept at reading minds.

"Sure, we deal in abstractions like percentages all of the time in medicine. Assuming we find a donor that proves acceptable, what are we talking about in terms of survival?" Everything else aside, that was the one thing I needed to know.

She threw a verbal left jab and connected, with a chilling effect on my overloaded brain. "With a good match, let's say with the brother, and because her age is under 40, age is important also, anywhere from a 20-60% success rate at 30-60 months. The figures vary from site to site, and may get better as time goes on, but that's what it is right now."

So many percent at so many months, hardly reassuring figures, was numbing. Let's say we were lucky and reached the averages. What would Kendra and I have left? Three years, maybe five? We'd allowed too much to slip away already, but 30-60 months, if that's what it was to be, well, maybe that wouldn't be too bad, if spent wisely.

Dr. Diaz wanted to take me on a quick tour of the Marcum-Whangpo facilities but I demurred, leaving that for Tony Howsam and Horace Carmichael. They would understand all of that better than I and I still wanted to meet with Bath and the Pan Unionists before returning to the Shangri La. They weren't having a convention, Fong knew that as well as I did, but when eight Americans descend upon one hotel all requesting adjoining rooms, and then slink about trying to be inconspicuous while spending too much money and drinking too much Scotch, they were bound to draw attention to themselves. And they had succeeded as I saw at once when I entered the lobby of the Regent to find two of Fong's constables stolidly watching the endless stream of traffic eddying around the front door and registration desk. One of them, pretending to be interested in the junks and cargo vessels plying the harbor, was standing at the far end of the lobby before the enormous glass windows looking out at Victoria Island. He was using the glass as a mirror to see what went on behind him. The other, standing at the entrance to the fine shops and boutiques extending to the left of the lobby, was studying the price tags on fine crystal and jade objects in one of JoElle's display cases. I don't know what his salary was, but he was in over his head. Just the same, he made eye contact and quickly looked away. Moments later, he took out a small black notebook, glanced at the giant Cartier wall clock behind the reception the desk, and began to make notes.

I thought of coming up with a diversion to throw them off, such as just turning around and walking back outside, but I knew that wouldn't work when I saw something even worse. One of Bath's men, it could only have been one of Bath's men, was headed directly towards me with all the subtlety and grace of a retired wheat farmer who suddenly finds himself driving his Winnebago the wrong way on the brickyard track in Indianapolis – while the Indy 500 is being run. Eddie saw him before I did and moved to make the intercept. Remembering Burrows warning about his violent temper, I held out an arm to restrain him, saying, "Easy, Eddie. I think it's a friend, more or less." And watched both constables writing furiously in their little black books.

It was Naroogian, Avram Naroogian, Pan Union's chief of security, the one Bath had told me was coming along in case of trouble in the lesser developed countries. He was well dressed, at least, in a dark pin-striped suit, not one of Harry Kee's, but acceptable although wrinkled as if he had worn it on the plane flight or had been sleeping in it. He hadn't been sleeping recently, though, as the first thing he wanted to talk about was that he had been waiting in the lobby 'for more than three hours.' For some reason, that seemed to irk him.

"You needn't have bothered," I said. "I was planning on calling Bath on a house phone. He could have told me what rooms you were in."

The notebooks were filling up fast. Naroogian, however, was totally oblivious to the presence of surveillance and only seemed interested in leading us to the elevators. Perhaps he was in urgent need of a bathroom. Certainly a three hour wait could leave you feeling uncomfortable, especially if one had been drinking coffee on the job, something I surmised from the coffee cup and saucer still sitting on the marble top of the small table he had been using as headquarters when we walked in. The dark swarthy Mr. Ngoc, for instance, could never have handled this assignment without being relieved at regular intervals, but then, was I jumping to conclusions about who Mr. Ngoc's employer really was?

Pan Union's big three were sequestered in a comfortable suite, all six feet propped up on a glass coffee table, several empty decanters offering testimony to an afternoon of drinking. A half empty ice bucket sat amongst glasses, some partially filled, others fully drained with nothing more than a thin residue of amber liquid or a melting ice cube coating the bottom. Wet rings of condensation had formed under the chilled glasses and an ice maker was burping away in another room suggesting that the day's activities had not yet been concluded. Fantus barely glanced in my direction, checked his empty glass, and heaved himself to his feet, padding barefoot to a sidebar where he opened a fresh bottle of Glenlivet and proceeded to reduce the fluid level substantially, transferring it from bottle to glass, no ice needed.

Bath merely waved in the general direction of the two remaining chairs, and I sat in one. Eddie chose not to be included in what may have been an invitation, moved to the doorway of an adjoining room and remained standing. No one offered either of us a drink or shook hands. They weren't friendly at all.

Eddie was staring through the doorway and inclined his head as if in inviting me to do the same. When I slid my chair forward an inch or two, I was surprised to see Corby, or was it Canby, whom I was accustomed to seeing behind her desk in Georgetown, talking on a telephone. Canby! That was the name. I had always assumed she was a receptionist, but here she was. An agent? Or hanky panky? Not too old for either one, I decided, but inasmuch as I couldn't hear what she was saying, I left that problem to Eddie and turned my attention to Bath. Or rather, he turned his attention to me. He went right to the point without any small talk. "Where have you been?" he demanded. Just like that.

"We were delayed last night in Tokyo. High winds. Winter weather across the Pacific. Perhaps you heard."

"The weather wasn't that bad. We flew across, too, you know." He was in an argumentative mood.

"Same ocean, different day. One day can make a difference in the weather," I explained. He wasn't interested in a weather report. Fantus went back to the bar, opened a fresh bottle of Old Crow, and placed it on the table. This was Bath's brand of medicine and he filled his glass, added an ice cube, watched the overflow run down onto his hand, licked his fingers, dropped an ice cube on the floor, and watched it bound away under the couch. Too much to drink.

"You didn't check into your rooms by noon," he accused.

"We're at the Shangri La."

"Yes, that's what we've discovered."

How many men and how much time did it take them to find that out? Maybe that's what Canby had been doing. Calling the various hotels and asking for us by name. He took a drink, leaned back as if about to fall asleep, and said, "We have to talk. To make plans."

I remained silent. I had already made plans.

He broke the silence by adding, "Plans about what to do in Bangkok."

Noncommittally, indicating willingness but no enthusiasm, I said, "If you think it's necessary. But it will have to be late. I have a 7 P.M. dinner engagement." I was hoping that Loretta Diaz would say yes when I called her to tell her that bit of news.

Canby hung up the phone and disappeared, appearing a moment later bearing a tray of a half dozen plates piled high with chicken bones, half eaten rolls, and greasy uneaten French fries. Obviously they hadn't gone hungry while awaiting my arrival. Nor thirsty, as Magellan, who as usual hadn't said a word, and Fantus, refilled their glasses, one more time.

Fantus was holding his ice filled glass against the right side of his face as if he was suffering from a severe migraine. "How did your meeting with the enchanting Dr. Diaz go?"

He ignored the withering stare aimed his way by Bath, but the message was clear. If they knew about the meeting with Diaz, they knew what had happened at Kai Tak. Someone was following and reporting. They had enough people here to do the job and could have hired locals if they needed more help. We would have to pay more attention to our surroundings. But Bath hadn't wanted me to know that. He was still glaring at Fantus, who seemed unworried, and took another drink.

"She's competent and the Marcum-Whangpo laboratory appears to be an excellent facility. I'm sure they'll be able to do everything we need done."

"And just what is it that we'll need done?" Bath asked belligerently. "I thought you brought along your own people to do all that. A Horace, what's his name? I thought he was the laboratory expert. We're paying for him. Why do we need anyone else?"

"If you check the fax Burrows sent, you'll find Dr. Diaz on there also. And Marcum-Whangpo. They're specialists. Carmichael, that's his name by the way, is more of a generalist. If we need help, we use Dr. Diaz." I still didn't think he knew about blood typing, Ken Green, and bone marrow transfusions. But I had to confess that I could easily be mistaken.

Watching them drink had increased my thirst. I walked over to the bar and found a bottle of white wine, held it up, and asked Bath, "Mind?" Without waiting for a response, I poured a couple of inches into a water glass. No wine glasses. These were serious drinkers, not dilettantes. A sudden clatter of dishes came from the direction of the hallway. Eddie never moved. It sounded as if Canby had dropped the tray.

No one had mentioned the shooting at Kai Tak and I had refrained from bringing up the photo of me taken in front of the Pan Union offices as I entered the limousine from one side, Bath and Fantus climbing in on the other. I remembered Bath saying, "Osten, why don't you get in from the curbside. Fantus and I will go around. Wouldn't want you to get hit by a car, would we, now that we need you." Then bending down to retrieve a carelessly dropped laptop, leaving me fully exposed to a conveniently positioned camera.

Suddenly more amiable, Bath asked, "We can get together then, after your dinner?"

Why not? I needed information as badly as they did. Especially from Magellan, who allegedly had been the first to make contact with the representative of Lee Duc Than, real or otherwise. "Let's make it 9:30, right here in this room if it's all right with you." I was sure it would be. They had gone to a lot of trouble to set up the recording devices, especially the one built into the ice bucket, and it would be a shame to waste all of that effort. I hadn't spotted the camera yet but it turns out Eddie had, almost at once. It was highly miniaturized, built into the telephone that Canby had been using. That's why she was trying to keep us in sight as long as she could. After she hung up, the other camera, the one I'd seen, the one still functioning from inside the buttered half eaten roll on the coffee table, took over. If you have high tech capability, use it; that was the Pan Union motto.

We were leaving when Bath asked, "Was there any excitement at Kai

Tak about the time you landed? Seems to me I heard something on television a couple of hours ago."

Eddie smiled. I tried not to. "Excitement? Not really. You know how crowded the terminal is about that time of day, but that's hardly exciting. Instead, it's annoying."

Bath and Fantus exchanged questioning glances. Bath persisted. "It seems to me, though, that I heard something about a shooting. Something like that. You didn't see anything at all?"

"Oh, the shooting! Sure, we were there when that happened. Someone took several shots at an Indian and hit his suitcase. Strangest thing you ever saw. The suitcase started to bleed, just like a person."

Bath was open-mouthed. "A suitcase was bleeding? How could a suitcase bleed?"

"It was bleeding musk. You could smell it fifty feet away, even with the wind blowing."

Bath was confused while Fantus, once again holding the cold glass against the side of his face, asked, "Why would anyone shoot at an Indian? That doesn't make sense."

I shrugged. "Who knows, Alex? Probably political. You know how volatile those political squabbles can get. Moslem versus Hindu, Sikh versus Hindu, Kashmiri versus Pushtan, there's no end to the possibilities. Some people hold grudges for thirty, forty years before seeking revenge. It can happen."

Eddie was chuckling as we passed Naroogian who appeared to be guarding a platter of chicken bones and empty dishes piled haphazardly at his side in the hallway. Canby was nowhere in sight and we still hadn't seen the remainder of the Pan Union party. It occurred to me that Magellan hadn't uttered a word. He couldn't be blamed for anything that way.

Loretta Diaz readily agreed to meet us for dinner and when she walked into the restaurant in a softly clinging red dress, revealing just the right amount of every curve, she had changed from the cool, competent white coated scientist to a desirable woman. Our table was the envy of every other as the maitre d' escorted her through the room, past a hundred ogling eyes, and seated her before an expanse of glass looking out over the harbor where a monstrous gray American aircraft carrier and its accompanying watchdog, a frigate, had hunkered down for the night.

The three of us stood to welcome her, three because Eddie had remained at the door "where I can keep an eye on things," and when Tony saw her, and she saw Tony, Carmichael and I became irrelevant. We ordered, we ate, we had wine, and we talked, Horace and I. Howsam and Dr. Diaz did the same, except that I doubt that they tasted, remembered or understood anything that was going on except what they felt for one another. Finally I signed the bill, motioned for Carmichael to follow me, clasped Howsam by the shoulder and said, "Stay as long as you like but don't forget, check out the facilities tomorrow."

Blankly, as if awakening from a dream, he said, "Facilities?"

"Yes. Facilities. Check them out. The facilities at Marcum-Whangpo, where Dr. Diaz works, remember? We have to use them. So check them."

He nodded, but his eyes showed no comprehension and he immediately went back to paying attention to the lady in the red dress. Hoping for the best, I left, Carmichael following along and reporting, as we went outside to find Eddie, "For crying out loud. They're holding hands now." I was surprised they had waited that long.

I had two assignments for Carmichael and this was as good a time as any to get him started on one of them. "You have a credit card with you? Good. Go down to one of the shopping arcades on Tsim Sha Tsui and find a camera shop. Get one of these," and I showed him an advertisement I had ripped from the room shopping guide back at the hotel.

"You want one this small? Just like this?"

"Like this or smaller, if you can find one. Make sure you know how to use it and ask for a demonstration to be sure. If they have any special gadgets that make it easier to hide, get them too. Pretend you're buying it for a spy because that's what we're going to do. Make a spy out of you."

He was delighted. "Great. Next to playing in the NBA, my greatest desire was to be a spy. Like James Bond. Unfortunately, I'm a laboratory technician."

I consoled him with a pat on the back. "Think about it, Horace. That's the perfect disguise."

As Horace disappeared into the night, Eddie shook his head, indicating, I gathered, that he hadn't seen any Pan Union people around so far. He accompanied me in the elevator as we went upstairs to retrieve my briefcase for the meeting where we would see Pan Union people on all sides. The only person in the hallway was a maid, her service cart parked opposite our door as she rummaged around on the lower shelf, found what she needed, straightened up, smiled, and pushed her load back towards the elevator, chewing on a bedtime mint intended for someone's pillow.

Eddie watched as she disappeared around the corner, then unlocked our door with the plastic card that have become the latest security gimmick in hotels, and commented, "She's working late."

By the time I had picked up my case and the two of us reached the elevators, she was gone.

The second meeting with Bath and his crew went better than the first. This time, surprisingly, Magellan did most of the talking, and just as surprising, he had something worthwhile to say. His contact in Bangkok had agreed to a meeting, he told us, and although he didn't promise to have Lee Duc Than there, he was ready to discuss things.

I asked the Explorer, "What's your reading on this situation, Fred? Is this guy on the level and do you have anymore information about where he may have stashed 'our patient'?"

"He acts as if he's got him on ice, but he wouldn't say where. But he must be confident that he can produce him because he asked for money, directly this time, and didn't back off when I told him we would have to see the merchandise before we would pay a cent."

"What was his response to that?"

"In effect, he said OK. He'd show us Lee Duc Than and we could talk to him. Just like that."

"Let's slow down a minute, Fred. Has he ever said how he got his hands on Lee Duc Than in the first place? After all, if this was a North Vietnamese official, no Thai lawyer could just drive up to Ho Chi Minh city and take him away. Things don't work that way. Not in real life. And if Lee Duc Than is as sick as we have been led to believe, would he have been able to walk, jog or take an oxcart through the jungle and make his way to safety? And those people don't hand out passports and plane tickets to someone who is supposed to know all about missing American POW's. Like I said, not in real life. So how did he get away?"

Fantus interrupted. "Osten, this Thai lawyer is legitimate. We know he has political connections in Thailand and is thought to have friends in North Vietnam as well. He probably knew about Lee Duc Than or Lee Duc Than knew of him and they got together. That could happen even in real life."

Was he going to tell me about the tooth fairy next? "Maybe, but then how do you explain the contact with Fred in, where the hell were you Fred when the contact was made? Uzbekistan, in the thriving capital city of Dushanbe?" That was a good one for the next trivia show on television.

"Right, I was in. . ."

"OK. Uzbekistan it is. Doesn't it seem odd to anyone that a Thai lawyer would make a phone call to you in Uzbekistan rather than walk into the American embassy in Bangkok? He could have done that, couldn't he? Just walked into the embassy and said, 'Gentlemen, I have this man from North Vietnam who wants to spill the beans and tell us everything we need to know about American POW's and God knows what else, but before I produce him, I want a little of that stuff called money.' Don't you think the duty officer would have done hand flips and called Washington, the Ambassador, the President, opened the door to the safe, and pulled out some of that stuff called money? Isn't that real life, too?"

That wouldn't explain Lee Duc Than number two and Ken Green, but I thought it was an interesting question just the same.

Bath was swirling another half filled glass of amber liquor and ice, careful not to spill any this time. He had changed his shirt and trousers, looked more alert than earlier in the day, and was clearly as puzzled as I was about the Uzbekistan connection. He seemed to like it here in Hong Kong spending $500 a day of the taxpayers money on a lavish suite and good liquor. He wouldn't relish the thought of wasting any portion of a career in Dushanbe. Fantus was frowning and not happy with Uzbekistan either.

That didn't deter Magellan, who rambled on. "Good point, Osten. He could have walked into the embassy, sure, but maybe he couldn't because I don't think he's in Bangkok at all."

A new wrinkle to the story and it caught my attention, although I must admit I wasn't surprised. "If not Bangkok, then where?"

"We asked for some help from the CIA and they called upon people they knew in the DIA and, using one of these new gadgets they have, they intercepted the last two calls from Chamburon Prima – the lawyer, and he was calling from Chiang Mai. Maybe all of the calls came from there, we aren't sure, but the last two did. They even know the phone number. Better yet, they got the room number. Room 4670 in the Royal Orchid Hotel."

That still didn't explain why they hadn't walked into the local police station or called the embassy in Bangkok. I had the feeling that Fred wasn't going to explain that, not right now, maybe never.

To my surprise, Bath, after sipping his drink, raised his glass in a toast, adding, "Fred did a magnificent job on this. He stayed with it, came up with a solid lead, and got word to us. It was good work."

I doubt that Magellan had heard kind words like this very often in his checkered career. I doubt that Bath had uttered kind words like these very often in his.

I suppose I should have said something nice, too, but what interested me was, "What are you going to do now?"

Magellan looked surprised. "What do you mean?"

"You know the hotel room the lawyer is in. Can Lee Duc Than be far away? Why not go to Chiang Mai, grab the lawyer, and ask him where his client is? Offer him a choice. Take the money and start talking or we'll break your knees and make you talk. Something like that. Send Naroogian. He should be able to handle it."

The Explorer seemed to have developed dyspepsia, grimacing as he replied, "We can't do that. You're the key, Osten. I promised to bring you along to treat Lee Duc Than like they asked. If we rushed in and acted like you're suggesting, we would have broken our word. We couldn't do that."

I have to give Bath and Fantus credit. They didn't burst out laughing and I didn't either, but I don't know why not. When was the word of this bunch of pirates worth anything? Even Magellan couldn't be that naïve. Instead of laughing, I did the next best thing and agreed with him. "You're absolutely right, Fred. Our word must be our bond and I'm sorry for having spoken so rashly. What do you suggest instead?"

I had detected the faint whiff of an odor to this whole thing back in Washington. Now the stench was almost overwhelming. But what about Ken Green? It was his handwriting, according to the General, and he should know.

None of them had an answer to my question so I asked another. "But Fred, we can't reach Chiang Mai for another two days, at the earliest. Even if they're in a hotel now, they could be long gone by the time we arrive."

Fantus shook his head vigorously. "Not so. As soon as Fred got word of where the lawyer was, we had men on it. They've been watching the room since yesterday and no one goes in or out that we don't know about."

It was a warning to me. I mustn't underestimate these people, I realized once again. They don't do everything wrong.

But Bath didn't seem entirely happy with the arrangement. "Osten's right, though. We should get to Chiang Mai as soon as we can. We could be sitting on an intelligence bonanza here and we don't want to risk losing it all."

None of them brought up the matter of Lee Duc Than number two and Ken Green, which was fine with me. I was willing to take this one Lee Duc Than at a time because, sooner or later, one of them should be with or near

Ken Green. Like Kendra had said, in the jungle, surrounded by yellow flowers. If I kept my eyes open and listened very carefully, someone was going to point me in the right direction.

To get to Chiang Mai, and it was obvious that's where we had to go, we first had to fly to Bangkok. Canby, no platters of chicken bones or microphones in her hands this time, went out to make reservations and came back to report that Bath and his Pan Union party were on a Northwest flight leaving at 10:45 A.M. Eddie, Carmichael, and I were on the 9 A.M. Thai International flight. Why the different flights? I didn't ask. Howsam, of course, was going to Malaysia, if he hadn't decided to get married before then.

It was long past midnight when we walked into the Shangri La and the lobby was all but deserted. The elevator was empty and the corridors quiet. Eddie carefully checked my room before going next door and opening the connecting door for the night. Thoughtfully, the night maid had turned down the bed and placed two chocolate mints on the pillow. Someone had added a vase of flowers, mostly yellow blossoms. No card. A quick check confirmed that there were no microphones or cameras either.

It was lunch time back in New York and I caught the General as he was sitting down to eat. Montgomery would have set the table, the usual half grapefruit, a lean beef sandwich on a single slice of unbuttered toast, a cup of decaffeinated coffee, and carrot sticks. He, too, would have fresh flowers, exactly like those on my bed stand, a standing order from Kendra, her favorite florist delivering them three times a week to, as she put it, "brighten his day." They did brighten the day and the night.

The General had no information, nothing helpful at any rate. "Still no match, according to Bertinoldi," he said resignedly. "And she's beginning to get depressed again. Mike, ever since you saw her, she's seemed more alert, cheerful, seemed to have her old fighting spirit back. But today, she looked depressed. It's been tough on her. All the drugs, the side effects, the nausea, all of that. Maybe when you get back, she'll brighten up again. You're good for her, no doubt about it."

I wanted to tell him, almost did, that maybe that was because we were in love. Or was it infatuation? She was still so much younger and that worried me, even in these circumstances. So did having the General as a father-in-law.

But the call wasn't entirely wasted. "Mike, I've been thinking. That number I gave you for AcChan in Bangkok. Don't use it. Don't call him. It's been changed."

That was a surprise. "How do I find him, then? Bangkok's a big city."

"I don't think that will be a problem. We have gotten lucky. You remember Broward, don't you, my old top sergeant from Korea? Montgomery was able to track him down for me. Broward has been around, served for five years in Southeast Asia, most of it in Vietnam and Laos, and he knows AcChan. They were together in 'Nam and Broward is sure his old comrade is kicking around somewhere in Bangkok or Chiang Mai even though he's moved a couple of times recently. By the way, Broward speaks highly of him, says he knows Laos like the back of his hand and is available for hire at the right price."

Was the General telling me to forget the name and number I had memorized and then burned back in his apartment? Or was he telling me to hire a mercenary?

"You still haven't told me how to find him. Or, for that matter, who or what he is."

I heard Green talking to someone in the background and when he got back on the line, he had more information. "Montgomery thinks Broward said he is a Meo, probably from Laos initially, but he lives in Thailand now. You know about the Meo, Mike. Fought on our side in Vietnam and when we pulled out, we sort of left them holding the short end of the stick. Just abandoned them, but some, like AcChan, got out and have done well elsewhere."

"About AcChan, General. Where elsewhere, specifically? That's what I need to know. Does Montgomery know that?"

"There's a big Cypriot, according to Broward. Owns a bar in Bangkok. Used to be a big hangout for American servicemen during the war. A real dive. Still doing a land-office business with returning American tourists looking for the old haunts, Europeans doing the Bangkok scene, a few natives who don't know any better."

He was wandering all over the map without telling me anything. "General, this Cypriot. He have a name?"

"Didn't I mention it? Name of Nick. Nick Valsidakis. The place is called Nick's Place. Ought to be in the phone book. Nick himself, he should be easy to find. Montgomery says he weighs over 350 pounds."

"What's the connection between him and AcChan? It doesn't sound like they trekked together in the jungle if he weighs that much."

"I don't know," was the answer. "Maybe they've done business or served in the army together. Or maybe AcChan just goes there to eat and drink.

Broward says Nick can find him and if Broward says it, believe it. And if you still have trouble finding either Nick or AcChan, get in touch with me again. Broward's getting old, like us, but he can still travel if he has to."

That "like us" was that a subtle hint that I was too old for his daughter?

"Say hello to Kendra for me," I said. Then growing bolder, I added, "Give her my love."

He didn't comment other than to say, "Bring Ken home for me."

For him? I was trying to do it for Kendra.

I ate a mint, unlocked the mini-bar, and drank a Diet Coke, checked to make certain the door was double locked, and went to bed. Eddie's light was still on in the next room and, as I fell asleep, I heard him rattling the pages of a magazine as if he was leafing through it at high speed. What was he reading at this time of the night?

I was up at 7, showered, shaved, dressed, and ready to travel when the bellhops came to pick up the luggage. Eddie was checking the room one last time as I stepped out into the hall and headed for the elevators. He called out, "Be right with you," as I turned the corner, waiting for him to catch up.

A maid, her dress much too tight and way too short, was leaning on her service cart, waiting for the elevator to the right. I pushed the down button and paused, looking back for Eddie. A bell sounded, the red down light flashed, and the door glided open, the car in front of me empty and inviting. Because of the early hour, there were no other guests waiting, and I was mildly irritated that Eddie was holding us up. I stepped inside, holding a hand against the edge of the door to prevent it from closing, because Eddie was still not in sight back down the corridor.

I suddenly gasped in pain as something heavy smashed into my side, slamming me backward in the car and causing me to lose my grip on the door, which started to close. I bounced off the back wall, managing to partially turn with my face to the door. The maid, the careless maid, had pushed her cart forcefully into the elevator and struck me a powerful blow just above the hip, a blow so powerful that for a moment I was having trouble getting a deep breath without pain. I thought about broken ribs, then became angry over the rude way a guest was being manhandled. In the next moment, I realized it was no accident. The maid was now pulling the cart back from my body, allowing me to breathe, but then, with the strain showing on her face, gathered strength and thrust the wheeled monster straight at me for a second blow. This time, knowing what to expect, I stuck up one foot and blocked it, my sole pushing back in the direction of the door in desperate effort. With both hands clasped upon the front edge of the cart, I shoved in the opposite direction. I saw instantly what the struggle was about. If the cart could be forced aboard the elevator, the door would close and I would be alone with a very strong maid. For what purpose, I could only guess. But as long as I shoved back and kept the rear wheels from entering, the door could not close, and I dedicated every shred of my being to keeping those wheels out in the hall. For a moment, it seemed an uneven contest. My hip was in pain from the initial blow, I was short of breath, and I wasn't in the best of shape. But for God's sake, I was losing a contest with a maid? Pinned between the unyielding back wall of the elevator car and the equally hard metal front of the cart, I made one more superhuman effort to win the battle and felt the cart steadily pressing harder and harder against me. This was one tough maid. Or I was one weak old man.

And just as I was about to lose it all, just as I expected to be slammed into the wall one last time, just as I had run out of strength to resist the unequal force pressing against me, there was a violent collision in the hall-way and the maid's head came flying over the front of the cart and fell onto a pile of assorted towels, Kleenex boxes, and toilet tissue, right in front of my startled eyes. The pressure of the cart eased and I was able to breathe again. I gave it a shove and it rolled off the elevator and back into the hall where I found Eddie sitting on top of a figure sprawled on the carpet, unconscious. I reached over and picked up the revolver that was lying just a foot away from the unmoving, outstretched hand.

"Yours?" I asked Eddie.

"No, his," he responded, pointing to the prostrate form he was sitting on. A large hematoma was forming on, yes, it was his forehead, and that explained the loss of consciousness. When Eddie, once again striking from behind, had leveled his target, he had brought head into contact with metal cart and the result was, well, it was the end of the attack, that's what it was. Of course, it was no maid. It was a bald man wearing a wig, which explained why the skirt was too tight, the skirt was too short, and why the maid's face was so hairy. The real maid, the floor maid, was found trussed in a closet on the floor below. She was under five feet tall, which explained the poor fit as the bald man had been forced to wear a dress terribly unsuited for him. He should have looked for a much larger maid. But I was just as distressed as he was. I should have recognized at once that something was wrong when I saw a short skirt, hairy legs, and a hairy face. In the old days, I would have reacted more quickly. Maybe the General was right when he talked of "old like us." Maybe I should wait for Eddie from now on.

Of course, Fong was almost the first man on the scene. He listened to my story, then had Eddie tell his version, wrote everything down, and then asked, "Weren't you leaving town this morning, Doctor?"

"Yes, Inspector. We were. We have a flight to Bangkok in an hour or so, assuming we are free to leave."

"Free to leave? Certainly you are free to leave. You are a victim or an intended victim, not a criminal. Why wouldn't you be free to leave? As a matter of fact, maybe it's best if you do leave. Our crime rate will probably go down. If we don't have victims, we can't have a crime. So when you leave, we will all breathe a sigh of relief. I may be able to take a day off I was promised three weeks ago."

Fong walked down the hall away from the crowd that had gathered, motioning for me to follow. A constable had helped the bald man to his feet and handcuffed him. Two others held him by the arms and led him away. He was still dazed, his eyes not focusing, and he walked right past me without any sign of recognition. I didn't know him either.

"I don't know what is going on here, Doctor. But I'm sure you are aware that in less than 24 hours, there have been what seem to be two attempts on your life. Foiled, both of them, by your interesting Mr. Chun who seems to have a flair for timely arrivals. The shooting at Kai Tak, well, one might say that was just a random act except for the little matter of your photograph in the shooter's pocket. So I don't think it was random. This situation here, a man in a maid's dress and wig, I don't think was a robbery or a mugging. I think it was more than that because this maid was trying to pull a gun from a stack of towels when Mr. Chun hit him. If I were to guess, I'd say it was more like another attempted shooting. Fortunately, Mr. Chun knocked the gun loose and he never got a chance to use it."

"Even so Inspector, don't you think it could have been a robbery? It certainly happens, doesn't it, that hotel guests are robbed?"

"No, Doctor, we like to think that things like that don't happen in Hong Kong, but the main reason that I suspect that this wasn't a robbery is simple." He held up a picture for me to inspect. I didn't need to take a close look this time. The big X showed up clearly from across the hall. "You see, he had this in his pocket. It is the same as the one we found yesterday."

They must have ordered them by the dozen.

"Go ahead and catch your flight to Bangkok, but be careful. Someone doesn't seem to want you to get there. And a suggestion, keep Mr. Chun on your payroll."

Fong provided us with a police escort to Kai Tak where Howsam and Carmichael were already waiting. They were standing next to a delivery man with Harry Kee garment bags draped across his arms. Eddie accepted the new clothing, mine, ready as promised, and handed Kee's messenger a beautifully Christmas wrapped package, with holiday stickers and tape, in exchange. It was just about the size of a gun and that explained the crackling paper I had heard the night before, just before falling asleep. He was wrapping, not reading.

As we walked down the ramp to the waiting plane he explained, "The hell of it is, boss, Harry Kee gets me a gun and then when I need it, I had it wrapped up like a kid's toy. So I had to tackle him instead of shooting him."

"Lucky for us, you didn't shoot. We wouldn't have been on our way out of town right now if you had done that. Instead, we'd have been in the police station answering questions such as, 'where did you get the gun?'"

"Like I said. From Harry Kee. He's a nice guy. Just loaned it to me for the day. Lot of good it did, though."

Later, apparently still thinking about the maid, he said, "Know when I realized something was wrong? Not because the cart was mostly in the elevator and banging back and forth. That looked odd and I wondered why it was stuck, and I couldn't see you so I thought maybe you had already gone down without me. But as soon as I saw her hairy legs, I knew she was up to no good, and then I saw you being banged around and I just reacted. I never saw such hairy legs on a maid before. And how about that crummy wig? Phony as the day is long."

He'd noticed everything I should have, except the beard. Concentrate, I told myself. Concentrate! This was no tea party we were going to.

Eddie fell asleep minutes later. So did I, but not before telling Carmichael, "Horace, keep your eyes open. If you see anyone with either a gun or hairy legs, wake us up." When I closed mine, Horace's eyes were as wide open as I've ever seen them.

# 8

Getting off a plane at Don Muang airport in Bangkok is like walking into a blast furnace. Even in winter. The humidity is crushing and the heat surges against your body in waves, almost demanding that you reverse yourself and retreat to the cool interior of the aircraft. Instead, we walked down the ramp onto the inferno-hot tarmac and began to sweat. We clambered aboard an open air trolley with canvas fringe on top and were towed to the terminal by a smoking tractor. I know they do it differently now, but that's how they did it then. Two Royal Thai Air Force jets, American made, screamed down the runway to our left, lifted into the air, clawed for immediate altitude, leveled off, and headed for Cambodia just over the horizon to the east. A mission, real or training? Who knows? Not far away, on that border, the Khmer Rouge are still engaged in the hideous practices of genocide, slaughtering civilians indiscriminately, and occasionally they stray across the border and the Thais hasten to remind them to stay at home.

After a cursory review of our passports, we were waved through customs and immigration. No one bothered to look at our luggage. I'd been to Bangkok on numerous business trips and since meeting JoElle, more than a few personal trips, and several months ago, she suggested, "You need a driver. One who knows the city, knows his car, and is reliable." If you've been to Bangkok and endured the impossible traffic jams, approaching terminal gridlock with each passing day, you know how bad it is. I expect that one day, a single car will enter the traffic system of the city and it will be the final impediment, the missing piece of the puzzle, and everything will come to a permanent halt. Meanwhile, she had located the perfect driver for me. Phrem Songinpone. He was a former Thai paratrooper, did know the city, and always seemed able to occupy the closest parking spot to any door. He was waiting there now, car parked on the sidewalk, with a uniformed military policeman standing guard. Old army buddy. Phrem himself was easy to spot in the crowd. He was the only one wearing a Green Bay Packer cap.

JoElle had been right about him knowing the city. Traffic jams were a challenge that he had learned to accept and overcome. He had a thousand shortcuts, slipped through unmapped and unknown alleyways, scurried across vacant parking lots, and once courageously drove through the courtyard and lobby of a crowded hotel to avoid a two hour wait at a clogged intersection. He earned every cent of his money. But that was in the city. Once outside, on the highways leading to the mountains up north or to the beaches down south, he was lost in less than ten minutes.

After squeezing all of our luggage into the trunk, we took off down the airport highway for the city itself. It was a compliment to his skill that we reached the Oriental Hotel some 90 minutes later, a remarkable achievement when you consider that we had driven almost 15 miles in bumper to bumper traffic that hadn't moved at all.

Eddie had spent most of the trip looking out of the rear window. As we got out of the car at the Oriental, he told me, "I didn't see anyone following us, unless they were doing it on foot. They could have easily kept up."

I went over a final review of my medical records as soon as we were in our suite. I had every note memorized by now and still hadn't any idea what I would be faced with when I finally saw Lee Duc Than, whoever he was. Drank more tea and ate another almond cookie, every bit as good as those in Hong Kong. This was one of the pleasures of the Orient that I hoped American hotels would adopt.

I was interrupted by Carmichael who reported on the use of his purchase at Tsim Sha Tsui mall. "Works like a charm," he enthused. "Look, it fits into the palm of your hand and there's room left over for a piece of pizza." And he showed me. I should point out that Horace has big hands, hands that easily grasp and dunk a basketball. Not everyone would have had room for a piece of pizza.

"Great," I said, "and as soon as you unpack, take the film down to the concierge and have him get it developed. We need it right away."

Which reminded me of the second assignment I had been saving for him. "Check on the package, too. It should be there."

It was. He was smiling broadly when he brought back the small, tightly wrapped box that had been waiting for us at the front desk. It had been delivered earlier that morning by an SAS pilot who had gotten it in Bahrain from a British Airways pilot who had received it in London from an American Airlines pilot who had taken it from a Delta pilot in New York who had brought it to the big city after accepting it from a skinny little man in a brown suit and scuffed black shoes just as he was boarding his 757 jet in Atlanta for a preflight check. The skinny little man worked for NIH, the National Institutes of Health. The package was carefully wrapped, unopened, and had been refrigerated aboard each of the aircraft in the galley and with dry ice. It contained one of a kind stuff and I immediately opened the minibar and put it inside.

Carmichael left to check out his facilities and meet the people at

Chulalongkorn University and Eddie and I went in search of Nick's place. It wasn't hard to find. It was as simple as asking Phrem to drive us there. He knew of it and made it clear he thought it was nothing but an overpriced tourist trap, although admitting to consuming a bottle of beer or two on the premises from time to time. "It's OK for a bottle of beer and to enjoy the bouzouki."

"They have good food, then?" I asked.

He looked at me questioningly. "I don't know."

"I thought you said you enjoyed the bouzouki?"

"The bouzouki, yes, the bouzouki is good. But you don't eat the bouzouki. You –," and he took both hands off the steering wheel to demonstrate, waving them left to right, then up and down in front of his chest, while the car bore down on a three-wheeled, open-air Tuk-Tuk, its four passengers and a driver staring at us in open mouthed terror.

Hurriedly, Eddie broke in, "The bouzouki, boss, it's a thing. Like a banjo or a mandolin, that a guy plays. Music. I think it's Greek," he added. "Maybe he better put on the brakes now before he hits those people in that golf cart up ahead."

Another asset that made Phrem so valuable was his remarkable grasp of English. Eddie had hardly mentioned the word 'brake' before Phrem applied it, put both hands back on the wheel, bringing the Mercedes to a smooth stop inches away from the rear of the Tuk-Tuk, whose driver yawned and smiled indulgently while his passengers resumed an animated discussion that had been temporarily placed on hold.

It was embarrassing to have the difference between Greek music and food explained to me by a security guard, but you have to swallow your pride in things like that, knowing that an opportunity was bound to arise later when I could do the same to him.

And as it turned out, the food was not the attraction at Nick's. It was Nick himself and the atmosphere of Casablanca type mystery and intrigue: dim lighting, sweet thick smoke, muted conversation, and high prices did nothing to diminish the appeal to wide eyed tourists, foreign correspondents hungry for atmosphere, and jaded embassy personnel whose offices and living quarters were nearby. Stubby, flickering candles stuck haphazardly into wax filled green glass ash trays decorated and provided illumination at each table. Overhead, a smattering of weak uncovered light bulbs tried, and failed, to cut through the haze of the cavernous room, built to resemble a cave, and coming remarkably close to actually looking like one. A small waterfall spouted from one wall, ran down to the floor and streamed away with a tinkling sound, mingled with an occasional splash as guests slipped on the narrow wooden planks crossing from one side of the artificial stream to the other, and fell into Nick's creek, as it had come to be called. It was difficult to see from one end of the room to the other, especially after coming in from bright sunlight, but the waiter who met us at the door seemed to have no trouble finding an empty table for us and stood by waiting for an order.

I ordered Singha beer. Local brand controlling 80% of the market. "Make it two," Eddie said.

The waiter was still standing and staring as if he didn't understand English. I tried again, pointing to Eddie, then to myself, and said, louder this time, "Singha. Him and me. Two Singha." He disappeared.

I had been wondering how to contact the owner, but I needn't have worried. Ordering two local beers apparently was the equivalent of leaving a wake up call for the proprietor. He was standing beside our table before the beer arrived. Dressed in black, all in black, even his sandals which I could see below his enormous bulging abdomen, he was all but invisible in the darkened room. As I had been told, he was a big man. An enormous man. Over three hundred pounds, considerably over.

"Gentlemen," he began, his voice not at all like Sidney Greenstreet, more like Peter Lorre, "I'm terribly distressed. When I saw two gentlemen like you walk in just now I said, 'businessmen, men of refined tastes and culture. Men who like Scotch, Bourbon, fine wines, the better things of life.' But Singha? You ordered Singha? What have I done wrong?" I was afraid he was going to cry. As the waiter appeared with the offending product, he picked up one of the open bottles and waved it around, waiting for everyone to sneer. I expected that boos directed at us might follow, but because of the darkness, no one could see. Because of the noise, no one could hear. "How can an honest man make a living selling this – this Singha?" He spat out the last word.

The table next to us, a table of four American tourists from the looks of them, all assorted electronic gear, designer eyeglasses, wrap around Ray Ban sunglasses on one woman, the latest bouffant hairdo on another, stylish clothes on all four, silly grins on their faces, they loved the act. This is what they had come to see. Nick was playing to his audience. This is what made him wealthy. Not the beer.

I picked up the second bottle of beer, the one he hadn't touched, took a drink, and very quietly said, "Sit down."

He handed the second bottle to Eddie, waved the waiter away, and sat down. Moments later, the waiter returned with a third bottle of Singha, placed it in front of Nick, and disappeared once more. The huge man drank from his bottle, almost half of the liquid disappearing somewhere, burped, leaned back, and said, "That's good beer." When I didn't respond immediately, he emptied the bottle and said, "I take it you wanted to talk to me?"

"Not to you. I want to talk to AcChan."

The waiter returned with a full bottle of Mekong whiskey and one glass. According to the price schedule posted by the door, it was the cheapest drink in the house. That didn't seem to bother Nick at all. He poured a glass and drank it.

"In that case, you do need to talk to me, don't you?" He was enjoying himself.

"If you know where he is, yes, I do need to talk to you."

Appearances to the contrary, this was no bumbling Cypriot merchant or restaurant owner who had gone to seed. He was instantly alert, carefully scanning the room to see if anyone could overhear our conversation, and talking softly. "Why? Why do you want to talk to him?"

"An old friend says he is the best man for a job I have in mind."

"If he's the best man, then your old friend must expect you to go into Laos."

"Let's just say it's an important job."

"AcChan doesn't come cheap. People who look for him know that."

"As I said, it's an important job and we'd be willing to pay."

I had his attention now. "A lot?"

"Let's just say a reasonable amount. We would certainly try to make it worth his while."

Nick fingered his glass, staring at the Mekong whiskey, not acting as if he wanted anymore. "And how much to his agent?"

"He has an agent?" I inquired. Did everyone in Thailand deal through agents?

"Yes, certainly, he has an agent."

"In that case, if the agent succeeded in putting us in touch with him, I am sure we could make arrangements to pay a – what should we call it – a commission?" I offered.

"If you did that, you probably could find AcChan and talk to him. Whatever. As long as his agent was satisfied that your intentions were honorable. About the money, that is."

"You mean about the money for the agent or the money for AcChan?" I asked.

"Both," he said emphatically.

"That seems fair enough. Would you be able to put us in touch with his agent?"

"Sure, that's easy. Won't be no problem at all." He finally decided to drain what was left of the whiskey, refilled the glass, watched with interest as the four Americans, fearing that the show was over, collected their gear and prepared to leave, arguing over whether to use Visa or American Express plastic to pay the bill, and only after the noisy foursome had stumbled over the bridge to the cash register did Nick beckon the hovering waiter, asking us, "Want something to eat?"

Remembering Phrem's parting warning, "Don't eat there," Eddie and I shook our heads no in unison. It wasn't just the flies and crawling insects, the indescribable odors, the bugs frying in the burning candles, it was just that I hate to eat what I can't see. It was too dark in the room to identify what might be on the plate. Eddie came up with a better explanation, one which I should have used, too. "Not hungry," was what he said.

Nick was undeterred. Maybe he had already ordered, maybe he always ate the same thing or maybe they only served one thing, but all he did was lean back, summon the waiter, and say, "Bring it." While waiting for 'it,' he asked, "About the money. How much you willing to pay?"

"That's something we should discuss with the agent, don't you think?"

"Discuss it with me," he said, brusquely.

"Why bother and then have to discuss it again with someone else?"

"Because I can fix it so you only do it once. With me." Another drink, wiping his lips with the back of his hand, wiping the hand on his black tunic, and leaning forward so that his face was a foot from mine. How he did this without toppling the table was a mystery. "Because I'm the man. I'm the agent. So talk to me!"

I wasn't surprised. In a movie, he would be the perfect Sidney Greenstreet, except for that squeaky voice. Overlook that; cast him in the role anyway. Eddie was the ideal Peter Lorre. And me. Who else could I be other than Humphrey Bogart?

While I was casting the movie, the waiter returned with a steaming covered dish, set it before his owner with a flourish worthy of Chasen's, was it still in business?, and removed the silver top. Exposed was a bowl of sticky rice, mixed with might have been bits of chicken or pork, or both, it was hard to tell, a sliver of green here and there, identity totally unknown, a fish head off to one side, just one, and shiny fragments that had to be endive or onion, maybe some garlic. With yet another flourish, the waiter produced first one egg, then another, and cracked both of them precisely in the center atop the pile of rice, the gelatinous white and yellow sliding like hot lava on snow down from the mountain top of rice to the valley nestled against the side of the bowl. With the satisfied air of a craftsman proud of his work, he then crumbled the egg shells, sprinkled the pieces on top of his culinary masterpiece, and walked away.

Nick contemplated the mess, picked up a fork, no chop sticks here, and proceeded to mix it into a single congealed mass that reminded me of the lobby floor of a famous pharmaceutical firm in New York, just off 42$^{nd}$ street. "Gimme a minute or two here, to eat," he said, coming as close to an apology as we were likely to hear. That's all he needed, a minute or two, and he ate it all. As he audibly crunched the last piece of white eggshell, he paused, "Calcium. Lots of calcium. Good for the bones. Need good bones to support the rest of me." In an aside directed to me, he advised, "When you get older, you gotta take care of your bones. Keep that in mind." I had been using Tums.

A napkin, the waiter had left one, replaced the hand this time, another belch, and he continued, "So you wanna get in touch with AcChan? That's gonna cost you 1000 bahts."

I had the sense that Burrows was peering over my shoulder as I spent some of our money. "Let's make it $20, American." About half of what he had asked for.

His eyes narrowed but his expression never changed. "How's the beer? Want another one?"

My bottle was half full. Eddie hadn't yet touched the one Nick had pawed earlier. I offered, "No, I'm still working on this one, but how about you? Can I buy you one?"

"That would be nice," he said, brightening, snapping his fingers to attract the attention of the vigilant waiter once more.

He sat for a moment contemplating the newly arrived bottle of Molson's, not the local brew, but imported all the way from Canada. The cap was still in place.

"Twenty five dollars would be nice."

"Well, to speed things along," forgive me, Everett, "let's make it $25."

He gave me a phone number and address, written on a surprisingly clean and professional appearing business card that said "Nick's Place" and below it, engraved, were the words, "fine foods and beverages." The Better Business Bureau would have jumped all over him back in my town for advertising like that. I noticed that the number and address were not the ones Green had given me back in New York. Down in the right hand corner of the white pasteboard was his logo, a small stringed instrument resembling a mandolin.

"When does your bouzouki player perform?" I asked, surprising him.

"You've heard of Viakos, my cousin? Wonderful. He's very good, I think, at making music. Come back tonight, every night. He may be here. He plays when he feels like it so come back any night to see if he felt like it."

We were walking to the cash register, Nick shuffling in his loose sandals, Eddie and I walking gingerly to avoid the creek, when I asked him, "What does AcChan do?"

Never breaking stride, he chuckled, the rumbling noise waking a German tourist who had fallen asleep at his table and forgotten why he was there with a sixteen year old Thai girl who was being paid 4000 bahts for her services, and replied, "I think you have a word for it in your country that may explain it very well. Tour guide. Yes, that's what AcChan is. A tour guide. Especially for people planning a trip to Laos." He leaned closer and I could smell the odor of garlic. "Remember, they don't like tourists in Laos. So you need a good tour guide."

The bill came to $30, plus, of course the $25 in cash already inside Nick's pocket. I thought that a little steep for two Singhas and a bottle of imported Molson, which the waiter was now putting back into the cooler for resale, the cap never having been removed. When I mentioned this to the pretty Chinese barmaid at the cash register, she smiled her prettiest smile and itemized it for me. "Your beers, sir, Singha, $5 American each. Cheap. One Molson, expensive beer from somewhere else, $10. And Mr. Nick's dinner, with discount, only $10. Cheap because you get owner's price. Thirty dollars. You understand?"

"What about the Mekong whiskey? Did you forget to put that on the bill?" I inquired.

She was dismayed. I should never have brought it up. "Oh, sir, I'm so sorry. I forget. Should be another $5 for Mekong. Very cheap stuff. Just another five."

I gave her two twenties, American. The waiter had earned his tip. Besides, someone had to pay for developing the film he had exposed while photographing Eddie and me. I wondered if I would ever get to see a copy of this one.

Phrem drove us to AcChan's address by taking Rama IV, swinging onto Soi 26, finding a half dozen shortcuts bypassing the crowded intersections around the elegant old Dusit Thani hotel and newer Sheraton, roaring through a bus parking lot scattering a dozen drivers and mechanics, and just when I thought we had it made, we were delayed a full ten minutes when traffic was stalled by an elephant and pickup truck, the elephant's foot resting on the hood of the rusted truck, with no one willing, or able, to resolve the impasse. The truck driver and mahout were shouting at one another, one on the ground looking up, the other perched atop the elephant's neck, looking down. Finally, the discussion ended, the mahout said something to the elephant, which removed its foot from the truck, and traffic slowly resumed, at a snail's pace.

AcChan lived in an attractive neighborhood, private homes interspersed with high rise apartments, all boasting security walls and surrounded by lush tropical foliage. Spirit houses adorned every gate side, attracting daily visits of saffron robed Buddhist monks subsisting on the offerings of rice and other edibles left for them each morning by devout believers. At AcChan's apartment complex we were waved through a ten foot iron gate by one guard and directed to a parking space by another. They acted as if they had been expecting our visit.

Children played in the late afternoon sun, splashing in a full sized swimming pool under the watchful eyes of several Thai nannies and a half dozen sun tanned, oil glistening expatriate wives, arrayed at intervals in lounge chairs, wearing as little as law and decency allow. Thai law was vague on the subject, so decency was the prevailing standard. None of them moved and, with eyes hidden behind wrap around dark sunglasses, it was impossible to know if any of them were awake.

AcChan had a spacious apartment on the eighth floor with a view of the Chao Prya river in the background. A man servant escorted us to a balcony from where we had a clear view of the towering cranes of the Port Authority of Thailand rhythmically transferring heavy loads from ship to shore, from shore to ship, in a never-ending stream of commerce testifying to the vibrant economy of one of Asia's rising powers.

He was taller than I had expected, much taller than what I had expected a Meo to be. He was lean and muscular, his skin a healthy bronze and his hair jet black. His eyes were such a deep brown that they had all but disappeared into the shadows of his prominent brows. His handshake was firm, his face lined and leathery as if he had spent much time outdoors. He may have started out as a hill tribesman, but he now moved in different circles, as a quick glance at the rich furnishings, the expensive paintings hanging from the wall, and the lush carpet covering the mahogany floors clearly revealed. He did well for a tour guide.

And he spoke perfect English. "Welcome to my home. It's fortunate that I happened to be in when Nick called." He indicated a chair and we sat down.

"He called then? I was wondering if he would."

"Yes, he called. I'm sure you were barely out of the door before he was on the phone describing what you were wearing, who was with you, and warning me that you were almost certainly on your way to pay me a visit. For which I thanked him."

"Did he offer to send a photograph over? A recent photograph to help you identify us?"

His face crinkled in amusement. Before answering, he leaned back and extended his long legs and watched the cranes at work in the distance. "They are always busy," he said. "Never a moment that they don't have cargo to move. It's good for Thailand. You were very observant back at Nick's, Doctor. Nick will be disappointed to learn that you spotted the camera. He takes pride in being able to collect what he calls 'data' without anyone knowing about it. But to be technically correct about it, no, he didn't offer to send a photograph over. He already has sent it over." He reached over to me and handed me my latest portrait. Not as clear as one might like it because of the haze and smoke, and the absence of a flash, but it wasn't a bad shot under the circumstances. Eddie and me, watching in fascination as Nick wolfed down a $10 meal, with discount.

"We came here directly from his place. How did he get a photo over here any faster?"

"Motorcycle. You know how bad traffic is in this city. Often a motorcycle is the only thing that moves. By the way, do you like the picture? Keep it as a remembrance of Nick's. I have others." He grinned when he mentioned Nick. "Did you like his place? The atmosphere? What do you call it, the ambiance?"

"My driver thinks it's intended for tourists. He warned us not to eat there, which was good advice from what we saw."

He agreed. "Yes, no one should eat there. I never have although I suspect that Nick took advantage of your visit to order a meal and add it to your bill."

He certainly knew Nick. "Yes, he did that, and went even further. He ate it. Which just goes to prove, I suppose, that he has forgotten what good food tastes like."

"On the contrary, he definitely has not forgotten that. Occasionally, perhaps every two months or so, when Nick has collected information that he feels may be of interest to me, I take him to dinner at a decent restaurant, quiet little places where we won't be recognized, and the owners always smile when they see him come in. They know the bill will be a big one as Nick has a gargantuan appetite and truly does appreciate good food."

How could they find a place where no one knew this huge man? "There are places like that, Doctor, places where they don't know him or don't remember seeing him after he leaves. There are many places like that in Bangkok."

Talking of food reminded me that we hadn't eaten. Another thing that reminded me was the growling of Eddie's stomach. Hunger did not seem to be AcChan's problem, however, as he continued, "How much did Nick charge you for my address and phone number? Twenty-five dollars! He is a larcenous man, isn't he? Actually, my phone number is in the phone book but I do change my address quite frequently. For instance, this place. I just moved here last week."

We passed a few more minutes in small talk; the weather, the traffic, the price of wines, and smoking, (both of us thought it a bad habit), while a manservant quietly served tea and almond cookies. When the tea was settled in a cup before him and he felt us to be at ease, he came directly to the point.

"I understand you want to find someone in Laos."

I was surprised. "Nick tell you that?"

"Yes, he did, but I knew it before he passed the information on just minutes ago." I wasn't certain he was going to tell me how he had come into possession of that knowledge but he relented, saying, "A friend told me. An old friend of mine, someone you know. He told me."

"And the old friend that we both know is?" and I waited.

He sipped from the Spode cup, savored his tea, and said, "Broward. He told me when I talked to him a week or so ago. We used Nick as a screen to see if you showed up and whether anyone was following you. You remember Broward don't you? From Korea where you served with him. I knew him, too. Later, when I served with him in Vietnam." He was studying the intricate pattern of blue hummingbirds that floated on the thin sides of the dazzlingly white cup, sides so thin that they were all but invisible. He seemed satisfied with what he saw and said, "Broward tells me you are looking for the son of a General. Ken Green, son of the man who was your commanding officer in Korea. Missing for fifteen years, he says. Is that possible?"

"That's essentially correct. You must have talked to Broward before moving because the address he gave the General to give me was the wrong one. Your old one. But nothing has changed since then."

"I wouldn't want to mislead you, Doctor. I talked to both the General and Broward three days ago. But you are correct in that nothing much has changed since then."

"Three days ago you were living here, but they gave me an incorrect address. Why?"

"For the simplest of all reasons. I must have forgotten to tell them about my move."

The look on Eddie's face was saying, "You're not going to believe that are you?" I answered silently, "of course not." It bothered me though, that everyone seemed to be talking to everyone else, except me. And I was the one they had asked to come looking for Ken Green. Well, don't whine about it, I decided. Take it one step at a time.

The first step was to tell AcChan, "I'm not sure if we'll be going to Laos. At least not right away. First we have to go to Chiang Mai."

He seemed surprised by the news. "Chiang Mai? If you look in the telephone directory you will find dozens of tour guides listed for Chiang Mai. Look under the heading 'Tour Guides.' They will put you in a minibus and take you sight seeing, shopping, to the restaurants, visit the zoo, swing by the night bazaar or drop you off at a carefully staged Kantoke dinner. You'll have a wonderful, but boring time. You don't need me for that. Any of the others could handle that nicely."

"I suspect that I'll need more than what a regular guide might be able to offer."

I had his interest again, although I don't believe I had ever really lost it. "How much more might that be?"

"I don't know, exactly. And I don't know what Broward or the General might have told you, but I'm told that I am looking for a sick man in a hotel room. One so sick that he needs a doctor and I'm the only doctor he's willing to see."

He repeated after me, as if doubting that he had heard me correctly, "and you're the only doctor he's willing to see? Do you believe that?"

"It doesn't really matter whether I believe it because that's only half the story. The other half is that he is supposed to have Ken Green with him, or Ken Green has him, or that they are linked together in some way. And it's Ken Green I've come for."

"I see. What about the men from Washington who are with you? Where do they fit into this?"

"The only man who is truly *with* me is this one right here," and I indicated Eddie. "I trust none of the others at all." I trusted Carmichael but he was sticking to the laboratory and didn't count as an operational asset.

AcChan had resumed his study of the hummingbirds. I examined my cup more closely and found it occupied by faint yellow butterflies, none of them moving but all of them so delicately featured that they seemed capable, had they a mind to do so, of flight. Yellow reminded me of Kendra and I realized why I was here all over again. His voice roused me from my dreams. "If there is a sick man in this hotel room, wherever it is, what do you propose to do with him?"

"Treat him. I'm a doctor and that's what I was hired to do."

"You've come a long way to do that. We have many fine doctors right here in Thailand. Why not let one of them handle all of this?"

"It's complicated. But I've been told that I treated this man years ago for the same problem and they want me to do it again. In fact, they tell me that the patient specifically asked for me by name. Apparently that's more or less the deal. I treat a man called Lee Duc Than. Ken Green comes out. We get a defector; a POW is freed. Everybody is happy."

"Not everybody, Doctor. Not the other side. They won't be happy at all. But even with that, then I suppose you should go and treat him, do the same as you did before, and try to take your Ken Green home."

"Except for one thing. As far as I know, I've never treated this man. I taught him when he was a student, but I never saw him as a patient. See my problem?"

He set his cup onto the tray. "Interesting." I didn't know if he was referring to the hummingbirds or my problem. In the distance, the silent cranes continued their endless swinging to and fro along the waterfront. It was becoming dark and lights had started to appear all over the city. Finally, he seemed to reach a decision. "All right. You may need my services in Chiang Mai after all. It's not a problem. I live there."

I looked around at the apartment. "You don't live here?"

"No, this is one of several places I use when I'm in the city. My home is in Chiang Mai. It's closer to the mountains where I always feel more comfortable. Bangkok, well, Bangkok is too crowded. Too many bad smells and too much rain. Of course, there's also the problem of traffic."

"When can we go?" I asked. "There is a certain urgency about this."

"Tomorrow, if you wish. I'm at your service, but tomorrow would be best as it would allow time for me to make a few telephone calls. Before I do that, though, tell me a little about these men you're working with. The ones you don't trust. What is their interest in all of this? I can understand an interest in Green. He's a missing American. But the other man. The sick one? What about him?"

"Supposedly he's a Vietnamese defector. Defected from the south to the north, was involved in keeping tabs on American POW's and reeducation camps for captured South Vietnamese soldiers. Educated in the United States. That's where I met him, but like I told you, I never treated him medically for anything. My associates in this project want this man, Lee Duc Than, and he offers information in exchange for my services. That's what they tell me."

"Who are *they*?"

"You want the name of the group? It's the Pan Union Trade Association from Washington, D.C."

"But they really are –," he prompted.

"The State Department. The other name is a cover or front, but they deal in information and work for my government. The name allows everyone to deny responsibility when things go wrong."

"You've worked with them before?"

"Yes, I've worked with some of them before."

"And yet you don't trust them?" he asked, his eyebrows raised.

"That's why I don't trust them," I explained, and he understood.

"There seems to be more here than meets the eye, Doctor. If you don't trust these people and if you're certain you've never treated this man before, then why are you here at all? Patriotism? Money? Adventure? Ego?"

"None of those. I'm here because I've come to find Ken Green."

"You've already said that. Why is he so important? I know you served with his father long ago and Broward has made it clear that you and the General have always been close, but why this obsession with the son? He's been missing fifteen years and he's an American. That could be reason enough to come this far, but there seems to be more. I have the feeling there is a personal interest in this beyond anything you've told me so far."

He had talked to Jordan Green. Hadn't the General told him the rest? "I don't just want to find Ken Green," I explained. "I need Ken Green. Rather, his sister needs Ken Green."

He was puzzled. "Needs him? After fifteen years, I am sure she would like to see him, but you said needs him. Why does she need him?"

Well, tell him the rest. If he's going gambling with me, he should know what the stakes were. "His sister, his twin, has a serious illness. The doctors treating her say it is likely to be fatal, unless. . .unless she gets a bone mar-row transplant. And he is the most likely compatible donor. So what I need is him. Or at least a blood sample from him to find out if the bone marrow transplant is feasible. If it is, then I must take him back. If not, then aside from his family wanting him back, it wouldn't matter."

"It sounds as if you have more than a passing interest in wanting the transplant to succeed."

I realized how perceptive he was. "I've known his sister for a long time. From when she was a little girl. I want to do everything I can to help her get well."

"And that's all, Doctor?" he asked. "Nothing else?"

Sure, there was something else. "I may love her," I confessed.

"May love her? You don't know? Isn't that unusual?"

I didn't know if it was or not. It was something I'd been struggling with for years. "I'm quite a bit older than she is," I offered, lamely, and wished I hadn't said it.

He didn't say anything at all for a while and all three of us sat quietly in the room, now almost dark as the sun had set across the river, hanging for a moment just above the tree line and then disappearing with a suddenness that plunged the city into night. "Yes, that is a difficult situation, one that not everyone understands," making it sound that perhaps he did. "Before we make our plans for Chiang Mai, Doctor, I want to tell you a few things I have discovered over the years about missing Americans in Laos and Viet-nam. Some of this is difficult for Americans to accept, and some don't even want to listen. May I?"

I sat back to listen to what he had to say and it turned out to be a lesson in how self deception can be self defeating.

"Americans," he began," continue to talk about the 2,800 missing men as prisoners of war. They claim that they'll never recognize Vietnam as a nation until every last POW is accounted for and returned. They act as if these men are alive somewhere in Southeast Asia, held against their will under horrible conditions. That isn't so. There are almost certainly none to be returned. Most of them are long dead in places no one can find, graves overgrown by jungle, covered by the water of a rice paddy, at the bottom of an old bomb crater or in the wreckage of a plane in places humans never go. That's wild country out there. Lots of places where humans never go. So your countrymen worry about missing Americans. Never stop worrying abut missing Americans. Maybe that's good but it's a terrible burden to bear.

"You see, there are thousands and thousands of missing Vietnamese, too, and even though they are missing in their own country, no one has been able to locate them either. And then there are many thousands of others, Laotians, Cambodians or my people and other hill tribes like my Meo – all missing. Lots of missing people. More than enough to fill thousands of homes with sorrow here in Southeast Asia as well as in America. But only in your country is it an obsession, bordering on a crusade, incorporated into your politics, and wrapped in a flag. Your people should accept it like ours have. There is no one left to come home!"

I knew the odds and couldn't disagree with what he was saying. Yet, he had to be wrong, and I told him why. "We have reason to believe that one American is still alive. Ken Green. I have to find him." I wanted to tell him that if there was one, there may be others. I didn't, because I really didn't believe that myself. About Ken Green? All right, so he was the exception to the rule.

AcChan wasn't surprised by my reaction. "Doctor, I respect your feelings. I can understand your motives. I am only pointing out that the stubbornness lives on. Americans will not accept, cannot accept, that the quest is futile. Whether it's 2,200 men or one man, the hope lives on."

There was no point in entering a debate. There was only one thing I needed to know. "Will you help me look for Ken Green?" Kendra had said her brother was in a jungle. And there was that letter back in New York. Dead men don't write letters and that's what I told AcChan.

He listened carefully and when I finished, he shrugged and said, "No, I haven't heard of dead men writing letters. I suppose I should go along with you to check into this intersecting phenomenon. There's always a first time for everything, isn't that what they say?"

"Then you concede he could be alive?" I asked, clinging to even the slightest hope.

"If he's writing letters, possibly," was all he was willing to concede, but at least that was something.

Then, before we left, he described how he had come to know Broward.

"I served with him in Vietnam. I was much younger than he was but he always seemed to know so much more than the rest of us, even though he was a stranger to our country. I had grown up in a small Vietnamese village just inside that arbitrary line called the boundary with Laos. One day, the Americans came to recruit as many men as they could. The Viet Minh, Viet Cong, Pathet Lao, Khmer Rouge, Cao Dai, North Vietnamese, and other sects and bandits had taken turns terrorizing our village for years, starting even before the Japanese left what had been called Indo-China in 1945. The American offer seemed like our best opportunity to break the cycle of violence and depredation that had been disrupting our lives for twenty-five years. They had an air of power about them, their planes filled the skies, their artillery could be heard thundering across all of Vietnam, and their men walked with confidence, an arrogance that in the early days of the war was unshakable. We talked it over, my three older brothers and I, and joined with several others from our village and perhaps twenty more from a neighboring hill tribe. We were Meo and they were Nung but all of us were considered to be good fighters and we got along fine.

"Money was a motive, none of us could deny that, but it wasn't the only thing that made us want to carry a weapon and march with the Americans. We wanted to strike back at the men who came by night to suck us dry, to demand our pigs, our chickens, our rice, and if the mood struck them, to seize our young men as recruits and our young girls as concubines. Better to fight them, we decided, than to submit.

"So when the men with the green berets entered our village offering money and guns, it was too good an opportunity to pass up. Our whole village paid for our decision, though, and a few weeks after we departed, the Viet Cong came and burned the village, killing almost everyone who had been left behind, including my mother, two sisters, and my grandmother. A clear warning to others. My father had died when I was a little boy and I don't remember him at all. So I was alone.

"Meanwhile, the Americans were training us, arming us with light infantry weapons and we were based at a place called Tchepone on what your people called the Ho Chi Minh Trail. It wasn't on the main road from the north but was a secondary supply route that went through Laos and then circled back into South Vietnam, well out of range of the big guns located at

192

several American fire bases scattered about the area. We were much more lightly defended than those positions but we did what we could and strung wire, laid Claymore mines, dug our bunkers and slit trenches, and settled in for more training and waited. Everyday, we went out patrolling with Americans and that's when I got to know Broward.

"One afternoon, as we were returning from a patrol, we were ambushed. Several men were hit but we managed to get back inside the wire. By the next morning, it was obvious we had been surrounded by North Vietnamese regulars who had decided it was time to remove this annoyance on their supply line. They hit us three or four times before noon and each time our 300 tribesmen and dozen Americans beat them off, but it was just a question of time before they would overrun the position. We knew that. They had more men, superior firepower, and were better trained. By then, there were dead and wounded North Vietnamese all around our perimeter so we were making them pay a terrible price, but they seemed willing to pay it and kept coming. Our radioman had asked for help but someone on the other end kept insisting 'hold the position for three more days;' they never said what difference another three more days would make, never explained it at all, but did promise to drop supplies by helicopter. No matter how hard our radioman tried to explain it to them, they didn't seem to grasp that we couldn't hold out for more than a few hours. Three more days was out of the question."

The tea was cold, the manservant had disappeared, and both Eddie and I sat listening to a story that could only have one ending.

"Broward finally took the radio and told some colonel that we couldn't hold the position any longer. We were almost out of ammunition, the enemy was through the wire in two or three places, and if we didn't get relief, it was all but over for us. We needed, he told them, gunships to sanitize the perimeter, ammunition, artillery support, and more men. Then we might hold out for a day. But forget the three days. It was out of the question.

"I was close enough to Broward to hear the colonel's response. 'You do that Sergeant. You hold on at least 24 hours and we'll send everything you need, and then provide your boys a ride out of there.'

"That's what he promised. What we got was one fast helicopter pass over the camp and three boxes of ammunition, two of which fell outside the wire into the hands of the enemy. What we got, in other words, was nothing. That's what Broward told them on the radio and someone kept telling him, 'you're doing good, boy, just hang on.' And Broward cursed the unseen colonel, called him names I haven't heard since, and the colonel, far away and safe, said, 'Sergeant, I could have you court-martialed for talking like that.' It turns out that that was the least of our problems because right about then, the black pajamas of the NVA were through the wire everywhere and killing everyone in sight.

"I was alongside Broward when he realized what had happened and I thought he had gone mad. He was cursing the colonel and screaming at the North Vietnamese and standing fully exposed alongside the bunker. He was firing his automatic rifle in full bursts and when it was empty, he threw it down and picked up another. I realized he had decided to die right there. But I wanted to live and I knew there was a chance. Not a good one, but it was better than nothing. One day on patrol, I had seen a deep gully that ran behind our bunker and disappeared into the jungle almost a half mile away. When I investigated later, on my own, wondering why we hadn't strung wire where it entered the camp, I found that we didn't need wire. Whenever hard rains battered the area, logs and other debris were washed into the ravine and had formed an impenetrable mass, more formidable than wire could ever be. In addition to that, the underbrush was thick and bristly, a natural barrier that would discourage attackers from making an entry from that direction. And so far as I could see, none had.

"I seized Broward by one arm and pulled him, both of us falling almost at once and rolling down the side of the gully. We were scratched and bruised by the time we hit bottom, but the brush effectively hid us from the view of anyone up above. If any NVA soldiers had seen us fall, they probably assumed we had been hit and tumbled into the jungle. But none of them appeared above us and no one followed us down. The next thing I knew, Broward had regained his feet and he was pulling me along behind him, down the ravine, in the direction of the stream that was at the other end. He was in full command of his senses once again. Eighteen days later, along with three others who had found the same escape route, we walked into an American fire base, half dead. The map showed we had covered more than 50 miles through trackless jungle. My three brothers –," he paused, still recalling the day, "my three brothers and all of the others, I never saw any of them again."

So like in Korea, Broward had been abandoned again, after a promise of help. Unfulfilled.

AcChan hadn't finished. "I continued fighting for the Americans. Why not? Where else could I go? My brothers were missing, my mother and sisters had been murdered, my village had been destroyed. A dozen Americans were missing that same day. Twelve. Have any ever returned home? I doubt it, although I admit I don't know. My brothers? Have they ever been heard from? No. Who will account for them? Who is looking for them? Not even me anymore. I went back once to see if I could find them. The jungle had recaptured the camp and had covered it over. There were no graves, there were no bodies, there was almost nothing except the tangled ravine Broward and I had used in our escape. There were memories, but that's all. I don't look anymore. I know, just like most Americans hoping for a miracle must know by now, that they died. If not on the day we were overrun, then on some other day when the enemy decided they weren't worth keeping alive any longer. Or on some day when a prisoner simply lies down and dies because he can't go on. I accept what happened and my people accept what happened. And then one day, the fighting was over and the Americans went home to take up their lives again. Not us. We had no homes. Those who still survived had to walk through the jungle once again, across Laos and Cambodia, hoping to make it to Thailand. Or take a boat and try to reach Hong Kong or Singapore, Malaysia, even the Philippines. But they didn't want us and were as likely to turn us away to drown as take us in. Me, I made it to Thailand.

"And as you see, that's where I still am. Life has been good to me and this country has provided a good home. Then one day, I was in Bangkok and had a chance to talk to Broward again. I still talk to him on the telephone from time to time and he is a good man. Always was. I asked him if he was ever court-martialed for speaking harshly to his colonel and he just laughs, although I am sure he has never forgotten how angry he was. One time, he said, 'No, no court-martial. The man never brought it up again, but someday I might.'"

AcChan seemed to have nothing more to say. He wasn't the only American ally to have felt the pangs of disappointment when cast aside as we rushed for home.

Abruptly, he said, "So, you want to go to Chiang Mai to look at a man in a hotel? Well, why not?"

He hadn't mentioned money, so I brought it up. We needed someone, I explained, to show us around Chiang Mai, cars, rooms, air transportation, guides, and someone to take care of – I found it difficult to find the exact word for what I had in mind, but finally decided upon – security.

Eddie added, "What we need is some guns."

AcChan smiled. "Mr. Chun, guns are dangerous. I hate to see you having to worry about guns just yet. What I can do, though, is provide men who already have guns. Now, if later we have to go elsewhere, Laos for instance, then we'll talk about guns again."

Eddie wasn't completely happy with that arrangement but for the moment, he accepted it as better than nothing.

As to the money, AcChan said, "I think I know what you'll need. I can take care of it but rather than try to set a figure now, I'll bill you."

Burrows would be screaming, "That's like signing a blank check, Osten. You can't do that!" Funny, I had a feeling that AcChan could be trusted to deal fairly with his customers. My record when it came to feelings like that wasn't perfect, but it was better than average.

I hoped my final question sounded like an afterthought although it had been rattling around in my suspicious mind since much earlier in the conversation. "By the way, did Broward ever learn the name of the colonel?"

"You mean the one who threatened to court-martial him?"

"Yes, that one."

"Well, nothing ever happened about the threat, but he knew. He knew all along. The man is still around. In fact, he has a suite just down the hall from you at the Oriental."

"Fantus," I said, although I had never known the Phantom to hold a military rank or wear a uniform.

"Fantus," he echoed, nodding.

One thing was obvious. AcChan had an excellent grapevine if he knew who was staying in what room at our hotel. Even I didn't know that.

He had another surprise for us. "Who followed you here?"

"No one," I told him only to have Eddie correct me.

"Not so, boss," he said quietly, as if he wanted to keep a secret.

It didn't work. "Mr. Chun seems to think someone did follow you, don't you Mr. Chun?" asked AcChan.

From the balcony, Eddie pointed, "See that motorcycle out there at the edge of the streetlight? It's across the street. See it? It was behind us all the way from Nick's place and then it pulled up here when we did, and hasn't moved since. The guy driving it hasn't even removed his helmet. He's just sitting there. Waiting."

"What color is the motorcycle?" asked AcChan.

"Light green. Kawasaki, big engine. Fast moving. Guy's helmet is blue."

"You have excellent eyesight," complimented AcChan. Turning to me, he asked, "Is he going to Chiang Mai with you?"

"Definitely. I need him. He's my medical assistant." It was time Eddie had a title.

With a smile, AcChan said, "Most doctors here in Thailand use nurses. But in America, you are always one step ahead in such things."

He walked to the elevator with us. "Where are you planning on going right now?"

"To the home of a friend near the Siam Intercontinental to say hello, make a few phone calls. Possibly for dinner."

"Fine. Tell your driver to take Sukhumvit Road and stay on it. Pay no attention to the motorcycle. It won't be with you for long. I'll be in touch in the morning from Chiang Mai. I'm going there tonight and will make all of the arrangements from my office. The motorcycle suggests it would be wise to do some planning today rather than letting it wait until tomorrow. Your tickets will be at Thai Airways in the morning. Just call them early and they'll tell you which flight you're on. Mr. Chun, it was nice to meet you. Try to stay close to Doctor Osten tonight. You never know when he'll need his assistant. Medicine is a very demanding profession."

Eddie had a one track mind. "Yeah, right, but don't forget what I said about guns."

I didn't mention the Kawasaki to Phrem and he accelerated smoothly onto Sukhumvit, was waved through the first traffic light by a khaki clothed policeman, and straightened out as we headed towards Siam Square. Behind us, I heard the squealing of skidding tires and the shriek of brakes followed by the dull thud that announces the collision of one vehicle with another. In the intersection, barely visible under the streetlight, a small taxi was sitting atop a motorcycle, while nearby, on the sidewalk, a helmeted figure in a torn leather jacket was struggling to sit up. The policeman had deserted his post and was ambling toward the scene.

Eddie looked back in satisfaction. "The Kawasaki ain't with us any longer."

"Isn't, Eddie. The word is isn't. Medical assistants must use proper English."

"Whatever. He isn't following us no more anyway."

Phrem, oblivious to the motorcycle and its misfortunes, continued down a nearly empty street, traffic finally having thinned out. Apparently the Bangkok rush hour was almost over, at just after 9 P.M. We proceeded in silence until Eddie asked, "What did he mean back there when he said I had good eyesight? Of course I got good eyesight. Especially in the dark. Remember, I work the night shift in a parking lot. I have to have good eyesight."

"I'm sure AcChan meant it as a compliment. He was probably amazed that you were able to identify colors in the dark. That's difficult to do."

"Oh, the colors. On the colors I was just guessing."

# 9

JoElle Montparnier lived in another impressive high rise, one block from the spectacular flowering gardens of Siam Park and the Siam Intercontinental Hotel. Like that of AcChan, her balcony offered magnificent views of the Chao Prya River and the brilliantly illuminated center of Bangkok. A never-ending stream of traffic flowed steadily, even at this late hour, on Rama I and Petchaburi Road. Everyone agreed that what Bangkok needed, badly, was a rapid transit system, either subway or elevated rails, speeding the masses to work everyday, reducing congestion, pollution, and commuting time. The water table was so high, it was feared, that subways would fill with runoff and be inoperable; elevated rails would spoil the view, and both were too expensive, land acquisition costs alone threatening to break the national bank. So gridlock lived on and detailed plans gathered dust in municipal vaults.

While the uniformed doorman phoned upstairs to report my arrival, I suggested to Eddie that he find something to eat. I hoped to dine alone with JoElle and didn't want company. Eddie had already made other plans.

He wasn't upset over having to find his own dinner. In fact, I found that he preferred it that way. "From what's been happening so far this trip, and like the guy said a little while ago, maybe I should stick close by. I'll just send the driver for some pizza while I wait down here and keep an eye on things."

"Pizza! You want pizza in Bangkok?"

"Yeah, why not? It's familiar and supposed to be good for you and I seen a Pizza Hut back a ways. It's better than that stuff with the raw eggs we saw in the bar."

Phrem didn't look thrilled about his mission to the Pizza Hut but he was always ready to carry out the toughest assignments, so he put on a brave face, took the money, and left, promising to "return as soon as possible." I took that to mean he would stop to get something else to eat, possibly from a noodle cart. Eddie sat down in the lobby to wait while I took the elevator upstairs.

JoElle was one of the complications in my life, a nice one, a pleasant one, but one, nonetheless, that meant the avoidance of making decisions, primarily because I didn't know what decision to make. The dilemma was that I might be in love with her, too. When I was here in Bangkok with her, I was almost certain that I was. When I was in New York, I was almost certain that it was Kendra, and in between, while traveling or back in the office, I couldn't make up my mind. Meanwhile, time was running out. Not theirs as much as my own. Until now. Now Kendra was in trouble. And I still didn't know the answer.

Let me tell you about JoElle. She was tall, her shoulder length auburn hair curling softly under at the ends, sometimes cut short, either way acceptable, had sparkling green-gold eyes that flashed and sparkled like precious stones, full sensuous lips, a perfect shape, tanned and trim, carried by perfect legs on a five foot seven frame that looked good in a business suit, great in casual clothing, magnificent in evening gowns, and sensational in a bathing suit. Her face? Extraordinary, beautiful, nothing out of place, nothing that I had ever found at any rate. A dozen times in the past five years I'd said, "this is the woman you want, isn't it?" And started to answer yes. Except for Kendra. I kept hearing myself ask the same question about her. Emotional gridlock. Romantic gridlock. It was appalling. That's what I mean about complications.

I had first seen JoElle at a reception at the British embassy five years earlier. Two weeks later, I saw her again at the Spanish embassy, both times in the company of a suave, smooth talking black haired junior South American diplomat. Very junior, one I disliked immediately. The primary reason for that emotion was that he was reasonably good looking and lucky enough to be with the most beautiful woman present at either gathering. Any unaccompanied man would feel that way. I had the urge to meet her and found myself fervently hoping that he would leave town. Incredibly, that's what happened.

Three weeks later, at the Oriental Hotel, attending some conference or other called by a World Health Committee my government had asked me to join, discussing population control in the Third World, a voice behind me interrupted nothing of importance. "There *are* too many people in the world, you know." I knew who it was before I turned around. I had already memorized the voice, had willed her to talk to me, and she had.

"Why do you say that?" I asked. She was even more beautiful than I had remembered. Small electric shocks were running up and down both legs.

"Well, for one thing, if there were fewer people, I might have met you sooner."

At the time, I thought it was one of the nicest things anyone had ever said to me. I probably would have thought that no matter what she had chosen to say. I found myself looking around to see if the tuxedo topped by axle grease was anywhere in sight.

She laughed. "You're looking for André? You were, weren't you?"

That laugh had welcomed me back to Bangkok ever since.

Without waiting for an answer, she said, "He's not here. Called away by his country, and most likely by his wife who may have heard of his scandalous behavior here in Bangkok. He had one, you know. A wife. Most men do." Scratch one minor diplomat. "What about you? Any wives?"

Before the evening was over and in subsequent evenings, I learned a great deal more about JoElle. She had been raised in old French Indo-China, then Cochin China, later called South Vietnam, near the city of Hue, where her father owned a substantial rubber plantation. She attended Catholic schools just outside the city, starting her first classes immediately after the French had returned to the country after evicting the Japanese in 1945. Being an infant, she remembered nothing of the wartime hardships, but the rigors and brutality of a Japanese prison camp were more than her frail mother could endure and, after she died, a Vietnamese woman cared for her. The same woman stayed on after the war to raise her when her father, Alain, who had survived imprisonment in another camp, returned to pick up the pieces of his life and to restore his plantation to prosperity. Despite the strict discipline of the nuns, maybe because of it, she became the ideal pupil, intelligent, obedient, a quick learner, a master of five languages by age 14. Two things were carefully concealed from the nuns; her passion for dancing and her love of a good party.

Then the troubles started all over again. Armed men, the aforementioned Viet Minh or Viet Cong and others, came calling. They intimidated rubber workers, damaged the trees, burned homes and factories, looted and raped, those actions always a tradition to be observed, and then they started to kill. All of this was in the good name of revolution, of course, to rid the land of the evil foreigners and make it a better place to live. The verdict about the latter is still not in, but clearly they accomplished the first. Among the foreigners to depart was JoElle's father, selling his land at a fraction of its worth and lucky to get it. Down in Saigon, he found employment with the rubber company he had once supplied with raw materials and, as the killing moved from countryside into his once peaceful neighborhood in the city, he tired of it and moved again, to Singapore, still with the same company but in a more hospitable environment.

Alain Montparnier had expected JoElle to move with him and she did, as far as Saigon. There, finishing her education at the refined British School for Girls, she went to work for Air France, was an instant success on the reservations desk because of her flair for languages, and her beauty didn't hurt either. She had numerous 'boyfriends,' many of them Air France pilots stopping over for a day or two, but most of them had wives back home, too. She knew that and what's more, decided that being a wife was exactly what she wanted out of life, just like those housewives back in France. Dating an already married pilot wasn't likely to lead to the altar and children, so she was wary of them all. Then, inexplicably, she fell 'in love' with a hard drinking French diplomat almost twice her age, a friend of her father's who had known the family since their plantation days, and in a weak moment she said yes to a half hearted proposal of marriage. It was a disaster, lasting three months with her ineffectual husband drunk the entire time, even at their wedding. Even his government, one which often turned a blind eye to misbehaving civil servants, was distressed by his behavior and called him home, permanently. JoElle stayed behind and he notified her two years later that he had sought and obtained a divorce, uncontested. Good riddance.

By then, Air France, recognizing talent when they saw it, had promoted her, placed her in charge of VIP travel to and from Vietnam, and she encountered a dashing, macho Australian, was swept off her feet, and found herself married once again. Problem was, he was already married, had neglected to mention that he had a wife and three wee ones back in Melbourne, and three weeks later, shamefacedly admitted to his transgression and begged out of the relationship. Lawyers were able to work out the details.

Concluding that perhaps she was marrying in haste, quantity rather than quality, she deserted Saigon, which was about to fall to the bad guys anyway, and selected Bangkok as her next port of call. Thai International Airways signed her on, gave her the vital job of luring European tourists to fill the numerous flights they were scheduling from places like Frankfort, Amsterdam, Munich, and Vienna. Paris, too, of course. Then one day, she took note of the fact that the flights were 90% filled with males between the ages of 28-44, most of whom were buying package tours that included a beachside hotel room already equipped with one or more of Thailand's lissome young women from up north, and seldom visited the forests and waterfalls that were the other natural attractions she had hoped to sell. SEX, she concluded, was what she was selling, not tourism. She decided to go into another line of work.

What she did was start her own business. Gems. Thailand had a lot of them. What few the country didn't have were available in nearby Burma, Cambodia, even in Laos. Rubies, emeralds, sapphires, onyx, opal, many others. High quality and low prices. And it turned out that many of the same men that had come on sex tours felt guilty about having so much fun and bought stones to take home to the little lady who had kept the home fires burning. That wasn't all they took home, in many cases, but that's another story. As far as fine gems went, JoElle once again proved how rapidly she could learn and in no time at all, a stop at her store became a must for tourists and travelers alike. Business was so good that she created her own brand, GemElle, opened new shops around Bangkok, and within five years, her name was seen in fine jewelry shops from Singapore to Hong Kong, from Taipei to Tokyo, the capitals of Europe, and finally, the ultimate success, her own shops on Rodeo Drive and Fifth Avenue, as well as the Miracle Mile in Chicago.

In a word, JoElle was wealthy. Still beautiful, as beautiful as ever, and 46 years old. She looked years younger, partly due to a personal trainer, but mostly because of hours of rigorous exercise, a healthy diet, and good genes. Still unmarried. Any men in her life? I didn't know. I didn't know if I was in her life.

Unlike AcChan, she hadn't waited out on the balcony. When I stepped off the elevator, she was in her open doorway, wearing something dark green that seemed to cling to all the right places, suggested much, but revealed nothing. Her kiss made me wish I had come here first. It made me feel as if I should stay. The view from her balcony was even more impressive than I remembered and there was a gentle evening breeze that brushed away the oppressive lingering heat of afternoon. Down below, the Mercedes was parked at an angle allowing an unobstructed view of the front door. There was enough light to see Eddie and Phrem in the front seat. They were both eating pizza, so Phrem had not stopped at a noodle cart after all.

A maid unobtrusively placed a tray alongside the couch, poured tea, offered small rolls and fresh fruit, and withdrew. No almond cookies.

Reluctantly, JoElle, her fingers entwined with mine, said, "Your office called. They want to talk to you."

It wasn't the best way to start a romantic evening. But Marge wouldn't have called unless it was important. At least, I didn't think she would.

I reached the office easily enough, but Marge was on a coffee break and Clovis answered. Her perky voice sounded sincere enough, but when she offered to put me on hold or have Marge call me back 'in a little while,'

I pulled rank and ordered, "Not in a little while, Clovis, get her on the phone now."

I must have struck the right note of firmness because she replied, still perkily but startled, "Oh, I didn't realize it was you Doctor Osten. I'll buzz her and she'll be right with you." And in another moment or two, she was.

"Doctor, I have several bits of news for you." Marge never had messages. She always passed on 'bits of news.' "First, you remember the leaves and twigs and stuff Mr. Burrow's friend sent to us from Malaysia?"

"Yes, of course I remember it. That's one of the reasons we set up this trip. To get more of the stuff, as you call it. That's where Tony Howsam is now. In Malaysia. Should have arrived there a few hours ago. Why? What about it?"

"Well, right after you left, we got some more. A big package, a big box, really. Just chock full of the stuff."

"That's good, I guess. I don't understand how those things are getting through the customs people but, as I said, that's good. Have the lab start analyzing it, see what they can extract and identify."

"They've done that."

"Already? That's quick. Seeing they've already done that, ask them if they'll have a report for me by the time I return."

"They've done that."

"They've done what?"

"Got the report for you. It's right here. I've got it somewhere." I heard papers rustling in the background and I could visualize her digging through my packed in-basket, which would be waiting to challenge me when I returned to the office. I wondered if computers were the answer. Would they make things easier? Marge was back, triumphant. "Here it is."

"How is it?" I asked. "Getting pretty full?"

Confused, she answered, "What's getting full? The report?"

"My in-basket. Getting pretty full?"

"Your in-basket? No, there's not much there. I found the report under the newspaper. I'm on a coffee break, didn't Clovis tell you, and I took the report with me and then lost it under the paper while I was reading the sports page. It's right here. The report."

Marge was a pro basketball nut. She would have been reading about the Piston's game from the night before. Bill Laimbeer was her hero.

"If you've got it right there, read me the summary. I may as well find out the news, good or bad, right now. Who sent it up, by the way?" Up because the laboratory was down, our offices on the top floor, naturally.

"Arlie Vicelio. He sent it up."

Arlie Vicelio was our chief of analytical chemistry. We had paid a small fortune to lure him away from academia, but he had proved to be worth every cent of it. Obviously, he hadn't wasted any time in turning his staff loose on the new samples sent in by good old Jack. Usually that was a good sign. If Arlie was hot on a project, it was usually one full of promise. Another thing, Arlie's group was paid bonuses for productivity, based on profitability, and maybe they could smell bonus money lying in the trail up ahead. "OK, what did he say."

"I'll try to summarize."

"Marge, you don't have to summarize. Just read the summary. Arlie always writes a nice neat summary at the end of each report. Look there. That's what I want to hear." I could smell fragrant cooking odors from somewhere in the apartment as JoElle's cook began to prepare dinner. My stomach was growling as badly as Eddie's had earlier, and I hadn't had the opportunity to silence it with pizza.

By the time she was halfway through the summary, which seemed to be several pages long, it was apparent that we had struck pay dirt. The needles contained taxol, we knew that from earlier reports, not massive quantities, but enough to make them worth further study. The bark contained taxol, as suspected, and was worth pursuing. But it was the globule, the tiny red fruit, of which we had received only a few in the first shipment, that came up a winner on the slot machine of chance. The red berries were loaded with taxol. The extractant from this puzzling pea sized appendage, a berry we had not found replicated on other species of yew trees we had studied, was calculated to contain 72 TA units per millimeter, the TA being a measurement we had devised in our laboratory, the initials standing for tumor activity. Tumor activity meant killing malignant cells. Our best previous TA level had been 16 units from an Oregon yew and we had been considering that to be commercially viable and medically useful. A reading 4.5 times greater was analogous to bringing in a gusher in a newly discovered oil field.

I could hardly restrain my excitement. "Marge, have you shown this to Burrows? Does he have a copy?"

"You know he seldom wants to be bothered by scientific reports. He gets the ones about money – sales and things."

"I don't want to sound mercenary, Marge, but this is about money. It's what we've been looking for. So get a copy to him. Meanwhile, tell Arlie you've talked to me and I want everything run again and confirmed. By different people. Then send some of the material, the raw material and especially the small globules, down to Howsam's lab and have his people repeat the work. I don't want the two labs talking to each other about it. Make that clear. They are to do it independently of one another. Even though Tony isn't there, his staff can do it." These results were almost too good to be true. I needed to know there had been no mistakes.

"Arlie's people will think you don't trust them if you do that," she warned. "They're very sensitive, you know."

She was right, of course. Arlie's analytical chemical staff and Tony's microbiology laboratory were in perpetual competition with one another. For the most part, that was a healthy thing to have, but there was professional jealousy in our organization like in most others. Part of it was that Tony and Arlie could see a single opening up ahead, one promotion, just one level higher that they could reasonably aspire to – and that was my job. They both wanted it; only one could get it. But they would both have to wait. I had no plans to retire just yet. Meanwhile, there were other considerations.

"Marge, listen to me very closely. This is not a matter of trust or jealousy. This is a matter of not going off half-cocked. This might be the biggest development in the history of Osten-Burrows. Both Arlie and Tony know that the TA assay is a tricky one. It's new and there is always the possibility of an error in interpretation or technique. We can't take that chance. We have to be absolutely certain that we have it right before we commit our resources to the project and ask Clozyme to come along with us. If we get it right, do it right, and come up with the right answers, we could be looking at big bonuses next year. I'm talking big, big bonuses. Explain it to Arlie in those terms, both the scientific and financial ones. He'll understand."

Even from 12,000 miles away, I could hear the rising excitement in her voice. "Sure, I can do that. Arlie will go along. He's always been cooperative. We get along fine and talk every morning while having coffee." I knew they talked while having coffee. I didn't know how well they got along. That part worried me. Arlie was from LA. He was a Laker fan. He hated Laimbeer.

"Sounds good to me," I told her, hoping for the best. "Don't forget to get the report to Burrows right away."

"I can't today, but I will as soon as he gets back," she promised.

"Back from where?"

I knew what her answer would be before she said it. "Playing golf."

"Marge, isn't there snow on the ground?"

"Not in Atlanta. He flew down there to play in some kind of a tournament. He'll be back tonight, he said."

"All right. Put a copy of the report on his desk and attach a note that says I want him to read it and then in the morning you march in, point to it, and if necessary, stand there scowling at him until he does." Marge could do that. She had a fierce scowl that worried Everett. "Then, if Arlie's group and Howsam's lab confirm the initial results, fax copies of everything to Bernard at Clozyme. He needs something more than a newspaper story to pacify his stockholders and this might be just the thing. Tell him I'll call as soon as I get back."

She was making notes of everything I was telling her. The notes would be neatly typed and on my desk when I returned, red checks to the right of each item meaning it had been faithfully executed; red checks to the left meaning something hadn't been clear, nothing had been done or somebody had fouled up. I always followed up on the check marks to the left first. I was about to hang up when she interrupted to tell me, "I have two more bits of information for you. First, a Doctor Bertinoldi wants you to call. Let me give you his number."

She read it to me and I copied it down. It was a number that I didn't have. "Second," I prompted, eager to make the call to New York.

"Second, well, I'm not sure of the second. I may have gotten it wrong but he hung up before I could ask him to repeat it."

"Who, what, and when, Marge, just the essentials."

"I'm not certain I have the essentials because what I've got doesn't make much sense to me. Maybe it does to you." She seemed to be having trouble making sense herself.

"Try me. What was the message?"

"This man said, I think, to tell you to 'be careful.' Sounds dumb, doesn't it? 'Be careful?' You're almost always careful. Why would anyone want to tell you that?"

"Who called and said that? Did they say anything else and when did they call?"

"There wasn't a they, Doctor. It was just a him. One person."

"You're right Marge. I shouldn't be using the plural. Let's try it again. Him. When did he call and did he say anything else?"

"No, he didn't say anything else. Just asked for you and when I told him you weren't here, he said to let you know to be careful. That's it. About the when, he called right after you left to catch the plane for Tokyo. I should have mentioned it when you called last time but my note was in your overflowing in-basket and I missed it. It slipped my mind. I forgot to make a note."

"I thought you said the in-basket was empty?"

"It is now, after I cleaned it out. That's how I found the message."

"You didn't recognize the voice?" I didn't think she had.

"No, I don't think I ever heard it before. But he gave me a name and I wrote it down. Maybe that would help, but it's a funny name."

She must have been studying her handwriting, I could hear her breathing on the other end of the line, then, "I think what I have here is S. Porer, or maybe Plorer, maybe even Porter. S., just an initial, then whatever that last name is. Know anybody with a name like that?"

By that name, no, I didn't. But I did know a nickname that came close. The Explorer. Fred Magellan, using a name he hated, but one that he knew I would recognize, had called me to suggest "be careful?" Careful of what? Things like gunshots in the terminal at Kai Tak or a hairy legged maid with a killer cart in the hotel or a Kawasaki rider in a blue helmet? Things like that? What else did he have in mind or did he know? Strangely enough, the Explorer was here in Bangkok, his room just down the hall from mine. If he was so worried about my safety, why hadn't he just dropped by for a little chat? I would more than happy to talk to him.

"Thanks, Marge. If he calls back," and that wasn't likely to happen, I knew, "check on that name, will you? And try to keep the in-basket empty so that we don't lose anymore notes." I gave her my phone number at the Oriental and Carmichael's at the University and said good-bye.

Her closing words were, "Don't forget. Be careful."

JoElle was sipping white wine out on the balcony. A glass, mine, stood untouched alongside her. I waved, indicated one more call, and dialed Bertinoldi. Apologetically, a nurse explained that he hated to be interrupted when he was making rounds with staff and resident physicians. "Do it anyway," I advised. "He called me."

They found him and he sounded annoyed and in a hurry, which is his usual state, but his manner changed when he found out who it was. "The General wanted me to call and let you know that she's rallied. Her fever is all but gone and her appetite is much better. These are good signs. She even got into a spirited argument with the General himself today and I was more worried about his blood pressure than I was about hers. His face was beet red when he left here."

The news about Kendra was encouraging. But what had she and her father been arguing about? I must have asked because I heard Bertinoldi saying, "Politics. Just politics."

"Politics? They both belong to the same party, believe almost all the same things. How could they be arguing over politics?" I was mystified. It wasn't like Kendra to disagree with the General over a political issue. She generally gentled him into believing that he was right, then got her own way.

"They weren't arguing about the party. It's my understanding that they're both Republicans. They were arguing over whether the General should enter the primary for the Senate seat. There's one open this year and the party apparently wants him to go for it."

That was no surprise. There had been rumors of a political future for Green for the past several years. He would be a good fit. A retired General without a blemish on his record, an attractive man with that indefinable quality that spells charisma, something all candidates need today because of television. "Well, I can understand that," I told Bertinoldi. "He'd probably be a good candidate, but I can see why Kendra would be against it, with her illness and Ken still missing. She wouldn't be able to help in the campaign and I'm sure she feels the stress on him would be more than he could bear."

I wondered if the sound I heard was a chuckle, something that Bertinoldi had never attempted during our short acquaintance. "You must not know this woman at all. You have it wrong. She wants him to run. Insisted on it. 'Run,' she told him, 'you're the best candidate they'll find.' And he kept insisting that he couldn't do it, wouldn't do it, and he finally stormed off, like I said, his face beet red."

That was strange. I had always assumed the General would be most receptive to the idea of a Senate seat.

I wasn't going to have the opportunity to ask Kendra about it, either. "She's having more blood drawn for tests," Bertinoldi advised when I asked about calling her room. "Then she goes to physical therapy. You should try again in a day or two."

I decided to try one more call. I had no more success in reaching the General than I had in reaching his daughter. From a half world away, Montgomery's voice was crisp and efficient, but he was of no more help than Bertinolodi. "The General is out and I'm not certain when he will be back. Yes, certainly I'll give your message, Captain. Do you wish him to call you back?" To Montgomery, Jordan Green was always the General. As far as he was concerned, Green had never been anything other than in command. I was the Captain, a rank of long ago and it no longer applied, but in Montgomery's eyes, I was destined to rise no higher.

I hung up, joined JoElle for my wine, and we ate dinner outdoors. Later, the night having become cooler, she stood, crossed arms clasped to her bare shoulders, looking out at the river. From behind, I covered her hands with mine and she leaned back, resting against me. Her fragrance, one I had never been able to identify but which I associated with the soft enchantment of Bangkok nights like this, warmed us both. I kissed her lightly behind the left ear, then the right. Without turning, she asked, "Do you love her, Mike? Are you afraid you might lose her?"

She knew about Kendra, just as Kendra knew about her. I couldn't lie, but I wasn't sure what the truth was, so I compromised. "She's the General's daughter. He's an old and dear friend."

She arched her neck and looked back at me in amusement. "What an answer. An old and dear friend. Yes, I'm sure the General is, but his daughter is not so old and she's much better looking. In fact, she's very pretty. Were you trying to evade the question?"

Sure, that's what I was doing. It didn't appear as if I was going to get away with it as she turned to face me, her body pressed close against mine, and I did the only practical thing under the circumstances. I kissed her. After a while, she pushed me away and looked up. I was thankful I was still several inches taller, having just started to worry about the statistics that showed men losing height as they aged, reminding me of Nick's tip on calcium. Still a little breathless, she said, "That wasn't the answer I was expecting."

"It was the best I could come up with." Which, in a way, it was.

I left shortly after, before life got any more complicated. Before I did, though, she gave me something to think about. "You say you're looking for the General's son who's been missing for fifteen years? That's interesting because one of my gem buyers who travels the north for me, occasionally swings into Laos and Burma, has come back with a strange tale of a white man who has suddenly appeared up there. From out of the blue. No one seems to have seen him. No one knows where he came from. And no one knows what he does but the rumors are that he deals in gems. To make it more interesting, just as mysteriously, a new source of stones has suddenly opened up, apparently from Laos. We've even been buying some of the new merchandise through middlemen and they are of high quality. Now sometimes a story like this is nothing more than smoke, a rumor that can't be traced, and often it simply indicates some overactive imagination has gone into overdrive. Or it may be a smoke screen for someone dealing in drugs, an activity much more likely to be found in Laos than fine gems." She meant illicit drugs.

What did this have to do with Ken Green? Probably nothing and I told her so. But just the same, I agreed to meet with her gem buyer in the morning. "I'll have him at our corporate office at 9 A.M. His name is Choprindonakh," she said, "but just call him Chop like I do." Another kiss and I was back in the elevator.

Eddie was erect in the passenger seat, wide awake, holding an empty pizza box across his knees. A crumpled Mr. Donut sack lay at his feet. Phrem was sound asleep in the back, but he awoke instantly, clambered into the driver's seat, and was ready for departure. As I climbed into the back seat, I stepped on two Coke bottles lying on the floor. I had been upstairs slightly more than two hours and they had trashed the car with fast food containers and soft drink bottles. Had there been any doubt about it, I realized now, civilization had come to Thailand.

# 10

Bath was displeased. He was trying to restrain his anger but his flushed face and lips tightly pressed together were a dead giveaway.

"I did not send a man on a motorcycle to spy on you. He was there to protect you. Have you forgotten what happened in Hong Kong? You're an American working with us on a project and I have a responsibility to protect all of my men, even you."

His concern was appreciated. It might even be true. "So it was your idea to send a man along to keep an eye on me?"

"No. It wasn't my idea. It was my idea to not allow you to go anywhere at all, but instead, Naroogian suggested that we send someone along to keep an eye on you. Just to keep you out of trouble."

"And to help if I did get in trouble?"

"Certainly. But what kind of help could he have been in that first dive you went to? I've told all of my people to stay out of there. It's off limits. From what we hear, Valkidis is involved in questionable activities all over Southeast Asia. If anything had gone wrong inside that place, there was little our one man could have done to help. Maybe call the ambulance, that's about it."

Feigning surprise, I told him, "The food wasn't that bad."

"The food? You didn't eat there? I've never heard of anyone eating in Nick's place. But even if you did, you got out of there alive and the next thing we find is you're in the home of a man of disrepute. This AcChan. A soldier of fortune, some say, trying to pass himself off as a legitimate businessman. You stayed there until after dark and then when you leave, that damned taxicab almost killed the man who was following you."

"The man following us? I thought you said he was the man protecting us?"

Bath threw up his hands in exasperation. "Osten, the man had to follow you to protect you, didn't he?! How else could he do it?"

"And then he lost us. So he couldn't protect us and despite all of the dangerous places we went, nothing happened, except to your man on the bike. So maybe we weren't in any danger in the first place. By the way, how is he? The man who collided with the taxicab?"

"He's still in the hospital. I don't think anything is broken, but apparently he has a concussion. He'll be all right."

So, according to Bath, Nick was involved in 'questionable things' and

AcChan was a 'soldier of fortune trying to masquerade as a legitimate businessman.' He was certainly right about Nick, if reselling previously owned beer and eating everything in sight are crimes, but I wasn't sure if his reading of AcChan was correct. I had the feeling that there was much more than met the eye when it came to him. Probably more important, they didn't seem to know about JoElle.

"Then you walk into the hotel at this late hour, announce you're on a noon flight to Chiang Mai, when we already had reservations for all of us at 3 P.M. Magellan is trying to change that now so all of us can go with you. You're not cooperating, Osten. Not at all. And then that little thug of yours, Chung, beats up one of my men in the hotel lobby just now. What is going on here?"

What was going on was AcChan had made one phone call and gotten the reservations, message waiting when we walked into the Oriental. Just after I picked up the note at the desk, a 270 pound gorilla came charging across the lobby as if he planned on having us for a late night snack. Bath didn't believe the gorilla part. "Stokes! He doesn't weigh any 270 pounds, does he?" Fantus nodded, yes. "Well, you have to keep your man under control, Osten. I can't have my men getting hurt."

"Chun," I repeated. "The name is Chun. And he didn't beat up anyone. Like you said, we do remember Hong Kong and not knowing what Mr. Stokes had in mind, Eddie took the necessary precautions. Mr. Stokes was much too big for Eddie to hit effectively while he was erect, so first he kicked him in the shins, then knocked him down when he bent over. We're sorry about that. I've already apologized to the Oriental Hotel general manager for Mr. Stokes' screams, screams which brought many people running. I was surprised that many people were still up and about at this time of night. Like I told the manager, it's behavior like that, screaming in hotel lobbies at midnight, that gives Americans such a bad reputation overseas."

Bath wasn't sure whether I was serious or not. He fell silent. Magellan reported moments later. He had been unable to change the reservations. We made eye contact for a moment as he said, "We'll leave three hours after you, after all. The early plane, the one you're on, is full." Was he passing a message? Another 'be careful,' for instance, or was it my imagination?

Fantus was off in a corner now shuffling through a stack of blue folders. Priority stuff, the first ones I'd seen since we had departed Washington. He handed them to Bath who shuffled some more and finally selected one for inspection. He flipped through single spaced computer printouts and then, to no one in particular, muttered, "This says he's still there."

Fantus nodded. "He's still there. Hasn't moved much in the last four days. There's still no sign of anyone else. He goes to the restaurant or brings food back to the room, makes a few phone calls, and waits. It looks like he's waiting for us, like he said. We have the phone tapped so we know who he calls and what he says. Mainly calls Fred or the restaurant. Once or twice called some woman, asked her up, but she never showed. Doesn't mention Lee Duc Than except when he talks to Fred. Then that's about all he talks about. Lee Duc Than and money."

Magellan had been trying to interrupt and finally broke in. "I doubt that Lee Duc Than is in the room at all. Our people have never seen anyone except the maid and room service go in and out. And the room service just delivers food for one. Other than them and the repairman, no one has been in the room since he rented it."

Fantus looked up immediately, demanding, "What repairman? What was he supposed to repair?"

The question caught Magellan off guard and he went on the defensive. "They said a guy with a toolbox so I supposed he was a repairman. That's who usually carries toolboxes. But obviously I wasn't there so I don't know what he repaired or who called him."

Fantus was angry. "Christ, Fred, who do you have up there watching the room? The idiots shouldn't have allowed anyone to waltz in there carrying a tool box without checking it out. Who called him? They should know if the phone line is tapped, shouldn't they? Did they hear our pigeon call for a repairman? What was he to repair? That's basic stuff, Fred. How come these clowns don't know how to conduct a basic surveillance? Who did you say they were?"

He hadn't been given the opportunity to say, and for a moment I thought Magellan would run out of the room and hide, but he hung in there and replied, "Dirkens and Disbrow. They went up two days ago, as soon as we pinned the location down by satellite. They have Thai help but they're in charge."

Dirkens, Disbrow, weak shinned Stokes, a battered motorcycle rider, Magellan, Bath, Fantus, Naroogian, and Canby; that made nine, plus the hired Thais. Pan Union was underwriting an expensive payroll on this project. Plus us, the consultants.

I decided to offer some advice. That's what I was being paid for. "Look, it sounds as if you have our man under full time coverage. This shouldn't really be a big deal, should it? Let's stop fussing about a repairman and what he repaired," I had a theory about that but they didn't need to know what it was, "and go up and pay a visit. Either he has Lee Duc Than with him or he doesn't. Either Ken Green is there or he isn't. If Lee Duc Than is there and he's sick, I'll try to get medical care for him. If Ken Green is there, we'll try to bring him back with us. If no one is there, we'll reevaluate our options and do something else."

Bath and Fantus were passing silent messages back and forth and neither appeared happy with my scenario. Bath explained why. "The problem with all of that, Osten, is that you'll be in Chiang Mai three hours ahead of us. What's to stop you from rushing in and trying to grab our man by taking things into your own hands? Maybe that's why you were meeting with the soldier of fortune today. Maybe he's supposed to help you."

Hoping to set their minds at ease, I laid it out for them as simply and honestly as I could. Simple they might understand. Honesty would be a stretch. "First, you have two men and their helpers watching the room. Call them and tell them not to allow me to do that. If they don't have enough people to do that, have them hire some more. Second, I don't want Lee Duc Than. I wish I'd never heard of him. I want Ken Green. If you get Lee Duc Than, you've come up with the intelligence find of the decade. If you recover Ken Green, you'll all go home heroes, rescuers of a missing American, something no one else has ever done. Either way, your careers take off. Me, I'm trying to help a friend. I already have a career."

That wasn't the whole truth. I wanted more than that. I needed Ken Green's bone marrow. For Kendra. They didn't have to know that.

They bought it, but as a precaution, they also made the phone call to Dirkens, or maybe Disbrow, they didn't say.

The next morning, all packed and ready to go, I met with JoElle and Chop at her office. Chop was a gold mine of information. There was indeed a white man, most everyone assumed it was an American but no one knew for sure, involved in precious stones up north. No one knew where he had come from. He was just suddenly there or at least the rumors were suddenly there. No one knew how old he was, or what he looked like and no one claimed to have seen him. He was just there. How did they know? The grapevine. Messages from the jungle and they were often reliable, Chop said.

JoElle looked better than ever.

There were at least twenty empty seats on our 'full' Boeing 737 when it lifted off at noon. Magellan hadn't tried too hard to get seats on it or had he wanted to get seats on it?

Tommy gun toting paratroopers greet most flights into Chiang Mai. This is rough country up near where the borders of Thailand, Burma, and Laos all come together in the so-called Golden Triangle. It's drug country and, a little farther to the north, it's where the poppies grow and the opium flows. Drugs and smuggling were the major underpinnings of the booming economy and, although the Thai government had made efforts to stamp out poppy fields, efforts to have the farmers grow potatoes for fast food french fries and strawberries for shortcake were falling far short of success. The cold hard facts were that opium was more profitable than anything else and, as in our country, farmers grow what the market pays for. Across the border in Laos, no one was making any effort to stamp out anything, except freedom.

Chiang Mai was Thailand's second largest city after Bangkok. It had been built in the Middle Ages, but don't let that fool you. The city, once surrounded by a massive water filled moat and a 12 foot thick brick wall, now boasts a decidedly modern center with palatial hotels. Western style fashions and entertainment abound and mingle with traditional Thai culture and food. Tourists arrive by plane, bus, and train to sample the pleasures and they are many; mahogany furniture, hand-crafted by skilled artisans, many of them as young as 13; gemstones polished to perfection, many of them smuggled across the border from Burma or as the military junta ruling it prefer, Myanmar; silver plates and artifacts, much of this also smuggled from neighboring countries; delicate Celadon pieces, lacquered jewel boxes, umbrellas, and the finest silks, spun right before your eyes, and then converted to high fashions while you wait, and much more. Should it happen that the average tourist became tired of the dazzling sights of the city itself, as AcChan had suggested, it was possible to locate tour guides who, for a price, would take you into the hills to visit hill tribe villages, leaving the impression that you had lived as the natives lived. That was an illusion of course, for once the guides put a village on the itinerary and the tourists arrived, the village was no longer the way it had been, and all that was left was the perception of a people as we wished them to be, not the way they had really been. Finally, if bored with night life, shopping, and sight seeing, many visitors turned to what they had come for in the first place – purchased sex. It was a risky thing to do, but that didn't deter many, who often paid twice, in cash while in town, and in misery after they got home.

But just as it was in Hong Kong, we hadn't come to shop or tour. We were on business and we used our three hour head start on Bath and his crew to good advantage. At our appearance in front of the terminal, a large taxi-cab pulled out of line, to the annoyance of other drivers who shouted and did what taxi drivers do in our country, honked their horns, but we did as we had been instructed and got in. Without directions from me, the driver sped onto the two lane highway, turned suddenly onto Charoen Muang Road, crossed the Ping River on Nawarat Bridge, made a sharp left onto Kotahasan Road following the walled city's moat, another tire squealing turn led to Chang Lar Road, from where, moments later, we whipped through Suan Prung gate into the old walled city itself. Two blocks away, as planned, Eddie and I exited and climbed into a black Volvo which reached cruising speed in the crowded, narrow street in a matter of seconds. Like Phrem, this driver knew his city, as he careened, twisting and turning through a maze of streets, alleys, and lanes, finally bursting through Chang Puak gate, exiting onto northbound highway 107. Two miles outside the city walls, we suddenly braked, rolled into a driveway all but invisible from the road because of towering trees and thick shrubs, passed through an elaborate wrought iron gate attended by an armed guard, drove directly into an open doorway and came to a halt as the doors closed automatically behind us.

AcChan was waiting upstairs in his warehouse, tea and almond cookies already in place. No one, not even a man on a motorcycle, could have followed us on this crazy ride. "Someone tried," AcChan reported. "You lost them at the Ping River bridge."

Through an enormous one way window making up an entire wall of his modern office, I watched as a score of men and women scurried about down below, loading and unloading motorized carts that coursed up and down vast aisles of thirty foot high automated shelves. I could identify, even from this distance, popular brand names of consumer products, pharmaceuticals, electronic equipment, hardware, and soft goods of every variety. Brand names from the United States, Europe, Asia, and others, presumably local merchandise carrying the difficult to read Thai hieroglyphics. Conveyor belts running horizontally were carrying merchandise in an endless stream toward an open end of the vast structure where men and women were packing everything into cartons and loading them onto waiting trucks. It was well organized hustle and bustle, a throbbing, pulsating commercial enterprise, and AcChan acknowledged it as his without waiting for me to ask.

"Yes, in addition to being a tour guide, I also have this little business to keep me occupied," he said, deliberately understating the size of his operation. He didn't waste further time on the warehouse, however, and without pausing added, "There are two men, maybe three, watching the hotel room. They have as much subtlety as a rhinoceros in a cage of canaries, and were just as easy to spot. I wonder how they expected to remain invisible when one of them is just about the only black man in Chiang Mai, and he either sits at one end of the hall or walks up and down in the hallway outside the room he is supposed to be watching. Neither one speak any Thai by the way, which is a major handicap when they try to ask questions. The second one, he's hopelessly lost or bored and sits and dozes almost all day and night in the lobby. It's as if he doesn't have a room to sleep in. They have a third man, we think, and he seems to be Chinese, and he does seem to be staying under cover. Maybe he's running the telephone tap in the basement and, so far, we haven't identified him for sure. He may have help on the tap so we can't discount the possibility that they have an additional person or two on the team. But overall, this bunch seems to be inept, not very skilled in their business. I would think that American intelligence services would be better than this."

What made him think this was American intelligence at work? It also made me remember what the General once told me in Korea: "Never underestimate your enemy. It could be fatal."

But were they the enemy? They were supposed to be my friends. My co-workers on Operation Patient, which if everything went according to plan, was about to go into high gear now that we were in Chiang Mai.

I took a cookie and poured tea, no man servant or maid having appeared to handle that chore. "So, you've had someone look the situation over. Is there anyone in the room with this man, the lawyer, whatever he is?"

"He's a lawyer, that much is true. Not a very good one, perhaps, and he has been involved in some questionable cross-border schemes in the past, but recently he has been behaving himself as far as we can tell. We sent a man in there and managed to get a look at the room, two rooms actually, connecting doors, and there is no one in there except the one man. Makes you wonder why he has two rooms, doesn't it?"

"Yes, it does. By the way, what did your man fix?"

"Fix? What makes you think he fixed anything?"

"He had a toolbox with wrenches, things like that."

He leaned forward, elbows resting on the desk, and blinds slowly moved from either end of the window and blocked the warehouse activity from view. Maybe it wasn't one way glass after all. "Nothing. He didn't fix anything because there wasn't anything broken. He just went in, took a good look around, and came back out after twisting a pipe or two under the lavatory. But the man in the room didn't want him to leave. He wanted to talk. He seemed lonely and glad for the company. But you weren't here when that happened so someone else saw my man go in and reported it and they told you. I'm impressed. Maybe they're doing better work than I thought so we won't take anything for granted from here on."

"I agree," I told him. "We can't afford to take anything for granted, especially since I don't really know what this all about, even now. Having said that, how many men do we need to cover us at the hotel?"

"Depends upon what you want covered. The way it looks now, you'll be going into a hotel room with your associates to talk to one man. That's it. If you're going to find the others, this Lee Duc Than and Ken Green, you'll have to go elsewhere. Probably by car. That's easy. We'll follow. If, however, you suddenly head out to the airport, that's harder. I'll have to know where you're going, make phone calls to get somebody there ahead of you, and send others to follow. I can do that, but like I said, it's harder. Let's think of the car first. For that, I'll have three men plus myself and two vehicles. That should be adequate. We'll watch as you go into the hotel room and then wait to see what happens from there."

This was his operation and I could find no flaw in his planning so far. "What if this is all a scam?" AcChan wasn't sure what scam meant, from the expression on his face, so I continued, "A fraud. What if this man is simply trying to blackmail the American government by pretending to have information when he really doesn't have any? A hoax."

"That's a crime even in our country, Doctor. We should report something like that to the proper authorities and allow them to act on it." Of course, I should have known that.

"But then what do we do about finding Ken Green?"

"In that case," he said, biting into a delicious cookie, "we come back here, sit down and talk about what we should do next." He motioned to Eddie, who was standing near the door, as usual, listening to the conversation, "What do you plan on having Mr. Chun do while all of this is going on?"

"He's my medical assistant, so he stays with me. He carries my medical bag with any necessary supplies just in case we find Lee Duc Than in the room." Which, of course, was not likely.

"Fine. That's a good idea," AcChan decided. "My ideas, they sound all right to you?"

"Sounds reasonable, unless we go by air. How will I get word to you?"

"Well, I hope you don't see us around so that's a good question. Let me give you a number to call in case you have time to get to a phone. Just remember, the possibility that you won't or they won't allow you to have access to a phone. So memorize the number. I suggest Mr. Chun do the same, and then, if you can't use it, somehow leave a message at the front desk of the hotel, and I'll retrieve that. Think of a reason to approach the front desk and pass your information to whoever steps forward with a hand extended in greeting. It will be one of my men. I'll have the message in seconds. Well, maybe a minute or two. OK?"

It seemed OK to me.

Eddie and I returned to our rooms in the Chiang Mai President hotel on Changklan Road, not as elegant as the Chiang Mai Royal Orchid, not as new either, but all of the rooms were air conditioned and I didn't anticipate being there for long. It was conveniently near the Royal Orchid, yet we would avoid being in the same building as our intended target, or with the Pan Unionists either, for that matter. When the black Volvo dropped us off at the front door of the President, one of AcChan's men slipped out of the passenger seat and followed us inside. The car moved into the parking lot and took a position from where the driver could see the front door, the sun behind him. Eddie noted the action and said, "We're covered."

After a shower and shave, they do wonders for your spirits in the hot tropics, I sat down to read the morning Bangkok Post Thai Airways had thoughtfully provided each boarding passenger earlier in the day, and found that the Pistons had smashed the Knicks the night before, 114-99. Marge would be beaming this morning or was it yesterday morning? Especially since Laimbeer had scored 20 points, gathered nine rebounds, punched someone, and been ejected. That was the way to play basketball. I noticed that the paper referred to them as the Bad Boys. A new nickname.

We went over to the Royal Orchid for lunch, the black Volvo trailing our cab all the way, two men in the front seat. I ordered the thick German tomato soup and black bread and ate it on the outdoor terrace. Eddie had a hamburger.

I didn't intend to break my promise to Bath, but that didn't mean scouting had been ruled out. Leaving Eddie to keep an eye on an American half asleep in a comfortable chair in the lobby, a potted palm hanging over his head and obscuring his view of the elevators, I walked down to the lower level to see if I could find anything interesting. Like a wire tap setup. What I found instead was a large black man standing alongside the cash register holding a book. A large red sticker with 439 bahts printed on it was obviously the price. According to the morning Post rates of exchange table that translated to about $21.95 American. He kept saying, "How much is this?" and the clerk kept repeating, "Puut thai mai dai," which means, according to my rudimentary knowledge of Thai, derived mostly from a restaurant guide furnished by Shell Oil, "please speak slowly."

This could go on for hours, and while it was, the hotel room wasn't being watched. Not good. So I helped out. I stepped up and tapped the cover of the book he was holding, saying, "Nii raka towry" or "How much is this?"

The relieved clerk beamed, the impasse broken, and she responded, "Sii roi sam kow bahts." Four hundred thirty nine bahts, just as the tag said.

Her customer still appeared confused. He obviously didn't comprehend what he was expected to pay so I told him, "Bahts, you know. Thai currency. You probably have some in your pocket, but if not, you might try giving her $22, possibly try $25, in American. Or you could use a credit card. The sign says they honor just about any piece of plastic you have." As AcChan had pointed out, he didn't speak Thai. Couldn't read it, either.

He fumbled for his wallet, extracted several brightly colored Thai bank notes and thrust them at the clerk, thanked me and hustled off almost forgetting the book which he had laid down while counting the money. He thanked me when I handed it to him and disappeared up the stairway, headed for the lobby, where I was reasonably certain he would waken a startled colleague and tell him who was in the book store. Both of them would take out their photographs, the ones with the large X, to reacquaint themselves with my features, and get down to business. They might as well. It was almost time for their boss to show up.

Bath's man had good taste in books, though. He had just purchased a copy of *A Midsummer Night's Dream* by William Shakespeare, a classic.

A half hour later, Eddie called the airport and learned that the 3 o'clock Thai flight from Bangkok had just touched down. We sat in the Royal Orchid bar and sipped lemonade while awaiting the arrival of the Pan Unionists.

We didn't have to wait long. Bath, Fantus, Magellan, Naroogian, and two other men I hadn't seen before trooped inside like an invading army. The sleepy American had roused himself from underneath the palm tree and rushed forward to meet them, trying to grasp Bath's brief case, only to be brushed aside as Bath would have none of that. He must be protecting his precious blue files, I reasoned, nothing else being that important.

And they had no reservations. None. The clerk went through his files again, and again, and then called for the manager. Bath was fuming, stamping his feet, pounding on the counter, as he declared, "Of course I'm sure we made reservations. Didn't we make reservations?" he demanded, glaring first at Fantus, then Magellan, as both hurriedly turned away to inspect the labels on their luggage, which had just been carried in from a mini-van parked by the front door. He faced the manager once more and said, "Canby made the reservations." Something which made absolutely no impression of the manager as he had never heard of Canby in his life "This is ridiculous. Check again."

No reservations.

Coming up unobserved, I asked, "What seems to be the problem?"

"Osten! So you're here." I wondered why he was surprised at that. "Can you believe it? These people say they have no reservations for us. We made them two or three days ago. Canby made them, damnit, and they have no record of it. Gross incompetence, that's what it is."

"Well, this is the busy season, you know, so mix-ups will occur. With so many tourists crowded into town this weekend for the Mae Sa Valley baby elephant walk, I'm not surprised to find it difficult to get rooms." Baby elephant walks were held just about every week of the year and a few tourists did schedule it for a visit, but as a matter of fact, the one for this week had been canceled so it wasn't a factor in Bath's problem. I didn't think Bath knew anything about the walks, however, and I was right.

"A baby elephant walk! What the hell is that? Why would that mean we don't have reservations?"

"What name did you make them under?" I asked.

"Mine. My name. Bath. For all of us. Six rooms."

Six rooms! They weren't even going to share rooms. There goes more of the taxpayers money.

I turned to the clerk who looked vaguely familiar. Was he, I wondered, one of the men whom I had seen working in the warehouse just a few hours earlier? "You don't have reservations for Mr. Bath?"

"No sir, no reservations for Mr. Bath."

"What about reservations for Mr. Magellan or Mr. Fantus?"

"No reservations for those gentlemen, either."

"A Miss Canby by any chance?"

"No, no Miss Canby," the clerk said, and I detected a grin as he said it.

AcChan! Had AcChan done this? Was this a game, a pulling of the tail, a tweaking of the nose? If so, then, "What about reservations for a Mr. Towel, or possibly Mr. Towle?" and I spelled the name both ways.

To Bath's relief and evident surprise, the response was, "Yes, sir, we do have reservations for Mr. Towel. Six rooms. Are these the people?"

"They are. Yes, this is the Towle party."

Bath was standing by with a look of pain on his face. He repeated what he said a moment before, "This is ridiculous."

"Mistakes happen," I consoled him. "Do you want the rooms?"

"Hell yes, I want them."

So they registered and when the clerk examined the signatures, he inquired, "Am I to understand that Mr. Towle will not be with you?" Obviously Bath was using the name Bath. Or something else.

"He's here in spirit if not in the flesh," I answered for the group and I swear that I saw the clerk wink.

Frustrated, but not defeated by events at the front desk, Bath now assumed his leadership role and issued his first command of the day. "Fred, have someone bring the bags to the rooms at once. We have much to do and little time to get it done."

He asked, "What room are you in, Osten? We could meet in yours if we have to."

"Room 214 at the President. Not here."

"What do you mean, not here? Why are you doing this, Osten? Why are you always staying somewhere else, traveling on different planes, eating in different restaurants, meeting with different people? I get the feeling you're not being cooperative and this is a joint operation. Have you forgotten? Joint! Means together. We work together. How can we work together when you're always somewhere else?"

And he was right. I wasn't being cooperative. So I decided to do better, starting right then, although I first ignored his question, let it run right past me, and said, "If you want to get together and start moving, how about doing it right now? If our man is upstairs, let's get him."

He considered it, looked as if he was ready to do just that, when he spotted Magellan and Fantus disappearing in an elevator with the two unknown Pan Unionists. "They're going up to their rooms. Let's do the same and then all get together for one final briefing. In my suite." He had managed to get a suite after all the confusion at the desk? "That sound all right to you," he asked. I nodded. "How about you, Avram?" Naroogian nodded. "Then that's what we'll do," he declared and headed for another elevator. "Tell everyone, Avram. Thirty minutes. My place." He looked at his Movado and left.

Safely settled in a suite, Bath began issuing new orders once everyone had assembled, closer to 45 minutes later, but still within a reasonable period of time as these things go. "All right. Our targets are in room 4670. We're two floors above. We'll take the elevators down as a group and knock on the door."

"What about the stairway?" asked Naroogian.

"No, not the stairway," Bath stressed. "We'll take the elevator."

Naroogian tried again. "I don't mean I want us to take the stairway. I mean will we have anyone covering the stairway in case they try to escape?"

I couldn't imagine anyone wanting to escape if they were waiting in a hotel room for us to bring them money. Especially if they'd been waiting for so long that they had become lonely, so lonely that they were willing to talk with bogus repairmen.

Bath saw it differently. "Good point, Naroogian. Raise Dirkens and Disbrow on the intercom and tell them to watch the stairway at each end. Don't let anyone go up or down until they get further instructions from me. I don't want anyone messing this up but us." I wondered if he was aware of what he had just said.

Naroogian demonstrated why he had been brought along as the security chief with his next question. "What if they refuse to open? Want us to kick in the door? Rush them?"

Bath was still thinking about his response when I interrupted. "Why won't he answer? In fact, isn't that what Magellan and he have been talking about? Our coming to see him for a discussion of mutual interest? Ours, people. His, money."

Bath apparently only paid attention to one question at a time. Naroogian's had finally registered and his decision was, "If he doesn't open, kick it in. Kick the door open. Will that be a problem?"

We all watched as Naroogian calmly walked to the nearest door, the one to the hall, opened it, checked the door frame and lock, closed it again, pushed on it with both hands and announced, "Piece of cake."

Bath was pleased and relieved. "Fine. Any other questions?" There were none and we trooped to the elevator, waiting a full five minutes for one to arrive. This time Fantus suggested taking the stairway, an idea promptly vetoed by Bath because, "They'll have sealed the stairways by now." Apparently Dirkens and Disbrow took their orders so seriously they wouldn't even allow their own boss to pass. Or had they booby trapped the stairs?

When we finally arrived on the fourth floor, an elevator having arrived in due time, Eddie was waiting for us. Bath recoiled, stepping back inside the car as if he had just stepped into a patch of poison ivy. "What's he doing here?"

"Mr. Chun? He brought my medical bag, just in case we need it, as you can see."

Eddie obligingly held up the plastic imitation alligator skin bag crammed with all manner of things that I might actually need in an emergency, even if this wasn't likely to be the time an emergency was declared. He shook it and the long supple neck of the stethoscope snaked its way through the half open top, as if wishing to prove my point. We proceeded with our mission, Eddie falling in at the rear of the column.

Room 4670 was two doors down the hall from the elevator. Bath nodded to Fantus who knocked, once, twice, three times and we all stood silently in the crowded hallway, waiting. Nothing. Not a sound except the breathing of one of the unknowns from pan Union. He was wheezing. We were lucky we hadn't walked down. He wouldn't have made it. Naroogian seemed to have better hearing than the rest of us and whispered to Bath, "I hear them. They're hiding something or going out the windows. We'd better get in there before it's too late."

I still heard nothing, but admittedly, my hearing isn't as acute as it once was. Everyone moved aside as Bath stepped up and knocked sharply on the door, shouting, "Open this door. At once."

Without offering anyone the opportunity of responding, he turned to Naroogian and ordered, "Kick it in."

Apparently kicking in doors isn't as easy as it looks. Especially when they are made of heavy wood secured in a stout frame and fastened with decent American built Sargent locks. At the first kick, the door trembled but held fast. The second kick, delivered with a resounding whack, resulted in modest splintering of the wooden frame just above the lock, while third and fourth kicks weakened the structure even more, shattered shards of wood flying loose with each blow, several nails suddenly exposed, the lintel drooping overhead, but the door was still closed. Naroogian was breathing heavily now, almost as hard as the wheezer, and had developed a noticeable limp, probably a bruise on his right foot, the one he had been using as his primary battering ram.

Pushing the remaining man with no name forward, he motioned at the door and said, "There, Larry, I've loosened it for you. Go ahead. Finish it."

Two more kicks did it, the door flew open with a crash, and as everyone dashed inside, I took my time, stopping to check on the damage the American taxpayers were going to have to pay for.

The room was empty. Fantus, though, was the first to spot the connecting door to the second room and, with a whoop, he charged through, the rest following in a pack. Room two was empty as well, even with a 24 hour watch, well, almost a 24 hour watch allowing for time in the book shop and nap time. It was clear Dirkens and Disbrow would have some explaining to do before the day was over.

You don't kick a sturdy door down at midday in a crowded hotel without attracting attention and while we were standing around wondering what to do next, two security guards and a dark suited, grim faced young Thai whom I assumed correctly to be a representative of the owners, rushed in and mingled with the rest of us. We were soon joined by three khaki clad policemen nervously fingering the unbuttoned holsters at their sides. There was quite a lot of chatter going on, questions were being asked, explanations offered lamely, and no one seemed certain of what the next move should be, when the missing piece to the puzzle walked in. He was carrying a sack of groceries in a brown paper bag under one arm and a six pack of cold Pepsi in the other. He stopped just inside the door, backed out when he saw it hanging from one hinge, checked the room number, and nervously stepped back inside to ask, "What happened to my room?"

Naroogian reacted faster than anyone else and reached out to grasp the startled little lawyer, who once more backed up so hurriedly that the loaf of French bread, which had been sticking up from his sack like a missile ready for launch, was tossed into the air and fell at Magellan's feet. He stepped on it. But Naroogian had captured his man and all we had to do now was explain to the police, security guards, and general manager of the hotel what we were up to. Then arrange to pay the bill, to pay the police and to pay the security guards. When that was done to everyone's satisfaction, we could sit down with Fred's Thai lawyer and find out how much money it was going to take to find out what was really going on.

What we discovered was that Chamburon Primavitavit had simply gone out shopping, needing groceries. The Pepsi had been an afterthought. It seemed like a good move and I walked over to the six pack, freed one, held it up questioningly for the lawyer to see, and when he nodded in assent, I opened it and took a drink. It was every bit as good as the lemonade we had enjoyed downstairs and fresh Thai lemonade is among the best in the world. Naroogian, who had worked up quite a sweat in kicking down the door and then collaring our man, took a second bottle, and drank it. I took out five dollars and handed it to Cham. Fantus was right. The name was too long. When Eddie took a third bottle, I added another two dollars and hoped that it was enough. The lawyer seemed to appreciate our honesty, but seemed bewildered by our hastiness in kicking down his door.

Once the police departed, Fantus examined the contents of the shopping bag. Nothing remarkable. Bottled water inside, Pepsi in a separate container, now half empty. A box of Ritz crackers, a small packet of laundry detergent, single dose size that Thais often used, and a can of tomato soup. Why that, with the wonderful tomato soup they served downstairs in the restaurant? The detergent made sense. He had been hanging around waiting for us to arrive for so long I suppose he had to wash up a few things. Probably needed a change of underwear.

Now that we were there, however, it seemed as if the lawyer had lost his voice. He sat there with nothing to say.

And Bath, predictably, had no patience with that. None at all. Instead of being the refined American from the State Department, one who, if I were to guess, had won as many awards and commendations for heroic acts as his companion, Fantus, he snarled at the miserable little man sitting on the couch, surrounded by people twice his size, except for Eddie, of course. They were about the same size. "All right, you little creep. We don't have all day. Where have you hidden Lee Duc Than? Tell me. Right now."

It was a bad imitation of an intelligent interrogation, the kind you would expect to see in a cheap B movie or network television show. "Bath," I suggested, quietly so Chamburon wouldn't hear, "do you remember how good cop, bad cop works?"

"Huh?" he said.

"Good cop, bad cop. Remember?" I wasn't sure he had ever known so I didn't know if he had anything to forget.

He surprised me. "Oh, sure. What do you want me to be?"

As if there was any doubt. "Be as bad as you wish. Then let me have a go at it."

But Chamburon short circuited our operation asking of Bath before he got back to his bad cop routine, "You must be Magellan."

"No, I'm not Magellan. I'm Bath. I'm in charge here." Always the big man.

"Where is Magellan? I've talked to him and he told me he would be here. He seems like a reasonable man." My respect for Chamburon went up significantly. He had already figured out that Bath was not.

Since stepping on the French bread, Magellan had disappeared into the other room. Now Bath shouted, "Fred, get in here. Talk to this man. Find out where Lee Duc Than is. We have to know, right now. Tell him we brought the doctor he wanted. That's him right there." He jabbed a finger in my direction.

Fred got off to an inauspicious start. Sheepishly, he stood before the couch and confessed, "I'm sorry about stepping on your bread."

Not having seen it happen, Bath reacted as if they were talking in code. "What are you talking about? Stepping on bread. What does that mean? I don't want to hear anymore about bread. Just ask him what I told you to ask him."

Once again Chamburon broke up an aimless exchange by co-opting the conversation. And this time he got right to what was on his mind, not Bath's. "What about the money, Magellan? You promised money. You know you did."

Magellan didn't reply. He just looked at Bath, who sighed and said, "Of course, the money. It's always the money. Anywhere you go in the world today people ask about how much money they can get for even the most worthless information. So once again, we come to the money."

This was pointless and a waste of time. Of course they had promised money. That was the lubricant that enabled voices to speak clearly, the motivation for one man to flee his country and betray it to another, and the reason why lawyers like this one were willing to sell one human being to another. At least, I hoped he had one to sell – Lee Duc Than, and that he could lead us to a second – Ken Green. So, tired of the game with Magellan, I said, "Cut it out Bath. Tell the man how much money his information is worth. It's in your budget somewhere. Just get on with it."

Magellan was the first to respond, although I watched Bath carefully. He was angry. Enraged would probably come closer to it. Looking like he was now, I knew it would, indeed, be dangerous to underestimate him. "As you know, Mr. Bath, we talked about twenty five thousand dollars; five thousand for Mr. Chamburon here, and twenty thousand to help resettle Lee Duc Than. Plus medical care for him, of course, arrangements for him to be brought to the United States, debriefing and relocation, all extra." From previous experience, I knew the 'all extra' could easily run upwards of a quarter of a million dollars.

"I recall all of that, Fred. Don't dwell on it. I also recall the conditions that accompanied the offer. This man is to deliver Lee Duc Than to us alive and we get to talk to him. No Lee Duc Than, no money. Make sure he understands that."

Chamburon had no difficulty in understanding it at all. He proved that by responding eagerly, "I can take you to him, for now, at any rate. He can talk. So when do I get the money?"

We were making progress.

"First things first," pontificated Bath. "Where is he and how long will it take to get there?"

"Not far. Maybe fifteen-twenty minutes out on the Old Chiang Mai-Lamphun Road near the Nong Hoi market. He has a room on an island in the Ping river. He was doing well maybe a week ago but I haven't seen him recently so maybe that's changed."

Bath frowned. I was thinking, "What the hell. Is he in a hospital? Is he that sick?"

Whenever I go on a trip, I always read up on the medical facilities in the areas I visit. Where the hospitals are, which ones have good emergency room facilities, what kind of reputations the hospitals and doctors have, that sort of thing. You never know when you'll need the information, and when you need it, it's likely to be in a hurry. I'd done it for this trip. Had all of the information in my head for Bangkok, other Thai cities, and had made a point of checking on everything I could find on Chiang Mai. It sounded as if Chamburon was telling us that the man he called Lee Duc Than was in a hospital, but was there a hospital on an island in the Ping River? There was something there, what was it, and then I remembered, and what I remembered wasn't good.

Directing my questions to Chamburon, I asked, "You say he's in a hospital on an island in the Ping River? A patient there?"

"Yes."

"Not in one of the other hospitals in town?"

"He was first. Then they sent him to where he is now."

"Well, that's it then, I guess," I told my audience, finally remembering clearly what it was I had almost overlooked when reading about Chiang Mai and it's many medical facilities.

"That's what, then?" demanded Bath, and for the moment, savoring the knowledge but not thrilled by the prospects, I had the attention of everyone in the room.

I held the suspense as long as I dared, checking my memory one more time to make sure I got it right, and then told them, "He's in a hospital of sorts. Probably in isolation. He's in a leprosarium."

"My God," said a stunned Magellan, "you mean Lee Duc Than is a leper?"

Leper!

The word hung there, casting a chill over what had been, until then, a hot humid room with a poorly functioning air-conditioner.

Had I ever seen a case? Recycling my memory, scrolling back through gray matter instead of a hard drive, I concluded: no. Not knowingly. That didn't stop every eye in the room from focusing on me. I was a doctor. I was supposed to know about these things.

I do, from books, not practical experience. Leprosy is an infectious disease that has become associated with dread down through history. There was evidence of that dread in effect right now; Eddie gingerly holding my medical bag as if afraid that it had suddenly become contaminated, perspiration forming on Magellan's forehead as he wondered if just talking to Chamburon had exposed him to danger, the unnamed Pan Unionist door kicker backing out of the room as if he would just as soon have nothing more to do with Operation Patient, if leprosy was what it involved. From earliest times, lepers have been outcasts, banished from society, forced to live out tormented days of horrible disfigurement in out of the way hell holes, abandoned by terrified neighbors who didn't want to know of their existence. A handful of dedicated humanitarians fought to change these shameful practices but it wasn't until medicine understood that this was not a disease of the unclean, or a curse placed upon the dammed, that progress was made, and haltingly even then.

Leprosy is a disease caused by a germ. It's name is M. leprae, a myobacterium, identified as an acid fast bacillus. Another myobacterium, M. tuberculosis is responsible for another disease, once thought conquered but which has recently made a strong comeback, tuberculosis. TB. The germs look very much alike.

Tuberculosis can spread rapidly, especially among poorly nourished and overcrowded peoples of the world, such as in Third World countries, but it can and does prove to be contagious in Western countries as well, recently appearing with increasing frequency among the immune damaged subset of HIV positive patients, adding a new urgency to the need for increased vigilance.

Leprosy, also called Hansen's disease, although infectious, appears to be only moderately so, affecting less than 5% of close contacts – in our country, far fewer than that. Casual contact poses almost no risk at all. Try telling that to anyone. Mention leprosy and fear runs through just about everyone. Mention tuberculosis and most people shrug. It should be the other way around.

Leprosy probably is spread by way of nasal discharge from an active case to a susceptible individual. Once gaining entry into the body, the myobacterium can proceed to infect the skin, mouth, eyes, lungs, and adrenal glands, almost any organ unfortunately, and in a classical advanced case, it is not unusual to see entire fingers or toes so badly damaged that parts of them fall away, while huge non-healing ulcers scar the face and leave the patient permanently deformed. Nerves and muscles are damaged, the patient loses sensation from arms and legs, and ultimately, life is a living hell, a human being trapped inside the wretched shell of organic, minimally functioning wreckage. The brain marches on, leaving everything else behind. Little wonder the mere mention of the word brings with it dread, fear, and despair.

At one time, there was no cure. Isolation was the only available choice. Today we have marginally effective drugs, and while there still is no cure, if cases are found early, the disease may be halted, but never turned back in its entirety.

Had I come all this way to see a man with leprosy? I knew, for a fact, that I had never treated one with that diagnosis before. Why would anyone say that I had?

I dredged up some statistics from memory. What were there, in my country, maybe 2,000 cases. Not many, not in a country of over 250,000,000 people. But in Southeast Asia, how many? Some said millions, maybe 20,000,000, so wouldn't the physicians of Chiang Mai be more likely to correctly diagnose and treat this problem than I was? If so, what was I doing here at all, other than looking for Ken Green?

Chamburon was my only source of information at the present so I made use of him while he was still around. "How long has he been in the hospital?

This hospital. Have they told you what he has?"

"In a hospital? Two, almost three months now. When I first saw him, he had sores on face with yellow, sometimes green stuff draining. They got bigger and bigger. Got so big I said 'you go to see doctor' and he said, 'no, call doctor from America.' But I don't know name of doctor from America and he don't know it either, right away, so when he said, 'yes, I must see doctor now,' I took him. Doctor here say go to hospital and he go to one."

So he'd been ill with draining sores for several months, and got worse. "The doctor here in Chiang Mai, did he send him directly to the leper hospital, the one on the island in the river?"

"No. First he send him to hospital on Sidonchai Road and then they send him to place he is now."

"Have you been seeing him often? Visiting him and keeping in touch?"

"At first, often. But he seemed so sad. Didn't talk much, didn't say much. Just said get doctor from America. Kept saying, 'Get doctor from America.' And I say everyday, 'What doctor from America?' He don't know until two men came and then he knew."

If I was surprised to hear about two other bedside visitors, Bath and Fantus were shocked. Bath recovered nimbly and asked, "What two men? Where did they come from?" His abruptness silenced Chamburon who looked nervously from the impatient Bath to me, then to Magellan. Magellan squirmed uncomfortably. He knew, about the visitors, he knew. And had kept it a secret, not telling Bath and definitely not telling me. Why?

Chamburon ignored Bath, answered his questions, but did it talking to me.

"Two men. One Vietnamese man. One American. Or German."

"One white man. This is the one you think might be an American?"

"Yes, white, this American. Or German."

"Why do you think he might have been a German?"

"Many Germans visit here. Tourists. With their cameras and money, taking pictures, rude people, grabbing young girls, talking loud."

"Was this man doing that? Talking loud, grabbing young girls, taking pictures. Was he rude?"

Chamburon gave that some thought before deciding, "No. I don't think so. Didn't talk much at all. The others wouldn't let him talk much, maybe. Vietnamese man did talking."

"Who wouldn't let him talk?"

"The other men. The other two men with the guns. The ones who wanted to take Lee Duc Than with them in the car."

I had no idea of what he was talking about and although Magellan looked as if he had heard this before, the expression on his face said he didn't know what it was all about either. Bath and Fantus were still shocked by what they were hearing. They weren't pleased at all. I suspected that Magellan would have some explaining to do before this was over.

This time I asked my questions before anyone interrupted. "What are you talking about? What other two men with guns and a car and why did they want to take," I didn't know what to call the man in the bed, compromised by calling him, "your man with them? To where?"

Chamburon shrugged, rolled his eyes, clearly he wasn't certain of what had been going on himself. "Two men with guns. Maybe guards. Ran in and argued, big arguments with doctors coming, people running around and everybody angry. Then police came and Vietnamese man, American or German, and two men with guns leave in car, driving very fast. Two men with guns, maybe Vietnamese, maybe Chinese. Gone. Not come back."

Guards? Chinese? We weren't going to get much more from Chamburon. It was obvious he didn't know much more than what he had told us. Magellan knew only what Chamburon had told him so he wasn't going to be of any help either.

"When did all of this happen?"

"Two weeks. I only go back once since then. Lee Duc Than in different room now. All alone. Hard to find. Hard to see. He seems," he groped for an English word, didn't find what he wanted and said, in Thai, "mai berk barn," hoping that I would understand what he meant. Luckily I did. The night before, leaving JoElle, she had used the same phrase. When I asked her what it meant, she smiled and said, "Depressed. I'm depressed. I smile at your coming and frown when you leave. I'm depressed. Understand?"

The man in the leprosarium was depressed. Well, why not? It wasn't the kind of place that would bring smiles to anyone's face.

My audience hadn't contributed much to the proceedings and it seemed time to find out if any of them were still awake. Bath was the most likely candidate, he had followed every word of Chamburon's story without moving from one spot on the floor. "Have you any pictures to show him?" A reasonable request. Bath was a big believer in pictures. Hadn't he been liberally distributing photos of me in recent days?

His eyes darted from mine to Fantus, and back. "Pictures of what?"

"Pictures of Lee Duc Than, things like that. If Lee Duc Than is in the hospital not far from here, show him a picture and see if Chamburon can make an identification."

He'd forgotten to bring the pictures. "They're downstairs in my brief-case."

Neither Fantus nor Magellan offered any help so I called to Eddie, "Bring those photographs over here and show them to Chamburon." Eddie removed a large manila envelope from my medical bag and brought it over, slapping it into my hand as efficiently as if he were the scrub nurse on a heart bypass team. The first photo out of the envelope was our happy class dinner group in the restaurant parking lot. I held it up for Chamburon to see and he took it, walking across to the window where the light was much better. "See anyone you recognize?" I asked.

Chamburon studied the photograph carefully, ran a finger across each face, and then looked up triumphantly and said, "Yes."

He eagerly pointed to a tall figure in the middle row. Me. No one else. He had never seen anyone else in the picture, he declared emphatically, insisting on it even when I pointed to Lee Duc Than, Co Phan, Ho Phan Van, and Truang Van Dang. None of them were familiar. Not at all. He shook his head again and again to make the point.

It wasn't all that surprising. The picture was twenty years out of date. Faces could have changed by now, especially faces deformed by draining sores such as those Chamburon had described. That was fine, except that my face had changed, too, in twenty years and he had identified me. And he had seen the hospital patient *before* the sores developed, hadn't he?

I had additional pictures supplied by Marge, borrowed from the Alumni association, lifted from the photo album of an aging professor and a couple she had found crammed into the back of one of my file drawers. Plus one the General had insisted I take, just before I left his apartment. No, none of them looked familiar, he repeated over and over, except, twice more, me. And we weren't excited in me.

In fact, no one was excited by any of it and boredom was about to replace the lingering euphoria of successfully kicking down a door when Chamburon's face lighted up and brightened my day. I handed him a photo-graph of Ken Green, a twenty-five year old snapshot that had been his mother's favorite, taken on the day her son had been awarded first prize in public speaking at the exclusive Ramapo Hills Day School in suburban Haddonfield, New Jersey. Ken had only enrolled there the one year, Kendra not at all, as the slightly elastic budget of an Army officer could stretch just so far before snapping; but that one year, a glorious year as far as Leah had been concerned, was one they both treasured. This photograph was the crowning moment, a smiling Ken, holding up a calligraphically adorned parchment attesting to his oral domination of twenty-one classmates, his handsome face wreathed in a satisfied smile.

The lawyer paused, took a second look, and said, excitedly, with gestures, "Him. This is him. The American or German, this is him. By the nose and eyes I can tell. Older now, but this was him when young."

I hadn't expected anyone to identify the General's son from this photograph, the one Jordan himself had handed me a few days ago in New York. Did it mean that Ken Green had been here, two weeks ago, visiting a leper? And if so, where was he now? Or was Chamburon mistaken? After all, it seemed too easy. Kendra had seen visions of her brother in the jungle. He hadn't been seen in fifteen years, had been declared dead. Now, suddenly, was I ready to believe that he was in Chiang Mai, alive, last seen in the company of two Chinese men with guns? I wanted to believe it, but like I said, it all seemed too easy.

I scribbled a brief note on a business card, pretended to put it in the envelope with the photographs, handed the package to Eddie and palmed the note. My hand wasn't big enough to dunk a basketball but there was room for a small pasteboard. On the way through the lobby, I made a detour to the front desk and passed my note to an outstretched hand. I received one in exchange. Bath had gone on ahead, but Fantus was lagging behind and wanted to know, "What was that all about?"

Casually, but not too casually because that would make him more suspicious than he already was, I said, "A note for my office in case they try to get in touch with me. Telling them I'll be back in an hour or two." It never seemed to occur to him that I was staying in a different hotel.

Behind me, the desk clerk handed my card to a bellhop who hurried out of the front door ahead of us, passed something to the doorman who hastened across the driveway to touch an arm extended from the open window of a tan Volvo. The arm disappeared, the window closed, and as Bath's mini van nosed up to the curb, the tan Volvo coughed gently and came alive. As the crowded van pulled away from the entrance, the Volvo accelerated and passed it, headed out Sidonchai Road, crossed Mengrai bridge, and kept going once on the other side of the Ping River. An identical model, except for the color, this one being black, pulled out of the driveway and followed us at a discrete distance and was still there when we parked at the leprosarium. Was it was possible, I wondered, that AcChan also owned the Volvo dealership in Chiang Mai?

Things became more interesting at the hospital. The trail warmer, I suppose one could say, as a courteous man at the front desk confirmed, without hesitation, that they did have a patient by the name of Lee Duc Than. They also stated flatly that we couldn't see him. No one could see him. He was in isolation and the presence of the Pan Union contingent didn't seem to bring smiles to many Thai faces in the business office where the receptionist directed us. It was clear that they were still thinking about guns, arguments, and the improper decorum exhibited by the previous visitors to Lee Duc Than. The appearance and demeanor of our mob didn't seem to be an improvement. In fact, to a Thai, it may have been even more ominous than a confrontation with a single American/German, one Vietnamese, and two men of indeterminate ancestry, guns or no guns.

Foremost among the suspicions of the medical staff had to be the simple fact that we were, aside from Eddie, Westerners, and Westerners didn't visit lepers. Aside from a nervous journalist who had been given an assignment by a sadistic editor and a busload of tourists whose driver had taken the wrong turn, Westerners were a rarity at the hospital. Now here were seven of them with one Korean. And Chamburon.

Not that many of the our group were eager to pass beyond the front desk, but then the Thai staff wanted no one else to pass beyond it either, except of course, someone had to. The someone, it turned out, was me, and I was allowed through the barriers and led to the isolation area because I was the 'famous American doctor' that Chamburon had insisted was coming to see the patient. He had said it so often, and the patient, even in delirium, had repeated it with annoying persistence that the hospital staff had accepted that a medical man of some repute was on his way. They viewed my arrival as the second coming of Hippocrates and when Eddie showed them my medical bag, packed to the brim with all the proper trappings of the trade, nothing was too good for me.

They understood, accepted without question, that Eddie was my assistant and envious eyes were cast in his direction, especially by several comely nurses. How fortunate he was, they seemed to imply, to be employed by 'the famous American doctor.' Moments later, Eddie was ready to resign when he realized that being employed by 'the famous American doctor' meant he was going to be taken onto the wards where lepers actually lived and died. Bath and his crew didn't have that problem. They were ordered to stay where they were in the reception area and a uniformed and armed security guard took up a position by the door. Naroogian and the door kicker could have picked him up bodily and thrown him into the river had they wanted, but they were content to stay where they were and let Eddie and me do the walking.

While a white coated young staff physician led us down a flowered path to where they had secreted Lee Duc Than, I finally got a chance to read the note in my palm. "Call me. Important. A." AcChan! Well, that would have to wait until after we got a look at Lee Duc Than.

We'll call him that, but I had no way of knowing who he was. He was all alone in a small isolation cabin. A uniformed attendant at the doorway moved aside, allowing us to enter. Although the exterior of the building needed repairs and paint, the interior was clean and smelled of disinfectant with a trace of the ever present hospital odor of urine. It was sparsely furnished although the bed was serviceable, a single sheet stretched tautly over the thin form lying quietly, a carafe of water with straw on a bedside table, one straight backed wooden chair for visitors, and hanging from the wall at the head of the bed was an 18 inch brass crucifix. Was he Catholic? Why not, I remembered. Many Vietnamese were.

Emaciated was the first word that came to mind; terminal was the second, but then I reconsidered. The face was that of a terminal man, the skin tightly stretched and yellow across the bony substructure, the center missing, replaced by a monstrous suppurating sore that glistened and dripped yellow-green pus from the left cheek and chin down onto a dressing loosely tied across the lower face and neck. Several smaller sores on the forehead and right cheek, one of them involving the edge of the nose, completed the gruesome configuration. The odor of the rotting tissue could be detected from ten feet away. There was no point in comparing a picture of Lee Duc Than, or anyone else, to this apparition. There wasn't enough to compare. Except his eyes. His face was terminal, but as for his eyes, his eyes, closed when we first walked into the room, suddenly opened, seemed to shine, brightly, just for a moment, and was that a glint of recognition there, or was I imagining things? Then they closed. The breathing was irregular, shallow, but much faster than it had been moments before. He sighed and sighed again. But wait. Was it a sigh? I heard the sound again, leaned close, as close as I could without touching the massive sores on his face, and heard him say, I swear, at least I was almost sure he said, "Osten." Just once. My name. Then he said it again. "Osten."

I sent Eddie for Chamburon. It wouldn't hurt to have him here as I tried to communicate with this damaged man.

The doctor offered me the records, which were of no practical value as they were written, not surprisingly, in Thai. Murmuring my thanks, I asked, "What if I ask you questions and have you answer them for me? I can't read your records, which I'm sure are detailed and complete, because I am not familiar with your language." All true, except the part about the records being detailed and complete. I could see little evidence of x-ray reports, laboratory work, and in fact the entire record was but three pages long, not much for someone who had been admitted with a serious problem some two to three weeks earlier.

He was happy to oblige. Nothing was too good for the world famous American doctor and to give the young Thai his due, he did a good job. They hadn't done much in the way of the missing pieces, just one chest x-ray it turned out and almost no blood work, but he seemed to care about the patient and was able to recite the history and outline the care he had been given effectively and in meticulous detail.

Chamburon had arrived and I took him outside where we found a small bench under a fragrant pine. "Please sit. I need to talk to you about the patient," I told him. Away from Bath and Fantus, even without Magellan on hand, he was much more comfortable. In addition, he was informative.

I started by asking him, "Tell me what you know about this man. He's very ill and it would help if I knew when all this started, how it started, what you first saw when it began, and when you first met him. If I'm going to treat him, if anyone is going to treat him, we must know all of this. The doctors here are doing a good job but have you told them everything? If they don't know everything, or if I don't know everything, then this man may not survive."

"Is he going to die?" Chamburon wanted to know. I wondered if he was worried about his investment or showing genuine concern for the patient.

"He might. He's in very bad shape, like I told you. Tell me what you know. For instance," seeing he didn't seem to know where to begin, I tried to get him started by prompting, "why did a Vietnamese defector get in touch with you, out of all the people in Thailand, and ask for help? How did you get to know him? How did he know your name?" Those seemed to be easy questions and it turned out they were.

Hesitating at first, then speaking more freely, he told me, "Back when the war was on, maybe 1969 or 1970, I was doing business in Vietnam. For my clients. Business things, you know, selling things, sending things."

"You were dealing with the Vietnamese? Doing business with them?"

"Yes, but not me. Others. Men who wanted me to arrange business with the Vietnamese. I did that. Arranged business." Doing what lawyers do, I supposed. Drawing up contracts, doing the paper work, maybe the dirty work, for all I knew. Plenty of other Thais did the same thing even while we were using their soil as the base from which we launched air attacks against North Vietnam. But business is business. It was for Chamburon and, while doing it, he had encountered Lee Duc Than. Could be. Lee Duc Than had split his time and loyalties, half the war spent in the South as a government administrator, next appearing in the north with an even better job. So a Thai could easily have met up with him and done business, one side or the other. It didn't matter that much now, did it? The war was over.

He had been doing business with the north. He admitted it. "It was profitable," he explained.

"You were a front man for Thai business men?" I asked.

He confirmed it, indirectly, saying, "They didn't want to use their own names."

"That's what I meant. They used you as a front man so they didn't have to be identified."

"Yes."

"Did you travel to North Vietnam and meet with anyone there?"

"Yes, many times. I met many people, made many deals, signed many papers, and brought it all back for my clients. To Bangkok."

A small boat drifted lazily downstream, two men wearing broad brimmed Thai hats to protect against the sun, both faces in full shadow were all but invisible. They had Chinese features, I thought. A large black vulture floated gracefully overhead, riding a thermal ever higher into a perfectly blue sky.

"Did you meet this man, the one in there," and I motioned to the building where the ravaged man lay, "when you traveled in the north?"

"No, never. But I heard of Lee Duc Than often. His name was familiar and it was said he had come to the north after studying in America and working for the South for many years and all the while he was an agent of the North Vietnamese. When the fighting was over, he went back to the south and was an important man. I knew of Lee Duc Than. Everyone knew of him, but I never met him.

"Then one day when I was in Ho Chi Minh City trying to trade cement for lumber and fish, we make a lot of cement in Thailand you know, a man called me and said he was Lee Duc Than. Said he knew I did business, what do you call it – so other people don't know about it?"

"Confidentially?" I suggested.

"Yes, that. Said he knew that and he had signed some papers of mine when I did business in the north and if I could do a favor for him, I could make some extra money. He said he must trust me, as a lawyer, to be, as you said, confidential. Some people forget I am a lawyer, but that's what he wanted. A lawyer. I knew his name. Good name. Powerful man, so I said yes. What did he want me to do?"

We both watched the water for a moment. The boat was almost out of sight but we watched as a dead dog, face down in the water, floated by. Behind it was a shape that could have been a human body but another glance showed it to be a large air filled plastic bag, or was it? A master and his dog out walking and both falling in? Ridiculous. Chamburon was still staring at the object as it moved past us. "Plastic bag," I said reassuringly. He didn't appear convinced.

He went on with his story. "Did I know anyone in the American embassy, he asked, that I could talk to? He needed to talk to someone. Finally he told me what he had in mind. Not right away though, he didn't trust me too much right away. Later, maybe four or five calls later, and on a second visit to Vietnam, he told me what he wanted to do. He wanted to come to Thailand and then later, to your country."

"Did he say why?"

"No, he never told me. He just said he wanted to leave."

Chamburon was answering my questions promptly, not hesitating, not speaking as if he had memorized what he was supposed to say. He didn't say, but both of us knew some of the reasons the man called Lee Duc Than was desirous of leaving Vietnam. The economy was a mess, planning was all but nonexistent, medical care was primitive, the infrastructure was deteriorating at an alarming pace, and there were too few jobs to support a rapidly expanding population. And for Lee Duc Than, if he was who he said he was, the political factors became important. If he had been a double agent originally, the men in the north must be wondering, "Could he be trusted now?" Sometimes the master can turn upon a servant in sudden violence and Lee Duc Than may simply have decided it was time to flee.

Chamburon's next words caught my attention. "One day, when we were

240

talking on the phone, he told me something else. He said he was sick. He said he needed to see a doctor and he wanted to see you."

"But you said he didn't know my name."

"No, I didn't say that. What I think happened is he couldn't remember your name. Couldn't remember then, but knew it once so all he could do was say, 'get me the American doctor.' Finally, he said 'the one from university,' and that had to be you."

"Who told you my name? If he couldn't remember it and you didn't know it, how did you come up with my name?"

"Magellan. He told me when I called him."

So this is where Fred got into the act. I wanted to hear Chamburon's version without Pan Union ears standing by so I urged him along by saying, "Yes, I was wondering how Magellan came into the picture. How did you happen to contact him?" He looked as if he didn't understand 'contact' so I tried again. "When did you first talk to him?"

"When Lee Duc Than said to call a doctor from university, I didn't know what to do. I had no friends at American embassy. I was on list of people who were not friends of America."

I could understand why. He had been dealing with the 'enemy' and it's easy to find your name on someone's list whenever you do that.

"But I had a cousin who did have friends, knew a man who had been in embassy maybe ten years ago, but was gone. I called my cousin and told him I needed help and he said for some money, he would try to find the man and he did." They were already divvying the pot.

"He found Magellan?"

"Not right away. My cousin had to ask. Many people he asked and they all said nothing so he finally went to the American embassy and told them he was an old friend with message from Magellan's son."

Which was a surprise. I hadn't known Magellan to be a family man. Puzzled, I asked, "What son?"

"No son. Just a story. Lots of Americans come here and meet girls and have sons and go home. So story is a good one. It could happen. You tell someone in embassy that American have son, they don't know whether he wants to know about it or not, so they look up name and send message and maybe he calls back. Asking, because sometimes they don't know either."

So that's what they did, passed on a message to the duty officer at the embassy, he called Fred and told him he had a message from his son and Fred, who must have been as surprised as anyone, and maybe secretly pleased, called back. To start this entire project rolling. It could happen, I supposed. It wasn't likely, but it could have happened that way. Maybe Fred hadn't spent every night in the embassy down in the communications room; maybe he had even visited Pat Pong or Soi Cowboy, two of the wildest streets in all of Southeast Asia during the Vietnamese war. Slightly less raucous today, they were still there. "So what happened then?" I asked.

"He called my cousin and my cousin told him to call me. He did, but he didn't say where he was, and right away he asked about his son. Then I told him about Lee Duc Than, even though he was disappointed."

I couldn't imagine Fred being disappointed about having the opportunity to get his hands on a high ranking defector. He wasn't. *That* he was excited about; not having a son, that was the disappointment. I tried to imagine Fred as a father and the image wouldn't focus. Teaching a little kid to play basketball, baseball, football, volleyball, even bowling, none of them seemed to fit. Badminton, maybe, but not the others.

Chamburon was plunging ahead with his narrative. He was working hard to earn his commission. Apparently Magellan told him to keep in touch with Lee Duc Than and if the opportunity arose, to help him get out of Vietnam. That proved to be surprisingly easy. Lee Duc Than was still an official in the government of Vietnam and was privileged enough to be included in a trade delegation assembled for a visit to Thailand. One evening after the meetings had ended for the day, he simply walked out of his room at the Rex Hotel, strolled a block or two in the dark, and casually made his way along Soi Suphang to Sukhumvit Road and got into the cousin's car. If anyone had followed him, they weren't quick enough to react before the escape was in full flower, the cousin turning onto Soi Akkami, followed it to New Petchaburi Road, and was on the road out of town. Before morning, they were in Chiang Mai.

"He wasn't sick then? Not when you first picked him up? I thought you said he was asking for me when he first called and that Magellan was the one who gave you my name."

"Sick?" He was flustered. Had something gone wrong with his script after all? "Yes, he was sick. A little sick when we picked him up, but he got worse after the men started looking for him. When we had to hide, he got worse."

"What men who were looking for him? Tell me about them. Was the American one of the men looking for him?"

He had hidden Lee Duc Than in a room above a restaurant in the old walled city. At first, Lee Duc Than had been willing to walk outside, eat downstairs, visit several wats, and attend mass three or four times. Then he started to lose his appetite, developed a fever, became pale, started to cough and then one day, forcing himself to eat a small lunch at an outdoor table, he was frightened by a car that passed slowly, circled the block, and returned again. He was convinced that the two men in the car were looking for him and when the car disappeared a second time, he got up and fled back to his room. His condition grew worse after that, his appetite shriveled to nothing, and his weight fell alarmingly. Then the sores on his face began to form. "Then Magellan said, put him in hospital."

"So Magellan knew he was in the hospital?"

"Yes, he said put him in hospital. Not this one. Another one. They looked at him and said take him away. To this one. This is where he has been for three weeks and he is getting worse. The sores are worse. He coughs worse. And he wouldn't eat so the doctors say 'feed him,' so I stayed and did."

Chamburon was going to a lot of trouble for $5,000. He couldn't have much of a law practice left if he was able to spend several weeks hanging around Chiang Mai helping to feed a sick refugee. That's what you get, I suppose, for winding up on someone's list. Why, I wondered, couldn't he have identified anyone from the photograph in the parking lot if he had seen Lee Duc Than before the sores became as disfiguring as they were now? Sure, Lee Duc Than was older now, weren't we all, but he had been able to identify Ken Green from a picture taken 20 years earlier. Why not Lee Duc Than?

He still hadn't told me about the men. "What about the men he thought were looking for him?"

"They were looking. They found him in this hospital. He was in the main building then and I was feeding him. The doctors said –"

"I know, they said you should try to feed him. Tell me about the men, Chamburon. The men. How many, who were they, when did they arrive?"

"I was feeding him. He eats better when I do that. Then two men came in. One is Vietnamese, thin, shaky on legs, but standing. The American, one in picture, tall, thin, hair on face, limping, dragging right leg. Dressed in good clothes, neat, clean. Both of them clean. Vietnamese man did talking, most of it. Lee Duc Than was angry, shaking his head no, but I didn't know what they were talking about. Then American started talking, but quiet and I couldn't hear him either."

Was this real, or imagination? Real, he assured me. "They thought I was nurse or orderly. Doctor made me wear white gown and mask when feeding Lee Duc Than so they thought I was nurse. Let me stay. Didn't look at me."

"They didn't recognize you as the man who helped Lee Duc Than escape?"

The idea of being the man who helped Lee Duc Than escape was one role he did not relish. Not with men with guns looking for both of them. "I had mask on."

Of course, he was fortunate enough to be in an isolation ward and the mask and gown helped. Once again, all of this for $5,000? Risk your life, if that was what we had here, for so small a sum?

Ken Green and the Vietnamese man had chatted amiably enough with the patient but that all changed when the Chinese, or whatever they were, arrived shouting and waving their revolvers. "What did they want?" I asked. "Why were they so upset?"

"They were tired of talk. They wanted Lee Duc Than, right then. To take him, lift him out of bed and take to car outside. American or German, man, said, 'No. He is sick. Leave him alone.' Chinese tell him shut up before it is too late and then Vietnamese man say it is already too late because police must be coming and they were. Doctor outside in hall heard noise and called police and they came. Chinese men yelled and were angry but they all left in car just before police came. German man, too."

Here he was with that German man again. "Chamburon, let me ask you. Why do you refer to the American, the man you told me was Ken Green, as a German? He's an American."

"Maybe. But I know some German. We have lots of Germans here in Thailand and they –"

"Yes, I know what they do. They're rude and all that, but why do you call him a German?"

"I know German words. And this man speaks in German."

Ken Green speaking German! He hadn't when he died fifteen years before.

"What about the Chinese men. How do you know what they were saying? Do you speak Chinese?"

"A little. But do not need to know Chinese when they yell and wave guns. Know when men are angry. Besides, I know Chinese curse words. They used many of them." Chamburon obviously was multilingual. Many

Thais were.

"And after they left, these men, Lee Duc Than was moved down here?"

"Yes. The doctors say he is safer here."

I doubted that. *They* were safer with him here. That boat, for instance, slowly cruising back upstream right now, with the powerful motor mounted on the rear, that boat could be at the dock within thirty seconds at full throttle. Two men could dash up the path and be inside the isolation room in another thirty seconds. Safety for Lee Duc Than was somewhere else, not here. The two men seemed uninterested in us as they motored past, their faces still obscured by shadows.

It was time for a review and apparently Fantus and Naroogian had decided it was time to find out what was taking me so long. They were walking determinedly down the path, closely pursued by an angry doctor in white, the stethoscope dangling from around his neck bouncing up and down as he pursued the two Pan Unionists. He finally tore it from his neck and carried it along in his hand. Back when I was a resident physician, we carried our stethoscopes in the side pocket of our long white coats. Around the neck was the fashion now and it had its disadvantages.

"The sores, Chamburon." Something in my tone alerted him. I was digging now, he knew, following a lead that had surfaced earlier. He wasn't clear what it was. I wasn't either. Yet. "Tell me when you first saw them and how big they were at that time."

Naroogian and Fantus had stopped to argue with the doctor a football field away.

Chamburon gave the matter of the sores some thought before answering, "He had small ones when we picked him up. Maybe this big," and he held his thumb and forefinger about a quarter of an inch apart.

"Were they open with green and yellow stuff coming out of them then?"

"No. Not then. They were bumps about this big," and he held the same two fingers closer together than before. Call it one eighth of an inch. That high. "Then they got bigger and stuff was in the middle."

"But they grew fast," I said. "If they were small when you first saw him outside his hotel and they are huge now after only, what is it, four weeks at the most, they grew fast?"

"They grew fast," he agreed.

"What about the cough? Was it bad at first?"

Naroogian was still arguing with the doctor but Fantus had left them and was headed in our direction.

"Just a cough, like this," and he forced a dry cough, obviously intending it for a sample. It was a hacking nondescript cough that wasn't very informative.

"Do you know ai-luk?" I asked, pulling a Thai word out of the hat, actually one I had found in the Thai-English medical dictionary we had in our office. I wasn't certain I had it right, whether it meant a deep cough or cough deep, whether I had the words in the right order. But Chamburon responded as if he and I were in the same medical school class.

"Ai luk? Cough. Yes, he did that. All the time. Kept me awake in hotel after cough got worse. Yes, cough very much, just before we see doctor. Cough like this," and he gave me another one. Deep, rattling, prolonged, and then finished a bravura performance by spitting on the dock.

Fantus glared at Chamburon and the Thai lawyer shriveled within himself. He had been talking to Magellan but by now he had come to understand that any payment for his services was dependent upon either Bath or Fantus, or both, not Magellan. As far as I was concerned, I had what I needed, for now at least, so when Fantus snapped, "How long do you expect us to hang around here waiting while you talk? Shouldn't you be examining the patient or something?" I was all sweetness and light.

"That's an excellent idea. I'm glad you thought of it. Would you like to help me while I do a physical examination right now?"

He decided he would stay down here by the river with Chamburon while Eddie and I did the honors. Eddie wasn't thrilled either.

Before leaving them, I pointed out onto the river. "Keep an eye on the boat."

"What boat?" Fantus asked, his eyes following the line of my arm, sliding off my extended fingers to look directly at the long tailed boat which was making a slow turn towards the opposite shore.

"That boat. The one with the two men in. They keep passing back and forth as if watching something interesting ashore. Like they're watching us."

Fantus peered into the sun, squinting for a better look, then covering his eyes with a hand before saying, "Maybe they're fishing."

"Maybe, but I don't see any lines. No poles either. So just keep an eye on them." If nothing else, that would keep them busy.

When I went back inside Lee Duc Than's room, Naroogian was standing next to Fantus who was pointing to the craft, now broadside again and headed downstream once more. Naroogian covered his eyes to look into the sun and then said something to his companion. Chamburon was sitting on a bench, the only one uninterested in the boat.

The young Thai physician who had been pursuing Fantus and Naroogian had stayed by the door and was waiting to translate the Thai notes into English. The record was a slim three pages because they hadn't done much. He had Hansen's disease, leprosy, they had decided, apparently based upon his facial disfigurement, the skin lesions having been considered enough to make the call. They said the patient was 45 years old, and he looked thirty years older right now, but 45 was what Lee Duc Than should be if the University's records could be trusted. His temperature had been high when he was admitted, staying up around 102 degrees for a week or more, but now had stabilized at 99.5 or less. He was anemic, had too few red blood cells, hemoglobin, and platelets and that was about it. A small sketch of the skin sores had been made when he was admitted and comparing it to what was there now was frightening. They were spreading rapidly and now half of his right cheek was eaten away by a angry red cavity filled with pus, the upper end of it creeping against the lower eyelid. If it spread much further, I could see that the eye itself would be endangered. The right side of his upper lip was eaten away and a massive ugly purplish swelling had left his face lop sided, grotesque, a fitting mask for Halloween. Or a Stephen King horror story.

A second smaller sore was eating into the left nostril, with swelling of the eye on that side leaving him with virtually no vision at all, just a slit for the left eye and nothing at all from the other. His neck was swollen and he was having trouble swallowing. When I donned gloves and palpated the neck, I found a chain of hard, painful lymph nodes extending from the collar bone to the angle of the jaw on both sides. I knew they were painful to the touch because that was the first reaction from him I had seen. He winced. I murmured an apology and he tried to smile which made the wounds gape even more. I was afraid Eddie would throw up. He would need more training as a physician's assistant before being ready for cases like this one.

Lee Duc Than coughed, a wet rattling cough, a true ai luk from deep inside the lungs and he tried to bring up the thick choking mass of phlegm lodged deep inside. He fought it, struggled to breathe, to clear the airway, and lost, the tenacious greenish yellow glob sliding back into his chest from where it had come. He was warm, gasping, pale, exhausted, and a ghastly gray. The whites of his eyes, when I pulled the lids down as gently as possible using sterile gauze to protect both of us, were a sickly yellow.

If I were a Thai doctor faced in this clinic with this man, I could understand making a diagnosis of leprosy. He was in a hospital where they saw a lot of it, had skin lesions that could be part of it, was rapidly deteriorating, was sick, and was here in Southeast Asia.

But for a moment, let's pretend we were in the United States and someone brought him into the clinic there. What if he walked into a medical clinic where no one had ever seen a case of leprosy? What if I had seen him? What would I have called it? And what would I have done that hadn't been done?

What about the skin lesions? Think. Of what? An infection, spinning wildly out of control, something like a bacteria, yeast or fungus that had started caseating and eating away flesh. Even the dreaded flesh eating bacteria was a possible candidate, I would have thought of that before leprosy, wouldn't I? Why not things like blastomycosis, histoplasmosis, actinomycosis, nocardosis, erysipelas or anthrax? And if the patient was suffering from malnutrition, whatever the reason for that might be, his immune system might be damaged and then we would have a new set of names to contend with: staphylococci, streptococci, even the common cold sore could go crazy once in a while and herpes simplex would become a risk to the immunocompromised patient. One of those, that's what I would have thought of first, or all of those if I had nothing to work with, like I did now. So what would I do back in my clinic?

Shorten the list. That's what I would do.

An older Thai doctor had appeared at bedside. He stood quietly and watched. Through the only window, I could see Fantus and Naroogian looking out towards the river, shading their eyes against the sun. The door kicker walked over to them carrying field glasses.

I touched Lee Duc Than's bony hand reassuringly and then slowly inspected each finger in turn, first one hand and then the other. The nail beds were pale and the nails needed cutting but were clean. I lifted the sheet and looked at his toes. Normal fingers, normal toes, ten of each. All there and intact.

I held out my hand to Eddie, recovered now, having fought back the earlier nausea, and he stepped forward with my medical bag as if he had been trained for this all of his life. I removed the stethoscope, my otoscope, several sterile tongue depressors and the small white container that had made the circuitous trip from Atlanta via a half dozen airlines. At the very bottom of the bag, invisible until I removed the last of my many tools, was the handle of a revolver. A .38 from the looks of it. Where in the hell had Eddie gotten a gun?!

I handed the bag back to him and he was the picture of innocence. Maybe this wasn't one of my tools. Perhaps this was one for the assistant. I was every bit as innocent as he was.

I used a light to carefully examine the lesions on Lee Duc Than's face, shined it into both eyes, and observed the prompt narrowing of the pupils. In response to my request he managed to open his mouth and I inspected the bleeding, tender gums and oropharynx. I listened intently to his chest, first the front, then the back, the younger Thai physician and Eddie propping up the patient, one of them on each side, in order for me to do so. I felt the apical heart beat, compared it to his radial pulse at the wrist, took his blood pressure, all the while under the watchful gaze of the Thais. I could hear the gossip tomorrow. "The famous American physician does all the same things we do." Of course, we all know what to do. The rest is hype or a gut feeling.

Lee Duc Than coughed. Coughed again. Deep and harder. I took out cloth face masks and put one on, handed another to Lee Duc Than and Eddie helped him put it on. The older Thai doctor was Thanukavit. He was the man in charge. Trained in Scotland, he spoke excellent English with an accent reminiscent of the Highlands and whisky. He was more than happy to put on a mask and listen to the chest, removing his own stethoscope from around his neck as he did so. I used a surgical marker indicating the area of interest and he finally listened to it after first moving his shiny head piece from place to place to familiarize himself with the patient's background noise.

I used a disposable syringe to make one small injection just under the skin of the right arm, removing a small amount of material from the Atlanta package, leaving enough for two more tests should they be necessary. From a vial supplied by our own Osten-Burrows laboratory, I took another small amount of test material and made a second injection on the left arm. I finished the test procedures by making two small abrasions with a tiny needle just above the second injection. On one, I placed a drop from a bottle marked positive control; on the other, a drop from a bottle marked negative control. Thanukavit watched intently and was more than willing to guard both drops for the next ten minutes, making certain that the patient didn't accidentally wipe them away in moving about the bed.

I suggested making cultures from the lesions on the face. No argument. I had culture media and we inoculated it. The younger physician hastened to carry the specimens to his laboratory; I kept others for Carmichael and Diaz. We collected sputum specimens, getting Lee Duc Than to cough and cough harder, this time raising the slimy material that had once before escaped back into the cavity where it had been hiding. Specimens to their lab; specimens for Carmichael. Biopsy? From these lesions, these spots here, here and there? Thanukavit frowned, seemed reluctant, weighing the cost, perhaps, or the previous oversight.

"It's possible that this case will prove to be so interesting," I said, "that we will want to present it at the World Conference on Infectious Disease, possibly at another also, the World Conference on Immunology, and if that happens, you would be one of the main presenters, should you be interested." He was.

"I will ask the surgeons to do the biopsies for us at once," he responded eagerly.

We got all of the specimens and samples that we needed, in each case one for them and two for us; Carmichael one, Loretta Diaz a backup. Before we were done, I had to promise that the surgeon, too, would be on the program. Of course, both he and Thanukavit would have all expenses paid. Now all I had to do was find the program.

Even more important, though, was to make a diagnosis. He could have leprosy. The local doctors had put him here, in the leprosy hospital, but why? According to the history that Chamburon had related to me within the last hour, the man being called Lee Duc Than had not been all that ill when he defected. Coughing, yes, a little. It steadily progressed and was now severe. The skin sores had been small and then grew rapidly as time went on, not very much time to my way of thinking. The involvement of his nose and eyes was appallingly evident, but that had all occurred since he had reached Chiang Mai. I knew that, but did Thanukavit and the attending doctors here know that? Had they gotten the history from Chamburon or had they simply inherited a sick man sent over in a debilitated state from another hospital, as Chamburon had implied?

The same thoughts might have been bothering Thanukavit as he asked, "Do you think this man has leprosy?"

I told him, truthfully, "sometimes, Doctor, a complicated case like this is difficult to diagnose. If I had seen this man in the United States, I would not have made a diagnosis of leprosy. Here, the chance of it being leprosy is higher, but on the basis of the history I have, and because of the way his fingers and toes are, I doubt that I would have made that diagnosis in your country either."

He was perplexed. "What did you find wrong with his fingers and toes?"

"That's just it. Nothing. With the sores on his face as far advanced as they are, I would expect to find other parts of him to be damaged as well. Especially the fingers and toes. They aren't, however, and that could be significant."

Thanukavit knew that, recognized that as peripheral nerves died as a result of leprosy, the skin and muscle tissue of the fingers and toes becomes dull and lifeless, and in time, there is nothing left to do but surgically remove them before they decay and fall off. There was nothing wrong with the fingers and toes of our patient. Instead, the areas of infection were on the face, the large eroded areas on the cheeks and lip an angry fiery red, not dull and lifeless, and the center of each cavity filled with raw tissue and green pus. Regional lymph nodes of the neck were swollen, tender, and hard, the way you would expect to find them in an acute infection, not what you would find in leprosy. Thanukavit was listening intently as I laid out my case, point by point. He wasn't ready to agree but I had the feeling that he had not closed his mind to other possibilities.

"Then there's the chest," I said. "You listened to it when I did. In my clinic, we would want an x-ray of that chest at once. What do you think?"

"An x-ray. Yes, certainly an x-ray. I don't know if we have taken an x-ray recently." According to the record I had seen, they had taken one two weeks earlier, but from the chest sounds we had just listened to, he needed another. Thanukavit remedied that oversight at once, ordering the patient taken to the main building where the radiology facilities were to be found. Unfortunately, he was advised by a junior physician, the films wouldn't be ready until the next morning. The technician responsible for developing film had left for the night, taken the only key, and no one knew his telephone number. We were in luck, however. The man who took the films was still there.

I had one more important task to perform before they took him away. Stripping off the first pair of latex gloves, I discarded them in a red biohazard container, identical to the ones we use back home, and put on a fresh pair. Reviewing my three by five inch blue cards filled with notes copied from the full medical records of the Vietnamese patients I had seen 20 years earlier, I took out a half dozen sterile glass slides and several sterile swabs. Patting Lee Duc Than reassuringly once more, I reached over and took his left earlobe firmly between my right thumb and forefinger and squeezed. A pea sized pearl of white matter suddenly burst from a small pore. It was thick, adherent, the consistency of a semi-dried glob of Elmer's glue, with just enough liquid content to allow me to collect bits of material on four of my swabs, smearing each in turn on a fresh glass slide, which I air dried by waving about, placing them carefully into small plastic envelopes. I handed the envelopes to Eddie who inserted them into stronger manila envelopes with a hard cardboard backing for added protection.

Thanukavit was watching my latest maneuver with interest and frowned when I finished by lifting my glove encased forefinger up to my nose and sniffing. There was the distinctive odor I had expected to find and, although I hadn't made the final diagnosis, I was quite certain that I had identified the man in the bed.

And we hadn't found Lee Duc Than!

I didn't tell anyone, not yet; there was still too much to do and some things were best kept secret. If they were secret, that is. We had our laboratory specimens, we would have our x-rays by morning, we had made biopsies, and now it was time to get everything back to Carmichael and Lorretta Diaz. And then get on with the main part of the project: find Ken Green and the real Lee Duc Than.

Just before they wheeled the patient away, I gave him a second small intradermal injection just above the two control tests we had administered earlier. The negative control was entirely gone, not a trace remained. The positive control, on the other hand, was red and in the center a half inch welt, a small hive had formed. I was satisfied. That was what I had expected.

He was looking at me, his one eye a slit, the second only slightly better, and he knew who I was. As soon as I squeezed his ear lobe, I think he understood that I had identified him as well. He was saying, soundlessly, "Well, now you know. What do you intend to do about it?"

In fact, I hadn't decided how to play this hand. I didn't know whether to raise or call. To try to improve my hand by drawing a card or to stand pat. I chose the latter.

He wasn't going anywhere. Not as weak as he was and as horrible as he looked. But he wasn't safe where he was either. It seemed prudent to safeguard the patient but Bath didn't think it was such a great idea. "It's not our problem. Let the hospital staff protect him. Who the hell is he, anyway? Have you figured it out yet? Is it Lee Duc Than?"

The questions were perfunctory, asked because he was expected to ask questions, and if he didn't, it would look suspicious. He didn't look suspicious; he sounded suspicious. My problem was I wasn't sure whether Bath thought it was Lee Duc Than or someone else. Until I knew what he really wanted to know and why, I wasn't about to help him.

"I don't know," I told him. "But we have all the specimens we need and after we get reports on all of that, and after seeing what the x-rays look like, I should be able to tell you more."

"What do you mean, tell me more," he challenged, "you haven't told me anything yet."

In that, he was correct.

"You have enough men to put a guard on him tonight. Do it. I don't want anyone accusing us of jeopardizing the safety of a man who might be able to tell us about American POW's. That would be inexcusable. The hospital can help, but we need men we can trust, Americans, like us." Now, if that wasn't a cheap appeal to patriotism, nothing was. He bought it. Then again, maybe he did and maybe he didn't. He assigned Dirkens and Disbrow to the first shift, to start as soon as the x-rays had been completed. The hospital was willing to assign a security guard, making a protective threesome, and that was comforting.

The message from AcChan had still not been acknowledged and I phoned him immediately upon my return to the President. "Stay there. I'll be over in twenty minutes," was his response.

That left me with enough time to call Kendra, as Bertinoldi had suggested. "She'll be by the telephone tomorrow," he had said. "The nurses will make sure of that. She'll be expecting your call." I couldn't reach her. I talked to a dozen nurses and each one had a different excuse. She was there, but either in x-ray, or getting a test, or in therapy, or away from her room. She wasn't anywhere or she was everywhere or nowhere. But not within reach of the telephone line. It was like making a telephone call to find it answered by impersonal voice mail; like calling Social Security for help, or an insurance company trying to clear up a snafu. It was frustrating. "We'll tell her you called," echoed in my ears, and that wasn't what I wanted and I didn't think that was what Kendra wanted. I wanted to hear her voice, to ask her how she felt, to know if it was true that she had rallied; and to tell her that I was near the jungle, where I was ready to start the search for Ken. I needed her, not the voice of a nurse. And hanging up, heard again, "We'll tell her you called." Thanks. Thanks a lot.

I fared no better with her father. "Not in," said Montgomery. "Is this Dr. Osten? I'll tell him that you called." Thanks. Thanks a lot.

When I called my office, I got Clovis. "Oh, Doctor, you should be happy you're not here right now. An ice storm. The roads are slippery and no one was able to get to work. The parking lot is a skating rink. Really, three or four of the security guards brought skates and are playing hockey with some people from the lab. I tried to avoid them and slid into the ditch alongside the pond. You know the one. I may never get out until spring. Marge? Not here. You know how bad her driveway is when we have ice. She'll get in later with a cab. Mr. Burrows? He's at Cypress Point or someplace like that in California. It's charity golf for the Wild Society or something. No, I don't know about Tumor Activity reports but Marge will when she gets here. I'll tell her you called. Oh, Tony Howsam called from somewhere. He got there. And Horace called. He got there, too, wherever it was he was going."

"Yes, I know, Clovis. They both came with me. So did Eddie."

"That's nice. I'll tell all of them you called. And I'll tell Marge, too. I hope your weather is better than ours. Ours is bad."

I stood holding the phone for a moment after the line had gone dead. Was there something wrong with the connection or had she been hit in the head by a hockey puck?

With the luck I was having on the telephone, it was a blessing that AcChan was knocking softly on the door before I dialed Bertinoldi. He wasn't alone. He introduced his companion, a short, stocky man with a shock of red hair, who was obviously not a Thai or hills tribesman. "Jock McLemore. He's with the American drug people," which I took to mean the DEA, Drug Enforcement Agency, or some comparable agency. "I wanted you to talk to him before we plan any visits across the border. By the way, he thinks you must be the man his father remembers from Korea."

McLemore? Korea? The man with the wrench, the man who salvaged a water pump from the burned out truck and was able to get us back on the road once more? And he had a son who was at least thirty years old. Well, that figured. Time does fly. I hadn't heard from McLemore, the elder, since Korea. But he obviously remembered me, just as I remembered him and the events of that one lonely night on a dark road.

We shook hands, settled down in comfortable chairs (the President furnished chairs a cut above the average for comfort), and waited for room service to deliver tea. When the fragrant liquid was safely in hotel cups, none of the fine china here, tendrils of steam lazily curling into the air, AcChan asked, "Did you find your man?"

"No. We found a man, a very sick man, but not 'our man.' Not Lee Duc Than."

"I didn't think so."

"You were there, I suppose?"

"Yes, I was there. Got there before you did, as a matter of fact. You did well by handing my man a message in the hotel. Once we knew where you were going, I went there and had another car follow."

Eddie poured tea. There was no end to his capabilities. AcChan savored his and said, "One of the best things the British ever did. Tea. Afternoon tea. Very civilized. Gave all of the British expatriate merchant types the time to sit around each day and think of new ways to colonize the world for the benefit of those resource poor little islands. It was when they started to drink whiskey that it all fell apart."

After another sip, he leaned back and said, "So you discovered that the man in the hospital isn't Lee Duc Than." It wasn't a question. He stated it as a fact.

"That's correct," I acknowledged, without elaborating.

McLemore had been quiet so far, contemplating his tea as if he were hoping to change it into the British beverage which AcChan had tied to the downfall of John Bull. It wasn't happening and he wasn't drinking.

"Jock, tell Doctor Osten what you have been telling me." To me, he said, "Jock has been in Chiang Mai for almost two years. Obviously, with that hair, his cover was blown within a week of arrival so he has spent most of his time collecting information, observing and reporting on the local scene. Reporting, that is, to his superiors in Bangkok and Washington. Who comes and who goes and what they seem to be doing in Thailand. I think you'll be interested in what he has to say."

"Officially, I'm an engineer," McLemore began. "Sent to Thailand to consider building a semiconductor factory to manufacture computer chips. The labor is cheap, the land even cheaper, and the tax structure very favorable. I really am an engineer, college degree and all. And I really do know computers and this wouldn't be a bad place to build a factory for that very purpose. I already have located the acreage, negotiated contracts which will never be signed, and if you're interested, I could be talked into leaving my current position and taking one with your company to proceed with the plans I have worked so hard to develop. What you may be more interested in, however, are several things I have seen and others that I have heard in the past year. Just as AcChan says you've heard, there does seem to be a strange

Westerner somewhere up here in northern Thailand or Laos. Mysterious fellow, never seen, often talked about. Nobody knows what he does. Has even been rumored to have visited Chiang Mai. He wasn't around two years ago, but he is now."

His description matched what I had heard at breakfast back in Bangkok. Ken Green? Why should we think that, aside from the letter he had sent. But surely Americans were not unknown in this part of the world. And if no one knew what they were doing, they were described as mysterious, dangerous or crazy. By now rumors about me had probably begun to circulate.

Of course, Chamburon had identified Green in the old photograph back at the hotel, but what did that mean? It could mean that he had been here, visiting the hospital. That's what it meant. Or it could have been a false lead. Blind alley.

"At the same time, during the past two years, we have been interested in a pair of Americans who have made a dozen trips to Chiang Mai, always by helicopter, and have traveled extensively in the north for two days or more at a time. We've watched them but never questioned or detained them although their actions have been deemed to be 'suspicious' by several of our field agents. We've never followed them or searched their luggage either. They could be innocent travelers, they could simply be doing their job, we just don't know."

"Or they could be something else altogether," I suggested.

"Yes," agreed McLemore.

"Like dealing in or smuggling drugs. Something like that."

"Conceivably, yes."

"They must know we have DEA agents in the area who would be interested in frequent visits to this hot bed of drugs and yet they keep coming and showing up on reports. It doesn't seem to bother them?" I asked.

McLemore took one sip of his tea and made a wry face. He didn't spit it out but swallowing it was an effort. "Jeez. You don't have a soft drink, do you?" Eddie opened a Pepsi for him and he drank half the bottle with one swig. "No, these men aren't bothered by that, as far as we can see."

"Because? It wouldn't be because of who they are or what they are, would it?"

He finished the Pepsi with a loud gulp. "You're way ahead of me. We have been told to leave them alone. They're with the government, ours, Bangkok says, and we are to keep hands off. Some kind of mission."

"State Department, I suppose?" I said.

"Right. State Department."

"Would their names be Fantus and Naroogian?"

"You wouldn't happen to have a little bourbon or scotch, would you? I'm thirsty as hell," he said, appealing to Eddie. Eddie promptly supplied one or the other with ice. I didn't know we had either one. Finally satisfied, McLemore said, "You're half right. Batting five hundred. But it's Fantus and Bath, not Naroogian."

Which surprised me. Hadn't Bath said they always sent along a security man to dangerous places like this? In the Fantus-Bath tandem, who was security? Or was this a special assignment? Calling for special arrangements?

I was still pondering the significance of this information when AcChan said, "Now I have some additional information. What if I were to tell you that we may have another witness? A witness who says they saw an American beating up on an old man about 10 days ago. Way up north in an obscure area where hardly anyone ever sees an American. In a waterfront dive, I'm told. Would this interest you?"

"Should it? You know I'm looking for an American who was declared dead fifteen years ago. Is there any reason to believe that this sudden flurry of American sightings has anything to do with that? Or do we have an isolated event totally unrelated? This is your country, AcChan. What do you think?"

"Let me tell you about the witness and how it came about," he said, not answering directly. "One of my men was born in a hill tribe village clinging to the side of the mountains north of Chiang Mai. He went to visit an ailing father two days ago and the entire village was talking about a woman who had just arrived from across the Mekong River. She was telling of what she had seen one night; an American, she thinks, hitting or beating, she wasn't clear which she thought it was, an old man who was crying and screaming for help. Even though there were several other men around, no one lifted a finger to assist and they finally hauled the beaten man inside the only building around, slammed the doors, and turned out the lights."

"That's interesting. You say this woman just arrived and what she described took place a week ago? That would have been a week or so after Chamburon says he saw Green here in Chiang Mai. Could you go from here to there, up in Laos, in a week?"

AcChan nodded. "Depends mostly on how you made the trip. This woman walked, that's right, walked. If Ken Green was with the people that caused all of the problems at the hospital, don't forget they had a car. Sure, they could have reached the Mekong in a week or less."

"All right, then. What do you suggest we do?" McLemore was listening, but not participating other than to finish his drink and ask for a refill.

"I suggest we drive up to the village and talk to the woman. See what you think of her story for yourself. Show her your pictures. The main reason I suggest that is because I don't have any other place to start," he confessed.

"I have to go to the hospital first thing in the morning," I said.

"Do that. As soon as you finish, get in the car with us and we'll go into the hills. It's a Meo village of old allies of yours, like we talked about before. It would be good for you to see how they live these days. Bring Mr. Chun along. We'll leave Bath and his people behind. I don't believe they would be welcome where we are going." In a Meo village after Vietnam, probably not.

"How will I recognize your car? A Volvo again?"

No. No Volvo for this trip. We're going into very rough country. No roads at all part of the way and only trails the rest of the way. We'll have a Land Rover. Two of them. You know what they are, don't you?"

"Expensive Jeeps. Sure, I know."

"Jeeps! Jeeps are junk. A Land Rover will get you there every time. That's another thing the British did right. Tea and Land Rovers."

"There must be more than that," I corrected. "What about Shakespeare and the Magna Carta?"

"OK, so they could write, too," he conceded.

I agreed to meet AcChan at the hospital at ten in the morning. McLemore hadn't said much more, mumbling "good night" as he went out the door. Hanging around Chiang Mai and reporting on the local scene wasn't going to be good for his health if he stayed much longer and continued drinking.

"How's your father?" I asked as he prepared to leave.

He grimaced. "Dead. Heart attack, I guess, three-four years ago. Just before I came over here."

That's the risk you run when asking a question like that, but once it's asked it can't be withdrawn. I said, "Sorry to hear that." And meant it. The Korean vintage McLemore had been a good man. I hoped his offspring would prove to be as versatile and endure.

I should have known that Bertinoldi would be out to lunch. I called, or tried to call him, as soon as AcChan and McLemore left but had no success in reaching him, which left me batting considerably below .500 in that category. I propped up a couple of pillows on the bed, took out more medical reports and several reprints from journals that I needed to review, read until my eyelids were too heavy to keep open, and fell asleep. Just before that happened, I heard Eddie in the room next door rattling papers once more. Christmas presents again? That reminded me. I had completely forgotten to ask him where he had found his new gun.

# 11

I didn't ask him about the gun the next morning, either. Instead, Eddie surprised me by asking, "It was the ear wasn't it?"

"The ear? What about the ear?"

"I don't know how you did it, or exactly what you did, but when you squeezed that ear, you knew that Lee Duc Than was someone else. That he isn't who they say he is. There was a clue there and it gave you the answer. Right?"

It was a very astute observation and I hadn't expected Eddie, or anyone else, to make a connection. I wasn't absolutely certain, of course. In medicine it pays to be cautious, and that's why I had ordered x-rays and proceeded with the laboratory tests. But if I were a gambling man, I would have been willing to give good odds that the man we had in a hospital bed was definitely not Lee Duc Than. It probably was . . . . I almost told Eddie who it might be and then decided not to. Do it right. Wait for the results of the tests you've already ordered.

The chest x-rays showed extensive bilateral infiltration of the upper posterior segments of both lungs with two obvious cavities in the left one where fluid levels were easily identified. The injection given in the right arm a day earlier was already showing peripheral inflammation; the one on the left showed no reaction at all, but I hadn't expected anything to show up there for a week or more. Frankly, with what I now knew, I expected no reaction at all in that area.

Thanukavit and I peered through a powerful scanning microscope and both saw the perfectly stained acid fast organisms. The young Thai laboratory director agreed. The routine blood count revealed a leukopenia, not enough white blood cells, very few platelets, and a frightening anemia, the hemoglobin hovering at just above 7 grams, less than half of what a normal healthy male should have.

Cultures taken from the massive sores on his face were already heavily colonized with streptococci and staphylococci organisms, and growing abundantly on specially treated plates were the mycelia and colonies of molds and fungi. It was clear that this was a mixed infection, a fast growing one, and not typical of the indolent, slowly progressive pace of Hansen's disease. Maybe this was the flesh eating monstrosity that had recently been reported from several other mini-epidemics in Africa and Asia. Whatever it was, though, it needed immediate treatment or this man would not survive.

The clinical picture was further clarified by several of the nurses and attendants who had cared for him since his arrival at the Ping River hospital. "Yes," they agreed, "he coughed a lot," and sometimes they reported that when he coughed he brought up massive globs of bright red blood, spraying it over the bedclothes and himself. Or when it was really bad, on them. Once or twice he had coughed so hard, the blood had splattered the wall alongside his bed from where it was scrubbed the next morning by an anxious orderly, vigorously applying large quantities of detergent to erase the last vestiges of coagulated blood and phlegm. They produced a missing piece of the scanty record, the temperature chart, which showed fever spiking as high as 103 degrees on many days, dropping to near normal levels later in the day, and then rising again at night.

Thanukavit and I sat in his office to review the record one more time. He had none of the oak framed plaques that adorned the walls behind Bertinoldi's desk, or mine, too, for that matter. In their places were a metal framed portrait of the King and Queen, and an aerial view of Chiang Mai, a red arrow crayoned onto the glass covering marking the location of the hospital. A small spirit house perched on a tall pole could be seen through the window. Two saffron robed monks, shaved heads reflecting the early morning sun, were outside, carrying bowls, foraging for the day's rations.

"He's debilitated. Badly malnourished," I said. "He hasn't been eating. His appetite failed him several weeks ago before he came into the hospital." I didn't want him to think I was criticizing the care. I needed his cooperation. "His immune system is not functioning well and he has become susceptible to infection. Any small break in his skin will become infected and the infection spreads rapidly because he can't fight it off. That's what happened to his face." Thanukavit was paying rapt attention and now nodded in agreement.

"And in his lungs, here," I tapped the upper lobes of both lungs on the displayed x-ray films, his eyes following closely, "we see infiltration and fluid levels. Cavitation." I held up a slide, one we had looked at together through the microscope, "While here we have acid fast organisms. On the arm, a positive skin test already."

"Yes. I agree. I see all of that," said Thanukavit. He was kind enough to ask, although I am sure he had formed his own opinion as I had been talking, "What do you think it all means?"

"Doctor, you're the expert on leprosy. I'm not. But I don't think he has leprosy. I think he has tuberculosis, pulmonary tuberculosis, a serious and advanced case, complicated by the malnutrition. Serious and life threatening, highly contagious, but despite that, treatable.

He wasn't arguing my diagnosis when he asked, "What about the face? Don't you feel we are justified in considering leprosy or do you feel it is cutaneous tuberculosis?"

It was a reasonable question. The diagnosis is not always easy and I told him so. "I think it has been growing too rapidly to be leprosy. I suspect that it is a mixed bacterial and yeast infection and neither TB or leprosy are directly involved. Indirectly, because of his lack of appetite and poor diet, the TB could have left him vulnerable to this massive infection, but if we treat the underlying disease, improve his nutrition, and get him started on antibiotics at once, we might see dramatic improvement." He might also die, I realized, because it was late in the game to be starting treatment.

This had to be humbling to Thanukavit. To his credit, he didn't try to pass blame to anyone else, and I'm sure other staff physicians had made most of the decisions which I was now saying had been incorrect. He simply remained silent for a moment longer and then said, "You said treatable. How would you do this in your hospital?"

"We would do it just about the same as you would in yours. First, I would complete the sensitivity studies on the organisms cultured from his face to find the most effective antibiotics to treat them. I'm sure your laboratory is already doing that." I wasn't sure but I knew they would start on it within minutes as soon as Thanukavit left his office. "While awaiting those reports, I would start intravenous ceftizoxime and an antifungal agent. Then, in order to treat the tuberculosis, I would follow the guidelines set up by our Public Health Service and hit it with just about everything we have: isoniazid, rifampin, pyrazinamide, and streptomycin. That could change, too, after the laboratory reports are back, but start with them all."

I wrote the orders for the initial drug schedules, made notes in English on the chart, and was assured they would be translated and added in Thai, and then advised, "Doctor, make sure everyone who has worked with or come in contact with the patient understands that he is very infectious. He is a risk to others. They should take all necessary precautions: mask, gown, gloves, disinfectants, separation of his bedclothes, dishes, silverware, all of that, and it would be wise to follow all of his close contacts on your staff with chest x-rays and tuberculin testing." I made a note to do the same with Chamburon.

I had no idea whether Thanukavit's budget would allow for all of the drugs I had suggested. I had no idea how much they would cost, but knew it would be a lot. I didn't even know if he could obtain all of them, but this was a joint operation so I made a generous offer on behalf of my joint partner. "If you have trouble paying for these drugs or in finding a supply for any of them, let me know at once. If I'm not available, call this man at Chulalongkorn University. Tell him your problem and let him work on it." I gave him Horace's number. He needed something to keep him busy. "If it's the money part, paying the bill, just send it to the American Embassy. Write on the bill, 'approved by Mr. Bath, Pan Union, special fund, Operation Patient'."

Thanukavit was making notes. He seemed relieved. He smiled as a white robed Buddhist nun passed us on the flowered path. There were flecks of gray in her short hair. The river was placid this morning as we walked towards it on the way to the isolation cabin. A small one man boat was being oared slowly upstream close to the near shore. Another, farther out, was working its way against the current, much lower in the water, identifying it as one headed for market laden with fresh watermelons and mangoes.

Disbrow was wandering around outside the cabin, shouting, waving his arms, and stamping his feet. From time to time, he would glance at the open book in his hand and start over, repeating what he had just done. Both arms akimbo, he froze into immobility when he saw us and stood, a statue in the park, the only thing missing, a pigeon on his head.

Thanukavit watched, a worried expression on his face, fearing he was witness to the return of the men with guns. "Shakespeare," I explained. "I suspect he's a thespian practicing for the neighborhood theater group back home." Othello I could understand, but what role would he have in a production of A Midsummer Night's Dream?

Dirkens was inside, asleep, and awakened only after we had passed him in his chair and were standing at bedside. "Where's Disbrow?" he demanded. "Did he screw up again?" I didn't think that deserved an answer, but I glanced outside and could see Disbrow down on the dock where he had resumed his acting career. This pair needed relief. They were obviously overworked.

Disbrow had an audience. A third American, a Pan Unionist I presumed, was sitting under a tree on a folding chair, looking bored. But he was awake. Sitting on the ground ten feet away was a Thai security guard, so the hospital had sent one down after all. He was propped against a tree. They were both watching Disbrow who seemed unconcerned and, in fact, may have appreciated their presence. They were looking at him as if they thought him crazy.

We didn't stay long. Looked at the patient, listened to his chest, and took his pulse. I told him we would be starting medication, told Dirkens we would be back in a few minutes, and left. Eddie asked, "Why are we coming back in a few minutes?"

"We aren't. What they know may hurt them." I don't think he got it.

On the way back to the main building, I told Thanukavit, "You should change your records. Get the right name on the chart. You'll need it for the bills you send to the embassy anyway."

He was surprised. "What do you mean? This man is Lee Duc Than. That's what we've been told. That's all we know."

"He's not. That's what someone wants you to believe, so that's why they've used that name. Maybe it's the patient himself. Maybe it's someone else. But the name is Co Phan. He's Vietnamese, that much is true, and he went to the United States and attended the University. All of that is true. But the records show that he is living in Seattle, Washington, right now and that isn't true. He's laying in bed down in that cabin. And he has tuberculosis."

The third Pan Unionist, still without a name, watched as we walked into the main building and disappeared from sight, then hurried over to the cabin, presumably to talk to Dirkens. I was hoping Dirkens would tell him we were coming back in a few minutes. We weren't. We went out the side door and got into a waiting Land Rover.

As soon as we had seated ourselves in the back, the driver pulled away from the hospital, closely followed by a light colored Volvo. The driver concentrated on driving, not talking, and apparently knew where he was going, so Eddie returned to a subject that seemed to fascinate him; Co Phan's ear.

"All this stuff about tuberculosis and infections, that was a blind alley, right? It was the ear. That's what told you the guy wasn't Lee Duc Than."

So I told him. "My old records show that I saw three Vietnamese students back at the University, all of them 20 years ago. One of them came in to see me because he hammered his fingernail and had blood underneath. You know how painful that can be. So I drilled a hole in the nail, drained the blood, and relieved the discomfort. Before he left the office, he pointed to his left ear lobe and said it hurt; said he had a lump there, and wondered what to do about it. What was causing it. I took a look and sure enough, he did have a small hard lump there but it didn't look like a pimple. It wasn't red and swollen, it was just hard, and when I squeezed it, thick white fluid came out of it. The stuff smelled rancid, like cooking oil gone bad, and that was typical of what is called an epidermoid cyst. A lot of people have them, scattered about the body, usually on the upper trunk, scalp, sometimes the face, even an ear lobe, like this one. They aren't serious, you don't have to do anything about them, just express them every once in a while if they hurt, although you could surgically remove them if you wanted to."

"Express them? How do you express them?" he asked.

"Squeeze them. Squeeze the foul smelling stuff out of them. That's what express means. Squeeze."

"So that's all I did twenty years ago. Squeezed it and made a note. Yesterday, imagine the coincidence. Here is a man claiming to be Lee Duc Than who has an epidermoid cyst in exactly the same place as another man named Co Phan had a long time ago. Same spot. My conclusion, and I hope it's the right one, is that he isn't Lee Duc Than at all. Just says he is. But I don't know why. That is something we still have to find out. That and who actually is living in Seattle using the name Co Phan."

Then I had a question for Eddie. "Where did you get the gun?"

A blank stare, although he looked nervously down at my medical bag, which hadn't left his hands since our arrival in Thailand. Maybe in bed, but other than that, no. "The gun?"

"Yes, the one in my bag. Or do you have more than one?"

"No, just that one. I didn't know you saw it in there."

"Sure, I saw it. Where did you get it?"

And that's when I discovered that Harry Kee had a men's clothing store in Chiang Mai, a branch of the one in Bangkok, which of course, was itself a branch of the main store in Hong Kong. In a manner of speaking, he had established a franchise, custom tailored clothing and guns, and Eddie was rapidly becoming one of his best customers.

Four miles outside of town, we passed a second Land Rover parked alongside the road. After another two miles, we pulled over and five minutes later, the second vehicle pulled up behind us. We transferred from one to the other where AcChan was waiting. "No one followed you," he said, "but I didn't think they would. They're all at breakfast."

"A little late for breakfast, don't you think?" I said as I took a look at my watch. 10:30 A.M.

"Not if they're waiting for someone who didn't show up, it isn't."

"Who failed to show?"

"You. They think you're coming to meet with them after you see the patient. That you're going to tell them who he is, what you're going to do about it, and see what you plan to do next."

"They never invited me. Nor did I promise I would meet them. In fact, we didn't talk about this morning at all."

"Blame me. I'm the one that passed them the message. I should tell you, Doctor, that I'm not impressed with the way your associates operate. They don't seem to have the right kind of mind for the business they seem to be in." He didn't tell me what the message was, instead motioned to his driver, saying, "You haven't met Bip yet. He's from the hill village where we're going. His English isn't too good but don't worry about it. Mine is." And he laughed.

"About breakfast," I reminded him.

"Yes, breakfast. You know they did leave men at the hospital last night. Big guy, walking around all night like he was giving a speech, and the other one like he was practicing his sleep. In the middle of the night, another one came and just sat there on a chair, swatting mosquitoes outside under a tree. By the way, did you seriously consider the patient to be in any real danger?"

"He was dangerously exposed in that cabin and until I know what's going on, and until I can recognize friend from foe, yes, in answer to your question, I did consider him to be in danger. Still do."

He thought about this for a moment and said, "Well, you may be right. I thought you might have been overreacting a bit but under the circumstances, I suppose we should keep an eye on him. Just in case. I'll take care of it." He spoke to Bip in Thai, or was it Meo, and then returned to our conversation. "The new man, he was the one who was supposed to call Fantus this morning. Right after you saw the patient."

"Then they know I'm late for breakfast by now because I've already seen the patient. So he's called them and they're wondering where I am."

AcChan was enjoying himself. "I don't think so," he said. "I called Magellan's room this morning and told him I was the Thai doctor in charge of the case and that the patient had taken a very bad turn for the worse and that the American doctor would be detained, delayed indefinitely, but would come to meet with them as soon as he could. Most of all, though, I assured him that they needn't worry. Their men were here and doing a fine job. Incredibly, he believed me. About all of it, even the good job part."

"Maybe, but don't forget. All they have to do is phone the patient's cabin and they'll find out I've been there and disappeared, and that the patient is unchanged, so they'll be looking."

"Let them. They don't know where to look by now. But they won't call the room and find out. Don't worry about that."

"Why not? There's a phone there. I saw it."

"Not working. We fixed it in the main building. And while Dirkens was asleep, regrettably, someone slipped into the room and stole his cellular phone. There's a lot of theft in Chiang Mai, you know. Can't leave things expensive like that lying around when you're taking a nap."

"What actually happened?" I asked. You don't slip in when three other people are watching a room.

"The security guard. Remember him?" I nodded. "He works for me," AcChan explained. "He took care of things."

Eddie had been listening intently to every word AcChan said. "Neat," he said in appreciation of a job well done. "I like that. By the way, my name's Eddie," and reaching across from the back seat, tried to shake Bip's hand. Bip, surprised, almost steered us into the ditch. Thais are not big on shaking hands and after some hesitation, Bip gingerly allowed his to be touched and quickly returned to his driving. "So," Eddie said, "tell me about the village. What goes on up there? Any action?"

He sounded as if he thought he might be going to Las Vegas. And clearly, he had taken a liking to Bip.

Bip looked confused, not understanding much, if anything, of what Eddie had been talking about, and AcChan said, "Like I said, Mr. Chun, he doesn't speak much English."

Eddie scowled in disappointment. "Damn. That's going to make it harder to talk to him. By the way," he said turning to AcChan, "you can call me Eddie."

I soon found out the wisdom of utilizing a four wheel drive vehicle for this journey. The village was some 70 kilometers northwest of Chiang Mai, passing by several ancient temples, or wats, along the way. Tourist buses fought for space in overflowing parking areas, disgorging hordes of polyester clad visitors, most toting Japanese cameras and clicking shutters to photograph everything from the spectacular golden roof of a temple to the most obscure insect hauling away fragments of yesterday's lunch. I understood why Chamburon had German on his mind. When we paused at one roadside temple, almost everyone was speaking in Teutonic tongue.

When the road ended, we struggled along a trail. When the trail ended, we slogged along a track, almost invisible to the eye, but by carefully following wandering tire tracks through the swampish ground ahead, we kept going. When the track and tire marks came to an end, we clambered over rocks, forded several streams, eluded the grasping tentacles of hanging vines that entered the open vehicle, groping for victims, trying, it seemed, to tear one loose and carry the unfortunate back into the dark overhanging canopy of massive trees, from where there could be no return. The sturdy springs and frame of the Land Rover groaned in protest, the durable metal sides brushed away limbs and thorns that savaged the paint, while the throaty engine growled defiance as the proud product of Britannia moved implacably uphill. Suddenly, we crossed one more hand hewn bridge of logs laid across a torrent of water, lurched up a slippery bank on the other side, and broke out of the jungle to find a village spread out below us in a small valley.

It wasn't much, this hamlet, home to 200 to 300 Meo. Maybe thirty to forty small one or two room wooden buildings; usually one room for cooking, eating, and living, and another for sleeping. Sleeping mats lined the plank floors, anywhere from ten to fifteen in a home, and the interior was warmed, winter and summer, by coal or wood fires which cast a pall of smoke and soot over the inside of buildings and left the valley shrouded by a perpetual haze, worse on hot, humid days, just like back in Los Angeles. Thai smog. There was little furniture aside from a table and several chairs but even here, far away in the mountains, television was changing the way of life. In most of these homes, flickering black and white screens, high up on a shelf along one wall where it was easy to see, brought the world as seen through CNN or America as seen through Gunsmoke.

Outdoors, small black, white, and brown piglets wearing colored neck ribbons scurried about underfoot in search of food and exercise. If they had known what fate was in store for them, they would have scurried right on out of town and into the jungle where their chances at survival were no worse. Every home seemed to have a radio, and a mixture of Thai music and the voice of news echoed from almost every windowless structure. The throb of a generator higher up on the side of the forested mountain revealed the source of the village's electricity. Shallow wells provided water and pit privies served as toilets. Often they were side by side. There was no evidence of urban planning or basic sanitation. The pig corral, for larger porkers, sat almost squarely in the center of the largest cluster of homes, the better to protect this richest of all assets from the depredations of jungle cats and wild dogs that roamed the forest by night.

And incredibly, even here there were other four wheel drive vehicles and camera wielding tourists walking in a mixture of pig dung and mud down what passed for the local shopping mall, seeking the bargain of a lifetime, but more likely to pick up a case of hepatitis, malaria or gastroenteritis instead. I asked AcChan, "How did they get here? There was no road."

He repeated my question to Bip and relayed his response. "He says he took a shortcut. There is a trail on the other side of the village that takes longer." That explained it, of course. I still didn't see any Pan Unionists. None that I recognized, at any rate. I did notice a small artifact for sale, an attractive miniature yellow ribbon wearing piglet, an inch or so long with tiny erect ears. Ostensibly made by the Meo villagers, a bargain at 80 bahts. Barely visible on the bottom, in small, faint letters, were the words 'Made in China.'

The house we were looking for was on the other side of the village, a quarter of a mile away, further up the slope. "Up there," AcChan indicated, "that's where we'll find the woman. And here, this would be a good place to leave Mr. – Eddie. He can keep an eye on things down here and alert us if anyone suspicious enters the village. Both the shortcut and trail end here so this is a good place to mingle with the tourists, look like a shopper, and keep the eyes open. You see anything unusual, give us a whistle."

Eddie didn't take to the idea immediately. "I can hardly mingle with the tourists. Most of them, all of them, are white, and I look more like some-one who lives here. Most of them are talking German," even up here, I had noticed that, too, "are carrying cameras, and traveling in pairs. A man and a woman, usually, but not always." I had noticed that, too. "And I don't have a camera, can't whistle, don't speak German or have a woman," he con-cluded.

"No problem," AcChan said, and he quickly overcame all but one of Eddie's concerns. He produced a camera from a canvas bag on the seat along-side him. "Just click this to take all the pictures you want. It's easy. And this is better than whistling," he promised, handing him a small compact radio. "Just extend this small antenna," demonstrating it, "push the button and start talking. When done, push the button again and listen for one of my men who'll be on the other end up above." I looked where he was pointing and the second Land Rover was already parked up on the hill near the house. They must have taken the long way around and gotten there sooner than we had, despite the shortcut. "As far as talking German, just grunt a lot and say things like danke, gutten tag, jawohl, and nein. That should get you by nicely. As for the woman, I can't help you. Pick one up. Steal one from a tourist but

269

don't do it to a native. They really get upset over things like that."

"What about this radio? Who will be listening on the other end?"

"One of my men. Here, let me show you." AcChan took the radio and demonstrated by pushing the button marked SEND. "Gennu, are you listening? Say something in English. Over." He pushed the second button marked RECEIVE and held the instrument away from him for us all to hear. There was a moment of silence, then the buzzsaw of static followed by a hoarse voice saying, as if from a great distance, not wasting any words or effort, "I speak English." The radio fell silent once more.

Eddie took the radio, pocketed it, and carried the camera across the street to see what kind of bargains he could find." OK boss, I'm ready to mingle. But don't leave me here. This place has no paved parking lots. It's not my kind of town."

As he mingled and we proceeded up the hill, AcChan asked, "Where did he get the gun?"

"How do you know he has one?" I thought it was still in my medical bag back in the hotel. I should have known better.

"I saw it when he was putting the radio in his pocket."

Eddie needed deeper pockets. "You've got to understand Eddie," I explained. "He works for us as a security guard, at night, in a neighborhood where there recently has been some trouble. He carries a gun at work so naturally he feels that he should have one here. Especially after what happened in Hong Kong."

"I do understand Eddie," he said. "I can understand why he wants to have a gun. I often feel that way myself. What I was asking was, where did he *get* the gun. He didn't get it from me. I doubt that you brought it with you. So he got it here. In Thailand."

"From Harry Kee, well, actually I suppose from someone in Harry Kee's store."

"Harry Kee? The clothing guy? That's a surprise. I get a lot of my clothes from that store. These pants and shirt, I'm sure they came from Harry Kee's. I like shopping there. Good merchandise and good prices. And he also supplies guns! That's interesting. I didn't know that, which proves you can learn something new every day."

"An old Chinese proverb, I believe," I said.

"Are you sure?" he said with a grin. "I thought I read that in a business magazine. Maybe it was *Forbes*. Are you sure you're not quoting from Malcolm Forbes, the original, or even Bernard Baruch?"

He seemed to have a good grasp of American culture and a decent sense of humor. "About guns," he continued, "don't let it worry you. Up here, a gun is sometimes helpful. I've got one, Bip has one, even he has one," he said referring to the driver of the second Land Rover. Proving he understood English, the driver pulled back his light jacket and sure enough, under his right shoulder, in a tight holster not unlike what I suspected Bath was wearing, was the handle of a gun. "As a matter of fact," AcChan said, after a moment of reflection, "I guess you're the only one without a gun. We'll have to do something about that."

We talked to the woman outdoors, in the open, under a grove of apple trees, sitting at a wooden picnic table. I understood the risk of long range microphones picking up our conversation and cameras recording the event, but it was far better out here than indoors surrounded by at least a dozen others in the choking smoke and stifling heat. Bip knew the woman, talked to her in a dialect I had never heard before, and spoke to AcChan who told me, "She is willing to talk to you but she doesn't think what she saw will be of much help. It was just a brief look and it was dark and rainy."

The hill tribesman driving the second Land Rover was our interpreter. He placed the radio on the table in the RECEIVE mode in case Eddie should call. I looked out across the valley, from this vantage high enough to see a half mile of brilliant red flowers stretching in every direction. A dozen men and women were stooping over the plants, busily engaged in tending to them. It was too far to see exactly what they were doing, but every so often, one straightened up and carried a large basket to a waiting cart pulled by a placid water buffalo. "What's the crop?" I asked.

"The usual. It's what they rely on for cash up here. Poppies." He was noncommittal. Non-judgmental. That didn't mean he wasn't concerned. His voice sounded concerned.

Poppies could wait. The woman was more important right now. "Will she be in trouble for talking to us?" A good question, I felt, as I wasn't sure how the drug lords of the poppy fields down below would view our visit. I could understand now why AcChan and his men were armed. This was not friendly country to men asking questions. I wondered what the people spending their hard earned dollars, pounds and marks on 'Made in China' junk would think of their visit if they knew of the poppy fields carefully kept from their sight. Probably nothing, I decided. They probably wouldn't care.

"I'll take care of that. The people that count know that we are here for something else. Not drugs. I'll remind them of that again after we leave. She shouldn't have any trouble and neither should we. On the other hand, if Bath or any of his people came up here, I couldn't guarantee they would ever leave alive. So we did them a favor by allowing them time for a late breakfast." If that was good enough for AcChan, it was good enough for me. Another old proverb.

Her name was Simi Si. She was just over five feet tall, had raven black hair, and delicate features that were more in keeping with a Thai or Vietnamese stock than Meo. Nevertheless, she had been born in a mountain village much like this one, only hers was in Laos, and had lived there most of her life until she had made, as she put it to the interpreter, a mistake. The mistake was in marrying a lowland Laotian who had arrived in her village to cut timber, stayed when he met her, and then after she had agreed to marriage, demanded that they move to, and she spat out the words in anger, 'down below.' The lowlands. By the river. She bore him a child, he had started to drink, beat her, abused her, swore at her, and then, with no one in the village to protect her, her family far away having moved to Thailand, he finally cast her out. Threw her aside.

When that had happened, about two weeks ago she thought, she had nowhere to go except Thailand. Her family, the survivors, had fled across the river to escape the vengeance of the Pathet Lao for having chosen the wrong side in the never-ending Vietnamese and Laotian civil wars, and she followed on foot, alone, except for her baby. She couldn't leave her baby. And didn't. She was safe here, she thought, as her husband would never cross the river looking for her. Why not? He was a coward, that's why and besides, she didn't think any of the villagers back in Laos would tell him a thing. They despised the man, she said. They would tell him nothing. Even though she didn't think they knew where she had gone. She hadn't told a soul. Just picked up her baby and left.

"How old is the baby?" I asked.

She brightened at the question and quickly replied, "Three months, a little bit more. And a very good baby. Cried very little." He was crying now, softly behind us in the crowded house. Or was it another baby? There could be more than one.

"Ask her what she saw. About an American, back up by the river."

Suddenly Bip took over the questioning, which slowed us down as he first heard my request by way of AcChan, relayed it to Simi Si, and then the process went into reverse. She responded to him, he spoke to AcChan and then AcChan told me. It took time but Bip was sensitive, his voice kind rather than abrupt as the previous interpreter had been, and I was fascinated both by the story she had to tell and the way she was telling it. She was speaking to Bip as if they were lovers, their eyes locked as one, his voice soft and reassuring, her response frank and open. It took no more than five minutes to realize we were watching two people falling in love. If I hadn't needed information, I would have excused myself, taken AcChan with me, and allowed them to be properly introduced. We didn't have the luxury or the time, so I listened, fascinated as much by the way the story unfolded as by the story itself.

"It was very dark. It had been raining. When the lights came on, she was surprised and when she saw the beating, she became frightened," was the way Bip started. He spoke a few more words to her and she responded with a five minute narrative during which he listened intently, sitting silently. Somehow, without moving, Bip seemed to draw ever closer to Simi Si as she was speaking, a gesture of comfort and reassurance which seemed to bolster her confidence.

After she had fallen silent, he relayed what she had told him to AcChan who then told me, starting by saying, "You realize that often, talking in this way, something gets lost in what is it called? – the translation – but this is what he just told me. Like he said, the wind was blowing and it had been raining. The river was very rough with large waves and the rain had just stopped when her husband walked up behind her and hit her in the side of the face. He was cursing. He called her a dumb cow and hit her again before she even knew what was wrong. Then she realized he was angry because she had forgotten one of his shirts back on the riverbank where she had been washing their clothes. She must have forgotten it when the rain started and although she gathered up everything else, the one shirt, his favorite which he needed for a trip, had been left behind. He was so angry that he threatened to throw the baby in the river if she didn't bring it back right away. She was afraid he might do that because when he had been drinking, he was capable of doing anything. Drinking made him mean. She'd seen him do mean things like strangle a dog, tear the head off a chicken, kick a young boy whom he didn't like, and, of course, beat her whenever he felt like it." The man sounded like a real nice guy.

AcChan continued. "She always did the laundry down at the river's edge by a dock at the only store. The water is shallow there, less leeches, less chance of encountering snakes or crocodiles."

The Professor's wife used to complain of having to make do with an automatic washer and dryer, considered that too much of a burden and hired someone to come in and do her laundry. Try a couple weeks in the jungle, America, and see how you like them leeches.

"So she was afraid that he would harm the baby and she picked up the infant and ran out into the dark. She knew that she had left the shirt on rocks near the dock, rocks she used to pound the clothes clean and beat the water out of them when she was almost done, and she hurried back hoping to find it. Luckily, the rain had eased, she was able to find her way back, and was terrified that someone would have come along and stolen her husband's shirt. Then she would be in for a very bad time.

"The dock is in front of a dark, old building. She calls it a store but says it is many other things. They sell beer and whisky, gasoline for boats that come up the river, people eat and drink inside, too, so it's a kind of a restaurant, tavern, store, fueling depot, all rolled into one. Maybe even more. She thinks you can get women there, you know, men get a woman there, and maybe even drugs to smoke or use in ways that, she says, make you dreamy or wild. She's never been inside so she really doesn't know what goes on behind those doors, her husband told her he would beat her like she had never been beaten before if she ever went inside, but that doesn't stop him. He goes there all of the time, to drink, eat, and maybe to get a woman. She thinks."

Bip interrupted and angrily said spoke a few words to AcChan. "He says the husband is a – what's the right word here? – well, let me clean it up and say he thinks the husband should be taught a lesson."

I raised an eyebrow. "Do you think Bip is becoming emotionally involved here?"

"Maybe. You must admit that she is a pretty woman. I bet if we sent her down below to join your Eddie, he would be very happy with the choice. They would make a fine looking couple."

"Possibly," I conceded. Actually, I knew Eddie would approve, but he would have to fight Bip for the maiden's hand. "But let's get on with what she saw. Enough about the lost laundry."

"I've got the rest of the story. It's my fault we're taking so long getting to it. I want to make certain you understand all that happened here. Let me continue." He did.

"She was walking along the edge of the riverbank trying to find the stones which served as her laundry board when she approached this building, whatever you want to call it. She had just spotted the shirt, a white spot on the rocks, and had started over to it walking cautiously because it was easy to slip into the river here and she was carrying the baby. Then she heard voices, loud voices, and a thumping noise as if someone was beating on a door. Naturally, she looked to where the sound was coming from, it seemed to be from the side of the building, and suddenly a light came on, a much brighter light than she had ever seen on any building before. In her village, they still use lanterns so this was something different. It lit up the whole area and she saw three or four men, they seemed to be the ones making the noise, and they were dragging another one, one who didn't seem to want to go inside. But they got the door open and when he still didn't want to go, the big man, she calls him an American, took a fist and hit him, once or twice, she's not sure, and then they dragged or carried the poor man inside, swearing and shouting as they did so, the door slammed shut and the light went out, and she saw and heard nothing more."

"What did she do then?"

"Grabbed the shirt and ran home with her baby. Thank God, she says, the baby never woke up despite the wind, rain, and noise because if the baby had cried, they would have seen her and maybe beat her too."

"Thank God, she said? God, not Buddha?"

AcChan solemnly explained. "Missionaries found many of these lonely villages fifty years ago. She's a Christian."

That explained that. "Then what did she do?"

He looked at me curiously. "What do you mean, then what?"

"What did she do when she got home? I presume she went home. Did she tell her husband, or call the police, or tell anyone at all? Did she go back the next day to see what she could find? Did she tell anyone at all about what she had seen?"

Bip put my questions to her and this time, while he was talking, she watched my face closely. Was she seeking approval, fearing to find disapproval there? Had there been something in my tone of voice that had threatened her? She was a very pretty girl, just as AcChan had said. There was a fading but still noticeable yellow-purple discoloration along the jaw line on the left side of the pretty face. Her husband had left her something to remember him by.

"No, she never told anyone," AcChan reported. "As a matter of fact, when she ran back into the house, her husband hit her again because she had dragged the shirt in her hurry and it was muddy. The baby started to cry and he hit her, ordering her to make the child stop. Noise, especially the baby crying, bothered him. And she had to wash the dirty shirt again because he needed it in the morning. So she never went back, never told anyone, until now. About the police, you must be joking. What police? Up there, the only law that counts is the law you make for yourself. Usually with a gun. Your Eddie might feel right at home across the Mekong. He could be the law if he had a gun. Either him or a local war lord. Most people would prefer Eddie."

"Why did he need his shirt? A business meeting?"

AcChan beamed appreciatively. "You ask very interesting questions, Doctor. Yes, why would a man living in this kind of village need his white shirt? A festival? A date? A party? Or as you suggested, a business meeting? Let me ask."

Surprisingly, it could have been a meeting. He delayed his departure for a day because the shirt hadn't dried, but then packed it and left, as he did once or twice every month, for a journey up the river, where she thought he cut mahogany, smuggled across one border from Burma, and destined for another, into Thailand where it would be made into fine furniture and works of art. "Most men don't wear white shirts while sawing logs," I pointed out.

AcChan agreed. "That's true. At least, I don't know any. Maybe he does other things, too. Maybe, knowing the area we're talking about, he may have some connection to a crop grown in a field like that one out there," and he waved his arm in an arc to include the valley filled with red blossoms." After he had left the village, she put together a few belongings, wrapped up the baby in a backboard, slung it over her shoulder, and took off. She crossed the Mekong River after a long walk, and finally, incredible as it seems, after a journey of 250 miles, mostly in jungle and some of it on foot, she came here. Once in Thailand, she was able to ride a bus and someone brought her to the base of the mountain in a truck. She walked up and here she is."

"When did all of this happen?"

"She's not certain, but she thinks it was about two weeks ago. She lost track of time in the jungle."

Two weeks ago was about the time that Ken Green, according to Chamburon, had been in Chiang Mai.

We walked back to the Land Rover, leaving Bip and Simi Si alone for a moment. "Why did she think the man was an American?" I asked.

"Another good question, Doctor. I was afraid you were slipping. She called him an American because he looked like one, she said, and because he talked like you. Spoke English."

"Not German?" I wondered.

"No, not German. Just English. He even swore in English. Of course, you have to understand that Simi Si doesn't speak either language. I don't know if we can accept what she said about language as the gospel truth. And she couldn't identify him from your pictures either. Bip showed them to her and she says it was too dark, she was too frightened. Just doesn't know."

Eddie was standing no more than 200 feet from where we had left him. He hadn't purchased a thing. The piglets, however, had impressed him, and that seemed to be what he had been watching rather than looking for Pan Unionists. He was impressed by how nimble they were, how they were fond of darting between the feet of tourists and natives alike while chasing one another, and then announced, "the only other interesting thing I saw while you were gone was the drug dealer."

AcChan had been lagging behind, waiting for Bip, but he suddenly took an interest in our conversation. "What did you see?"

"Over there, by the blue pickup with the canvas top, see it? See the guy fifty feet to the left standing there with a duffel bag? With the fatigue pants and the funny cap? He's been talking to the truck driver, the one that brought up half a dozen tourists a while ago, and he slipped him something. My guess is it was money and he wants a ride back down the mountain – him and his duffel bag."

I saw who he was referring to. "Why do you assume that he's peddling dope or carrying dope?"

"That's the way guys in our parking lot act when they're peddling dope. Sneaky. Slipping money to one another. Making deals. Like those two."

I was mildly shocked. Not about these two guys, as he called them, on a mountain in Thailand, but about his bald assertion that something similar was going on in our parking lot. Just outside our door, a few blocks down the street from the University, in the heart of America, things like this were going on? Sure, it's the culture.

Without being obvious about it, AcChan took a long look at the man with the duffel bag and then turned away to face me, his back to the man under suspicion. "He's probably right. The Thai government knows all about the poppy crop and what it's used for so the area is heavily patrolled by the Border Rangers and military. They watch the jungle trails but much of the raw opium is moved by helicopter or taken down with loads of tourists. The tourist trade is important to the economy, so many of these trucks go up and down the mountain without being stopped more than once or twice a year.

The drivers add an extra passenger for the downward portion of the journey, throw on a duffel bag of raw material, and make a nice little profit."

As we watched, the duffel bag was casually stuffed under one of the passenger benches along one wall of the covered back, the passengers climbed aboard, among them the khaki clad man who sat on the tailboard, feet dangling, ready to leap off in an instant at the first sign of trouble. We followed them at a distance of a hundred yards or so, and because there was no room to pass on the twisting road, we were still there just before reaching the first military checkpoint midway between a popular wat and the mountain top. The leading truck slowed, the newest passenger leaped off, removed his duffel bag and both disappeared into the underbrush by the side of the road. The red bereted soldiers waved the tourist vehicle through, took one look at us, and ordered everyone out of the car. They lifted the hood, crawled underneath with long flashlights on poles and checked the springs, exhaust system, and shock absorbers. They removed the seats and inspected them one by one, peered into the glove compartment, map case, and ash tray. Ran a finger around the cup holders, lay flat under the steering wheel and looked under the dashboard, tapped the gas tank, checked the oil and removed the radiator cap. Finally, in a move born of desperation, the young officer in command had the spare tire pulled and the air let out, before accepting defeat and saying, "You may go."

AcChan, calmly standing by during the search, paid them a compliment. "A diligent and thorough search, Lieutenant. Very well done. Thank you."

Once we had resumed the journey, I dared breathe once again. I had been worried that they might search for guns. Apparently the thought never entered their minds.

In the wat parking lot, we saw the pickup and the duffel bag again. The driver and extra passenger were saying good-bye, once again something exchanging hands.

AcChan saw the look on my face and anticipated my question. "He walked around the road block and they picked him up on the other side. Watch, now. He'll put the merchandise into the trunk of another vehicle."

Less than two minutes later, he did. A green Toyota pulled into the parking lot, the driver walked into a shop across from the wat, and the extra passenger waited a moment longer and then casually walked past the car, took out a key, opened the trunk, placed the duffel bag inside, and slammed it solidly before leaving. Five minutes later, the driver returned, carrying a bottle of Pepsi, got back behind the wheel, and drove away.

"Can you remember what those men look like?" AcChan inquired.

"Possibly. But why should I? I don't plan on doing business with either of them."

"Maybe not," he said. "But your associates do. They do a lot of business with them."

"Which associates?" I asked, although I had a feeling I knew.

"You remember what McLemore told you about Bath and Fantus? How they are frequent visitors? Well, those two men you just saw have been in the welcoming committee on more than one occasion. The one with the Toyota, especially. He often drives for them. The other one, his name is Burun by the way, often meets them at the airport. Carries their luggage. In between, he practices by carrying duffel bags."

"OK. I'll try to remember what they look like," I told him. And then I asked a question that didn't need to be asked. "What do you suppose they get together for?"

AcChan stared straight ahead before answering. "Makes you wonder, doesn't it?"

It was a question I should have asked Fantus when we got back to the hotel. It would have been easy as the three of them, Bath, Fantus, and Magellan, were all waiting in my room at the President. Bath, in particular, had a strained expression on his face, one you might find on a man who has just spent a fortune to recarpet the living room only to find that his dog has peed on it.

"We waited for you at the Royal Orchid and you never showed up for breakfast. Now here you are sneaking into a hotel room hours later. I suppose you have an explanation for all of this?"

What I needed was a shower to wash off the dust of the trip. I didn't need Bath crying all over the room. "May I correct something you just said? You said sneaking into a room. We did not sneak into a room. We used our key. You, on the other hand, did sneak into our room. Where's a policeman when you need him? Eddie go call a policeman."

Eddie started towards the door and I am reasonably certain that he was on his way to do just what I had instructed him to do, but Bath held up a hand and said, "Hold it. Let's not be hasty. What I want to know is where have you been?"

"All right, Eddie. Give them a minute or two. After all, they didn't kick down the door this time so perhaps this is a friendly call."

Perhaps. It was difficult to visualize Bath and Fantus visiting Chiang Mai on a regular basis and consorting with men who I assumed to be dealing in illicit drugs. I had nothing to go by other than AcChan's assertion that this was so, backed up by McLemore's information. Why wasn't that enough? Because no matter how shady the Pan Union bunch might seem, they did represent our government, at some level, and the General still maintained close ties with the organization. That didn't mean they were clean, but I still wasn't ready to accept that they weren't. In the back of my mind was the certain knowledge that I could never trust Fantus. Bath was no better. I looked at the third member of the delegation and pondered Magellan's role. If he had one.

I laid it out for them as simply as I could. Might just as well shake the tree and see what falls out, I decided. "We went up into the mountains looking for Lee Duc Than and Ken Green."

Bath reacted at once, demanding, "Are you telling me that the man in the hospital isn't Lee Duc Than?" He asked the question, but I didn't get the impression that it came as any surprise.

"That's correct. I'm 99% certain that the man is not Lee Duc Than." I didn't have to tell him that my records showed that I had never seen a Lee Duc Than in the first place. But for the moment, that was irrelevant. The man in the hospital was someone else.

"His name is Co Phan," I told them. "He's Vietnamese and I have no idea why he was using someone else's name. Perhaps when he's feeling better, he will be able to shed some light on that. For now, we'll just have to wait."

I didn't tell them about the tuberculosis. Let them think the man still had leprosy. They were less likely to bother him.

Fantus turned suddenly on Magellan. "Fred, you've done a sorry assed job on this whole situation. You're the one who did all of the negotiating with Chamburon and led us into this mess in the first place. How do you explain this? You heard what Osten just said. What about it?"

Like Bath, Magellan hadn't seemed surprised at my revelation either. For that matter, all three of them could have been auditioning for a role in Disbrow's little theater group. Fantus was all bombast and noise, but was he really surprised? I didn't think so. Had everyone but me known who the man was, and if so, why the charade? Why wait for me to announce, hey, folks, we don't have a Lee Duc Than, we have a Co Phan? So, what were we planning for an encore?

I couldn't see what the argument was all about. If someone had called and offered me a tantalizing tale of intrigue and adventure, not to mention the possibility of being a hero, wouldn't I have been taken in just as badly as Fred? Wouldn't we all? Wasn't it conceivable that that's why I was here? That I had been hoodwinked, too?

They stopped arguing as soon as I told them I was going to go into Laos with AcChan. "Why?" Fantus asked. "Why him and why Laos?"

"To do what we have to do. Find Lee Duc Than and Ken Green. Nothing has changed regarding those two, has it? But now we have a lead that we didn't have before. Chamburon says Green was one of the men involved in the confrontation at the hospital. Now we have reason to believe he was seen again in Laos by at least one more witness. It's obvious that if the trail leads to Laos, we can't waste our time sitting around here. That's the why Laos. The why AcChan is easy. He knows Laos. Has traveled it and knows his way around. We need him."

Ignoring AcChan for a moment, Fantus seemed more interested in the witness. "Who gave you this new information?"

"That's confidential, Alex. I promised to not reveal any names right now. That was a precondition for the meeting. Let me just say that the information seems reliable. It has to be checked out. That's why we need AcChan. He has contacts where we need them."

"Before you go running around on anything like that, tell me where we fit in," Bath demanded. "After all, this is a joint operation and we're paying for it. Which reminds me. Where in the hell did you get the authority to have the leprosarium bill us for Co Phan's treatment? They sent a bill to the embassy marked for my attention and I'm catching plenty of heat over that, I can tell you."

Good for the hospital. They were doing just as I recommended. "Look, Bath, we came over here with the understanding that I would try to find and treat people who claimed to need medical care. Specifically, one Lee Duc Than. Now I'm reasonably certain that this man isn't Lee Duc Than but none of us know why he claimed he was. Until we know that, we don't know what this is all about. So we can't let him die. He has to be treated. The treatment he needs costs money and we'll pay. That's the deal. After all, this is Thailand, not the United States. We're getting a bargain. The hospital bill is probably less than a tenth of what it would be back in New York. Let's not argue over the bill, shall we? If you don't want to pay, then I'm going back home. I have plenty to do and finding a sick man without being able to treat him doesn't make sense to me. So either we pay the bills as they come due or I'll catch the next flight home. I'm not going to be responsible for helping you find a man, watching as you use him for your own ends, and then leave him lying in some decaying rat hole." It was an empty threat, but it rang true.

In the silence following my impassioned declaration, I could hear Magellan wheezing once again. Finally Bath held up a placatory hand and said, "Don't get so excited. I don't understand why you're so excited. You're just like the financial officer at the embassy. He was all excited, too. But he owes me one, so I'll get it approved. Now just calm down and tell me about the rest. Where do you go, who's going, and how?"

Now I knew one thing for certain. They didn't want me going home yet.

"Eddie and I will cross the border and go into Laos. We're not certain where we have to go. AcChan is still working on that. Naturally, he'll be going along with some of his men."

Bath asked, "Where's Naroogian? Get him in here." He wasn't far away as he was in the room five seconds after Magellan went into the hall looking for him. "Avram, what about this AcChan? You've looked into his background. What can you tell us about him?"

"He's a mercenary. Hires out to the best bidder. That's the word we pick up all over. Has excellent cover because he pretends to be a legitimate businessman." Naroogian seemed confident of the accuracy of his facts.

"And he's expensive," added Bath, making it likely that this was not the first time he and Naroogian had discussed AcChan.

"Very expensive," agreed Naroogian.

They both paused when I asked, "Is he any good?"

Reluctantly, Naroogian admitted, "They say he's effective at what he does. But they say he's expensive."

"If he's good at what he does," I said, "he should be expensive. Why hire cheap mercenaries when so much is at stake? Anyway, I've made a commitment to him. We've signed him on."

"You've hired him? Already, without consultation?" Bath was dumbfounded.

"Like I said. We need him. He's given me a budget to work with and I guess you'll need to get this through your financial man right away. Hope he owes you more than one because otherwise you're going to owe him. The price covers it all, even the helicopter."

Bath looked surprised. "You're going in on a helicopter?"

"No, not in. Out. We'll need to be lifted out by helicopter. Think that can be arranged?" The question was directed to Fantus, the man with the almost perfect record of never coming back to pick up anyone needing a lift. He didn't react at all.

Bath was more concerned about the total cost than the helicopter. They were a lot alike in that respect, Bath and Burrows. Only in that one respect. I could see no other likenesses at all. "Are you trying to tell me that you have committed us to pay for this mercenary and his crew to go into Laos with you, complete with a helicopter? Is that what you're saying?"

"That's what I'm saying. AcChan and about eight to ten men, and all of the equipment that he feels we need. Plus the helicopter. Hope you can find one." From what McLemore had told me, I didn't think that would be a problem. Just in case, though, I added one more stipulation. "Make sure it's a big one. Big enough to carry twenty people. If we take in a dozen, and then find Lee Duc Than and Ken Green, it's obvious we need that much room. Looks like you'll need an old Huey war horse, something like that."

The idea of a private airlift seemed to appeal to Bath. "I can get a helicopter. Don't worry about that. Some people I know owe me. Isn't that right, Alex? We can get a chopper?"

"I'll work on it," he promised.

"Because this is a joint operation, as you keep reminding me, I suppose you'll be coming along."

He didn't keep me waiting for a decision. "No," he answered at once, "I'll be needed back here to plan and supervise. I shouldn't get too far from base."

"Then who do you suggest we take?"

He didn't even look at Fantus before replying and, needless to say, Alex didn't volunteer. Clearly, he wasn't going. Apparently this decision was going to take a little while to make, and in the meantime, Bath returned to the money. "How much is this going to cost us? What did you promise him?"

"I didn't promise him a thing. He quoted a price for eight men, weapons, equipment such as food, uniforms, boots, medical supplies, all of the things he thinks we need based upon his experience. For one week. He says a week will be enough time. He says either we do it in a week or we won't get it done at all. After that, he expects the Laotian military, the Pathet Lao or some local war lord will be climbing all over our butts and we will be lucky to get home at all."

"And that will cost – what?" Bath asked, curious about the cost of hiring and equipping a small army.

"A total of $74,382.88, American."

He gasped. Even Fantus blanched. Naroogian, on the other hand, seemed unsurprised. Perhaps being in security, he appreciated how expensive things like this could be.

"You can't be serious. Over seventy four thousand dollars? How did he come up with the odd amount – the 88 cents?"

"Bath, I have no idea. I told him what we wanted to do and as a businessman, he sat down and came up with that figure." That was not strictly true. I had tacked on the 88 cents just for the hell of it.

"And there was one other condition. Payment, in full, is to be made in advance. He was absolutely firm about that. So you'll need to talk to the financial man right away."

He stalled. "Osten, what's your opinion? Will we find Lee Duc Than? If we spend this much money, do you think we'll even find him?"

"If I didn't think we could find him, I wouldn't be preparing to spend a week of my time looking. Yes, I think we can find him." In fact, I didn't care about finding him. I was only looking for Ken Green. Lee Duc Than was of little interest to me. I added, "If there is anyone out here who can find him, I suspect that it is AcChan."

He made his decision. "Take Magellan, Naroogian, Dirkens and Disbrow with you. Naroogian will be my eyes and ears and Fred is good at communications." He didn't say why he was sending Dirkens and Disbrow. I had my own idea about that.

"About the money . . . ?" I asked, letting the question finish itself.

The money no longer seemed to be a problem.

"I'll arrange to have the money paid to AcChan in the morning. I'll set it up with Lothar Bray at the embassy. He owes me."

Everyone, it seemed, owed Bath. For what? Meanwhile, who did he owe?

At any rate, with the money problems out of the way, Bath was eager to be moving on and he sent Fantus off on one errand, held a whispered conversation with Naroogian, then sent everyone out of the room before asking me, "Do you trust this mercenary? AcChan. Do you trust him?"

I didn't know the answer to that. I didn't know because I really knew very little about the man. He had been a name until two days ago, referred to me by the General, and his story of serving with American forces in Vietnam was credible. The little I had seen of him since had been favorable. He seemed to know what he was doing but there were many unanswered questions. I knew that. Once we crossed the Mekong into Laos, we would be in his hands. Would I rather have him with me than Fantus? Bath? Magellan? The answer was a resounding yes. What about Naroogian? The verdict was still out, but he was Bath's man. A cautious vote for AcChan. I would prefer to take the field one more time with the General or Broward, than any of them, but they were too old and had remained behind. They had sent me in their place. And quite frankly, I was too old. Did I trust AcChan? I had no choice.

"I trust him," I answered.

"Do you trust him with your life and my men's lives?" Bath said dramatically.

Did I? I gave it more thought, answered, "I trust him." Up to a point. I didn't trust anyone completely. Maybe Eddie. No one else.

Bath persisted. "Has he ever worked for the DEA, for the Thai government, our government?"

The DEA question was an interesting one, wasn't it? I didn't think so, but he did have an acquaintance in the DEA. The red headed McLemore. About the rest, I couldn't say. Too many unknowns. Even I realized that, but Bath was fishing. Clearly, he was fishing.

"With your connections at the embassy, you should be able to find out things like that." I wondered why he hadn't already used his connections to find out everything there was to know about AcChan. Or had he tried and come up empty? "Meanwhile, I'll talk to a couple of my sources and see what I can come up with."

"What sources?" he wanted to know. My having sources made him nervous.

"Look, you have your contacts. I have mine. Let's see if we can come up with anything. Meanwhile, send him the money so we can get moving. We're wasting time."

"So you won't tell me who you're going to talk to?" he decided, more worried now than he had been before. I ignored him and he left. That left me with only one problem. I really didn't have anyone to talk to.

So I called the General. This time I was lucky. Montgomery picked up the phone on the first ring, which suggested that he had been standing by expecting a call from someone else, but he had the good manners to sound pleased when he heard my voice, whispered to the General, 'It's Osten,' and handed the phone to Jordan Green.

He sounded exactly like the man who had inspired soldiers in combat, more like his old self than he had been in several years. His voice was crisp, sharp, clear, and authoritative. I was ready to take back what I had been thinking about him being too old for this new campaign. If he had told me to take that hill, any hill, right now, I would have done it. "This you, Mike?" he barked. It had to be Kendra. That had to be why he sounded so upbeat.

"Mike, you wouldn't believe it. Whatever that damn medicine is that they're feeding her, Bertinoldi told you what it was, didn't he?, well whatever it is, it seems to be working. She's looking better, gaining weight, has color back in her face. Mike, she's looking like her old self. God, man, I wish you were here to see her."

He sounded so excited, I wanted to jump on a plane and fly home to see her. In the back of my mind, I kept hearing Bertinoldi saying the same thing about Kendra, but I also kept hearing him say that it might be a temporary reprieve. Then suddenly, the General himself put things back into perspective. "What about her damn brother? Found him yet?" Too many damns. He'd been drinking.

He had been doing that lately, especially when under stress, and it was a habit he had acquired since retirement. He had rarely touched liquor in any form in his younger days. And never while wearing the uniform.

Finding Ken Green, not going home, was still the top item on the agenda. Mine and Jordan Green's.

While I had him on the line, I took the opportunity to ask about AcChan. My instincts said to trust him but my mind said, 'Why?'

"You said he was in the army," I reminded the General. "Whose? Ours or someone else's?"

Green paused while thinking about it. "I'm not sure if he was ever in our army. He was an auxiliary, a hill tribesman recruited by the Special Forces like lots of others. Meo, I think, but we signed up several different groups over the years – Karens, Lisu, Nungs, as well as Meo. Most of them made good soldiers and let's face it, they worked cheap. After we left the battlefield in disgrace," Green had never accepted the fact that we hadn't won a clear cut victory in the rice paddies, jungle, and hills of Vietnam, "many of them fled to Thailand. They didn't have much choice if they were to escape the vengeance of the Viet Cong and North Vietnamese, and once they arrived in Thailand, some joined the Thai army. AcChan, I think, became a paratrooper. The Thais loved them. They fought where they were sent unlike the peace loving Buddhists that make up the bulk of the army and won't hardly fight at all. Yeah, I think that's what Broward told me. He was a paratrooper. But I know for sure that they were together for a while in Vietnam."

And that checked out with what AcChan himself had told me earlier.

The General continued, "I hope you can work something out with this man, Mike. Broward says he's first class, a good soldier. Smart and tough. Broward has never given me a bum steer in all the years I've known him. He was one of the best topkicks I've ever had and if he says AcChan is a good man, then he's a good man. You can bet on it."

That's exactly what we were doing, I reflected. Betting on it. Betting lives on it, for that matter.

I should have asked where Broward was, where he was living right now. But I didn't. It didn't seem important at the time.

Abruptly, Green interrupted himself in mid-sentence, saying, "Hold for a second, will you Mike? I have another call coming in." Then silence until Montgomery came back on and said, "Dr. Osten, the General has been called to another phone and wonders if you could call back tomorrow at about this same time?"

I told him the problem. In 24 hours, I was hoping to be across the Mekong river into Laos but he still didn't put the General back on the line, coolly informing me, "I'll certainly tell him that, Doctor, as soon as he is free." And then he, too, was gone. I stood holding the dead phone in my hand, now nothing more than a useless piece of plastic and metal, an electronic marvel gone dead, and put it back on, as they used to say, the hook. In fact, it was a modern Scandinavian design that, when placed flat on a hard surface, knocked itself out. No hook needed.

Apparently angered by my unspoken description of it as a useless piece of junk, a strident ringing shook it and I watched as it slithered along the gleaming freshly waxed table top and threatened to throw itself floorward. I saved it from self destruction by picking it up and finding Carmichael on the other end.

"Remember how you always complained that every trip out here you lost to the Union Oil guys in basketball?" he started, words tumbling out in a torrent. He sounded as happy as a clam inside a shell protected by an electronic lock, for which he had the only code. "You remember that?"

I knew what he was going to say next. Whenever Horace mentioned basketball and sounded happy at the same time, he had been in competition, and he was about to tell me that the losing streak was over. He did.

"We beat 'em, trounced 'em, as a matter of fact. Something like 94-70, maybe worse. They got so mad they walked off the court with a couple of minutes to go and left us grinning and high fiving all over the place. That should make you feel better, right? Now that you've beaten them?"

The Union Oil guys he was referring to were drillers, wildcatters, managers, men who worked on the drilling platforms out in the Gulf of Siam. They loved a good game of basketball and took on anyone who came along foolish enough to challenge them. They were known to ferry in their best players by helicopter if the challenge looked formidable, just go with whoever was ashore on leave for the average game, and when I defiantly prodded their operations manager, an old friend, into a contest, I'm sure they sent people who had no hope of ever playing against anyone else. In other words, they scraped the bottom of the barrel, which was a kindly act, as they beat us every time just the same. I didn't know who they had sent to play Harold's aggregation, but having lost, it wouldn't make it any easier for us the next time I ventured onto the court in shorts.

I didn't mean to break his mood, but I felt obliged to ask, "Who was on your team, Horace? You and who else?"

"Me, a couple of men from the lab here at the school, and Phrem rounded up several more, two Thais and a graduate student from Taiwan. Plus an Aussie that he found somewhere. Great guy. Says he played some ball in the states. College. Division III. Then there was that tall redhead shooting baskets when we got to the gym and I signed him up. German. Lot of Germans around here, you know that? He scored 18 points, grabbed a bunch of rebounds, made it easy for me to score 40 points or more. Had a great day, if I must say so. So you won and broke the curse."

It was nice of Horace to share the honors with me, but as near as I could see, I deserved none of the credit. Forty points from Carmichael, 18 points from a redheaded German, an Aussie with college experience. Where were these people when I needed them? Why couldn't Phrem recruit this caliber of talent instead of the five foot five Thais that he usually hauled in to give me a hand? So I didn't feel bad about making a point. "Did you see me out there on the floor, Horace? Do you recall?"

"On the floor? No, you weren't there. You couldn't. You were in Chiang Mai. But it's your team, you know. You always arrange the games and the Union Oil coach asked about you. Seemed disappointed when he found you couldn't be there. So it's your team. And you won."

I bet the Union Oil coach was upset when he found I wouldn't be there. Better me than Carmichael, from his perspective. I persisted. "Horace, did I get to play? Make it into the lineup and all that?"

There was a lengthy silence while Horace used his Ph.D. to ponder the matter. Tentatively, as if answering a tricky question on a pop quiz, he conceded, "No you didn't get to actually play because, like I said, you were there. Not here."

"If we have the time when I get back, can you round up this same group and schedule a return game?" I asked, hopefully.

"Oh, sure. They'll want another crack at us and they'll stack the lineup with new people. Count on it."

"Think I can crack the starting lineup? Can you replace one of your Thai or Chinese midgets and get me in there?"

Knowing that I approved the size of his annual bonus probably affected his judgment and enabled him to overlook my advanced age and limited ability, he seemed genuinely enthusiastic as he said, "No problem at all. It will be a big help to have someone on the floor that understands the game, calls the plays, and gets me the ball. That last one, getting me the ball, is the key. I laid off in the second half tonight because I figured there might be a rematch. Never showed them what I could do inside. If I have to, I can score 80 points without hardly breaking a sweat."

I suspected that he could. Made me eager to get back to Bangkok and then I realized that when I started thinking of Bangkok, I was thinking of JoElle, not basketball. Possibly I was finally getting my priorities in order. Which made me realize that Horace must have called about something other than a basketball score. He had. He'd heard from Howsam.

"Tony called from somewhere in Malaysia. He's excited. Says maybe old Jack stumbled onto something big. Who's old Jack, by the way, one of our people that I haven't met? Well, whatever," he went on without waiting for an answer, "he says there are huge groves of an unusual yew tree way back in the highlands, in places you'd never expect to find them. He's already sent back crates of limbs, buds, fruits, ground scrapings, just about everything you can think of. He says what's interesting is that where those trees are thickest, nothing else is growing. No underbrush, no weeds, no flowers, no fungi, no nothing. You know how the needles cover the ground in a pine forest and how quiet it is when you walk through a place like that? That's the way it is, he says. Almost spooky. Nobody cuts the trees down because they burn very poorly and the lumber is so coarse and knotty that it isn't of much use. Besides, the place is so remote that it's hard to get into and harder to haul anything out from. But he's mapping it and sending everything out to Hong Kong and the office like you told him. I called Marge and told her to expect all sorts of things in by air within 48 hours. So that's good news, don't you think?"

It was and I told him so.

"You're in contact with Diaz? No problem with communications to Hong Kong?"

"None at all," he said. "all I have to do is pick up the phone and push a few buttons, just like home. I did that a few minutes ago and that's really why I'm calling. She says the laboratory specimens you sent, the slides, show a lot of acid fast organisms. Her pathologist identified them as the tubercle bacillus. She says the patient almost certainly has tuberculosis and they should be able to confirm that when the cultures are done. Another week for that, though. Meanwhile, she says, be careful around the patient. The bugs look virulent, contagious as hell, and if he coughs in your face, you could have a real problem. She says to take every possible precaution to avoid that. Strict isolation is essential, she says."

"That's pretty much what we thought when we looked at the specimens in the hospital lab," I told him. "That it was contagious looking."

"No, that's not what she said at all. She didn't say it was contagious looking. She said it was contagious as hell. Her exact words. There's a difference."

He was right. There is a difference and I made a note to once again warn the hospital personnel to practice strict isolation to protect the staff. "OK, Horace. Thank Dr. Diaz for me and tell her I'll be in touch as soon as I get back from the trip up north. Then call the office and tell Marge to distribute the samples as soon as they come in from Howsam. I've talked to her about it and she knows what to do. Now, as for me, I'm going to be out of touch for a while. Might not have a phone nearby and we may not find it wise to use a radio so you won't hear from me. Maybe a week. Maybe ten days. We aren't sure. But I will be trying to get more laboratory specimens to you and I want you to forward them to Diaz at once. I'm counting on you to be available so don't get hurt playing basketball."

"How are you going to get lab specimens out if you can't call?"

"I'm not sure yet, but we'll find a way. There's always a way." I realized that I was being excessively optimistic, for my own benefit as much as his, because I doubted that the Laotian postal service would have a branch office where we would be going.

After I hung up, I called Bertinoldi in New York. He didn't sound nearly as enthused as the General regarding Kendra's condition. She was, he said, "holding her own, doing as well as could be expected, better than she was, but we're still hoping for improvement in the blood picture." He had used most of the medical clichés which I had frequently resorted to myself when I was trying to avoid telling the full story to the worried parent, family member or interested others, the full story often being the patient really wasn't doing well at all. Evasive, that's what he was being. Evasive. Or was it just my imagination?

I called JoElle and she was still awake, listening to music, she said. Her voice floated softly across the miles and I could visualize her smile as I told her of Carmichael's big win on the basketball court. "It wasn't in the morning Bangkok Post," she said. "At least, I don't think it was. All that was there was a football score from your American playoffs. What you call football, although the rest of the world thinks football is something else."

And as she mentioned football, I thought of field goals and that led me to goal posts, and that gave me an idea how to get laboratory specimens back to Horace. I would have to check it out with AcChan. That lifted a load from my weary shoulders, brought a smile to my face, and when we said good night, I knew that if I were back in Bangkok, I wouldn't be playing basketball with Horace. Not this night. I'd be listening to music.

But before that, there was still work to do in Chiang Mai.

# 12

Eddie was fascinated by the gadget Magellan was fumbling with the next morning. By fumbling I mean twisting one of several dials, then another, clicking small switches and pushing a half dozen black buttons, all the while wearing a bemused expression of puzzlement. Nothing happened and he continued to turn dials and push buttons in frustration. What appeared to be a stubby antenna protruded from one end of the foot square black box while at the other end a concave plastic saucer, six inches in diameter with four silver concentric circles, each one a little larger than the other, radiated from the center to the edge. That part of the apparatus resembled the front burner on an old electric stove, the dials and buttons reminded me of parts resurrected from an old food blender, the kind touted on the early black and white television programs in the 1950's. Despite its appearance, I suspected it had something to do with communications, Fred's specialty, remember?

He was sitting on the terrace in bright sunshine, a bowl of untouched breakfast oatmeal next to a half empty glass of orange juice on the table, with Eddie an attentive audience of one. Eddie's plate was empty and he went back for seconds of scrambled eggs, bacon, hashed browns, toast thickly lathered with butter, and a bagel with cream cheese. An all-American all-cholesterol type of breakfast. He always ate the truck driver's special and I'd seen the laboratory reports from his pre-employment physical examination. Blood pressure 108/68 and cholesterol 176. Disgusting. I had the waiter bring me orange juice, tea, a slice of melon, and another of pineapple. Let's just say I was watching my weight and everything else.

Magellan was still muttering to himself and turning the whatever it was over and over, tapping on it, trying every button and switch one more time. Without success. Keeping one eye on Fred, I used the other to scan the morning Post, flown up on the early flight from Bangkok. The good news was that the Pistons had hammered the Bulls, 122-90. Marge should have been happy last night, I thought, as I read that Laimbeer had scored 15 points and pulled down 12 rebounds. Make that the night before last, I corrected myself. It took that long for the news to get here. JoElle had been right, though. There was no mention of Carmichael's performance against Union Oil. As is so often the case, local sports coverage was inadequate.

I looked up as Eddie speared a sausage on his fork, used it to point to Magellan's machine, and asked, "What's that?"

While I'd been reading the paper, Eddie had apparently gone back for sausages and biscuits.

Magellan was hard pressed to come up with a name for a moment, then said, "This? It's a radio. Sort of."

"Funny looking radio. Never seen one like it. What's that round thing on the end?" this time pointing with a rolled up pancake leaking syrup. He'd gotten pancakes, too. The hotel was justly famous for its breakfast buffet. I asked for another piece of pineapple.

Moving quickly, Fred pulled the black box away just in time to avoid dripping maple syrup. Patiently, he said, "antenna." His fingers traced the circular pattern in the plastic dish, touching each of the four silver disks in turn, "This part receives the message." Grasping the stubby six inch rod on the opposite end, he pulled and extended it to a full three feet. Tapping it, he said, "This sends the message."

What Fred had was an old, very old, and almost totally outdated transmitter-receiver designed to tap into the advanced global positioning satellites that our government has thrown up to communicate with friends and agents, and to spy upon enemies and their minions. The problem was, it was obsolete. New ones were one tenth the size, ten times as powerful, and could fit into a coat pocket or small briefcase. So why did Magellan have one like this? And what was it for? So we could communicate with friendlies or for Bath and Fantus to use to find us, no matter where we went?

He flipped the POWER switch one more time and nothing happened. All of the dials remained blank, everything was as flat lined as the cardiac monitor during coronary bypass surgery. None of the red, green, and amber lights scattered across the face of the instrument showed any sign of life. His hand groped for a small hammer lying nearby, as if considering the traditional American method of persuasion on a balky machine – give it a good hard rap and see what happens.

I thought of mentioning the two small objects partially hidden behind the oatmeal, but instead decided to spread strawberry preserves on a piece of toast the waiter had brought without prompting on my part. This gave Eddie the opportunity to pick them up and ask, "What are these things?"

Magellan stopped what he was doing, forgot about the hammer, put the orbital positioner on the table, folded both hands in front of him, and said, "Batteries."

"Little rascals, aren't they," said Eddie. "What are they for?"

They were little rascals. Less than the size of a regular postage stamp and not much thicker. Tiny wafers, light as a feather, made in Silicon valley by a company that layered sodium, silicon, phosphorous, cadmium, mercury, with an outer micron thin coating of nickel, the whole thing triggered by a secret catalyst fully capable of sending a signal several thousand miles, transmitting nonstop for more than a day at a time, and receiving signals from a satellite hovering far overhead, open for business 24 hours a day. What a paradox. Obsolete hardware, the most advanced technology, all in the same package. Did it work?

"Fred," I suggested, "why don't you try those batteries in place of the ones you're using and see if things work any better? Maybe the old ones are worn out." From the look on his face, I knew that Fred knew that there were no batteries in it at all.

He picked up his toy, snapped open a center panel, took both batteries from Eddie, and put them into place. As expected, there were none to remove, a point that Eddie noted at once. "Hell, man, you didn't have no batteries in there. Do you suppose that's why it wasn't working?"

Magellan pushed the POWER button once again and this time there was a sudden surge of electrodes and a flashing of lights with loud, persistent beeps audibly escaping from the machine. Two Germans having a morning beer at the next table clasped their heads as if in acute pain. "Fred, do you see that dial over there next to the red switch? Turn it to the left. Soften the beep. We don't want it that loud, do we? Sound travels far at night and we never know who'll be listening, do we. Turn it way down. To low. Very low." He did and the beep was tolerable.

One German got up and lurched to the men's room. The other pushed away his beer and tried coffee.

"It's working now," Magellan reported, proudly.

"Sure it's working now," Eddie retorted. He finished his last sausage. "But it would still be a dead duck if you hadn't of put those batteries in, right?"

Magellan didn't answer. He picked up his spoon and started eating the cold oatmeal. Eddie got tired of waiting so he finished off his last pancake and went to get more coffee. I was left to ponder the question: How good was Fred, really, at 'communications?'

AcChan, on the other hand, was much better organized. Dressed in what I could only describe as safari casual, an epauletted khaki jacket, an Australian bush hat, soft leather boots shined to a high gloss that would make any first sergeant smile appreciatively and keep the recruit from KP for weeks, and underneath, a gaudy Jim Thompson silk shirt in variegated colors of orange, green, and purple and a floral pattern that defied description, he was tilted back in a comfortable chair watching workers scurrying about the warehouse floor below, right where he had been the a day earlier. "One way glass," he confided when he saw me looking at the drapes. "I only pull them when I want to avoid distractions or for decorative effect."

Without preamble, he said, "I don't think we should fly to Chiang Rai."

The day before he had warned me, "Don't confuse Chiang Mai and Chiang Rai. Many tourists do. They're different cities. We're in Chiang Mai now. For a number of reasons, I want to jump off on this trip from Chiang Rai. It's closer to the border, we will be able to find everything we need up there, and there will be fewer prying eyes to contend with. We'll fly up."

Now he was changing the plan. "I know," he continued. "I told you we would. It's easy to do, as Thai Airways has frequent flights but those prying eyes I told you about – I got to thinking. They'll be at the airports in both cities and a group like ours, a mixture of Thais, hill tribesmen, farangs like you, me, your Mr. Chun, is going to attract attention. I'd rather not have that. The rumors about us have already brought in one visitor asking what kind of war I was going to start. I'd just as soon not have any more."

I recognized that we were a motley crew but I hadn't anticipated that we would suddenly have attracted a following. "What kind of rumors and who was the visitor?"

He didn't sound worried about either problem as he replied, "The rumors? One, that we are planning on a raid into Laos. That's what he called it. Two, that we are trying to locate a helicopter or two to pull it off. Neither of which is altogether incorrect, as you know. The visitor? An army colonel. Just asking. Friendly and polite, but asking. I've known him for years so that probably made him more friendly than if it had been a stranger."

"What did you tell him?"

"I told him it would be just a little war. Nothing serious and I promised that we wouldn't involve the Thai army in any event. He laughed, because he knows I won't involve the army, at least I never have, but just the same, I think we can assume army eyes will be watching the airports and checking on the location of helicopters the next few days. So I don't think we should fly, because army eyes are one thing. Other eyes are something else."

I was curious. "What other eyes?"

"One set is obvious. Bath and Fantus, although their own people will be with us so they shouldn't have a hard time keeping track of where we are.

And then there is Huy Thacht."

At first I thought he was saying high tech and I wondered what that had to do with our taking an airplane. "No, not high tech," he explained. "It's a name. Huy Thacht. He's a self styled warlord who considers the land across the river to be his. Actually, he's nothing more than a bandit and dealer in drugs with a band of cutthroats following him. There are dozens more like him, but he may be the most dangerous of all. We've never met, face to face, but I've seen the results of his work in numerous villages along the border. What he calls himself is irrelevant. What he is, is a murderer, as well as a disgrace to the human race."

"And he has people watching the airports?"

"He has people watching everything. That's how he stays in business. So we won't fly. We'll go by trucks. That way we'll be invisible."

Three trucks, to be exact. "They'll carry charcoal to Chiang Rai and bring back a full cargo of cotton, potatoes, and lumber. Part of the cargo going north will be us. I have trucks going out every night so no one will pay any attention to these three. We'll load everything here, depart after dark, leave town on route 105, and pick up national route 1. Here, let me show you on the map." He spread a large colored map of Thailand and Laos, our planned route already heavily marked in red crayon, across his desk, and then pushed a button, the drapes once again soundlessly covering the glass wall with a tapestry of tiny blue hummingbirds exploring the mysteries of the delicate orange and yellow blossoms of the Asian Bird of Paradise. Apparently he didn't wish to be distracted.

His finger followed the marking crayon as he continued his narrative. "See, we go southeast almost 80 kilometers until we meet Route 1 at Lampong. From there we head north, another 80-81 kilometers, to Ngao. Notice how the road twists and turns here, and it's hilly, so the trip will be slower, but our drivers are skilled and know the way so we'll be all right. The road improves after Ngao and another 50 kilometers brings us to Phayao where the road straightens out and we have an easy run into Chiang Rai. By then, it'll be morning and we won't be able to get out and wander around. Even here there are eyes. Look over here," and he pointed across the map to the Burmese border. "Just 60 kilometers away is Fang. Ever hear of it? It's a hotbed of opium smuggling. All kinds of smuggling, but drugs are the worst. Back at the end of World War II, Chinese Nationalist soldiers who had been stationed along the Burma road and in south China were pushed out of their own country by the Communists, or just chose to leave, nobody is quite sure, and they settled here. Complete with guns and officers and what you would call in your country a business plan. Governments in the area, including Thailand, weren't capable or willing to interfere, so they put the plan into effect. Raising poppies and harvesting opium and supplying the world with vast quantities of drugs. Very profitable. Local governments cut a deal. Don't bother us and we won't bother you and nothing could have satisfied the warlords more. Since then, and remember this all started over 40 years ago, they have stayed on, succeeded by a new crop of warlords when the old ones died off, and the deal wasn't a bad one except for the people who had lived here before all this started. It's been rough on them, from time to time, when they get caught in the crossfire between warring bands, but on the other hand, it's brought more money into the area than ever before so perhaps even their standard of living has improved from the world's nasty habits."

"Do you expect to run into any of these charming people?"

"When you cross the river, you always expect to encounter them. You'd rather not, but they're always around somewhere. And the one we are most likely to meet, like I said, is Huy Thacht."

I nodded. Forgetting the Burmese border, he returned to Chiang Rai. "I own a warehouse in the city. We'll drive directly to it and hole up inside. I've given the workers the day off. I think the manager told them it was in honor of the spirits of the mountains, something like that, and it may even be true as they have a lot of holidays up here in the north. At any rate, there won't be anyone around but us, and we'll provision for the trip and make our final plans. After dark, we'll get back in our trucks and take the road out of town, going 30 kilos to the village of Thoeng, turn north for another 15 kilos, and follow an unimproved road eastward, I suppose it would be more accurate to call it a trail, until we come to the Mekong. That's the border. That's where we leave the trucks and they turn around and go back. We splash across the river, on foot, arrive in Laos on the other side, move into cover before dawn, look around, find a safe place to stay for the day, and then get going after dark once more. That's when the fun starts."

He looked at me, apparently seeking approval, then asking, "How does it sound to you?"

I didn't know about the fun starting after we crossed the river but I was reasonably certain that it wasn't going to be much fun hiding under a cargo of charcoal in the back of a truck. It could be worse, I thought. The cargo could be chickens, pigs or manure.

The General said to trust the man. All right, I'd trust the man. "It looks fine," I said, rolling up the map. "But remember, the trip to the river is your show. This is your country. On the other side, we have to make joint decisions, you and I."

He didn't hesitate. "If there's time," he cautioned, "yes, we can do that, unless one of us can't act or isn't there to act. Then the other one will have to act alone."

"Why couldn't one of us act?" I asked although I was pretty sure I knew the answer to that.

Tactfully, he said, "Maybe you're in one place and I'm in another when something happens. Or maybe you get hurt or I get sick. Things like that. Then we have to act alone."

"Is that likely to happen?"

"Anything can happen. You know that."

"What if we both get sick, or hurt, as you put it, at the same time? Then what?"

"Bip. He's my second in command and will take over. I've already talked to him about it."

"Bip? He doesn't speak English. How will Naroogian and the other Americans understand what he wants them to do?"

"I was watching him and Eddie together. They seem to understand one another without words so maybe he can be the translator. Using hand signals. Bip is very good at that and Eddie seems to be picking it up. In an emergency, you'd be surprised how effective hand signals can be and they don't make any noise."

He was smiling when he said it but he was dead serious.

"I'll tell Eddie," I said, holding up the cylindrical map now secured with a rubber band around its middle. "Mind if I look this over to check times and distance?"

"Not at all. Just keep it. I've got more."

When we assembled just after dark, a dozen of us in all, everything went smoothly. Naroogian, Disbrow, and Dirkens stood together off to one side, while Magellan, clutching a black bag protecting his satellite transmitter was by himself, thirty feet away. I was wondering if he had remembered the batteries or whether he had any spares. He looked at me as if he wanted to speak, but remained silent.

Three Thais, wearing light blue trousers and matching shirts with a golden AC logo on the left sleeve and gold braid highlighting a single shirt pocket, were standing, military style, by their trucks. They were obviously our drivers. Two others, wearing the same matching blue uniforms without braid on the pockets, were carrying double barreled shotguns. When AcChan arrived moments later, he was carrying a FN89 NATO assault rifle with a fully automatic 28 shot clip in place and three more attached to his bush jacket where he could get at them in a hurry. I knew a skilled rifleman could reload in less than one second which meant AcChan, all by himself, was a small army. He was wearing no uniform and no logo, either, unless you wanted to describe the black and gray camouflage striping as a uniform. Maybe it was, for his line of work.

He had Eddie, Magellan, and me get in the first truck, the one where he was riding up front. Naroogian, Disbrow, and Dirkens climbed into the second while the third was occupied by just its driver and shotgun wielding guard. We found plenty of space behind fifty pound bags of charcoal and with the canvas tarp stretched across the top, it was a relatively snug, although somewhat dusty, little hideaway. To talk to AcChan, we simply had to rap on the window between us and the cab and he could open it for a chat. "There's food and water in those containers and if you need to relieve yourselves along the way, use the empty tin cans. Don't look out from under the canvas. Your pale faces can be seen for miles. We won't be stopping between here and my warehouse in Chiang Rai so try to settle down and get some sleep. Don't worry about trouble along the way. We can handle it," he said, raising his rifle to make the point.

"What about the army? What about the colonel who was asking questions?"

"He went away happy. Smiling."

"What did it cost you?"

He wasn't offended by the question. "Money, of course. Not much. You can still buy a colonel reasonably. Generals are much more expensive. It's all in the cost of doing business."

"Now that you've given him money, won't he be even more convinced that you are up to something, how should I put it, illegal? Won't he want to watch more closely?"

"Not at all. He wished me a safe and happy journey and told me he was going to be home tonight watching kick boxing on television. Big championship match. Said we won't even have to worry about traffic tickets." He laughed as he said it, as if we didn't have a worry in the world.

"Why do you say that?" I asked, suspecting that traffic enforcement wasn't considered a high priority in Thailand, especially up here in the north.

"As he was counting the bahts in the envelope I gave him, he assured me that none of his men would even see the trucks with my logo on tonight. If you can't see them, you can't stop them, and look, right here on the door, on the hood, on the canvas sides, and on the tailgate, see that gold AC? My logo. All over the place. So the trucks are invisible and the best part of it is that the colonel's men handle all of the roads from here to the border."

It sounded as if we would indeed be invisible, and so it seemed as the night went on. Several military vehicles passed us as we headed east and even more went by after we turned north towards Chiang Rai. None of them showed the slightest interest in us. In fact, several times our drivers exchanged waves with smiling paratroopers and everyone seemed to be on friendly terms. So we weren't exactly invisible, but no one seemed to care what we were doing. Which was fine with me.

My concern soon centered around the swaying stacks of charcoal that surrounded us. Would a sudden stop bring them tumbling down upon us? And even if that didn't happen, would we choke to death on the gritty dust that swirled about the rear of the truck, about one of out five bags having broken, allowing the pulverized contents to escape into our small cubbyhole? One thing I knew we wouldn't have to worry about from then on was that our pale faces could be seen if we peeked out from under the canvas. Even without a mirror, just feeling my face with my fingers, I could tell that I had become as black as the night outside. Eddie complained of his eyes itching. Magellan couldn't stop sneezing. I felt in need of a shower.

But we were vastly more fortunate than Dirkens, Disbrow, and Naroogian. At the last minute, AcChan, ever the businessman, had filled an order for 72 breeding chickens and a monstrous pile of caged hens and a single rooster, leaking feathers and waste, and squawking with every turn and bump in the road, threatened their environment with aural and air pollution through the night. They envied us the luxury of nothing worse than coal dust in the lead truck.

The third truck was indeed carrying pigs. Six pigs. Plus two of AcChan's men. None of us envied them at all.

It wasn't the best of roads and the journey was slow, and sometimes tortuous. We encountered stretches that made mother's old fashioned washboard look pebble smooth, we splashed through waterlogged crossings without bridges, and zigzagged back and forth across twisting mountain roads with a switchback every quarter mile. And then, shortly after I had finally dozed off, I suddenly came awake with a start as the horns of all three trucks erupted, the sound as loud as the tornado sirens mounted at home just outside the front entrance of the research building. I lifted the canvas and stared out into the darkness, expecting to see a full fledged assault on our convoy. Eddie appeared alongside me, a revolver in his hand. I looked to the right and then to the left and there wasn't a person to be seen, not a light in evidence and then, as suddenly as they had started, the horns went silent. The welcome sound of transmissions being engaged meant we were about to move again but didn't stop me from rapping on the window just above my head and it promptly opened.

"What the hell was the noise?" I asked AcChan, his face dimly outlined by the dashboard lights.

"The horns?"

"Yes, the horns. What other noise was there? I thought we were supposed to be invisible. Invisible people don't stop in the middle of the road and make that much noise in my country."

AcChan gestured to the left side of the road. "See those two peaks over there? You can see them against the skyline. Lots of phis living there. Spirits. Truck drivers always stop here and pay respects to the spirits. It's good form, as the British would say. It's good luck, the Thais say. Actually, there's a spirit house just off to the side of the road and one of the drivers hurried over with some rice for the spirits' breakfast. If they're happy, those spirits, they can make us happy."

"I can understand the rice, if the spirits get hungry. But don't they sleep? Do they really want horns blaring at them all night long?"

"Sleep?" He was serious and considered his response carefully. "I've never thought about spirits sleeping. I've always assumed that whenever I needed them, they would be there. I think they're a lot like your angels. Always on duty so they stay awake just in case you call."

"Anymore spirits expecting us to drop by tonight?" I asked, "Or will we be able to go nonstop from here?"

He asked the driver something and then said, "Couple more places up ahead where we leave rice, but no more horns. Maybe you can get some sleep now."

"Yeah, we'll try," I said and the window closed as soundlessly as it had opened.

I punched a broken charcoal sack into shape and stuck it under my head as a semisoft pillow. Trying to ignore the sharp edges of briquettes pushing against my neck and scalp, I made another attempt to fall asleep. Eddie's voice from the darkness delayed the process. "You know, what he said was interesting. I never thought about angels sleeping before. I hardly ever thought of angels at all before, matter of fact. Do you think angels sleep?"

I opened one eye but wasn't sure whether the shadow I was seeing on the other side of the truck was Eddie or just a fallen charcoal sack. I talked to it anyway. "I'm not sure whether angels sleep or not, Eddie. But I do. I'm going to try right now."

I was still trying when he asked, "What about God. Do you think He ever sleeps?"

Now he had me thinking about it. Just like AcChan, when I needed to speak to God, I had always assumed that He would be there, regardless of the time of day or night. Maybe that was unrealistic, but it was equally unrealistic to think of having to make an appointment with a deity. After a while, I came up with a temporary solution at least. "Maybe they work out a call system like we did in the hospital. Some of the angels are awake while others rest and take turns later. Maybe eight hours on and sixteen off, something like that. And if God is asleep when someone needs Him, the angel on call evaluates the problem and makes a decision about calling the Boss. That might be how they do it."

He was silent for a moment and then said, "That could work."

I was hoping he wouldn't ask whether God might be of another gender and, while worrying about an answer to that one, I fell asleep. I woke up later, suddenly, without cause, and glanced at my luminous wristwatch dial. It was after three A.M. and Eddie was snoring softly right where I had thought him to be. Magellan was invisible in the dark. I stretched and looked into the cab through the closed window where I saw AcChan, wide awake, his rifle at his side, looking straight ahead, as our headlights drilled a tunnel through the inky blackness, fifty to a hundred feet at a time.

The warehouse in Chiang Rai was a miniature arsenal. If AcChan had been surprised to discover that Harry Kee had found a weapon for Eddie, Harry Kee would have been astonished at AcChan's inventory of modern weaponry. Assault rifles, machine pistols, light machine guns, handguns of every description, grenades and grenade launchers, antitank rockets, land mines, flares, smoke and stun grenades, even mortars, with an assortment of ammunition to fit them all, were neatly arrayed on metal shelves. All were perfectly maintained, clean, gleaming with oils, carefully wrapped in felt and linen, and smelled like good weapons should – ready for use, lethal, dangerous. Field packs, already provisioned with rations, water, medical supplies, high caloric wafers and gum drops, plus large squares of Swiss chocolate, were lined against one cement block wall. Everyone changed from casual clothing to the same black and gray camouflage that AcChan was already wearing and found matching tarps and slouch hats on another rack. We donned no-skid boots with steel toes and soft leather uppers that, despite thick soles, waterproofing, and jungle readiness, were amazingly light.

Dirkens lifted one foot and said, mockingly, "Stylish. Real nice. Just what I always wanted to wear to a party."

"The party you'll be going to is being held in a jungle swamp," AcChan reminded him. "Your party shoe will have to keep your feet dry, warm, prevent you from slipping in the mud, maybe even protect your foot from falling logs. It should do even more, but unfortunately, it won't protect you completely from poisonous snakes, punji sticks, and land mines. You step on one of the poisoned sticks and it penetrates the sole, you might die. You step on a land mine, boom, there goes the boot and your foot. Both. Even the steel toe won't help then."

Dirkens took another look at his foot, as if trying to visualize what it would mean to have only one. Or none. He laced up both boots without another word.

AcChan and Bip picked out weapons for everyone; then demonstrated how they worked. The Thais needed little instruction. They seemed familiar with whatever they were handed. Dirkens and Disbrow were a different matter. It was clear that they had no desire to be here; they didn't want a weapon and they showed no interest in how the AK47's worked. They sat sullenly, children dressed in costumes for a Halloween party, not willing to get their noses wet while bobbing for apples. In disgust, AcChan turned to Naroogian, saying, "They have a choice. They either decide to help or they stay here until we get back. They're your men. Talk to them." He walked away with better things to do.

Naroogian had needed no help. He had picked up his own AK47 and checked it carefully, inspected the barrel and the firing mechanism, checked the ammunition clips, and was very much a professional in his element. He glared at the recalcitrant Pan Unionists and after a moment of silence, barked, "Pick up those damned weapons. Do it now!"

Following AcChan into another room, I looked back and saw that they had obeyed the order and Naroogian was busily explaining how the rifles worked. Basic training.

A wooden crate in the other room occupied our attention for the next few minutes before AcChan spun on me and said, "What about you? What kind of weapon are you going to carry?"

I didn't think it was the right time to make some comment about the Geneva Convention mandating that physicians didn't carry weapons into combat. AcChan would brush that aside as unworthy of comment, which it was. After all, the Germans started that nicety of warfare on the road to extinction in the death camps of World War II; and the Japanese certainly didn't seem to be bothered by any of its provisions when they orchestrated the Bataan Death March, beheaded captured American pilots or brutally worked thousands of Allied POW's to death building the infamous bridge over the River Kwai at a site not far from where we were at that moment. And as you know, I carried a weapon with me in the Congo, so I was going to do no less in the unfriendly terrain AcChan promised we would find across the Mekong. I chose a Glock. German, fifteen shot clip, three extra clips. "That should keep trouble at bay until we can come to help you." I noticed that he didn't say, 'if you get in trouble.' The way he said it, the 'until we can come to help you,' sounded as if he was certain we would encounter trouble.

He showed me how to use the Glock. Later, when no one was looking, I walked back and renewed my acquaintance with the AK47 and an Israeli Galil as well. We'd met in the reserves some years earlier.

Eddie and I unpacked the large, specially ordered crate and I read the manufacturer's operating manual taped to its stainless steel side. It seemed easy enough to use and we repacked the machine and its supplies, this time encasing it in light polystyrene foam rather than the much heavier wood, inserted medical supplies that I might need, a guess, really, because I wasn't sure what I would need them for, added loaded film cassettes, sterile tubing, and a dozen soft plastic liters of intravenous fluids, and we had a traveling medical clinic ready for the road. Almost. As further protection against rough handling and the elements, we wrapped everything with a hundred yards of tight waterproofing, strapped it, attached long, sturdy aluminum poles along each side extending 30 inches both in front and back, secured them, and stood back to look at what we had created. It resembled a Pharaoh's traveling chair from Egyptian antiquity, only in place of an exalted ruler, our litter bearers would be carrying a piece of modern technology that would enable us to diagnose and treat, I hoped, ailments that we still had not confirmed but were nonetheless likely to be confronted.

"What we need now," I said, "is a couple of strong people, very strong ones, to carry this."

"What about Dirkens and Disbrow?" Eddie suggested. "They don't want to do anything else."

"Mr. Chun, Eddie," AcChan said, laughing, "you have an interesting sense of humor. I doubt if those two could lift it off the ground."

I stepped between the aluminum handles and tried to lift one end. It didn't budge. AcChan watched as I tried it one more time, only to give up in defeat. "It's heavy," I reported.

"Don't worry about it," he said reassuringly. "I've hired the men to lift it. They'll get it done."

Aside from the guard that AcChan had posted at the front door and another by the telephones, ("no phone calls," he had warned everyone, "they could be traced"), everyone had moved to another room and laid down on sleeping bags to rest up for our nighttime crossing into Laos. Everyone that is, but AcChan, me, Eddie, and Magellan, and the man that drove his van up to the building, placed a ladder against the side, climbed onto the roof, and came down through an opened skylight.

Magellan was puzzled. Eddie had awakened him quietly and now he was listening to my proposition. When he realized what I was asking him to do, he looked around nervously. "You want me to bypass Fantus and Naroogian? And Bath? That would be the end of my career. They'd throw me out so fast I wouldn't have time to clean out my office. They'd take my name off the door and erase the files. I'd be nothing. I could kiss my pension good-bye. I can't do it."

I held up my hand to slow down the torrent of words. "Fred, you've been in Uzbekistan for years so you don't have an office with your name on the door. Possibly, considering some of the things Pan Union has been involved in, the best thing that could happen to any career is to have the files wiped clean. Then you couldn't be blamed for anything. They can't take your pension away and besides, you're a young man. You could start over."

I didn't know about the pension and he wasn't so young, but I figured a little lie never hurts when used in a good cause. "And, most important of all, we don't want you to bypass Fantus and Bath. All we want to do is have you create a backup system of communication in case something goes wrong. A backup that Naroogian wouldn't know about. You're the perfect man to do it. You have the experience and knowledge to make sure we don't get stranded in the jungle. That would not be good."

The combination of flattery, especially being 'the perfect man,' and the risk of being stranded in an inhospitable place, had a certain attraction to it that Fred found hard to resist. "You're not trying to double cross Bath? All you want is a backup?"

"That's it. A backup means of communication. In other words, we need a second transmitter in addition to the one you already have. That way, if anything happens to your primary set and you can't communicate with the satellite, we'll have an option. That is, if you can make one."

"Of course I can make a transmitter. I've been to college. I've had courses in radiotelegraphy and all that stuff."

"What about a receiver? Can you make one of those as well?"

"Sure, it's just as easy. But there's no way I can do it."

"Why not?" I asked.

"No parts. I don't have the parts, all the pieces, all the stuff that you need."

Throughout our discussion, the small Thai in coveralls had been standing silently off to one side. He approached when I beckoned and stood staring at both of us as I said, "He has the parts. On the roof. After you assemble them into a receiver and transmitter, we're in business."

Now that we had reached the critical stage, the part where one had to put up or shut up, Magellan was much less confident. "It's been a long time since I did anything like this. I'm not sure I remember everything. I'm not sure if I even remember what parts you need."

"I can understand that Fred. It's the same thing in medicine sometimes. You tend to forget some of the details but usually, like bicycle riding, once you've learned it, it's something you never lose. I'm sure you can do it, that's why we asked you first. But if not. . ."

"If not? What do you mean, if not? Do you have someone else?"

"Yes, certainly. We don't put all of our eggs in the same basket on anything as important as this. That's why if you can't, or don't want to, Eddie will do it."

Which must have come as a shock to Eddie. Without any change in his expression, though, he said, "Right. I had all of this stuff in college, too."

And that apparently tipped the scales, helped Magellan reach a decision. "As long as I won't be betraying Pan Union and Bath, and you promise that this is only a backup system, then I'll try. Maybe Eddie can help if I have any problems."

"You'll do that, if he needs help, won't you?" I asked Eddie.

"Be glad to," was his answer.

We started to unload the treasure trove of parts hauled down from the roof, spreading them out across a massive conference table in the locked second floor offices of the warehouse. It was hard to realize that this mass of electronic gear was available this far away from what we consider our advanced society but AcChan had assured me that everything we needed, and more, could be obtained on site and this diminutive Thai was proving him right.

Magellan finally got around to asking, "Let's say I get this put together, all these semiconductors, transistors, wire, switches, what do I do then? Who does it communicate with? What's the purpose? Who has the receiver?" He seemed to be sorting the pieces into small piles. With a marking pen and sticky notes, he labeled one pile A, another B, and so on until he had reached Q. That seemed to be as many piles as he was going to need.

I told him what he already knew and then added a little more. "Fantus is supposed to be acquiring a helicopter to come in on your signal and pick us up. You'll be sending him the signal using the black box you already have. If he doesn't show up or if we need a special pickup, we have to be able to send out another signal on this new transmitter. What I want to suggest, if you don't mind, is that you build it right into the existing transmitter. That would be clever and would effectively hide it from prying eyes and mean that you won't have anything else to carry. It would simplify your problems and solve ours."

He was puzzled. "What do you mean, build it into the existing transmitter? How am I going to do that?"

I showed him exactly how from a blueprint sketched by the Thai who had finished delivering his merchandise and was already back on the roof, preparing to leave. "See how it works? You can assemble the transmitting portion here, inside the black box where there is plenty of space. Then just run these wires along the back, attach them to the edge of your dish, like so, and you will be able to use the same antenna to send either the message to Fantus or the backup, if needed."

He examined the sketch, picked up his satellite communicator, if that's what it was, inspected it, and said, "You think that's possible?"

Eddie, who had been following the conversation, said, "Not only possible. It's ingenious. Should work perfectly."

Buoyed by Eddie's optimistic assessment, Fred said, "Well, let's see what we can do, then."

To my surprise, he actually assembled something, hiding it cleverly inside the original black box. Two hours later, after carefully picking and choosing from the assorted bits and pieces he had in front of him, he stepped away from the table and said, "There. That part is done. Now for the easy part. Making a receiver. Have to make sure it works on the same frequency. That's the tricky part. How far will it have to transmit, by the way? I assume you have some idea?"

"I'm guessing maybe 20-30 miles. We won't have to reach out for a satellite but we will have to guide a plane in, should that be necessary. Can you rig it to do that?"

"Twenty to thirty miles? Yes, I guess we can do that," and he started rummaging about in his pile of pieces once more. "If I get a receiver to work, who gets it?"

"The Thai electronics wizard that brought you all of these goodies. We'll give it to him to put into the hands of the backup pilot."

He worked diligently for another hour, stopping once to repeat, "If Bath finds out about this, or Naroogian, you understand that I'm in serious trouble. Naroogian is here to keep on eye on all of us; you, me, Eddie, AcChan, all of us. He's to report regularly, tell Bath if anything funny is going on, and this is definitely not what they had in mind. They find out about this transmitter within a transmitter, it's me they'll send, not a message."

"They won't ever find out, so don't worry about it. The only way they could find out was if you told them. And you're not going to do that, right?" I was sure that sooner or later, he would.

"Of course I'm not going to tell them. You think I'm crazy?" he sputtered as if offended by the very idea.

He appeared to be just about done with the second part of his project when I asked, "You say Naroogian is to report regularly to Bath? What is he going to use to do that? Your satellite transmitter?"

"Yeah, I guess so. What else could he use? I've got the only transmitter so when he makes a report, he'll have to let me know."

"That's what I figured. Has he done that yet? Asked you to send a message for him?"

"Funny you asked about that, because no, he hasn't. Which is surprising because I know Bath told him to report at least once a day. This is the second day and we haven't sent anything back yet. So I figure he'll be asking me to turn everything on, maybe as soon as he wakes up. I hope when I added these other things in here, I haven't screwed it up. That would be hell. It would be a dead giveaway that I've been messing around. That could cost me my job."

All the while he had been working, he had been wearing bifocals. Now he removed them, applied several drops of cleaning solution to the charcoal smeared lenses, and carefully polished them with a clean handkerchief. "How long have you been wearing glasses, Fred?" I asked, as I had never seen anything on his face before.

"Only for reading, that's all," he said defensively. "Or close work like this. I was wearing contacts but last night on the truck, I dropped one of them into the charcoal dust while I was trying to take them out. Have you ever tried finding a contact lens in several inches of charcoal dust, at night?"

"You didn't find it?" He shook his head. "You should have told us. We might have been able to locate it using a flashlight."

"He said," meaning AcChan, "no lights. So I didn't bother. But now I have to wear this pair of glasses and I don't like it."

"They don't look bad, Fred. They look fine."

"It's not my vanity that's hurt, Osten. Without my contacts, I can hardly see in the dark. I might as well be blind when the sun goes down. Last night, for instance, when all that noise started and you were talking to AcChan, I looked out and couldn't see a thing. Nothing. I missed it all."

"No, you didn't Fred. You didn't miss a thing. There was nothing to see."

He had put his glasses back on and was holding the transmitter up to the light. Apparently satisfied with his work, he did the same with the receiver, blowing several small specks of white plastic off the black plastic wrapped case. He examined the blueprint closely and then shrugged. Pointing to the now nearly bare tabletop he said, "Why do you suppose I have these four pieces left over? According to this, we had just enough pieces to make both parts."

"I don't have any idea, Fred. Do you suppose it'll work as it is?"

"I don't know but I suppose we could try it." He didn't sound overly anxious to do that, but he didn't have much choice.

"Have you put batteries in?" I asked.

"Of course I have batteries in. It won't work without batteries," he responded indignantly.

Eddie reached across the table and handed him an object which Magellan glanced at and hurriedly added, "Well, what I mean is this transmitter here, see this one, the one I just made and stuck inside the other gadget, it runs off the original batteries. And this receiver, the one I was just finishing, I hadn't put the batteries in yet. Eddie just gave 'em to me. Here, let me put them in." And he did.

He continued to look at his handiwork with a mixture of pride and apprehension, finally reaching around to the side and flipping a newly installed switch. Nothing happened. "Damn," he said.

Eddie said, "Turn on the other one, too."

Magellan was startled and then suddenly reacted as if stung by a yellow jacket. "Oh, sure, thanks Eddie." He picked up the receiver and pushed the single button on its front. A small red light began to glow, 10 seconds later there was a faint hum, and he flashed a triumphant smile of relief and said, "It works."

"For my information, Fred, exactly how does it work?"

"That's easy. When the receiver picks up the transmitter's signal, it starts humming. As the receiver approaches the transmitter, the hum becomes louder and louder. If it's on a plane and it starts moving in the opposite direction away from us, the humming becomes weaker and gradually fades away. When they circle and come back into range, they pick it up again."

"What range do you think it will have?"

"I don't know. Fifteen to twenty miles? That's just a guess."

"Not the twenty or thirty I was talking about then?"

"I don't know," he repeated. He sounded worried. He really had no idea.

Eddie pointed out what could be a problem. "How far apart are they now?"

Magellan looked at him as if wondering what the question meant. Then I saw concern in his eyes. "A couple of feet. Why?"

"The hum is pretty faint for a couple of feet. You sure anyone is going to be able to hear it from fifteen miles away?"

"Maybe not. I'll work on it when I get a chance."

Magellan put his equipment back into the black bag. AcChan took the newly built receiver for delivery to an unknown airplane pilot and as Eddie and I walked downstairs, he said, "He didn't do a bad job. I was worried about those leftover parts, too."

"What do you know about what kind of a job he did? Isn't that a little out of your field?"

"Not really. Didn't you know? I really did take courses in that stuff in college. I thought you knew. I thought that's why you said I could do it if I had to. I think I could have. But he didn't do a bad job, anyway." Once again, Eddie had amazed me.

By then it was almost dark, everyone was awake, had been fed, and it was time to go.

# 13

Fifteen of us huddled under rain pelted ponchos as dawn struggled into existence the next morning. Rain slanted down from gray, wind driven clouds scurrying hurriedly across a leaden sky as if eager to find new places to deposit moisture that had been accumulated on a long journey. The quagmire under our feet was already testing the performance of our water proof, all-weather boots. I wiggled my toes inside the left boot and was rewarded with the feel of still dry cotton. I didn't bother wiggling anything inside the other boot. An hour earlier, crossing the river, my right foot had slipped into a hole and I had been feeling moisture ever since. I was waiting for the right time to change into a dry sock, but the right time wasn't when it was raining this hard.

We were sheltered by enormous trees fifty yards back from the river's edge, thick underbrush all around providing excellent cover. AcChan had sent three pickets out to screen our position although with the foul weather, and because of the apparent isolation of the area, I doubted that they would be necessary. I was wrong. Shortly after daybreak, a small one-man boat was visible through the mist and rain, bobbing along on choppy water, and it slowly drifted downstream, its occupant unaware of our presence. Ten minutes later voices, not more than fifty or sixty feet away, just below the knoll we had chosen as our assembly point, alerted us to possible danger. We listened and waited and the voices, like the boat, seemed to fade away.

Shortly after, one of AcChan's scouts crawled into our position, cradling his rifle to keep it out of the mud, reported and then disappeared once more. AcChan, crouching low and speaking softly, whispered, "Three men. Following the trail along the river and now they're just sitting along the bank. Waiting for something or someone." Needless to say, we remained where we were, quietly.

Crossing the river had been no problem. It was shallow, easily forded at the point the trucks had left us three or four hours before. Even the pharaoh's chair was easily carried over, two huge hill tribesmen simply picking up the aluminum handles and marching stolidly through the foot deep water carrying this engineering marvel, its power pack, and all related equipment, to the other side. They were sitting now, one on each side of their cargo which they had carefully set down on a tarp and then covered with another. I had never used this machine before, had never heard of the company that made it, but was about to put it to the ultimate test. In this place, everything was about to be given the ultimate test.

Voices again. Was it my imagination or were they closer than before? I heard safeties clicking off rifles on each side, saw Bip and AcChan tense, and then suddenly relax. A sentry reappeared and AcChan listened and then said, "They're leaving. Going back upstream, using the trail. We'll be going the other way, down river." He spoke normally now, the danger over.

We had planned to travel only at night, but with the rain certain to mask our sounds and keep most people inside, AcChan decided to move shortly after noon. "This is a remote area," he explained. "Especially down-stream from here. There is no settlement until we come to the small village where we want to go. The one where Simi Si lived. Just beyond that is the store where we hope to find a lead to your Ken Green. We'll go around the village, check out the store, and see what we find. It'll be dark when we get there and I should have a chance to talk to the two men I sent up to keep an eye on things."

This was news to me. I hadn't known anything about two men arriving ahead of our main party. He must have sensed my unease because he reas-sured me, "Don't worry. Both of them know this area. They were born here. As a matter of fact, most of the men I brought know this area. We've worked around here before."

I didn't ask what kind of work that had been but I doubted it had been as tourist guides. It didn't exactly look like Disneyland or Las Vegas. But who knows? Many travelers are becoming jaded, hungering for new scen-ery. If the rain ever stopped and the sun came out (remote possibilities), this might be just the place.

Four mud wrestling hours later, both feet soaking wet, I knew that no, the tourists wouldn't come. The greenish black mud dragged each foot back into the ground as if we were walking in a sea of molasses, each step re-quired herculean effort and left us bathed in sweat as a scorching sun re-placed bath temperature rain. We removed our ponchos, loosened our shirts, and were wringing wet from perspiration and the continuous drip of water from rain soaked leaves overhead. Dirkens slipped and fell, stumbled again as he was helped to his feet by Naroogian, and then squealed in terror as he saw a three inch shiny black object fastened onto his wrist. Bip moved up from the rear of the column and with a vigorous shake of the head and flash-ing hand signs warned against that kind of outburst. He said something to Eddie, that's right, said something, and walked away. His message was clear. Keep quiet.

Eddie relayed it to Dirkens and then pried the object loose from his wrist. "Leech" he told him. "Bip says there are a lot of them around here. Try to stay out of the water. They won't hurt you. Just pull them off, like I just did."

An hour later, we had covered no more than a mile and were a soggy mass of disheveled camouflage clothing. Our canteens were empty and our thirst was unquenchable. Except for the tribesmen carrying the x-ray machine. They didn't seem to be sweating at all, were moving as if 200 pounds of dead weight was as light as a feather pillow.

We struggled on, desperate for water, until a sudden subtropical nightfall drew a shade over the glowering sun. We had managed to bypass the village and now, sinking back into another grove of covering trees, we paused to let weary muscles recover while AcChan sent three men to the river to fill the canteens. He warned, "Drop in two of the blue tablets you all have, shake thoroughly, and wait fifteen minutes before drinking." Not everyone complied. Off to one side, Dirkens lifted a full canteen and drank deeply, his blue tablets still in his pack.

"You heard the man," I told him. "Blue tablets, wait fifteen minutes, then drink."

Sullenly, he responded, "Yeah, I heard him. Maybe I'm just thirstier than the rest of you." But he took out his blue tablets, added two and shook the canteen halfheartedly, hardly paused, and drank some more.

After our break, we moved out in single file, going more slowly now as this was the stretch of river where we knew the store to be, where Simi Si had done her laundry and left her shirt behind on the night she saw the strange events at the side door. We came to a sudden halt when AcChan, at the head of the column, dropped to one knee and held up a hand, prompting every man in line to do the same. Then I saw the shadow on the trail ahead and realized that AcChan had gotten to his feet and walked forward to exchange whispered greetings with a newcomer.

I moved forward and heard, rather than saw, someone behind me. Not surprisingly, it was Naroogian following Bath's orders to be the eyes and ears of Pan Union. AcChan ignored him as he said, "This is Wanchai. He was born about five miles from here and lived there most of his life so he knows this area very well. I sent him up here three days ago. He says we're almost to the tavern. By the way, as you know, we haven't known exactly what to call the place: store, tavern, inn, the latter, that's a stretch as you would say, and he says what they call it up here is a parn-khar with bia and lao witska-ki. In other words, a store, a shop, selling, among other things, beer, whiskey, and more."

"What we might call a party store," I suggested. "Or a strip mall in one building selling a little bit of everything."

Even in the dark, I could see him smile. "I've seen party stores in Hong Kong. Maybe it's a party store. Cigarettes, candy, soda pop, beer, whiskey, and a lot more. But not a mall. I've seen malls in Hong Kong, too. This is not a mall. To have a mall, you need running water. Here the only running water is rain running through the roof. Let's call it a store and let it go at that."

Wanchai had some interesting things to report. He'd been inside and bought a couple of beers. Looked the place over and in turn was carefully looked over by the proprietor who thought he recognized him from before. Was asked where he'd been, how come he was back, what would he be doing now? And noticed that two or three others sitting around a filthy room at battered tables looked at him just as carefully, and with as much interest, as the proprietor. He had the feeling that he wasn't really welcome, not just for the price of a beer or two.

"What's even more interesting," AcChan told us after listening to more of a tribal dialect that I didn't recognize, "is that at least two men sit at the bottom of a staircase leading up to a second floor. They never leave it except to go outside to answer the call of nature, and even then they are replaced by another. No one goes up or down those steps unless the men say so."

I was puzzled. "How does he know there are men sitting at the bottom of the stairway all the time if he's only been in for a beer?"

"He's been there only once, but I sent two men up to look things over. The other one, Hjuang, he got a job in there."

I was surprised. "They hired a stranger? When, according to Wanchai, they're cautious?"

"Hjuang looks safe. Some years ago when he was a little boy, he stepped on a land mine. Scarred his face and tore off part of his foot and he still has metal fragments in his hip so he looks bad, limps, and people think he isn't all there. But he's all there. Very sharp mind and strong body but nobody thinks that. They see what they want to see. And they see a man who is safe. But he works for me. So he wanders about cleaning the place, emptying the garbage, washing dishes, things like that. But he can't go up the stairway. That doesn't mean he can't watch to see who does. So he's done that and he's told Wanchai that three or four times a day people come – Thais, Laos,

Burmese, Chinese, once in a while even men like you, Westerners, speaking several different languages, come by boat and go up, stay a while and then come back down, and leave. Sometimes they bring things, sometimes they take things away, and always they have lots of money. They spend a lot of it buying witsa-ki, whiskey."

"What kind of things do they bring and what do they take away? He have any idea?"

"Bags, he says. Big bags. But he doesn't know what's inside."

"What about you, AcChan? Do you have any idea what's inside?"

"Sure. I have ideas. I bet it's about the same one you have."

Naroogian, who had been listening silently, suddenly interrupted, "This isn't any damned party store. We should go in there and take a look."

AcChan waited a moment before making any comment. "Osten," he said finally, "he's impatient and wants to go inside and take a look."

"I know," I responded. "But I don't believe any of us have been invited."

"Yes," AcChan observed, "that's a problem."

But Wanchai wasn't through and we stood listening as he continued with his report. It was apparent that he had been a busy man since his arrival three days earlier. He had fished down on the river bank, met other fishermen and exchanged stories with them. He had wandered about the village and gone back into the bush on obscure trails that he remembered from childhood, still finding farmers working hard to coax a few reluctant vegetables from small plots of acid jungle soil. Pigs and chickens fled at his approach and men and women stared at him curiously, a mixture of fear and friendship, and were more than willing to talk, quietly, always peering over a shoulder as they took the money that lubricated their vocal cords. They all had stories to tell, and most of the stories dealt with the store. Even Hjuang, while emptying the garbage, had come across a young man with a fascinating story.

"What would we like to hear first?" he asked. I deferred to AcChan. He was the one who would have to listen and then translate everything into English for me. He asked several questions of Wanchai and then said, "I think we should talk to some of these people and see what they know. One of the fishermen lives nearby and usually fishes about this time. He should be out on the river soon and Wanchai thinks he can interest him in having a meeting with us. Let's get everyone under cover and out of sight and wait until he shows up."

That didn't suit Naroogian at all. "It's a waste of time. Let's walk in there and look around right now," he urged. "We don't have to talk to anyone. If they're there, we'll find them. That's it."

He seemed to be in a hurry to find Ken Green and Lee Duc Than, but AcChan vetoed the idea. "Let's not make a mistake here. I doubt you'll find Green and the Vietnamese defector inside. But there is information to be gathered in this area and taking a little time to do it is the best way to approach the problem. Let's talk to the fisherman."

It made sense. If we blundered into the store and word got out that a band of marauders was loose in the jungle, it wouldn't be long before human blood hounds would be tracking us down. That wouldn't help our cause and even Naroogian backed off after a moment, apparently having thought about it and deciding to accept AcChan's method.

"What makes this fisherman interesting," AcChan confided as we moved deeper into the brush, "is that he told Wanchai something very similar to what Simi Si told us back in the hill village. There were lights and a sudden outburst of some kind one night, maybe the same night, two or three weeks ago, just outside the store. It's worth hearing what he saw."

"He'll talk to us? To strangers?"

"Wanchai says he will. For money, of course. Money is a universal language, even up here where there is almost nothing to buy. They save it and when they go to market towns, some as far as fifty kilometers away, they can buy what they need, things to make clothing, to cook in, shoes, a radio, a gun. Money is just as important to them as it is to you and I. They just don't see much of it."

So once again, we took cover in thick underbrush, ten foot high elephant grass, and once again, it started to rain. It rained so hard that I removed my canteen cup and held it skyward, within minutes collecting an inch of fresh water, replenishing a dwindling supply while huddled under my poncho, listening to the beat of rain all around. With nothing else to do, I opened a packet of dried rations and enjoyed mouth sized bits of salted ham, with crackers, cold lima beans, and a one inch square of delicious milk chocolate. Not quite as sumptuous a meal as I'd enjoyed a week earlier in Hong Kong, but under the circumstances, who was there to complain to? When I had finished, I carefully dug a deep hole in the soft earth and buried all remains of my feast, covered it completely, and packed leaves and fallen twigs over it in accordance with AcChan's instructions. Not as an environmental measure, but instead a much more practical reason. To avoid detection and pursuit.

I wasn't even aware that Wanchai had left us until I saw him suddenly reappear and report to AcChan. "He's found the fisherman," he told me. "He's willing to talk but doesn't want to come this far into the trees and it's better that he doesn't. I don't want him to see how many men we have and especially how many Americans are with us. Someone else may come along and make him a better offer. You know what I mean?"

I understood perfectly, but Naroogian, who had been sitting quietly a few feet away in the darkness, didn't. Or maybe he was just being difficult. Without mincing words, he said, "If you talk to this man, I go along."

Without hesitating, dealing with the Americans being my show, I flatly told him, "You don't go. You heard AcChan. We don't want him to have any idea how many Americans are with us. If he sees me, that's enough. If he sees you, he may start to get ideas. You wait here."

It wasn't going to be that easy. "Look," he snapped. "Bath said to stay close to everything and I can't stay close if you run off in the dark to talk to people when I'm not around."

He had started to rise and I reached out and lightly touched him on the shoulder. "Sit back down, Avram. Let me go over this one more time. Bath could have come along himself. But he didn't. He sent you along, with the others. But he didn't put you in charge. I didn't put you in charge and AcChan didn't put you in charge, so you aren't in charge. I am. AcChan and I will talk to this man and when we get back, we'll tell you all about it, and that's the way it is. Do you understand?"

I felt the tension in his shoulder, heard the anger in his voice, and could see just enough of his face by the dim light to see the hostility that he couldn't mask. Or was it fear? Was he enraged or was he terrified? Or was he playing a game? It didn't matter. He wasn't coming along.

"How do I know I can trust you?" he finally responded. "How do I know you'll tell me what you find out?"

"You can trust us because we're all on the same team. Have the same motivation in being here, don't we?"

He sank back against the tree. "Sure, Osten, we're all on the same team. I almost forgot." He didn't sound entirely convincing.

The fisherman was waiting by the water's edge. His name was Lo Dan and he had been working this stretch of the river for fifteen years. By this time, after all those years, he had become part of the local scenery, like a meter reader or telephone line man back home; seen but not seen, part of the background, someone of no importance. Someone who was just there. Every night, rain or shine, unless the wild winds of the monsoons drove him to shelter, he drifted gently downstream dragging two or three lines behind him, baited with small fish, bits of crab or other choice baits with which he hoped to attract the huge channel fish that lay in wait, deep, against the bottom. Some nights he was lucky and caught one or two; other nights unlucky and he went home empty handed. When he caught the big ones, he sold them, occasionally to the people in the store, more often to a fish buyer who visited the village every two or three days and took them to Vientiane, or somewhere, he didn't know. How did he prevent the fish from spoiling in the heat? Salt! If he didn't have salt, and sometimes he didn't, he dried them in the sun if the sun was shining, but there were times when it didn't, like when it was raining, and then the fish would spoil. Unless they ate them, and if the fish was big enough, sometimes they were you know, they had a village feast. He provided the fish, others the potatoes, the squash, the pineapples, the rice, mangoes, papayas, bananas, mangosteen, jackfruit, custard apples, plantain, litchi, and rambutan. Everyone contributed whatever they could find or grow and it was a banquet for them all, 100, maybe 200 people sometimes, and it was like a party. It was bad to not sell the fish but it was good to have a party. No one went hungry at a party.

For twenty bahts, he told us of the night when the normal routine had changed; when the lights on the side of the store had suddenly flared in brilliance, he was surprised because he didn't even know there were lights on that side, had we ever seen how bright those lights were?, and he saw the men, several of them, all tangled together, fighting, and even though he was far away on the water, he could hear voices raised in anger. It ended in a shout or scream, he wasn't sure which, and the door slammed and the light went out. Did he stay around to see what happened next? No, he did not. He wasn't crazy. It wasn't wise to ask many questions around there. Everyone knew that. Sure, he went inside from time to time to sell a fish, but that's all. To sell a fish. Maybe to buy a beer, just once in a while, because if they did business with him, wasn't it right that he did business with them? Men at the bottom of the stairway? Yes, always. He didn't ask why there were there. They were just always there. It was said they worked for the man from Luang Prabang, whoever he was, although some said they took orders from a warlord in Fang. But as for him, he didn't know. Would he recognize the men he had seen outside in the light? Maybe. Probably not. But one of them was like him, he said, pointing to me. An American.

I listened as he spun his story. When he seemed to have run out of anything more to say, AcChan turned to me and said, "Anything else you want to know?"

"Ask him how well he knows the river upstream from here. He seems to fish mainly downstream. See what he knows about the country to the northwest. And ask him how big his boat is."

"You have anything specific in mind?"

"Not really. Not at this point. Just collecting information. Then find out where he lives and make sure Wanchai knows how to get in touch with him again. Give him the twenty bahts and a bonus of five and tell him there's more where that came from if we need to talk to him again. But he must not talk to anyone about us. Make sure he understands that. If he thinks the men in the store are dangerous, make sure he realizes we are even more dangerous. If he talks, we come back and take the money away. Make sure he knows we aren't kidding."

AcChan hesitated before relaying my message to Lo Dan. "Something wrong," I asked.

"Kidding. I'm not sure what kidding means. Goats, little goats, having little goats. How do I put it to him so we both understand?"

Evidently AcChan had mastered the English language but had missed out on some of the more common slang expressions and idioms. "Serious, that's what it means. Just tell him we're serious about this. We mean business."

"What do you mean business? You mean you're going to do business with him? Buy fish?"

Another breakdown. "Look, just tell him that he must not tell anyone he talked to us or even saw us. Like I said, we mean bus – just tell him that. He'll understand."

"If I just tell him that we'll take the money away if he talks about us, he'll understand."

"Fine. Just tell him that, but don't forget about asking the other questions first. Let's get our money's worth."

It turned out that Lo Dan knew the river like the back of his hand. He could, he proudly boasted, identify every tree and bush, as far as four days of poling upstream and a whole day drifting downstream. He seemed to feel they were equivalent distances. How many miles or how many kilometers was that? He didn't have any idea.

It was left to Naroogian to come up with the best guess. After we had, as promised, briefed him on our conversation, he slipped down to the river bank, watched the flow eddying by, and decided, "Looks like four to five miles an hour. How long does this guy float in a day? Eight, ten hours, maybe. So he could drift as much as 40-50 miles. He says it takes him four or five days to cover the same distance going against the current. I make it he moves about one mile an hour, against the current. That sound about right?" Apparently working on a problem had a soothing effect on him. He was no longer belligerent and seemed to have rejoined the team.

AcChan accepted the assessment. "That sounds about right to me," he said. Wanchai had listened and mildly disagreed. He insisted that with maximum effort, a good riverman could move faster than that, but without any way to test either thesis, we accepted Naroogian's analysis. Surprisingly, no one asked why it mattered and although I had the early glimmering of an idea, I still couldn't have given a good answer had I been asked.

Naroogian for his part was amazed by the price we had paid for Lo Dan's information. "Twenty bahts! You expect a man to keep quiet for twenty bahts? You're lucky he even talked to you at all. That's what? A dollar?"

We were hidden in the underbrush with a view of the side door of the store. Wanchai had gone back inside to see if anything had changed or if Hjuang had acquired any new information. Eddie spoke up from behind a nearby bush. "Hey, what's wrong with a dollar tip? I look forward to getting every dollar tip I can. Sometimes I get more, but even just a buck – it helps."

Where was he getting tips? In our parking lot? I asked.

"Sure, right in our parking lot. I used to get a lot more before I moved to nights. You'd think it would be the other way around, wouldn't you? That people would appreciate my being there at night, but they don't. They just want to get in their car and get out of there so even when I walk them out and open the door for them and watch while they drive away they may say, 'Thanks, Eddie,' but no tip. But not Burrows. He always tips. A buck at a time. Howsam, too. Always a buck. Even old Doc Garrison in pharmacology. Another buck. It all adds up."

He was making me feel like I was living in another world. I had never tipped Eddie or any of the other parking lot guards in my life unless you count the twenty or fifty (once) dollars I slipped them with thanks at Christmas. But tip them, for sitting in a comfortable guard house watching a bank of television screens panning the perimeter of our campus, at the current $13 an hour plus benefits? No, I had never done that. "I didn't know you were accustomed to receiving tips, Eddie. Especially from Burrows. Howsam,

I can see Howsam doing that. He's single, makes a lot of money, so that doesn't surprise me. "I realized that I was also describing my own situation, so added, "Have you been upset that I haven't tipped you?"

"Not at all. Never expected a tip from you. I never went to get your car and pulled it up to the door like I did for the others. Rain or shine, when they came out, I would go and start their car, drop it off right in front of them, three feet away, and open the door. That's why they tipped me. For the special service. You always walked over and got your own car. No tip expected. None needed."

I felt better, happy to hear that I hadn't been stiffing him all of this time. What puzzled me though, was why Burrows needed anyone to drive his car to the door when he had the first parking place next to the door, not twelve feet from the door to be exact. That meant Eddie was driving Everett's car, what?, nine feet, and was being paid a dollar a trip. Based on mileage, that was a more than livable wage. By comparison, Howsam and Garrison were getting much more for their money. Both of them were parked at least fifty feet from the exit.

Two men walked onto the porch and the glow of cigarettes flared and dimmed as they puffed away. Wanchai was illuminated in the light of the open doorway briefly and both smokers eyed him warily as he wiped beer foam from his mouth and walked downstream away from us. No one followed. "That was the signal," AcChan explained. "He'll walk until he's certain no one is trailing along and then circle back. It may take him the rest of the night. So we wait."

And we did. Shortly after daybreak, it wasn't Wanchai that made an appearance. Instead it was Hjuang, opening the side door and carrying out cases of empty beer bottles that rattled against one another as he limped under his burden, stumbled once or twice, and added them to a growing pile of crates at the rear of the building, alongside a shed from which the throb of a motor had resumed after being silent for several hours. On his next trip, he dragged a heavy metal container across the pitted ground, gouging chunks of black mud as he went, and dumped its contents onto a five foot high mound of garbage, from which, although it was almost the length of a football field away, the odor of rotting fish could be detected on the prevailing wind, blowing directly into our faces.

I was concerned about the continued absence of Wanchai but AcChan didn't appear to be worried. "He'll be back. Like I told you, he will make certain that no one is following before he circles back in our direction. Meanwhile, if anything unusual goes on inside, Hjuang will come outside and dump dish water by the side door."

We waited another three hours and the sun was high in the sky and hot before we saw Wanchai again. He wasn't alone, this time. Walking behind him was a slim young man whose age I guessed to be about 18 or 19 – although many of these Thai, Lao, and hill tribe people looked much younger than they were so he may have been quite a bit older. Wanchai spoke to the newcomer and he approached AcChan, making a proper wai, both palms together, hands raised to the level of the chin where they lightly touched his face and were lowered slowly, bowing at the waist as he did so. Respect. AcChan immediately returned his greeting, his gently clasped palms raised only to the level of the upper chest as was fitting for the elder of the pair. Respect returned. All very fitting and proper, here in the bush, just as in Bangkok. His name, Wanchai told us, was Ha.

Ha had a story to tell and Wanchai had taken the time to detour to his village and bring him back to relate it to us. As usual, he told it to AcChan who relayed it to me, with Naroogian standing by. He was part of the loop once again.

"He saw almost the same thing the fisherman saw," AcChan reported. "He saw the lights, heard the shouting, all of that, but admits that he probably heard more than he saw. He says his girl saw it all, at least she was his girl then. He's afraid he lost her."

I was puzzled. "How come his girl saw it better than he did? How far away were they?"

"He was as close as we are now. Closer. See those bushes not far from the door? Where the grass is soft and thick, and then a clump of bushes? They were there."

"If they were that close," Ha was staring at the bushes AcChan had described, and he seemed sad as he did so, "how come he didn't see things very clearly? As clearly as his girl did?"

"They were having sex," AcChan explained, "and he was on top while the girl was on her back. His back was to the door so he didn't see. She was looking right at the lights and saw everything."

I understood the problem.

"Ha says the girl felt sorry, very sorry, for the old man. He was crying and they hit him."

If she had been that close, directly under the light as it came on although hidden by the brush, she might be the one to identify our pictures of

Ken Green and Lee Duc Than.

"What about the girl? Can Ha arrange for us to talk to her?"

They talked quietly and I sensed disappointment. "He doesn't think so," said AcChan. "Her father found out what they had been doing, they'd been doing it more than that one time, and he threatened to kill him if he ever saw his daughter again. Of course they all do see each other, almost everyday because the village is a small one, and it's impossible not to see one another, but he doesn't dare talk to the girl or come near her. He really fears the father. Says he has a bad temper, owns a knife and a gun, and he doesn't want to take any chances."

Young love. It seldom runs smoothly. "OK, so he doesn't want to take any chances. What about Wanchai? Could he take a chance and try to talk to the girl? Show her one of our pictures?"

Ha, AcChan, and Wanchai carried on a three way conversation and finally AcChan shrugged and said, "Wanchai says he'll do it. I'm not sure what he has in mind, though, and I'm a little worried. First he asked if the girl was pretty and Ha said yes. Then he asked how big the knife was and Ha told him only a small one, an eight inch blade, maybe a little bigger, and Wanchai laughed and said he'd take the risk."

I wondered if Wanchai had romance on his mind but I was curious about the gun so I asked. "Doesn't he want to know about the gun? Shouldn't he be as concerned about that as he is about a knife?"

"Wanchai has never worried about guns. He has always feared dying from a knife. He has a lot of little superstitions like that. Many Thais do. Besides, Wanchai has always fancied himself a ladies man, I think you call it." As if that explained everything.

"How are they going to find the girl? Ha will have to point her out, won't he?"

"He's willing. He still has affection for her even though he's scared to death of the father. Just to be safe, because although I doubt that this man is really all that dangerous, I'm going to send Bip into the village with them. Bip isn't a ladies man and he isn't likely to scare easily and he's not doing anything laying here in the bushes so he may as well get some exercise." I gave them copies of the photos of both Ken Green and Lee Duc Than, sadly out of date, of course, after all of these years, and they headed into the woods, Ha leading the way.

Hjuang never dumped dish water, but two hours later, Bip and Wanchai still absent, he once again limped outside, walked down to the river's edge and sat on the flat stones used by village women to do their laundry. He proceeded to light a cigarette, took off his shoes, and dangled his feet in the water, slowly moving his toes back and forth (five toes on the left foot, only two on the blast-damaged right), and leaned back in satisfaction. A hard working man on a well deserved break. No one, except us, seemed to pay him any attention as he lighted a second cigarette. I could hear him coughing as he inhaled deeply. AcChan cautiously crawled towards the bushes the young lovers had used for their moments of pleasure, the tops of the head high saw grass barely moving as he silently made his way across the fifty yards separating our trees from his destination. Hjuang threw his cigarette away and stood up, and carrying his shoes in one hand, made his way back to the side door, pausing at the bushes, stepping inside the protective ring of greenery, unzipping his trousers, relieving himself, all the while talking as if to himself. He re-zipped his trousers, crossed to the building, leaned against it as he put on one shoe and as he was preparing to put on the second, a shout from inside sent him scurrying through the door still carrying it in his hand.

AcChan returned in the same slow, cautious manner, only after reaching the relative safety of the trees sitting up, grimacing, "Do you know how close he came to my head with his," he groped for the English word, then settled on Thai, "patsarwa?" I suspected he meant urine. Even from a distance, we had seen what a close call it had been.

I was more interested in what Hjuang had been saying while he did what he did.

"He had something to say, but he didn't have to almost drown me. I'm lucky I was only splashed. He told me of someone else we should talk to. A kid, he said. Name of Goong. Lives up the jungle trail alone with his mother. He's told people that he saw something interesting here one night, but no one believes him because everyone thinks he's strange. Tells a lot of stories that you can't believe, does unusual things, often thinks he sees things that don't happen. Yet, maybe this time, he really did see something."

"Goong? Isn't that an odd name?"

"Odd name? Goong? What's wrong with it? His mother probably named him that when he was little, even when he was born. That's what it means. Little. Actually, it really means shrimp but like you, we think shrimp are little. But maybe he's not so little anymore. Maybe he grew up."

"How old is he?"

"Nine, ten years old, Hjuang doesn't know, but he's heard the men in the store talk about him. He steals bottles from the pile back there and brings them back a couple of days later and sells them again. Up until now, they've humored him and given him a few bahts because they know his mother has no money. But now, they've heard rumors that he's been talking about seeing something unusual by the building one night and they want to talk to him about it. They want him to shut up. Having him talk to other people has made them unhappy."

Suspecting that they might want to do more than that, I suggested, "In that case, we should talk to him first. You mentioned trail. Do you know where it is?"

"Sure. There aren't that many. Over there," he was pointing back towards the river and waved his arm in an arc, from north to south, "that's the river trail. You can go up the river or down the river. Back there," and he motioned to the garbage pile behind the store, "That's where the jungle trail starts. Meets another one from the village just before the rise in the ground where the trees seem taller, and ends about a mile further on. Nothing for a trail to go to after that. River trail, jungle trail. That's it."

We couldn't go looking for Goong right then. We were still awaiting the return of Bip and Wanchai from their mission to the village. When they rejoined us, I was surprised to see that Ha was still with them. He had pointed out the girl as she walked down to the river to help her younger brother pull in a net and Wanchai had waited until she was on her way back before approaching her. Apparently his reputation as a ladies man was well deserved as he struck up a conversation with her almost without trying and had her laughing at his small talk before they had gone fifty yards. When he asked her if she would be willing to do him a favor, she peered suspiciously at him, fluttered her eyelids in a manner worthy of the experienced coquettes of Paris, and asked, "What kind of a favor?"

She seemed disappointed, Wanchai thought, when he asked her to look at a photograph he was carrying. Maybe, he thought, she was expecting him to ask for something else. But he just showed her the photo, like he had been told. She took it, studied it, and looked very attractive as she tucked her lower lip up behind her upper teeth, something he had always found appealing in pretty women. Ha nodded in agreement. Apparently he did, too.

Did she recognize the man in the photo? AcChan said, "He doesn't think so. She said the man she saw at the store was older. Much older. She didn't know if it was the same man."

"What about Ken Green. She recognize him?"

AcChan talked to Wanchai and said, "Same problem. Maybe, but the man she saw, the American she calls him, was much older."

And then an enraged wild-haired man, snorting like a water buffalo and built like one, came out of a nearby house and ordered the girl to come with him. He glared and snarled at Wanchai, hurled one furious look at the terrified Ha, and followed his daughter into the house. Apparently he didn't need an eight inch knife to protect the honor and virtue of his daughter, as sullied as it already was, and both Wanchai and Ha had decided that they had gotten all of the information that they were going to get. Bip had watched from nearby and his report to AcChan was direct and to the point. When he had finished, AcChan told me, "Bip thinks we should recruit the father. He is as strong as an ox. He also doesn't think the girl really recognized anyone but was just trying to lead Wanchai on. Flirt, I think you call it."

Disappointed, still without an identification, we decided to leave Bip in charge of our small force watching the store while AcChan and I went looking for Goong. We cut through thickets of bamboo and picked up the jungle trail out of sight of the building, without meeting a soul. In fact, it had been a tedious and boring day watching a jungle clearing and a muddy river. Aside from swatting insects and sweating, and the mission of Wanchai and Bip to the village, we had accomplished little. Four men from the village had taken the river trail and entered the front door, staying inside twenty minutes or so, and then departing. Every half hour, one or two men from inside came outside and smoked a cigarette and then went back into the shadows. Perhaps they had a no smoking rule inside, although I couldn't imagine health considerations entered into it. Two boats slid into the dock, one powered by a small outboard, the other gliding by downstream. The operator of the first carried a battered red can to the rear of the building, knocked on the side door and Hjuang appeared, filled the container from a fifty five gallon drum with a hand pump, carried it back to the boat while the owner went inside to pay or drink or both. The drifting fisherman went inside after carefully tying his frail single man boat to the dock and came out in minutes carrying two bottles of beer. He untied the boat, got in, paddled strenuously for a minute or two to regain the main current, opened one bottle, drank it in two or three massive draughts, then tossed it overboard and opened the second, drinking more leisurely now that his thirst had been slaked. Almost one whole day, six customers, hardly a thriving business. But perhaps they did more business after dusk.

And long before darkness, we found Goong. We were lucky. There were very few homes, none of them more than rough shacks away from the collection of buildings that made up the village, and we hadn't gone far until we came to one with a small collection of empty beer bottles sitting alongside. The lopsided building appeared ready to topple onto one side, a moss covered roof sagging in the center as if ready for collapse, and a stove pipe projecting not more than 12 inches, barely clear of the rotting boards and mildew, a dirt floor, one doorless entrance and two small unscreened windows without glass, marked it as a place barely fit for human habitation, one not qualified for an FHA loan. Despite that, someone was at home as oily black smoke was pouring from the chimney.

Goong wasn't a shrimp any longer. He was close to 50 inches tall, not bad for a ten year old Thai or Lao boy. He was sitting just inside the doorway and almost certainly had heard us coming despite the wet ground and silence that marked AcChan's movements. Further back in the gloomy, smokey interior was an old woman dressed in black. She squatted impassively on her haunches and watched, without saying a word.

Interestingly, Goong wasn't frightened; merely curious. He took in AcChan's assault rifle and our camouflage clothing at a single glance, his gaze lingering on my face for a moment longer and then returning to AcChan, as if aware that if there was to be a conversation, it would be with him.

He admitted to his name, saying yes, he was Goong. Refused to answer any questions about the empty beer bottles, denied having ever been to the store, never saw lights at the place, and certainly knew nothing about a fight, shouting, and any foreigner. Nothing at all. The place was 'evil' he said. Wanted nothing to do with it.

A twenty baht note bought us the information that his name was still Goong, that he regularly stole bottles from the store, why not, they had a lot of them and he needed the money (although they didn't pay very much to get them back), and that yes, he had seen something strange one night when he had been at the store. For another twenty baht, he suddenly remembered what it was he had seen. He was in the bushes alongside the building. No, not the clump where Ha and his girl were, he knew what they did there, he was back a little further, and no he wasn't there to watch them. He had come, frankly, to steal some bottles. It was a good night for it. It had been raining and the wind was blowing and the men from inside wouldn't come out in that kind of weather. They never did. And the wind would cover any noise he made although he never made any because he was good at moving quietly. Almost as good as you, he complimented AcChan, and seemed to mean it. Oh, yes, he had been in the bushes and was waiting for his chance to steal some bottles but he had the sudden need for thorng, he repeated the word several times, and AcChan said in an aside to me, "Bowel movement. He had to go."

He was right in the middle of it when the lights had come on and he had jumped and almost soiled himself, which would have been a mess, and he was frightened because he thought the lights meant that they had discovered him and were coming for him and he was in a bad way because his trousers were down around his ankles so he couldn't run very fast, if at all. Certainly, if they caught him, they would beat him. Once before, they had caught him and beaten him and he didn't want that to happen again.

"Ask him exactly what he saw?" I said.

AcChan did and reported, "Well, here's something for you. He says he saw it all. Three or four men by the door, lights on, some pushing and shoving, and then the others picked up the old man and carried him inside. They did that, he says, because the old man was sick and having trouble breathing."

I was surprised as was AcChan. "Are you sure that's what he's saying? Nobody hit anyone; no one was angry."

"That's what he's saying. Let me ask a few more questions to see if there's anything else." But there wasn't. There was no fight. No one struck anyone. A man was sick and the first aid team picked him up and carried him inside. According to Goong, just friends helping a man in distress.

But was Goong reliable? What was it that Hjuang had told us? "He's a little strange. You can't always believe the stories he tells so people don't pay much attention." And viewed in that light, the story he had just told us was a little strange. No one else, not Lo Dan, not Simi Si, nor Ha and his girl, told the story in this way. They had seen something different. Or had they? And yet Goong didn't look strange, he didn't act strange, and he didn't talk strange. He looked at us coolly, in command, without a care in the world now that he had currency in his pocket.

AcChan had been processing the information just as I had and he finally said, "I don't think he's lying. Not deliberately. What he told us is what he thinks happened."

"Do you think that maybe, in the middle of a bowel movement, he became frightened and imagined some of what he just told you? Like he said, he wouldn't have been able to run very fast if they had started to chase him so his mind would have been on escape, not observation."

"It's possible," AcChan conceded. "But he thinks what he told us is what happened. We could talk to him for a week and he won't change his story now."

I showed him our traveling photos of Lee Duc Than and Ken Green. "This one," I asked, pointing to Lee Duc Than, "was he the sick man?"

Couldn't tell, he told me. He was laying down, the others were carrying him, and he never saw the face clearly. Ken Green? See him there? This one? He looked at the second photo. Didn't know. Too much confusion, besides they all look alike. Who all looks alike? Americans, like you, and he pointed to me and laughed. Showed him the picture of Bath, one Horace had taken with the mini-camera in Hong Kong. Just for the helluva it. And he laughed again. Said something to AcChan.

"I know," I said. "We all look alike, we Americans."

AcChan shook his head. "That's not what he said this time. He said they don't all look alike after all. He says this one he's seen, several times, down at the store. Comes in a boat. Comes with other men and some of them are Americans, too."

I let that soak in before very slowly asking AcChan, "What do your instincts tell you about what he just said this time?"

"I think he thinks that what he just said really happened. He could be wrong, but we have to consider that he might be telling the truth. If he is, things have changed."

The old woman in the shadows suddenly said something that neither AcChan nor I heard clearly but Goong looked at us with concern. "Someone is coming. You should leave before they see you." Before either of us could move, he had darted out of the clearing and disappeared into the thick brush surrounding the shack. AcChan moved in the next instant and I followed.

"This way," he hissed, and we both hurried into the same thicket of brambles which had closed like a curtain behind Goong. And crouched there we watched as two men went inside the shack, listened as they threw things aside, and then stormed out empty handed. They looked about in anger, then returned to the trail and started back to the river.

Goong hadn't been more than twenty feet from us throughout and as they departed, he crawled back and said, "Men from the store. Looking for their bottles."

They had indeed been men from the store. The same ones that we had watched smoking cigarettes on the porch. But I didn't think they had come looking for bottles.

The old lady was unharmed, still sitting exactly where she had been earlier. Before we left, AcChan warned Goong, "Stay away from the store. They might hurt you." He gave him another twenty bahts along with the advice.

"He won't, you know," he said as we went back, staying off the trail this time and going much more slowly through the woods. "He'll go back again and again until he's caught. Then they really will hurt him."

While waiting for night to fall, I had time to think about what Goong and the others had told us of the events of two weeks earlier. Obviously, something out of the ordinary had happened, and I wasn't surprised to find differing versions of what it had been. That's often the problem with eyewitness testimony. We tend to see what we want to see, filter events through our biases, and when surprised, as our witnesses must have been, they could easily have misinterpreted what happened while trying to adjust to the unexpected.

What was clear was that a Westerner, a white man, a foreigner, probably an American, had been involved. Had he been attacking an older man or trying to help a sick man? Different versions. While we were at it, I began to wonder about the description of the other principal involved, the man the American struck or carried inside the building. Witnesses said he was old, they all used some variation of the term, but Lee Duc Than, if it was him, wouldn't be old by our definition of the term. What had he been, no more than 30 when he was attending the University, possibly younger? A year, possibly two, in the United States before returning to Vietnam and that was less than 20 years ago. So Lee Duc Than would be, give or take a year, no more than 50 years old. Could our witnesses be seeing Lee Duc Than and calling him old?

"It's possible," said AcChan. "First of all, Americans have a difficult time in determining how old many Asians are. Vietnamese, like Thais, often appear to be younger than they are so Lee Duc Than may have been older than 30 when you first saw him in the United States. Did you check with the University about his age?"

I admitted that I didn't know. "So he could have been in his early thirties, let's say. Now about 20 years later he could be in his fifties instead of about 50. And that makes a difference."

"How could a couple of years make that great a difference?" I asked him.

"Well, how old do you think the woman in Goong's hut was?"

"His grandmother? Probably early to late sixties, at least."

"You see, there is the problem. Why do you assume it was his grandmother? Because she looked so old, I'm sure. No teeth, face wrinkled, hands deformed, hair thin. Breathing heavily. But it wasn't his grandmother. It was his mother. When she warned him that someone was coming, she used the possessive form of speech and said 'khorng shan but shai,' my son, not my grandson. She looked older I grant you, but I doubt that she was more than 40. It's a hard life up here. People age very rapidly, the diet is often inadequate, and medical or dental care is simply not available. They work hard, are subject to many tropical diseases and parasites, and although they look younger than usual at the beginning, in a few years, they look much older and you can easily be misled when you come here from your country. So your Lee Duc Than, especially if he's ill, could look much older than you might expect." Something new to consider. The problem was, no one had yet identified anyone seen in the altercation at the door; not Lee Duc Than and not Ken Green, and we had no way of knowing if we were even close to finding them.

If there were any answers in this neighborhood, the best place to ask was inside the store. It was also likely to be the least friendly place in the neighborhood as well and I was amazed, after learning how many people had watched from the darkness as the events at the door unfolded two weeks earlier, late at night, that no one had yet reported our presence to the men inside. We had been camped nearly on their doorstep for eighteen hours, had sent men into the village asking questions, and visited Goong, and so far no one had bothered us. So far as we knew. And that seemed unlikely.

All that was about to change. AcChan wanted to hit the place right after dark. "No one has been going in all day and Hjuang hasn't reported any problems so we should go in and see what we find," was his reasoning.

Naroogian didn't want to wait at all. "Send Wanchai back in for another beer. If everything looks the same, let him sit there and nurse it along for ten minutes and we'll come in and take over. If something looks wrong, he can come back outside, give us a signal, and do what he did before. Go down river and come back and tell us why he called it off."

I didn't like either plan. Sending Wanchai back inside would look suspicious. From what he had told us, they were already looking at him coolly, a stranger, one who had appeared without explanation with money to spend. People fitting that description are seldom welcomed with open arms even in our country. Why should they be in Laos where everyone along the river had a somewhat shady reputation, especially if they had money? On the other hand, I wasn't thrilled at hitting it shortly after dark. Sure, the best time was in darkness, I knew that, but the hour or so after sunset was likely to be a time when villagers came for a beer, either because they worked in the fields during the day or preferred to stay in the shadows, like us. We didn't want to involve innocent people in something that could turn violent and AcChan assured me that our presence would lead to violence. "I haven't told you everything," he finally admitted as the three of us struggled to reach a decision. "Bip and I know this place. I should say, we've heard of it before. It is known as a center of, for want of a better term, you could call criminal activity."

He didn't elaborate and we compromised. We would wait 90 minutes after full darkness and then go inside. We watched as the sun dropped behind the towering rim of massive trees to our west, settling first into the dense foliage of the laburnum, then sliding lower into a canopy of pines before disappearing entirely in a last magnificent blaze of orange and purple behind the irregular shapes marking the hills and mountains giving shape to the river valley. Inside the building, dim lights appeared, shadows were seen moving from place to place, and twice, as a figure passed a side window, AcChan murmured, "Hjuang."

Then, with no one in sight and absolute calm on the river, even the waves having decided to take the evening off, AcChan glanced at his watch and said, "I think it's time, Doctor. If you're ready."

Before I could answer, we heard the throbbing noise, just a faint hum at first, growing louder and louder, coming towards us and we saw the running lights of a boat out on the river, curving shoreward now, headed for the dock. Bip hurried to alert the men, who had already moved to their preassigned positions, ready for our grand entrance into the only beer parlor in town.

"We have visitors," observed Naroogian.

We did indeed, three of them. One leaped nimbly to the dock carrying the docking cable, a second gunned and reversed the engine bringing the boat smoothly alongside the derelict old dock where it could be tied down, and the third sat casually in the rear, waiting until the boat was securely tied and had stopped rocking back and forth, and then stood and strode purposefully to be helped ashore by the crewman who was waiting with an extended hand. The front porch light came on and the two cigarette men, Goong's would-be adversaries, came outside to wait. From the erect way they were standing, I wasn't sure if they meant respect or if they were fighting back fear.

Both of them made a wai, the traditional Thai greeting, as the new-comer approached them. He disdained a response, ignored them, and walked inside. The crewman who had leaped ashore went back aboard and threw a large bundle ashore. Then another, a third, and fourth. He shouted some-thing to the men on the porch and they hurried to help him, each picking up a heavy sack and starting back to the store, one of them stumbling clumsily as if the load was far too heavy for him. The crewman bounded ashore once more, seized the remaining two bags on one end and started dragging them behind him, finally disappearing inside, leaving the third man alone on the boat. He promptly lit up a cigarette.

"Interesting luggage," said AcChan.

"Looks a lot like the package we saw up in the hill village," I added. "Duffel bags."

"It probably is. They buy them by the gross up here and package prod-ucts in them. I suspect you know what the product is by now?"

"Unless things have changed in the last few days, I suppose it's raw opium."

"Right. Raw opium. I would say we're looking at some kind of a deliv-ery. I don't know where it came from, but I can guarantee you I know where it's going."

"You mean this place sells more than beer and fish?"

"That's right. But they aren't going to sell this load here. This is a transit point. The boat has been to a raw opium processing plant, some-where downriver from the direction they came. They drop it off here. In a day or two, maybe less, maybe more, another boat will pick it up and there will be one, two or three more drops before it leaves the country and arrives in Bangkok or Hong Kong, and then on to the real factories, the laboratories in Marseilles, France or Brindisi, Italy, or somewhere else, and turned into that very salable product, heroin. Much of it destined for your country, Osten. For dollars. What they do inside here might be to sell some opium, let you smoke it and sleep off your troubles, but that's not what they have in mind. The payoff is to get it out of Laos and into the countries of the west where the current crop of your affluent suburbanites thinks it's great fun to turn on, drop out, get high. When they ruin their lives and those of their children, as they will, it won't seem to be nearly as much fun. Meanwhile, a lot of very vicious people are making fortunes on the stuff. Those bags, this boat, these men that just arrived, that's what I was referring to as criminal activity a little earlier."

All the while he had been talking, I had been thinking. Listening, too, naturally, but thinking. "AcChan, we need the boat."

"You have something in mind?"

"I'm not sure, but I just know we need the boat. It will make us more mobile, for one thing."

"Sure it will, but where are we going?"

I shrugged. "I don't know," I confessed. "I just feel that we should take it. If nothing else, we can sink it."

"Great. We take it to sink it." He thought for a moment and then said, "We can take it and I must admit that the idea of sinking it if we can't think of anything else to do with it appeals to me, too. But we won't be dealing with amateurs. Someone may get hurt. They'll have guns."

"We have guns, too, and there are more of us."

"You're guessing on that. We're not certain how many men are inside right now."

"Unless we have all gone blind, there should be no more than three men inside, that's all we've seen, joined now by three more from the boat. That's six. We have fifteen, plus Wanchai and Hjuang."

"You've overlooked the room upstairs. The one that's always locked. We don't know who, or how many, are in there. Even Hjuang doesn't know."

"I'm guessing no one's in there. If there were, Hjuang would have seen someone, heard someone or been able to tell us something about the room. No one stays invisible in a room for days at a time. They have to use a toilet, go outside, walk around, make noise, fart, do something."

"I think you're wrong about that. We're going to find at least one man there, with his radio."

That surprised me. "What radio? How do you know there's a radio?"

"By the antenna. The big one sticking up on the roof. You can't see it now, it's too dark. But it's there. I was sure you'd seen it."

I was chagrined. I didn't gnash my teeth in anger, but I well might have. I had missed the antenna and I couldn't explain it. Like in Hong Kong, when the would-be maid surprised me with an attack cart, my concentration had failed me. That hadn't happened in the good old days and I wondered if it was a sign of advancing age or carelessness, neither one a good sign out here in the jungle.

AcChan didn't dwell on it. "So you want the boat," he mused.

"Undamaged," I told him.

"Of course, undamaged. That makes it more fun when we sink it," he said wryly. "Eddie, can you reach Bip and get him to come up here?" Then AcChan made his final plans for the attack.

Bip and two Thais were to crawl silently through the tall grass to within twenty yards of the long tailed craft and then make a sudden dash across the open ground to the rear where the lone man stood guard, his position still clearly marked by the intermittent glow of a cigarette.

AcChan with me, two of his men, and Magellan would wait near the side door until there was commotion at the boat and then burst inside. If the door was locked, AcChan assured me he would kick it in. Unlike Naroogian's failed promise at the hotel, I had no doubt that the result would be different this time. Meanwhile, Naroogian himself would lead a Thai, Disbrow, Dirkens, and Eddie through the front door, while Wanchai was dispatched to the far side of the building. Our instructions from AcChan were simple and direct. "If anyone shoots at us, shoot back." A Thai rifleman was ordered to stand watch on the village side, another at back to protect against surprise from the jungle trail, while Hjaung was our inside man, our secret weapon. Our limited forces were deployed and ready for action. Except for Dirkens and Disbrow who were dismayed at AcChan's instructions.

Until now, they had grudgingly worn jungle camouflage, carried assault weapons, trudged through oppressive heat, and battled ferocious insects feasting on their blood, all without voicing a complaint. They hadn't however, considered that carrying weapons often meant having to use them and that using them could lead to violence and suddenly they were stricken with an attack of conscience, or was it reluctance, or something far worse?

"What do you mean shoot them?" asked Disbrow, plaintively. "You mean, shoot these people we just saw go in the building? We can't do that, can we?" he asked, apparently addressing his question to Naroogian, who remained silent.

"They're your men," AcChan told him. "Do you want to explain the situation to them? Or should I?"

At least Naroogian didn't disown his Pan Union associates. He didn't exactly praise them either. "You heard the man. He said if anyone shoots at us, we shoot back. Makes sense to me. Otherwise, maybe we'll have to be carried back home in one of the sacks we just saw them take inside. Got it?"

Dirkens wasn't convinced. "Avram, what are you saying?" He asked, pleadingly. "I can't believe you mean this."

Clearly, Naroogian was wishing he had left these two behind. They were not, the psychologists would say, properly motivated. But then, why should they be? I was looking for Ken Green; I had a reason for being here, motivation, desire. AcChan was being paid and there could have even been more than that. Eddie was with me, and Naroogian himself? I wasn't sure. But he would do what had to be done to stay close to me, of that I was certain. But Disbrow and Dirkens? They shouldn't be here and they knew it as well as I did. They were fish out of water, better suited for performing Shakespeare in a community theater or napping beside a pool than for carrying heavy backpacks and fully loaded rifles in Laos. Violence didn't become them. It scared the hell out of them.

They found no sympathy from Naroogian, their company foreman. "Like I said, you heard the man. You've had weapons training. You've been drawing a paycheck, a good one for too long without working very hard, now earn it. Go in that building and do your damned job. Just follow me. It isn't that hard. Probably nothing's going to happen anyway." We should be so lucky.

Dirkens still wasn't convinced. "I don't feel right about this, Avram. I'm going to file a grievance."

"Fine, you do that. If it makes you feel any better, I'm not too happy about this either, but you go ahead and file the grievance while I just do my job. Put it in writing and send it through channels."

"How can I do that? I don't have the forms and there aren't any channels out here."

"How come I never thought of that?" said Naroogian sarcastically. "If you can't do it here, do it when you get back to Bangkok, or better yet, in Hong Kong or even wait until Washington. Just stop whining about it and get on with the job. OK? You understand?" He ended the conversation by walking away.

Dirkens and Disbrow stood alone, looking at one another, and fell silent.

They had a point. I had been wondering about the legalities of smashing in the door of a private building in a foreign country myself. It wasn't something we would normally do back home, but then, as AcChan had pointed out, this seemed to be a place where 'criminal activity' was the norm. But was it? Was anything illegal going on, did the duffel bags contain opium or were they filled, perhaps, with nothing more sinister than coconuts? Were men keeping people from going upstairs because of criminal activity or because the lady of the house was embarrassed because she hadn't made the bed? And did any of that, bad housekeeping or simple lawbreaking, justify our planned forced entry without a warrant? Maybe not, but we were definitely going inside just the same. Perhaps I could have called it off, just walked away. But even if I did, I wasn't certain that AcChan would have walked away with me. I knew what I hoped to find. Information about Ken Green. I didn't know what he hoped to find, but I was certain it was more than that.

The plan wasn't perfect. No plan ever is. None ever allow for all the possibilities of error, the uncertain responses and actions of the participants on either side, all of the unknowns. Such as Disbrow stumbling and falling down as he came through the front door, dropping his rifle, and knocking down a Thai rifleman in the process. Forgetting all of his previous instructions, Dirkens stopped to help his fallen comrade, leaving Eddie and Naroogian alone to immobilize a startled group of three men sitting along a bar of rough pine planks supported on empty barrels. Two others sat motionless, drinks before them on a scarred round table. A bartender turned open mouthed to stare into the business end of Naroogian's AK47 and made the mistake of reaching for and raising a monstrous handgun, only to scream in agony as Hjuang, standing beside him, struck the threatening arm with a full bottle of beer, breaking both bottle and bone, the gun clattering to the floor from where it was retrieved by Hjuang. Showing practiced experience, he cocked it, leveled it at the remaining patrons, none of whom showed the slightest inclination to reach for the guns within easy reach of every one of them.

The Keystone Cop entry of the Pan Union commandos at the front door probably helped us as we crashed through the side entrance. Two men, sitting comfortably at one moment in wooden chairs tilted back against the wall, were distracted by the commotion at the other end of the room and, as they started to rise, they found themselves lying flat on the floor, looking up into AK47's and FN89's, a sight to discourage any effort to right themselves. I could only admire how AcChan had leaped forward, kicked the back legs from under the already unbalanced chairs, and left their occupants on their backs, wondering what had hit them. As a rifleman covered them, we bounded up the stairway, AcChan first, me following, and Eddie, appearing from somewhere, right behind me. The sound of smashed doors, falling chairs, and the bartender's piercing scream had alerted someone on the second floor because as we neared the top of the steps, the door was thrown open from inside and a startled man, gun in hand, was slammed aside by AcChan who knocked him down and kept on going. I dodged the falling body and went through the door as AcChan fired twice, both shots slamming into a radio transmitter where a dark skinned man was sitting, hurriedly turning dials and speaking into a microphone. Metal and plastic flew across the room as AcChan struck the still humming set with the butt of his rifle, and as the sound faded and the lights dimmed on the control panel, the finely instrumented piece of equipment went dead. AcChan's next shot blew a hole in the third man in the room, the one in the corner who had just fired a bullet from his gun, a bullet than whined when it passed less than a foot, I felt it was more like less than an inch, from my left ear. I knew Eddie had been right behind me and as the shooter slumped to the floor, a blood stain spreading across the front of his chest, I spun, expecting the worst. Eddie was still on his feet, breathing hard, pale, in shock, and I looked for the wound but didn't immediately see any blood. I reached out to support him as he said, "Geez, boss. That was close. Went right over the top of my head. You OK?"

Things settled down nicely after that. The radio operator sat quietly by his useless piece of equipment, both hands tightly clasped on his head. There was no expression at all on his face. I examined the man on the floor and not surprisingly, having been shot at close range, he was dead.

The operation outside had gone exceedingly well. No trouble at all and we had the long tail boat, undamaged, just as ordered. Now we assembled all of the prisoners downstairs under the watchful eyes of Bip and three Thais and we went looking for the duffel bags. We didn't have to look far as they were found in a locked room just off the bar area and we brought all four of them out for inspection.

They contained a brown resinous material, resembling the moist clay children in day care centers use to amuse themselves, only it smelled different. Not a nice clean clay smell, more of the smell I remembered from going into grandmother's root cellar when I was a boy – damp, moldy, the smell of moist earth, potatoes going bad, aging rutabagas and turnips, home brewed beer. AcChan pulled off a pinch and tasted it. "Bitter. Tastes like it, Bip. Smells like it, too. How much do you think there is in each bag?" he asked me.

I peered inside the open bag and removed a dinner plate sized mass of gray-brown material, approximately two inches thick, the soft exterior still impregnated with flattened poppy leaves, many tiny black seeds, bits of twiggy debris from the parent plant and an occasional insect. Each plate was separated from the neighboring one by a more modern innovation, waxed paper. I estimated the weight at a pound, slightly more or slightly less, I wasn't sure. I scratched the surface and it had formed a firm crust. I pushed harder and found the mass to be soft and pliable, the inside soft and mushy.

"Opium?" I asked.

AcChan confirmed it. "Opium. Raw stuff. Lots of it."

We counted sixty plates to the bag and estimated each bag contained 25-30 kilos. For which the farmers in the hills had probably received the equivalent of $25 US. By the time it was processed and purified, transported and marketed, these same bags would bring, depending on the market value at any given time in the many countries where it might be sold, from five to six million dollars. A product of the world economy, an example of the global market at work. It sounded profitable, but there were all the usual expenses, of course. Many people derived a living from this raw material as it worked its way down the chain of supply, all the way from the underpaid farmers, who were happy to receive anything at all, to the transhippers like our sullen captives in the store, to the processors and laboratory technicians, to the middlemen who smuggled it around the world, and finally to the drug lords who distributed it in major cities everywhere, and their allies, under-age kids who helped push it on street corners, entertainers and sports stars who actively flouted it as a life style, and corrupt public servants who made it all possible. Of course, there were risks in the business just as in any other. For example, the dead man on the floor upstairs.

"If you were worried about what we were doing here, Osten, rest easy," AcChan told me after we finished examining the contents of each bag. He must have sensed that I had been worried. "As I told you. Criminal activity. These bags prove it."

They seemed to, but was it against the law in Laos? Was breaking and entering, and shooting people, against the law in Laos? Was there any law in Laos?

Of more immediate importance, I decided, was the radio. "Did they get anything out by radio?"

AcChan said, "We'll ask."

The logical man to ask was the one we had found sitting in front of the set when we burst into the room and he didn't want to tell us. He sat, hands still atop his head at a table downstairs and glared at us without responding at all. He had the straight black dark hair I associated with a Vietnamese, but his face was fuller, his nose broader, the forehead shorter and his lips noticeably fuller. I had no idea what nationality he might be, and so far, he hadn't responded to questions in English, Thai, Lao or several hill tribe dialects thrown at him by Bip. Oh, he could understand the questions, you could see that by the flickering of his eyes when they were asked, but he wasn't going to answer.

Despite his silence, AcChan was still trying to elicit information from the radio operator, who I was certain had been the man treated with respect by the locals when he had arrived by boat less than an hour before. If so, he was a man of some importance. AcChan tried Chinese. There was still no response.

Across the room, Disbrow was seated on a bench trying to wrap an Ace bandage around a swelling ankle. He was our only casualty, a victim of misjudging the height of the threshold. He seemed to be in pain, which wasn't helped by Dirkens who was leaning over trying to give advice on how to apply the elastic dressing.

Eddie had been upstairs looking for anything of interest and he came back carrying a black satchel and his arms laden with paper boxes and file folders. He dropped the satchel and kicked it in my direction. "Take a look in there," he said.

What was in there was $500,000, exactly, in American $100 bills, all brand new, crisp, and tightly wrapped with new rubber bands each enclosing 50 bills, exactly $5,000 per packet, 100 packets in all. With curious eyes from around the room watching, I counted, wrote down the figure and handed it silently to AcChan. He nodded and stuffed the note into his pocket.

He walked back to the radio operator, who was still not acting as if he realized that he was a captive. AcChan made it clear to him that he was. He pointed to the money and said, "We've got what we came for. We thought it would be more, but we'll take what's in the bag. Unless you want to tell us where the rest of it is. I don't believe in deadlines and I really must be going so either tell me right now what I need to know or I'll just have my assistant take you, all of you, outside and shoot you. We can't be bothered with prisoners." As if to give emphasis to his statement, Bip stood up, checked the clip in his rifle and moved to stand beside AcChan.

I didn't know how serious he was about this and I hoped it was a ploy to loosen tongues, so I decided to help out and see where it took us. "You're right, it's time to get out of here. We can't be bothered with prisoners."

AcChan looked up in surprise and said, "I'm glad you agree."

Naroogian heard me and said, "Well, then, let's do it and get a move on." I was afraid he really thought it was a good idea. So were the prisoners. Unfortunately, so was Dirkens.

He had taken over the wrapping of Disbrow's ankle, Disbrow apparently having failed to do a satisfactory job of it, and when he heard us talk of shooting the prisoners, he lost his grip on the leading edge of the elastic and it sprung loose, completely unraveled and fell limply to the floor. "Avram, you can't talk about shooting prisoners. Shoot them? All these people, just sitting here having a beer! We can't shoot them. There must be a law against it or something." He looked imploringly at Naroogian. "You can't let them shoot anyone. This could get out of hand."

He found no support in Naroogian. "You get a better idea?" he growled. "What do you want to do with them? Sit here and drink beer? Play cards? Wait until their friends come along and shoot you?"

I thought that summed it up neatly, although I was sure there had to be other options. In any event, Dirkens thought about it for a moment, then bent over and picked up the fallen Ace bandage and resumed wrapping. In a lower tone, he asked his companion, "It wouldn't be right to shoot anyone, would it? You wouldn't do that, would you?"

Disbrow appeared to be unimpressed. He had his own problems. "Wrap the damned ankle, will you? It hurts like hell and I want to be able to get up and walk out of here with everyone else."

"Anyone else have anything to say?" I asked, scanning the room. The Thais took their lead from AcChan, not me, so I was talking to Eddie and Magellan since the other Americans had already made their contributions. Eddie's eyes were as wide as saucers, I still didn't see how the bullet upstairs had missed him but perhaps that was the advantage of being only 5 feet plus a little, but he had nothing to say. Magellan was holding tightly to his two transmitters and smiled weakly as if he would have liked more than anything in the world to be able to turn on one of them and ask for instructions, from someone, anyone. He couldn't so he stood there, and continued to smile. Maybe he couldn't see as he wasn't wearing his glasses.

That seemed to clinch it for AcChan. "All right, then, we'll shoot them. None of them speak English so they can't be of any help to us and this one, who could be of some help about the radio, he won't talk at all. Take them outside, line them up, and get rid of them." I heard the safety click off Bip's rifle and two Thai riflemen moved up to support him. How far was this going to go?

The click of the rifles seemed to galvanize at least one captive, the broken-armed bartender. "No!" he screamed. "I speak English. Good English. What do you want to know? I can help. Just fix my arm and I can help you."

I had been afraid it was going to come to that. My orthopedic experience was rusty. I wasn't sure what to do for the arm resting crookedly on the table in front of the sweating Lao. Plaster, proper materials to work with? Aside from the Ace bandage already, almost, wrapped around Disbrow's ankle, we didn't have much. But there was always something and I looked around for anything I might be able to use to make him comfortable.

AcChan, though, was cool to the offer. "I don't know, Osten. Like I said, we have the money so we don't need any help, do we?" He was playing his line skillfully, using just the right lure, fishing for the big one.

From behind him, coolly, much too coolly for the situation he was in, the radio operator said, "Don't play games with us. I speak English. I suspect I'm the one you really want to talk to so why don't you ask me your questions?"

"I've already done that," AcChan replied. "You didn't give me any answers."

"Ask me again. Maybe you'll get lucky."

"Maybe. We'll see."

The radio operator looked relieved. I noticed that he was sweating, too, every bit as much as the bartender. Maybe he wasn't sure that AcChan had been playing a game after all.

While AcChan, Eddie, and Naroogian took the suddenly talkative captive upstairs for a private conversation, I found newspapers and magazines and a few fragments of wood and used them to make a decent splint for the broken arm after trying to set the ends of the shattered bones back together. It wasn't the best looking job I had ever seen, but it was the best I could do at the moment. Surprisingly, when I finished, he thanked me.

Then I went over to the bench, took the much worn Ace bandage away from Dirkens and wrapped it tightly around Disbrow's puffy ankle. No thanks from him. After I had finished, Dirkens opened two beers, handed one to Disbrow, and started to drink the other. He didn't offer one to me.

# 14

"He talked," AcChan told after he came back downstairs. "Told us what he knows or what he would like us to think he knows." We were standing on the porch near the front of the store and could see the shadow of the long tail boat still tied to the dock bobbing gently on the swells of a placid river. The running light on the stern flickered and caught my attention until I realized that it was nothing more than one of AcChan's men moving from one side of the craft to the other, hoping to detect oncoming river traffic long before it spotted us.

"He says he's originally from Jakarta. Mother a native of New Guinea, father from India. Was raised, he says, in Indonesia, living in several different places over the years, including Paris, London, Vienna, Singapore, and now lives in Bangkok. A real cosmopolitan type of man. I believed the mother and father part, largely because of the color of his skin and there wouldn't be too much reason to lie about that, but the rest of the story is probably fiction. Creative fiction. Mostly, if not all, lies. He was just passing by in the boat, he says, and was thirsty so they stopped by for a beer and something to eat. The bartender, he seems to be the manager as well, asked him if he knew anything about radios when he put the beer in front of him. Seems as if he had this radio, a big one, and it wasn't working. So he was eager to find a man with technical skills to look at it. That's not always easy in remote areas like this, he told me, so even though his skills are limited, he agreed to take a look at the set. So our thirsty Mr. Suchep, that's his name by the way, according to him, Vijay Suchep, had just gone upstairs to see if he could be of any help when we arrived, knocking people about, shooting, frightening everyone, especially the poor man who was in the room with him who foolishly tried to use a weapon Mr. Suchep had no idea he possessed.

"You're probably wondering about the money," AcChan continued. "He was amazed himself. He had never seen that much money. Real American money. Had hardly ever seen American money before and couldn't imagine what it was doing in that satchel. Then I had Eddie search him, and to his surprise, although not to mine, we found another $11,000 of this currency stuffed into his pockets. All $100 bills. 'Oh, that,' he explained. Expense money. Just money to pay his bills along the way. He noted that a lot of places in Laos don't accept credit cards like they do in the tonier joints he usually hangs out in, so he carries cash. Didn't even realize it was American cash. Just something to use as he traveled about. He suggested that should I

344

care to, I could have it. He could always raise more. Which led me to believe he was offering ransom."

"Or a bribe," I suggested.

"Whatever it was, I took it and added it to the rest. Then we went back to the matter of the man with the gun. Just an acquaintance, had only encountered him three days earlier in Vientiane, and they agreed to travel together for safety and companionship. They'd been warned about bandits before they departed on the trip so most surely the poor man had armed himself against just such an event. When we broke in, he must have assumed we were bandits and had acted in self defense, hoping to prevent a robbery. He inquired, at that point, 'you're not bandits are you?'"

"How did you answer that?" I interrupted.

"I scoffed at the suggestion. I told him on the contrary, that we were a photographic expedition for an American magazine gathering material for an upcoming television travelogue on the beauty and joys of travel in southeast Asia. I don't think he believed me."

"What about the raw opium?" I asked.

"I was just getting to that. He was appalled. He just couldn't believe his eyes when we brought out those bags and opened them. He had no idea what was inside. Sure, they had been on the boat on the trip from Vientiane, and I doubt that the trip started there, by the way, but they belonged to his unfortunate traveling companion, no he didn't even know the poor man's name, isn't that a shame, who is lying over there dead. He saw them put aboard, four?, he thought there had been only three, and assumed that it was something the man sold, a product, samples or perhaps even his luggage, but he hadn't asked and the dead man had never told him and now he never would, would he? Suchep himself? His business? Teak. He buys it. Was going upriver in search of prime stands of teak that he hoped to purchase, cut, and ship back to Thailand where it would be turned into expensive furniture for rich Americans and Europeans who were demanding more and more of it while there were fewer and fewer trees to be found. His work was hard, but he did a service to everyone by traveling in places like this trying to make American homes more beautiful. Sure, sometimes he smuggled teak logs into Thailand, everyone did. But after all, it's only a little crime, not a real one. Not like smuggling drugs or selling drugs, right? That's when he winked."

"So that's what he had to say? Aside from his parentage, did you believe anything at all?

"No."

"What did you do when he winked?"

"I stood up and remained quiet for a while. Then I said for telling all those lies, we would shoot him anyway. I suspect he thinks we won't, but he's not sure. His lips became very pale. He looked worried. Naroogian's reaction was interesting. As I was leaving the room, he went over and slapped the man hard on the back of the head. 'You lying bastard,' is what he said. But he looked pleased. Not about hitting the man in the head, which really didn't do any damage, but pleased about what he had just heard. And he knew the man was lying, just as I did. I suspect if questioned again, Suchep might tell some other kind of a story."

We went back inside where our captives were all in one group again, closely guarded by alert Thais and Naroogian. Suchep was seated on a chair, hands before him on the table, glowering at everyone in the room. The bartender-manager was watching him cautiously, his splinted arm supported by a makeshift sling fashioned from the only table cloth we could find in the place, but seemed even more wary of AcChan. I took out my photographs again and showed one to him. "Ever see this man?" AcChan translated. He shook his head no. "What about this one?" holding Ken Green in front of his face. Once again, no.

AcChan reached across the table and pulled on his hand, twisting slightly. "What did you use to make this splint, Osten? Maybe if we pulled it off we could make a better one from our tent pegs, if it isn't too tight." And he pulled harder, the taped wrapping unable to keep the fractured bones from rubbing against one another. The result was pain, and sweat began to pour from the injured man's forehead once again. "Doesn't seem too tight, Osten, let me try once again," and he grasped the end of the splint more firmly. He didn't do anything, just held it, and the bartender glanced at Suchep, looked back to AcChan, and decided we had the guns and it was his arm.

His memory improved. "I saw them, maybe," he admitted. "Two weeks ago, once or twice before, too, in here." He tapped Lee Duc Than's picture, saying, "He was sick and looks older. But maybe it was him. This one," pointing to Green, "is older. Both are older than pictures, but this one is thinner. Face different, but I think it might be the man." He avoided looking anywhere near Suchep, who was glaring at him murderously. I was glad we had the guns. From across the room, Naroogian was watching carefully. He looked almost as angry as Suchep and I wondered why that should be. He didn't try to strike the bartender in the head, however, so perhaps I was reading his expression incorrectly.

AcChan looked at me with a gleam of satisfaction. He was saying, silently, progress, at last. He leaned close to the bartender and asked so softly, I barely heard him, and I was only five feet away, "Where are they now?"

Eyes downcast, not daring to risk a glance at Suchep, he replied, "They say that way," and he motioned towards the back of the building. "I've never been there so I don't know for sure."

"Who says 'that way'?" AcChan wanted to know. "And you've never been where?"

"People who talk. Men who come in here from the river. That's what they say when they have too much to drink. But I've never been there and I don't know where it is." He was evasive, fearful of giving us any information, just as fearful of withholding it.

But AcChan was persistent. "Give us a name. Tell us where they are." His hand was once again grasping the splint.

"The place is called Yellow Garden. That's where they are," he whispered as he carefully removed AcChan's hand and moved a few inches back from the table.

It was clear none of the other captives had anything to say. They sat sullenly as they were questioned each in turn and one of them spat at AcChan instead of replying and for that, earned himself a rap on the back of the head delivered by Bip, not Naroogian.

We had a name but no idea where it would lead us, if anywhere. But one thing was clear; we had to be leaving the store, as soon as possible, and I reminded AcChan of the urgency. "They may have sent a message before you blew away their radio and we could have visitors at any time. We should be moving out."

He didn't argue. "You're right, we've wasted enough time. Eddie, take a man or two and collect everything that will burn. Pile the furniture, any wood you can find, papers, all of it right in the center of the floor here. Put the duffel bags in the center of the pile. There should be gasoline and fuel oil out back. Bring some in here and saturate the pile with it. Get it ready to burn. Then blow up the generator. We won't be using it and we don't want anyone else to use it for a while either."

Next he instructed Bip to collect anything we could use to bind the captives. He came back with rope from outside, a roll of sturdy twine from the boat, discovered a dozen roles of the ubiquitous duct tape under the bar, and produced ten pairs of lightweight but sturdy plastic handcuffs from his pack. "Tie them together, hands behind their backs, the rope looped around their necks, tightened with tape, so that we have them in a single file. You know how to do it." And Bip did, indeed, know how to do it.

AcChan saw me watching the operation and said, "I borrowed the idea from the Viet Cong. They showed many of us how to move prisoners along with the least possible trouble. Tie them up, tight, and if they give you any trouble, shoot them on the spot. Make sure you tell them that, Bip. Just so they understand the rules. Especially him – Mr. Suchep. Right, Mr. Suchep? We want to make sure you understand the rules." Like I said, I was glad we had the guns and not Suchep because the look he gave us was decidedly unfriendly.

"While we're waiting for all this to be done, let's look at the map. I've been up here and thought I knew the villages in this area but I've never heard of one called Yellow Garden. And I don't see one on this map either," he said after another five minutes of searching. "Maybe Wanchai or Hjuang will know something by that name. Both of them were born nearby."

He turned to another Thai rifleman standing near the door and ordered, "Go outside and relieve Wanchai. Have him come in here." Then turning to me again, he asked, "Well, it's your decision. What do you want to do with the prisoners? Drag them along with us as we go hunting for Ken Green or send them back?"

"Send them back where?"

"Across the river. Back to Thailand," he said.

Puzzled, I said, "Who wants them there?"

"Who wants them here?" he challenged.

When he had instructed Bip to tie them up, I had assumed he meant to leave them here, at the landing, as we pushed on. Now I realized that it was a poor idea. They would surely be free in no time, either on their own or by threatening or buying a villager to cut their bonds and then they would be as menacing as ever. So we had to do something but before we could consider that question, Wanchai suddenly burst through the front door, dragging a reluctant figure behind him. It was the love smitten Ha.

"He was hiding outside and I saw him in the bushes. I didn't think he had come out of a window so I didn't shoot, but I didn't know what to do with him, so here he is."

Ha looked around, eyes wide as he watched Bip and another Thai tightly binding a long column of men together, took in Eddie and his men piling furniture, duffel bags, papers, and planks into a giant pile and splashing gasoline over it. He finally said, "I heard shooting, so I came to see what was happening."

"You should have stayed in the village," AcChan told him. "You could have been hurt. Did any others come with you?"

"Many others. Including Prathorn, the wild bull. He's out there. Maybe his daughter, too."

AcChan turned to Wanchai and said, "I want you to go out there and round up whoever you can. Send them back to the village. It could become dangerous here. But before you go, do you know of a village named Yellow Garden? Anywhere in this area? Anywhere at all?"

Wanchai thought about it and finally admitted that he did not. He left to carry out his assignment and we went back to the map only to be interrupted by Ha who asked, "Are you looking for Yellow Garden? I know where that is. I've been there."

AcChan and I were looking at one another in disbelief. AcChan fired questions at the youth who listened and answered, "No, I don't know of any village by that name. It isn't a village. Yellow Garden is a place. A very pretty place."

Get the whole story from him, I suggested, and AcChan and he carried on a lengthy conversation which he relayed to me something like this.

"Yes, he's been there, numerous times. With Noi. You know him, don't you?, Simi Si's drunken and abusive husband. Sometimes he drinks too much and has to go there but he's afraid to go alone. So Ha goes with him. Gets paid for it, leads him through the jungle along a trail that's hard to follow at night, takes him to the edge of the jungle where he has to stay behind because Noi doesn't want anyone to know he needed help, doesn't think it would be safe for either of them if the people living in the big house knew someone had been with him, so he hides in the brush, watches as Noi goes up to the fence, is passed through the gate, and goes into the house. Often he sticks around until twilight because it's so pretty, as he told us."

"What's so pretty?"

"Yellow Garden. The spray, the spray of water that leaps high into the air and picks up the sunset in orange and yellow tones, reflecting off low lying clouds on many nights, lighting up the sky. And the flowers. He says the valley below, all around the big house, is filled with yellow flowers, as far as the eye can see. The yellow flowers and the yellow spray, that's Yellow Garden. It may not be the official name and it isn't on the map, but it's what Noi calls it, as do many of the others who live in the big house, according to Ha. At least that's what he says Noi told him."

"So Yellow Garden is a flower garden," I concluded.

"No, not really. The flowers are separate and just add color to the spray. The flowers are what he looks at while he waits for the spray."

"What the hell are you talking about?" I said, exasperated. "What spray?"

"Sorry. Thought you understood. The spray from the water striking the rocks. Yellow Garden is the name of the waterfall. A big one."

"A waterfall! We're looking for a waterfall?"

"Apparently. Although Ha has never seen it."

"Why not? He's been there."

"He's been where he can see the spray. And the top of the waterfall. From a distance on the other side of the big house. But he's never seen the bottom where the water strikes. He's been told that's what happens by Noi but there are mountains on one side and the river on the other and the fence in between so he's just watched from where Noi leaves him and then returned home, unseen, each time."

"Well," I said, "it looks like it's time to talk to Noi and see what he can tell us. Perhaps we can hire him to lead us there."

"That won't be possible. According to Ha, Simi Si's husband is already at the big house. He went up there three days ago and hasn't returned. He usually stays for a week at a time so isn't due back for several more days."

I was curious. "What is this big house he talks about? Who lives there and what does Noi do there? In fact, what does anyone do there?"

It took a while and more translation but I finally got my information. "The big house is just that. A big house. Ha makes it sound like something out of the Mississippi plantation country, a place where you would see fine ladies in crinoline dancing with handsome gentlemen in uniform, although I suspect he's romanticizing a bit."

It sounded as if AcChan was mixing Gone with the Wind and Georgia with something else, but I did get the picture, even if it was misleading.

"He's not sure who lives there," he continued. "Noi doesn't want to talk about that. He does talk about how he hires people to work there. Goes out, he says, and finds men and women to work on the farm. Always seems to be needing more people so they must be awfully busy on that farm."

"What kind of a crop do they grow?" I asked.

"Ha says he doesn't know. I think he does, but he's young and pretends he is still naïve. But I bet if I gave a cynic like you a guess or two, you could come close."

I bet he was right.

"Can Ha show us where this waterfall is on the map? It's laying right here and that would help us find the place."

AcChan took him to the colored map spread across the bar and pointed to our position, showed him the mark for the village, drew a finger along the river bank, and asked where Yellow Garden might be. Ha shook his head. "Not this river," he objected. "The other river."

"What other river?" he was asked. "Show us on the map."

"I can't," he replied.

"Why not?"

"Because the river isn't on the map! It should be here," he insisted, drawing an imaginary line westward from the building, towards the mountains clearly shown fifty to sixty miles away. The mountains were there; the river wasn't. AcChan hastily pulled several more maps from his pack and examined each of them. None showed a river.

"These are excellent, current maps. Military and geological survey maps. I don't understand it. None of them show a river where he says there should be a river. Where's Wanchai? Get him back in here."

Five minutes later, relieved from crowd control duty where he had been sending curious villagers back to their homes, without much success, everyone wanting to hang around to see what was going to happen next, Wanchai looked at the maps and solemnly told AcChan, "Bad maps. They don't show the river. It should be here." He drew an imaginary line just north of where we were and then headed due west towards the mountains. "I'm sure it's still there," he added. "It was there yesterday when I left the store and walked downstream away from you before circling back. That's how far I walked. Down to the river. The one not on the map."

"Interesting," murmured AcChan. "Ha, do you know Lo Dan, the fisherman? Do you know where he lives? Will you go ask him to come up here for a moment? Perhaps he can explain where our river went."

"You won't have to go far to find him," Wanchai said. "He's right outside with all the rest. I'll go get him."

LoDan didn't use maps; he didn't own any and didn't bother looking at the one AcChan placed in front of him. "Of course there's a river going towards the mountains," he said. "I fish in it once or twice a week. How big is it? Big enough. Not as big as the one in front, not as wide, maybe not as deep, but it has some big fish in it. Sometimes the best fish I catch come from there."

"Would a boat like the one by the dock be able to go up the river?" asked AcChan, never doubting for a moment that a fisherman would have passed up an opportunity to examine our prize of war out front.

"I could go anywhere with a boat like that," Lo Dan countered. He sounded as if he was dying for a chance to demonstrate what he could do with the long tail boat and its powerful motor.

"How far upstream is the waterfall?" I asked.

He shrugged. He didn't know. He'd heard there was a waterfall somewhere up there but he had never gone that far.

"Why not?"

"Less than a day's poling upstream, the fishing isn't good. Too many crocodiles."

"What happens? Do they eat the fish?" I asked.

He shrugged again. "I don't know, they might. But they eat people if you fall overboard. Those are big crocodiles. Then, there are the men who shoot at you when you go that far up the river. They are worse than the crocodiles."

"What men? Why do they shoot at you?"

"They don't want you to go up the river. That's why." That made sense and you didn't need a map to figure it out.

"Find out if he thinks he could slip by the men who shoot at you, in the dark, using the long tail boat," I suggested.

AcChan translated once again and responded, "He doesn't know. He's never gone up the river in the dark. But he thinks he might be able to do it, if he was quiet and the night was dark enough. I take it you're planning on traveling upstream to see a waterfall?"

"I don't know. It's an option. If Ha could show us the trail, maybe we could send the equipment on the boat and save ourselves a lot of heavy lifting and time. But to do that, we'd have to hire Lo Dan and Ha and I'm not sure they'll take the job."

"It never hurts to ask. There is a high rate of unemployment up here and you might be surprised how easy it is to add men to the payroll." AcChan motioned Lo Dan aside and talked to him in low tones. He did the same with Ha and then returned to where I was waiting, smiling. "Like I told you. They need work so they'd be more than happy to do what you asked. Lo Dan is eager to try a boat like the one we've just requisitioned and Ha is familiar with the trail and he figures we'll pay more than Noi, so why not?"

We even hired Prathorn, the wild bull, and another husky hill tribesman, assigning them to ride the boat upstream and carry the x-ray machine and its supplies from the boat landing near Yellow Garden to the big house. We needed them as replacements as AcChan had decided to assign the other two tribesmen to Wanchai, part of an escort taking our captives back across the river. About that, I once again inquired, "Who are you sending them back to?"

"Wanchai will find someone to take them off his hands. If he has to, he can use the $500,000 as an added inducement."

"You're sending the money back, too," I said, surprised. That was a lot of money for a businessman to be tossing away.

"Think about it, Osten. What would we do with it up here? There really isn't any place to spend it."

I was thinking about it. Entrusting that much money to Wanchai didn't seem like the smartest move in the world of finance, unless AcChan knew a lot more about Wanchai than I did. Which he surely did and he didn't seem to be worrying about it in the least. But then, he rarely seemed to be worrying about anything.

"All right. So you send them back under guard with a bag of money. They meet who? The Thai Border Police? Aren't they going to be interested in why some of your men, armed to the teeth, happen to be traveling with eight men trussed with ropes, handcuffs and duct tape, and have a half million dollars in a black satchel?"

"Those are good questions and the Thai Border Police, if that's who they encounter, almost certainly will ask exactly those questions. That's why I want to make sure Wanchai is along. He answers questions like that better than anyone else."

I argued that Dirkens and Disbrow should be assigned to the group. AcChan wasn't thrilled with the idea. "I want them to move fast, Osten. They would only slow the group down."

Neither Disbrow nor Dirkens liked the idea either. "I don't want to leave the main party, not while my ankle hurts," complained Disbrow. Dirkens looked on helplessly and didn't have anything to say.

Naroogian settled the matter. "They stay with me. They're my men and they go where I go and I'm going up the river." That seemed to settle the matter, although he added, as an afterthought, "Magellan goes with me, too." Of course, Magellan and his transmitter.

Ten minutes later, the column of captives guarded by Wanchai, Hjuang, two tribesmen, and a Thai rifleman headed upriver back towards the ford where we had crossed two days earlier. "Move as fast as you can tonight and try to cross into Thailand by dawn," were AcChan's parting instructions. "If you're close to the border when it becomes light, keep going. If you have to stop, hide, stay quiet, and make it very clear to everyone that if they make any noise, or if you are discovered during the day, they are the ones who are likely to be hurt." Then they were gone.

It didn't take long for the rest of us to be on the move after that. Lo Dan topped off the fuel tank on the motor of the long tail boat and received a crash course in how to operate the craft from an unexpected source – the boatman who had piloted it to the dock earlier that evening. He had seen how things were going, recognized that AcChan was the new boss on the block, and volunteered his services. AcChan accepted another recruit, but didn't think him trustworthy enough to issue a gun or to give him control of the boat. Instead, he was relegated to a consultancy, his hands tied behind him, and an anchor tied to his right ankle. It was made clear to him that should he get out of line, Prathorn would cheerfully pick him up and throw him into the river, from which it was unlikely he would ever return, the depth being over thirteen feet. As a backup, AcChan had Lo Dan's small pole boat tied behind the larger craft where it would be towed along obediently like a puppy on a leash, just in case we needed it.

We loaded the x-ray machine and other materials aboard, tied the volunteer securely to a stanchion amidships, anchor snug around the ankle, watched as Prathorn, the second recruited tribesman, a rifleman, and then at the last minute, Dirkens and Disbrow were assigned a seat. By Naroogian!

Dirkens led the protest this time and was finally silenced when Naroogian thundered, "Stop whining and shut up. Disbrow can't walk and we have a long walk ahead of us. Miles and miles. So I'm doing him a favor and giving him a ride. You go along and keep him company. You're armed, you're in good company, and it's an easy ride. So what if the others don't speak English? You and Disbrow talk to each other and follow the lead of the Thai with the rifle or the guy running the boat. I assume they know what they're doing. At least he," indicating AcChan, "seems to think they do. If he trusts them, you can trust them."

He didn't convince either Pan Unionist but it didn't matter, because once they were settled in the boat, Lo Dan gunned the motor and they pulled away from the dock, steered for the channel and then made a giant loop heading back to the north where the river that wasn't was located. Just before we untied them from the dock, AcChan issued his instructions to Lo Dan and his rifleman. Stay to the north bank, use the motor at normal speed for the first hour, then cut it way back and crawl slowly at trolling speed until well past the place where the gunmen were supposed to be. In the dark, they should be able to slip by, but if not, gun the motor to full speed and head towards the waterfall. Take cover along the far bank before dawn, and stay there, hidden and not moving until we radioed them to come in to the boat landing below the big house, which Ha assured us was there, or gave them other instructions. AcChan made the Pan Unionists feel a little better by handing Disbrow a radio. "You can send with this by pushing the red button. Don't push it unless you're under attack. Keep the green button depressed. This is the one you need to pick up instructions from us. Got it? Don't send any messages. They can use the transmission to track your location if they have the proper equipment. Just listen for us. You'll be fine." They didn't look like they were believers.

With the captives on their way and the boat out on the river, we finished packing our gear, took one last look around at the store, and burned it down. Bip threw the torch that landed squarely in the center of the gasoline soaked pile and it burst into flame with a roar. We watched spellbound from the edge of the clearing, standing on the jungle trail, as flames, clearly visible through the open doors and windows shattered by the force of the blast, darted about the interior, tongues of orange seeking out and devouring everything in their path, lighting up the night like had never been seen along this stretch of the river, visible for miles. With a rush, a wild torrent of fire tore through the roof and escaped into the night, licking at the soggy roof, consuming it, black oily smoke boiling into the sky above the humpbacked roof, uncoiling as it reached for freedom, and mingled with the lowering storm clouds once again assembling just behind the ridge line to the west.

Reluctantly, we turned away from the spectacle and started a slow climb away from the river, passing quickly into thick trees, past Goong's hovel, where I thought I saw a quick glimpse of him hiding in the same thicket he had used earlier in the day, and headed west. I glanced back once, just in time to see the roof collapse amidst a shower of sparks and flaming embers thrown high into the night, and several booming explosions shattered the quiet of the forest. None of the villagers would be asleep tonight. Without looking back, AcChan, just a dim shadow immediately ahead of me, said, "Looks like we may have missed something. Ammunition, fuel, bombs, something." Two more explosions cut him short. In the silence that followed, he observed, "Definitely. We missed something. Careless of me."

Aside from the shuffle of feet on the trail, the squeak of wet leather boots, and the occasional sound of metal against metal as weapons contacted packs or canteens, there was almost total silence for the next two hours as we pushed hard to put as much distance between us and the river as we possibly could. Ha seemed to be an excellent guide with superb night vision. He led us on a straight path at first, towards the ridge line, then we began to veer slightly south as we climbed higher. The higher we went, the more the trail began to turn back on itself, and despite the coolness of the jungle night, we were soon sweating heavily once more. After a while, I became aware of a new sound in the sky, the staccato beating of a helicopter, one that seemed to be coursing erratically back and forth, as if looking for something. Us?

AcChan sensed my question once again as he stopped and listened. "They could be looking for us, Osten. But you never know up here. If they have infrared equipment, they'll spot us even if we go into hiding so we might just as well keep going. Let me know if you feel like stopping for the night. We could any time now."

I had already passed the time when I should have stopped. Both legs were about to cramp and each step was threatening to be my last. But pride and possible embarrassment kept me going, until I realized I could go no further. Humbly, I managed to catch up to AcChan, fall in beside him, and in almost a whisper, suggested, "Maybe this is far enough. If we get a chance, maybe we should stop and rest." As a final attempt to salvage some dignity I had added the 'maybes,' but I could easily have left them out of both sentences.

He expressed no surprise. He simply said, "At the top of this rise, where the trees thicken, among those rocks, see, against the sky, that looks like a good place. We can set up camp, rest, eat something, and wait until morning to see what the land up ahead looks like." He left me behind as he hurried forward to tell Bip and Ha of his decision.

I wasn't the only one who had reached the point of fatigue. From behind me, Naroogian's voice asked, "Is this guy crazy? He'll kill us all with this pace."

Before I could answer, we had reached the rocks and AcChan was signaling the column to halt. We moved away from the trail, into the rocks fifty feet higher up and more than a hundred feet to one side. Most of the men opened rations, the first food in almost twelve hours, and then spread tarps on the damp ground to rest. Sentries were posted and the camp fell silent as sleep overtook most of the party. I was restless, trying to find a comfortable position on the uneven ground, and kept thinking of Ken Green, Kendra, poppies, opium, and what it was all about. Was Green involved in growing the yellow flowers, was he still a prisoner, what would we find at the water-fall ahead? Nothing, Green, Lee Duc Than or an ambush? I didn't ask one other important question, because it no longer seemed relevant. The one that went what was I doing here? What difference did it make now? I was already here, and there was no turning back. My body needed sleep, but my brain wouldn't permit it.

And that's the way I was when AcChan silently appeared out of the darkness. "You asleep?" he asked, although I was sure that he had been watching me toss and turn fitfully.

"Not yet. Anything wrong?"

"I don't think so. The helicopter was a problem for a while there, be-cause we don't dare light a fire that would give us away, but other than that, no, nothing's wrong."

"Who do you think it is? Fantus?"

"I doubt it." He sat on his haunches staring up at the darkened sky, silent now, a sky that had cleared and sparkled with stars scattered like dia-monds across a black velvet tray inside a jeweler's display case. "He doesn't have to look for us. We're going to radio him and tell him where we are, remember. So it's not him. Could be military, a patrol or someone hauling drugs, or smugglers, or just a stray civilian. Hard to say. The safest thing to do is stay out of sight."

"Well, thanks for the update. You'd better get some rest yourself," I suggested. "You've had a long day like the rest of us."

"I didn't come by to bring you up to date," he said, surprising me. "I came because Bip is worried about you."

"Bip? What's he worried about?"

"The way you're laying. He says it's bad to lay that way."

"The way I'm laying? I'm just laying here on a tarp spread over the ground in an effort to stay dry. It's uncomfortable but other than that, what's wrong with it?"

"Your head. It's pointing to the west. That's unlucky. He says you should change it and have your head pointing to the east. If you don't want to do that, try it with your head to the north. Even that is better than to the west.

Safer."

I couldn't see what difference it made which way your head was pointing and although it was hard to see many of the men who had fallen asleep around me in the darkness, as near as I could tell all of them within sight seemed to be sleeping with their head to the east. "Apparently Bip has superstitions, too, like Wanchai?" I asked.

"So it seems. As I told you, Thais have many superstitions. Being a Meo, I don't have that problem."

"I see. Let me ask you, then, which way are you planning on sleeping tonight?"

He grinned. "With my head pointing east. I'm not superstitious, though. It's just to make Bip feel better."

He was suddenly gone, disappearing into the darkness before I realized he was no longer beside me. I got to my feet, turned around, and laid back down, this time with my head pointing east. A few feet to my right, I heard Eddie mumble, "Well, I might as well turn around, too, if it's luckier that way." I heard him moving around in the dark, answered his "good night" and fell asleep, awaking three hours later to a faint dawn, the light coming from in front of me to see the sun just breaking over the massed green of the jungle canopy behind us. I never did find out if sleeping with your head to the east was lucky or not, but apparently it enabled one to fall asleep quickly, and that was reward enough. Eddie had already risen and was on sentry duty, sitting alongside a huge boulder fifty feet away, watching the trail.

AcChan allowed several of his men to light miniature alcohol stoves and we enjoyed hot tea and canned biscuits for breakfast. There was the usual bustle and movement seen in any camp, men tending to bodily functions, spitting, coughing, but no talking, no laughter. Gear was reassembled, tarps folded, all waste collected and carefully buried further away from the trail, and then the area where we had slept was carefully brushed with limbs to remove, so far as possible, all traces of our having been there. It wouldn't fool an experienced tracker, but anyone giving it a casual glance would have seen nothing out of the ordinary. Perhaps a small party had once stopped for lunch. Nothing more, if that.

Bip resumed the point with Ha immediately behind him and we were on the trail again. We had gone a mile, maybe slightly more, when dark clouds began to form over the hills directly ahead, and the sun, which, at first light had offered the promise of a dry trail, succumbed once again to the onslaught of the monsoons and the rains returned to the land. Out came the camouflage ponchos and slouch hats and we moved on, lifting wet and muddy feet, one after another, to plant them again onto a waterlogged track made by the foot ahead. It was impossible to hear any sound but that of the rain against our rubberized protective clothing, the dripping of water from the leaves overhead, and the occasional clanking of metal as one man or another shifted his pack in a futile search for a comfortable position. It was noon, just after, when Bip suddenly dropped from sight in the tall grass alongside the trail and AcChan raised an arm, indicating HALT! Everyone froze in place, crouched down following AcChan's lead, and waited as Bip rejoined him to report.

"Bip has seen men in the valley below, coming our way. We'll move back there," indicating higher ground a hundred yards or so to the left of the trail. "It's higher ground and we'll have a better field of fire from there if we need it. Hurry now, everyone off the trail."

We were there, under cover, rifles at the ready, when a dozen or more men slowly worked their way up the steep ground along the slippery trail, heads down, keeping the rain from their eyes. They were dressed in black waterproof covering similar to ours, were spaced ten to fifteen yards apart, and moved methodically, with chilling precision. Each man was armed, most with automatic weapons. The point man was relentlessly scanning both sides of the trail, his head pivoting first right, then left, then looking straight ahead, alert for the slightest indication of danger. He paused momentarily at the exact spot we had left the trail and stared at the mud under his feet. He looked straight ahead at the trail in front of him, finally waved his arm, and the column moved forward, disappearing around a bend in the trail.

"He's not sure about footprints," AcChan whispered to me. "He thinks there may be some but the rain is washing them away so he's not sure. Our camp, too, the rain will wash away all traces. See, sleeping the right way made us lucky."

He was right about the rain. It was now coming down so hard that I was worried that it would wash the garbage from our camp site out of the ground and float it down onto the trail. I didn't bother to bring that up. If it was a problem, I was sure AcChan had considered it and made plans to cope with it.

We were ready to move back to the trail when suddenly, there on the track immediately below us, were three more men, a rearguard. Two of the men stopped and looked directly uphill at our position. I held my breath. Had any of our men, thinking that the danger had passed, exposed himself to view?

The three black coated figures stood on the trail for another minute, not moving, and several safeties clicked off rifles to my right and left. Everyone was waiting for AcChan to make the first move and so far, he was just watching. Then, down below, first one man and then another, struggled to light a cigarette, cupping the thin white sticks against the wind and rain, in an effort to keep them dry. The third man suddenly walked into the brush, right at us, then stopped, dropped his trousers and performed what was most likely a highly satisfactory bowel movement, one that almost precipitated a burst of automatic rifle fire that would have made this his last act on earth, had he come another five feet up the hill before doing what he had to do. His two companions called to him, threw away soggy butts, and moved after the rest of their party before he had finished. A moment later, still pulling up his pants and dragging his rifle, he scurried after them.

Taking no chances, we stayed right where we were for another thirty minutes, then sent Bip and two men down to scout our back trail to see if it was clear. When they returned to report that it was, we resumed our trek towards Yellow Garden. This time, Bip and two riflemen moved further ahead, giving us more of a buffer in case we encountered another party on the trail. Just in case, AcChan also sent two men back as a rear guard.

"Who were they?" I asked.

"If I had to guess, I'd say from Yellow Garden. If I had another guess, I'd say they were headed for the store in response to a radio message they received from our know-nothing radio operator. A little slow, probably because they weren't sure what the message meant seeing we cut it off before he was finished. Another guess would be that it wasn't their helicopter last night because if they had a helicopter, why send men on foot? They could take them by air."

"Maybe, but isn't it possible it's raining too hard?"

"That's a good point. Maybe they're grounded. Which is a break for us. See how lucky sleeping right turns out to be?"

"What does this mean as far as we're concerned? Having armed men to the east, Yellow Garden, where there are presumably more armed men, to the west, and us in the middle?"

"Osten, you know as well as I do what that means. We are more or less surrounded. It also means that we're almost certainly outnumbered. The sixteen men that just passed us are more than we've got altogether and there are certain to be others at Yellow Garden. But we have the element of surprise. And the boat out on the river, if it hasn't sunk or been discovered."

He was silent for a while as we walked on in the rain. Then he cautioned, "Don't get your hopes too high about finding Green or Lee Duc Than. They may have been moved or they may never have been there at all. We may be chasing phantoms, but we'll find some answers once we get inside the wire and into the big house to take a look."

"You figure we'll make it inside?"

"Sure. We'll get inside. It's finding a way out that might be the hard part. I know we've been told that Fantus will come for us. You've been told that, haven't you? But you know what a poor record he has in picking up people in need of a ride to safety. So we should be thinking of an alternative, just in case, wouldn't you say?"

That didn't need an answer. AcChan had his own reasons for not trusting Fantus; I had mine and neither one of us had to say more.

It took us the rest of the afternoon to struggle the final five or six treacherous miles. We halted once when Bip discovered a land mine planted almost squarely in the center of the trail. Two more were found just to the left and another to the right where someone trying to avoid the first mine would be likely to walk in going around the danger. With Bip directing traffic, we carefully sidestepped the explosives and moved ahead. Ha was surprised. He had never seen mines along the trail before and Noi had never seemed worried about stepping on any in the many trips they had made together. "They're new," AcChan decided. "Put in today by the party we saw along the trail. They are suspicious that something is going on and wanted to leave a little message for us in case we slipped by them."

"What does that mean?" I asked and realized I was beginning to sound like an amateur. I knew what it meant. We had to be cautious from here on.

AcChan took the question seriously, however, and said, "It means that Bip is very good at avoiding traps like that. I wonder if they have anyone as good?"

"Why should that matter?"

"Two can play this game. Bip put down a mine right alongside theirs before he left. We'll see if they can find it before someone steps on it. It's a dirty weapon, one of the worst, but if they want to play with them, they should know they're taking a risk. So if they have a good man on the point, they'll be fine. If not, boom."

If it bothered him, it didn't show.

It was about then, despite the incessant beating of the rain and the water cascading upon us from the trees overhead, that I heard it again; the rhythmic clip-clopping sound of a helicopter, slowly moving from east to west and back again, hidden from view somewhere inside the leaden, moisture saturated clouds. I was confident that if we couldn't see them, they couldn't see us, and I motioned to the sky with a thumb and AcChan acknowledged with a nod, saying, "Somebody's still up there."

"Looking for us?"

"If they are, they'll have to get awfully lucky, won't they?"

"Unless, like you said, they have infrared sensors aboard. Then they could see us even in this kind of weather."

"Sense us, Osten, not see us. Even with infrared, they wouldn't see us, but they would know someone was down here on the ground giving off heat. That would allow them to pinpoint us, follow us, be waiting for us somewhere up ahead. So let's hope they don't have that gadget on board."

If they didn't, I was thinking, why would they be out flying around on a day like this? But those thoughts were interrupted when the small radio attached to his pack emitted a faint beeping sound while a small red light began to flash insistently on the dial.

AcChan reached behind him and removed the receiver, flipped a switch and said, "A2." I wasn't able to make out any of the faint transmission, the voice scratchy and garbled as if coming from a great distance, and AcChan's response was brief, after which he turned to me and said, "Disbrow. They hear the chopper out on the river and they're worried. I told them to get back under cover along the bank, that's where they're supposed to be anyhow, and to stay there until they hear from us." He was silent for a moment and then added, "That was stupid, him calling. I told him not to break radio silence and that we'd call him."

"Are they all right?" I asked.

"So far. If nobody heard the call, they should stay that way, but if they keep talking on the air, they could wind up being crocodile food."

"I hope you didn't tell them that. Dirkens seems worried enough about crocodiles as it is."

"No, I didn't tell them that. I just told them to stay quiet or they could get killed."

I grimaced. "That must have made them feel better, I'm sure."

Naroogian had seen AcChan on the radio and he hurried forward to find out what had been going on. "Disbrow?" he asked. AcChan nodded. "You call him?" said Naroogian.

"No, he called me. He was worried about the sound of the helicopter."

"That damned idiot," Naroogian snorted, plainly angered. "He could get killed if that helicopter was monitoring your channel."

"Exactly. That's what I told him," AcChan replied calmly. "I told him to stay off the air until we called him."

"Well, I hope he listens this time. He does some of the dumbest things. I don't know why Bath would send along a pair like that."

I'd wondered that myself and couldn't stop from asking, "Did you ever consider it was because they do dumb things like that that they got sent along?"

Naroogian took a hard look at me, wiped the rain from his face, and tugged his slouch hat further down until it was almost touching both upper eyelids, and said, "Yeah, matter of fact, I have considered that. More than once."

# 15

The final several miles went smoothly and uneventfully despite the rain. It was pitch dark and we were stumbling along in single file, all eleven of us, with Bip on the point and Ha immediately behind him, when the village youth suddenly touched Bip's arm and pointed to a faint light, dead ahead, down below us. We all saw it then, and moved forward cautiously for another quarter mile where we saw a second, third, and then a whole string of lights at two hundred foot intervals, illuminating a fence that sparkled like a twinkling band of Christmas tree lights along Main Street downtown in Anywhere, USA. Rain, not snow, made it glitter, and I thought that softly, in the distance, I could hear the strains of Silent Night, Holy Night rising from the foggy air, but that surely was just my imagination.

This fence was the boundary. Down below was our objective. Yellow Garden. What would we find? Ken Green, Lee Duc Than, Noi, merchants of death or nothing? Nothing at all?

AcChan passed around night glasses to Naroogian and me and we took a look at our target.

The waterfall was not in view. "Farther that way," Ha indicated, sweeping his arm to the north, in the direction of the river. Out there on that same river was our flotilla, one large boat, one small boat, six men, and all of our equipment. That is, if still undetected by a predatory airborne hunter.

What we could see with the glasses, although not as picture perfect as a daytime scanning, seemed peaceful enough. There was a large main house in the midst of a broad expanse of grass, not a tree within two hundred feet, and then only small ones. No bushes, a few low shrubs almost against the house itself, none more than 18 inches high. A wide verandah extended around the two sides of the house we could see and appeared to go all the way to the third side opposite our view. Four windows with shutters opened from the front and a large double french door seemed to be the main entryway. The roof seemed to be of curved interlocking tile, the construction frame with broad wooden siding, painted white. A plantation house. I was looking forward to a better view by day, although by then I hoped to be inside.

A football field length away were two barn like structures, one a single story with large hinged flaps hanging down along its sides, reminding me of tobacco barns I had seen in Kentucky, the flaps raised to allow the freshly harvested weed to cure or dry in nice weather, lowered again to protect a precious crop from inclement weather. The second, much larger two story building, was like a dairy barn, gabled roof, three small windows on the ground level, two above on a second level, with a large door at either end. Three large trucks, a small tractor, and a Japanese pickup were parked to one side. What appeared to be a BMW was parked near the house. What was strange about seeing it there was that there was no road. None. None to have driven it on to get it here and none to drive it on now that it was here. A fourth small building could barely be seen behind the main house; from inside came the throb of a smoothly functioning generator, obviously the power source of the kilowatt hours flowing through wire into the multiple fluorescent lamps lighting the perimeter in such a pleasing manner. What was less pleasing was what the lights showed upon closer inspection; a perimeter, not of Christmas tree beauty, but of incipient harm, a perimeter comprised of jagged yawning teeth, a war zone protected by wicked coils of razor wire. Plus, it seemed reasonable to assume, additional land mines.

The wire was eight to ten feet high, enclosed an area roughly the size of three football fields, and there were but two gates in evidence. One was almost directly below where we now lay, a guard house wrapped in wire, bathed in floodlights, the gate securely closed and locked with a massive chain wrapped around concrete anchored steel posts, one lonely guard tilted back in a chair, his AK47 rifle across his lap. Tilted back, yes; asleep, no.

On the other side of the enclosed compound, we could make out a second gate and guard house but we were too far away to see it clearly. AcChan sent Bip on a scouting mission. "Go to the left around the wire. Ha says you can do that without too much difficulty, and slip up to that other guard house. How many men? Is it the same as the one below us? See if you can spot any additional problems: mines, sensors, dogs, mobile guards inside, anything like that. And see if you can find a way to get inside without blasting our way through. Take a man with you as backup."

Eddie immediately volunteered. "I'll go. I know what to look for and I'm used to spending time in the dark back home in the parking lot."

I didn't see the connection between our parking lot and what appeared to be a fortified compound but I could see that Eddie was eager to go, so when I raised no objection, AcChan simply nodded, then motioned for one of his riflemen to accompany the other two. As they set off, I said to Eddie, "Be careful. Let Bip lead and don't take chances."

I wondered what the cost of Workmen's Compensation coverage for something like this would be. I knew Burrows would go crazy should he ever find out what one of his employees was doing on this night. Make that two. I was still on the payroll, too.

Of course there had to be another gate into the compound. The one leading up from the river where our boats would dock if all went right. "No," Ha said. I don't think there is a gate and fence back there. There is just a trail, according to Noi. They usually guard the dock and don't worry about anyone coming ashore anywhere else."

"Why not?" I asked.

He said something in Thai, beyond my basic linguistic capacities of his native tongue, but AcChan helped out. "Too much water, too wet, except for the trail. I suspect it is what you call a swamp. Can't walk through it."

In that case, our men probably couldn't come that way either, especially carrying a heavy x-ray machine. "We'll have to clear that trail, too, AcChan," I said, "before the boat comes in."

He nodded and I could see him mentally counting his men, assigning tasks, and wondering how to get it all done with limited resources.

I heard movement next to me and wasn't surprised to find Magellan lying there, breathing hard as if he had spent more energy than he had planned on crawling from one spot to another. "See anything?" he asked.

"Take a look," I said and handed him the glasses. After a perfunctory scan of the perimeter, he handed them back without comment. It was evident that he hadn't come over to scout the farm.

"When I've had a chance, I've been working on the transmitter. The one I built in Chiang Rai. The special one. The one hidden inside the main one." He was speaking softly as if he wanted no one to overhear us. Naroogian was a hundred feet away and was no threat for the moment.

"I remember, Fred. I remember that it seemed weak when you tested it and we need it to transmit 20 miles or more. How's it coming?"

"Well, I've been working on it but that hasn't been easy with all the rain and with Naroogian watching me all of the time. I don't think he trusts me but he hasn't said anything. Has he said anything to you?"

"About a transmitter? Not a word. Do you think he suspects you've made a second transmitter?"

"I don't know, but I'm worried about it. Don't you see? Naroogian is security. He's Bath's security chief. He reports to Bath. If he finds I've done something like make a second transmitter, instead of just carrying the one to contact Fantus, I'm in trouble. You have no idea how much trouble that would be. For me. Even for you."

I thought he was through, which disappointed me, but after a moment he said, "Who is that second transmitter supposed to contact anyway? You never said. I tested it with the receiver I made and then you took the receiver and I never saw it again. So if I send a message with the new transmitter, where will it go? Who gets it on that frequency? It's for someone to come and get us out of here, isn't it? Right?"

"I never said that, Fred! We don't need anyone other than Fantus for that. Isn't that his job? To get us out of here? That's what you have the original transmitter for. We don't need a duplicate for that. You send a message to him and he comes in with his magic carpet and poof, just like that. He arrives and whisks us away to safety. That's how it works, isn't it?"

He was staring at me as if he couldn't believe what he had just heard. Fred, as well as many others, must have been aware of Fantus' shoddy record when it came to performing heroic acts of rescue. He certainly knew that I had witnessed a couple firsthand. Lamely, he admitted, "Sure that's the plan, but I thought you might have an alternative in case something kept him from arriving."

"Fred, I am certain that Fantus will get us out of here. Absolutely certain. So, no, I do not have an alternative air evacuation proposal. I need your second transmitter for something else. I'll let you in on the secret. Keep it a secret. Your transmitter, it's for the blood."

His mouth gaped. "Blood! What blood? What do you mean we need it for the blood?"

For a man who had been exchanging messages with Chamburon about a sick man needing help, only to find that it was the wrong man, and who was now engaged in a hunt for the real Lee Duc Than, he seemed to have little understanding of what was involved in diagnosing and treating sick people. We did it by looking, naturally, and by examining the patient, using the tools at hand: stethoscope, ophthalmoscope, blood pressure cuff, the x-ray machine floating about on the river, the hands, and sometimes the nose, but it almost always required more than that. Blood. Blood to test for the right cells, the wrong cells, the chemical components, too much of one thing, not enough of another, to unravel a mystery, to find a clue, to point the way, making it possible to give the illness a name, to bring it down to the level of understanding, and to expose its vulnerability.

"Blood, Fred," I said, "to help us identify the man and diagnose what's wrong with him. Like in doing blood tests. We don't have a laboratory with us," not completely true as I did have the equipment and supplies to run a number of rudimentary tests on Lee Duc Than, should he be there, but I didn't have the technological skills or equipment to do the match for a possible bone marrow transplant, something which Magellan didn't need to know, "so I need to collect blood specimens, have them picked up and flown back to our laboratory technician in Bangkok. He's set up to do it, time is important, and we need your backup transmitter to make sure it gets done."

"There's no way my transmitter can send a signal all the way to Bangkok," he said, skeptical about buying the story. "I'm lucky if we get the twenty miles you asked for."

"I understand that, Fred. That's why we've asked the pilot to fly over this area every afternoon at 2 P.M., making a large circle to cover the grid where AcChan thought we could most likely be found, and we'll start transmitting. When he hears us, he calls, follows your signal in, lands and picks up our specimens. Four hours later, they should be in Bangkok and in another four hours, we ought to have some answers."

Fred was still dubious about the plan. "Why go to all that trouble when all we have to do is radio Fantus, have him come in and take us out as soon as we find Lee Duc Than? Why hang around any longer than we have to?"

Which was good thinking, a sentiment that I shared completely. So I explained, "Remember Co Phan? The man we left in the hospital in Chiang Mai? We thought he was Lee Duc Than at first. Let's say that he had been. He was so weak and so ill that we couldn't have moved him had we wanted to. It probably would have killed him. But we needed laboratory work to help identify him and to decide what to do for him. No problem. He was there, in a hospital. They had all the facilities we needed. That's not the case here. There are no facilities. None. The nearest are back in Bangkok, so if he's ill, critically ill, we're going to need help to decide our best course, medically for one thing, and from the standpoint of safety for another. That's where you come in."

He liked it. He liked being needed. Who doesn't? But I didn't want him to buy the whole story, not all of it. I wanted to leave the door open for a little doubt, to tickle his built-in insecurity and to activate his sense of self preservation and denial of blame, so I added, "Of course, if Lee Duc Than could travel, and if we find Ken Green there as well, we might just call in the plane and instead of sending out lab specimens, put them aboard and send them back to Bangkok with protection. That's what we might do. Then call in Fantus and the rest of us could leave. That would be the best of all."

I left him to wrestle with how much, if any of that, he might want to report to Naroogian.

Bip and Eddie still had not returned and I was tired, had seen as much as I was likely to find profitable from the ridge line overlooking the lighted guard house, so I crawled back through the grass to rest my back against the trunk of a comfortable tree. A soft mat of fallen needles cushioned me and I looked up in wonder at the towering pine tree responsible for coating the forest floor with velvet. I hadn't expected pines here, not in this climate, but I was indeed sitting in the midst of a grove of massive straight trunked monsters, their odor reminding me of home, the scent of fall in the countryside, as colored leaves floated down from sunlight deprived oaks and maples in advance of the chill winter winds, the neighboring white pines serene through it all, safe in the knowledge that their green foliage was to remain, a splash of color on an otherwise soon to be bleak landscape. What kind of pines were these, I wondered, and had no answer because I couldn't see the nearest limbs, twenty or thirty feet overhead, lost in darkness.

And then I remembered what kind of work I did for a living and reached inside my multi-pocketed jacket to remove small plastic specimen bags, filling several, some with scoops of soil, others with dried needles collected from the ground, and then another to accommodate several one inch densely packed cones that had fallen from high in the forest canopy. To this bag, not yet quite filled, I added several twig fragments, taped everything tightly using clever self sealing devices, and slipped them into another, more spacious pocket built into the all-purpose trousers.

Naroogian must have been watching. "What did you find?" he asked. I hadn't heard him move in the darkness but he was there.

"Dirt," I told him. "Real dirt, like this stuff here," and I scooped up another handful of pine needles and soft, moist soil and slowly let if run through my fingers. "It's the business I'm in."

"Yeah, I saw you putting it into plastic bags. I'm in the same business, only I put mine down on paper. They call them reports."

I knew what he meant.

Waiting is always hard. Waiting in the rain, like now, was harder. Fortunately, while inserting the plastic bags into a flap pocket for safekeeping, I discovered another piece of milk chocolate I had previously overlooked. It melted gently inside my mouth and the taste of Switzerland provided ten minutes of pleasant diversion. It also put me to sleep and I awoke with a start when AcChan touched me and said, "They're coming back." Obviously, he never slept.

AcChan had been confident that Bip would find a way through the wire, but he was wrong. It wasn't Bip, but Eddie, who found it.

"I didn't see any listening devices," he told me, AcChan and Naroogian, the three of us gathered in a tight circle around him with Bip crouched nearby, hanging on every word even though he wasn't supposed to understand any English at all. "I think there are alarms at the gates. It looked like it on the far side. We were able to get close enough for a good look without being spotted. I suppose they can turn them off and on like you do with a security system in the home or office. But it's over there, boss, where they screwed up. On the other side of the fence. It's lower. We can get over it. At least, I can get over it, at a place two hundred feet or so south of the guard house. I go over the fence, go back to the guard house, knock out the guys in there, turn off the alarm, and open the gate. Piece of cake." Hadn't Naroogian used the same description just before his abortive door-kicking fiasco back in Chiang Mai?

As for Eddie, I had no idea what he was talking about and I wasn't sure he did either. AcChan had listened to this brief report and was looking at me as if waiting for translation from another language, even though he spoke perfectly good English. I suspected it was the 'screwed up' and 'piece of cake' that were giving him the most trouble.

"He says they made a mistake of some kind across the way. He thinks it will be easy to get over the wire and inside," I explained.

AcChan nodded. "I heard him say that. But he didn't say how he was going to get over the wire."

"You have a plan, I suppose," I asked and Eddie assured me that he did, waiting until after I had said, "even if the wire is lower over there it will tear you apart on contact. This kind of wire is wicked stuff. How do you propose avoiding that problem?"

He smiled happily as he replied, "Easy, boss. There'll be no contact. None at all. I'm going to jump it!"

I looked down at the lighted wire below us, the vicious cutting edges glistening in the wet rain, and grimaced. Even if the wire on the other side of the fence was not as high, there was no way that Eddie, or any of the rest of us, was going to leap over it to the other side without suffering grievous wounds in the process. I stared at him and said, "Jump it? You can't jump it! What are you talking about? It's eight feet, maybe more, high. Must be about the same on the other side."

"It is. Sure. But that won't be a problem. Just get me a pole, a nice strong one, and I'm up and over."

"What kind of a pole?"

"A pole. Like I said, nice and strong. Like in pole vault." There was absolute silence as the three of us stared at him and Eddie pressed on, apparently intent on selling an idea that sounded more like suicide than rescue. "Maybe you don't remember from my resume, but I was an athlete in high school. Track. Ran the 440, 880, relays and, because it was a small school, also did the pole vault. I was pretty good. Finished second or third almost every year in the conference meets and I had speed, strength, and finesse and wasn't bad, if I say so myself. So that's all I need for this job. A pole. Find the right one, I run, I go up, and swoosh, I'm over. The other side. Hit the ground, do a barrel roll, up on my feet, take out the guards, and let you in. That's it."

He was crazy. I could only conclude that a tropical disease had struck him down in the darkness and that he had lost his mind. I looked at Eddie and saw a security guard who was out of shape, out of his element, hadn't vaulted in years, had no idea how to, as he put it, take out the guards, and who almost certainly would fall flat on his face or in the midst of the wire and be cut to pieces, unless he put this idea out of his mind at once. Eddie looked at me and came off as a self professed commando ready to carry out an act of derring-do, not a worry in the world, just something he did every night on duty in the parking lot. But I knew better. He was my responsibility and I slowed him down, or tried to.

"You've been out of training, you haven't vaulted in years, it's raining, and we don't have a pole for you to use." None of that seemed to matter.

"Boss, it's the best way. Maybe the only way. Besides, Bip agrees," he declared. And Bip, the hill tribesman who wasn't supposed to speak English, seemed to have followed every word and was nodding vigorously as if in full accord with the plan.

I was ready to continue the argument when Eddie suddenly said, "I know you're worried abut my being injured. I can understand that, but don't worry about it. What I'm going to do is cheat."

That got my attention.

He explained how. "They've been doing some kind of construction on the other side of the fence, outside the wire. Looks like a bulldozer has been pushing dirt around and digging a trench. Big one. Goes way back away from the wire. But in a couple of places they piled up dirt almost right to the wire, just about as high as the fence itself. That's where I can cheat. I get a running start outside the wire, run up to where the pile of dirt is, stick the pole down and fly over, coming down on the other side, across the sharp stuff, and there I am. Inside. Just get me a pole, and swoosh, it's done."

Swoosh? He had swoosh on the brain. Here he was, lean as a greyhound, laden with forty pounds of equipment, wearing mud caked boots and wet clothing, and just like that, without a practice run, he was telling me he was going to vault a barbed wire fence that was capable of ripping him to shreds if he slipped or fell short. Burrows would go absolutely stark raving mad over the Workmen's Compensation liability I was discussing with one of our employees, especially since I was actually considering it. The problem was, as I knew, that if anything went wrong, Eddie would be in deadly peril. And I'd been in enough unusual situations in a long lifetime to also know that something always went wrong. Always!

I wasn't the only one giving it serious consideration. So was AcChan. Speaking for the first time, he breathed new life into the idea. "It might work," he said and I wondered how he had come to that conclusion. I had been wracking my brain and I couldn't think of a single reason to assume that it had the slightest chance of success. Eddie could slip and fall on the run up. That wouldn't necessarily be fatal as he would still be outside the wire and we could run like hell if he made noise as he fell. Or his pole could fail to hold in the soft, wet soil, and then he could just as easily fall into the center of the razor wire with catastrophic results. He could break bones upon landing, he could be knocked unconscious or just twist an ankle and not be able to move. All of that, and more. And what about once he was inside? How did he get rid of the guards that he so cavalierly assured us he could do? He couldn't, that's what I decided, and was about to say 'Forget it,' when AcChan preempted me by adding, "We should think this through."

"The guards," he answered when I brought up how Eddie, the security guard, was to take on an armed camp by himself, "may be no problem. I have something that might work on them."

Then I had another idea, floated it half seriously to see what kind of reaction it would raise. "Why do we assume that these people are unfriendly? What if we just walked up to the gate and introduced ourselves? Explain we are here hunting, fishing, looking at the sights, something like that, and see what they do?"

Naroogian and AcChan looked at me as if I was the one losing my mind, not Eddie. Naroogian was the first to respond. "Jesus, Osten. They'd start shooting. That's what they'd do. You're not serious, are you?"

Not quite willing to give it up, I said, "Look, this could be a prosperous farm in an out of the way place. Naturally, they're cautious. Everyone knows there are bandits and drug dealers, smugglers, war lords, and God knows what else up here, so they take precautions. They put up a fence, lock the gates, arm the guards to keep people like that away. But we're respectable and mean no harm. Let's tell them that. They may invite us in for breakfast." I didn't believe it, but I wondered if anyone else did.

"While you were sleeping a while ago," AcChan said, calmly, as if talking to someone who might be ill, "I did a little scouting myself. This is a prosperous farm and I saw a small field of sunflowers where they seemed to be harvesting an excellent crop of seeds. They seemed to be feeding most of them to the birds, the large flocks that congregate in these pines. They eat a lot of sunflower seeds. No money in that, though. Then I saw where they were growing a few vegetables and a small plot of herbs, even tea. Mostly for their own use, I suspect. No money in that, either. Then I saw the large field that is hard to see from here, even with the night glasses. Huge field. Stretches from one side of the fence to the other, except for the area right around the house and outbuildings, and if you look closely with the glasses, the same kind of crop is growing outside the fence over there in the general direction of where the waterfall is supposed to be. Ha says that is correct. The same crop inside and outside the fence. Huge crop."

I suspected that I knew the answer when I asked, "What crop?"

"Poppies. That's the cash crop. They make opium from them. If we went up to the gate, Naroogian is right. They'd start shooting. This is a fortified base camp. Not an innocent dairy farm in your Midwest." So we went back to considering Eddie's plan once more.

"OK, for the sake of argument," I conceded, "let's say Eddie gets inside, although I still don't see how he'll do that without breaking his neck."

Across from me Eddie nodded, up and down, then turned his head from left to right, did it again, as if checking to see what a broken neck would feel like. For the moment, everything seemed to be working normally and he paused to listen as I continued, "What's he going to do now? The guards are armed, they're two of them, and he's bound to make noise of some kind or at least be seen when he approaches the guard house. They'll shoot first and ask questions later and the element of surprise is gone. We might just as well blast our way inside as take that kind of risk with his life."

AcChan held up a small canister about the size of a push button spray underarm deodorant, and said, "Maybe this is the answer we need. I've used it a couple of times and it works."

"What is it? Shaving cream?"

"No, not that. More effective, I hope. It's a gas. Works fast."

"A gas? Is it lethal?"

He looked at the container as if considering the impact his answer might have and then replied, "Lethal? You mean does it kill? I guess the answer is sometimes, it might. I've heard that if someone is what they call hypersensitive to it, the heart stops, but usually no, they just fall unconscious in three or four seconds and stay that way for several hours. A few simply become disoriented and see the man who sprayed it but they can't do anything about it and stay that way for hours. It's pretty good stuff. Name of tribromofluorcarbatetra – I can't read the name in the dark and the label is rubbed off right here. But it puts them to sleep effectively and it may do the job."

"You've used it?"

"Sure, we've used it. It works better if your target is in a closed room, but it works."

I pointed to the guard house below. "That is not a closed room. The windows on all four sides are propped open and there is a stiff breeze right now and a lot of rain, so will it work under those conditions?"

He agreed it was of some concern. "I've been thinking about that. Eddie won't be able to spray the gas into a heating or air conditioning duct because there isn't any and he won't be able to just dash over to the window and spray them because, as you say, he'd be exposed in the lighted area and they'd see him. So after he jumps the fence, he has to crawl to the shack, staying low and out of sight. Then, suddenly, he leaps to his feet, sprays one of the guards right in the face and as he falls, he does the same to the other. One right after the other. They're both down. He kills any alarms by throwing the switch, opens the gate and we're inside with him."

Just like that! Eddie was nodding affirmatively. I guess that meant he could do it. I wasn't so sure.

But assuming we were inside, what next? AcChan explained that as well. "See that long low building over there, a hundred yards or so from the main house? The one with huge window flaps that can be opened? That's where they process the raw opium and compress into those flat plates we saw in the duffel bags. Shouldn't be any problem there. I doubt that they have guards in it or around it. It's just a workshop. See the two story building? My guess is that that's where the armed guards live, probably on the first floor with the workers, the ones who care for and harvest the poppies or work in the processing room, living up above. I doubt if any of them have weapons. Our problem is with the men on the first floor. One good thing is that at least sixteen men have been sent out to see what happened at the river. We won't have them to deal with until they see what a mess we made and turn around and come back. There may be a guard or two down at the dock like Ha suggested, and there may be a few wandering around in the dark that we can't see. Those are the risks we just have to take if we're going inside. The main house, you're wondering?" I was. "I don't know. There will be armed people there, I'm sure. I don't know how many. We just have to rely upon surprise and speed to neutralize their numerical advantage, if they have one, and they probably do. By hitting them in the dark we will have the edge, no matter what. But it all depends on being able to take the sentries out quickly."

So Bip, Eddie, and a hill tribesman went looking for a pole. "About twice my height," he instructed, "thirteen or fourteen feet long," thus giving himself the dimensions the Detroit Pistons had long been seeking to play at the low post. Twice his height, honestly measured, would have been much closer to ten and a half feet. "And strong," he added, "it has to be strong and as light as possible."

They were back in less than thirty minutes, appearing silently from the tangle of jungle immediately behind us carrying a slender, twelve foot long, inch and a half thick limb of one of the toughest woods I had ever encountered. It would bend, but not snap. It was incredibly supple, yet strong. Eddie pronounced it to be "perfect."

AcChan identified it as tamarind. "It will hold him. Interesting tree. Has a beautiful red-striped yellow flower. You may have seen it growing around my warehouse in Chiang Rai. Also has a nice fruit, tastes sour, too acid, some complain, and not everyone likes it. But it makes a good laxative. Better than your prunes."

Because of the water, heat, and other tropical causes of cramping, one thing we didn't need right now was a laxative, but you could never tell when that information might come in handy when back in the comforts of civilization.

Eddie was practicing where to position his hands on the twelve foot pole to gain the best leverage as I returned once more to his assigned duties once inside the wire. "Why won't they see him even if he crawls through the lighted area? They're not blind and they aren't asleep."

"If that seems to be likely to happen, we'll do like Eddie is doing by jumping the fence where it isn't as high as it should be. We'll cheat."

"Cheat?" I asked. "How do you propose to cheat?"

"A diversion. We'll create one to draw their attention."

"What kind of a diversion?"

It turned out that the plan was still not complete. He frowned and said, "I don't know yet, but we'll think of one."

For a time, we had forgotten the real reasons we were all gathered here, in a driving rain, in the darkness and mist of a dreary night, tired and hungry, and we were entirely focused on one objective, vaulting a man over a fence, the rest of us getting inside to join him. Of course there was a lot more than that involved; Kendra and the General, even the rescue of Ken Green should he be there, those were my reasons. AcChan? Maybe money – or was it a chance to do damage to a drug empire? Eddie thought AcChan sincerely cared enough to do just that. Naroogian? A job, an assignment from his boss or something else? I didn't know. Magellan? Redemption for a career that had gone nowhere, a last chance to do what had always eluded him in the past, to do something correctly, to succeed in the field, to win a commendation, a plaque to hang on his office wall? And Eddie, a security guard, a former high school athlete making a comeback in a field event that he hadn't tried in a decade and a half, for what? Because it was a challenge, a barrier to be crossed, something that had to be done to prove he was as big a man as any of us? Whatever it was, we were now committed and had passed to the point of no return.

We left two riflemen to take out the single guard below us in the original guard house and circled the wire, following the path Bip and Eddie had traveled earlier on the scouting mission.

On the other side, Bip carefully dug the insertion point for the pole and packed it with a flat stones to hold it securely after Eddie planted it at the end of his run, starting his leap. Eddie continued to experiment with hand holds and then, at AcChan's urging, stripped to his shorts, and allowed the gas canister to be taped to his left upper arm with the ever present roll of duct tape. "You'll be lighter, won't be carrying all the wet clothing that could slow you down, and should be able to fly further," AcChan explained.

All Eddie said was, "Makes sense."

I knew now, once he had stripped and been equipped with the gas canister and pole, that even were I to suddenly announce that I was calling the whole thing off and we were returning to Bangkok, that the project had taken on a life of its own and no one would accompany me. They would remain to watch the jump and take part in whatever followed. And so would I.

As we made final preparations, safely out of sight and sound, two hundred yards away from the brightly lighted second guard house, Bip passed out the final piece of equipment for each man – inch wide strips of yellow ribbon, ribbon that glowed eerily in the dark, reflecting the distant light bouncing off the wicked razor wire outlining the perimeter of the fortified position we were about to breach. Silently, AcChan demonstrated that we were to tie each ribbon around the left arm, even Eddie's, and we moved closer to the wire, ready now for the moment that we had been waiting for.

"So we don't shoot our own?" I asked AcChan, pointing to the ribbon now secured on my arm.

"That, too," he responded. "But mainly it's an old Thai warrior tradition. Today is Monday. Monday is yellow ribbon day. If Thai warriors go into battle on Monday, they wear yellow ribbons for bravery and to be successful. Other days, different colors, but on Monday, yellow. You don't have to wear it, being American, but it can't hurt."

"Does it always work?"

"Always, the Thais think. Especially if you fight hard and smart, and when you have a freshly cut laburnum tree with you. Then it works best."

He seemed to have his trees confused. We hadn't cut a laburnum. It had been a tamarind.

He corrected me patiently. "No, the tamarind is for Eddie to use. Laburnum is the tree of bravery. All of our men have a piece to carry. Here is yours, just a small piece, but it should be big enough to work." And he handed me a three inch twig of dark gray wood, freshly cut, still exuding the sweet fragrance of the tropical forest from where it had grown. "When they went to find Eddie's pole, they also discovered a perfect laburnum and we all have a piece to carry. The laburnum and yellow ribbons, that's a good combination. We will do well tonight."

I accepted it and quickly reached inside my water logged jacket to find a dry pocket to store the newest token of good luck. And it worked almost at once. While putting the twig away in a dry place, I discovered yet another unsuspected piece of milk chocolate, which I unwrapped and ate.

Now it was time. Eddie had used almost all that remained of the duct tape to fashion a usable grip on the pole, a foot or so from the top, and it seemed to meet his exact specifications. He nodded. He was ready. "What if they hear me land or see me coming? What then?" he asked.

"If that happens," AcChan replied, with no emotion, "we shoot the guards, blow the gate with grenades and come in anyway." He paused, waiting for objections or approval.

Stating the obvious, I said, "If that happens, we lose the element of surprise."

"Not entirely," he decided after reflecting for a moment. "Remember, we'll be going in just before dawn when most everyone should be asleep. It'll still be dark, there will be noise, shooting, explosions, and smoke, possibly fire. We probably are going to have some very confused people in there, so we'll still have an advantage. Maybe not as big an advantage, but it won't be as bad as you might think."

Well, we'd come this far, allowed Eddie to eagerly finger his makeshift pole in anticipation of a too long delayed vault, and there was no sense in turning back without completing the house call Pan Union had hired me to make. "Let's go in," I decided and AcChan deployed his small force without further delay.

Eddie had his assignment. Take out the guards at the gate. The two men we left on the other side of the wire were scheduled to eliminate the single sentry below them. AcChan, a rifleman, and Bip were to take the dormitory where he expected to find the majority of heavily armed and dangerous men. I was to accompany Naroogian and Eddie to the main house while Magellan and a rifleman were to tackle a neighboring smaller building only fifty yards away. "What do you think that is?" I asked.

"Don't know. Maybe what you would call a guest house, or a maid's house, or just another house."

He suddenly became aware of Ha who was standing by without any assignment, thought about it for a moment and then said, "When we get inside, run as fast as you can across to the other gate and open it. One of the men we left over there should join you and sweep the inside of the wire looking for any other sentries we've missed. The second man should go back down the main trail to watch for the return of the sixteen men who passed us earlier. As soon as you've checked for additional sentries, hurry back to us at the main buildings and we'll clear the trail to the river so the boat can come in. Everyone got it? Know what you're supposed to do?"

There were no questions. What could anyone say? Either it worked or it didn't and it wouldn't take long to find out. Before we broke up and put the plan into action, it occurred to me that I did have a question. "How are we taking out the guard on the other side of the compound? The one inside the wire, all alone guarding the gate?"

AcChan was genuinely troubled. "Unfortunately," he admitted, "he has to be shot. I thought of other ways but we don't have any other way."

"If you shoot him, there goes the silence we were counting upon. Unless you brought a silencer."

"We did, in a manner of speaking. At least we have something almost as good, and in some ways, better. Both men we left over on the other side are well trained with a silent weapon and that one we did bring along."

"What weapon?" a curious Naroogian asked.

"A Thai warrior crossbow. Used on a target from close range, just out of the ring of light, it will be effective and silent. Very silent."

An attack using a crossbow, a pole vaulter, nerve gas, and yellow ribbons, plus small pieces of wood; some of the old, some of the new, and a lot of the bizarre. I wondered if anyone had thought to bring along a rabbit's foot?

And just like that, it stopped raining. One minute it had been pouring, and the next, nothing. It took me almost a full minute to realize that water was no longer beating against my head, had stopped running down my face, and it meant, I recognized, that with the din of heavy rain no longer offering a protective shield of background noise, the men in the guardhouse were more likely to hear Eddie as he splashed to a landing inside the fence. AcChan sensed the danger and snapped out his final orders, sending his men to their preassigned jump-off positions and asking Eddie, "Are you ready?"

The small man in shorts, a canister taped to one arm and a yellow ribbon tied onto the other, was apprehensive, swallowed bravely, and hesitated. Champions going into competition always have butterflies, feel the pressure, and wait for the surge of adrenaline to kick in for maximum performance. That's how Eddie looked. He was already soaking wet, smeared with multicolored mud, was grasping a slightly crooked tamarind stick, it wasn't as straight as it had first appeared, and his thin, slightly bowed legs didn't seem sturdy enough to carry him fast enough, and far enough, to hurdle him over and across the fence that lay directly in front of us, jaws open and waiting. Nervous but determined, I decided, and wondered if he would go through with his vault. Then to my amazement, he said, "I better be going, boss, before I wet my pants." Memorable lines come and go, this didn't rank up with the best such as "I shall return" or "Don't fire until you see the whites of their eyes," but for a spontaneous effort by an underweight security guard, it wasn't bad.

At the end of our runway, Bip was kneeling and pointing to the stone fortified hole in the ground, the insertion point for the tamarind pole. "Put it here," he seemed to be saying with signs, "ram it in solidly, then keep running and rise as the pole lifts you, in a giant arc, and land softly," here Bip was pantomiming as if he were cradling a baby in both arms, "on the other side."

Eddie nodded and seemed to be saying, "Catch the pole when I drop it so it doesn't fall onto the fence and make noise," and backed down the runway to find reasonably solid footing. He hefted the pole several times above shoulder height, checked the wind, fortunately blowing from the west and directly behind him, which would be a help, and started running. No practice run, no warm-up, no margin for error. Holding the pole level, straight ahead of him chest high, he flashed by me, already puffing from the exertion, and AcChan directed a tiny beam of light from a torch, invisible to everyone except his two night goggled riflemen, two hundred yards away where they had taken aim at the sentries, ready to fire if Eddie failed in his attempt to clear the fence. Or if they heard him.

The former high school track star reached the end of his run, slipping once or twice along the way and losing a little of his momentum, slammed the pole smartly into the insertion point, his feet still moving, and suddenly, feet scissoring wildly, he was airborne, soaring into the night, disappearing from sight, flying at and over the fence, and silence. He disappeared. Not just from view. He disappeared. Entirely. There wasn't a sound, not the splash of water that I had feared, no noise from the wire, no screaming in pain, no shooting, and no shouting. Nothing. Just silence. I could still see the wire reflecting the light from the guardhouse, and there didn't seem to be a body impaled upon it, but as for Eddie, he wasn't anywhere to be seen. Ground and darkened sky merged into one massive dark hole and somewhere in it was Eddie. Injured, dead or already crawling towards the guardhouse to use his gas canister on sentries who remained in unconcerned postures exactly where they had been before Eddie's takeoff? As I waited, I realized how stupid the idea had been. And I had approved it! It was simple, I realized now. We should have gone to the gate, blown it apart, and shot our way inside. That's how they do it in the movies.

We waited for another ten minutes, hoping for some sign that he had made it safely across. Bip had caught the pole and was still holding it, looking at AcChan now, expecting orders to move, impatient as we all were, to find out where the missing man had gone. I was afraid that I had sent an almost naked security guard, who should have been safely patrolling our parking lot back at the office, to an early grave. AcChan kept checking his watch and slowly moved the assault party along the fence until we were as close to the gate as we could come without being visible in the lights. But those lights were no longer what concerned him. In minutes, dawn would be breaking and dawn out here came up with a suddenness that would leave us exposed and unprotected with no place to hide.

He made eye contact with me, then motioned to Bip, and both removed grenades from their belt pouches and started moving ever so slowly towards the gate. He was about to fall back on our second option, blast our way inside.

He halted, rifle at the ready as a guard suddenly stood and walked nonchalantly to the gate, unlocked it, walked outside, and kept on walking, the gate hanging open behind him. For a moment, I expected to see the hand of Eddie behind this unexpected event, possibly holding his gas canister threateningly, forcing the guards to do his bidding, but that wasn't the case. He wasn't there. I didn't know what was happening until AcChan, who had remained absolutely still with me immediately behind him, stiffened and whispered, "He's going over to a rain gauge. He's checking to see how much rain has fallen."

And sure enough, fifty feet further on, over a small rise, we could make out the small tank with a measuring device in its side, the kind our own weather service uses to measure rainfall. As he neared the gauge, the guard was out of sight of his companion and the instant that happened, Bip, who had been silently stalking him unseen in the fading darkness, struck him on the back of head with Eddie's tamarind pole. He went down like he had been shot and stayed there. As the first sentry was falling, AcChan was already reacting, flying across the embankment, riding the mud to the bottom as if on water skis, bursting through the wide open gate, and holding his rifle against the head of the remaining sentry before he could make a move from his chair. One look at the rifle and AcChan's face convinced him that he didn't want to move from his chair and he raised his hands, staying right where he was.

The only sound to be heard was the sucking of thick mud as it clawed at the boots of our men passing through the gate and the soft order AcChan murmured into his hand held radio. I suspect that the guard at the second gate was struck by a silent missile from a Thai crossbow moments later. We were inside. Ha hurried away to carry out his assignment and I went to look for Eddie. "Five minutes, Osten, that's all the time we have," AcChan warned.

Which meant ten.

It turned out five would have been enough. I found the mud smeared figure fifty yards away, a motionless body sprawled, almost invisible, against the ground. I knew it had to be Eddie. Who else would have been jumping fences at this time of the morning? Fearing the worst, serious trauma at the very least, I hurried forward, aware that my medical bag was somewhere behind me in Magellan's possession. When I was ten feet away, I halted, raised my Glock in alarm, as the figure, which had been lying motionless, suddenly moved and then stood erect, saying, "Boss, is that you? How'd you get inside? I haven't knocked out the guards yet."

He was a sorry sight. Blood was running from a laceration on his scalp, apparently the result of striking something when he landed, and more blood was coursing down his left arm where the canister – I looked about, he didn't seem to have the canister – had been taped. And that, it turned out, had been the problem.

He'd made it over the wire, with plenty of room to spare. "Too much adrenaline flowing I guess," he explained, and when he struck the ground, the canister had been torn free from the usually reliable duct tape, bounced off his head, and then disappeared in the darkness. He'd been searching for it ever since, crawling over uneven ground through deep puddles and, in the darkness, hadn't found it.

I heard movement behind me, spun with the Glock poised for full automatic fire, and found Magellan standing there, holding the missing canister. He held up both hands in supplication, as if afraid I would shoot when I saw who it was, and quietly said, "Here it is. It was in the mud right over there."

"Jesus," I said, taking my finger off the trigger to his obvious relief, "where did you come from?"

"I followed you. I've got his clothes, remember?" No, I didn't remember, because I had never known who had his clothes.

"Good," I told him. "Give them to him so he can get dressed." That, I reflected, wasn't going to help much. The clothes were soaking wet and Eddie was both wet and muddy, and there was no way to dry off, but being dressed in wet clothes was better than being naked as I realized for the first time that Eddie had also lost his shorts in the landing. With all the mud he had picked up, I hadn't noticed until now. Then Magellan surprised me. He reached into my medical bag, pulled out a small dry towel, tossed it to Eddie who used it to dry enough skin allowing him to slip on his shirt and pants and rejoin the human race, fully clothed, almost.

"You had a towel in there," Magellan observed. "Hope it was OK to give to him. It was, wasn't it?" Even here, he was afraid of being blamed for something going wrong.

"No problem, Fred. It was good of you to think of it." It was, because I'd forgotten.

As soon as we returned to the gate area where the others were waiting, AcChan took in Eddie's presence with a glance, then waved his arm over his head, pointed towards our assigned objectives, and everyone moved as if on cue, which I guess we were.

The light was improving rapidly and our immediate objectives were clearly visible in the lingering morning mist. Monday morning, a yellow ribbon Monday for Thai warriors, who would be successful in battle on this day wearing the proper ribbon and fortified by a twig of laburnum, "especially," as AcChan had explained it, "if they fight hard." We'd soon know, wouldn't we?

AcChan, Bip, and a rifleman angled to the left, headed for the largest building inside the compound, the one he called the dormitory, where he surmised the armed defenders were likely to be asleep. As I ran, I watched the rifleman veer to cover the rear of the building while Bip and AcChan headed directly for the main entrance. Then I was suddenly too busy with our own target to follow their movements any longer.

A half-dressed, muddy camouflaged Eddie, shirt flapping wildly behind him, bare feet splashing through the mud with his boots tied together and dangling from his neck where they slammed into him with every step, and blood still running down his face from a bleeding scalp, was gamely keeping up but obviously had still not fully recovered from his sudden collision with the ground after his vault across the wire. He had overlooked the soft landing enjoyed by competitive jumpers, the air cushions or foam pillows waiting to receive them, and had fallen back to earth onto a landing area of hard, although muddy ground, and scattered rocks which had bruised and bloodied him instead. He was breathing hard but holding his rifle at the ready and did his best to stay even with Naroogian and me and was right with us when we halted one last time, crouching at the edge of the flower garden, fifty feet from a broad wooden porch that ran across the entire front of the house before disappearing around to the far side as well. The house was painted white, neat shutters accentuating the eight windows spaced at neat intervals, and a huge wooden door barring entry into the building. Rotting stumps between us and the house were all that remained of the forest giants that had been put to the ax to allow a clear field of fire in case of attack, the grass was trimmed and cut low, and there were no shrubs or bushes of any kind to provide cover from this point on. The place looked like a Georgia Civil War plantation, but when we found out later that the shutters were of thick steel, the door was doubly reinforced, and that gun slits had been thoughtfully provided on all four sides, we realized it wasn't a peaceful farm. It was, in fact, a fortress.

And this Monday morning, whether it was because of the yellow ribbons on our sleeves or the absence of the owner and sixteen men we had passed on the trail, we were lucky. Aside from the men at the gates, there were no sentries, no prowling dogs abroad in the darkness, and someone had neglected to close the steel shutters, had forgotten to close and lock the sliding steel screens across the front door, and the building lay before us, open, inviting, apparently occupied by a sleeping garrison.

Eddie winced as I grasped him by the shoulder. "Go around to the rear. There must be a door back there and come in, staying low. Remember, we'll be coming in the front."

"Do I shoot?" he asked.

"If someone shoots at you, yes, you shoot. Just don't shoot us. We're the ones with the yellow ribbons."

"What about me?" he asked. "I don't have a ribbon anymore. It must have fallen off when I jumped."

"Don't worry about it," Naroogian said, not sounding as if ribbons of any color were going to bother him although he was conspicuously wearing his. "I know what you look like. I won't shoot you." He started to rise, impatient, and said, "Let's move it, Osten. I don't want to be here when it's completely light." He was right.

"Let's go," I said and dashed for the door. Naroogian beat me by ten yards and Eddie disappeared around the side of the house.

This time Naroogian got it right. He raised his right leg, kicked, hit the sweet spot and the unprotected door crashed inwards, Avram stumbling after it, and me one step behind. We found ourselves in a large room, couches, chairs, a mahogany table, bookcases, lamps. Off to our right was another room with an even larger table, a dining table, from the looks of it, with matching chairs and hutch, dishes neatly stacked inside, fully stocked wet bar, everything in readiness for the next social event or a visit from the neighbors. It looked, in fact, like a living and dining room you would expect at home, except for one thing. There was no television set, none. In its place was a radio, a small receiver, a German made Brundig with short wave capabilities indentical to one Burrow's had back in his stylish office. It sat on a small table alongside a hideous floral patterned, overstuffed chair that reeked of dampness and mold. Piled high next to it was a stack of cassettes.

For a moment, the only sound was the ticking of a restored Seth Parker grandfather clock, the burnished pendulum rhythmically swinging back and forth in regular cadence. It was exactly 5:27 A.M. The sudden crackle of gunfire outside startled me, and you can hardly expect to kick in someone's door and start shooting nearby without waking whomever was in residence. I heard sounds to the right as if someone was stirring and there was a crash from the left as if someone had fallen out of bed. Naroogian motioned to the door on the right and pointed to himself to indicate that it was his. I took the one to the left, partially hidden by an alcove, threw it open, and almost fired a burst from the Galil assault rifle into my own image that suddenly appeared in the floor-length mirror directly opposite the door. Startled by my own unshaven, mud-smeared apparition, I almost failed to turn in time to see a figure stumble from the far side of the bed, reaching into what appeared to be a jumble of clothing lying on a bedside chair. Even in the dim, early morning light, he appeared to be naked so it seemed reasonable to assume he was groping for a pair of shorts. I realized how wrong I was when I saw the barrel of a revolver protruding from the place a leg should be when he raised his arm and pointed it at me.

Instinctively, not from training but just from the instinct of self-preservation, I pressed the trigger and the Galil responded with a burst of gunfire that raked the back of the chair, the seat, the wall, and burrowed into the mattress, sending feathers, clothing, wallpaper, and shoes flying in every direction. I had forgotten I had set the Galil on full automatic and when I lifted my finger and the gun fell silent, the chair was reduced to kindling and the naked figure had gotten the message, slowly raising his hands and allowing the gun to slip from his fingers where it tumbled onto the floor. Somehow, he was still holding the shorts aloft. Maybe as a token of surrender.

Despite all of the shooting, I seemed to have missed the man, although he was standing silently, drunkenly, not daring to move, when I heard the sobbing. It was coming from a young woman who was sitting up against the teak headboard in the midst of a sagging, well worn mattress, now bullet-damaged as well, with a thin sheet pulled tightly against her chin and peering out from above the tattered white linen with wide, terror-stricken eyes. I didn't know if she had a weapon under there or not and I couldn't see both hands, so I reached over and snapped the sheet from the bed and left her uncovered, in the same state as her companion – naked.

The roomed reeked of the stale smell of sweet smoke, an opium pipe lying openly on the nightstand just beyond the chair that would never be used again. I motioned to my captive to drop the underwear and he flipped them onto the mattress where his party companion of the night before scurried to put them on. They were much too large but she was operating on the understandable principle that some covering was better than none. It wasn't easy to keep my eye on a captive and watch a second dress herself with one hand, the other attempting to modestly conceal her tiny breasts.

She had just finished the task when Naroogian rushed in, herding a single male captive into the room. Unlike my prisoners, his was wearing underwear. Nothing else. Just underwear. Apparently, no one bothered with pajamas. Too warm.

"This is it?" he asked. "Just these two?"

"This is it and I see you've come up with one."

Naroogian looked quickly around the room, noted the smashed chair and riddled wall where heavy, steel-jacketed slugs had ripped into the wallpaper, and said, "What was all the shooting?"

I motioned my Galil in the direction of the man still standing with both hands held high above his head and explained, "He reached for a gun."

"You seemed to have missed," Naroogian observed, sneering.

"Not exactly. Notice, he doesn't have his gun."

Naturally, Naroogian had seen the girl still in bed and, leering in her direction, he said, "These two seem to be suffering from an acute shortage of clothing. What the hell is she wearing?"

"His shorts, I guess." I didn't tell him how they had come into her possession. I made it clear then that they were to get dressed, first moving very slowly around the side of the bed where I could retrieve the fallen revolver. To my surprise, there was a veritable small arsenal of rifles, pistols, shotguns, and more than plenty of ammunition that had been just out of my sight on the floor at the head of the bed, some of the weapons tucked away under the bed, one of them an assault rifle lying with an empty vodka bottle on top. When I was close enough to see my captive close-up, I could see that both pupils were pinholes in the exact center of his eyes and he was still not certain what was happening. Which was lucky for me. Had he not partied on drugs and vodka the night before, his reaction time might have been swifter and while I was standing in front of the mirror, he might have been able to give me the opportunity to see myself get shot.

I tossed their clothing to them and they started putting it on. Eddie joined us to report there had been no one in the back rooms, a kitchen, storage area, and another bedroom, all empty. He scooped up the weapons and ammunition and hauled them to the front door where he stacked everything alongside a Chinese made knock off of the Russian army rifle that Naroogian had collected in the other bedroom.

Naroogian had our three captives sit on the floor, facing the wall, hands on their heads, and we left Eddie to guard them while we investigated what lay at the top of an unlighted stairway leading to a second floor. Naroogian in front, me behind, we were halfway to the top when another rattle of gunfire erupted. It came from the direction of the dormitory. We paused, waited, and it was quiet again so we went ahead, reaching the top to find, as below, a door to the right and one to the left. I went right. Empty. Naroogian went left, disappeared briefly, and then I heard him calling, "Osten, you better take a look at this."

He was standing just inside the room, a dim light barely outlining a bed in which lay a man, an old man from all appearances, his face skeletal, skin drawn so tightly over the facial bones that it seemed likely to split if he should so much as try to open his eyes or speak. He lay amidst a wrinkled sheet, his feet propped on a pillow and the sheet fitted snugly under his chin. There was a three day stubble on his face, but his hair, although long, was still black, neatly combed back as if it had been washed and combed regularly. Despite the grim appearance of the room and its occupant, the usual ammoniacal smell of urine stained clothing and bedding was absent. The floor was clean, the walls, now being washed by the pale light of a new day's dawn, were freshly painted, free of mold, and the one window sparkled with cleanliness as the sun fought to rise above the forested horizon. It was obvious someone was caring for this man, despite his weakened condition.

I saw her then, an almost invisible figure laying back in a chair in the far corner of the room, a place the light had not yet reached, her almond brown eyes staring at us in surprise and fear as she took in our unwashed uniforms, our weapons, our unshaven faces, and listened to our strange voices. Despite our sudden arrival, our kicking in the door, the shots fired directly below where she lay, and the menace that our weapons brought into the small room, her first concern was for the man in the bed. In perfect, slightly accented English, she pleaded, "Don't hurt him. Please don't hurt him."

Concern for the man and fear written all over her face.

I could understand the fear. Hearing gunshots from inside the house, and now from outside as well, is hardly the way anyone wants to start a day. Naroogian was simply standing and staring at the girl when I reassured her, "We're not here to hurt anyone. Not him. Not you."

She seemed to relax slightly and I looked at her more closely. Thai, maybe Vietnamese, I decided. Young, maybe twenty, twenty-one, although sometimes it was hard to tell. And pretty. Very pretty. Beautiful, I decided. Maybe I'd been away from Bangkok for too long.

"What's your name?" I asked.

"Somchai," she answered. A Thai name, not Vietnamese.

"And this is?" I indicated the man in bad.

"He is my patient. I'm his nurse. He's very sick."

"Yes, I can see that. But what is his name?

"They don't want me to know, so they have never told me. But I know anyway."

"If they haven't told you, then how do you know?"

"He told me himself. Sometimes when he is very sick and his fever is high, he talks to me as if I am his daughter. He calls me his 'little flower' and other names he remembers from his younger days, when he had a daughter. And when he is sick, very sick, so sick I didn't think he would ever come back from the land of the living dead, he says his own name, as if he is afraid of losing it, and asks me to repeat it, to sing him a song from his childhood. But I can't because I don't know what the song is and he has tears in his eyes, begs me to sing it, and holds my hand until he falls asleep again. He was a nice man then, when he was younger, and had his daughter, when she used to sing to him. But I can't, because I don't know what the song is."

She was genuinely distraught. I caught the glistening of tears in her eyes as the sun rose higher outside the window. Aside from that one burst of gunfire, it remained quiet. Too quiet. Naroogian was fidgeting uneasily across the room. He wanted to return to the lower level, go outside, and see what was happening. So did I.

"When this man is sick, has a fever, and talks to you, what does he say his name is, Somchai?"

"His name? His name is Lee Duc Than."

This was Lee Duc Than? This skeleton that breathed was the man we had been looking for? The message saying that he needed medical care was not in error. This man was near death. Medical care might have arrived too

388

late.

And if this was Lee Duc Than, what about Ken Green? Where was he? They were supposed to be a tandem. Find one, had been the supposition, and you will find the other. He wasn't in this building, so he must be in another or not here at all, in which case I would be back to square one in the search for Kendra's donor.

But five minutes later, I breathed a sigh of relief. We found him, sitting on a chair in the small building next to the big house, a Thai rifleman holding a rifle unswervingly aimed at his chest, and Magellan standing nearby, not certain what to do next, still holding his dual transmitter, his pack, my medical bag, a rifle, a slouch hat pulled low on his head and another stuffed into his belt, Eddie's I suspected, and the gas canister. He was loaded like a beast of burden.

I recognized Green at once, even though it had been sixteen or seventeen years since we had last seen one another. He had been missing for fifteen years, after all, make that reported dead for fifteen years, and yet he still had the same eyes, the same dramatic golden-green he shared with the General, the same face, leaner, and lined now where it had been full and unworried before he fled New York to join the army, a touch of gray appearing at the temples, a scar on the forehead that I didn't remember, but it was Green. Older, sure, weren't we all, and as he stared at me now I wondered if he wasn't thinking the same thing. Poor old Osten, getting older, something like that.

Naroogian followed me into the room and took in the situation. Magellan seemed relieved to see him and hurriedly reported to Pan Union's security chief, "He claims to be Ken Green, but that's all he'll say. What do you think? Is it Ken Green?" He didn't ask me, which was odd, as I was the only one who had known Ken Green in his previous life.

Naroogian jostled Magellan out of the way and stood in front of Green, removed a plastic envelope from an inner pocket, extracted a photograph from it, stared at it, and asked, "Are you Kenneth Green? Captain Kenneth Green of the United States Army?"

Green ignored him and looked at me instead. "Mike, nice of you to drop in. Just happen to be in the neighborhood?"

I laughed. It wasn't a bad line for a dead man. "No, Ken," I replied. "I just thought it had been too long since we'd had a chance to bore each other with stories, so I came up with some new ones and here I am."

The no-nonsense Naroogian repeated his question. "Are you Kenneth

Green?"

Green glanced at him as if he had heard questions like that too often to allow one more to bother him and asked me, "Who is this?"

"Ken, this is Avram Naroogian, an American like yourself, who represents Pan Union and who has come along to help retrieve you. I'm not sure why he wants to know your name but I suppose it has something to do with making sure your back pay is figured correctly." Actually, I suspected it really did have something to do with the United States Army, a fact confirmed almost at once as Naroogian persisted in asking his question.

"Is your name Kenneth Green?"

Green continued to ignore him and Naroogian turned to me and said, "His name is Kenneth Green. I heard you call him that."

"I called him Ken, Avram, no last name. But what difference does it make?"

Naroogian seemed satisfied that he had found his prey and announced smugly, "In that case, Captain Green, I am to inform you that you are to consider yourself in my custody and that any attempt to escape will be dealt with in the harshest possible manner."

I thought that at my age I had heard just every bizarre twist of fate, but this one was a new one. I thought it ironic that Naroogian had just arrested a man officially declared dead. Even the army couldn't be that desperate for manpower.

I suppose I was mildly outraged. Only mildly because to be frank about it, Naroogian was running a hollow bluff. He was one man against many, but I refrained from reminding him where we were and who held the balance of power. AcChan did and AcChan was working for me. I think.

Green didn't seem to care. He already knew where he was, where he had been, and didn't seem to be concerned about the bluster of a lone American representing, well, who was he representing? I decided to find out.

"What are you talking about?" I demanded, sounding more annoyed than I was. "We've come a long way to find a missing American and you take him into custody. Into what custody and by whose authority? For God's sake, Naroogian, the man has been a prisoner of the Vietnamese for 15 years; don't you read your own reports, look over the records in your office and use common sense, every once in a while?"

He bristled in response. "This may come as a shock to you, Osten, I know his father is a personal friend of yours, we know that, but does this man look like a prisoner to you? He's sitting here in a nice little bungalow, all alone, well dressed, plenty of food around, and we have reason to believe that he has been traveling, certainly down to Chiang Mai, maybe elsewhere. Sound like a prisoner to you? Prisoners live in jails, don't eat regularly, wear torn, dirty clothes. Not Green here. So I ask again, does he look like a prisoner?"

I didn't answer, but I had to admit Green looked reasonably comfortable. I had been wondering about that myself. But before I would have made an arrest, I would have taken the opportunity to sit down and talk to him. Not Naroogian, obviously.

"So," he continued, "I'm taking him into custody, bringing him back, and we'll have the whole matter examined in detail. It's my responsibility."

"Who made you responsible?"

"My government. The United States."

"Specifically, Avram, what branch of government do you represent? Could I see your credentials and badge, permitting you to make an arrest on foreign soil?"

"If this man is a deserter," he replied, making no effort to produce credentials, "I need no warrant or badge. I have been ordered to bring him in. You shouldn't be questioning me like this, Osten. You've worked for the government, still are, right now, and know you do what you're ordered to do."

I had worked for the government, yes, still was in a manner of speaking, but had never known that my authority extended to making arrests in the jungles of Laos. I had assumed, and still believed, that I was on an errand of mercy, looking for a missing American, hoping to find a potential blood marrow donor, and helping a sick man along the way. How far off the beaten track could anyone be?

I decided to explore the matter in more detail. "What of Lee Duc Than? Is he in custody, too?"

"He is, yes. Those were my orders. Take them both into custody and bring them back for interrogation. After all, he was a double agent. A spy. Operating on American soil."

"And your orders were issued by whom?"

"Bath. He's the man in charge."

"And what did Bath tell you to do if they wouldn't come voluntarily or, as you put it, they tried to escape?"

He shifted his feet nervously, looking around the room, counting the numbers. Less confidently now, he said, "He said to bring them back, but if they wouldn't come, if they tried to flee, to use whatever force necessary to prevent that from happening."

"That's what *he* said. But how much force would *you* actually use?"

"What Bath said was, and this may sound harsh to you, but what he said was, 'shoot them.'"

It did sound harsh, almost barbaric. Green listened, sitting calmly, making no comment while I asked, "How do you propose to do this? Alone or with help?"

"What do you mean?" he countered. "I have help if I need it. Disbrow, Dirkens, Magellan, you. You're Americans. All of you are supposed to help me." His voice trailed off in uncertainty, as mine would have, too, if I had just recited a team roster with as many weak links as his. Already, Magellan was edging towards the doorway as if wanting nothing more to do with any of us. Disbrow and Dirkens were still out on the river and, even if present, their value was questionable to say the least. My loyalty to his mission, as Naroogian already recognized, was suspect. Recognizing that his position had weakened, he lowered his rifle, and said, "For right now, while we sort things out, we can have Fred keep an eye on him and the three others we have next door. I don't suppose anyone will try to escape while shooting is likely to occur. Especially if we put them under guard."

Perhaps Lee Duc Than wouldn't be able to escape, not in his condition. And Somchai would stay with him. But as for the others, even Ken Green, I wasn't so sure. But then, if he wanted to escape, why had he let us know that he was alive in the first place?

# 16

AcChan's plan of attack had been almost perfect. Surprise was total and the only shooting, aside from my burst in the bedroom, came when two guards wandering back to their barracks from a night at the airstrip, something we had missed completely on our earlier reconnaissance, blundered into Bip and AcChan as they approached the dormitory from different directions. Seeing Bip dimly outlined against the brightening dawn, one of them shouted a greeting, thinking that a comrade was up and about earlier than usual. Bip disillusioned them at once, firing a short burst from his AK47, sending one tumbling to the ground with a leg wound, the second immediately dropping his rifle and raising his arms as high as he could. Another burst of gunfire was loosed by AcChan who was entering the front door at that very instant. Finding six sleeping figures still in bed, he fired half a clip of ammunition into the air, waking them to a state of utter confusion, and freezing them to their beds as they, too, stared down the barrel of his weapon. He was supported by the rifleman who had entered from a side door and stood at the ready, and they were joined shortly by Bip and his prisoners, one dragging his injured companion, whose cries of pain were more than enough to convince the others to stay where they were.

There was a tense moment when a dozen more men and women came tumbling from the second floor where they had been awakened as bullets from AcChan's warning shots tore through the wooden floor, some passing within inches of their heads where they slept on the bare planks. These were the workers, unarmed, standing nervously now, watching as Bip and the Thai rifleman collected the arms and ammunition stored neatly in gun racks along both sides of the dormitory. The prisoners were herded into a small empty room at the west end of the building, tied with rope, cord, and tape, and placed under guard. Like AcChan's warehouse in Chiang Rai, this building was an arsenal. There were huge quantities of automatic weapons and ammunition, including two Chinese model light machine guns, hand grenades, two mortars complete with fifty rounds, and three shoulder fired Russian grenade launchers. In another locked room were two one-man shoulder fired missiles. Behind another padlocked and chained door was a room bulging with burlap sacks and duffel bags, some empty and others filled, exactly the kind we had seen filled with opium down at the river.

Within minutes, AcChan had the second floor residents, men and women alike, hauling empty sacks and bags outside and filling them with dirt that they were digging from a circular area some fifty feet from the main house. When each bag was filled, it was hauled to the porch and stacked against the side of the building.

AcChan saw me watching the operations and explained. "Those are the workers being held here against their will. I told them to help us and we'll get them out of here. As you can see, they want to leave."

"What are they doing?" I asked.

"Filling sandbags and making a trench, at the same time. The sandbags will protect the house against gunfire and the trench will provide cover in case they use mortars or attack while we're here."

I began to understand what he meant. "You're turning this into a fortified position! Against whom? Where do you expect the danger to come from?"

"For starters, the sixteen men we passed on the trail yesterday. It isn't going to take them long to find out we're not at the river and then they'll be back. In addition, according to the sentry we captured on the way back from the airstrip, there are more men there and by now they know something has gone wrong here. They have a radio and can call for help. So I suspect we will have visitors later today or tonight. And until I hear from you that we can try to move, we had better prepare for the worst. So that's what I'm doing."

"What's the airstrip for?" I asked. "Any sign of a plane or helicopter?"

"We haven't checked it out yet, but will try to get a look. It's further west, towards the falls, between the falls and the mountain out there to the south, and like I said, appears to be more than adequate to handle smaller planes, almost certainly helicopters, and that could be the source of the chopper we heard flying overhead. They have a control room, lighted runway, fuel, a sentry house, so it's a problem. But at least we don't have one other problem. I just talked to the boat. They're all right and coming in to the dock with your equipment. The trail is clear from here to the landing and Ha and two of my men are down there already. They should have the things you need up to the house in another hour. Once you have everything, how much time do you need to determine how long we'll be here?"

That was the key to everything. How soon could we leave. As far as Green was concerned, he looked capable of leaving right now. He was limping, ever so slightly, but it wouldn't prevent him from walking to safety. Lee Duc Than was another matter. I had no idea what was wrong with him and that's where the equipment would be helpful, but even after I knew what the problem was, he was so ill that he would have to be stabilized and treatment begun before we could safely move him. A day, a week, I didn't know. I told AcChan and he accepted it, saying, "That's your end. Try to make it as soon as you can but until then, we'll have to make do with what we have."

I told him about my problem with Naroogian. He listened soberly and after I was through, he said, "He doesn't understand the situation we're in. Like many men do, he is trying to overreach. When the time comes, let me handle it. Stay out of it."

I wasn't sure that would be possible, but it seemed like a good way to leave it for the moment.

So I turned my attention to Lee Duc Than. He was the key to leaving, and the person who could best help me understand his problem seemed to be Somchai. She was a nurse and had been raised in the northern Thai village of Mae Chan, not far from the Burmese border. When sixteen years old, she had been recruited by an older man to work in Bangkok, but the work involved certain physical intimacies that she preferred to avoid, and despite having a contract, signed by her parents who had already been paid a fee for her services, she walked outdoors on her third day of employment and continued walking, aimlessly, through hopelessly congested streets, breathing the polluted air so different form that in her native village, until she found herself, alone and destitute, across from the parking lot of the famed Oriental Hotel. She was there when expatriate business executive Harry Clarkson went inside for lunch and, because she had nowhere else to go, she was still there two hours later when he came out after lunch, which had included four martinis, one less than his usual quota. He had seen a pretty little Thai girl on the way in and now saw a ravishing beauty as he left, alcohol having that effect upon Harry, and he decided to take her home to his empty house, his wife having just the day before returned to visit her family in Australia. Somchai understood his invitation to join him in the car, and accepted somewhat reluctantly not knowing what else to do, but vigorously rejected what he had in mind once they reached his home and he led her into the bedroom.

Already numbed by alcohol, further saddened by her refusal and his lunchtime failure to sell a backhoe to a promising new customer, Harry fell asleep, Somchai curled up on a couch in another room and in the morning, when he was somewhat more alert although nursing his usual headache, he was surprised to find that she had poured fresh orange juice, made coffee, placed buttered toast and jam in front of him, had straightened the messy living room, and had a smile waiting for him as he entered the kitchen. Until then, he had forgotten about the girl, about bringing her home and wasn't sure what had happened after they got there, although he was almost certain he had struck out. Then it struck him that beautiful and available Thai women were in abundant supply, but what his wife had been looking for for three years was someone to cook, clean, and serve as a nanny to their two small children. In fact, one of the reasons she had decided to go home on an extended visit was his failure to come up with the ideal candidate for the job. Could it be that this one was the answer to her prayers, even if not his? And you never knew, of course, perhaps one day she would change her mind about him.

Six weeks later, his wife due to arrive back from Sydney, he began to harbor doubts about his hasty decision. What would his wife think to find this girl ensconced in the home, albeit properly assigned to a small maid's room off to one side of the kitchen, cooking, cleaning, and doing the laundry? What his wife thought when she did return, was exactly what Harry had in mind when he first met Somchai and brought her home. She was almost immediately inclined to throw her out, and possibly him as well, but then a first glance showed the house to be clean, the laundry freshly done and properly stowed after ironing, the meal on the table a fragrant assemblage of spicy odors and tasty morsels, and she decided, "I'll take care of this in the morning."

But by morning, Harry's bedroom ardor had so impressed her, true ardor in place of perfunctory performance that had marked much of their married life, that she concluded that perhaps she was being a bit hasty in concluding that something was amiss, so she decided to wait a few more days. By then, although Harry was cooling down slightly, still better than before but slowing just a bit, her children seemed to have fallen in love with their nanny, and that had never happened before, so she decided to have Somchai stay on, on probationary terms, of course, and marveled that Harry had been so perceptive of their needs, so skillful at finding exactly the right person, a combination housekeeper, cook, and nanny that they had so sorely lacked since their arrival in Thailand. As for Harry, he was both delighted and disappointed, at one and the same time.

And a year later, when Harry was reassigned to Kuala Lumpur, he talked to a good Thai friend of his who knew the Chief physician at Silong Hospital, a man who had seen Somchai one night when Harry and his wife entertained a large group at their home. He was impressed more by her beauty than by her other skills, a mistake easy enough to make, and assumed that

Harry had hired her for ulterior motives and never had a doubt about what they were. Naturally, he harbored many of the same motives and agreed to help train her as a nurse. His motives were no more fulfilled than those of Harry, but he lived up to his end of the original bargain and Somchai, displaying an uncanny ability to learn and an amazing aptitude for nursing, completed her training, graduated, and earned the right to her title and the wearing of the white uniform and cap still favored in much of Southeast Asia, even as it disappeared from view in the western world. In time, hoping to return home, or at least be nearer to her parents and six siblings, she went to Chiang Mai, took a job in the hospital just off Suthep Road, and one night, while shopping late at the night Bazaar, she accidentally met Ken Green. It was just like that, she admitted, their eyes locked, he talked to her, discovered she was a nurse, told her he needed one to care for a sick old man, offered her a job, and she took it.

"Why?" I asked. "Why would you accept a job from a foreigner, a stranger, at night, when you didn't know him, or what the job was all about, or even where it was?"

Until now, she had been speaking English, but suddenly she reverted to Thai and said, "Rak." I scrolled through the memory files of my mind trying to identify the word, drew a blank, and once she had recognized my problem, she clarified, in English. "Love," she said. "I fell in love." I took that to mean in love with Ken Green. I found myself wondering what his motives were.

At first, about a month ago, Lee Duc Than had improved. She had given him antibiotics and urged him to drink more fluids, fed him from foods she prepared in the kitchen. Then one day, Ken told her that he and Lee Duc Than had to go into Chiang Mai, it was important, and she would remain in the house awaiting their return. She didn't want to stay there alone, not exactly alone as there were others always about, and one especially, the son of Lee Duc Than, whom she didn't trust and disliked from the first day she laid eyes on him, troubled her more than all the rest. He wanted the same thing so many men were after, and although she thought she had made it clear that she wouldn't go to bed with him, she still wasn't sure he would leave her alone once Green departed. But more than that, she feared for the safety of Lee Duc Than. His health, she was sure, was too fragile for the kind of trip they were contemplating. But Green assured her that she wasn't to worry. They would, he said, take a helicopter from here to Chiang Mai so the trip wouldn't be arduous, no more than two hours or so, and come back the same way. And apparently that's how it almost worked out, but on the way back, there was so much rain and fog over the landing strip that they hadn't been able to come all the way by air and had to land elsewhere, down near the river, she thought, and that's when it happened.

"What happened?" I asked.

"He got worse." She elaborated. "He was very sick when they got back. He is almost never able to speak, eats nothing, drinks nothing, only what I can force down him, and rarely opens his eyes. He no longer asks me to sing to him, no longer tells me stories, and I've been begging them to take him to a hospital where doctors can treat him. I don't know what to do anymore. But although Ken is willing, his son won't consider it. Ken says he can't take the chance. Not right now. I'm afraid the man will die."

"You said that's when it happened. What happened down at the river when he got worse? Is that when Ken hit him?" I asked her.

Her head snapped up in shock. "Hit him! Like in anger? Ken would never hit him."

"Some people who were there that night said that's what he did, Somchai. They said there was cursing, shouting, anger, and finally Ken hit him. What can you tell me about that?"

Her eyes wide, nostrils flaring, she declared, "He would never do that. This old man is a friend. He saved Ken's life, not once, but maybe twice or three times. Ken would never hit him. All I know is that Lee Duc Than got worse and when they brought him back, he was as sick as he is now. He isn't going to get better unless he is taken to a hospital." In that, I agreed.

It was at that point that we were interrupted by Ha and the man he would wish to be his father-in-law. They were struggling up the stairway carrying a heavy burden, bringing me a piece of equipment that might help answer some of the mystery surrounding Somchai's, and now my, patient. The x-ray machine, a rarity in this part of the world and certainly one of the first to be taken on a house call in Laos. We even had hauled along a portable generator just in case, but it turned out that the power supply in the compound was more than adequate for our needs, as the throb of a heavy duty generator, and the presence of lighting everywhere, proved that the power supply was uninterrupted. I wondered why it hadn't been cut off by now or was it inside the wire and under our control?

Somchai thought the portable x-ray equipment, complete with compact prepackaged cassettes, and self contained darkroom and developers, taking up less space than a 17 inch television set, was nothing short of a miracle. She had seen nothing like it, nor had I, until now. She eagerly helped as I took films, some with Lee Duc Than lying flat in bed, others with him propped up to permit A-P and lateral exposures to be made. Surprisingly, when I asked him to hold his breath to give us a better view of the lungs, he responded and did so. But that effort, and the pushing and prodding that we did in order to make the best possible films, pushed his frail body almost to the breaking point. His breath came in rasping sobs, became irregular, starting and stopping, sometimes absent for twenty to thirty seconds at a time and I feared that he would never breathe again. His pulse, too, was irregular, rapid, with numerous extrasystoles, the thready beat visible against his chest wall between the fourth and fifth ribs, rippling against his pale skin, faint and fast, then suddenly pausing, followed by a return of a hammering beat, the 200 thrusts a minute indicating the appearance of tachycardia. His blood pressure was a surprisingly normal 110/68 and when I checked for veins to withdraw blood samples, I found good ones on the inside of both elbows.

I indicated the right arm and Somchai fastened a tourniquet above the vein, I swabbed it with an alcohol pad, uncapped my syringes with their sterile, use-only-once B-D needles, and filled my tubes, one after another, eight in all, made blood smears, four of them, air dried the latter, labeled with date and name and inserted everything into an eighteen inch master container that was the size of, and resembled the shape of, a thermos jug you might take to work. I asked Somchai to collect a urine specimen, handed her the container if Lee Duc Than could supply it on his own, and the catheter if not. Then I went to find Ken Green. I hadn't talked to him yet about supplying specimens and I didn't want to keep the pickup service waiting when they arrived. I wanted to get what I needed with as little wasted time as possible because I knew Lee Duc Than needed help that shouldn't be delayed much longer.

Someone had brought Green over from the other building and he was sitting downstairs on a couch, guarded, if you could call it that, by Eddie. Eddie of the bruised face, damaged shoulder, and an arm hanging loosely at his side. Someone had washed the blood off his face and the bleeding had stopped, for now, although the laceration was still gaping, the entire left side of his face turning color, red, some blue, some black. The hanging arm worried me and I touched his shoulder and asked, "That hurt?"

"Hurt? Yes, but I can use it," and he raised his arm head high, making a fist, demonstrating his fitness for duty. And wincing in pain.

My medical bag was lying on the floor beside him, apparently where

Magellan must have left it. I pointed to it and asked, "Is everything in there? Everything we need? We didn't take anything out or leave it someplace else?" I emphasized the everything and anything, and I was sure Eddie understood because when he answered, he did the same.

When I had the information I needed, I suggested, "Why don't you go upstairs and lay down for a while? Rest that arm. I'll come up later and patch your head."

He wearily picked up his rifle, tucked it under his right arm, and started up the stairway, the butt end of the gun bouncing off each step as he went. I held my breath, hoping that the safety was on, otherwise the AK47 would start discharging at any moment. A minute later, he reached the top step without opening fire and I started to breathe again. Across the room, Ken Green did the same.

I didn't handle it properly. I just came right out and asked him for blood samples without explaining why, and he became furious, as furious as I had ever seen him. I understood why, but before I could say anymore, he had shouted, "Damn you. I don't use drugs, and I don't have AIDS, and you can't come in here and demand blood specimens on me after all that I've been through. Go to hell."

At the time, drugs were a big problem and AIDS was just becoming a big problem although both were much worse in Asia than in western countries, and I was surprised Ken knew anything at all about them, having presumably been locked up in a prison camp for all these years.

"You want blood from me, get me out of here. I'm a prisoner, as much a prisoner here as those laborers you have out there digging fox holes and filling sand bags. Just what the hell are you planning on doing? Fighting a war? You're here, you have enough men to get out, why are you digging in to stay? You want a blood sample in case I get wounded and you need to give me a transfusion?" he said wryly.

I motioned to the couch, where moments before he had been sitting and in front of which he was now standing, his face having turned from marked pallor to a bright red flush. "Ken, we're not talking about drugs and we're sure not talking about AIDS. What I should have talked about first was Kendra. I need a blood sample from you to see if it matches Kendra's."

He sank back onto the couch warily. "What has Kendra got to do with any of this? Why are you trying to match her blood type?"

My first impression had been that Ken Green looked all right, that he was healthy. Naroogian thought the same. We had both been wrong. His face was almost the same, thinner than what I had remembered, sure and with more lines in it than ever, but his arms seemed to have all but wasted away. What had once been finely shaped biceps were flat and soft, there was skin hanging loosely from the back of both arms where once solid muscle had been in command, and his thighs, even though covered by loose fitting twill trousers, were no more than half the size they had once been, back when he played football, ran track, and skied, had a sport for every season of the year. Back in the days before his falling out with his father, back when we had all been younger, happier and healthier. Back before he developed the limp, been infected by malaria, and been under attack by parasites. But that was then and this was now. Now he didn't look as good as I had origi-nally thought.

I tried again, this time saying, "She's sick, Ken. Kendra's sick. She has a blood disorder that sometimes turns into leukemia. She's in the hospital, been there for several weeks, and is getting weaker. A week or so ago, she started taking a medication that is temporarily helping, holding off the seri-ous complications, but we desperately need to find a blood type that matches hers, and so far no one has come up with it. Her doctors have looked at thousands of specimens, computer printouts, and tried everything they know, but the best bet is you. Her sibling. If there is a chance of an acceptable match, you're it. No drugs, Ken, no AIDS; what we're interested in is the blood type. Will it match Kendra's at an acceptable number of critical points? If it does, then we may be able to save her life with a bone marrow trans-plant."

He was silent for a long while. "Mike, I doubt that even the General would come up with a crazy story like this to shame me into coming home, and if he did, I doubt that you would be a party to it. If you say Kendra needs my blood, then I believe you." He held out both arms. "Take what you need."

I needed a lot, sixteen tubes in all; red ones, blue ones, green, lavender, brown, black, white, and orange. Plus smears. Safely nestled into another red jug, ready for the journey to Carmichael. I called for Ha and sent him off to look for AcChan, letting him know we were ready for a pickup.

The timing was almost perfect. According to the original plan, a pickup plane was to be orbiting somewhere in our vicinity at noon, waiting for a signal that would bring it over us. This was the first opportunity for Magellan to activate his jerry-built transmitter and I'm sure he received that news from AcChan with considerable apprehension. Part of the problem, of course, was his fear that Naroogian would discover what he had done, in violation of Bath's instructions. Fred seldom, if ever, went against company policy, but in this instance, for reasons perhaps not clear to him and certainly not to me, he had seemed to be willing to break the rules. His other major concern involved a more basic emotion: embarrassment. He was afraid that what he had made wouldn't work. It had been one thing to talk bravely about how good he was with electronic gear, but now, when the time had arrived to flip a switch, he was afraid of seeing ridicule on the faces of those who would gather around to judge his machine, and him, as a success or a failure.

Eddie was back on his feet, still shaky, still hurting, still unbandaged, but willing to accompany the Explorer as AcChan instructed, "The two of you take the transmitter to the high ground back there along the river trail. The signal should carry well from there. Turn on the power at exactly twelve noon, that's ten minutes from now, and keep sending until the plane either touches down or is waved off. Then turn it off to conserve your batteries. Got that?"

Magellan nodded, even while looking at his gadget laden piece of equipment, a transmitter buried inside a transmitter topped by a Pan Union supplied satellite dish, and true to form, said, "It's not my fault if it doesn't work, you know. I didn't have time to test it, not nearly enough time."

"It's too late to worry about that now. We have to use what we have and what we have is in your hands, right there. Just do what you're supposed to do." With that, AcChan, with much of his own to do, turned and walked away.

The ever optimistic Eddie patted Magellan on the back, looked at the river trail, and started up the gradual slope to the high ground. "Don't worry about it, Fred. We know it works. It worked fine back in the warehouse, didn't it?" Which was something I was still unsure of, all the while knowing it didn't matter, one way or the other.

AcChan was checking on our sandbagging operation and the trenches. Bip and Naroogian and two riflemen slipped away to see if they could safely scout the helicopter pad and landing strip, one of the riflemen carrying the red jugs and another a long box holding a surprise package of telescoping aluminum rods and wire. I went back upstairs to see what I could do about making Lee Duc Than travel ready. That was going to be the major challenge for the rest of the day.

I found his blood pressure had dropped even further, his skin was dry, as were the mucus membranes, his eyes seemed glazed with a film. His heart beat continued to race at near 200 per minute, his breathing was shallow, and he was lethargic, although responding feebly to the deep pain reflex. He had been unable to pass a urine specimen, as I had feared, and Somchai had passed the catheter and added the specimen to the rest of our collection. Having used the catheter, I knew that we would now likely face another problem, a urinary tract infection, and I made a note to add the appropriate antibiotic to his treatment program to take care of that possibility. Before Somchai packed the sample, I had looked at it and saw that it was scanty, highly concentrated, mahogany colored, and that further confirmed the presence of hypovolemia – he was dehydrated.

I analyzed one of the tubes of blood we had retained for spot study using the portable chemical analyzer that came packed with the x-ray machine, and the readings showed an increased hematocrit, elevated BUN, and higher than normal serum creatinine – all pointing to the same thing. Dehydration. Somchai confirmed that he had been unable to take more than an occasional sip of fluid for days, obviously had been given no intravenous fluids, and was now showing the result of fluid deprivation.

She assisted me in setting up a makeshift intravenous apparatus using a bulbless disconnected floor lamp as the holder and attaching the plastic bag of isotonic saline to the tubing inserted into a small vein in the back of his left hand. We watched the fluids necessary for life slowly drip into him and I laid out my program for the rest of the day. "This is the schedule for adding glucose, vitamins, antibiotics to the intravenous line," I told her, producing a carefully itemized list, the times for each to be added underlined in red, the amount underlined in green. "Do you understand it?" She did, she assured me, and with that temporarily under control, I went looking for Ken Green once again.

On the way, I stopped to look at Disbrow's ankle. It was discolored and swollen but it was nothing that wouldn't heal with time, say, fourteen days. I gave him a packet of ibuprofen and sent him back to the dormitory where he had been assigned guard duty. Dirkens made it a busy day at the office by checking in with an upset stomach and, he confessed, diarrhea. I was surprised all of us hadn't developed that, because we had long since run out of safe water and had been forced to treat the bountiful ground water with chemical disinfectants that made it taste wretched. It turned out that Dirkens didn't like the taste, his preference being for Perrier or something similar, so he had, he admitted, been drinking untreated water straight from the river for the last two days. I gave him a sulfa compound, knowing that it wouldn't help much, and added an over the counter bismuth to try to settle his stomach. That wouldn't help much either. I suggested that he try using the chemical tablets and he just looked at me as if I didn't have any idea how difficult that would be. He went back to guard duty as well, although the idea clearly didn't appeal to him.

Another stop took me to the dormitory where I examined the man Bip had wounded earlier that morning. He was lying in a bunk, one arm tied to the metal frame, his left leg wrapped in what appeared to be a bloody towel. On closer inspection, it turned out to be somebody's underwear. The blood was his; the underwear may have belonged to someone else and I could only hope that it had been clean before being used as a dressing. Underneath the wound, I was almost certain that bones had been shattered so I resolved to have the x-ray machine hauled down here and use it one more time. As long as we had it, use it. The bleeding had stopped so I scrubbed the wound carefully with a germicide, applied a layer of mucopiricin which may or may not help but was all I had, changed the dressing, putting on a real one from my bag, gave him an injection for pain, which must have been considerable although he wasn't in shock, and told one of our alert riflemen to tell the wounded man we would be back to look at him again later. I don't know if he understood or not, but I was certain none of the captives did, even though they had all been watching me treat their wounded companion as I worked. They probably hadn't expected to receive medical care, just as I hadn't expected to provide any, but you do what you have to do, I always say. Besides, way back in Washington, I had talked about making a house call. I hadn't expected it to turn into a clinic.

AcChan was directing the placement of a light machine gun in one of the newly dug foxholes when I went back outside. He crouched behind it, swept the gun from side to side, and seemed satisfied. "Good field of fire," was his only comment.

"We may need it," I told him. "I doubt that we'll be able to move Lee Duc Than today. Tomorrow, maybe. Depends upon how he responds. I've got him hooked up to intravenous fluids now and that may help." He didn't seem surprised by the information. "Any sign of a plane yet?" I asked, realizing suddenly that I had forgotten all about Magellan and his signals. Not that it mattered. No one would hear them.

"Not yet," AcChan responded. "What about Green? You want to send him out? I could have the plane land and pick him up."

It was tempting. It made sense to fly him out of here and back to Bangkok where he would be safe and the testing could be done. If he was the match we were looking for, he could be on his way back to New York in less than 24 hours. On the other hand, how safe would it be to try to fly him out?

"There's a risk," AcChan confirmed. "If the plane lands, it may not be able to take off because the runway may be too soft. I'm not sure about that. And there is the possibility that there are people up on the hill over there just hoping to get something to shoot at. Us, that would be nice, but shooting down our plane, that would be even better."

"How many people could leave on the plane?" I asked, wondering if we might be able to evacuate Somchai and Dirkens along with Green should we decide to make the move. In that case, Dirkens could ostensibly be going along to guard Green, hopefully satisfying Naroogian's fear that he would somehow manage to escape.

"They could take two. It's a four passenger plane and they have two men aboard, one to fly it, another as backup. But it's a gamble, Osten. A big one. We may be able to get your specimens out of here but I'm not so sure we should try having them make a landing."

We both watched as the laborers continued to pile sandbags higher along the front walls of the main building, leaving room enough so that the steel shutters could be closed in case shooting started.

I made my decision. Dirkens had come in with us and he would go out with us. He was, after all, an extra rifle and it was clear that we were spread thin as it was.

We both heard the faint sound of an engine off in the distance at the same instant. AcChan spoke into a radio that he quickly removed from his pocket and gave directions in Thai to an unseen listener. He listened for another minute or two and then said, "They see the strip." Then, "They see the pickup apparatus. They'll circle to the west, loop back, and make a run to the east for the pickup. You sure this is going to work, Osten?"

It had worked before, so I was hoping it would work again. What we had, what Bip and the riflemen, accompanied by Naroogian, had done was take two long aluminum poles, pound them a foot deep into the ground ten feet apart, and attach a delicate nickel-iron cable between them, fastening it with a fitting designed to snap free when brushed with the trailing hook, firmly attached to the belly of the approaching plane. The finished product resembled a football goalpost, in miniature. Using lightweight, all but un-breakable magnesium and polycarbonate clamps, a rifleman quickly attached both red jugs, filled with specimen containers, to the crossbar and Bip added a half dozen three foot long, one foot wide, blaze orange Velcro flags to the uprights, from where they snapped briskly in a ten mile an hour breeze, forming a perfect target for the plane to identify. We saw it then, a single engine craft flying low between the compound and the river, headed west. Just short of the falls, the spray barely visible in the distance, it turned sharply left, swung left again, and lined up on the runway, dropped lower and headed directly towards the flapping orange flags. The hook descended from the plane, the pilot waggled his wings, leveled off, heading directly at the cross-bar, eased off on his power ever so slightly, waiting for hook and cable to make contact. As they did, power was increased, the nose tilted skyward, and the frail uprights shuddered and fell as the cable was torn free. Simultaneously, both jugs leaped upwards where they were trapped by a spring device that appeared out of nowhere, and in less time than it takes to describe it, both red specimen containers were pulled safely inside the plane.

There were men with guns on the mountain, just as AcChan had suspected, and they had watched all of the preparations in silence, had watched the plane make its run without firing, assuming, I am sure, that it was going to land. Now they recognized their mistake and gunfire raked the landing area, angrily seeking the soft sides of the rapidly ascending airplane. The crackle of gunfire galvanized our force, armed men and laborers alike. Everyone dropped to the ground or sought shelter in a foxhole, the trench or one of the buildings. I could see puffs of smoke across the runway, clearly marking the positions of some unseen gunmen. Then there was another sound, the flat boom of a mortar tube being fired, and I watched fascinated as a flash of fire erupted on the far hill, just to the right of the still visible smoke, and then another and a third explosion rocked the site. Two of our riflemen were manning a mortar from the far foxhole and had used the smoke from the hillside to return the fire. Suddenly, everything was quiet again. A minute or two later, AcChan stood up and walked back to the main building. Seeing him, the laborers resumed filling sandbags and piling them in a rapidly increasing mound around foxholes and the house. They seemed to be working with more urgency than they had earlier.

Once again, inside the house, AcChan was on his radio. In answer to my unasked question, he said, "No, they didn't hit the plane. Your stuff is on its way. The only problem now is the helicopter. It's out there somewhere and I hope it doesn't run across our air force, but the pilot is good enough to avoid that, I think. It's a good thing we didn't ask him to land. They probably would have hit him once he was on the ground. In fact, they probably could have hit him if they had crept a little closer to the edge of the field instead of staying up there on the side."

"That was quick work with the mortar," I complimented. "Do you think we hit anyone?"

"Probably not, but that wasn't bad, was it? They'll have to keep their heads down during the daylight now that they know we have someone who can shoot back. My worry is that they may have some mortars up there, too. Then this could get to be an interesting affair. Because they can see us better than we can see them, being on the high ground."

The high ground. He was talking of taking and holding the high ground, just like the General had advised many years before. Some things don't change.

Naroogian had been crouching in a ditch at the edge of the airstrip during the pickup and ensuing action, and he came running back to the main building now to join us. "What the hell was that all about? I thought the plane was coming in here to take some of us out and all it does is yank something off a clothesline and keep going." Which wasn't a bad description.

"The laboratory specimens, Avram," I told him. "They picked them up. I thought Fantus was in charge of taking us out of here? Isn't that your understanding?"

"Exactly. That's exactly how it will be. With a helicopter. You heard Bath." He seemed to believe it. I was surprised that he didn't ask who had arranged for the pickup plane to stop by.

I left AcChan and Pan Union's security chief to work out details of our nighttime defenses, both of them agreeing that we were likely to find nocturnal visitors on our doorstep, and went upstairs to see how my nurse and patient were doing. There was still no visible change, although I had been hoping that there would be, and Somchai was standing by, watching the intravenous fluids run. She had already changed from one bottle to another as I had instructed, and was preparing to add the antibiotic when I walked into the room.

I watched as she bent over to adjust the flow, slowing the rate of administration, and marveled at the delicate line of her neck, back, and thighs. Ken Green, a prisoner, wasn't he, is wandering the night bazaar in Chiang Mai and meets this lovely girl, asks her to work for him in the dismal place, and she accepts? Says she falls in love with him, a man officially dead for fifteen years, and has been here ever since caring for a man she never knew, and who thinks she's his daughter! Incredible.

Maybe it was time to talk to Green. To clear up some of the many mysteries, but first I had Eddie bring my medical kit up from downstairs and took out the remaining vial from the mystery pack hauled to us by the airline relay all the way from Atlanta. The nitrogen stabilized plastic vial was intact. I snapped off the top of the ampoule, pulled a test dose of the cloudy material into a disposable syringe, and injected 0.5 ml. subcutaneously using a 27 gauge needle, puncturing the skin midway between the elbow and shoulder. Lee Duc Than gasped, his arm pulling away from the pain, something he had not done earlier when we had withdrawn blood, and inserted the original intravenous needle. I considered that a good sign.

Eddie was standing behind me, his face flushed, and I wondered if the excitement of the day was overwhelming him or whether he was reacting to his earlier injury. His scalp had stopped bleeding but he still looked like he had gone one too many rounds with a heavyweight, and lost. "Were you surprised it worked?" he asked.

I misunderstood the question. I thought he meant the intravenous was working or that the injection we had just given was working, but he meant something else, as I discovered when I looked at him quizzically.

"Magellan's thing. Were you surprised it worked? The plane heard it and came in just like it was supposed to. He kept saying, 'It won't work, I didn't test it enough, I don't know what I'm doing,' over and over, and then all of a sudden there was the plane. So it did work. He was so surprised that he forgot to turn the batteries off and I had to remind him because we probably are going to need it again. Right?"

Now if only Naroogian heard of it, and believed it, the Magellan caper would be a success. Eddie's face was flushed, more than I had thought, and when I felt his forehead, it was warm. He needed another nap and some ibuprofen. I bandaged his head and told him to find a bed.

And seeing that none of us had slept much the night before, or the night before that and the one before that, a nap was on my mind as well. But incredibly, something better was at hand. Running water, a bathroom, and a shower, with razors standing by. I used the ground floor facilities and came out fifteen minutes later feeling like a new man, although a very tired new man, ready to don my wet and muddy camouflage uniform. It was missing, and in its place was a clean khaki shirt and a pair of tan twill trousers identical to those Ken Green was wearing. They fit, a little snug as if I should consider the diet once again, but if I stayed in Laos eating this food much longer, that wouldn't be a problem. I had my own dry shorts and socks and once I had fully clothed myself again, I looked in the full length mirror I had almost blasted with an assault rifle earlier that day and was satisfied with what I saw. I would be a better target now, wearing these clothes than my jungle fatigues, but sometimes you have to take risks like that.

Green was in what I called the living room, no longer guarded by anyone as security measures seemed to be becoming progressively lax despite all of Naroogian's bombast about Bath's orders, shooting people, and escape plots. "I see the clothes fit. I figured you might like to change to something a little less foul smelling than what you were wearing and Somchai has been doing regular laundry since she came." I wondered if she was going down to the river bank like Simi Si to beat things clean against the rocks. Not at all, he said, they actually had a washing machine. Old fashioned kind, but it worked. I had glanced in the kitchen and they also had a refrigerator, a microwave, an electric stove, as well as the radio, one kind to listen to and another to send. The latter was up at the airstrip. That's what electric power generation can do for you. Makes life easier, brings civilization to the jungle. How long before air conditioning, dish washers, VCR's, television, and cellular phones? And fast food? And this was a prison? If so, it must be a federal prison.

My only reply was a rather flip, "Feels great to be clean again. I like to change clothes every week or so, on a regular basis, now that I've gotten used to it."

Thoughtfully, he replied, "I can understand that. Not so long ago, I didn't have a chance to shave or clean up, or change clothes, at all. Not at all. I was filthy." I assumed he was talking about a different prison.

I seemed like as good an opportunity as I was going to get. "Let's talk about that, Ken. Those years when you were missing. It's been fifteen years, I suppose you know that, and everyone back in the states were told you were dead. I don't know if you knew that, and obviously you weren't, but what happened? What happened after you were shot down and how did you wind up here?" Then, as if it mattered, and it might have, I amended my statement. "I should say everyone but Kendra thought you were dead. She told me often that she 'talked' to you while you were missing, even after you were officially declared dead, and she kept trying to convince the General, your mother, the war department for that matter, that it wasn't true. And me, for a long while, she tried to convince me of the same thing. And obviously, you aren't dead so she was right all along. Tell me what happened."

I was afraid he was withdrawing into himself and, where moments before he had seemed ebullient, pleased to see me wearing presentable clothing he had been able to provide, now a cloud passed across his face and he stared out the unshuttered windows at the darkening green of the hill where hostile riflemen were almost certainly peering through field glasses with malignant intent. Our own laborers were still working with the efficiency of warrior ants engaged in dragging a dying grasshopper, piece by piece, into the nest, their pieces the filled sandbags, the nest the main building they were fortifying. The entire front and west side of the house was now protected by a three foot high wall of sandbags and the trench extended across the entire south wall and then flowed in an arc east and west as well. AcChan obviously expected the main assault, if there was to be one, to come from the direction of the airstrip and mountain although he didn't entirely neglect the rear or river side either. Three deep foxholes were being dug there and now his riflemen were making smaller, shallower ditches at irregular intervals to the south and north, busily installing something and then covering it up.

"Mines," he mused. "They're laying mines. You really do plan on staying here to fight, don't you? It's a mistake, Mike."

A mistake, maybe, but from the grim determination of the workers and our men, I knew they intended to have everything possible done by nightfall and that wasn't far off.

He finally turned away from the mountain, saying, "I suppose you think it all started when I was shot down. Everyone would think that. But it all started long before that. Long before."

I settled back in my chair, indicating that I was willing to listen. I heard a single rifle shot from far off and then another. Too far off to be any of our people. Snipers. None of the laborers slowed their steady pace. No one took cover. For the moment, also, no one fired back.

"You know my father, I should call him the General, I suppose, better than I do. I remember him coming home from one war after another, one country after another, always the hero to the eyes of a little boy, with medals and ribbons, commendations and promotions. The bars of a captain, the gold oak leaves of a major, then they changed the leaves to silver and said he was a Lieutenant Colonel, then the eagles on his collar and a full colonel. Followed by stars. A General. He was and still is a General, I suppose. Funny, though, I always thought of him as the General. Even as a little kid. My Dad, the General! Do you know what it's like to have a General for a father?" he asked as if that was a burden he wouldn't wish upon anyone, not his best friend, not his worst enemy. It was a rhetorical question and he didn't expect an answer, not that I could have given him one. My father had never served in the military, had owned a small business and struggled to find the money to help me through college. But he'd always been there, at home, when I came from school, watched me when I played football and baseball, offered encouragement when I struck out or threw an interception at a critical point in the game, and stood proud when I graduated, both from high school and college. I liked having him around, often called upon his moral support and learned by listening and watching as he lived his daily life. And he made enough money to enable my mother, who inherited more, to buy land, raise grapes, and produce wine. In Switzerland. Then he died, much too young. That was the only kind of father I knew, and I was certain that having a General for a father would have been much different. But would it have been more of a burden to him than to me? Or to Ken?

"I admired him, I guess," he continued. "He was home often enough and we lived together at several of his duty assignments when I was small, but later, when I was in high school and then in college, I saw the way others looked at me when they found out my father was a military officer. He was a pariah to too many, despised by too many, hated and ridiculed by too many. Even my friends. His crime: he was a military officer, the lowest form of life in America according to many. I thought that was unfair. He was just doing his job, I argued. But when the war in Vietnam turned ugly, when we participated in the murder of its president, when we became involved in atrocities such as the killing of prisoners and civilians, when all of it was documented, and when our leadership denied culpability, denied that any of it had happened, and kept saying there was a light at the end of the tunnel, my admiration turned to hatred. I wanted the General to say the stories were wrong, that they were all lies, and that we didn't do these things, and he wouldn't. He insisted that the military was an honorable profession, that in war, bad things sometimes happen that even well meaning men can't control, and seemed in a state of denial that I considered cowardly. That's when I began to hate him. More and more.

"At first, Kendra and my mother were the buffers, smoothing over the worst of the differences between us. I think they more or less agreed with him that it was a privilege to serve your country in time of need, Kendra more than my mother believing it, she always was so much closer to him than I was, but I felt that the people living in Vietnam should decide for themselves who was to govern them. If they chose the Communists, so be it.

Why was it our problem? Well, you have to understand, he had been there for two tours of duty and was going back for another. So he felt strongly about love of country and duty, honor, all of that stuff. And one day, we were arguing and I shouted, 'What do you want me to do? Join the army and become a killer like you?' I wanted to withdraw those words the minute they were out of my mouth, but it was too late. First of all, Jordan Green was no killer. I knew that. He was, though, something even worse to the people I ran with. A patriot! Sure, that was worse," he added, as he saw my eyebrows rise. "Much worse. Because patriots think they're right and everyone else is wrong, don't they? They see it in black and white and their country is always on the side of God. There can't be any discussion. None. Later, I began to realize I was just as bad. Bull headed. We couldn't communicate, but I think now that he tried much harder than I did. I just wouldn't give him a chance. So I wanted to apologize for calling him a killer, but I couldn't. I couldn't say the words and he stood looking at me before replying, and hurting me when he did."

"Ken," he said, "it's a matter of honor. I'm proud to serve my country. It's what I do. Your friends have little honor, less respect, and probably even less courage because it doesn't take much courage to write anti-war graffiti on the walls of public buildings, to throw rocks and bottles at police during protests or to scream obscenities at those who try to exercise the rights of free speech. Those aren't acts of courage. Those are the marks of cowardice."

"Of course, he was referring to me. Those were some of the things I had done. I hadn't been comfortable with mob action, but because my friends knew who my father was and I wanted their approval, needed it, I had to be as vociferous and outrageous as any. Maybe more so. It was my personal badge of honor."

How much the two of them were alike. The General talked of honor, his honor in serving country, while his son sought honor in street demonstrations. Honor to one, dishonor to the other.

He was standing by the window now, still intent on watching the mountain outside. The foliage was too thick and the distance too great to permit easy observation. "I'm surprised that we didn't come to blows," he was saying. "Our arguments became that violent. And all the while I was skipping classes, drinking more than was good for me, and experimented with pot. All of us, the student radicals, were essentially out of control. Our personal life a mess; our academic life a sham, most of us staying in college to remain out of the draft without the courage to truly stand up and defy what we called a fascist regime."

Perhaps what they needed, it seemed to me, was exactly what the General had been encouraging: discipline, hard work, pride in themselves. But there was little chance of that happening in the America of those days, maybe not now, either.

Without explanation, or it was possible that in his mind he had explained, Ken suddenly said, "Then one day after a particularly brutal argument with the General, which left my mother in tears, something that shamed me, I stormed out of the house, went down to the Federal Building, and enlisted in the Army. I'm not sure why, I mean I know why the army, I didn't like the idea of spending a life aboard a ship of any kind, but what I don't know is why I signed up for anything at all. I had a deferment, I was safe, could have stayed in school wrapped in a cocoon of comfort, and no one would have looked askance. Thousands were doing it all across the country. Instead, I signed up. Impulsive, stupid, stupid, stupid. Just to get even but I don't have any idea how I was hoping to get even. It was to shock the General and then I realized that's what he wanted me to do and I had finally lost.

"Army, yes. That's what I joined but I sure didn't want to march and drill anymore than necessary and I didn't want to crawl around in Vietnam in rice paddies and collect leeches. I'd seen enough of that on television. I was smarter. I wanted to fly helicopters. I made that clear and soon I was in Fort Rucker where they taught me how."

I couldn't believe how much dirt the laborers had dug from the front yard, how deep the trenches and foxholes were, and how many sandbags they had filled and stacked as a protective barrier against the house. Green was looking at the same thing, shaking his head as if amazed at what he saw. "Do you have enough men to hold this place, Mike? You know they're going to come take it back tonight, don't you?"

Noncommittally, I said, "They're probably going to try."

Ken was watching AcChan walking the perimeter, Bip in tow immediately to his left, both of them gesturing, pointing, digging into the soft ground with their heels, and several times forcing small orange flags mounted on slim wires into the ground as if to mark the spot. For what?

"Another officer, you can spot them a mile away," Green said. Not in anger. Statement of fact. "He in command?"

While answering, I noticed another rifleman stringing wire from one orange flag to another, bending down as if to make a connection and then moving on, wire unraveling behind him, to the next flag. This one, was it still a Monday, a yellow one. The lucky one. Would we be changing ribbons at midnight?

"He's in charge," I confirmed. "But about the officer thing, I'm not sure. He's a free lance businessman. Used to be army but retired now." Was he? Interesting, Eddie said cop; Green said officer. I said businessman. Whatever he was, he had better be earning his pay or we were going to have trouble getting out of here. Our position was looking more and more like a closed box. Custer at the Little Big Horn had been no worse off than we were. At least he could have ridden out on horses. We had nothing but feet and a slow boat. Plus a sick man.

The sun had swung around from behind the mountain and was working its way to the west, its late afternoon glow shining brilliantly upon the massive fields of poppies we could see from the window. Those poppies interested me as much as anything. I wondered if Ken would ever get around to mentioning them.

Not right away he didn't. "I found that I liked flying," he was saying. "I took to it naturally, handled a helicopter as well as anyone in my class. I was assigned to Vietnam. The war was in high gear and just about every new pilot in our class was sent there. A few received other assignments and just before orders were issued, I was called in for a little chat with the Major. I could go to Korea, he told me, all I had to do was say the word. Korea! I could see the fine hand of my father behind that, taking me out of the line of fire. I didn't want any favors from him and if the offer hadn't been made with something of a wink, an air of conspiracy, if the orders had just come out that way, I probably would have accepted it as fate and gone. But I *knew* it was my father, calling in an old chip from a friend somewhere, and I said no. I would go to Vietnam. That was my preference, the Major shrugged, and that's where I went. Smart move, right?"

I didn't think that deserved an answer.

"I flew my missions like everyone else. Took men in and took them out of landing zones. Sometimes they made no contact with the enemy and other times they came back beaten and bloody. I flew by night and by day, did recon missions, and sometimes hauled VIP's, civilians, government officials here to get their 24 hour look at the war and go home to report on how well we were doing. Took Red Cross people around the country and hauled entertainers in and out of distant camps where the girls could shake their trim bottoms at woman hungry GI's and unknown comics told dirty jokes that would fall flat in the typical cheap club that had stopped hiring them years before. Everyone had a racket, everyone had an angle, everyone but the grunts doing the fighting and dying.

"And then one day, I received a call from my father. He was back in the country. Wanted to get together. Let bygones be bygones, I guess. I hoped. We did get together for a few minutes off to one side at Ton Son Nhut. I was flying out of a base near Da Nang but I hitched a ride down to Saigon, shared a drink with him, and we decided to make it dinner next time. It was OK, we talked about home, Kendra and mother, and didn't really argue much. Amazingly, I was looking for his angle, racket, whatever, and he didn't seem to have one. He seemed interested in the country, in the Vietnamese, in the people and how they could be helped and what we should be doing to make their country prosper and survive. To me it seemed ridiculous. Was he the last man in Saigon who thought we could make a difference? Was he that naïve or was I that cynical?

"So we had dinner again and this time we started arguing again. It's so long ago now that I can't even remember what it was, but I'm almost certain it was something stupid. Maybe about how naïve he was, I'm afraid it may have been that, because with all of his worldly experience, I couldn't imagine he didn't see how bad things had become, but whatever it was, I became enraged, angry at myself mainly, stormed out, and took a cab back to the airfield. The next thing I knew I was back at my base, flying again, three, four, five missions a day, ducking enemy fire and battling balky engines and bad weather. A week later, on what had been described as a routine mission in the highlands, I got hit. One minute I was flying at five hundred feet, aiming for a clearing up ahead where I was to drop off a three man team on some kind of mission, something I'd done dozens of time before, and the next I heard a loud bang and fought to control the ship as it started spiraling down toward the jungle below. I couldn't save it, although I tried to land upright. Even that failed as we toppled onto one side, but I must have been thrown clear, unconscious. By all rights, I should have been squashed by the helicopter as it toppled, but I wasn't and I came to laying in the thick brush fifty feet away with another American alongside me. I recognized him as one of the waist gunners. He was still unconscious and had blood coming from an ear. The chopper was burned, my skin was singed where it wasn't covered by clothing, and I could see three bodies in the twisted wreckage. The other two men aboard were nowhere to be seen and I gathered that they had either run off or been captured, in any event neither the escapees, if there had been any, or the Cong, if they had been on the scene and left, hadn't seen the two of us, but how they could have missed us, I don't know.

"My wounded companion, a machine gunner on his first mission, I never knew his name, was badly injured. He came to after dark but was delirious and by morning, he had died. There wasn't a thing I could do to help. I had no radio, no medicine, no water, no food, no map. Nothing. I piled brush over his body and decided to walk away despite dizziness that made it hard to stand, even harder to walk in a straight line without falling down. I concentrated on selecting a tree, bush or rock, and headed for it some fifty feet away. When I reached that immediate objective, I would select another marker and try to reach it. At each landmark, I was forced to stop and rest, so as you can imagine, I wasn't moving very rapidly and had no idea where I was going. I just wanted to be moving, away from where I was. So I kept going. I don't remember what I did when night fell again, whether I slept or just kept on wandering. I remember how thirsty I was and I finally succumbed to a raging need and drank water, kneeling like a dog, from a puddle along the trail although we had all been warned against doing that.

"I guess before noon the next day, if I remember where the sun was in the sky after all this time, exhausted, dizzy, a ringing in my ears, still dazed from what must have been a blow to the head suffered during the crash, I took a break along a faint trail, and when I opened my eyes and tried to stand, I found myself face to face with three men dressed in black pajamas. They were jabbing at me with rifles and telling me, I guess, that I had better stand up right then or be shot. For a moment, dying seemed like the best option, but then, upon second thought, I decided, to hell with it, not now, maybe later, and stood up. They pointed me in the direction they wanted to go and here I am, fifteen years later. Almost everyday since then, Mike, I've wondered if I made the right decision. Maybe it would have been best if I had just allowed it to end right there, on a trail in the jungle, years ago. But it didn't, so now you tell me, what happens next?"

What made him think I had the answer? Except for Kendra, I didn't know what happened next. He could be the answer for her. I didn't know about him. But why not just go home and try to pick up the pieces, as unlikely as that seemed right now. I wasn't talking only about the emotional psychological aspects of the problem, the scars he would have to overcome to return home to face his father, to accept the loss of his mother, and to confront the serious illness of his sister, but the practical aspects of the problem as well, the little matter of our getting out of this place in one piece. In that respect, that one thing hadn't changed all that much for Ken Green, not yet. He was still a prisoner.

We were interrupted by Somchai who brought a pot of tea and two cups. I suggested she bring a third and join us in a brief break and we sat, three of us, silently watching as the sun set at the far end of the mountain, darkness overwhelming us suddenly as so often happens at this latitude. As quietly as she had come, with a lingering look at Ken Green, she returned to tend to the patient and moments later, she called to me from the head of the stairs, and I hastened to join her, fearing a setback in Lee Duc Than's condition. Instead, what she proudly showed me was a small wet spot soiling the sheet underneath him. He had wet the bed, a good sign, indicating that the fluids were beginning to correct the dehydration, a hesitant first step on our way out of here. She produced fresh sheets from a closet and we pulled off the old and replaced them with the dry and I went back downstairs to see if Ken could be encouraged to continue with his story. I wanted to hear as much of it as I could without the burden of Naroogian's heavy hand over the proceedings, and he was still outside somewhere with AcChan.

He seemed eager to keep talking, as if there had been no one to listen to him for far too long. At first they prodded him with rifle butts, forcing him to stumble across the rough terrain, always in a northerly direction. He remembered enough of his survival training courses to look for the sun in an effort to orient himself in case an opportunity for escape presented itself. But none did. He was too weak, too confused, hurt too much to even think about it for the first three or four days and after that, it was too late. They blindfolded him, tying a smelly black rag over his eyes, almost choking him when they covered his nose as well, and then bound his arms tightly behind him. Now it was almost impossible to walk at all. He was able to see a little, his feet mainly, below the blindfold, but instead of stumbling on the trail, he was staggering, unable to maintain balance, and for that he was regularly beaten, kicked, and pushed, often falling to the ground where he was beaten steadily until somehow he regained his feet and lurched forward once more. If they wanted to kill him, he wondered, why didn't they just do it? He no longer cared.

And then one day, maybe ten or twelve days after he had been captured, they came to a base camp. He must have been a sight, his burns festered and draining pus, his torn clothing reeking with the stink of excreta and jungle filth, his feet raw and bleeding as they had taken his boots away, but all he knew was that someone pushed him to the ground where he sat, unable to see, while he listened to a hundred strange voices all around him. Then he was hauled to his feet once more, forced inside what he thought was a tunnel, and when the blind was torn away from his eyes, he sat there blinking in the light to find an officer of the North Vietnamese army sitting across from him at a crude wooden table

They knew who he was; they had taken his identification tags and he saw them laying on the table in front of the officer. He was asked to give his name and he did more than that. He gave them his name, rank, and serial number. A soldier standing behind him struck his shoulder with a wooden club and the question was repeated. The same answer, another blow. But that wasn't all they wanted to know and the first blows were just a warm-up to the real thing.

Where was his base? Name, rank, serial number. A beating.

Where was his home? Name, rank, serial number. Another beating.

Who was his commanding officer, who were his parents, where did he go to school, what did he do before joining the army? To each, the same response. Name, rank, and serial number. After which the same. A beating. Sometimes on the shoulders, then the feet, moving to the chest, the groin, on the back of his hands. Until he hurt everywhere and individual blows lost their meaning, each one becoming nothing more than a segment of agony that seemed to go on forever. Finally, after he had told them nothing more than his name, rank, and serial number and absorbed a day long ordeal of beatings, they dragged him through the tunnel, above ground once more, and then threw him into a nine foot deep pit covered by cross hatched bamboo. His new home was open to the sky above, nothing but mud below and when it rained, as it did almost everyday for the next three weeks, he was afraid the water level would rise high enough to drown him or that the walls would collapse, burying him in mud. And then he began to hope that one of those would happen to spare him the endless rounds of questions and beatings that continued day after day, night after night, seemingly without end. There wasn't an inch of his body free of bruises, scabs, and maddening sores, and any places spared by the club were quickly discovered by voracious night flying insects that hovered just above the bamboo lid, dropping down to make a meal of whatever remained of his malnourished body. But he knew that they weren't planning on killing him, having discovered the limits of his body, how much abuse it could absorb, and stopping just short of going too far.

They fed him once a day by throwing a piece of rotting fish into the pit, adding a cup of watery slop, sometimes containing an identifiable bean and other objects that he couldn't name. A handful of rice once or twice a week, a cup of water twice a day, dropped down on a string and at first, in his eagerness, he spilled half of it as he tried to capture the dangling cup, the guard sometimes mockingly keeping it just out of his reach. The sun was merciless on some days, the rain without pity on others, and he was either crouched in mud, hungry or sitting in a rapidly drying hole with dust from the ever-present feet overhead choking the breath out of him as he sweltered in filth. He had no idea how long this went on. Weeks became months and then he began to wonder if he had lost all track of time. How old was he now? How long had it been? Did it matter?

Much, much later, as he was awash in his own excrement, his body a mass of pain and sores, so battered that even swarms of hungry mosquitoes and other biting insects had disdained him for the past 48 hours as too unworthy of their attention, he saw, dimly outlined against the glare of a bright sun hanging directly overhead, a uniformed figure staring down at him. He heard him say, "Take him out of there and bring him to me. But clean him up first."

The cleaning up was cursory, but they allowed him to wash in a bucket of water, even offered a scrap of soap to use, and gave him a pair of the familiar black pajamas to wear for the upcoming interview. His own clothing, what was left of it, apparently was discarded, as he never saw his ragged uniform again.

Another table, his dog tags once more laying before the questioner, a different one this time. Slightly older, perhaps, neatly dressed, without military rank or decorations, straight black hair, serious, one gold tooth visible on the left upper jaw.

"You are Kenneth Green of the United States Army?" he asked.

Name, rank, and serial number. Even now it was still the only answer he ever gave.

"Yes, yes, we know," was the reply. No anger, no beating as had usually happened by this time and Green became aware that the two of them were alone in the room. No one with a club was standing behind him. This was different!

"Once, many years ago, I met your father, the General. He wasn't a General at that time, of course, but I felt he was destined for great things even then. I'm sure he has been worried about you since you disappeared.

Three years is a long time to wonder about what happened to a son."

Three years! It had been three years? Three years living in a pit in the ground. He was astounded. It couldn't be, but then it must be. Why would this man lie?

But even more surprising was the revelation that his father was now a General. When they had last seen one another in Saigon, Jordan Green had been a Colonel. Now this man was referring to him as General. And he realized that he may have become a pawn in a bigger game than before. A bargaining chip, a trade: information for the son of a General. Would anyone be willing to make the deal? Wryly, he doubted it. They had picked the wrong man. The General would make no deal.

But there was no talk of a deal. There were no threats. The war was going badly for the Americans, Ken was told, and the American people were tired of the war, just wanted their soldiers to come home. Wouldn't he like to go home too, he was asked. Like the others. Why, even now celebrities, movie stars, writers, former government officials, all of them opposed to the war, were visiting Hanoi and being treated with the greatest courtesy, so why did some misguided young Americans, like you, continue to come to our country to make war against the peace loving people of Vietnam, when all my people want to do is live in their own country, free from foreigners, free to raise families and to trade with the rest of the world, taking their rightful place among the nations of the world? That's all.

Ken Green didn't know how much of this was true. He was thinking, but he remained silent. He fell silent once more, in the room at Yellow Garden. It was fully dark outside now and I walked over to the front windows to pull the blinds tight although the only light on the first floor of the building came from a dim bulb in the small back room off the kitchen. A quick glimpse revealed that the perimeter lights were on, the razor sharp wires of the barrier once again gleaming as twenty four hours earlier. They looked wicked but, I reflected, hadn't kept us from coming inside. And unless AcChan had sent men to block the gates, there was nothing to keep anyone from just walking in. They didn't even need a pole vaulter on their team.

Before resuming a seat across from Green, who was back on the couch, I said, "The man who hauled you out of the pit? It was Lee Duc Than?"

Ken appeared surprised as if he hadn't expected me to discover his secret. "Yes. It was Lee Duc Than."

When the interview was over, they hadn't taken him back to the pit. Instead, the guards marched him, without a word, across the vast compound, past many more foul smelling pits where other unseen prisoners still lay, to a small building surrounded by a bamboo and wire fence. An eight foot high metal gate barred the way to freedom but otherwise it was the first reasonable place of confinement he had seen in what? – three years of captivity. That idea, the three years, shocked him beyond belief. Three years missing and he had no idea where it had gone. The war still smoldering somewhere, people still dying, for what?

He had better clothing, started to receive decent food, nothing elaborate and still not much of it, but it was edible. He was in a room with a plank floor, a real floor rather than mud, and one small unbarred window almost at the top of the wall next to the ceiling. If he stood on his toes now he could see the tops of trees at the edge of a thicket some distance away. They gave him a blanket, that's all, and there was no bed, nothing to sit on save the floor, and no table. It was a bare room, a room with a view, and it was luxurious compared to what he had endured for so long.

He saw Lee Duc Than again three days later and immediately repeated his name, rank, and serial number. Habit. But he hoped they wouldn't send him back to the pit. When his interrogator asked if his food was better, his room acceptable, he said, not meaning to, "Yes, it's better," and immediately felt guilty because he had betrayed himself, or so he thought.

Lee Duc Than liked to talk of America, how he admired Americans, enjoyed their food, literature, and educational opportunities. "I went to school in your country," he told the surprised Ken Green. And he asked no questions. He did the talking. All of it. Ken listened and was puzzled at this strange turn of events. On a fifth visit, he thought it was, each visit occurring irregularly at a week to ten days apart when guards came to bring him to the main building where he was allowed to sit in a real chair and finally, treated to a cup of tea, real tea, he learned that Lee Duc Than enjoyed American pizza, had dated his first American girl there, and he finally discovered where the 'there' was: my town, my university. The place where I once taught and the same place where I now lived and worked. And it was the place he had met, he told Ken, Jordan Green. At my invitation, the General, not a General then, of course, had come visiting and when I asked him to talk to my students, he consented to do so and there, in an informal roundtable, he met the younger Lee Duc Tan, presumed student, real life double agent, now North Vietnamese official. What a small world.

I thought back. It could have happened. Lee Duc Than was there, we knew that. Jordan Green was there, I had invited him. I even remembered us all sitting around the conference room, was that Green to my right, Lee Duc Than across the table off to one side? Maybe. But there was still something wrong. I could see them in the room together, sure, easily, but I still couldn't visualize Lee Duc Than in the clinic, in my office, as a patient. He'd never been there. Memories can fail, but records don't lie. Or do they?

Ken was still talking, but his voice had changed. When I looked up, I could see tears in his eyes. "I didn't mean to," he was saying, "it just happened. At first I listened to Lee Duc Than talk. I refused to respond to or acknowledge anything he said. He didn't seem to mind. He talked on and on without paying any attention to my reaction. Talking of America and the war seemed an obsession with him. But I was lonely. One day, I started to talk and I couldn't stop. I told him everything. I told him about my unit, where we had flown and why, where I had been trained, and all about my anti-war activities while in college, about the conflicts with my father, how much I missed my mother and Kendra. Even admitted that I missed the General, a little. Lee Duc Than seemed embarrassed and I wondered if he really cared about any of it. It was as if the information that I had just given him was without value, and maybe it was as it was all out of date by then. Who cared where I trained and where I had flown? The war had gone on and on and all of that was changed. Finally, he said, "Perhaps I should tell you, I should have told you before. Your mother, she has died. Long ago. A couple of years now. It was wrong to keep it from you.'"

"I didn't cry then, not in the room where Lee Duc Than could see me, but that night back in my cell, I did, for the first time since my capture. It was the first time I had been able to muster tears in place of despair or anger, but now they splashed down across my face in an unending torrent. Just that one time. I never cried again, but that night I felt the anguish of deep personal loss and wondered why God had chosen this cruelty for me, and for her. More for her. She deserved better than I had given.

"I never expected to be released. Lee Duc Than talked of release once or twice, but there always seemed to be something holding him back, a caution that he never explained, and I finally despaired of it ever actually happening. I was reconciled to dying in some prison camp, locked up and hidden from the world forever. Probably to the camp I was in, I decided, as it seemed as if I had been there forever. Actually, it was probably closer to a year, maybe eighteen months. Some prisoners find a way to mark the days, keep a calendar of sorts, to keep track of time. I didn't. From the earliest days in the pit, I had lost all track of time and now it didn't seem to matter.

Until they moved me. They came in the middle of the night, tore the thin blanket off me while I was asleep, and forced me to my feet once more. There were three of them, carrying truncheons and although I considered fighting back, I had become older and wiser and simply went along with the plan. Maybe, I thought, someday, I'll get even. I haven't yet."

That happened three more times over the years. A sudden move, no reasons given, always a long walk along jungle trails at night, which made him think that fighting was still going on and that not everything was going well for the North Vietnamese regulars. American or South Vietnamese planes must still have been overhead or they wouldn't have skulked through the jungle like frightened rodents. Then one day, they moved again, this time in broad daylight, riding brazenly along a road in an open truck and he knew that they had finally either reached North Vietnam proper or that the war had ended. In fact, both were true.

For another five years, he lived alone, confined to one room, guards peering through peepholes every hour or two, always accompanying him on a one hour exercise period inside a small walled compound. Guards changed at regular intervals, none remaining on site for more than ten weeks before disappearing to be replaced by new faces. They never talked, never uttered a word, and the two or three times any guard evinced the slightest interest in him, the man was replaced within twenty four hours, as if an unseen presence was monitoring every move, every look, every action, every thought that took place in his place of confinement. The replacements were always stone faced, sullen, and silent, and they, too, would be replaced by others who looked just like them. The only escape from this loneliness, this isolation, was a monthly visit from Lee Duc Than. No matter where he was held, and he assumed it to be somewhere near Hanoi, the small, soft spoken Vietnamese, who often seemed fatigued when he arrived for a visit, appeared every fourth Tuesday, precisely at noon, and stayed until he had nothing more to say. At first, Lee Duc Than did all of the talking, told of his stay in America, his days at the University, finally even revealing how he had taken money from his South Vietnamese employers while actually serving his North Vietnamese handlers. Then one day, he simply went north to start working openly for the men from Hanoi, the outcome in the war being obvious now to everyone but the Americans who still thought they had propped up a viable government in Saigon. That's when, poring over the lists of captured Americans, he had come across the name Ken Green and it didn't take much investigation to satisfy his suspicion that the son of a high ranking American officer had fallen into their net. At first, he told Ken, he had hoped to use that information in some way to benefit his country, but in fact, North Vietnam no longer needed any help from sources such as that, having already won the war on the field, so he had started calling on the young American. And found that he enjoyed it!

No one protested or thought it irregular when Lee Duc Than asked that a prisoner, a helicopter pilot, be transferred from his incarceration in a tiger pit to better accommodations. After all, Lee Duc Than was a ranking official who dealt with prisoner of war matters. If he wished to move one of them from one place to another, or interrogate him personally, who would object? It was his business. If he moved the man from one place to another, each one slightly better than the one before, who cared? Allowing him more freedom than other prisoners? Why not? Perhaps this one was cooperating. But at the same time, everyone was told, he was to see no other Americans and no other American captives were to see him. Because, as far as the world was to know, none of them existed. None. There was to be total denial.

One day in the summer of 1980, ten years after Ken Green had disappeared from the sky over Vietnam and was considered a dead man by his own government, this ranking North Vietnamese official, his place in the hierarchy seemingly secure, started his monthly visit with a surprising question. "Some time ago you told me that you had studied mining and geology in college. Is that correct?"

Green was startled. He hadn't remembered any such conversation but was aware that over time, although he continued to believe in the illusion that he hadn't revealed any information about himself or his family to Lee Duc Than, was aware that he had, in fact, from time to time, done exactly that. The loneliness was so overwhelming, the temptation so great, that there were times when he knew he had talked, as if his tongue and soul were defying the orders of his mind to stay silent. Afterwards, when he realized how far from name, rank, and serial number he had strayed, he consoled himself by saying, "What harm could it do?" Nothing they could learn about him now would have any effect upon the situation, politically, militarily or personally. He, too, had started to think of himself as a dead man. And without realizing it, Lee Duc Than had become the father that he missed when he was a child. Someone to talk to, to look up to, and to please if given half a chance.

"Yes," he said. He had, but that was so long ago and he had never graduated with a degree, that all important piece of paper, what good would it have done him after all, so his knowledge of rocks, soil formations, oil bearing strata, geological formations, all of the things he should have spent more time on, had more than likely eroded like topsoil in a Midwestern flood. His concern did not bother Lee Duc Than.

"If I bring you books, will you be able to recall what you say you've forgotten?" he asked. He coughed, brought up thick mucus which he collected in a tissue, disposed of it in a nearby metal container, took another from the small packet in his hand, and resumed his seat. He coughed a lot, seemed pale, had been losing weight, and that had begun to worry Green. If anything happened to Lee Duc Than, he reflected, what would happen to him?

Books! Real books! He hadn't been given a book to read for ten years. He had been given nothing to read for the entire time of his captivity, not a scrap with a printed word on it. Several times, he had seen small pieces of paper inside the compound during an exercise period, blown there by the wind, but before he could pick up any of them, it was always snatched away by an ever alert guard. No newspapers, no magazines, no letters, and now the offer of books. He had begun to wonder if he could still read and had been reduced to composing his own books, books of the mind, memories of days gone by, as they had never allowed him the use of pencil and paper either. On some days in the dusty yard, he scratched words in the sand, his name to see what it looked like, Kendra's, a number or two, only to have them wiped out by the boot of a smirking guard, who then hurried him back inside as a form of punishment for attempting to exercise his mind, which they apparently were trying to destroy. Almost succeeding.

So the offer of books, no matter what kind of books, was a welcome one indeed. And the books arrived. Books on basic geology, as if he were starting college all over again, geography, soil formations, and then, one day, books about the identification of gemstones, the techniques of mining for gemstones, the polishing of gemstones, the marketing of gemstones, and the worldwide distribution of gemstone producing areas. As he read, his quarters slowly improved even more. A chair and table were brought in by puzzled guards one afternoon following Lee Duc Than's visit; a lamp was next, oil, no electric outlets provided, a mattress pad allowing him for the first time to sleep off the bare floor, another blanket, and surprisingly, a Chinese Celadon figurine which arrived with a shipment of books that no one ever acknowledged sending. It was followed by a tiny, intricately carved teak statue, three inches high, depicting a sitting Buddha, delivered by a stoic guard, the same one who broke all the rules by teaching him numerous words of Vietnamese in exchange for a limited vocabulary of English. It was, Ken realized, unusual behavior for a guard, something that had never occurred at any previous stops along the prison camp trail.

There was a bigger surprise ahead. Two weeks later, on a Monday instead of the usual Tuesday, Lee Duc Than appeared early in the morning. Even the guards were flustered by his arrival, hastily beckoning Green from his room and taking him to a small office where he had never been before. Lee Duc Than was already there. They greeted one another normally, the Vietnamese smiling warmly, indicating a chair across from the desk where he was seated, but then his manner changed, his pale face taking on a serious conspiratorial air, as he whispered, "Read this," while pushing a small piece of paper across the desktop. It was clear that he was concerned that their conversation was being monitored. Had all of their conversations over the years been overheard, Green wondered. Were all of his words on tape, a record of his failure to stay true to his own code of silence? Shame and embarrassment, a violation of the military code, a betrayal of his father who would never have talked to the enemy, no matter what the circumstances.

'Collect your belongings,' said the note. 'You leave tonight. For Laos.'

Tonight! Laos! So soon and a specific destination, after all of these years. His belongings were his books, his Buddha, his figurine, and what he now considered to be his tattered honor. His blanket, of course. His security blanket. In the past, he had never been allowed to keep anything when he was moved, but this time, the two guards who came for him helped him carry the books to a waiting truck where they were loaded and then all three jumped up into the canvas covered back, an American made vehicle with faded U.S. Army markings on the sides, and they roared away into the darkness with a bone crushing jolt, suggesting that the driver may not have been familiar with multiple gears. Five days later, travelling first by truck, then on foot, and finally by a small boat powered by a sputtering outboard motor, they arrived in Laos, here at Yellow Garden and both had been here ever since. "Not quite free, not quite prisoner," he said, and before I could ask him to elaborate on that comment, Eddie, still flushed, but clean and bandaged, opened the front door and slipped inside, closing it quickly behind him. Before he did, I caught a brief glimpse of a rifleman in a foxhole to the left and another to the right, a third in the center stationed alertly behind the light machine gun that had been sighted earlier in the day. In the reflected light from the gate houses, I saw a crouching figure running quickly between the dormitory and the solid warehouse building nearby. It looked like AcChan.

Eddie peered outside from behind the blinds and then turned, saying, "AcChan thinks we should move the man from upstairs down here. He thinks it will be safer. He also said to tell you he sent the boats back out onto the river." He stood as if waiting for an answer. "Do you need any help before I go on patrol with Bip?" he asked.

Ken had been staring blankly as if unaware of Eddie's presence. Had he come here five years ago expecting freedom, only to be disappointed again? Had our coming made his situation even worse?

Eddie was standing by and I sent him back into the night by saying, "No, go ahead. Green will help me move Lee Duc Than." I didn't know if he would or not, but it seemed important to involve him in some way with the night's activity, as it was bound to concern him, his freedom and Kendra's, before it was over.

Eddie disappeared the same way he had come, a shadow out the door, and I started for the stairway, wondering if Green would follow or not. Without a word, he did.

At the top of the steps, I went for the jugular, verbally. "So," I said, "Lee Duc Than allowed you to go free, to come here to Laos, to help him grow poppies, produce opium, and you got started in the drug trade. Was that the price of freedom, Ken?"

It was as if I had struck him in the midsection. He stopped three steps from the top and just stared at me, his face an unreadable mask, pale, then changing to anger. Very real anger.

"I don't deny the poppies, Mike. Obviously, anyone can see them. They grow poppies and process opium here, yes, but not me. Haven't you seen the piles of dirt, the bulldozers, the mine, the shafts, my work? Haven't you seen what I've accomplished? My God, we've torn up half a mountain, we've dug and dug, we've extracted a fortune from the soil, and we're still doing it. That's my work. The mines. Not the poppies. They belong to Huy Thact."

Huy Thacht! A warlord, one AcChan had warned we might encounter. So Yellow Garden was his nest and we had taken up residence in it. I wonder if either of them knew it yet.

What Green was telling me, I hadn't known. Of course, we'd seen dirt piles. That was how Eddie had gotten over the fence, the bulldozer operators having carelessly allowed dirt to accumulate too close to the wire from where it could serve as a successful launch platform. But as I'd spent the day inside, for the most part, and because it clearly wasn't safe to wander about on the mountain, I hadn't seen shafts, mines or bulldozers, and thus had no idea what kind of work Ken had been engaged in. Although I had an idea, and he confirmed it when I said, "You've been digging for gemstones? That's why Lee Duc Than brought you the books?"

"Yes, stones. Valuable ones, for people to wear on their necks, wrists, and fingers to look pretty. That's what I've been doing in this Godforsaken place for the past five years. And I've done it well. Stones, not drugs, so you can go back and tell the General that his son isn't into polluting the minds and souls of young people. He's trying to make them happy with beautiful stones. That's all."

He still cared what people thought, what the General thought, what I thought.

Suddenly, trembling two steps below me on the staircase, he began to sob and leaned wearily against the wall as if in despair. "Not drugs, Mike. Not drugs. Stones, Mike. Just stones." His shoulders were shaking uncontrollably and as I stepped down to where he was, and embraced him to help him to the top of the staircase, he cried out, "Oh God, I want to go home. Mike, help me, I want to go home so badly. Please help me." His tears were real. I felt mine beginning to form as I listened to this cry from the heart, torn from deep inside, born of the anguish of fifteen years, and it was then that the first shots of the night rang out.

Instinctively, expecting to feel the impact of bullets striking the building, I crouched lower, pulling Green with me. I saw Somchai crawl into the hallway from Lee Duc Than's room above. AcChan's advice to move the patient made more sense than ever and I realized that we couldn't remain huddled like this any longer. Especially when there was a sudden rattle of gunfire just outside the building, on the left front where one of our riflemen must have found a target, and then the tinkle of breaking glass from below and the thud of slugs hitting above us convinced me we had wasted too much time as it was. I straightened and headed up the stairs to the top, shouting to Ken Green and Somchai as I went the last few feet, "We have to move Lee Duc Than right now." We did it by simply picking up the light mattress with him cradled inside, and as Somchai carefully held aloft a functioning 12 drop a minute intravenous bag, needle still securely anchored in a small vein by copious layers of adhesive tape, we eased him down the staircase and found him a more secure location just off the kitchen. Somchai attached the plastic container to a handy doorknob, a temporary expedient but one that worked well, and using my flashlight, I checked and found the fluid to be running smoothly with no evidence that the rapid shuttle from one floor to another had done damage to either patient or equipment.

Scattered rifle shots could still be heard in the distance now. The nearby foxholes had fallen silent. In the momentary silence, as we watched Lee Duc Than breathe and while I was checking his pulse, Somchai reminded me, "The other one is still up there. The soldier."

I realized that she meant Dirkens whom I had last seen lying in the second bedroom, seized with cramps and nausea. He was crouching in a corner and recoiled in fright when a beam from my probing flashlight discovered him. He was unable to see who was behind the glare and one arm was extended in supplication, as if saying, don't hurt me. He was terrified.

Speaking softly, I was able to induce him to coming downstairs with me and finally left him, sitting in a corner opposite Lee Duc Than. Clearly, he was not going to be of any help this night, although he still clutched his rifle as if it was his favorite teddy bear.

My own rifle was in the front room where I found Green after things had settled down once more. My Glock was snugly holstered at my side and both were loaded. I was wondering how soon it would be before I would have to use them.

I took another quick look outside and was startled to see a string of red and blue lights in the direction of the mountain, something we hadn't seen the night before. Probably because of the mist and fog, I decided. Further west, there was a blinking red light, obviously perched atop some sort of a radio tower, all of them, including the dim light in our back room and the gate lights, so the power was still on. And if the power was on and there was a radio tower, there had to be a radio somewhere, and I was willing to bet that messages had been flowing in and out all day long. From Huy Thacht, say, and to him. Telling him about visitors to his home.

I was hoping to see AcChan, to give him the information Green had revealed about the owner of this choice piece of property, but when the door suddenly flew open, I saw Naroogian instead, and he saw the rifle leveled at him and said in mock horror, "I surrender. Or are we on the same side?"

He looked around, took in Green standing to one side, Somchai in the kitchen doorway, and asked, "Anyone hurt?"

"Not in here," I told him. "How about outside?"

"I don't think so. They seemed to be shooting at the floodlights mounted on the roof line of the buildings and in a few of the trees. AcChan figures they're trying to knock them out so we'll be blind when they attack. From the sound of all the breaking glass, they got some of them but I don't think they got them all, although they had the advantage of knowing where all of them were, this being their place to start with."

"Where is AcChan? I've been busy in here," I didn't tell him what was keeping me busy was the Ken Green story, one that I'm sure he wanted to hear before anyone else, "and I have no idea what's been going on outside."

"AcChan? Our leader? He's been everywhere. One time I look he's out checking the wire, next he's moving the prisoners to the cement block building out back, then he's checking to see if the mines have been set, the guns are sited properly, the foxholes are deep enough, and now he's getting all of the laborers under cover. They're scared to death with all of the gunfire."

"Talking of scared, you've got the same kind of problem in the back room."

He didn't try to conceal his disgust. "You mean Dirkens? Is he still shitting his pants? It isn't diarrhea that he's got. He just full of crap and when he gets scared, it all runs out. Unfortunately, we need the bastard, we need his gun but I don't suppose he'll be able to help, right?"

Just another question that didn't need an answer and none was called for when Naroogian walked past me into the back room where I heard him talking to Dirkens, who might have mumbled a reply, but I wasn't sure. Naroogian was back in less than a minute to report, "What a prize. He threw up. Stinks like hell."

He turned his attention to Green who was back on the couch, apparently his favorite place. At home, we'd have a television right opposite, in the corner, a remote control at hand to click from one channel to another. Here there was but a single channel, no picture, just grim reality.

"He giving you any trouble?" he asked, as if a man sitting on a couch was likely to be a problem.

"No trouble," I told him. "Just sitting and waiting. He wants to get out of here just like we do."

Naroogian didn't agree. "You sure of that, Osten? Really! Those are his friends out there, the ones doing the shooting. They're not our friends, you know. These are the people he's been living with. Him and that China doll back there with Dirkens."

"Avram, I don't know if you're aware of it or not, but bullets fired in our direction aren't able to discriminate. They could hit Green or Somchai just as well as you or I. If this gets ugly later tonight or tomorrow, before we get out of here, I intend to see that Green has a weapon to defend himself. He's an American, wants to go home, and by God, I intend to see that he gets there."

I don't know if he was influenced by my passionate little speech or not, but he didn't raise much of an objection to giving Green a weapon, warning only, "You do that, give him a gun, he's liable to shoot you in the back. Consider that, Osten. And if you give him a weapon, he better make sure he doesn't point it in my direction because I'm not nearly as forgiving and I'm liable to shoot first and ask questions later. If you get what I mean." He said that directly to Green, not me, but I think we both got it. Despite his words, though, it was clear that Naroogian also recognized that before this night was over, we might need all of the rifles we could find. "And then, as soon as possible," he added, "I want to talk to this missing American, just like Bath ordered. I'm sure he has a story to tell us, wouldn't you say?"

I would, because he had already started telling it to me.

Naroogian paused before going back outside as if he wanted to say more, decided against it, ending with, "I'll tell AcChan you're looking for him," and was gone.

I stayed low for the brief time the door was open. Who was to say we were the only ones with night vision goggles?

From behind me in the dark, I heard Ken ask, "Who's Bath?"

It surprised me. I hadn't been sure he was listening to anything Naroogian had to say, staring vacantly and sitting stiffly all the while Avram had been in the house, but apparently he had. The name Bath intrigued him. "I guess you might say Bath is the man we work for," I answered. "At any rate, he is the man who raised the money to pay for the expedition. From the government, of course, not his own. Want to see what your benefactor looks like?"

I'd been carrying the photos Carmichael had made in Hong Kong days before wondering what use they would be, and not expecting much from them now, I took a photo taken outside the hotel, not especially flattering but good enough to capture his main features as I saw them: reptilian eyes, greasy hair slicked straight back, thin aquiline nose, and slightly receding jaw – not a pretty picture, but it was Bath just the same. They say pictures don't lie, and although that is a myth, I was surprised at the truth that sprang from this one as I played my flashlight beam upon his features and held it out for Green to inspect. He took it, looked at it carefully, and then handed it back, walking over to the blinds once more to peer cautiously from a corner.

Would he, like me, prefer to be outside, where we could see despite the darkness, where we could hear despite the silence, and where we could feel the air against our skin, instead of being inside, trapped in prison of our own making, away from the sights and sensations of the drama unfolding around us?

Still looking away, he asked, "You work for him?"

"No. Not really. He's paying some of the bills but I'm working for myself. For you, for Kendra, maybe even the General."

"That's good because if you were working for him, I would be tempted to use that gun lying over there to shoot you in the back, like your Mr. Naroogian was talking about."

I glanced at the rifle still leaning against a chair and started to move towards it, cursed myself for a fool, stopped, and asked, "Why? Why would you be tempted to do that?" After all, I still had the Glock inches away at my side.

Green was in no hurry to answer. He continued to look outside, finally releasing the blind and walking back to the couch where he sat once more. "Why? Maybe because I don't like the way he looks, or that he has access to government money, or that Naroogian takes orders from him. Maybe, but mainly because I know the man. I've seen him several times and I don't like what I know."

I wasn't sure what he was talking about. Was it possible that Ken had seen Bath fifteen years ago in Vietnam or on a trip to Chiang Mai in more recent days? Or even before ever coming to Vietnam while still at home, possibly when the General entertained him as a guest, if he ever had. After all, Jordan Green and Bath had known one another for a long time.

"I see him every once in a while, most recently not more than three weeks ago. He flew in with a helicopter and took out his usual load," he said. "Some gems, some opium. Whatever sells."

He paused once more, as if gathering strength. "He's a regular visitor. Name is Towle, though, not Bath."

Without comment, I handed him another glossy photograph, light illuminating the second face. "Sure, I've seen this one, too. Flies the helicopter. Usually stays with the plane while your Mr. Bath negotiates. They're buddies. Partners, maybe, but Towel or Bath, whatever his name is, seems to call the shots. He's the boss. Interesting financial backing you have here, Mike. What I don't understand is, why didn't they just fly you in rather than sending you on foot, doing it the hard way?"

While he was asking that, I was asking myself why we needed Magellan's decrepit transmitter to send a signal when the helicopter pilot already knew his way to the landing pad? Meanwhile, I held out my hand and took back the second photo, tucked the picture of Fantus back into an inside pocket, hidden from view once more, alongside his partner, Mr. Bath.

So Bath and Fantus were visitors, flying in and out of this jungle paradise on business. What a surprise!

AcChan's sudden reappearance didn't leave me much time to evaluate this latest information. It had no particular bearing upon our present situation, but certainly would be a factor in any planned evacuation by air. Especially since those plans involved a helicopter piloted by Fantus.

AcChan bent over to look at Dirkens as he came through the back room, asking me, "What do you think? Useless? Or can we use him?"

"Use him for what? He just sits there leaking from both ends. If that can be of any help, factor it into your planning. Otherwise, cross him off the list. Not available for duty."

"That's a pity. I need every man I can get. Under the circumstances, I should have had him taken back out on the river with the boats. But we'll make do with what we have. If they don't hit us from every side at once, we may be all right. If they do, we're in trouble. They'll come through the wire anywhere they want. They don't have to worry about making noise like we did so they'll just blow it and come in. I had expected them to be tossing grenades by now, using rockets and mortars, they've got some up in the hills according to the prisoners, but they haven't so I expect they're waiting for instructions from whoever comes in on the plane."

He saw my look of surprise when he mentioned the plane. "That's right, you don't know about the radio. They have one down on the landing strip in an operations shed. You can see the radio tower from here tonight. A while ago, they were talking back and forth to someone who wanted to know what the situation was here and they told him, and if we got the message right, they are planning on sitting tight until the head man gets here. The head man, when he gets here, is going to make the plan to finish us off."

"We should have blown the radio or turned off the power while we had the chance," I said.

"No. I wanted them to talk to one another so we could listen. And I want to leave the lights on as long as possible. In a way, it blinds them more than it does us. They tried to knock out the floodlights but failed to get them all so we still have a way of illuminating the compound and the light will be in their eyes, making us hard to see. The man I left on our back trail has come back and reports that the sixteen men we passed on our way in are back. They may have a couple of new men with them. The prisoners we took the other night and the sentries from the gate confirm there are at least another twenty men stationed at the airstrip and on the slope of the hill looking down our throats. When Huy Thacht arrives, he'll have several more men with him. So to say that we're outnumbered is an understatement. But I've been able to do a little recruiting of my own." I must have expressed surprise because he went on to add, "Laborers. Three of them. Just about everyone in this part of the world knows how to use a weapon and three of the men have been pushed around far enough and are only too eager to shoot back. We have plenty of weapons, so they'll be outside, two of them in foxholes to the west of the house, one of them accompanying Bip and me back to the airstrip.

"The way I figure it is that we have thirteen men to hold the building and hang onto prisoners we've already scooped up. When the attack comes, I want you and Chun outside on the south side, the front, of the house in separate foxholes. Each of you will have a trained rifleman with you. The third foxhole you've seen will be occupied by a machine gunner. Let's hope he can get by without an assistant. Another of my riflemen will be opposite the only door leading from the cement clock building where the prisoners are being held. They shouldn't be a problem as they've all been tied tightly but if anyone tries coming out of that door, they're dead. He'll also be able to cover part of the west side of the building. Backing him up will be two laborers with assault rifles in slit trenches to his immediate right. That's where the attack will be coming from, I'm sure. The south and the west. That's where they have their strength.

"However, just to be sure, I've put a single rifleman on the east side of the building where he has a clear field of fire all the way to the edge of the jungle almost three hundred yards away. I don't expect them to try to cross that much open ground. Meanwhile, I've posted Naroogian and Disbrow to the rear, looking towards the river. As you know, there's just the one narrow trail coming up from the dock and when we last looked, there was no danger from the quarter. There still isn't if LoDan's report can be believed. He's down there with one hill tribesman, Ha, and the boatsman we captured back at the store. We've decided to untie him and give him a gun and hope he uses it against Huy Thact's men and not us.

"Give Green a rifle and have him backing you up at the front door, ready to move to the east windows if I'm wrong and they send an attack from that side. Have Magellan at the back door, although I don't know how much good he'll be inasmuch as he can't see in the dark. Have Somchai stay with Lee Duc Than and Dirkens, who is useless. Worse than useless. A liability.

"Counting everyone we'll be able to deploy on our defensive perimeter, we've got thirteen men, including Green and Magellan. I figure, from what we can piece together and what we've seen, they have anywhere from forty to fifty. Of course, we also have four men back down by the river with the boats. But the numbers may not be as bad as they seem," he said as if my morale needed a boost. "Well dug in defenders have an advantage, especially if they have enough ammunition to lay down a heavy curtain of fire at the first sign of trouble. We do, and I suspect the men that will come tonight will cut and run if we do that as I doubt they're very well motivated. I know that they aren't as well trained as my men and I just wish I had brought a half dozen more. But even so, these thugs are used to attacking unarmed civilian villages, abusing women and children, and they aren't accustomed to finding a fixed defensive position in the way." Even as he was speaking, I knew he was thinking of his fixed defensive position that had been overrun so many years before when he and Broward barely escaped with their lives. He looked at me as if reading my mind. "Any suggestions?"

I noticed that he hadn't specified any assignment for himself and none for Bip. "Don't worry," he assured me. "We won't miss any of the excitement. Bip and I are taking Prathorn and one of the laborers who knows the area and will go deep into the jungle. We'll head west towards the falls and then circle south to approach the far end of the landing strip where we plan on hunting snakes."

"Snakes?" I asked.

"One snake in particular," he explained. "The head snake. The one coming in on the plane."

"Huy Thacht? He's coming in on the plane?"

"How did you find out that this is his place?"

"Right there," I said, pointing to Green. "It isn't a secret."

"That's where you're wrong," he corrected. "It is a secret. This is a man, a nasty Vietnamese renegade who thinks nothing of killing, who we've hunted for more than fifteen years, but never knew exactly where he could be found until now. We know he comes to Bangkok, has a home in Bangkok in all likelihood, another home, according to rumors, in Hong Kong, yet another in Manila, and travels with impunity because no one knows what he looks like. Now I've heard his voice on the radio, he says he's coming, and I want to be there to greet him. The best way to kill a snake is to cut off its head. So tonight, Bip and I will be snake hunting. That's our job."

"How do you know he'll be on the plane?" I asked. "Why couldn't it be someone else, a second in command?"

"Some things you just know, Osten. Huy Thacht travels the world over. He's been reported almost in my backyard in Bangkok, like I said, has been seen, says Interpol, in France, some say in the Caribbean, possibly even South America, although so far he seems to have stayed out of the United States. But this is where his fortune comes from, so I suspect he'll come, himself, to take charge of recovering his home. My chief concern is that he may just say, 'who needs the house? I'll build another one. Just blow it up.' Then his men could use the mortars and rockets they have to pound us into a pile of rubble. If that happens, I've told Naroogian to pack up and move everyone down the river trail and use the boats to get away. You'll have to make the best of it with Lee Duc Than. There could be one problem with that plan, though, and it's Naroogian himself. He says if they start using heavy stuff on us, he wants to use Magellan's transmitter, call in Fantus and go out by air."

"That's never going to happen," I responded. "You know that. Fantus is not coming."

"Of course I know that. And you know it, too. But does Naroogian know it? He may think that's an option."

For the second time that evening, Ken Green, who had listened without comment while we had discussed our plans, supplied a remarkably useful piece of information. "They won't hit us with anything big. They'll be very cautious."

AcChan and I both looked at him with interest. "Why do you say that?" I asked.

"Huy Thacht, the man you call the leader. He's not only the leader, like you said, but he's Lee Duc Than's son. He won't want to kill his father, so he'll move cautiously, don't you think?"

Both AcChan and I were silent, assessing this bit of the puzzle, fitting into the larger mosaic of the nighttime chess game that was about to commence. I was the first to speak. "If Huy Thacht is Lee Duc Than's son, why didn't he call in a doctor for someone so ill? That doesn't make sense."

From the shadows across the room, Somchai spoke softly. "He doesn't believe in doctors. He believes in spirits. Good ones and bad ones. You pray to the good ones, through Buddha, asking for assistance. If you lead a good life, you stay healthy. If you fall ill, Buddha helps to heal you."

"That's fine, Somchai, but it obviously isn't working. They brought you in to help; why not a doctor, too?"

"Ken brought me here," she corrected. "But Huy Thacht did not want me. He felt I would do more harm than good because I was not a believer in the power of Buddha to heal illness. But after I was here, he couldn't let me leave because I had seen too much and knew too much so he ordered that I stay. Which is why I am still here."

Not entirely true. Huy Thacht wouldn't allow her to go, perhaps, but would she leave if she could? The way she looked at Ken Green made me wonder. I had seen the look of love before and she had it.

Ken himself, said simply, "I was the one who made her a prisoner. I tried to help and should never have asked her to come here." He was lying, as the look on his face clearly demonstrated.

It took AcChan to put the new information into perspective. "We may not be playing from as weak a hand as I feared," he said. "This changes the rules. If they don't use heavy weapons, we have a good chance of beating them off, even with our limited manpower."

He looked at his watch again, the third or fourth time since he had come into the house, as if expecting something to happen at any moment. "Bip and I will be leaving shortly," he said, "but before I go, I want you to know that the captives are in the cement block building, all of them tied tightly, the door barred and a rifleman in a foxhole looking directly at the opening. If anyone comes out of the building, he will shoot. The laborers are locked in the other end of the same building. In the morning, we'll likely allow them to leave. They're not tied. One of them volunteered to go with us on the snake hunt."

"You have to allow them to leave," Green said. "Otherwise, they'll be killed."

"What do you mean?" AcChan asked.

"Ever since I've been here, a new group of laborers are dragged in from neighboring villages at four to six month intervals. They are worked hard and then replaced by new ones. It goes on and on."

"So it's slave labor. They work the people hard and get new ones. What's new about that?" I asked. "Goes on all over the world in unenlightened societies."

"Except this is different," Green responded. "When they bring in new ones and get rid of the old, they don't just send them back home where they came from."

"They don't?" I said, and I didn't need to ask what he was going to say next.

"No. They take them out and shoot them. They want no one going out of here talking of what goes on."

"You've seen this happen?" AcChan wanted to know.

"Many times," Ken affirmed.

"Then they were never planning on allowing you to leave either, were they? You know even more than the average laborer," AcChan said.

"In that case," I pointed out, an easy thing to do as it seemed rather obvious, "they wouldn't want us to leave either, would they?"

"An excellent observation," agreed AcChan. "Very well put."

The hum of propellers overhead halted further conversation. AcChan referred to his watch once more, and nodded in satisfaction. "Right on time," he said. The roar of the engines, multiple, two, was loud and as we peered through the covering blinds once more we watched as blinking wing lights dropped lower, lined up on the blue runway lights, glided smoothly, and touched down, nose headed westerly towards the operations shed.

Watching, frustrated, I said, "We made it too easy for them by keeping the runway lights on."

AcChan was unperturbed. "Not at all. I wanted them to get down. I want to make it hard for them to take off again." He spoke softly into a small handset, listened to a scratchy response which I couldn't decipher, and then suddenly said, "Now." For a moment nothing happened, then the earth rolled, the building trembled, and an enormous fireball erupted at the far end of the field. A shock wave slammed into us and a window broke somewhere up above, a dozen smaller explosions blossomed across the landing strip, and one of them, near the end of the runway, seemed much larger than the others. I didn't know if it was my imagination or not but it seemed as if I could see flames leaping and dancing across the wings of an airplane.

Up on the mountain, the light of the radio tower had disappeared. Out on the field itself, although brightly illuminated now by the several fires still burning, I saw that the runway lights had been extinguished. The double strand of blue was missing. The dim bulb in the back room had gone out while the gate house, brilliantly lighted moments before, had vanished in darkness. I had been counting on the floodlights in case of attack and meant to ask AcChan about them when he suddenly picked up his rifle and said, "Time for me to be going. Get everyone else into positions, too. The night's activities are about to begin. By the way, how did you like that boom? That was the operations shed and radio. No more messages from there. Maybe we got the plane, too. I hope so, but if not, we've still got more work to do. Now remember, if anything goes wrong, get everyone back to the river on the boats and go downstream. To where the store was. Got it?" he asked, looking at me. I must have looked worried because he said, "That bit about anything going wrong? Just an expression I use. I don't expect anything bad will happen, so good luck."

And he was out the door into the darkness. I saw his outline briefly as he hurried down towards the wire where three other shadows rose up to join him and then they all vanished.

I turned to Green and said, "Get Dirken's rifle and do what AcChan said. Cover the front door and windows. Keep Somchai with you." He hurried to the back room to find a weapon. Magellan was already crouched behind sandbags by the rear door and just outside, I saw Naroogian and Disbrow settling into a fresh foxhole. Further left, a single rifleman was huddled in his lonely shelter, guarding the isolated flank, looking down the trail towards the river, our presumed safety valve.

Lee Duc Than was unchanged and Dirkens lay where he had been earlier, a foul smell marking the spot. The odor would keep him safe from attack even if the bad guys broke through our perimeter.

I went back to the front, saw that Somchai was well protected by the overturned sofa, something Green must have arranged while I was in back. He, with a rifle, was in position alongside her. Outside in the damp air, I saw two men already in the foxhole to the right, knew I should go to the left, ran, and then rolled as I had once been trained to do. That had been a long time ago and as I was untangling myself from the bottom, trying to pull my rifle free from under one leg, and wiping mud from my face, finally working myself free and sticking my head cautiously over the edge of the hole, I heard a voice saying "You OK, boss? You landed pretty hard." It was Eddie, peering down anxiously. He had decided to share his foxhole with me, sending his original partner to join another of AcChan's men in the hole to our right.

It was quiet for more than an hour. Flames still lighted the sky to the southwest where whatever remained of the operations building was still burning. Twice I thought I saw moving figures outlined briefly against the glow of the fire but by the time I called Eddie's attention to what I'd seen, they had disappeared. We knew that there were people out there, just beyond, and possibly inside, the wire. After all, they'd been shooting at us off and on since early afternoon, so it was eerie to crouch in the shelter of a wet foxhole and look out at the shadows dancing crazily, first on our left, then to the right, followed by sudden movement straight ahead – to find nothing there. Tree limbs waving in the wind, moonlight darting in and out from the scattered high clouds, and maybe more. Twice Eddie was convinced that he saw someone walking directly at us and once I almost fired at an apparition that rose from the ground and launched itself across our field of vision, fading away with the rustle of, what was it, wings? A night bird? Owl? But why did it take flight? Merely off to hunt or startled by something else? And then again, nothing.

"How'd you like those explosions?" Eddie whispered after one false alarm.

"I guess they did the job. AcChan said they blew the operations shed and radio tower but I don't know what the rest of the explosions were. The ones out on the landing strip itself."

"Mines," Eddie confided. "After it got dark, he took a couple of men and they planted mines up and down the runway, hooked them to a battery and plunger, and when the plane was touching down, he blew the whole thing up. Maybe he even got the plane. I think that's what he had in mind. Be ironic wouldn't it, if we used their own mines to blow their plane up?"

Ironic, maybe, but simple justice all the same.

Something had caught Eddie's attention. "Is that something moving over there? To the left of the building, remember, about where the flower gardens were before we dug them up? Look, right there, is it moving?"

As I stared where he directed, I saw nothing at first. A moment later, everything seemed to be moving, it was as if a circus troupe of clowns and tumblers had suddenly entered the center ring and I threw off the safety, ready to depress the trigger, only to find that not a thing was moving at all. Nothing. Slowly, finger poised over the trigger guard, I asked, "I'm not sure. What do you think? Anything there?"

Eddie was aiming at the same spot in the night and stared hard before deciding, "No, I guess not. Sometimes in the dark, your mind plays tricks on you and you begin to see things that aren't there. Happens to me all the time in the parking lot at the office. Course, there I've got lights all around the lot, not like here where we turned them all out."

"What do you mean we turned them all out? I thought we blew them up when we knocked out the radio and shed."

"They went out at the same time. That was the plan," Eddie explained. "Make them think the lights are out, but they aren't. We've got the generator right back behind us and it's fine, so when we need lights, we can turn them on again." As he talked, he was still staring at the spot that had been bothering him earlier. "Damn," he muttered. "I'm still not sure that something isn't moving out there."

I looked again, first directly at the spot, then taking another angle slightly off center in hope of picking up movement. Saw nothing. Heard nothing.

Then I heard Chun sliding slowly down the muddy side of his foxhole, heard him splash into the two to three inches of water that had accumulated in the bottom almost as soon as it had been dug into the waterlogged soil, and he clawed his way back up to where his head could once more see over the edge. Fortunately, I had been able to find a toehold in the wall where I lay, was able to keep my feet just out of the water, and smiled as I heard him begin to slide once more. "Geez," he said, "anybody got a hook to hang me on? I keep sliding down and can't see."

He crawled back once again and now, clearly aggravated, he decided once and for all to clear up the mystery of movement out on our immediate front. "They've got some flares over in the other hole. I'm going over there to see what they think. I'll be right back."

This time, without making a sound, he was up and over the edge, leaving me alone in the dark. I hadn't realized how lonely it was until then. Or how dark.

That changed a moment later when, with a bang and a whoosh, something soared into the sky, exploded high overhead and hung there, lazily drifting downward, an intense bright light, with the brilliance of a hundred headlights, turning the entire scene before me into daylight. It was so bright, it hurt the eyes. Obviously, the riflemen in the neighboring foxhole had fired a flare. The buildings were boldly outlined, the ground illuminated by a ghostly orange-white glow, the razor wire glittering two hundred yards away, the grass a pale gray, the denuded areas, stripped to fill the sandbags we now crouched behind, emerging as darker patches, some of them almost black, looking like dried blood, I had just about decided, until I looked once more and realized that the black patches were moving, standing up, and coming straight at me.

A rifle in the other foxhole reacted before I did, thankfully, because I had not reacted at all, but when I heard the crash of automatic weapons fire to my right, more firing from west the side of the house, and the chatter of the machine gun from somewhere in front of me, my own muscles started to respond and I found myself leveling the assault rifle and pulling the trigger. Once again, it was set on full automatic, a clip emptied and without thinking, I popped in another. And kept firing, just as AcChan had instructed. I was dimly aware that figures in front were still coming, then one slumped and fell, and another, a third stumbled and slumped to the ground, and then the floodlights blazed on behind us and we could see fifteen, maybe twenty black clothed men standing transfixed in the glare of near daylight, stunned, blinded, and they turned and ran. Two more tumbled like empty sacks as they failed to outrun the bullets spitting from our angry AK47's, a third almost reached the wire when he suddenly was thrown forward and hung there, impaled by the shining steel coils, twitching, then falling silent. For a moment, there was silence, then two or three shots echoed from behind the building, and then there was silence again.

The flare sputtered, fell lower in the sky, then went out. A minute later, the floodlights were extinguished, leaving the scene in darkness. Crickets, noisy just minutes before, night birds, calling back and forth to one another earlier, had fallen silent, all manner of creatures wisely hiding from man's violence against fellow man, even now, afraid that it might begin again at any moment.

There was a scrambling outside the foxhole and a small figure climbed the sandbags and tumbled in, head over heels, an entry no better than mine earlier that evening. Even before he sat up and retrieved his rifle, Eddie was asking, "You OK, boss?" I was as relieved as he was to find that both of us were still in one piece.

He looked over the edge again and, like me, could see nothing. "The men in the next hole didn't know if anyone was out there either. They were talking about it like we were, so when I came over, they decided to shoot a flare and look what happened. Lucky they did it when they did."

I knew some of the attackers were down, I'd seen them fall. The riflemen next to us were uninjured, according to Eddie, and I wondered about the rest of our holding force, but the line seemed to have held and I hated to give up the shelter of the foxhole to check for casualties. So I stayed where I was. We'd wait a while longer, maybe for AcChan to return, before venturing too far afield.

"What about the night glasses?" I asked, thinking that they could help us view the effects of the gunfire, check for casualties, and to see what kind of danger might still be nearby.

"AcChan and Bip took them," he answered. "They were going to use them to get as close as possible to the airstrip."

And five minutes later, they may have been as close as they needed to get because suddenly, to the south, where the fires had been burning brightly earlier and had now been reduced to an occasional flicker, there was a sudden blast of gunfire, the rattle and clatter of many weapons all firing at once, and although it lasted no more than 30-60 seconds, I realized it had been one of the most intense firefights I had ever heard. Just when I thought it was over, two loud explosions ripped through the night, once again the sky flared brilliantly, and then it all ended and darkness enveloped us once again.

High overhead, I was aware of the faint sound of a jet engine and, looking up into a suddenly clear sky, I saw the lights of a commercial aircraft, some 31,000 feet above, floating smoothly through the night. Looking at my watch, I decided it was Lufthansa, right on time, a nightly flight from Tokyo to Bangkok, still an hour from making its descent into Don Muang International airport outside the Thai capital. How nice it would be, I thought, to be aboard, above all of this, making plans for the next day, finalizing the business strategy to be employed to close the big deal, make the sale or to just relax, knowing that someone else was making preparations for the trip to the nearest wat, the shopping center, or making reservations for dinner at the Normandie grill in the world renowned Oriental Hotel. Or even better, to be on the return flight, back to the United States to Kendra, bringing Ken Green and his lifesaving bone marrow. Or to just stay in Bangkok. Lean back, relax, breathe easily, and enjoy JoElle's company. Then reality intervened. I couldn't have it all. I had to pick and choose, but if I could choose, it would be to go elsewhere, away from the bleeding and dying that seemed to have overtaken this forlorn spot, this, what was it, Yellow Garden? To somewhere with music, soft lights, laughter, sparkling eyes, eyes like Abby's, one's that could light the darkness with happiness, kisses that could melt the frost of a January cold wave, memories to make one smile, and I felt the tears instead. For Abby was gone, gone long ago and far away. Struck down in the effervescence of youth by runaway cells callously attacking her vibrant body, stealing her vigor and energy, spreading by night and by day, and then, inexorably, killing. I knew their name, written it down, memorized it, and I'd been searching for the weapon to destroy them ever since, sending men and money out into the world looking for the elusive answer.

And as if to mock me, a new renegade had made its strike against Kendra. Leukemia. It couldn't be allowed to win, not like the cancer that had killed Abby. Not again.

I had to get Ken Green out of here.

# 17

AcChan returned shortly before dawn. I didn't hear him, nor did I see him, coming. One minute, I remembered scanning the darkened compound, still warily watching the faint shadows that moved as if alive, vanishing like wisps of fog blown away on a gentle morning breeze whenever I tried to focus on them. The shape of a crouching man, the hiding places of furtive men, bodies that I imagined lay all about, turned out to be bushes, shrubs, and flowers. Or our own sandbags, casting long tendrils of darkness across the mangled grass over which the attack had come. I didn't recall falling asleep, although I was aware that my eyelids had grown heavy and was conscious of the lack of sleep all of us had endured. My eyes burned, stung, and I closed them, just for a moment or was it for more than that? When I opened them again, to my embarrassment, AcChan was beside me in the foxhole. Three feet away, slumped against the bottom with water over his ankles, was Chun. Sound asleep. I quickly glanced at the second foxhole but saw no one moving in that direction either. If AcChan considered falling asleep a dereliction of duty, he never brought it up, asking instead, "What happened here when the shooting began? Anyone hit?"

I still had no idea because since the attack several hours earlier, I hadn't moved from my sheltering sandbags. But we did, at first light, cautiously moving out to see what damage we had inflicted the night before. It turned out to be considerable. Three of the attackers lay where they had fallen, one still claimed by the wire that had impaled him. It was obvious others had been hit and at least two had apparently been dragged back outside the wire, judging by the blood and scuff marks on the soft ground.

Surveying the scene, AcChan said, "I don't think they expected the foxholes. They saw us sandbagging the building all day and figured we would be holed up inside, so when they started the attack, they were surprised to be hit from here. If we'd of been inside behind the shutters, they would have been able to crawl much closer before they were exposed to our gunfire. With the foxholes this far outside away from the building, they ran into heavy gunfire where they didn't expect it. They broke and ran, as I suspected they would."

They had, I wanted to say, but not before they came much too close for comfort, close enough for me to smell the garlic of one man's evening meal, the sweat of his fear as he moved into the danger zone where we lay waiting for him. Was he one of the casualties? Maybe, it was impossible to know.

Amazingly, we hadn't suffered a single casualty. Not one. True, we had been dug in and were defending a position, always easier to do than attack, but we had not been overrun. It hadn't even been close. Naroogian said the probe from the rear had been a light one, a few shots, nothing to see, although the riflemen in the foxhole on the back side of the house said he saw numerous figures in the dark and had opened fire on them. Several shots had been returned but no one had any idea of what casualties had been suffered on either side, except for the known dead and wounded. Disbrow, Naroogian boasted, had fired his weapon a "few" times at the fleeing enemy, and he may have hit someone as there was blood on the grass not far in front of their position.

Inside, Lee Duc Than seemed stronger, opening his eyes when I entered the room and taking in my face as if straining to remember. At first, I thought he might attempt to speak, but didn't, then managed a weak smile, directed at Somchai, not me.

Once more, I tried to dredge up memories from the past, a record, a visual image of having seen him before, but nothing came through. Give it time, I told myself, after all, my last view of Lee Duc Than had been twenty years ago and sometimes, even now, I forgot my office phone number and, even worse, never did manage to memorize my DEA number needed for writing prescriptions. Why would I remember events that far back any better? I satisfied myself that the IV's were running properly, checked his temperature and pulse, pinched skin between my forefinger and thumb, concluded that skin turgor was better, and went looking for AcChan.

He was considering an evacuation. "We hurt them last night. No doubt about it, but they'll be back. They know how many men we have and they know it's not enough to defend a sizable perimeter. They know where we have our firepower, where the foxholes are, and they won't be taken by surprise this time. I expect they'll have more men by tonight and we should be gone by then."

He made it sound as if he hadn't cut the head off the snake. That the snake, even if wounded, would be back. "I'm afraid we missed him," he admitted. "It wasn't a total waste and if we'd had more mines, we probably could have blown the plane sky high as it landed, but we used what we had and what we had didn't entirely cover the length of the runway. When we exploded the mines, we damaged the plane, so badly that I doubt it ever flies again, but missed the head snake. We got the pilot, we could see him still trapped in the cockpit, and maybe the co-pilot, too. But I'm afraid Huy

Thacht and some other people got out safely. We got close enough to do some more damage when we opened fire out there during the night, but as far as the head snake goes, I'm afraid he's still slithering around in the jungle."

And madder than hell, I was willing to bet.

Bip interrupted to report on the condition of the prisoners who had spent the night locked in the cement block structure, securely bound. None of them had been injured in the furious firefight. It was a different matter for another man, a prisoner brought back from the raid on the air strip. "He was hit in the chest and although I didn't think he was bad last night, Bip says he isn't doing well. I would like to talk to him to see who came in on that plane and maybe if you took a look at him, you could help enough to make that possible." It sounded as if I had acquired another patient.

Eddie found my medical bag behind the overturned couch and we went to play doctor once again.

A single rifleman was on guard, the captives under his watchful eye in a room Ken had identified as the gem sorting room of the mining operation. The man with the broken leg was the closest to the door so I paused to see how he was doing. Earlier, optimistically, I had spread mucopiricin over the broken skin, hoping to prevent an infection, but now, inspecting the dressing, I saw that it had turned bright yellow-green and exuded the unmistakable odor of infection. Broken bone, infected skin, the threat of osteomyelitis, and I was working in a room contaminated by billions of bacteria, hordes of viruses, countless tropical parasites, and had nothing with me except what was in my precious medical bag. And that wasn't much. I reached for it, groping for scissors, fresh sterile dressings, and a vial of antibiotic, ready to give him an injection to slow down the purulent spread. I was aware of a commotion behind me and turned just in time to see a stocky, dark Lao, who had appeared to be securely tied to a massive wooden sorting table just moments before, rise to his feet holding a heavy wooden club over his head, and smashing it against the head of the guard, who, distracted by another Lao suddenly shouting from across the room, was looking away and never saw the blow that felled him. His rifle clattered to the floor and was immediately snatched up by a second captive, also unexpectedly free, who leveled it at Eddie, now holding the only other weapon in the building, a rifle, useless at his side.

Menacingly, the armed captive was waving the rifle recklessly and talking in a language neither Eddie nor I could understand. I didn't need to understand it to know that he was demanding that Eddie put his rifle on the floor. The guard was unconscious, not moving, and I was afraid that he might have been killed, even though the first prisoner was standing over him as if ready to use the club again.

The room suddenly became deadly quiet and, in the silence, I said, "Eddie, I think he wants you to lay down your rifle. I think he means to shoot you if you don't."

"I know that's what he means, boss," a surprisingly calm Chun replied. "But I'm not sure that's the best thing to do. I was thinking maybe I should try to shoot him first."

He didn't have a chance, but the armed captive was unsettled by our conversation. He had no idea what we were saying either and didn't like the situation any better than we did.

"Eddie, this is what I think you should do. Put the gun down slowly so he doesn't get nervous and do something stupid. Then I'll go ahead and fix this leg and we'll see what we can work out. After all, they have us, but in a way we have them, too. Maybe AcChan can work out some kind of a deal."

"OK, boss, if you say so. I just hope you have everything you need to fix that leg in your bag. I think I packed everything you need." I certainly hoped so.

As he slowly lowered the rifle to the floor and raised his hands, I pantomimed to the frenzied captive that I still wanted to fix the leg of his wounded comrade. "Is it OK?" I asked, pointing first to the leg, then to my chest and then to the bag. He got the idea, appeared surprised to have the offer, and nodded, grunting at the same time in what I took to be assent. He took his eye off me for a moment to mutter something to his companion, who laid down Eddie's rifle, and went to the next prisoner in line and began working to free him from his bonds.

Well, a break is a break, I always say, and I rummaged about in the bottom of my fake alligator skin satchel, finding the antibiotic just about where I thought it should be, felt the gauze at my fingertips, and a syringe just to the left. I moved past them and touched the cool steel of the Walther P38 that had been nestled there for so much of the journey. I didn't bother taking it out of the bag, just closing my fist around it, finding the trigger guard, snapping free the safety, and picking up the entire bag, peering deep inside for a missing ingredient, I pointed at the Lao and fired, right through the plastic bag.

I suppose that could have slowed the bullet or thrown off my aim, I wasn't an expert on ballistics so I didn't really know, but what I had in mind was causing damage, and that I did. I felt immense relief when I heard the muffled blast from inside the bag, felt it jerk free from my hand, and was even more relieved when I saw his knees buckle, the look of surprise on his face, and the slow descent as he stumbled backward to the wall, sliding lower until he was seated as if at rest, the rifle loose on his lap. Eddie bent down, picked up his rifle, and pointed it at the second captive who immediately ceased untying a third companion and stood there, astonished, and then raised his hands. The door flew open at the far end and AcChan was inside, positioned in a classic fighting crouch, his gun pointing right; Bip immediately behind him, his gun swinging left.

It took a while to get everything sorted out once more. Predictably, AcChan blamed himself for the episode, although I couldn't see why. We didn't have enough manpower to defend ourselves and adequately guard a dozen captives but I guess his reasoning was that he should have brought more men with him. I wondered if Bath would have been willing to pay for any more or was even now doubting the wisdom of paying for any at all.

At any rate, AcChan personally supervised the inspection of each prisoner's bonds, had more rope employed to tie them securely, and I went back to attending to the injured, including the one I had just added to the growing casualty list. He was in shock, a thin trickle of blood running from a wound in the right upper chest where the bullet had entered between the second and third ribs, and when I put a stethoscope on his chest, I heard noises that were far from normal. But it was what I didn't hear that concerned me most. There was absolutely no sound from an area directly under the wound for three to four inches in each direction, and when I percussed the same area, tapped on it with my fingers, there was dullness indicative of something solid underneath. He was either bleeding inside the lung or the lung tissue, the right upper lobe most likely, had collapsed. Neither was a good sign and he needed immediate trauma center care. What he had was me and it had been many years since I had cared for the victims of bullet wounds and knifings, commonplace events during my residency, but had disappeared from my practice long ago. But I could recognize shock and I still had intravenous fluids, so that was a place to start. I had drugs to raise the blood pressure, antibiotics to fight infection, and medication for pain. What I didn't have was oxygen and I had no idea where to find a surgeon. He needed that most of all.

Somchai started the IV, I injected the morphine, and then went to look at the shattered leg. The bullet had struck midway between the knee and ankle and the swelling and discoloration were appalling. Once again, I considered bringing the x-ray machine down and taking films but then caught myself. What good would it do? The leg was broken, I was dealing with a compound fracture, and my orthopedic techniques were rusty as well. So a picture would show where and how badly the bone was shattered; what good would that do the patient or me? None. I had nothing to set it with, no better off now than I had been with the broken arm back at the river. So I did what I could. I cleaned the leg thoroughly once again, collected three sturdy two foot long, inch thick slabs of teak, and splinted the extremity to reduce movement of the bone ends, raised the leg above his heart to reduce the swelling, and injected an antibiotic. He grimaced whenever we moved him or manipulated the leg, but otherwise remained silent.

I moved on to check on the condition of AcChan's little snake, the man wounded at the firefight by the airstrip during the night and brought back for the information he might be able to provide. I had just started to examine his upper arm when Bip called AcChan aside and spoke rapidly to him in Thai, then left again. "Dirkens is missing," AcChan said. "He left the back room during the night, while all the shooting was going on, and walked out the back door."

"Out the back door?" I questioned. "Magellan was at the back door. He couldn't have just walked outside past him."

"Magellan says he did. Just walked right by without saying a word and headed for the foxhole where Naroogian and Disbrow were supposed to be."

"Well, did they see him?"

"Not a trace. Never saw him at all. Neither did my men on the side of the building. Of course, everyone was pretty busy."

"So what does Naroogian think? Where did he go? Green had his rifle so Dirkens wasn't even armed unless he got a gun from somewhere else."

"Naroogian thought he probably went to the river and tried to find the boats. That he might have felt safer down there than where the shooting was."

I supposed it was possible, but when I had last seen Dirkens, he was huddled in a corner holding his abdomen, trying to control his cramping and diarrhea. He didn't look like the kind of man to suddenly take a walk in the dark looking for a boat. "Did he ever show up at the river?"

"Bip checked. They haven't seen him, but of course I told them to stay on the far side, in hiding, so I suppose he could be down by the dock unable to find them."

"Can you spare anyone to go take a look?" I didn't want to leave an unarmed man in the open all day, not in Dirkens' condition.

"Bip is taking care of it," he assured me.

The arm wound had bled heavily, so heavily that I suspected the bullet had struck an artery. Someone had wrapped it tightly with gauze and the pressure had succeeded in slowing, but not entirely stopping, the bleeding. So I added more dressings, applied more pressure, and was hopeful that he would stabilize. AcChan was questioning him as I departed.

Eddie had returned with more supplies he had found in the x-ray packing case. Blankets to cover and warm the men in shock, ampoules of norepinephrine to add to the normal saline IV to increase the blood pressure of the man with the chest wound, and surprisingly, a single tank of oxygen which I had forgotten was among our gear. I held off on starting that, the setting in a dusty warehouse didn't seem appropriate, and I asked one of the husky hill tribesman who had lugged the x-ray machine most of the way from the river if he would help carry the wounded man to the main house where Somchai could watch him and Lee Duc Than together. Our own little hospital. He did better than that. He knelt down, grunted once, and picked him up. With Somchai trailing along holding the IV aloft, he carried him to the house, deposited him in one corner of the back room, then went back for the man with the shattered leg, putting him in the other. The man with the arm wound walked up on his own power an hour later after AcChan had finished with him. We were running out of hospital space.

Dirkens hadn't gone to the river. He hadn't gone far at all. He was no more than a hundred yards from the rear door, his body lying just over a small knoll covered by tall grass, invisible unless you walked right up to it, which is what happened. He was face down, just off the river trail, the one he had followed to the house less than two days earlier. There was a bullet wound in the middle of his back and it was a fair assumption, I felt, to assume that this had been the cause of death.

"Sure, I saw him," Magellan was saying. "I heard him behind me, turned and saw who it was, and then there was some confusion outside and I looked to see what it was, and next thing I knew, he was gone. I thought I saw someone out by the foxhole, but I couldn't be sure. Then I saw something move over there," he said, pointing to the fence, which was west, "and next thing I knew, the lights came on and I was blinded and I couldn't see a thing. Had no idea if it had been Dirkens or if I had seen anything at all. Then there was some shooting and I forgot about him until later. This morning, really, was when I realized he wasn't in the back room and hadn't come back into the house."

"You forgot about one of your own men until this morning when the last you had seen of him, he was walking outside, unarmed, in a firefight?" I was incredulous.

"I don't know. I guess maybe I thought he was with Naroogian. It wasn't my fault he left or didn't have a gun." Always eager to be absolved of blame, Magellan was at it again.

"You saw him, maybe, headed that way?" I asked, pointing to the fence. West. The Explorer nodded, yes. "Then how do you explain that his body was found almost directly north of the house, just off the trail?"

He wrestled with that for a moment, concluding, "He changed directions?"

An amazing conclusion. "And Fred," I asked, "how come you were blinded by the lights when the lights were behind you and aimed directly at the area we found Dirkens body? He should have been clearly visible in the light; it was as bright as daylight out there."

Uneasily, he replied, "I don't know, Osten. I was blinded. That's all I can tell you." Well, he did have poor eyesight. We already knew that.

"Did you fire your gun last night?" AcChan asked him.

"No, I didn't really have a target. Never got a chance." I didn't doubt that that was the truth, at least the part about firing the gun.

Naroogian and Disbrow, according to their version of the night's events, never saw Dirkens at all. Never heard him, saw him or had any idea that he had left the safety of the house and was out roaming around. No, the lights hadn't blinded them, they both agreed. On the contrary, the lights made the back of the house as bright as Candlestick Park. Sure, they had some shooting, they'd seen some figures coming through the wire, and like they had told us earlier, Disbrow probably had hit one or two with a well placed burst from his AK47. Did we want to go over and look at the blood? Naroogian made it sound like they had been hunting deer in Minnesota. You know, I think I hit that one, partner. Want to go with me while we track it?

"You didn't see Dirkens at all, then?" I asked once again.

"Of course not," Naroogian emphasized, irritably now, tired of going over the same old ground, "If I'd of seen him, he would have been safely inside the foxhole with us. After all, he's one of my men." He emphasized the 'mine,' glaring at Magellan, who didn't seem inclined to argue. Maybe he didn't want to be responsible for funeral expenses.

"How do you explain his getting shot?" I asked.

"What do you mean, explain it? Hell, Osten, there was shooting going on here last night. A lot of it. You heard it; you were here. So one of the men coming across the wire got him. As simple as that."

"Maybe, Avram. That's a possible explanation. But the men coming through the wire would have been in front of him. Dirkens was shot in the back. The only people behind him, so far as I know, were his friends." Naroogian glared at me angrily and was about to reply when he did a sudden about face and stalked off.

AcChan and I looked along the fence for signs of blood from Disbrow's wounded buck. There weren't any. The fence was intact, the wire still glittering dangerously in the morning sunlight. AcChan's rifleman stationed in back had seen no one climbing the wire, no men in black pajamas roaming inside the defensive perimeter to his rear, although he admitted he could have missed something as he tried to help out with the attack from the front.

The back wound bothered me. Even in Laos, the deliberate shooting of one man by another would be called murder. Unless you were being threatened, I reminded myself, like I had been earlier in the warehouse. But who might have done the shooting? And why?

Those questions remained unanswered, for now, but I did hope to get answers to the next one. "What do we do with the body?" I asked Magellan. He looked at me in confusion, as if not having any idea what the problem was. "The body, Fred. Do we bring him home with us or bury him here?" I preferred taking the body back where an autopsy might shed light upon the manner of death and direction of the wound, but there were practical problems galore with that, as I well knew.

When Magellan finally recognized what I wanted to know, he never hesitated. "Bury him here. We can't even think about taking him home with us. Nobody can ever fault us for making a decision to bury him."

"Well, somebody might. For instance, does he have a family? Wife, kids, anything like that? What would they think about leaving him here?"

"I'll ask Naroogian. He'll know what to do. Like he said, it was his man. Not mine." He wasn't going to fight over funeral expenses, just like I thought.

And Naroogian did come back to consider the problem. "I don't know if he had a family. The records are all back in Washington in personnel. Canby might know but she's in Chiang Mai or Bangkok, maybe even back in the office by now, so we'll check with her later. So bury him here. What did you have in mind, Osten, a hero's funeral back in Arlington National Cemetery?"

No, I hadn't been thinking of that, but I had wondered if a little respect to a countryman would be too much to ask. Even if he hadn't been much help. But what difference did it make now? I shrugged and said, "It's your call, Avram. If you want to bury him here, just do it."

As I walked away, he reached out and grasped my arm. His face was flushed in anger and his voice cold, threatening, deliberately set several pitches lower than normal in an effort to terrorize, the whole act so transparent that I almost broke out in laughter. "I know about the secret transmitter that you had Fred build back in Chiang Rai. I know how you used it to call in the plane that hauled out your laboratory specimens, that's what you said they were anyway. I know about all of that, but don't plan on using that transmitter again. I found it and dismantled it. There is just the one transmitter left, the one that I control, the one that Bath gave us to use to signal Fantus. When we're ready to leave, I'll have Fred contact Alex and he'll come and get us. Got that? That's the way it is."

He was serious. So Fred had told him about the transmitter after all. Good. I had figured him to be predictable. I brushed the hand away and said, "I've got it. But what do we do if Fantus doesn't come? He has a history of not being the most reliable man in town, as you may have heard, so how do we know he'll show up on schedule or at all? And if he did come, how will he land without getting shot to pieces? I bet those men on the hill have already established a bonus fund for the lucky devil who knocks down the first plane or helicopter that comes in to help us. Give the man a cigar," I exclaimed, in a very poor imitation of a carnival barker.

Just calling attention to the possibility of snipers on the mountain was enough to cause him to look in that direction and move uneasily, placing more of the warehouse between him and any watching telescopic sight atop a rifle. While he was distracted, it seemed like a good time to ask, "By the way, how did you find out about Fred's second transmitter? I thought he did a good job of hiding it inside his original one? How did you find it?"

"Do you think I'm stupid? The minute that plane started circling the field, I knew something was wrong. No small plane just accidentally stumbles onto an isolated landing strip like this one without someone making contact with it and telling the pilot where to go. So I started wondering. About Fred. After all, he did have a transmitter, I knew that and he guarded it and carried it around like a baby, but I knew he couldn't be using that one."

"Why not?"

"I'll tell you why not. I didn't trust him. Bath didn't trust him. So we gave him bad batteries. He can't use it until I give him some good ones. Yet, after that plane swooped in and picked up whatever you had hanging on the washline, he seemed euphoric. Now that's not Fred. He and euphoria don't mix. So I smelled a rat and the rat was Magellan. All I had to do was ask him and he fell apart. Admitted everything, how you told him to build a second transmitter, AcChan supplied the parts, and then yesterday, how he went up on the knoll, back there where we found Dirkens, and turned it on. To tell you the truth, he didn't think it would work so he was amazed when it did. So was I. But it's gone now and the only transmitter he's got is the one I'm responsible for. I'll make the decision to send signals, when and to whom."

"It sounds as if none of you have much faith in Magellan. Why not? Isn't he the man responsible for us being here, haven't you entrusted him with communications responsibilities? Didn't he, for that matter, build a radio from scratch?"

"What a joke, Osten. Bath kept him around because he didn't know what to do with him. Still doesn't and finally just gave him the communications expert designation to justify keeping him on the payroll." It never seemed to occur to Naroogian to ask why Bath would want to keep Magellan on the payroll.

"Let me say it again, Avram. When Fred gets the word from you to send a message, who's to say the transmitter will work even if you give him the batteries? And even more important, what assurance do you have that anyone will respond? After all, does Bath really care about any of us getting back? Will Fantus appear? Or are we expendable, all of us?" I didn't think it would serve any useful purpose to tell him that Ken Green had seen Bath and Fantus at Yellow Garden, doing business. Of course, it was possible that he already knew.

He didn't reply to my mostly rhetorical questions and walked away where he joined Magellan who was walking between the house and the warehouse. Fred stopped and waited for him to come abreast. Sure enough, cradled in the ever present canvas sack was his transmitter, the legal one, a small antenna protruding from a partially opened zipper.

Later, AcChan listened as I explained what I wanted to do. He shifted his feet several times while I made my points, one by one, and then said, "Let me get this straight. You want to take Lee Duc Than back to Bangkok and put him into a hospital. You also want to take the man you shot back so that he can get decent medical attention. You feel that we should take the man with a shattered leg along because you're afraid he'll die of infection if we don't. Of course we have to take back my injured man because he has a concussion. You would like to take Dirkens body back because your army prefers to bring its casualties back home for burial. Anyone we've missed? How about the laborer who cut his foot with a shovel? He's limping badly. Or the pregnant woman, his wife, I guess. Have you seen how big her stomach is? She may have the baby at any time. Shouldn't we take her along, too?" In fact, I had seen the advanced pregnancy and was hoping that one of the other women would have been through the midwife routine by now. If not, Somchai was going to have to help.

Although he sounded exasperated, I knew AcChan had been giving the evacuation careful thought. Taking along the casualties was going to make it more difficult for all of us, but I couldn't leave them behind. The captive with the arm wound could be left behind; but the others, far worse off, had to taken out.

He was quiet for quite a while before saying, "It's a matter of how much room we have on the boats." Of course it was and I recognized that it would be a tight fit.

"We've got a long tailed boat. That's about it. The dugout canoe won't be much good but we can tow it with a rope. With all of the injured, we really need a hospital ship with a gunboat for escort. The other big problem with taking all of the injured and sick is how to get them to the river bank. We can't use the pickup truck or the BMW they had by the warehouse because the minute we move either vehicle, anyone watching from the hill knows we're up to something. So we have to carry everyone and we don't have that many men. Not enough to carry and protect our column."

"I understand that," I told him. "But if what Green says is true about the fate of the laborers, then we can't leave them here."

He looked at me in astonishment. "Hold it! We do not have room for another dozen men and women."

"I'm not suggesting we take them on the boats. What we should do is use them to carry our wounded to the boats and then see that they get across the river safely and have a chance to escape on the other side. That's a better deal for them than leaving them here to be shot."

AcChan was counting. So was I. "I figure we can take no more than eighteen people in the two boats. Twelve in the long tail, six in the dugout.

And that's pushing our luck. We'll be overloaded and any sudden maneuver, somebody getting excited or careless, we could find ourselves dumped into the river. And as near as I can count, you're asking us to take twenty-four people. Six too many. Plus the x-ray machine, which takes up the same amount of space as two people."

The problem of the x-ray machine was easily solved. "Leave it here. We'll even leave the extra film and instructions. Let this be my charitable contribution to the new Yellow Garden Community Hospital." I wondered if Bath or Burrows would find a way to take a charitable deduction from taxes for my good deed. It also reminded me that I still hadn't found time to carefully review the chest films we had taken on Lee Duc Than.

I counted up my evacuees and came up with twenty-two, not twenty-four. AcChan didn't seem surprised at the discrepancy. "Who do you have going along?" he inquired.

I listed them: five riflemen, the hill tribesman, Ha, the fisherman who was out on the river with the boat, Ha's prospective father-in-law, Magellan, Naroogian, Disbrow, Bip, Green, Lee Duc Than, Eddie, the leg wound, the chest wound, AcChan, and me. Somchai, of course, I didn't think we could leave her behind. And Dirken's body. Twenty-two.

AcChan had been counting as I ticked them off, using his fingers, went through them twice, and when I stopped, held up the first two on his right hand and said, "That's twenty-two."

"Exactly. Twenty-two."

"You forgot two others, so when you add them you get twenty-four, like I said," he corrected.

As far as I knew, I had forgotten no one and I told him so.

He disagreed and made his point. "Yes, you forgot two. One, the man you found sleeping with the woman in the downstairs bedroom. Simi Si's husband. He goes back with us. He has a lot to answer for. They say he was the man who recruited villagers to work here, kidnapped them might be a better word, and you know what Green says happened after that. Most of them were killed. So he goes back. The other one is the man with the arm wound. Can't leave him either. We didn't get Huy Thacht but we got one of his gunmen and he has too much information to be left behind. That makes twenty-four. Six too many." Information for whom?

I yielded on Dirkens. "We'll bury him here. Magellan and Naroogian don't seem to care and maybe they're right."

AcChan looked around in deep thought. "We can do that. Strangely enough, this is a beautiful place, not a bad place to be buried at all. Last night, when we went to the landing strip, we caught a brief glimpse of the waterfall in the moonlight. It was strikingly beautiful. A developer could probably turn this place into a world class resort; swimming in the river, golf out there where the poppies are growing and where Green was digging for gemstones, it already has an airstrip that could be enlarged, and if people get bored, they could always dig for rubies. Nice little souvenir to take home. Charge enough money and get a good advertising agency and you could probably fill several hotels with Japanese, Chinese, and American tourists. Plus Germans. They go anywhere. Especially if you throw in a little sex."

I wondered how serious he was, about a world class resort. Viewed in the sunlight, without anyone shooting at us, it did seem to have possibilities. Then I decided that the neighborhood would have to change, though, before anyone would invest the necessary capital. Well, maybe not the neighborhood as much as the neighbors.

"We could bury Dirkens over there by the tree near where he fell," he suggested. And it was a nice spot. Grassy, shaded almost all day long with a good view.

So we had the number down to twenty-three.

It didn't take long for the number to shrink once again.

At midmorning, Naroogian appeared with Magellan in tow and interrupted AcChan in the middle of a conversation with Bip as both stood watching two laborers digging Dirkens' grave. Neither American seemed interested in the burial. Naroogian didn't bother to wait for an opportunity or invitation to speak; he simply said, "We've wasted enough time around here already. It's time to call in our helicopter and leave. I'm having Fred activate the transmitter and send the pickup signal. I want to be in the air by noon and to do that, we must have everyone packed and ready to board in less than two hours."

AcChan stared at him, motioned to me to come closer from where I had been watching the grave diggers, and said, "We're burying an American, your man, over by the tree. Would you like to say something over the grave before we close it?"

"We don't have time for ceremonies," was the answer. "Just get ready to move out. Fantus will land inside the compound so he won't be exposed to the gunfire from the mountain. I'll display a landing panel for him and he knows what to look for. By the way," he said, as he started to move off, Magellan almost bumping into him as he trailed closely behind, "Disbrow and I will be watching Lee Duc Than and Green closely to make sure they don't try to make a break for it." Naroogian, I concluded, was from another planet. Lee Duc Than was barely alive; Ken Green was desperately hoping to go home, to see his farther and sister, and neither was in any condition to make a break for it, as Naroogian seemed to think they had in mind.

Neither AcChan nor I made any comment and finally, Naroogian handed Magellan two small objects, ordering, "Here, put these in your damned gadget and call for the helicopter."

Sheepishly, Fred did as he was told, managed to pop both power sources into a front slot. I could see his mind churning frantically, wondering, will this work, did I damage it when I installed and then uninstalled the other transmitter or was this a dud even before that? He started to extend the telescoping antenna, pulling it to a maximum of four feet, and then fumbled for the ON switch, stopping in confusion when AcChan said, "Hold it. Not here. Not now."

An angry Naroogian sputtered, "Why not? Why not now? He's my man and I've told him what to do, so why can't he turn it on?"

"Don't get excited," AcChan said, soothingly. "He can turn it on but he should do it over there, on the rise from where he sent the successful signal yesterday. The ground is higher and there are fewer obstructions to worry about. The signal will be stronger and stronger is better."

Mollified, Naroogian turned on Magellan and said, "Go over there and turn it on like the man said. Why'd he have to tell you twice how to do it? Once yesterday and again today? Can't you remember anything? I thought you were the expert. Act like one!"

Chastened, Magellan hurried off to take up his new position. As far as I could see, it didn't seem to matter where he stood to send a signal or whether he sent a signal at all. If Fantus had been flying in and out of here for some time, as he had according to Ken Green, he knew exactly where to find us, didn't he?

AcChan raised the issue, obliquely, by saying, "Do you really think it matters if he sends the signal or how strong the signal is?"

"Of course it matters. Why wouldn't it matter?" Perhaps Naroogian wasn't in on the secret. Or perhaps Naroogian didn't think we were.

AcChan made it as clear as he could, saying, "Because Fantus isn't coming, not now, not ever. You're wasting your time."

Naroogian didn't respond, merely hefting his rifle and striding through the tall grass to where Magellan was standing, his transmitter held shoulder high as if an extra twenty-four inches would throw the signal further into the atmosphere. He was holding the receiver as close to his ear as he could get it, waiting for the return signal that AcChan had correctly predicted would never come. Neither of them noticed that the red lights on the dial weren't displayed. Either the batteries were in backwards, not working or the equipment was a total waste.

We buried Dirkens and I said a prayer over his grave. Eddie and Disbrow joined me in the briefest and simplest burial service I could ever recall having attended.

I next saw Naroogian in the main house where he had been attempting to interrogate Green with little success. First of all, Ken was on the couch, covered by a blanket and shaking violently, suffering from a malarial chill. I'd been wondering why he looked pale, seemed weak, and without energy for much of the day. Now I knew. His illness, and the obvious symptom of it, seemed to have completely escaped Naroogian. Green was looking out into space, his teeth chattering, his limbs shaking uncontrollably, and I knew that we had another medical problem on our hands, one that could wait, would have to wait, until we got back to the United States to treat adequately.

Exasperated at his lack of progress, Naroogian walked away, saying to me, "He won't talk. I'm not surprised. He has plenty to hide. His story about being held here as a prisoner won't wash. We already know that he was in Chiang Mai several times, maybe Bangkok once. And we know that he was down at the river store beating up the old man in the other room. We know that and knowing that, I can tell you that I don't believe he's a prisoner. I believe that he's a part of this operation and this operation is drugs. So I'm not surprised he won't talk." How did he know Ken Green had been in Chiang Mai? Or Bangkok?

Before he left, he warned Green, coming back to a familiar theme, "If you don't talk to me now, you'll talk when you get back to the States. You're still on the Army's rolls so they can hold you as a deserter. They can lock you up for years."

"You sure of that, Avram?" I asked. "It was my understanding that the army lists him as dead. They officially notified his father of that two or three years ago."

He may not have been listening. "Notified him of what?"

"Death. Specifically, the death of his son, Kenneth Green, who, the papers say, died in the service of his country. That means that if he is dead and the army considered him to be dead, then how can he be on the active duty rolls as a deserter?"

He thought about it for a moment, shrugged, and said, "Hell, I don't know. It's all too complicated for me. You know and I know he isn't dead. He's sitting right there." For the first time, he also seemed to notice that Ken was shaking, hesitated as he took that fact in, and pressed on. "He isn't a prisoner of these people because now we've got him and we're going to keep him. I guess my job is to take him back to Washington and let someone else sort it out. Now, if you'll excuse me, I'm going to go and get a haircut."

For a moment I thought I had misunderstood. "Haircut? Did you say haircut?"

"Yes, a haircut. Frankly, looking at you and Green, I must say the two of you should consider it as well. And Chun. Have you looked at him? For God's sake, his hair is hanging down in his eyes. We should all have gotten haircuts in Bangkok before leaving on this crazy trip. Did you see the prices there? Only half of what they charge in Washington!"

Evidently, I hadn't misunderstood, but where and why he was getting the haircut was a mystery. I hadn't seen a red and white striped pole anywhere in the neighborhood, nor was there evidence of a hair stylist's salon. Not even a regular plain old barber shop.

"Disbrow," he explained. "His father and grandfather were barbers back in Poughkeepsie and it was only natural the kid learned the trade. Back home, he moonlights on weekends and picks up a few bucks. He even set things up back at the office so he can cut hair when he has nothing else to do." His job must have been important.

That took care of the where. The why was easier. "Bath likes his people to be neat and trim, just like him. I don't want my hair looking like it does now when we get back to Bangkok."

The fact that Naroogian's hair was just above brush cut status didn't seem to have registered.

Behind us, where the blanket-wrapped Ken Green was still shaking uncontrollably on the couch, he said, "What day is this?"

I had been worried that Green was disoriented and now I was afraid my suspicion was about to be confirmed. "Wednesday," I told him and waited to see why it mattered.

For the first time, he looked directly at Naroogian and said, "Don't do it."

Avram stopped half way out of the door and turned back, surprised. "Don't do what?"

"The haircut. Don't get a haircut."

"What do you mean, don't get a haircut? Why not?"

Green made a conscious effort to control the shaking which was making his voice sound like a radio with static and said, "Superstition. There is an old Thai saying that he who has his hair cut on Wednesday is sure to meet disaster before the day is out. So don't do it."

Naroogian looked from Green to me and shook his head slowly. "I thought I'd heard everything, but apparently not quite. You ever heard that, Osten?"

"Never had but I'm not an expert on old Thai customs or sayings. I can tell you though that Thai barbers always take Wednesday off."

Naroogian was suddenly in better humor. "Of course they take Wednesday off. They've gone to all the trouble of spreading rumors like that so who would be crazy enough to get a haircut on Wednesday?" He was still laughing as he went outside.

For a moment, I thought Green might shout another warning to him but instead, he suddenly took an interest in the length of my hair, seemed to stare at the back where it was curling just above the collar. "Don't worry," I reassured him. "I'll wait until I get back to Bangkok before I get it cut." Why not? I saw no need to impress Bath.

In the back room, Somchai was keeping a watchful eye on our patients. Lee Duc Than was sleeping, probably the best thing I could hope for under the circumstances. I'd looked at my copies of his x-rays and knew that I needed help in evaluating them, but wouldn't get that until we opened a phone line, either here or from Chiang Mai. By now, I was certain the blood canisters and the pack of films were in the hands of my experts and help should be waiting once we got out of Yellow Garden. At the site around the small injection I'd made the previous day, there was the start of a tissue reaction. I was pleased, made a note and sketch of the size of the erythema and induration, and spent the next thirty minutes checking on the wounded.

Meanwhile, outdoors, AcChan was putting the final touches on the afternoon's performance for our presumed audience. "They're watching every move we make from up there on the mountainside. We hit them hard last night, harder than they expected, and they're not sure how many men we've got. They were given a bloody nose when they attacked the main house and then later, we surprised them at the landing strip, so by now, they're confused. I'm sure they think we have more men than we do. And I'd like to keep them thinking that way until after dark. So I'm going to use an old trick, one used by a General of yours in the American Civil War. What I'm going to do is send out small patrols, one after another, in different directions. Then, after they go a short distance, they'll turn around and sneak back, change clothes and go out again in another direction. As many times as possible. I want to make a dozen men look like fifty."

"Can you pull something like that off, without them catching on?" I was skeptical and it was taking a risk because while these patrols were out circling aimlessly, our defenses would be seriously depleted and an attack launched right then could imperil the perimeter.

"I think it'll work, unless they've sent a patrol of their own down close to the wire where they can ambush us. That could be costly, but it's a risk I think we should take," he explained. He was the military commander of the operation, so despite misgivings, I gave my approval.

"You picked this up from our Civil War? I didn't know you were a student of American History," I said.

"I'm not. But I have studied tactics and that one has stuck with me through the years. Always wanted to try it. This seems like a good time. Actually, I suspect tactics are a lot like medicine. You can learn from just about anyone if you're willing to select the good stuff and forget the bad. For instance, how many American generals study the campaigns of Taksin, one of Thailand's genuine war heroes? He took back the old capital of Ayuthaya after the Burmese had occupied it in 1767. The Burmese were a hated enemy and it wasn't bad enough to lose Ayuthaya to them, but they then took the opportunity to loot the temples and palaces, and not content with that, they burned the place down. As you know, the old capital was quickly reclaimed by the jungle and it still hasn't been fully restored. At that point in the struggle, Taksin took command of the Thai forces and in a series of brilliant campaigns, he outmaneuvered the more numerous Burmese, drove them out of the country, and avenged our earlier defeats. He won it by outflanking and outthinking the enemy and when it was over, Taksin set himself up as the king down in Thonburi, a city across the river from the village that grew and later became what we now call Bangkok. I just hope that I do better than Taksin in the next few hours."

I was puzzled. "What do you mean do better than Taksin? It sounds like he did all right."

"Not really. Sure, he became king and everything and that was good. But then they said he went crazy and the people got rid of him."

"What do you mean got rid of him? How do you get rid of a king?"

He shrugged. "Got rid of him, just like I said. Tied him in a velvet sack and beat him to death with sandalwood clubs. That's how they got rid of Thai kings in those days. Crazy, isn't it?" It made me wonder who would want to be king of Siam or had things changed?

He caught sight of Naroogian, seated in the open on an ammunition box with Disbrow busily snipping at his hair. "Speaking of crazy, what the hell are they doing?"

"Naroogian wanted a haircut and Disbrow is his barber."

AcChan looked at me in disbelief. "Isn't this Wednesday? Don't they know you never get a haircut on Wednesday? It's bad luck!"

"Green told Naroogian not to do it."

"Well, what did he say to that?"

"Not much. Mostly he just laughed."

"He's a fool. I hope he realizes what a chance he's taking just for a haircut. Especially since prices are so cheap in Bangkok and Chiang Mai. He should have waited. And frankly, don't you think he should be worrying about Fantus? Magellan is still standing up on the knoll like a telephone pole, waiting. By now, if his batteries were working and if the transmitter was really a transmitter instead of a stage prop, don't you think he should have heard something?"

Of course he should have heard something. I felt it was time to correct AcChan about Magellan and a telephone pole. "He's more like a Christmas tree without lights," I proposed.

"What do you mean?" AcChan challenged.

"When he turned on the switches, none of his control panel lights were illuminated. I don't know if the batteries are dead or if he, in fact, had a stage prop, but whatever it once was, it isn't working now."

AcChan thought about it for a moment and then said, "Well, I don't suppose that bothers you too much, does it?"

"Not at all. I don't see that it makes any difference in what we have to do."

Minutes later, I watched the first of our two and three man patrols form up and set forth in the clear view of anyone interested in watching from outside the perimeter wire. Each of the groups was soon lost in the thick underbrush as some headed for the mountainside, others went west towards the waterfall, more to the east, and another group followed a drainage ditch straight to the landing strip. Each patrol went just so far, then under cover reversed itself, came back by another route to reemerge by the warehouse and form up to repeat the process, this time leaving in another direction. Over and over again, our dozen men, the riflemen, Bip, AcChan, Eddie, a hill tribesman, even Ha and several laborers who had agreed to participate in the charade, began to look more and more like a full strength military platoon, a force much stronger than it really was, and I was hoping we would be able to mislead Huy Thact and his hired guns.

I went back to my foxhole of the night before; Somchai was armed and inside the house with Green who had a rifle, but I had no way of knowing whether he would use it. One rifleman was guarding the prisoners and Magellan was standing almost motionless on the hill behind the house. Aside from Disbrow and Naroogian, we were the defense garrison. And they were busy, at the moment Disbrow, almost done, was brushing the hair off Naroogian's collar. The three shots that rang out interrupted the pastoral scene, two bullets kicking up dirt right at Naroogian's feet and a third striking the wooden box he had just vacated. He stumbled, fell to the ground as Disbrow, despite the bad ankle, dashed for cover to the nearest foxhole, thirty yards away. He left his rifle behind.

I was certain the shots had come from the mountain, could see no evidence of the precise location and, with no target to select, held my fire. Back by the ammunition crate, I could see Avram lying flat on the ground and knew that he must have been hit, badly. Moments later, I was astonished to see him leap to his feet and make record breaking time as he threw himself into the foxhole alongside Disbrow. I saw a second rifle lying uselessly amongst the barber's tools and realized that neither the barber nor his customer would be of any help if we were under attack.

But there was no attack. Not then. There was more shooting as our patrols moved about, especially when any approached the landing strip which Huy Thacht's people seemed determined to make clear belonged to them. During one lull in the afternoon's activity, Disbrow furtively crawled from the foxhole, retrieved both rifles, and crept back to where Naroogian waited. During another, Green came outside, carrying his AK47, and joined me. Magellan had taken a seat on the ground, trying to keep a tree between him and the mountainside. At least, from where he was, he could see the rear of the house and I hoped he had enough sense to let us know if anyone approached from that side.

When AcChan returned, he was elated. "I think we have them confused. I'm sure they have no idea how many men we have down here and some of the credit for that has to go to Naroogian and Disbrow."

I couldn't see how they had earned even the slightest measure of praise and I told AcChan so. He came back with the rejoinder, "Osten, they're worth their weight in gold. Make that rubies," he said in recognition of where we were.

"They're lucky they're not dead. Didn't you hear the shooting? They were almost hit."

"That's just the point, don't you see?" I didn't. "Here we are, small groups of men coming and going, trying to fool them into thinking we have more manpower than we really do. Will they buy it? Maybe. Maybe not. Until they look down from the mountain and see, well, what do they see?"

When he paused for a breath of air, I continued for him, "They see two nuts, one of them cutting the hair of the other one, that's what they see."

"Wrong, Osten. Wrong. They see a garrison so secure that they have men to spare, men who can sit in the open and improve their appearance. It was obvious, if you were looking at it from their point of view, that we have so many men, not all of them have to be on guard duty or patrol at any one time. Even Magellan helped. From a distance, he looked as if he was trying to soak up sunshine and develop a suntan."

I hated to spoil AcChan's enthusiasm and I didn't, although I tried. "Maybe you see them as heroes, but the disaster you predicted almost occurred. Naroogian nearly got shot."

"Osten, that was no disaster. That was a near miss. If there's going to be a disaster, it won't be anything they walk away from. They simply don't understand how dangerous it is to tempt fate. The spirits don't like it."

Later, after our last patrol had returned and everyone had taken up defensive positions once again, AcChan suggested that every second man try to sleep for an hour or more, the alternates remaining alert and then trading off. All of us were operating on too little sleep and it was an excellent idea. "They won't attack during the day," he said confidently. "It'll be after midnight again and this time they'll have more men and come from several directions. I'm sure they want to get Lee Duc Than out of here safely so they won't use rockets or mortars on the buildings, but they may use them to blast the perimeter or take out the foxholes. They'll make a hell of a racket when they come, you can bet on it."

"But we'll be gone when they get here, won't we?" I said.

He nodded. "I hope so. I'm certainly counting on it. But a lot of that depends on you. Can you move your casualties, especially Lee Duc Than?"

"He's as good as he's going to get for now. He needs a hospital. That and a lot more, but we'll move him. Same for all the rest. We'll move them all."

Seeing Magellan still crouched behind a tree, AcChan said, "What do you think? Should we call him in? Nothing is going to happen. He's never going to make contact with Fantus."

"Sure," I agreed. "Let's at least allow him the luxury of a foxhole. He can pretend to be sending messages from there as well as from where he is."

Bip drew the assignment. He walked nonchalantly from the main building to the tree behind which Magellan had found shelter. Sort of found shelter might be a better description as it was a small tree and part of Fred protruded from one side and more of him was uncovered on the other side, but shelter is a relative thing. With his back pushed firmly against the trunk, he *thought* he was out of sight and that was more important than whether he actually was. Bip paused at the base of the tree, spoke calmly to Magellan, who had no way of understanding Thai, but seemed to understand he was being invited to join the rest of his group. He hastily crawled from the tree toward the nearest foxhole while Bip gathered up the forgotten transmitter, rifle, and assorted canvas bundles that Fred had left behind.

I marveled at Bip's coolness when he knew that he was in the sights of more than one marksmen well within rifle range. "He was taking a chance," I said to AcChan.

He shook his head in disagreement. "Not really. Remember, they had their best man shoot at Naroogian a little while ago and he missed two sitting targets. Just now, Bip and Magellan, they were moving, slowly, to be sure, but moving. Being a sniper is an ego thing. With lots of people watching, you don't want to make a fool of yourself. So, having missed once, and probably chewed out by Huy Thacht for failing to connect on an easy target, the shooter probably rationalized it by saying let them go. We'll go down there tonight and get them all."

And in order to avoid that fate, I started to make the preparations for a medical evacuation. The first thing we needed were litters, three men requiring them; Lee Duc Than, the man with the shattered leg, and the one I had shot in the chest. AcChan's rifleman was making rapid progress in recovering from his concussion and the wounded Lao could walk, his shoulder no longer bleeding. We needed people to carry the litters and AcChan easily recruited the laborers, a promise of freedom the only reward any of them needed. I briefed Somchai on what we needed to watch for on the trek to the river and once on the boat, making her aware of the importance of carefully recording the vital signs of each patient and alerting me to any changes that seemed abnormal. This was something she had learned back in Chiang Mai so I was repeating familiar ground, but she nodded eagerly, looking forward to seeing the last of this grim outpost.

During a lull in the late afternoon, and after musing over past and present events, I said to AcChan, "You know, I'm sorry to be leaving so soon."

"What?" he asked, in what I believe to be genuine surprise.

"I mean, I'm sorry to be leaving without ever having seen the water-fall. Yellow Garden. And I didn't get to see Green's mining operation. Didn't even see the vast fields of poppies out there to the west."

"See what I told you?" he said. "I can see this place becoming a tourist mecca. Tours of the mines, poppy fields, all the rest. I'll book you on one of my first trips. Might be in ten years, but I'll see that you have a seat on the plane and a suite in the resort. Just a modest down payment will hold the reservation." He sounded serious and then proved it by describing the mining operations he had seen up close.

"I don't know if Green was responsible for this project or not, but who-ever was did a good job. They managed to haul five or six bulldozers in here and they dug into the mountain and exposed a rocky projection that follows the base of the hills, from near the waterfall, all the way to the eastern edge of the landing strip. Probably three or four miles. A major piece of excava-tion. They've peeled off the overlying topsoil and then used explosives to loosen tons of rock. The gems are everywhere, small ones, large ones, mainly rubies and emeralds but I saw sapphires, opal, tourmaline, peridot, and oth-ers as well. They had, you might say, a gold mine here without any gold. But they weren't content with all that booty. In addition, they raised poppies and produced raw opium, so, not satisfied with one business, a legal one, they turned to a second, an illegal one. If they owned the land, and they might not, they were fools to dirty their hands. If they don't own the land, then having dirty hands isn't a problem to them. I guess they figure money is money. It doesn't matter where it comes from, just how much of it they can collect for themselves."

"You almost sound like you approve."

AcChan hastened to assure me, "I don't disapprove of making money. Neither do you or you wouldn't be in business. What I don't like and can never accept is the dirty money, the money that comes from corruption, the rot that destroys lives and is approved by the wink and nod of politicians who share in the loot. Gems are fine, even if many of them are smuggled from one place to another. I can even accept the corruption that accompanies that. It's the drugs I want to stop. The people that deal in the drugs, like Huy Thacht, have to be stopped."

We were interrupted by Naroogian who had finally decided it was safe enough to venture forth from his foxhole. His hair neatly trimmed, recovered from the near miss of a sniper's bullet, he came out to ask, "I don't see any preparation being made to leave. Fantus should be here at any moment and none of you have made any effort to get ready for a liftoff."

Arrogance or stupidity? I couldn't decide which. He seemed rational but just to be sure, I asked, "What time was Fantus supposed to arrive?"

"He said two o'clock," he answered, annoyed. "Maybe a little later. Two-thirty."

I checked my watch. "It's five to four. The helicopter is a little late."

Surprised, apparently having lost track of time because of the afternoon's excitement, he was looking at his watch when AcChan said, "Osten, he doesn't understand. There is no helicopter. There will be no Fantus. Bath never intended to take us out of here. That's why we have to take care of ourselves."

This was heresy to Naroogian and he spun away and went in search of Magellan, who was still huddled safely in a foxhole. There was a brief conversation, complete with waving arms and a shouted order, after which Fred picked up his discarded transmitter and slowly made his way back to the knoll, in a crouch all the way. Once again, he tried to shelter his two hundred pounds behind a tree built to protect no more than half that. He flipped switches, held the transmitter at shoulder height, and resumed his hopeless search for an answering electronic response.

An hour later, as the last rays of sunlight slanted across the ridges and jungle to our west, turning the high clouds that had formed during the late afternoon into a dazzling display of pinks, purples, oranges, and reds, we made our preparations for a trek to the river. Our movements were covered by the sudden darkness that enshrouded the valley as Lee Duc Than and the two wounded men were strapped onto litters, ready for the trip. The man with the chest wound was pale and gasping for air and I was afraid that continued internal bleeding had compromised his breathing beyond repair, but his only hope was surgery and we had to get him back to a hospital for that to occur. The shattered leg was no worse, his temperature was holding at just over 100 degrees, and there didn't seem to be as much of the purulent drainage I had seen earlier. Despite his age, Lee Duc Than was doing better than the other two. His eyes were open and for a moment, I imagined that he recognized me. In which event, he was way ahead of me. I still couldn't remember seeing him, although I kept imagining him sitting with me, with Jordan Green together at a seminar, long ago. A student, OK, I could accept it. A patient? No recollection and no record. That was the problem.

He coughed, sagged back against the litter still lying on the ground, perspiration evident on his forehead, and he was warm to the touch. The back of my hand against his skin seemed to rouse him and he looked at me and said, weakly but in surprisingly clear English, "The cough. It's worse."

I hadn't expected him to speak at all and it was a moment before I responded. With a platitude, I'm afraid. "I know," I said, "but once we get out of here, we'll see what we can do about it."

He looked at me, earnestly trying to establish contact although his eyes seemed to have difficulty in focusing, but finally he replied, "My" – pause, not enough breath to continue, "loving son" – longer pause, trying to refill bronchi depleted of oxygen, "may not want" – even longer pause, wheezing distinctly heard as the bronchi collapsed upon themselves, "you to succeed." He shuddered and gasped, drawing in air as if through a constricted garden hose, sounded even worse when he exhaled.

As if drawn to his side when they saw the effort he was making, Green and Somchai were now standing over the litter, deep concern evident in their expressions. "So Huy Thacht is your son, as Green says?" I asked.

Lee Duc Than simply nodded, too exhausted to speak. He raised a thin bony finger and pointed to Somchai, a question in his eyes. "Yes," I told him, "she is going to leave with us. Ken also." He seemed satisfied then and his eyes closed. The rattling and wheezing continued. He coughed once more and a fleck of blood appeared at the corner of his mouth. Somchai promptly leaned over and wiped it away with a soft cloth she was carrying.

His hand reached out and grasped her wrist. Making a concerted effort, he managed one deep breath and said, clearly, "Trap. Three miles." That was to be it for a while. He seemed to have lapsed into unconsciousness.

I looked at Green who had been listening and watching. "What trap, Ken? What three miles?"

"I don't know for sure, but once when we went to Chiang Mai, we went by boat. Somewhere downriver, maybe fifteen or twenty minutes after we shoved off from the dock below the falls, we saw several men on shore. They waved, our boatmen waved back, and it's where the river narrows so perhaps they guard the river approach at that spot. It makes sense. Maybe

Lee Duc Than is trying to warn us of that. A trap."

I hurried to brief AcChan and he agreed that a trap was not only possible, but likely. "Sure, they'll guard the river and the best spot is where it
narrows. That could be a problem. Think about it, Osten. See what you can
come up with while I finish my work here." I wasn't sure what work he had
in mind but I did start thinking about the problem of ambush. After all, it
confirmed what LoDan had told us much earlier. If you go too far up the
river, he had reported, men shoot at you. Logically, that also applied when
you went back down.

Green was some help. Not much, because despite being in charge of
mining operations, he apparently hadn't been allowed to roam about
unescorted. "No, I haven't had many opportunities to go to Yellow Garden
and actually see the falls up close," he told me. "I wish I had because from
this side of the river and up on the mountainside, it's a beautiful sight. "No,"
he decided after a moment's reflection, "I've never seen sentries up at the
falls. I don't see why they would put any there. The danger is from people
coming upstream from the store, not downstream over the cliffs and through
the jungle. There are no roads or trails back there and I've never heard of
anyone coming from that direction. So I don't think they guard the falls."

I asked more questions and to his credit, he answered them straightfor-
wardly, actually seeming to know far more than he thought he did. I hoped
that he was accurate and, just as important, telling the truth. The latter, in
fact, seemed to be the lesser of the two problems as he would be in the boat
with us. If we ran into a trap in the darkness, a bullet could find him just as
easily as anyone else.

"What do the falls actually look like?" he mused in response to another
question. "Well, it's about ninety, maybe a hundred feet high, a double falls,
really, with the south flow of water half the size of the north, spray towering
almost to the top of the falls itself, and the roar makes conversation almost
impossible. Some say, several say, that there is a cave underneath the north
flow extending back an unknown distance. Most of the Thais and Lao don't
want to tempt fate and explore because they fear spirits and, even more,
they are terrified of crocodiles. The river is full of them downstream and
they think the big ones have all moved up to live in the caves. Maybe they
have. I don't really know."

I had an idea, roughly formed, and decided to discuss it with AcChan
before revealing it to anyone else. As I moved away from the litter, Lee Duc
Than's hand came up in a gesture that stopped me. He had been close enough

to hear Green's description of the falls and I wondered if he was about to add something to the discussion. He whispered something, I didn't catch it, and leaned closer. This time he said it again and I wasn't sure whether he was speaking in English, Thai or Vietnamese. What had he said? It sounded like, what? Then I straightened up and frowned. It sounded like emerald. A stone, a green one, yes. But also the name of a restaurant, a coffee shop frequented by students at the University. Me, too, I'd gone there, I'd had coffee with my students there, many times after an early morning lecture. Was he asking me of that? Was this a sign of recognition?

I touched him and watched as his eyes opened again and locked on mine. "Coffee, at the Emerald?" I said. Then I remembered. He always drank tea. He was the man with the tea, always sat to the left of one of the Vietnamese women in the class. I suspected then that they were spending more than a few daytime hours together. "Tea," I made the correction, "at the Emerald. You remember?"

He nodded and closed his eyes. It was difficult to tell because of the darkness, but I thought I saw a small smile on his lips. The smile revealed a single gold tooth.

The Emerald was still there. It had become a dump, dirty, rundown, hardly able to pass the cursory inspection of bored sanitary inspectors from the Health Department. They allowed it to remain open, apparently operating on the principal that if you're dumb enough to eat there, you deserve anything you get. Like nausea, cramps, diarrhea or worse.

I wasn't sure that Lee Duc Than would want to go back once he saw the seedy neighborhood that now surrounded his diner. Then I looked around Yellow Garden and decided, why not? The Emerald may have become seedy but this place was downright tacky. And who was to say that one was more dangerous than the other?

But we could forget the Emerald. If I ever was able to return Lee Duc Than to town, I could take him to the Iroquois. It was still the same kind of place it had been when Abby and I had entrusted the care and feeding of our house guests to Andy Whitaker many years before. Good steaks, cold beer, crisp green salads with grilled salmon and mahi mahi on the menu for the diet conscious, placed there by Andy's son who managed the place now that Andy had retired to Palm Beach County, Florida. Retired? I hadn't realized Andy, someone I had always considered a contemporary of mine, was that old.

I found Naroogian and AcChan in a face to face confrontation back inside the main house. Naroogian was red faced and angry. "We're not leaving," he rasped. "The helicopter didn't come, I agree, but that doesn't mean it isn't coming. If it didn't come today, it will come in the morning. So we wait."

"You must be out of your mind," AcChan told him flatly. "There will be no helicopter. How many times do we have to tell you that? There is no helicopter. There was never going to be a helicopter. You're a fool to think that there was. The transmitter Magellan has been carrying around like a security blanket has never worked and was never intended to work. It was a fake, put together by someone who was laughing at you, at all of us, when he did it. Wondering, I'm sure, how anyone could be so dumb as to think something like that was going to work. When they gave it to you, saw Magellan take it into protective custody, they must have laughed even harder. And when they told you to sit tight until a helicopter came to pick us up, and you said 'sure,' they must have become hysterical. They're back in Chiang Mai still laughing. Most likely having a drink."

I thought AcChan had summed up the problem neatly, touching all of the salient points. Naroogian didn't buy any of it. "We wait until morning," he countered. "I don't care what you say."

"If we stay here tonight, there will be no morning for any of us," AcChan warned. "They'll overrun us as easily as the tide washes away a child's sand castle on the beach at Hua Hin. Gone without a trace."

Unwilling to yield, Naroogian said, "They tried that last night and we beat them off. We'll do it again."

AcChan shook his head. "No, we won't. Not tonight. Last night was then. This is now. Tonight they'll come with more men and more firepower and they'll sweep over us, just like I said. I know how it goes. I've been in positions like this before and we won't win. So we leave now."

Yes, and once before he had been waiting for Fantus to pull him out, just like now. Only Fantus didn't come. Just like now.

"I can't keep you here if you're afraid," Naroogian continued recklessly, "but Magellan, Disbrow, Osten, and Chun stay with me. Green and Lee Duc Than, too. They're ours. They go out with us in the helicopter."

AcChan walked over to the window and peered outside from behind the blinds. I could make out the figures of Bip and a rifleman in the nearest foxhole, the wire still visible in the background as if one of the gate lights had been left on although everything else was dark, the floodlights turned off for now. Softly to me, he said, "Tell him, Osten. Tell him what you think of his plan."

Loudly enough for Naroogian to hear, looking directly at him so there could be no misunderstanding, I said, "He has no plan. Instead, he has a death wish. We're leaving with you. Chun, me, Green, and Lee Duc Than, the four of us. I can't speak for Magellan and Disbrow. They'll have to decide for themselves. But it's time for the rest of us to leave, so let's get the hell out of here."

Naroogian exploded. "This is an outrage and you can't get away with it, Osten. I won't let you. If I have to use force, I'll use force to keep Green and Lee Duc Than. Those are my orders and I expect you and the others to back me up." He fumbled for his holstered sidearm as if to actually draw it but stopped and stood absolutely still as AcChan motioned to Bip who had suddenly appeared in the doorway behind us with his rifle leveled at Pan Union's security chief. Had AcChan summoned him while looking out the window? Two riflemen moved into the room from the rear door and everyone stood waiting for instructions.

"Anyone who wishes to stay, can stay," AcChan said simply. Eddie had also joined the crowd in the living room and when AcChan spotted him, he said, "Chun, find Disbrow and Magellan and get them in here. We need a decision from them. What about you, by the way? Know what this is all about?"

"I'm not deaf. I been listening. My decision is simple. The boats, I go with the boats. I'm not waiting for any helicopter." He disappeared, looking for the remainder of Pan Union's depleted force.

Magellan gave the same answer. The boats. Now. Not later, if ever, by air. Trembling with suppressed anger but conscious of the threat of Bip's rifle, Naroogian was dismayed. "What do you mean, you want to leave with the rest of them? You've been sending a signal all afternoon calling for a liftoff and now you tell me you want to leave, before our own people get here to pull us out?"

Magellan shifted uneasily and looked in my direction. "Tell him why you want to leave Fred. He doesn't seem to understand what's going on."

Still not certain of where the real power lay, but suspecting that for the moment, it was where the rifles were, Magellan was surprisingly frank. "I'm not sure this thing is working," indicating the transmitter, still loosely held under his left arm, the antenna momentarily pointed directly at the floor. "As a matter of fact, I'm wondering if it ever did work. I've been inspecting it and there seem to be missing parts. Worse, some of the wires aren't connected to anything. It may have been defective when they gave it to me."

"What are you talking about?" demanded Naroogian. "No one would give you a defective piece of equipment. That's absurd!"

"No, it's not," Magellan insisted. "I should have checked it when I got it, but I assumed it would be working, so I didn't."

Still skeptical, frowning, Naroogian moved threateningly close to Magellan and said, "What about that other transmitter you built back in Chiang Rai and hid inside the official one? The one you used to call in the airplane to pick up the laboratory specimens that the good doctor here tells us were so important?" He threw a venomous look in my direction while waiting for Magellan's reply.

Magellan, belatedly showing comprehension if not a lot of technological prowess, admitted, "I don't think it worked either. Maybe I didn't have the skills to make it, or possibly the parts were fakes, or defective, but, although I hate to say it, it probably didn't work at all." He was risking the wrath of his coworker, but had gotten it right.

Naroogian was a hard sell. "What are you talking about, Fred? It had to work. The plane came in and made the pickup. Have you forgotten already? How could it have found us if it didn't locate your signal? It came in right after you turned on the transmitter."

Magellan was doing better. He came up with an answer, not one that Naroogian wanted to hear, but the right one. "I think there's another radio," he explained. "Someone has another radio and they sent the signal."

"There was another radio, the one we blew up down at the landing strip, but we didn't use it. . ." he left the sentence dangling as he faced AcChan, suspicion on his face, and finished, "so you have another radio."

"Not one, but two," AcChan confirmed. "We've had them all the while. And ours work."

Obviously shaken by the information, Naroogian was momentarily silent, but recovered quickly and made an effort to seize the initiative once again. "So you've made me look like a fool, relying upon Fred's useless apparatus when you knew that it wouldn't work and were able to bypass it even if it did. OK, so I am a fool, but why can't we use your radio to call in our helicopter and get us out of here? If yours works, prove it. Call for help."

AcChan shook his head. "No. That's suicide. No helicopter or plane could come in here without being shot down. The captives tell us they have heat seeking missiles, they know how to use them, and they can hit anything trying to land here. In fact, they're close enough to the runway that small arms fire would likely shoot down anything trying to land. We won't be going out by air. We're going by boat and we're going now."

"Not me, I'm not leaving," Naroogian insisted, stubbornly.

"You're staying here alone?" asked AcChan.

"Not alone. Disbrow is staying and we'll be picked up just after dawn, regardless of radio messages."

He seemed confident of that and I decided to find out why. He answered, "How do I know the helicopter will come then? Simple. Before we left, I made arrangements with Bath that if he hadn't heard from us by now, he would send help at first light Thursday morning. That's tomorrow. All we have to do is make it through the night."

Disbrow had been listening to this without reacting. His face was expressionless. "What about it, Disbrow?" I asked. "The river with us or the possibility of a flight in the morning?"

He hesitated, mulling over his options, and then surprised me. "I'll stay with Naroogian. My ankle hurts too much to walk." I hardly needed to point out that one doesn't walk in a boat, only the less than half mile to the dock, and personally considered it a lame excuse, but if that was his decision, he would have to live, or die, with it.

With that settled and a rifleman assigned to keep an eye on the disgruntled Naroogian, who was still seething over what he obviously regarded as treachery from fellow Americans. Particularly Magellan. That was something they would have to work out upon their return to the relative civilization of bureaucratic Washington, assuming of course, they both made it back. Meanwhile, the rest of us could continue our preparations for departure.

I took the opportunity to outline my ideas about avoiding the possible ambush to AcChan. "About two miles, maybe a little more downstream, the river narrows. Green says they usually have guards there so we have to assume they do now. We have to eliminate them and the best way to do it is from shore. But once we leave the compound here, we all have to leave at once and some of us can't huddle down on the dock while others go overland to find and take out the guards. It's too dangerous. We'd all be sitting ducks if they decided to come into the compound, found it empty except for Naroogian and Disbrow, and then hurried on to the river where they could find us all in one bunch."

"You have a plan or is this just for my information?" asked AcChan.

Maybe he was getting edgy. Not enough sleep. "I have a plan," I told him. "This is it. Everyone but three or four of us board the boats. Those men go downriver, find the guards, and eliminate them. They will be able to surprise them, I hope, by coming up from behind while the sentries are looking out towards the water. That's where they expect trouble. Meanwhile, the boats go upstream towards the falls, using the motor on the long-tailed boat, actually going under the falls itself where Green says there is a cave. Should be able to hide there unseen for an hour or two, and then come back downstream following the far shore and creep past the dock in the dark so even if Huy Thacht has sent men to the dock, by then we might slip by, come to the narrows, wait for a signal light, and come ashore to pick up the raiding party. Going downstream after we leave the cave, we won't need the motor because we can drift on the current. If anyone has occupied the dock, and if they see us, we'll turn on the motor and go as fast as we can and hope for the best. And of course, if they start shooting, we can always shoot back. We should be all right if they don't have a boat they can use to chase us."

"They do," AcChan said and I wondered if my plan was about to fall apart. "But they can't. Can't chase us. Lo Dan spent his time waiting for us by knocking holes in three of their boats he found. He doesn't think there are any others."

Did that mean he thought the plan might succeed? "You're going to need the motor when you leave the dock and start upstream towards the falls," he pointed out, "because you'll be towing the dugout and the current is too fast for anyone to pole effectively against it. That will make enough noise to be heard. They could cut you off at the falls."

He was right. The motor could give it away.

"But I don't think they'll hear the motor above what I have planned, so it might work." I didn't know what he had planned, but whatever it was, it sounded promising. "Besides, remember, our boats got by in the rain and darkness on the way upstream a couple of days ago. Maybe we could slip by once again, but I think you're right. We should try to take their position out to reduce the risk. Bip and I, we'll take the guards. Maybe one other man. The rest go on the boats."

I was disappointed. It was my plan and in it, as it developed in my mind, I saw myself to be one of the men destined for the foot work, walking to the narrows, stalking the guards, and hadn't thought much beyond what happened once we found them. AcChan instinctively knew that was only part of the problem. Once they were located, they had to be removed. Subtly, not directly bringing it up, he used age as the reason for the change. "It's your plan and you have experience in handling things like this, leading groups of men," he reasoned, making it sound reasoned, at any rate. "You're not as familiar with the jungle and the wet ground along the river as we are. It will be a hard hike. Let Bip and me do it." I knew what he meant. They would take the risk because there was likely to be killing. He tapped several of the laborers who had assembled alongside the column and indicated they were to follow him back towards the main building. He motioned to Bip and two riflemen and all three quietly slipped away into the darkness, headed towards the dock. "Your plan is very good," he said. "It should work. Wait another ten minutes and then start for the river. Bip is going ahead and I'll be bringing up the rear." I was going to reply, to say something like be careful or good luck, but never got the chance. He was there and then he was gone, and we started the ten minute wait, the longest ten minutes I ever remembered.

We moved along the river trail, single file, a rifleman in front, me directly behind, a rifleman to the rear, the litters and their bearers, with Eddie, Magellan, Somchai, Green, and the walking wounded between. Aside from the shuffling of feet in wet grass, the occasional muffled squeaking of canvas against litter frames, and the unexpectedly loud rasping breath from both Lee Duc Than and the man with the chest wound, there was total silence in the night around us. Minutes later, I heard wheezing behind me and wasn't surprised when Magellan said, "Could we slow down a little? I'm having trouble keeping up." Fred often wheezed under stress, probably wasn't in the best of shape, which would make him wheeze even worse, but this wasn't the time nor place to slow down. Besides, with litters and walking wounded, we weren't moving all that fast to start with. I started to worry that it wouldn't be the sound of the motor that betrayed us; it might be heavy breathing.

Brusquely, I told him, "Use your inhaler and keep quiet." A moment later, I heard the hiss of a medical canister and in less than a minute, the wheezing had ceased.

I had other things to worry about as well. Would Lo Dan and the boats be there or would he have decided the risks were too great and simply gone home? Maybe, I concluded, he would think it an even greater risk to have AcChan track him down in the village should the boats not be there. And the money. He had been promised what was a sizable sum of money to be there. He'd be there, I decided, and went on to the next problem. Bip, where had he gone? And AcChan, what was he doing? And the noise of the motor?

How could we cover it? And Kendra. How was she doing? And then we were at the landing where Lo Dan was waiting, the long tailed boat bobbing gently on the swells of an otherwise quiet river, the dugout docilely tied to its stern.

I explained the plan to Lo Dan, told him of my concern about the sound of the motor, and waited while he watched as we loaded the boats, carefully packing litters and prisoners first, making sure everything was secure, the prisoners tied, the injured and sick made as comfortable as possible despite the cramped confines of two small boats. Ha translated for me, had passed on my message, now asked me, as Lo Dan finally spoke, "How far to the falls?"

"Maybe a kilometer, a little more. When we reach the first falls, on the far side of the river, there is a cave directly under the water, and we have to go into it."

"How long can he use the motor?" Ha asked.

"Maybe three or four minutes, maybe longer if AcChan can make enough noise to cover the sound." I was guessing that he had something like that in mind. "At the start, to pull away from the dock, can we pole the boat?"

Lo Dan looked at me as if I was crazy, having already counted and noting twenty-one bodies about to fill his two crafts, but then had an idea of his own. "Give him some help and he might be able to get away from the dock without the motor."

"What kind of help?" I wondered.

"Cut some poles, about twelve feet long, eight of them. Everyone who can grabs a pole and helps to move the boat. He says if we get away from the dock, get it moving, then he can use the motor for four or five minutes, turn it off, and we can pole the rest of the way to the falls. He thinks." Nobody was sure of anything anymore. They always left an out. Like Magellan.

We cut poles, Lo Dan found eight that were acceptable, and every one of them looked like Eddie could have used it for another vault. Three riflemen, Prathorn, Ha, the boatman captured when we seized the long-tailed boat who had quietly sat by all this time until the anchor had been removed from his ankle, and the other hill tribesman were assigned their stations, four on one side and three on the other of the slender craft. LoDan himself took the eighth pole and gave the others a crash course in boat poling. From the stern, he would both pole and steer and he declared us ready for departure.

As suddenly as he had disappeared forty-five minutes earlier, AcChan was back. Nodding to Lo Dan, he asked me, "He know what to do?"

Without thinking, I answered, "I think so." It was catching.

"We'll be leaving now to go down the river bank. I've talked to Noi about where the guards are likely to be and we'll try to surprise them. Take this radio with you and when we've cleared the shore, I'll call. Head back downstream, floating on the current, until you get past the dock again, and then start the motor and pick us up. I'll signal you with my light when I hear you coming. Got it?" I was tired. Lack of sleep. He was fatigued. No sleep. I could see the weariness in his eyes.

I was still puzzled by one thing. "How come Huy Thacht didn't have anyone down here on the landing? It doesn't make sense. How come no sentries?"

"There were some," he said, too casually. "Three. That's why Bip and his men came down ahead of you. Then signaled the boats to come in." He pointed to the water. Where the sentries had disappeared.

The laborers had finished their work and were leaving, taking a trail along the bank, headed west, where, according to a cautiously cooperative Noi, they would find a ford half way to the falls, enabling them to cross to the safety of the other side. They refused the offer of paper money, afraid, rightfully so, that possession of currency would mark them as men and women who had been in contact with undesirables, like us. They accepted our thanks and set off. Money, the eldest of the group told us, meant little. "Where can we spend it? We trade, fish, hunt, and just try to stay alive. We have no need for your money."

AcChan looked at his watch. "Wait five more minutes and then have everyone with a pole start using it. Get away from the dock, get it moving, and when you hear the noise, start the motor and go as fast as you can."

Before I could ask him what noise, I heard a commotion along the trail from the compound, a sudden harsh cry and flailing of arms and legs, and it was obvious that more than one person was involved. AcChan dashed away to the scene of the struggle, Bip immediately behind, with me a distant third. A rifleman was raising his arm to strike home with a wicked knife when his wrist was seized by AcChan and pinned in midair. Underneath, a Thai astride him, his face mud smeared and contorted in fear, was Disbrow. Lame foot and all, he had apparently decided to join us.

Seeing me, he managed to gasp, "Jesus, Osten, don't let him kill me."

AcChan defused the situation, speaking in Thai, releasing the rifleman's arm, and allowing Disbrow to regain his feet. He looked about miserably, sore ankle apparently forgotten.

"What are you doing here?" I asked, although it was clear he had decided to join us. For the record, I said, "I thought you were staying with Naroogian."

"I was. That was my original idea, but I thought, after the rest of you left, maybe we would go out and hide in the jungle or something and wait for help. But not that crazy bastard. He decided to crawl into a foxhole and said we'd shoot it out. He didn't even want to share a foxhole with me. Told me to get my own. So I crawled in and started thinking that it was stupid! Two of us against how many? Once I realized that, I decided to take off and join up with you. I was afraid that Naroogian might shoot me in the back when I left, but he didn't, and then when I got here, one of your men tried to stick a knife in me. This hasn't been my day."

The words 'afraid he might shoot me in the back' haunted me. Had Disbrow seen Naroogian shoot someone in the back? Or did he suspect that Naroogian might have done that?

Questions for later. For now, "Get aboard the second boat. It's crowded, but there's room."

He hurried in that direction only to halt when Eddie hissed at him, "Pick up your damned rifle. Nobody gets a free ride."

"Get going," AcChan said. "We're running late. I hope Naroogian didn't mess things up."

I know Thais aren't big on shaking hands, but I reached out and took his just the same. "I'll see you down below the narrows in a couple of hours," I said, exuding confidence that I didn't altogether feel.

He brightened, the fatigue forgotten for a moment, and laughed reassuringly. "Of course. A couple of hours. And don't worry. Take it from me. Bip told me this morning that nothing is going to go wrong today, especially for you and him."

Mystified, I asked, "What are you talking about? How can he say that?"

"He had a dream last night. You and he were hunting crocodiles in the jungle and you both fell into the water and were eaten. By a large crocodile."

I didn't know how that might feel to Bip, but being eaten by any size crocodile was hardly comforting to me. The fact that the river and, according to Green, the cave under the falls, were filled with crocodiles was enough to give me the chills about someone else's dream. Apparently AcChan recognized the look on my face so he hastened to explain. "You don't understand. That's good news. When a Thai dreams of dying, that means he's going to have seven consecutive years of good fortune and anyone with him when he dies shares in the blessings. And before seven years is up, if you're lucky, you'll dream of dying again and have seven more good years. So nothing bad is going to happen to you today or for seven more years. Count on it."

Well, that was better, but I was still a mite nervous about crocodiles in the river. Had anyone told them about the seven good years ahead?

Just then, the first explosion rocked the night behind us and a huge fireball soared into the sky. With all that noise, there was no need to worry about the motor and Lo Dan kicked it over and I jumped aboard as the long-tailed boat surged forward, tugging its load. By the time I was able to glance shoreward again, AcChan, Bip, and their companion had vanished.

# 18

We were able to keep the motor running for close to fifteen minutes, so loud and continuous was the noise that AcChan had thoughtfully provided for us. Over the continuing din of explosions, we could hardly hear the motor ourselves so I instructed Lo Dan to use it as long as we dared and only when the fireworks began to die down did he kill it and everyone took up their poles and went to work. Because of the unexpected surge of power, we had gathered more than enough momentum to reach the base of the north falls and glide under the covering veil of mist. From ninety feet above, water roared down, thoroughly dousing us as we passed underneath and then, once inside a spacious cave, became nothing more than a dull rumble, as if from a far-off passing train. Or, as Eddie said later, "like fifty open shower heads in the YMCA locker room." Once or twice above the background noise, I imagined, or was it real, the sound of small arms fire. Naroogian?

Across form me in the boat, Magellan was still holding his useless transmitter. "Throw it overboard, Fred. It's useless extra weight."

He was hesitant. "I should keep it. For evidence."

Evidence? Interesting. "Evidence against whom? You talk as if you expect there to be a trial."

Barely able to hear him about the roar of water, I think he said, "A trial. Yeah, mine," but suddenly, without another word, he held out both arms and dropped the transmitter soundlessly into the water where it immediately sank without a trace.

Eddie leaned close enough so I could hear him and shouted, "AcChan must have used the land mines to blow the place sky high. And the rockets. Wired everything together and set it off." After a pause, he asked, "What do you suppose happened to Naroogian?"

It was a question I had been asking myself. Actually, Disbrow's idea of hiding in the brush hadn't been a bad one. Huy Thacht may have assumed that we all had left by way of the boats and the two of them might have been able to get back safely, with a lot of luck, and if Disbrow's allegedly gimpy ankle hadn't given out. But now, what about Naroogian? I didn't know. I wondered if the small arms fire had been his swan song or a prelude to something else.

It was almost time to start our trip downriver. We would have to come out from under the waterfall to pick up any signal from AcChan, or so I suspected, although I wasn't sure. I thought of asking Magellan if we could pick up a radio signal from behind a waterfall, but I was almost certain his answer would be the same as mine. Not sure. Just as I prepared to tap Lo Dan on the shoulder and send him on his way, Eddie leaned close once more and said, "You want me to put these in your medical bag or in the canvas bag Magellan gave me?" Illuminated by my torch, I saw he was holding a dozen or more small plastic bags.

"What are they?"

"Samples of trees, leaves, dirt, flowers, stuff like you and Howsam bring back all the time. I've been picking things up along the way, especially inside the fence the last two days. Like this dirt I got from the bull-dozed area around the mine." He showed me a small bag bulging with what looked like soil, but it was hard to make out anymore than that. It was embarrassing. Eddie had been collecting scientific specimens while I had been forgetting to do the same, although I felt better when I remembered the specimens I had earlier tucked away in one of many jacket pockets. It was possible the trip wouldn't be a total scientific washout, thanks largely to his efforts, not mine.

He was showing me two more plastic bags, both of them larger than the others, and asked, "What do you call these things?"

When had he collected the dozen poppy capsules that were stuffed into these bags?

I couldn't ask then, it was too noisy and impossible to conduct a decent conversation, but later, he told me, "when Bip and I were out in a ditch that ran along the landing strip. There was a huge field of these things, most with yellow flowers, some with white, a few red. Flowers were falling off and the petals were laying all over the ground. These things looked interesting so I grabbed some. But I didn't know what the right stuff was. Was it the flowers, the seeds, these little black ones or was it this big bulb? So I just took some of everything. Notice how these little black seeds are pouring out of the top here, like they're in a salt shaker? Maybe more like a pepper shaker, really, because they're black," and if you shake the poppy, you'll see small black seeds coming out of the capsule head, just like he described it. Not pepper, and certainly not salt. Poppy seeds. You use them on your breakfast Danish.

Later I was able to tell him, when we were off the river and on our way back, "You may not know it Eddie, but this one plant is a treasure house of medicine. Unfortunately, it's mostly been discovered. Long ago. Morphine, codeine, heroin, raw opium, even more, all comes from this one plant. See this capsule, about two inches thick and almost that long, flattened on top and bottom, boasting a very smooth hard surface and these small holes you see on top? About the size of a small potato. The seeds, they're safe. Used in cooking. The juice, though, from the capsule, that's the stuff everyone wants. Workers, like the laborers we released, use very sharp knives to make small circular incisions in the capsule and the thick juice oozes out, dries in the air and is scraped free with a blunt knife in a day or two. That's the raw material, the stuff we saw pressed into flat plate like chunks, passed from processor to processor and in time, winds up as a prime source of the huge sums of money that fuel the crime business. It starts out as an innocent looking capsule growing with beautiful flowers in fields all over Asia, Southeast Asia, Africa, and the Middle East. It ends by leaving cities in America and Europe, all over the world, covered with blood stains, littered with the bodies of the dead and dying, with thousands of lives, millions of minds, wasted."

By the time I was done, Eddie was ready to throw them away. "Hang on to them," I suggested. "There's nothing wrong with collecting souvenirs. Not everything has to be converted to cash."

We came out from under the falls to find a glow still lighting the sky over the compound. Poling silently, our muscular seven forced a way through the swirling pond spreading out from the base of the falls and soon found ourselves picked up by current. The radio beeped once, twice, so softly that I almost missed it, but I knew AcChan was telling us to come through. Lo Dan took us as close to the north shore as he dared, staying just far enough out into the stream so as to avoid the monstrous trees that had fallen, prey to old age and high winds, with limbs and trunk extending twenty, thirty, sometimes fifty feet out into the water, a disaster waiting to happen if the boat strayed too close to a partially submerged snag. We were intent on watching the glow in the sky, listening to the occasional popping of a new explosion, perhaps grenades, ammunition, fuel oil, nothing heavy now. And then suddenly, rushing up out of the darkness, there was a break in the dark wall of jungle, an opening on the south shore, the dock from which we had departed almost two hours earlier. Clearly outlined against the glowing skyline were three or four men, men who had followed the trail from the compound to the river. Looking for us. They were no more than a hundred feet away!

Without a word being spoken, every man and the one woman aboard our two boats held their breath, crouched lower, the polers held their poles clear of the water, and even the man with the chest wound had fallen silent. Magellan wasn't wheezing and we drifted slowly toward the point of maximum danger. How ironic it would be for AcChan to have successfully cleared the supposed ambush site downriver only to have us run afoul of this one. And then one of the men threw away a cigarette, threw it away from us rather than in our direction and I realized they had their backs to us. They were looking back in the direction of the compound, at the fire! We were almost past, almost clear, almost free, another two hundred feet, then one hundred, drifting silently in the direction of safety, and then a shout, another, followed by a shot. Then another. Followed by a burst of rapid fire and I shouted to Lo Dan, "Start the motor." He didn't understand English. He didn't need to. He was already reacting, had leaned down and pulled once, twice, and the motor roared into life, the boat lunged forward, trying to escape. I was afraid that we might have thrown someone overboard, water was splashing ahead of us and alongside, and I was aware that automatic rifle fire was now a two way street. Several of ours were now sending a torrent of fire ashore, Lo Dan swung left and then right to make it harder for anyone to target our course, and a minute or two later, a wake rippling out behind us, we slipped around a bend in the river and were out of danger. At least for the moment.

I worried about the patients, worried about myself as I felt my heart beating rapidly and forcefully inside my chest. No pain, but it would be a bad time to suffer a heart attack. Predictably, I heard Magellan's wheeze start, and knew that the worst had to be over. He got worse under stress, yes, but always improved when terrified. The adrenalin rush was a tonic to his constricted airway; and now, no longer terrified, he was starting to gasp for air once more.

Miraculously, with all the firing in our direction, no one had been hit. The dugout had been struck and was leaking slowly as the wake from the lead boat washed up against the bullet hole in the prow. Disbrow was bailing and if it got any worse, we would have to slow down but for the moment, everything seemed to be under control. Fifteen minutes later, I spotted the quick flash of red off our right side, blinking once, twice, three times, the agreed upon signal and I responded, waited briefly for the acknowledgment and directed Lo Dan to head for shore. As we neared the bank, two figures stepped from the inky blackness, one of them catching the rope thrown by the tribesman, pulling it in, and bringing us to a halt. AcChan and a rifleman climbed aboard, causing some shuffling of the already crowded passengers to make additional space for them, and he ordered, "Cast off." The rope had been brought aboard so we started to drift into the current almost at once and Lo Dan started the motor, running it briefly before shutting it down once more when we reached midstream.

"Where's Bip?" I asked, hoping to hear that he would be joining us further downstream, but expecting something more sinister than that.

Wearily, leaning back against the side of the boat, AcChan replied in a voice that I didn't recognize as his. "He's not coming." No explanation. He was just not coming. Maybe not coming to avoid further crowding on the already overloaded boats. No. Maybe because he had something more to do on shore. No. Just not coming. AcChan's voice was near breaking when, thirty minutes later, he softly said, "I got careless." I didn't think he would continue but he did, collecting himself once more and adding, "We found the place and came up from behind three men. They never heard us and we took them out without a sound. I sent Bip to the river bank to signal you when you came into view, but I failed to check the area like I should have. There was a fourth one in the bushes, tending to a call of nature, wiping his, what do you call it, kon or ta-phok?"

Green, behind me, had been listening. "Butt, wiping his butt," he said.

AcChan seemed to have hardly heard, although he continued, picking up the story where he had left off, "When he finished and started back, he saw Bip and I guess Bip thought it was me and said something. I heard his voice, not thirty or forty feet away, realized that something had gone wrong, but before I could warn him, the fourth man reacted faster than I did and he shot Bip. I fired back and hit him but out of the corner of one eye, I saw Bip stumble backward and fall into the river. I ran down there and tried to reach him but couldn't. The last I saw was his body floating on the current and then he sank." He didn't say it, but he made it sound as though a crocodile had been in the vicinity.

Involuntarily, and I wished I could have choked on the words before they came out, I said, "So the dream was wrong. There was no seven years of good luck."

He looked up in shock. "That was a superstition, Osten. Bip believed in superstitions and that made it easier for him to do what he had to do tonight. And a lot of other nights. But you're partly right. Only partly. He had the dream but it wasn't wrong. It was how we interpreted the dream that was wrong. And I made it wrong, because I was careless. I won't be careless again." He fell silent, and was looking straight ahead at the river. Five minutes later, he was asleep. Exhausted.

I might have fallen asleep as well. I'm not certain because later, I recalled a voice saying, "There's another old Thai proverb. You escape from the tiger only to fall to the crocodile, it goes." And later, perhaps I dreamed this, I thought he said, "That part of the dream about you, Osten, that seven good years. It's intact. Don't worry about it. Not all superstitions come true, but most do. You're all right."

Then I definitely fell asleep because next, I was having dinner with Kendra in a small Italian restaurant just off Piccadilly Circus, enjoying a fine bottle of Soave and spicy pasta, the music soft and low and just sentimental enough to bring tears to your eyes, especially when you're with the woman you love, knowing that life like this was to go on for seven happy years, and I woke in terror, a beating in my ears, fearing that it would all end. Over, too soon.

The beating continued, it grew louder, and it was real. The helicopters roared low over our boat, pulled up sharply above the tree line around the next bend, the backwash lashing the river surface and rocking the boats. Was I the only one awake, I wondered as I reached for my Galil, snapped in a fresh clip and loosened my holster strap. In my mind's eye, I could see men pouring from the three helicopters and they would be waiting for us around the bend. It was to be a brief seven years but if this is where it ended, then it was time to go down with a fight. If Huy Thacht could assemble this force on short notice, we had run out of time. Our best chance at coming out alive was to head for shore, fight them in the jungle where better cover might offer us some hope. I looked back to AcChan to suggest we put in at once, not waiting until we rounded the bend ahead, and he said, "Put the rifle away, Osten. You won't be needing it."

I was surprised that he hadn't seen the danger. "They're waiting around the next curve."

"I hope so," he answered. "They're ours. Right on time. Landing by the store, or what's left of it. We're almost back to where we started this trip."

They were waiting, a dozen or more men, wearing dark camouflage identical to ours, although much cleaner. All three of the big birds were down, rotors still revolving slowly overhead. Two had landed to the side of the burned out shell of the store, a third between the dock and storefront. Lo Dan smoothly cleared the one channel and steered us to the dock in the new one, the long-tailed boat bumping once or twice, and a half dozen men leaped to secure it with ropes fore and aft.

The first face I saw was that of Wanchai, grinning at us from the dock.

When last seen, he had been headed downstream with a string of captives destined for "someone who would take them" as AcChan put it. Evidently someone had and he was back, in uniform, riding in style, with friends.

The helicopters were American made, olive drab in color, the only markings on them were three foot high bright blue stars on each side of the nose. No numbers, no names, no other insignia of any kind. I had never seen anything like them before.

It was daylight now, a gloomy overcast day with a threat of rain, but the helicopters had lured every villager from their home to the landing. Ha's girlfriend was one of the first to arrive, and she watched in awe as the burly Prathorn and the slim Ha stepped from the boat together, actually smiling at one another. Her face was a study in contrasts as first she was happy, then she was sad, first she smiled and then she cried, but finally, running to her father, she bowed slightly before him, an obedient young maiden, and then turned to embrace the embarrassed, but delighted, Ha. She had made her point. Just in time, too, from all appearances. She was at least six or seven months pregnant.

I thanked all of our volunteers, and Ha, especially, was beaming as he led his bride-to-be back along the path to the village. The last I saw of him was as he walked arm in arm with Lia, Eddie said that was the girl's name, and then both were embraced by an enormously muscled arm. Dad.

Not everyone returned to the village to a friendly greeting. When two armed men led Noi across the open area to a helicopter, he was greeted with angry shouts. One woman picked up a rock from the riverbank and launched it at the chastened prisoner, as head down, he was boosted aboard a plane and hidden from view. AcChan, hurrying from one helicopter to another to supervise the loading of his men and our wounded, paused to remark, "We're doing him a favor by taking him back with us. Simi Si's husband doesn't seem to be too popular in his own village."

"The price of fame," I murmured without enthusiasm. If wife beating brought fame and opium brought fortune, it would be easy to make a convincing case for anonymity and poverty.

In a matter of minutes, the helicopters were loaded, equipment secured, the pickets waved in from the defensive perimeter they had automatically established around the landing site, and the engines started. As we lifted off, nose down for a moment as with all helicopter takeoffs, the engine increased its power and we rose suddenly, swept low over the river, banked to the right, and started a rapid climb above the trees. The villagers below watched, the show over, a few waving, and then they began to drift back to their homes. I had observed that not a single item of value remained in the ruins of the store. They had picked it clean. Even the pile of empty beer bottles had disappeared. My guess was that Goong was sitting on a small fortune hidden back in the jungle.

"Will they be all right?" I asked AcChan, who was seated next to me.

Wearily, even despite the hour or so of sleep he might have been able to catch on the way back down the river, his face a mask of fatigue and personal anguish over the loss of Bip, he sighed, "I don't know. We use people, you know. Pay them a little money, offer them an opportunity to strike back against people like Huy Thact or Noi, to strike against evil, and then we fly away like this. They have to stay, so if evil decides to return, evil like a Huy Thacht, then yes, they can be hurt. Like the laborers. Green says many are shot. I suspect that they are. These people below? Will Huy Thact exact revenge? I don't know. I don't even know what will happen to Naroogian."

That surprised me. "You think Naroogian's alive? That he didn't get killed last night? I heard what I think was small arms fire back in the compound and I figured that was him. Making a stand."

"I heard it, too. But I don't know what it means. I wasn't there. But it helps to make my point. Maybe Naroogian was being used. By Bath. Or maybe Naroogian was using us. Could be either way. Or he could have been just what he seemed to be, a bullheaded stubborn man who decided to follow ridiculous orders because someone issued them."

"I don't believe that," I told him.

"Neither do I," he said. "Just wanted to see how you might respond."

Lee Duc Than was unchanged; still short of breath and coughing, feverish, eyes glassy, but he was able to speak when I took his pulse and blood pressure. "Everyone all right?" Did it without running out of air this time. Somchai was wiping his brow with a cool wet cloth. She had hardly left his side. I pulled up his sleeve and looked at the injection site. Much redder than yesterday, the margins raised and when I motioned, Eddie quickly came over and made a sketch of the size and shape of the lesion.

The wounded men were essentially unchanged also. The man with the chest wound had been gasping noticeably when we lifted him aboard but once we started oxygen flowing through a mask, he seemed to improve. He needed a surgeon to drain and correct the hemothorax that was threatening to snuff out his life. The infected leg was better and the antibiotics seemed to be doing their job. He needed a medical facility as well.

"There's a good military hospital in Chiang Mai," AcChan reported. "I've made arrangements to drop them there. Another forty minutes to our first stop to refuel, then an hour on the ground, another hour to Chiang Mai. Can they hold out that long?"

I shrugged. I didn't know. "They've come this far, let's hope another couple of hours won't be too much. But Lee Duc Than, I want to get him to Bangkok if I can. As soon as I can."

And in Bangkok I had help, a laboratory, Carmichael, and better communications. With luck, by now, there should be word waiting for me from Diaz, Bertinoldi, the General, everyone, plus the results of Ken Green's blood type, the latest on Kendra, and from Marge, for God's sake, I'd been gone far too long!

"No problem with Lee Duc Than. We can have him flown down by air ambulance. We'll set it up when we refuel and you should be able to depart as soon as you reach Chiang Mai."

We droned on, dipping lower, then veering sharply skyward, often skimming treetops and then bounding around looming mountains or avoiding mist that rose suddenly in front of us, the three helicopters forming and maintaining a perfect V formation in the sky, ours in the lead, the other two visible, one on each side, following precisely, matching each of our moves with a corresponding one of its own. The hillsides below were denuded of trees in many areas, thickly forested in others, broken only by small carefully tended fields. Near the air base where we were to land for refueling, the forest was gone, mute testimony to the implacable march of the relentless chain saw, erosion already clogging the once clear streams below with silt and mud, killing the fish, destroying the water supply for people who had lived for thousands of years in a pristine paradise. No more. Civilization was coming.

North of the base, as we jockeyed for a landing, I asked AcChan, "What did you use to stay in touch with the blue star people?"

Idly, as if not comprehending, he asked, "Use? You mean how did I contact the birds?" Then he suddenly smiled for the first time in a long while. "I'll tell them what you called them. The Blue Stars! They'll like the name."

He picked up his backpack and removed a small black box. Five inches by four inches. Plastic and metal. "You don't need anything very big to do it. Nothing as big as what Magellan was given. This does fine."

I'd seen them, even smaller. Global positioning satellite communicators. GPSC's for short. Gopsics to the military. Truly little black boxes. He watched me examine and hand it back.

"Nice little gadgets," he said. "I wonder how come you Americans are so good at thinking up things like that?" And he put it back into his bag.

We were almost on the ground when I asked one other question that had been bothering me. In fact, there were a lot of questions still bothering me but I had time for only one right then. "I know Fantus has a history of running an unreliable taxi service, I was left waiting on the street corner a couple of times when he never showed up, but you seemed absolutely certain that he wouldn't come. To tell you the truth, I was expecting him to appear, not to take us out of Yellow Garden, but to make sure none of us ever left because he must have suspected that if we got to Green, he would tell us about those Bath-Fantus visits in the past. But you were right. You kept saying he wouldn't."

The helicopter was settling onto the blacktop runway and we were jostled slightly as he replied, "Did I say wouldn't? Maybe I did. I should have said couldn't. He couldn't come. I was sure of that."

"What do you mean couldn't come? Why couldn't he come?"

He was climbing down from the plane with me behind him when he answered, and I stopped in surprise when he said, "Because he was dead. Still is."

Shocked, in disbelief, I saw that he was serious. "How do you know that?"

He pointed to our helicopter where an ambulance had pulled up close to the side door. "You remember the man with the arm wound we brought back from our raid on the landing strip? He told us. He knew all about it and it was confirmed by the helicopter commander. Fantus is dead. That's why I brought the man back with us. We want to question him closely and see what he knows and how come he knows. Most important, when he knew. But as far as getting a ride with Fantus, that's not going to happen. Not us, not Bath, are ever going to have the Fantus taxi service again."

Several uniformed men from the second helicopter had deplaned and were waving for AcChan to join them. Before he hurried off, as was his obvious intent, I said, "Why didn't you tell Naroogian about Fantus? I suppose it didn't matter much to the rest of us, we were leaving in any event, but Naroogian was staying, waiting for someone who was already dead to pick him up. He may have changed his mind had he known that."

It was difficult to read his face, his expression hardly changing as he said, "Maybe, but I doubt it. For one thing he didn't ask. For another, I'm not sure he didn't already know. May have known before we left Chiang Mai, before Fantus was dead. What I mean is, he may have known that Fantus was soon going to be dead and it happened."

Had he just told me that Bath, or Naroogian, or someone, had planned, or ordered, Fantus' death? Moments before, I had been wondering how many unanswered questions there were and now I knew there were many new ones to add to my list. AcChan was gone, in conference with what I assumed to be colleagues, of what, I couldn't even guess, but from the easy familiarity they enjoyed with one another, and the respect with which they greeted AcChan, I could only conclude that Eddie had been correct. Police or military, someone's, but whose?

I was filthy dirty, unshaven, unkempt, and Green was as bad, or worse because he had an unhealthy yellowish cast to his skin that couldn't be washed away. He was standing under a small canopy near a doorway leading to a room filled with white linen topped tables and chairs, almost all empty, and on the window a sign promised PEPSI. It was probably the officers club, I decided, and risking nothing worse than being asked to leave, I took Green's arm and steered him inside. Through large plate glass windows, I saw men and women in immaculate whites gently batting a tennis ball back and forth, not exerting themselves beyond the minimum in 95 degree heat and 98 percent humidity. I wondered why they were out there at all but perhaps this was the cool part of the day. While we waited for a seat, something I wasn't certain would be offered by a dubious, nervous Thai maitre d', a white coated waiter scurried outdoors balancing a tray filled with tall, cool, clear drinks, and the tennis players halted their contest and withdrew to the welcome shelter of the green canopied refreshment area, wiped perspiring faces with huge white towels, and prepared to recharge their batteries for five more minutes of aggressive combat. A Thai officer approached the door, glared at the maitre d', rolled his eyes in our direction and pointed to a table. We were seated.

A waiter was with us at once and eager to impress him with how much a part of the local scenery I had become, I ordered, "Narm manao. Song." Two fresh lemonades. His coat was white and stiff. So white it was blinding to the eyes; so stiff that any movement of his starch encased arms sounded as if a knight of the round table was drawing his sword. Our appearance, in contrast, was one of total dishevelment. His imperious look, waiters can marshal that look when they must, was a clear reminder that he was serving us against his better judgment But in due course, he brought the lemonade and it was delicious.

Alongside the helicopter, two men had wrestled a long black hose into position and were transferring fuel from an olive drab tanker truck into our aircraft. AcChan and two officers were talking animatedly off to one side and as I watched, a third man in uniform handed a thick manila envelope to another wearing the Thai insignia of a colonel who opened it, scanned its contents, and passed everything to AcChan. They continued talking without pause. Green was sipping his lemonade, staring off into space, and I saw Somchai appear in the open hatch of the helicopter. Perhaps he was thinking of her. I was thinking of Kendra. And JoElle. Both of them at once.

I broke into Green's reverie. "Ken, a couple of things bother me. You said you were a prisoner at Yellow Garden, yet there's no denying you left the place several times. You went to Chiang Mai, you went to the hospital where Co Phan was a patient, you met Somchai at the night market. You were seen at the store with Lee Duc Than. People are going to ask, if you had that much freedom, were you really a captive? They'll want to know why you just didn't walk up to a policeman in Chiang Mai, for instance, and say I'm a missing American POW and I want to go home. Or if you didn't want to approach the police, how about a doctor or nurse at the hospital before the others came? You might have asked them to send a message. I'm sure they would have done it. And when the police did come to the hospital, why didn't you stay there while the others, whoever they were, raced away?"

They were still pumping fuel and I ordered a second narm manao, not having realized until now how thirsty I was. Green decided to try a Pepsi. When the waiter returned with the two glasses, he conspicuously placed the bill on the corner of the table and tapped it, as if saying this is what you owe, I hope you're good for it. As a matter of fact, I wasn't. I hadn't any cash on me at all and I looked outside to see if there was any sign of Eddie. Usually he managed to secrete some money on his person somewhere and he was my best bet to avoid further embarrassment. If Eddie failed me, I would have to hit up AcChan for a loan. He had been handing out bahts all along the way and probably had a few left.

From across the table, I heard Green say, "Guilt, guns, shame, and Lee Duc Than."

Startled, I said, "Come again?"

"That's why I stayed. That's why I didn't go for help. Guilt, guns, shame, and Lee Duc Than. Mostly shame and Lee Duc Than."

I wondered if he would elaborate and he obliged me when he said, "Guilt. I felt guilty over the death of my mother. She was long dead before Lee Duc Than told me and I was a prisoner then in Vietnam, but the way I had left home, in anger, must have hurt her terribly. I felt that I had been responsible for her death. Guilt.

"Shame," he continued. "I was ashamed of what I had done to my father, to Kendra, and of course, to my mother as well. I had acted stupidly, recklessly, brought them so much pain for no reason at all. I was like the other radicals hiding in college, running away to Canada, screaming at the top of our lungs. We thought we had all of the answers, could solve any problem, get rid of racism, inequality, poverty, intolerance, all of it. What fools we were. What a fool I was. Especially me. I read the papers from time to time even at Yellow Garden, and I could see that many who marched with me, most, have joined the establishment now, cashing dividend checks, have found a safe haven in the institutions we threatened to abolish. Shame, because what I did was wrong. There was a better way. I just didn't find it. And for all that I wanted to do for my country, no one cares and no one remembers. Nor should they. I'm not even a name out of the past."

He was wrong, of course. He was going to be a name out of the past, had to be because of who his father was, because of Kendra's illness, because of his own fifteen year nightmarish journey, and most of all, because he would be denounced and reviled by some, honored and revered by others, and used for their own ends by the very men he had once called comrades. He would be news. He would have more than his fifteen minutes of fame whether he wanted it or not; whether he deserved it or not, it was coming.

"Guns, Ken, you said you stayed because of guns. What about them?"

"That's easy. Early on, I was in a tiger pit, behind wire and bamboo fences. The men outside had guns. Even later at Yellow Garden, they had the guns. I was allowed some freedom but was never out of the sight of my keepers; they never allowed me near a radio, I never got close to a phone, and they never allowed me to write or send messages. Even when I went to Chiang Mai, the guns went along. Sure I slipped them several times and caught hell for it later, but they were never far away or far behind. Even when I met Somchai, they were an arms' length away. At the hospital, I was able to lose them by taking a taxi, but they were right behind. And there was always the threat that they would harm Lee Duc Than if I crossed them.

That's where the guns come in."

It was obvious that Lee Duc Than must have played a major role in the whole story. He got to it next.

"Lee Duc Than? He saved my life. I would have died in prison in North Vietnam, just another nameless body thrown into a common grave except for him. When he first came to see me, I had decided to tell him nothing other than my name, rank, and serial number. Like I told you. Then I realized he really didn't care. He wanted to talk to me, not about me. Soon he had told me that some of his fondest memories were of his days at the University. He remembered you, said you had introduced him to the General, my father, and was impressed by that. He remembered girls he had met, talked as if he had fallen in love with all of them, found American girls fascinating, and was saddened when he was ordered back to Vietnam. He wanted to stay in the United States. He talked endlessly and in time, I began to talk to him and told him almost all of the things I had decided I would never reveal. One day, I realized he was a father figure, a substitute for the father I felt I had never had. More guilt. But then he brought me the books and I was obsessed by them. I read and read and was born all over again. It was a freedom even while locked behind walls. When he showed me topographical maps of what he called Yellow Garden and when he told me of what had already been identified as coming from there, I knew I wanted to make that my life's work. I'd lost fifteen years and now there was a chance to do something worthwhile. Not for money. I knew I'd never see any of that. I knew of Huy Thacht by then. Knew he'd get it. But for me, it was a chance to do something that mattered. That I could actually do something; engineer a mine, operate it, make it produce. I didn't care who got the rewards. Just doing, that was my reward. One day, somehow, Lee Duc Than pulled rank or something and allowed me to come to Laos. I have no idea how he did it and I've never asked. Three weeks later, he showed up and we've been here together. Both of us became prisoners. He a prisoner of his son who didn't dare allow him to leave, me a prisoner of them both, because Huy Thact would never agree to my departure, and to Lee Duc Than because I owe him my life. I couldn't desert him."

I knew what he meant. I had the same problem with the General. We both felt an obligation, justified or not, to the man we credited with saving our lives.

Eddie walked in. "Five minutes, AcChan says, then we leave. They're just about done with the fuel. Somchai says everybody is about the same except for the man with the chest wound. His skin is gray." Not a good sign.

I almost forgot, catching him as he was walking out the door. "Eddie, do you have any money?"

"Money? What do you need? Real stuff like dollars or some of this other stuff? Green, brown, yellow pieces of paper, different sizes and colors, what do they call them, bahts?"

The bill said 80. Assuming it to be Thai currency, I said, "Give the man 100 bahts." That should make him feel better about being forced to serve us instead of the tennis players who were now back on the court. One of the Thai women, nice legs and shape now that I had a chance to think about it, drilled a passing shot for a point to close out the set and her squat muscular male opponent didn't look too happy about it. They all retired for another glass of something.

"So you stayed out of concern for Lee Duc Than?" I ventured.

"Not really, Mike. I stayed because I couldn't leave, and then, on the one or two occasions when I may have been able to try to run for it, like in Chiang Mai, I didn't because I knew that Lee Duc Than had made me feel like a human being again. He had become my father. I couldn't leave him behind. I decided I would never leave Yellow Garden without him. Then you showed up and for the first time, it became possible."

Like I said, he stayed because of concern for Lee Duc Than.

The fuel truck had rolled away from the helicopter, ours, the other two were staying where they were for the moment. AcChan was waving from the open hatch as the rotors started to turn slowly. Green saw the movement and panic was written all over his face. He was afraid of being left behind. Was it because he was still not out of the reach of Huy Thacht or was it something else? Maybe I was wrong. Maybe he was afraid of going home.

Eddie didn't seem to be afraid of anything as he returned from paying the bill. "I gave him the 20 bahts as a tip. He seemed happy to get it." Which was probably true as he may have wondered if he would get paid at all.

We walked out into the blast furnace of Thai sunshine, were spun about by the rotor which had begun whirling in workmanlike fashion, and moments later, we were airborne.

"I've made arrangements for a Falcon Jet to meet us in Chiang Mai. You, Chun, Green, and Lee Duc Than will fly to Bangkok without making more than a momentary stop to switch planes. Can Lee Duc Than handle that?" AcChan asked once we were safely on our way once more.

"I'll check before we land but it's the best thing to do for him. He needs better care than we can afford and the best place to get it is in Bangkok, but for the moment, he looks all right. What about Somchai?"

"What about her?" he responded, glancing to the rear of the cabin where she still sat by Lee Duc Than. "It looks like she's doing all right, too."

"I don't mean that. Is she free to continue on with us and care for Lee Duc Than?"

"She's not a prisoner," he said in surprise. "If she wants to go and there's room on the plane, she can go. If you and Green want her." I felt that was a decision for Somchai to make and decided to talk to her before we reached Chiang Mai.

I watched as AcChan opened a small foil wrapped packet and removed a brown slab which he broke in half and started to eat. Still chewing he said, "Good. Want one?"

Expecting a tangy Thai confection or military power meal, I held out my hand while he reached inside a pocket and handed me one. GRANOLA, made in the US. "Nourishing stuff, low in fat, high in energy," he recited, hitting the highlights of the marketing campaign. I was as hungry as he was, not having eaten for two days, so I started chewing along with him.

"He tell you anything useful back there on the ground?" he asked, referring to my conversation with Green in the officer's club.

"Some, but I don't think he gave me the whole story."

He shook his head vigorously. "The whole story?! Forget that. You'll never know the whole story. Green won't tell you, even if he knows what it is, and it's certain that Magellan and Bath can't be trusted. Everyone has something to hide and it's my job, and yours, to dig out what we can use effectively and make sure the right people hear about it." Which of course, was what I was working on.

"You know what interests me about Green?" he asked. "Even more than the years he spent living in a cage and prison camps? Without going mad? What interests me is what he was doing in Chiang Mai when he went to see Co Phan and met Somchai. Remember, he had Lee Duc Than with him at the time. Seems to me, if they're both off the ranch, why go back to Yellow Garden at all? Ask him about that, will you?"

I did, almost immediately, simply moving back a few feet in the noisy cabin and resuming our conversation that had been interrupted back on the ground. "Why did we go to Chiang Mai?" he repeated in response to my question. "Lee Duc Than was looking for two old comrades of his. They'd gone to school in the States together."

"You're referring to Ho Phan Van and Truang Van Dong?" I asked.

"Yes, that's what he told me. They'd all served together in various government ministries in South Vietnam during the fighting. Lee Duc Than was in some political agency, he doesn't like to talk about it, while Ho Phan Van was in the War Department and Truang Van Dong was in the interior ministry, secret police type of job. As you know, Lee Duc Than defected. Went north."

"That may be why he doesn't like to talk about it. Maybe because being a traitor isn't considered heroic in our society unless you leave the other side and come over to us," I suggested.

Green considered it for a moment and had no comment. Probably wondering if any of that had relevance to his situation. "Anyhow, that's what he wanted to do. Find them and he heard one of them was in Chiang Mai. Sick."

Fine, an old warrior trying to arrange a class reunion with comrades. Why those two and why did Huy Thacht allow them to leave, as AcChan put it, the ranch?

"He didn't like me to be there when visitors arrived," Green explained. "Either I had to be confined to the house or taken away so no one could see me. Or so I couldn't see them. Once in a while, when they were going to use the house for a meeting, they sent me off like this, with guards, but kept Lee Duc Than, figuring I would come back to be with him no matter what. But this one time, because Lee Duc Than felt so strongly about finding an old friend in need, they allowed both of us to leave. Maybe, though, it was what had happened on the previous visit."

"What happened?"

"I hadn't been in the house, no one told us to stay there, so I was working up at the diggings near the west end of the field. I saw a plane come in, but Huy Thacht was coming and going by air all of the time so I didn't pay that much attention to it. When I finished for the day, we always had to come in at dusk with the guards making sure we were there on time, I heard voices in the main room, washed up in the rear, and then started upstairs to see Lee Duc Than. That's when I saw them and they saw me."

"Who? Who did you see?"

"Like I told you, the men in your pictures. Yes, those," he confirmed as I took them out once again. "You called them Fantus and Bath. I know the second one as Towle. Or Towel. It's pronounced the same but I don't know how he spelled it. All I know is that Huy Thacht was furious. He was angry at me, angry at the guards, angry at the two visitors and long after I had been taken next door, I heard him shouting. It was clear he did not want them to remember what they had seen. He made it equally clear to me the next day that I had never seen Fantus and Towel either. Or else. But from then on, when we were supposed to have visitors, he made sure I was out of sight or out of town, under guard."

I let it drop for the moment. Went back to the reunion. "So Lee Duc Than was looking for old comrades, his old classmates, his old South Vietnamese government buddies. Were they double agents, too?"

"Are you guessing or do you know, Mike? Because it was half and half. One of them, like Lee Duc Than, was already working for the North Vietnamese when you were teaching him about the good things in life." A strange way of putting it, I thought. "The other wasn't and never did. He wound up in reorientation camps, almost as bad off as I was, but survived."

Interesting. "Which was which, Ken? Who defected and who played it straight?"

"Truang Van Dong was the traitor, the secret policeman, kept the biggest secret of all. He was working for the other side."

"And?" I was leading him on.

"Ho Phan Van was legitimate. Worked for the South Vietnamese government, stayed to the bitter end and then ironically, was deprogrammed, rehabilitated by his old friend Lee Duc Than."

How much of this I could believe was open to conjecture.

Across from me, Green had started to tremble again and I feared he was about to have another attack of malarial chills. Suddenly he asked, "Do you know how far a mile is, Mike? How long it takes to walk it? I mean, you could say a mile is 5,280 feet and that most people walk it in fifteen to twenty minutes. But I mean for me, when they allowed me thirty minutes of exercise a day, confined to a fenced area 30 yards long, ten yards wide, surrounded by eight to ten foot fences. Bare ground, exposed to the sun or rain, either concrete hard or swamp mud, nothing in between. No matter how weak I was, or what the weather was, I walked, as fast as I could, I wasn't allowed to run even inside the fence, but I walked, back and forth, thirty yards one way and thirty yards back again, and when I had counted five hundred paces, I called it a quarter mile, one thousand a half mile, and two thousand one full mile. Three miles a day, thirty yards at a time, as fast as I could. Do you realize that's a ten minute mile, something I hadn't been able to do when in college when I was fit and healthy. But I did it in the camp, no matter how weak or sick. I had to, it was my only way to fight the system they were using to defeat me. Had they fed me, allowed me to rest and heal, I might have cooperated with them. But they didn't, so I walked to keep my mind from accepting defeat."

"And you did defeat them, Ken," I offered in hopes of consoling him. The trembling seemed to be growing worse.

"No, Lee Duc Than broke me. When he came into the picture and accepted me, allowed me to sit while he talked, he broke me. I told him everything. That was the main reason I didn't try to escape afterwards. I had shamed myself and my father. I knew that they would never have broken the General, no matter what they had done to him. He would never have talked."

I wanted to say, Ken, Ken, it doesn't matter. That was all long ago. Let's just get home and all that will take care of itself. And it would. But right now, he was still viewing it as a matter of honor, carrying the impossible task of trying to measure up to a father he had never known.

"That's what Lee Duc Than was good at," he continued. "Breaking men. He told me after we had come to Yellow Garden how he had broken his old friend Ho Phan Van. Didn't kill him, didn't want to. Just broke him. Reeducated him, made a new man out of him, a man of the people. First, he told me, it had been necessary to break his spirit, play mind games with him, destroy him physically and emotionally with starvation, selective physical punishment, and solitary confinement. Shortly after he had suffered what everyone thought was a heart attack, his reeducation was officially declared a success and he was released and told to report to another agency in Ho Chi Minh city, as a clerk. A year later, to the secret delight of Lee Duc Than, but to the dismay of other programmers and officials, Ho Phan Van dumped all the files in the agency onto an enormous pile, poured gasoline onto it, and set it afire. Then he urinated on the overstuffed furniture in the chairman's office and walked away. Some said he had died, his heart giving out again, but Lee Duc Than heard otherwise. He heard his old companion, he still thought of him as a friend, had made his way to Thailand.

"Of course by now, Lee Duc Than himself was in trouble. He had failed conspicuously with Ho Phan Van and the chairman could still smell urine in his sofa. No money for a new one in the budget. Then I disappeared. One day, I was in a prison compound, more comfortable than most but they had tolerated that at Lee Duc Than's insistence, and the next I was gone. Two strikes against him and he had seen enough baseball when living in the United States that he knew better than to stand around and take a third. He left for

Yellow Garden and that's where we both have been ever since. Until now."

The story was holding together well. I wondered if he had been able to rehearse it and knew exactly where it would have to go next.

"Then one day, out of the blue, Huy Thacht heard that someone in a hospital in Chiang Mai was calling himself Lee Duc Than. He decided to look into it, talked to his father, and finally agreed to allow the two of us, escorted, of course, by his men, to go see what this was all about. To tell the truth, I think he wanted us both out of there because another one of those mysterious visits was coming up and just a month before, I had seen a man arrive by plane, even spoke to him, and it was enough to send Huy Thacht into a towering rage."

Much too glib. Too smooth. Straining my credulity and I was willing to stretch it a long way for him.

"We came over the border without any trouble. You know how easy it is; you've just done it. Two guards accompanied us and Huy Thacht had more men in Chiang Mai. They were waiting for us to arrive. They had the car and we checked into the hotel, were assigned rooms and stayed there, closely watched. The next morning, Lee Duc Than and I went to the coffee shop for breakfast and while there, one of the guards was called away to answer the phone and the second seemed to be engrossed in a conversation with a pretty waitress." Pretty girls were always a problem, even with opium growing guards apparently. "Lee Duc Than saw that no one was paying any attention to us for a moment and he stood up, motioned for me to follow, and we went out a side door and caught a cab."

I interrupted. "Lee Duc Than could walk?"

"Then? Yes, he could walk. He didn't become seriously ill until later. When the cough got worse." I nodded and he picked up his story. "We found the hospital and asked to see Lee Duc Than. They showed us the room where the impostor was. Lee Duc Than took one look at him and started to cry. They embraced and both had tears in their eyes."

So he had found Co Phan, but why was he crying? The record showed that Lee Duc Than, Ho Phan Van, and Truang Van Dong had all worked together, even if on different sides, for the South Vietnamese government. Co Phan had been an academic, outside of government, not a close associate.

I let him continue while I thought about it. "Of course we couldn't get away with it. The guards knew where we were headed and they came rushing in, all bluster and noise, and I feared for our safety and everyone in the hospital seemed to come running. Maybe that's what saved us. At first, I thought Huy Thact's men might grab the patient and take him away with us but then, as someone said the police were coming, they hustled Lee Duc Than and me out of there. That's when he got sick. On the way back. I didn't know if we'd ever get him back alive. Naturally, Huy Thacht was furious. You don't want to see him when he has a temper. It's a sight to frighten anyone. Lee Duc Than's cough got worse and worse, he lost weight, and now he looks like that," and he pointed to the stretcher lashed tightly to the back wall.

"A few weeks later, he was so bad they sent me back to Chiang Mai to look for a nurse to care for him. That's when I met Somchai and asked her to come back with me."

Just like that, he was allowed to go back to a big city unescorted? "No," he emphasized. "Huy Thacht's men were there, never more than a few feet away. They were right at my elbow in the night market when I talked to Somchai. They were always there. They didn't want me to talk to anymore Yellow Garden visitors, and they sure didn't take any chances about my calling for help in Chiang Mai. When I got back to Yellow Garden with Somchai, I found that there had been another visit by helicopter, a big customer, Lee Duc Than said."

I was curious. "Why was Co Phan calling himself Lee Duc Than? What was the advantage in that? For that matter, if Lee Duc Than was on the run from the Vietnamese, wasn't it dangerous for Co Phan to use his name?"

"Maybe. But Lee Duc Than was surprised to find Co Phan in that bed. He expected it to be Ho Phan Van because the last we had heard, he was somewhere in Thailand and Co Phan was living in the United States. So Lee Duc Than asked him, 'Why are you using my name?' and he confessed it was an idea he had, one that might get him to the United States after all."

"What idea?" I guessed that it involved Chamburon and I was right.

Green explained, "CoPhan knew Lee Duc Than had been a government official, that he had been involved in reeducation camps and American prisoner of war registration and follow-up so he figured that the Americans would like to get their hands on anyone like that. He knew a lawyer, by reputation only, who had apparently handled some work for the National University in Saigon and he contacted him, told him he was Lee Duc Than, and asked him to make a deal with the Americans. Apparently, it didn't work because they hadn't arrived before we did. And we didn't do anything about it because Huy Thacht's thugs made so much noise when they arrived that we barely made it out of there before the police. Later, I guess Huy Thacht figured, what difference does it make? If someone is looking for Lee Duc Than, let them go to the hospital and knock Co Phan off."

"What about Ho Phan Van? Where is he?"

"Lee Duc Than thinks he died. He really did have a bad heart and he's afraid he may have passed away. We aren't really sure he ever arrived in Thailand. Of course, Lee Duc Than hopes he's wrong; that his old friend is in hiding and may still show up one day."

It was nice to think you could sentence someone to the rigors of a reorientation camp with just the correct mix of physical abuse and emotional turmoil, tinged with starvation, and still consider him a friend. You had to wonder if reciprocity applied.

If indeed Co Phan was in Chiang Mai, if Ho Phan Van was dead, a big if at this point, and if Lee Duc Than was really the man with us in the helicopter, then where was Truang Van Dong?

And Fantus and Towel, or Towle, not Bath, had visited Yellow Garden, not once but possibly several times, as had another, the big customer, that Green may or may not have talked to when they accidentally encountered one another. "How did you learn what their names were," I asked, "the men you call Fantus and Towel? You only saw them once or twice, you said, not much more than a glimpse, yet you're sure these are the men?" I was holding up their photographs again and he nodded.

"I'll never forget the faces. Of course we weren't introduced, but later I was listening when their names came up and I'll never forget them either. I suspected immediately that they were Americans and yet they never lifted a finger to help me."

Earlier he had said, "They didn't want me talking to anymore Yellow Garden visitors," but if he hadn't talked to Fantus and Bath, who had he talked to? The big customer? Customer for gems, or for opium? JoElle's buyer?

As he handed the photos back to me, I noticed the fine tremor in his hands, but he was not feverish although the sickly yellow of his skin still bothered me. As did the reddened eyes. "Why did Lee Duc Than cry when he saw Co Phan?" I asked abruptly.

"I thought you knew," he said, seemingly surprised. "When they were at the University, both of them in your classes for a year or more, they double dated. Actually they had a crush on the same girl, but sometimes Co Phan took her out and Lee Duc Than went with another girl. The next date, they reversed roles. I think Lee Duc Than was very much in love with her and if he hadn't already married and had a son, he would probably have proposed marriage to her and stayed in the United States. So even though they hadn't been that close after their return to Vietnam, they were still friends. Of course, Co Phan had been through reorientation too as he had been considered an unreconstructed, and therefore untrustworthy, academic. Lee Duc Than had been aware of that but hadn't wanted to intervene as it could only have made things worse."

It began to look as if Lee Duc Than went out on one limb, and only one, and that was the one holding Green. His Vietnamese friends were on their own and why not? They seemed to have remained friends just the same.

"The son you mentioned. That was Huy Thacht."

"Yes."

"So he's Vietnamese? How did he wind up in Laos?"

"He was in constant trouble at home, wanted nothing to do with his father, and joined an irregular militia army in Laos when he was fifteen. From there he went into drugs and built his own private army. Then he acquired Yellow Garden and apparently was willing to forgive and forget, if Lee Duc Than was, and brought his father home to live with him." As a prisoner it seemed, as much as a house guest. I wondered if Ken realized he was talking of a story remarkably similar to his own. Father-son conflict, resolved, to the advantage of, well, in this case, Huy Thacht. How would the Ken and Jordan Green story turn out?

"It wouldn't have worked out," I told him and smiled when I saw the mystified look on his face.

"The marriage of Lee Duc Than and his University girlfriend. Her mother would never have allowed it even if he'd been single. Trust me; I know."

As we touched down at Chiang Mai, red bereted paratroopers sur-rounded the helicopter and allowed no one within 200 yards of the craft. It may have been an unnecessary precaution as I could see no one showing the slightest interest in us, not yet, but AcChan cautioned me that it would be a different story in Bangkok. "The press will be there, cameras and all. There are rumors that an American POW is coming home from the Vietnamese War and that has set off a feeding frenzy. You won't have a problem here. No one will even be close enough to try asking any questions. In Bangkok, it'll be different. I'd suggest you keep Green from talking to anyone until he gets back to the States. Even then, keep him away from Bath and see that he talks to the military people first."

I was working on how to keep him away from Bath. Had been for some time already.

"About the Fantus business," I asked, "who killed him, when, and where?"

"I was wondering if you were going to ask. According to our prisoner, it happened right here in Chiang Mai, in his own hotel room, the night after we raided the store and burned it. The colonel confirms it. Someone waylaid him in the hallway, according to a single witness who is in protective custody, pushed him into his room, slammed the door, and fifteen minutes later when security arrived, he had two neatly placed bullet wounds in the back of his head. Execution style slaying, very professionally done, except for leaving a witness behind."

"Any idea who did it and why?"

He made a wry face. "Why? You knew Fantus as well as I did. He wasn't exactly a lovable man."

"Aside from that, any specific ideas?"

"Well, I can guess. Coming like it did right after we burned out one of Huy Thacht's bases, I'd consider that he had something to do with it, wouldn't you? Maybe he was angry over his losses, maybe he blamed Fantus for that, maybe Fantus was supposed to tell him we were coming or maybe he thought we would be somewhere else, I don't know. There are all sorts of possibilities. But one thing is clear, someone ordered a killing and you don't often do that to a friend."

If he'd narrowed it down to Fantus' enemies, the list was endless. He was correct, though, about Huy Thacht being the logical candidate. He may have decided to sever a business relationship permanently, without complications, not involving lawyers, contracts, and all those expensive items we take for granted back home. Then again, as I said, I could think of other candidates.

"You know what I think happened?" he asked. "What I gathered from our prisoner, Huy Thacht counted on Fantus and Bath to keep him informed of danger. From snoopers like us. Bath had contacts with the DEA, Thai police, and just about every other government agency you can mention. Plus your State Department, of course. Part of his deal with Huy Thacht was information for drugs and money. When we came into the picture, Bath was expected to keep tabs on us and pass the word of our movements to Huy Thacht. Remember the column of men we passed on the way to Yellow

Garden? They weren't going there in response to a call for help, like we thought. They were actually on their way to set up the ambush but we arrived before they did, because I deliberately misled Bath as to our timetable. We got there first."

"How come they didn't know that? They must have had someone reporting back to them?"

"They thought they did. Magellan. His transmitter may have looked weird but it worked. What we did when we had him install all that junk in Chiang Rai was inactivate it. I don't know how, but the man who brought all the extra parts was an expert. He knew what to do to make something not work and something Fred added did just that. Knocked him off the air. He wouldn't have known it but the gadget he was carrying was set up to send a brief signal every thirty minutes, whether he turned it on or not. Remember the helicopter that was flying around in the dark, even the next day in the rain and mist? It wasn't looking for us, as in seeing with the eyes, it was listening for us. With its ears. Naturally, it never picked up a thing, we burned out Huy Thacht's base, and Bath and Fantus had let him down."

"So he thought they had betrayed him?" I asked.

"Exactly, wouldn't you? He thought he had been double crossed by men he had accepted to some extent as allies or partners, so he hustled off to Chiang Mai to have it out with them, forgetting that he had only left a skeleton crew behind at Yellow Garden."

That would fit the behavior of a man that Green had described as having a violent temper.

"I don't know if Huy Thacht personally made the killing or whether he arranged it through his many contacts. More likely the latter but I suppose it depends upon how angry he was. At any rate, whoever did it went to the Royal Orchid Hotel, looking, I suppose, for Bath and Fantus, but possibly just Bath, who most likely was the most important of the two, and found Fantus in the hallway. You know the rest. Bang, bang," he demonstrated, a finger against the back of his head.

"Bath was lucky. He had been out on the town and came back to find police and army swarming around the hotel. Took one look inside Fantus' room, denied even knowing the Phantom, drove directly to the airport, and took a chartered plane back to Bangkok. He's holed up there right now, surrounded by the remnants of his depleted Pan Union force, wondering what to do. You and Ken Green are his problem. He's not sure what you may have learned but he has to be afraid of what Green could have revealed to you. Ken Green could destroy him. Obviously, he'd like to prevent that from happening and the best way to do that would be to destroy Green first. You see what I mean?"

Yes, very clearly I could see what he meant.

AcChan was staying in Chiang Mai, for now, to "attend to pressing business."

Magellan, Eddie, Green, Somchai, and I, along with Lee Duc Than, still on his litter, boarded the Falcon for Bangkok. As the throbbing Allison engines powered us into the clear blue sky, I sat next to Magellan and asked, "Fred, when you first received that phone call in Uzbekistan, were you convinced it was on the level? Right from the start?"

He frowned. "You mean when I first heard from Chamburon? I thought it was a little strange, I suppose, but yeah, I thought it was on the level. It sounded like we had a chance to get our hands on a defector from the North Vietnamese who had knowledge about American POW's and I knew there were a lot of people who would want to talk to a man like that."

It crossed my mind that the man who was able to bring him in from the cold might be in line for a promotion, making it easier to accept the premise of a strange phone call. "So what did you do then?"

"Like I told you back in Washington, I brought the whole thing to Bath. I thought he would be interested. And he was. Right away."

"Why would he be interested? Wasn't this something for the State Department or the spooks in the CIA, someone like that? Why Bath? After all, isn't he on the fringe of things at the Pan Union something or other?"

Magellan wanted me to get the name right. "Pan Union Trade Association. That's what it's called now."

"Sorry. Pan Union Trade Association. Why take this to them? Why not hurry into the ambassador's office in Uzbekistan or call someone at the State Department in Washington and say, 'I've just received this interesting call' and tell them all about it?"

I could see his mind thinking, no promotion there. After stumbling with a few false starts, he decided to say, "Well, Pan Union has a lot of connections in and out of the government, and I do work for them you know, for Bath, even though I was stationed in the embassy, so I guess I just naturally brought it to him. Seemed like the best thing to do."

"So you flew back to Washington and immediately told Bath about the call?"

"Yes. I did. But he didn't want to believe it. Said it was impossible I could have heard from Ken Green like that. Said he was dead. It wasn't until later, when I showed him the letter from Green, the one that had been forwarded from Vientiane to Bangkok to me, that he seemed to change his mind. He became agitated, as a matter of fact, acted as if he had been stung by a bee trapped in his crotch and wanted me to find out everything I could about both the letter and the phone call. Then he called in Fantus to help. You pretty much know the rest."

I doubted that. Doubted it very much.

Having concluded that I knew the rest, he didn't feel obliged to tell me anymore so he began skimming through an old copy of *House Beautiful* he found in the seat pocket in front of him. Ken Green and Somchai, like husband and wife, were dozing across the narrow aisle. Eddie was in the seat nearest the door and had his eyes wide open although he didn't seem to be looking at anything in particular. I took out my medical bag and went over to take Lee Duc Than's blood pressure. His eyes were brighter and they fastened on me at once. His skin was warm, but moist. I was hoping that we had corrected his dehydration with the intravenous fluids. He no longer seemed to have a fever so maybe the antibiotics were working.

Speaking without the difficulty he had demonstrated only 24 hours before, he asked, "Will you take me to the United States?"

I wrapped the cuff around his bony arm and puffed it up. Applied my stethoscope to the inside of his elbow and listened carefully, writing down 114/66. Not bad. His lungs were still rasping and I could hear numerous wheezes and rales. There was an area of dullness on the left side, down low.

He was still watching me intently. He never blinked when I asked, "Who are you?"

His gaze holding steady, he replied, "Lee Duc Than. You know me." Had both pupils constricted ever so slightly?

Maybe, I answered silently. Maybe, but you're lying if I can believe this test I made on your arm. It was redder than the day before, larger, the border raised noticeably, the center showing early signs of caseation. It was screaming out to me, "This man is not Lee Duc Than!" I was beginning to believe it.

As if he was reading my mind, he repeated, "I'm Lee Duc Than."

I didn't want to enter into an argument with an obviously seriously ill man but I couldn't refrain from pointing out, "About the United States. It might be difficult. You have no papers. We have only Ken Green's word about who you are."

Sorrowfully, he sighed, making it a question, "You?"

"I don't remember you. I can't recognize you. It has been too long."

He held up one bony hand in supplication, I thought, and then said, "Fingerprints."

Yes, of course, fingerprints. We must have gotten them at some point during his stay in the United States. He was willing to allow his fingerprints to make an identification? I looked once more at the skin test. Once more it screamed back at me, "This man is not Lee Duc Than."

Well, obviously, we had a problem here.

I looked carefully at the man on the stretcher. If this was Lee Duc Than, he should be younger than me. He looked much older. I took out my photos once more and studied them, comparing the face that others had easily identified as Lee Duc Than before I left University City to the man before me. Impossible to tell. The ravages of time and illness. The eyes were hauntingly familiar, had been earlier when I thought I could visualize him sitting around a table with Jordan Green, but were they, really?

"You treated me," he insisted. That again. The messages and now the patient always came back to that; my own records denied it. I didn't respond and then I noticed that the light in his eyes was fading, a rheostat dimming the bulb, he shuddered slightly, and was asleep.

Somchai had been watching and she now came over to sit beside him. Whatever else Green had done in Chiang Mai, he had found a compassionate caretaker for the patient, whoever he was.

Back in my seat, I found myself daydreaming of a place where Kendra and I were in the sun, the sky blue overhead, mountains towering high into the sky, snow covered peaks disappearing into the white clouds that moved endlessly from the horizon, gently spun cotton foam touching whipped cream, two glowing red eyes looking on as we walked, hand in hand, into an awe inspiring sunset. I awakened with a start and found Lee Duc Than staring at me, awake again, both eyes as bright red as the glowing embers of a dying campfire.

We avoided the first rush of media in Bangkok by deplaning at an empty gate far to one side of the main terminal. Phrem was there, with the car. Wearing a Packer game jersey, green and gold, number 5. The Old Paul Hornung number from the glory days of Green Bay football. No mystery. I'd given it to him.

Several judicious phone calls from Chiang Mai had smoothed the way for Lee Duc Than's hospital admission. Lumphini Hospital, a good one, and the ambulance journey was brief, the flashing lights having some effect this time, cars moving aside to let us pass. We followed in the Mercedes and as we moved, occasionally as fast as ten to fifteen miles an hour, only possible because we kept our front bumper within feet of the ambulance's rear bumper, Phrem grinned at me. "No gridlock yet. Maybe someday, but not today." It was his standing joke. Once, a year or two back, while we sat stalled in traffic on Rama IV, I had used the word to describe New York traffic at rush hour. He loved it, used it every chance he had, flaunted his worldly wise Americanism to fellow drivers, and waited for it to happen. Actually, he could stop waiting. Gridlock in Bangkok was a fact, mercifully on hold today so we were able to reach the hospital in near record time. A little under an hour, to go five miles.

Lee Duc Than was not the problem. One look at him and there was no argument that he needed immediate care. Green was something else. Not with the doctors, they could see the yellow skin and bloodshot eyes, recognized the signs of malaria, possible hepatitis and parasites. The problem was Green. He wouldn't stay. He finally did, one night only, he insisted, and I agreed, although I had a hunch it would be longer than that. They led him off to a room and it wasn't until then that I noticed a pretty nurse wrinkling her nose as she walked by, having first given Eddie a glance of interest, then hurrying away as if in search of something better. It was us, we looked awful, still filthy and mud smeared, and we, to put the best face on it, were giving off a bad odor. We reeked, in a word. I hadn't looked or smelled this bad since my escape from Korea. Somchai should have looked almost as bad but apparently she hadn't been crawling in as much mud, and besides, she was a girl and just naturally looked better. When I suggested she follow us to the Oriental for the night, she shook her head. No. She would stay with Lee Duc Than and Green. The ever accommodating hospital people with clipboards smiled and said that was just fine, recognizing that my personal guarantee of payment, in American dollars, was like money in the bank. "Just send all of the bills to the embassy. American embassy," I said. Smiles all around.

"And you'll have no trouble finding a place for the guards?" I asked.

"Guards?"

"Yes, the guards. Each man will have at least two. They will be here any time now."

The lead clipboard wavered ever so slightly, righted itself with dignity and firmness, and said, "No problem with guards. We have plenty of room."

I knew he was thinking, 'Why guards? Drugs, killers, maniacs, undesirables?' And also thinking, finding solace in it, 'that means even more money.'" As is often the case, money won out.

The guards, arranged by AcChan, his men in fact, arrived before Eddie and I left. Only three quiet men, neatly dressed in pressed khakis, dark hair, no nonsense type of thirty year olds, took up positions outside the doors that meant so much to me right then, Ken Green's and the mysterious still unidentified patient who called himself Lee Duc Than.

Eddie and I were ready for the Oriental but Phrem said, "No. Not the hotel. Madame Montparnier says you are to come immediately to her place. At once. We are late already and if traffic stays heavy, we will be even later." Impeccable logic.

Eddie had watched the hospital activities closely, after all, until AcChan's men had arrived he was our protection, and now he spoke for the first time since we had gotten back to town. "What do you suppose Magellan will do?"

I hadn't worried about Fred. We'd left him back at Don Muang airfield standing alone as we pulled away. I'd get back to him later. "I'm sure he got in touch with Bath. They should have a lot to talk about."

Eddie misunderstood, thought I was talking about a bath and said, "I could use one, too. I'm beginning to smell pretty gamy. Notice how that nurse turned up her nose at me just when I thought she might be going to ask me for a date?" We all had our problems.

I turned to Phrem. "We'll have to swing by the Oriental to pick up our belongings." We hadn't checked out when we left and I had nothing to wear, other than what I was wearing, and that wasn't fit to feed the hogs in.

"Everything is at Madame Montparnier's apartment," he said. "She told me to get them yesterday." All arranged. Phone call. Yesterday, while we were still on the river?

"You'll still have to take Mr. Chun to the hotel," I pointed out.

"No, his, too, at Madame Montparnier's place. Yesterday. He has the maid's room."

In an aside to me, Eddie said, "Do you suppose they gave her the day off or will we be sharing?"

He was overreaching. I hadn't seen him asleep for more than minutes at a time since I had chided him about falling asleep on the airplane over the Pacific, what was that, a week or more ago? So, if he had a bed tonight, any kind of a bed, he would use it for sleep, not frolic.

It turned out that the maid was there while JoElle wasn't. "Office," the maid explained. Which was fine as it gave me time to shower and shave and change into something clean, casual attire instead of jungle sloppy. Well worn Dockers, a comfortable polo shirt, slightly scuffed casual Florsheim mocs. Even after shaving, my face itched and burned and it was easy to see why when I examined myself in the mirror. Bites, dozens of them, on the face and neck, upper arms and legs. When Eddie had finished his ablutions, we discovered that he had even more. Bugs. Jungle pests. Too busy at the time to notice, too itchy now not to.

I went to the phone. Too early, much too early to call New York to report to the General, too early for Bertinoldi, too early for the office. Another two to three hours for that, but not too early for Carmichael who should be on the job in mid-afternoon Thai time. He was in! He rattled off his report as if firing a machine gun. He sounded starved for companionship. Turns out that wasn't it. He was in a hurry to get to the gym for a basketball game. "The samples arrived in perfect condition. We ran everything like you asked and forwarded backup specimens to Loretta Diaz. I talked to her today and she said all of the results should be in within twenty four hours." I paused and looked at the phone as if it had said something I didn't want to hear. The results should have been in 2 days ago.

I asked Horace about that and he hurried to reply. "Oh, I've got all of my results right here. Want me to read them off to you or would you rather that I bring them over a little later, after the game? It's the reports from Diaz and New York that we're still waiting for. I'll call Diaz right now to check on that and have her call you directly as soon as she hears anything more. Howsam? He's on his way back to the States right now loaded with stuff. Talked to him yesterday when he was in Hong Kong."

He didn't need to call Diaz and I told him that. I could do it myself and I did. She was in and confirmed that the final results would be available within 24 hours. Why so long, I asked. Just takes time, she answered.

"I've talked to Bertinoldi in New York," she confided. "He's cautiously optimistic."

That sounded promising. "Optimistic about what?" I asked hopefully. "Did he indicate that the blood type looked favorable?"

Maddeningly, she responded by saying, "He really didn't say what he was optimistic about, just that he was cautiously optimistic. I suppose he was talking about either the typing or the patient's progress. I should have asked." I agreed with that. She should have.

I suppose the word optimistic had lifted a little of the weight off my shoulders and I was in a forgiving mood, out of the jungle, clean, knowing that I was soon to see a beautiful woman, so I said, "Don't let it bother you. Bertinoldi wouldn't have told you much anyway. He resents anyone asking questions." Which wasn't unreasonable if you didn't have any answers.

Suddenly, she added, "Your Mr. Howsam is here this evening. We're going to dinner in an hour or so and he leaves for New York in the morning. Would you like him to wait around for you?"

According to Carmichael, my Mr. Howsam was supposed to be flying the Pacific right now on his way back to the office and here he was still in Hong Kong, so possibly out of perversity, I disappointed her. "No. Tell him to head directly back. I'll have plenty of time to talk to him when I return to the office. Right now, it's important for him to be on top of the TA 97-C project. It's hot."

She sounded disappointed and I knew why.

We broke the connection and I took a chance and called my office. Six in the morning and I didn't expect much, but you never know. Sometimes Marge was there early, scanning the technical bulletins from Arlie's and Howsam's crews, copying the financial figures for my attention, she knew I loved looking at daily sales figures while Burrows looked at the bottom line, the quantity for me, the quality for him, and once in a while, when the mood struck her, she warmed up my bagel and brewed a cup of tea when she saw me pull into the parking lot. She didn't have to and no one considered it demeaning. Like I said, when the mood struck her. It didn't always. Some days, if the Pistons had blown a big lead, I went down and filled her cup with coffee and brought it to her desk where we commiserated together, then got on with the day's work.

I should point out we didn't have titles at Osten-Burrows, save for me and Burrows. Those were mainly for business cards and the letterhead. Marge was either my personal assistant, administrative assistant, top aide, executive assistant, assistant director, something. Burrows had her listed on the TO as Marge, Osten's Secretary. But there was no pay scale for secretaries, and there were no secretaries despite what that said. We had a bunch of people, technical, professional, clerical, and laborers that had jobs and did them, adding and subtracting functions as we went to meet the exigencies of the day. We didn't fire people, we just moved them around and occasionally one walked in and quit. Didn't like being moved around. I wasn't aware of ever having received complaints from what is it, the Civil Rights Commission, but if we did, Burrows handled it. So far as I knew, we were a pretty compatible bunch of people. Not perfect, just compatible, most of us. And as if to prove the point, the phone was answered at 6 in the morning on the third ring. By Clovis.

"Oh, hi, Doctor Osten. Calling early this morning aren't you?"

"Hello, Clovis. Surprised to find you there. I was hoping to catch Marge. Is she there?"

"She's here."

Silence. "Is she coming to the phone, Clovis?"

"Oh, did you want her?"

"Yes, that's why I called. Remember, I said that."

"OK, I'll buzz her. She just went down to the other office," meaning Burrows,' to pick up the daily financial figures, "and should be back in a minute." Silence. "You been away, Doctor Osten?"

Away? For God's sake, I'd been in the office for no more than eight hours in the past three weeks and she was asking if I'd been away. My own, well, what was she? Maybe Marge's assistant.

"Do you see that office right behind your desk, slightly off to the right?" I asked her.

"Yes. You mean the one with your name on the door?"

"That's the one. Think now, have you seen me going in and out of that door for the past couple of weeks?"

"That's really hard to say, Doctor. You were always, I've told the girls this a thousand times, a quiet one. Coming and going, real quiet, not making a lot of fuss and noise like some other people I know, you know what I mean?"

I suppose that was a compliment. By her standards at any rate.

"But as far as your being here, I couldn't say because the door has been closed a lot and you could have been inside where I couldn't see you, know what I mean? But now that you mention it, I haven't seen you at lunch and your in-basket is getting awfully full."

My in-basket? I thought Marge had taken care of that!

Clovis mercifully disappeared once Marge came on the line. "Doctor, how nice of you to call. Bill scored 22 points last night and the Pistons were awesome. Just awesome. What can I do for you?"

In the next ten minutes, she brought me up to date. Things were going well, contracts were rolling in, new business, old business, unfinished business, all kinds of business. She touched upon it all. The technical directors were standing in line waiting for my return, each with a new idea, new product or improved budget, and she was scheduling them on an 'when and if' basis, was hoping the best man would win, and those terms left me wondering what she was talking about. Burrows? Happy as a clam in a stainless steel shell, one with a hundred year guarantee. Whatever that meant. The in-basket? Not to worry. She was taking things out as fast as they were put in. She didn't say what she was doing with any of it but the in-basket was 'clean as a whistle.' Which worried me as most whistles I had seen, usually in a referees mouth, were as dirty as could be.

I told her Tony Howsam would be on his way back by morning, she responded that no, he was already on his way, and I said no he was at dinner with Dr. Diaz and she said isn't it nice that he's fallen in love, and I said – well, you get the idea.

"That about it, Marge?"

"That's it. Well, that's not it. Just one more bit of news, two if you count the other one. A Doctor Bertinoldi wants to talk to you and so does a General. I think it's the one in New York who wants to be a Senator."

The part about being a Senator, that was news. "Thanks, Marge. Keep up the good work and say hello to Burrows if you see him."

"Oh, I'll see him. He's not out of town like you are. He's always here except when he's away and he looks real happy these days. Always does when business is good."

I'd noticed that myself. As I hung up, I wondered how things seemed to be so smooth and uncomplicated when I was away from my desk and so chaotic when I was behind it. And I wondered what anyone, other than me, would make of a conversation with either Marge, or God forbid, Clovis.

An hour later, Bertinoldi was in and he sounded like a broken record. Kendra, he said emphatically, was doing as well as could be expected, a recent blood count showing pancytopenia and macrocytic anemia, the new bone marrow specimen revealing poorly maturing myeloid precursors and megakaryocytic dysplasia and hypercellularity. He added, "a clonal abnormality, we figure it to be the trisomy 8 type, is present, but overall, she looks better, acts better, is eating better and her color is better."

On the one hand, using technical jargon, he was saying she was much worse. On the other, using clinical criteria, he claimed she was better. That was an inconsistency I could smell from 12,000 miles away. I pressed him for an explanation and he responded by saying, "She's better, if you know what I mean, but otherwise, things are the same." I had the urge to reach through the intervening miles of fiberoptic cable, place both hands around his scrawny neck, and demand a straight answer to a reasonable question.

Perhaps he sensed my unhappiness because he suddenly steered the conversation in a different direction. "Did you find the brother?"

Dumbfounded, I exploded, "What do you mean did we find the brother? We not only found the brother but I drew blood specimens, sent them to laboratories on two continents, including yours, and you mean to tell me you know nothing about it? By now, you should be telling me whether we've found the match you've needed for a bone marrow transplant. And you don't even know if the specimens were received in your lab?" By now, I was shouting. JoElle's maid peered through the doorway and silently withdrew, closing the heavy double doors behind her.

Sounding somewhat contrite, Bertinoldi confessed, "I've been away at a conference for a few days and must have fallen behind. I'll check on it immediately." I couldn't believe he had no one covering for him when he was out of town.

I did the best I could do, gave him JoElle's phone number, and told him to call back.

I was on a phone call roll. Montgomery answered at the General's apartment and Jordan came on the line at once. Having coffee and toast for breakfast, he told me and then asked, eagerness and concern in his voice, "Mike, tell me. How does he look? Is he all right?"

Was he more interested in Ken that Kendra? Had the old wounds been healed by fifteen years of separation? Had he overcome stubborn pride? Was he willing to accept a wayward son back from the dead?

"He looks good, Jordan. Thin, pale, has the malarial shakes from time to time, but he'll get over that. He's in the hospital now, getting checked over, but we should be able to have him on a plane in short order. We've already sent blood samples to Bertinoldi and Hong Kong for typing and I'd appreciate it if you would follow up with Bertinoldi to see that he completes his work without any delay." I didn't mention the delay that had already occurred. That could wait for a face to face discussion between Bertinoldi and me.

"They have the specimens, Mike," said the General, catching me by surprise. "Bertinoldi has been away but I've been in touch with a Doctor Caigle and he's promised to call when they have the results."

Why couldn't Bertinoldi have told me that himself?

"When will the two of you be leaving Bangkok, Mike? I want to see

Ken, want him to be here when I make the announcement. I want him by my side."

I could see the papers now: General welcomes son home from fifteen years of captivity in Vietnam. Pictures and stories, television appearances, features, requests for interviews. I wasn't certain that Ken was up to it, not yet. Maybe in a month or two, after proper diet and treatment, he could handle it, if he wanted to. I started to explain this to the General. He cut me off.

"Not that kind of publicity, Mike. Not for him. The announcement. Mine. That's what I'm talking about. I want him at my side when I announce my candidacy for the United States Senate."

I was speechless. He wasn't.

"I need him, Mike. Can you imagine the reaction of the voters when they see him standing alongside me, a man just released from the horrors of a prison camp, gaunt and emaciated, but still proud to be an American? Imagine the impact. The sympathy. This is an opportunity for me to serve the American people once again."

By using his son? Wasn't the spotless record of General Jordan Green enough to gain the approval of the voters of his state? He needed more? Was he going to stand before the cameras and say, "Look at me. My son was a prisoner of war. I deserve to be rewarded?"

Did he sense my feelings? Did he care about them? I couldn't tell because he made it clear when he said, "Mike, with him back home, on the campaign trail with me, I can't lose."

And I should have replied, "Oh, yes, you could, General. Consider this; was your son a prisoner or raising opium? Held in bondage or a defector? A hero or a smuggler?" Questions almost certainly to be raised in the months ahead. And leading the chorus at the head of the pack would be a shadowy figure called Bath, unless I was misreading the man completely.

What I did say was, "Jordan, before you do that, you should talk to Ken. He needs time to get his feet on the ground. He needs time to accept all that has happened and to get to know you and Kendra all over again. It won't be easy for him."

Didn't the General realize that they would put his son in a room, military and intelligence experts taking turns, and try to punch holes in his story, pick his brains, and if someone like Bath was pushing hard enough in the background, totally discredit and destroy him? The General must know that. He was an army lifer. Instead of an asset, the ticket to electoral triumph, Ken could easily be turned into a liability, disaster at the polls. Unless, and I considered the possibility, the fix was in. Did retired generals retain that kind of power?

He chided me. "Mike, of course I'm going to talk to him. That's why I want him home as soon as possible." Once again, he wanted to know, "When will you leaving Bangkok?" Then added, fixing a deadline as he did so, "we want to make the announcement Tuesday of next week."

This was Friday, I had to stop in Hong Kong, and it takes a full day to reach New York from there. We gain a day going back, international time zone, so what he was suggesting was that we leave in the morning. I wanted to get back so no problem there. But would his son be ready to travel?

"Don't waste time with doctors and hospitals in Bangkok, Mike," he ordered. "Get him back to the States where we can take care of everything."

I didn't promise miracles, but I knew I would try. I also didn't mention Somchai. I wasn't certain how she might fit into a Senate campaign, if at all.

Because it didn't seem he was going to bring it up, I did. "How's Kendra?" I asked. "What have you heard?"

"Caigle says she's doing well. Two days ago, last time I saw her before I had to leave town, she looked about the same. She wanted to talk to you, Mike. I could tell."

"I'll call her," I promised. "You should do the same with Ken." I gave him the phone number at Lumphini Hospital and I heard him repeating it for Montgomery who would copy it into the General's log.

I called Kendra's number and, of course, she was in the research lab. She couldn't come to the phone just then, maybe later. Could they have the number so that she could return the call? Is that the number? Where are you calling from? Thailand? Possibly it would be better, sir, if you called back later.

I understood. We're holding health care costs down.

AcChan was in his office. I could hear the din and hubbub of his warehouse in the background, as if he were walking around on the busy floor with a cordless phone, but I doubted that he would run the risk of electronic eavesdropping. "Let me tell you what I've done," he said without wasting time on pleasantries. "I have people covering Green and Lee Duc Than at Lumphini."

"I know. I've seen them."

"Good. They got there promptly then. I've also sent two men to the apartment, one to watch the elevator and the other to remain outside with your driver. Don't go anywhere tonight. You and Eddie should stay right where you are. Don't even think of going to the hotel. All of your things are at the apartment and we've checked you out of the Oriental."

"You obviously think we're at risk."

"Yes, you're at risk. Double risk. I don't have any idea what Huy Thacht or Bath might be tempted to try. They may go after you and Green, they may go after one another, I just don't know. Figure in the Lee Duc Than equation and it's even more explosive. After all, you're threatening to run away with Huy Thacht's father."

If he was Lee Duc Than at all. Which reminded me. I had to talk to Dan Emmet about those chest x-rays. He should have seen them by now.

Suddenly, I was listening to AcChan intently once more, "I have you booked on a morning flight to Hong Kong. The four of you, Chun, Green, Carmichael, and yourself. Everything is in my name for secrecy but Thai International security knows what's up and will protect you from the curious and keep crowds away if anything does leak out about Green. Lee Duc Than, from what I've seen, isn't able to travel and besides, he has no papers. That will take time if your government really wants him. I've pulled strings and gotten papers for Green, though, so he can leave. Security will have them for you at Don Muang. I'll pull Somchai up to Chiang Mai where we can protect her for now. Later, if Green or anyone else wants her in your country, we can see that she gets there. How does all of that sound?"

Rushed, that's how it sounded, but it eliminated the uncertainty of what would happen next. And it was guaranteed to make the General happy.

Not JoElle, however. She wasn't happy over a guard at the door. Gave the neighborhood a bad image, she said with a smile, and was downright unhappy to learn I was leaving at dawn. That brought on a frown. Even her frowns were very attractive.

"About the guard," she said, "wouldn't it be just as effective if we simply locked the door?" I assured her that both would be better. "About leaving in the morning, wouldn't two or three mornings give you more time to rest up?" Maybe, maybe not, I told her, and kissed her again.

We were interrupted by a banging on the door and took time out to allow Carmichael an opportunity to deliver his promised laboratory reports, a concerned guard peering over his shoulder. I took the folders, warned him to be ready for an early morning departure, consoled him as his face fell in disappointment, and said good-bye as he hurried away so as not to be late for his game. While I glanced at the reports on the balcony, sipping Australian chardonnay, barges and freighters surging up and down the crowded river, tourists and commuters flowing like frenzied red blood corpuscles through atherosclerotic streets down below, JoElle's maid served a light meal of fragrant spicy chicken and rice, fresh pineapple and peeled ruby grapes. The maelstrom below, devoid of sound and smell, threatening to turn the waterfront, if not the entire city, into a polluted wasteland, was proof of Thailand's arrival as a Tiger of the Asian economy.

She wasn't surprised when I put down the files, pushed aside my half eaten plate and told her I had to slip outside. I think she had suspected that I would be paying a visit to the Oriental before the night was over. "Didn't AcChan suggest you stay in tonight? With the door locked?"

"He did, but even AcChan doesn't know everything."

Bath answered on the second ring. "I'm coming over," is all I said. "I want to talk to you. Alone."

He hesitated, then, "Yes, I'll be here." Hesitated some more and added, "Alone."

JoElle's cook distracted AcChan's watchdog with an offer of food and he was sampling the chicken as I slipped by unseen, soft-shoed down the stairway rather than using the slumbering elevator, and used a side door rather than the front to catch the cab JoElle had obligingly ordered. Neither Phrem in the front seat of the Mercedes nor AcChan's second man, standing military erect by the front door saw me slumped low in the back seat as the taxi went down the circular drive and out into traffic. So much for watchdogs. Locks might, indeed, be more effective.

Two of Bath's Pan Unionists were in the lobby as I entered, both pretending not to see me and doing a poor job of it. Neither moved towards me as I entered the elevator but I was willing to bet one had a house phone in his hands before the doors closed. On the fourth floor, I tapped lightly at Bath's door and he opened it at once. He stepped into the hall, looked one way and then the other, satisfied himself that I was alone, and closed the door. In the lavish sitting room of his suite, he pointed to the bar and said "Help yourself. Take anything you want." No Canby, no Magellan, nobody to pour or serve. He was roughing it with self service.

"Not right now, maybe later," I told him. "I had a little something with dinner."

He had taken a glass into his hand and sipped. "I had hoped to hear from you sooner, Osten. To bring me up to date on our joint operation. It seems that Magellan, that was not a friendly thing to do by the way, leaving him at the airport, it seems that Fred doesn't know as much as I expected him to know."

Noncommittally, I said, "He got back then. Safely."

He nodded yes, tapped his foot on the floor, nervously drummed the fingers of his left hand on the back of the sofa, put down his glass, and ran his right hand through thinning hair that didn't seem quite as dark now as it had back in Washington. Perhaps it took a weekly visit with his stylist to keep the color from fading. "You aren't wearing a wire to record any of this are you?"

Strange he should ask, I thought, as my eyes scanned the room for evidence of listening devices or cameras. I didn't expect to find any. I didn't think he would want what we were about to say on tape or film.

"Now that you have Green and Lee Duc Than, what are your plans, Osten? What next?"

Did he really think we had found Lee Duc Than? Let's assume so. Don't debate it. I assumed he would know that we were leaving in the morning, despite the secrecy with which AcChan had shrouded our departure. Bath had contacts and there was no sense in underestimating him. Truthfully, I told him, "We're on an early flight to Hong Kong tomorrow morning. What about you?"

"We leave on SAS just before you do, to Hong Kong. Then back to the States." See, he did know. He leaned forward, hands on both knees and asked, "I'm not nearly as interested in your schedule as I am about your plans. What I mean is, what are you planning on doing once you get Green back to the States?"

I walked over to the bar and poured a small snifter of Napoleon brandy. I wasn't sure I really wanted it, but it was a good diversionary move, implying studied nonchalance, I hoped, and besides, the American taxpayer had paid for the stuff and I might as well have my share. "I'm not sure what you mean, Bath. I have to get back to work. I have a job. Green, what's he going to do? That depends upon him. Rest up, renew acquaintances, probably do what I have to do. Get a job."

He walked over to stand near me at the bar and freshened his drink. Scotch. "What about me? What has he told you about me?"

"Is that what you're worried about, Bath? Your trips to Yellow Garden? Does it bother you that he saw you there and can identify you as a visitor? A frequent visitor? That you saw him and knew he was alive and told no one? Something that makes those trips look highly suspicious, if not downright illegal. Is that what bothers you? Yes, he's told me he saw you there, you and Fantus. Much of the rest I can figure out for myself."

He swirled the ice cubes in his glass, still hadn't mastered the trick, and splashed some of the liquid onto the carpeting, and said, "I'll deny it, of course. You know that." Took a drink. "Then what you have is his word against mine and mine will be that he was a traitor. Not a prisoner but a defector, one who worked for a known double agent, Lee Duc Than, and when that became boring, he went into drug smuggling at Yellow Garden. That's what I'll have to say and I can make it stick. When I'm done, Ken Green will be known as the rotten American drug kingpin of Southeast Asia and he'll wish you had never found him."

The hell of it was he might be able to pull it off. The other problem I had was the feeling that I hadn't *found* Ken Green; it was almost as if some-one had drawn me a map and suggested, why not go there and take a look. Voila. Whattaya know. It's Ken Green. Bath took another drink and stood looking at me. My move.

"You can prove all of this without convicting yourself?" I asked. "You expect people to believe that an American who was seen going down in flames wound up as a drug czar after working against his own country for fifteen years, during which his own government gave him up for dead? You have all of this information, collected it by making visits to Yellow Garden, the home base of a known warlord and master drug dealer. Huy Thacht. That's your story?" The brandy was good. I settled back in a comfortable chair and studied the color of the fluid in the fine cut glass. "You think that'll fly, Bath?"

"Suppose my trips to Yellow Garden were part of an undercover opera-tion during which we collected all of this evidence, just like you said." He was thanking me for the help. "That explains the trips and how I learned of the continued existence of Ken Green. I can destroy him." He was challeng-ing me, on his feet again and leaning against the back of the sofa, spilling more fine scotch on the beige velvet finish.

"We," I said, "you mentioned we collected the evidence. Who is we?"

"Fantus. Alex worked with me."

"But Fantus is dead, isn't he? He won't be able to substantiate your story now, will he? What a pity he died at such an inopportune time." Bath returned to his seat and started tapping a foot once more. Then suddenly remembering, I exclaimed, "But there's always Lee Duc Than. If he regains consciousness and is able to speak, he may shed a lot of light on this whole affair. Green's role, your visits, all sorts of things. Yes, I'm sure many people will want to get at him, if he ever recovers." He was going to recover, I'd be willing to stake my reputation, not all of it, but a small part, on that. But Bath didn't know it. And I wasn't about to tell him.

His eyes narrowed as he wrestled with a new problem. He leaned back on the couch, tapping his fingers rapidly, and said, "Yes. There's Lee Duc Than to consider. What about him? Do you expect him to be able to talk?"

Noncommittally, I responded, "Well, as you know, his age is against him. The doctors will do what they can, but. . .," and by leaving the matter open ended, I may have given the impression that the patient wasn't doing well. What harm could that do? I wondered if Bath knew that Lee Duc Than, if I could believe my records, was actually younger than either one of us?

Pan Union's chief suddenly seemed to reach a decision of sorts. He replaced his glass upon the mahogany bar and stood in the middle of the room, declaring, "I could destroy him, you know. Completely."

"Destroy Ken Green. Why? What is there to destroy? He's already lost fifteen years of his life, his mother died while he was in a prison camp, his sister is critically ill, he's coming home to a country that he won't recognize, to a nation that hasn't been aware of his existence, the army lists him as having died, and he's alienated from his father. What's to destroy?"

He waved his hands in front of his face in irritation. "That's enough, Osten. You're going to make me cry. I'm not talking about Ken Green. He doesn't count, really. I mean the General. I know he's planning to run for the Senate, the word has been out for a week or more. He'll announce it in a matter of days. If I tell the people of his state that the General's son is a drug dealer and traitor, he can kiss his candidacy good-bye."

What Bath was proposing seemed straightforward enough. Quid pro quo. Ken Green remains quiet about Bath's trips to Yellow Garden. Bath forgets he ever saw Green. Neither one has ever seen the other. Fantus is dead, no problem there. I'm a possible problem, but without corroboration, all I have to pass on is hearsay. Lee Duc Than, he's the problem. If Huy Thacht can grab daddy and take him back to Yellow Garden, he's out of the picture. If, however, the elderly gentleman dies in the hospital, of natural or unnatural causes, that dilemma, too, disappears. Lee Duc Than would need more than one guard from this point forward and all of them should bring their own lunch.

"I'll talk to Green," I promised. The look he gave me was clear. Do that, it said.

We didn't shake hands or say good-bye. I have never made a practice of doing either with vermin. On the way out, I noticed that he was already partly packed for the flight to Hong Kong. His expensive Louis Vuitton bag was open on a foyer table, two or three dark suits neatly arranged inside, a matching overnight case standing beside.

Eddie Chun was waiting for me in the hotel lobby. Rather than being asleep, he was wide awake. One of AcChan's men from JoElle's apartment was standing alongside a nervous Pan Unionist on the far side of the empty room, the American nervously wondering what to next, but obeying his orders to stay where he was. Phrem and the Mercedes were just outside the door and as we sped back to JoElle's, Eddie took the opportunity to lecture me as if I were a small child. "Boss, coming here was pretty dumb. AcChan will be as angry as a dog with fleas when he hears about this. His men are lucky they don't have their ears cut off for letting you out of the building."

"I'll talk to him and explain. They'll be all right. How did you find out I'd gone, by the way?"

"I didn't find out you'd gone. I heard you go. The minute I heard the door to the hallway open, I said to myself, 'There he goes,' but by the time I got some clothes on, you were downstairs, pulling away in the cab. That was a good move by the way, scrunching down in the back seat. Phrem couldn't see you and wouldn't believe me that you were in there. But we were right behind, the guard with chicken grease all over his face following me, the other one staying with the apartment. We watched you when you went into the hotel, figured you could take care of Bath, so we stayed in the lobby and took care of his people. I hope you didn't mind."

I told him I didn't mind at all. He continued to amaze me. Certainly he didn't plan on spending his career as a security guard, did he?

JoElle was waiting. We set the alarm for five o'clock and went to bed.

# 19

Five o'clock comes too early, no matter where you are. When your body and mind tell you it should be late afternoon and you haven't had enough sleep, it's worse than usual. But after a shower, freshly shaved, hot tea, a warm croissant, and fresh pineapple, life didn't seem to be bad. JoElle was totally relaxed, radiantly beautiful in a clinging rust peignoir of Thai silk, her chin resting on one hand, a fork in the other idly pushing a wedge of vine ripened pineapple across her plate, a trail of juice marking its attempt at flight, and asked, "Your Ken Green, what will become of him?"

I didn't know how to answer. Would he become a war hero, home at last, freed from a prison camp? Standing beside his father, reunited at last, the General, another hero, announcing his candidacy for the Senate? Joining the candidate on the campaign trail, exciting the crowds, making headlines and great copy for the media, on the morning network news, the talk shows, the magazines, his picture everywhere, father and son. Together again! And a symbol of hope for the many American families who looked longingly across the Pacific, hoping to hear that their son, too, had been found, would be coming home, alive and well. It could happen, he could be that symbol, that hero, the clincher for the General's campaign. Or he could be a disaster, for the General and to himself. It all depended. On Bath, on the truth, on keeping his mouth shut, and maybe, I suddenly realized, on me.

I had asked AcChan earlier about the possibility of other missing Americans being found. He had simply shaken his head, sadly but firmly. "It's not likely, Osten. It's been too long. I don't doubt that there are a few Americans who never went home. But I doubt if they were ever captives, prisoners, wounded or lost. They simply never went home. Do you know what I mean?" When I didn't answer, he continued. "A few wanted to end a bad marriage. They never went home. Others found a new life here, with a new woman, or found a new friend – drugs. They never went home. I'm sure some went AWOL and didn't know how to end it and they hung around, still living in anonymity in Thailand, Malaysia, Hong Kong, possibly even in Vietnam. I've seen Americans hanging around the streets of Bangkok and other cities, drugged out, burned out, wasted. Are they missing Americans left over from Vietnam? Or are they Americans who fled your way of life and have been cast adrift over here? I don't know and most of them are in such bad shape that if you stopped them on the street and asked that same question, they probably wouldn't know the answer themselves. Think about it; you still have Americans missing from the Korean War. From World War II. There are always men who don't come home from wars and can't be accounted for. Only in America do people agonize over it endlessly and that's because in America, you still think there are solutions to everything when the rest of the world accepts that there aren't."

I didn't know what would happen to Green, but I knew he deserved better than what he had experienced the past fifteen years. JoElle readily agreed. She finally tracked down the tricky piece of pineapple and ate it. Her lips were sweetened by the abundant juice when I kissed her.

I was lucky and reached the General at home just before he left for a dinner engagement. When he heard my voice, he was concerned, "Mike, is something wrong? Is Ken all right?"

A simple yes sufficed and I went directly to the purpose of the call. When he understood what I needed, he asked only one question, "Are you sure you know what you're doing?" It was the same question I had been asking myself.

"It has to be done, Jordan. There isn't any other choice." I said, making it sound much more emphatic than I felt.

"In that case, Mike, I'll make a phone call or two and see what can be done. I have a few favors I can call in and this sounds like an appropriate time to use them." As an afterthought, "Kendra, she's doing as well as can be expected. Had a comfortable day. Nothing yet on the blood match." Incredible!

Everyone seemed to have a few favors to call in. I didn't. Not out here. I was going to have to rely on Eddie and Horace. They were on the payroll.

I said, "I'll be back," as I kissed JoElle one last time at the elevator, not caring that the Thai guard was squirming uncomfortably, trying to be inconspicuous and protective at the same time. I surprised myself when I said it. I was thinking, 'what about Kendra?' and I answered, "Yes, what about Kendra?' and a small voice at the back of the brain said, 'you are in love with her' while an insistent voice off to the left side of the brain said, 'you love JoElle.' Jeez! I was arguing with myself. I resolved the problem the same way I had since Abby's death. Sublimated it. Buried it, deep in the mid-cortex. I *did not* have time for a discussion of love at this time, I firmly told both of the contesting factions. I must concentrate on survival. They quieted down, survival being something both sides understood.

I had called the hospital and Green was ready, waiting at the door, a guard at his side. No luggage of course, no luggage and no papers. A man without a country. A man without clean underwear. We could remedy both, AcChan the papers, and "We'll pick up what you need in Hong Kong," I told him.

Lee Duc Than was no better, no worse. The injection site was clearly caseating, the tissue eroding, peeling, and an angry red color. His temperature was almost normal, he was still coughing, and I suggested to the bright young Thai attending physician trained in Scotland, a fellowship in Denver, that he biopsy the site, send specimens to the institute in New York, to Diaz in Hong Kong, and have his own pathologist read them as well.

"You think that is what he has then?" he asked, after I told him my tentative diagnosis, one it had taken me twenty years to make. "Don't feel badly about missing it," he consoled me. "It's a very difficult diagnosis to make with a single visit." He probably was thinking, "But I would have made it." That's the way we've all been trained to think. Positively.

AcChan met us at Don Muang. A half dozen media people, mostly, it seemed, from Australian publications shouted and tried to reach us, but police and airport security pushed them back and we boarded smoothly, seated in first class. He embraced me, shook my hand, damaging the image of the unemotional Thai in the process, and promised again, "Don't worry about Lee Duc Than and Somchai. I've already put additional security on them at the hospital. We'll keep an eye on Mme. Montparnier, too, although she may not need it. Just in case."

"Huy Thacht?" I inquired. "Will you get him?"

He looked at me with raised eyebrows. "Get him?"

"Perhaps a better way of putting it would be, will you arrest him?"

"That is an interesting way of putting it. What makes you think I could arrest him?"

"Eddie figured it out a long while back. He said you were a cop. He didn't know what kind and I don't either, but you are either cop or military. So you could arrest people. You've been doing it ever since we crossed the river up north."

"Perceptive, your Mr. Chun. Here all along, I thought I had convinced everyone I was a businessman. Just trying to make a living."

"You are a businessman, as far as I'm concerned. You have a contract with the embassy and I'm sure they'll be, I'd like to say, happy to honor it, but probably it would be more correct to say, willing to honor it. So hold them to it."

"Oh, I will, Doctor, you can rest assured of that. And there are even some extras that we'll include. They'll pay it. Don't worry."

He hadn't told me anything about what kind of a cop. When I repeated the question, he gave it some thought and replied, "Special kind. Special task force of several Southeast Asian governments to fight drugs at the source. The source of much of the world's drug supply comes from right up north where we were. We don't always win and we don't always lose and we don't always get our man or men, but we do keep trying. You can count on that. So I expect I'll get Huy Thacht, if he doesn't get me first. He knows who I am and I know him. That should make it interesting."

"I'm sorry about Bip," I said.

His eyes misted. "Bip was a good man. I'll remember him and I want to make sure that Huy Thacht does, too. But Huy Thacht is my problem. Yours was on the SAS plane that just left. He'll be in Hong Kong ahead of you."

He said good-bye to Eddie and Green and drove away in his own dark blue Mercedes, just missing a collision with Carmichael who arrived in a green taxi and ran at top speed to climb the outside alleyway and arrived at his seat puffing and out of breath just as they closed the doors. "It must be the humidity," he claimed. "I can't be out of shape." He took the cold glass of fresh orange juice offered by the Thai cabin attendant and gulped it down in a single swallow. She got another and he repeated the bravura performance. Holding the cool glass against his forehead, it reminded me of one of the deceased Fantus' more endearing habits, he said, "I saw it. Got a good look. Saw everything I needed while they were checking in. Make, model number, color, everything. Should be easy, just like you said. But they were checking in late and I had a heck of a time getting over to this terminal before you left. Phrem whistled up a cab for me and he drove right onto the field, all kinds of guys in khaki running after us."

Eddie was listening intently. Green was half asleep. Carmichael beat him to deep sleep.

An hour later, Horace was still snoring but Green had awakened. "Kendra says you could read her mind and she could read yours, back in high school and college," I said, and he appeared to be startled, not yet fully awake.

"She said that?"

"Yes. She felt that you and she were tuned into the same wavelength. She could tell what you had done at school, you knew what had been going on in her life, and that the two of you actually made a game out of it. She says for several years after you disappeared, she felt she was still able to see you. Until recently, those feelings were so strong she didn't accept the fact that you were dead."

"I wasn't," he said pragmatically. I couldn't argue with that.

He ignored the telepathy experiments he had conducted with his sister and went back to something that he apparently couldn't erase from his mind. "Maybe he wasn't a bad father. Maybe he was so dedicated to his career, his men, his life that he had to do what he did. I was like a lot of kids, hungering for affection, feeling shortchanged in the cuddling and affection departments. It wasn't that he never paid me any attention. He did. He held me on his lap and bounced me up and down, took me by the hand to the park, pushed the swings, waited by the pool while I learned to swim at the Y. I thought of all that in the tiger pits and realized it wasn't bad, that the problem was, I wanted more. Yet as I grew up, I began to feel he was rejecting me, that he hated me, and that I hated him. Why would I do that?"

If I knew Jordan, he was wondering the same thoughts back in New York. Probably had been for years. How does it happen that people grow apart and never get together again? What can make them whole once more? I wondered if it might be a Senate campaign.

"He's going to run for the Senate, Ken. Your Dad. I wouldn't be surprised that he wants you to be on the platform with him when he announces his candidacy and during the campaign to follow. Remember, you'll be an important figure back home. Your story will be told and retold on television and print. Everyone will want a piece of you for an interview. Just the story of your missing fifteen years is big news. Add that to the General's run for elective office and it's even bigger. Can you handle it? The exposure and the pressure?"

"Handle it. I don't know what you mean." He seemed genuinely mystified by the idea of being an integral part of a political whirlwind.

"The health part. The mental part. It will be grueling. Travel, speeches, and interviews. Can you handle that?"

"If I get some rest first and if the General asks me, yes, I suppose I could handle that."

I decided to bring it right out in the open again, see how he reacted, and asked, "What about things at Yellow Garden? Anything there that should best be forgotten? That you wish hadn't happened?"

He seemed surprised and puzzled. "Hadn't happened? I don't know what you mean."

I played the role of the eager investigative reporter. "Ken Green," I snapped, "I understand you were at a place called Yellow Garden in Laos. I further understand that at that place there was a man called Huy Thacht who is an internationally known kingpin in opium and heroin, that he is implicated in murder, slavery, and other crimes against humanity. You lived there, Mr. Green, and yet you say you were not involved in any of these activities? You were an innocent lamb amongst men without morals or scruples?"

He grew pale, his jaundiced skin turning to green as he caught the implications of what I had just said. "They'll try to use that against the General?" he asked.

"Of course, wouldn't you if you were an opponent? The question is, is any of it true, can you refute charges such as those should they be brought?"

He looked to be in pain. "Of course much of that is true. Huy Thacht is actively engaged in criminal behavior. Poppies were grown at Yellow Garden and processed there. Drugs were shipped across the world. But I had nothing to do with it. I developed the mining operations, worked with my books and hands to succeed, and we did. I was a prisoner. You saw the wire. The guns. Lee Duc Than knows this. Somchai knows this. You know this to be true also, Mike." Unfortunately, no matter how much I wanted to agree with this last comment, I was forced to admit to myself that I really didn't know that. Green was hoping, maybe, to convince me before the fact? And Somchai and Lee Duc Than were in Bangkok.

"One thing continues to bother me, Ken. When you went into the American consulate in Vientiane and left the note, why didn't you just stay there and ask for asylum?"

"What note?" he asked, astonished.

"The note. The one that got to Bath and the Pan Union people, the one your father confirmed was in your handwriting, the one that said you had Lee Duc Than and wanted to come home with him. The one that said you wanted me to come and bring the two of you in." I had always liked that expression, bring you in, since I first read it in the title of a spy novel years ago.

It was my turn to look astonished as he said, "I've never been near Vientiane in my life. I've never been to the consulate there or anywhere else. I've never written a note asking for help. They wouldn't allow it."

Shocked, I told him, "I saw the letter. Your father said it was from you."

"That's impossible," he said and I had no reason to disbelieve him.

While I was still working that out in my mind, he said, "We were able to read mind's you know. Kendra and I. Especially in college. She was always better at it than I was. I was never able to do it with anyone else and now I must have lost it altogether. Here she is, sick and hospitalized, and I never had the faintest inkling of her problem."

We descended into Hong Kong from the southwest, crossing Lantau Island, skirting Stone Cutter's Island, and lining up on Kai Tak's single runway after making a sharp right turn above crowded Kowloon. I looked at the bustling city below with its many shopping malls and told Horace what we would need. He still had his credit cards and as soon as we landed I sent him directly to Tsim Sha Tsui to make his purchases. Eddie and the luggage were dispatched by cab to the Shangri La, my warning ringing in his ears, one he repeated after hearing it. "You want me to keep a close eye, a very close eye, on the luggage? You expect some problem with the luggage?" He had the idea.

Green came with me to Harry Kee's haberdashery. It was time to find clothing suitable for the son of a Senatorial candidate. I wasn't surprised when Harry Kee himself hurried to meet us and then measured Ken for two suits, a sports jacket, shirts and slacks, matching ties, dress shoes and another pair for casual wear. Found him a combination topcoat-raincoat, a dark tan London Fog, all premium merchandise at premium prices. While one assistant toted up the prices, another finished the minor adjustments needed on one pair of pants, everything else right off the racks due to the constraints of time, and took the opportunity to tell Harry what else I would like to find.

Smiling, he glanced around his spacious richly appointed establishment to take in the dozen or more customers all being fitted and cared for, nodded to another assistant, and said, "Would you care to step into my office, for just a moment? We should discuss this in private."

His office was a blend of traditional dark mahogany and dark red fabric walls, expensive paintings, jade carvings, reminiscent of a fashionable London club where cigar smoke and Scots whisky would be most welcome. After we were seated in matching red leather chairs across a coffee table of teak and glass, he began by saying, "Your Mr. Green appears to be excited about going home." A man servant carrying an expensive humidor containing even more expensive Cuban cigars offered one to each of us. I didn't smoke but after looking at the wrapping, a Hoyo deMont Epicure #2, took one and before slipping it into a pocket said, "Do you mind? For an associate." Burrows. Harry Kee smiled, had no objection, took his own and lit up. The sound of automatic venting devices came on at once, the soft whirring ensuring that no odor whatsoever would contaminate the fine fabrics in the fitting rooms as the smoke was ushered through an intricate series of tubing and discharged outside into the afternoon air.

Kee's face was a picture of contentment but the look was deceptive. He was uneasy. "You understand, Dr. Osten, that this is something I normally do not handle. I must emphasize the do not. I choose not to."

He hadn't said he wouldn't.

"I can understand that but I was hoping that a man with your many contacts in Hong Kong, a man with an excellent reputation, could come up with what I need. I, in turn, want to emphasize that this is not for personal use, is not for resale, but is badly needed for an important business transaction. It is of the utmost urgency and I need it tonight or not later than very early tomorrow morning. Five or six o'clock. I recognize the problems that this might pose for you and I would, of course, expect to reimburse you for your trouble."

Flattery is never wasted and it is doubly effective when there is a price tag. Kee puffed thoughtfully, smoke spiraling above his head where it fell victim to the gentle air current to be whisked away. He seemed to be wrestling with a decision, or it may have been the price, because he finally said, "I may be able to help, but the cost would be significant. For what you need, perhaps as much as ten to fifteen thousand dollars, American."

I had expected it to be more. "I can't tell you that money is no object, Mr. Kee, as we both know that money is always an object, but that sum is reasonable." He smiled, leaned back, and puffed deeply.

It took another ten minutes to take care of the details and when I went back into the shop, Ken was sitting on a rosewood bench surrounded by wrapped packages and dressed in new slacks and a sports jacket. I handed the cashier my credit card and he swiped it through a machine, which took less than a minute to approve more than $3,500 in purchases, a minor miracle of technology and reckless affluence. I tucked the signed receipt into my wallet. Burrows would have to decide. Was this a gift or an expense? Hopefully the cigar would tip the balance in favor of reimbursement. It was even possible I could collect from Green's back army pay, if they decided to declare him alive again.

Eddie was to meet Harry Kee at the shop at midnight. I still had much to do, the most pressing of all being to find the ten to fifteen thousand dollars, American. I rarely carried that much cash around with me and my credit cards were all but tapped out.

Things had gone smoothly both at the hotel and in the mall. Eddie was checked in, the luggage gathered around him where he could see all of it, and Carmichael had purchased two sturdy Samsonite cases for Green's new wardrobe and a black Louis Vuitton bag, as near as I could tell, an exact replica of the one being used by Bath.

It was good to hear Lionel Smith's voice at the Hong Kong and Shanghai Bank. He was on the line, saying "Mike, how the hell are you and where the hell are you? I heard you went through town like a mystery man a week ago and I was hurt that you didn't call. The last time in, you said we'd go to Macao and hit the casinos. Still looking forward to it. And what's this nasty rumor printed in the South China News that someone took a shot at you at Kai Tak? That why you got out of town? A jealous husband or boyfriend?"

Don't let the name fool you. Lionel Smith. That's his real name, but his mother is Chinese and his father very British and Lionel is a true mixture, with a love for life and the good things it offered, as well as possessing a sharp financial mind that he must have inherited from the deceased Tristan Smith, along with a small fortune in stocks and bonds that Lionel had turned into a much larger fortune. Lily Smith, his mother, was very much alive, still beautiful, and probably breaking the heart of some fine gentleman at this very moment, a man hoping to marry beauty and money, only to discover one day that Lily had married once and decided that once and Lionel were enough. Lionel handled our banking, Osten-Burrows Inc., in the Far East.

A few pleasantries and I got right to the point. "Lionel, I need fifteen thousand dollars, American, this afternoon. In cash. Can you do it?"

"Ah hah," he chortled. "You've already been to the casinos and they've cleaned you out!"

"No casinos, Lionel. Not this trip. I just need cash."

"That much cash? What on earth for? Hey, not that your credit isn't good, Mike. It is. I had lunch yesterday with Tony Howsam and he says things are going well. Never been better, sales are up and you have several hot new drugs in the pipeline. You need money, we'll get you the money. By the way, I didn't dare believe everything Howsam was telling me. "

"Why not?" Tony was always reliable.

"He's in love. Never believe a man in love. Their view of life is distorted. Can't tell real from illusion. You knew about that, didn't you, Mike?

The girl from Macao, the Portuguese girl. Pretty, very pretty, and smart. Wish I had met her myself. Lily would have approved."

Love. I had my own problems with love. "About the money, Lionel? What about the money?"

"Oh, yeah, the money. That's no problem. What do you want it in? Big bills, little bills, huge bills?"

"How about one hundred dollar bills? A neat little stack of 150 one hundred dollar bills." There were a lot of one hundred dollar bills American floating around the Orient. Earlier in the trip, we had counted 5,000 of them up on the river. The unofficial currency of Asia.

"Got it. Do you want to pick it up, have me send it over, what?"

"Can you bring it to the Shangri La, like around six o'clock, and meet me for a drink in the lobby, by the piano player?"

"I can do that. No problem. I'll bring the paper work with me and you can sign it then."

"Ah, Lionel, no paper work and no signatures. Just a personal loan and a handshake. No record. Put it in a plain paper envelope, no markings of any kind, a rubber band around it. Don't lick the glue."

There was silence at the other end of the line while he digested the latest instructions. "Yeah, Mike, I can do that. What you want is, well, like you said, a personal loan, one that maybe can't be traced."

"Exactly."

He laughed, Lionel always saw the bright side of things, and said, "Sounds a little like some sort of spy business. A movie maybe? But, hey, let's do it. Anything else?"

"Actually, yes. Get some rubber gloves. Wear them when you put the money in the envelope."

More silence. "This is interesting. No fingerprints. No spit. No trace. Sure, I can get gloves. I'll see you at six. I'll be the one with the funny looking hands."

Leaving Eddie with the luggage, I caught a cab and took the tunnel over to Marcum-Whangpo on the Island. Seated across from Loretta Diaz, her desktop clear of everything except a slim manila folder, she radiated beauty and warmth wrapped in the professional's white laboratory coat. The beauty and warmth won out and it was easy to see how Tony might have fallen in love.

She had made copies of numerous reports for me and slid them across the desk. "First," she said, "the man in Chiang Mai. You were correct. He had tuberculosis and there is no sign of leprosy. You can see the results of the blood chemistries and cultures and here is the pathologist's report. We've been in contact with his doctors and they have transferred him to a tuberculosis center in Chiang Mai, continued the drug therapy you prescribed, and he is doing much better. He's eating, has gained weight, and his fever is all but gone. The other slides you sent from the material expressed from his ear was epithelial debris with keratin and a small amount of calcium. Nothing else."

"A sebaceous cyst, then, as I thought," I said. Which meant that Co Phan was not in Seattle, Alumni Association records notwithstanding. He was in Chiang Mai. "What about the patient in Bangkok? The one calling himself Lee Duc Than?"

She reached into a desk drawer and removed a second folder, much larger, and slapped x-ray films into viewing boxes along the side of one wall. "Here's what we have on him. These are the films you took in Laos, much better than we expected them to be by the way, considering that they were taken with a portable machine." Tapping two of the films, a lateral and anterior-posterior view displayed side by side, "right here, you can see diffuse pulmonary infiltration as well as large confluent lesions, there and there, and at first, our radiologists thought that these were metastasis from a distant primary tumor. Then they talked with your radiologist, a Doctor Emmett, and he reviewed the films and compared them to some taken many years ago. There were striking similarities. For instance, in both the old and new, there was hilar adenopathy and what Doctor Emmett described as a ground glass appearance. The major difference now is that the new films reveal much more extensive pulmonary changes, as if this is an ongoing process."

I interrupted. "Ongoing but slow, wouldn't you agree?"

"Definitely. Everyone was struck by that. Whatever it is, it's growing or progressing very slowly."

I scanned the work sheets, reviewing the blood count and chemistries once more. "Leukopenia, elevated serum uric acid, increased alkaline phosphatase and no eosinophiles," I said, more for myself than for Diaz. I went on to the next page. "Interesting," I muttered. "The ACE levels are elevated."

"Yes," she observed. "We noticed that. We've picked up elevated ACE levels in other patients such as those with histoplasmosis, acute tuberculosis, hyperthyroidism, even in lymphoma, so it may not be that important."

"Maybe, maybe not, but we're pretty sure this man doesn't have tuberculosis. He didn't react to the tuberculin test, the x-rays aren't typical of TB, and the cultures, it says here, are negative. We can rule it out. His thyroid levels are normal and a histoplasmin antibody test was negative. I see no clinical or laboratory evidence of lymphoma." She agreed. "What about the biopsy specimen from the injection sites on the two patients? The stuff that was carried so lovingly by the world's airlines all the way from Atlanta."

"I can show the slides to you in the lab if you'd care to go down," she offered.

I deferred. "I'm no pathologist. What did your own say?"

"There was nothing to see from the patient in Chiang Mai. No tissue reaction. Normal. On the other hand, the specimen from Bangkok was a revelation. Usually, you don't see this much tissue reaction until much later, but there was heavy infiltration of neutrophiles into the area, numerous huge monocytes could be seen, and there was extensive caseation and erosion along the margin of the specimen. We've made arrangements to have another specimen sent in a week and we'll take another look but meanwhile, I would have to say you were right once more."

"We're justified in making the diagnosis, then?" I asked. "He has sarcoidosis?"

"Almost certainly," she agreed. "Another biopsy or two would definitely confirm it, but even without them, I would have to say this man has sarcoid."

Which meant that Ken Green knew more than he had been telling me. Either he'd been lying or I hadn't been asking the right questions.

It was when I asked Loretta Diaz about Green's blood type that I sensed evasiveness. Tests, she said unconvincingly, weren't completed. Not here, not back in Bertinoldi's laboratory. "Maybe today or tomorrow," she expected to hear from him and about the same time, "we'll finish up here and compare notes."

She could tell from the look on my face that I knew she was avoiding a direct answer. I let it go when she asked, "You're returning to New York with Green in the morning? So soon? I'm sure by the time you get back, Bertinoldi will go over the results with you. He can bring you up to date personally." Clearly she was avoiding the issue, the bad news, and I was sure it would be bad coming from Bertinoldi.

She did, however, want to talk about Howsam. He'd been there, she confirmed, left almost two dozen specimens for analysis, and Marcum-Whangpo was already extracting and identifying them, especially one he had sent earlier from the Malaysian highlands which was already showing enormous inhibitory zones against fungi and bacteria. "Imagine," she exclaimed, "a single compound exhibiting activity against both, a combined antifungal and antibacterial antibiotic. That's exciting."

It was clearly a possible new product, assuming that side effects, everything had side effects, didn't wipe it out before it ever reached the market. I would have traded that bit of exciting news, though, for just the slightest hint that the search for a bone marrow donor had been a success.

When I returned to the Shangri La, I found Lionel waiting, already comfortably seated near the piano, listening to Chopin and sipping tea. I joined him, selected a strawberry covered something from the tray when offered, and held an inside pocket open as his gloved hand, not rubber, he had found a pair of Midwestern winter cotton ones somewhere, tucked the bulging unmarked envelope inside. I didn't think cotton conducted fingerprints, being somewhat new at this kind of business, but I doubted it. "You can leave the tip," he remarked as the bill came. Which I did, a generous one. Lionel and I agreed to meet for our visit to Macao on my next trip, date unspecified, as usual. He didn't ask what the money was for, knowing that I wouldn't have told him in any event. And, as it turned out, I didn't need it.

We were scheduled on an early morning flight for Tokyo, transferring there to a Los Angeles bound 747 and then flying on to New York after a change of planes to a 767. Bath and his depleted entourage were on the same plane. I saw him later that evening, at his request, at the bar in the Shangri La. He was obsessed over Ken Green. "I don't want this man to become a hero, Osten. He isn't one."

I knew that. Green himself never thought of being a hero. He considered himself a failure, a disappointment to his family and friends, and even more distressingly, to his country. He just wanted to return home and hopefully, find a life to make up for all that he had already lost. But his country was a strange place. It may not allow him to be the Ken Green of anonymity that I thought he would prefer and his own father was likely to be foremost among those demanding he be pushed front and center, as if to make up for lost time. And he still owed me; either the truth, or at the very least, an explanation for a story that just couldn't be. "Let it go, Bath. Let him go home and see how it all plays out." Good advice but Bath had too much to lose to take a chance on that. I knew it. He knew it. "Everyone is entitled to his fifteen minutes of fame. Let Green have his, then it will all die down and be forgotten." I was suggesting, subtly, that he leave Green alone. Bath wasn't into subtlety.

"The General won't allow it to die down, "he insisted. "Not running for the Senate, he won't. He'll keep it alive. You know that."

"Did it ever occur to you that if the General wins, he may feel he owes you a favor, Bath? After all, you helped bring his son back home." A lie, of course, because that was the last thing Bath had wanted to do, but a little white lie because my intentions were honorable. I wanted to get out of town with Green before things got ugly. I don't think I fooled Pan Union's chief at all.

He suddenly looked at his watch, a Rolex this time, and said derisively, "Sure, that would be nice, having a Senator owe me." He finished the drink in front of him and started out, "I'll see you in the morning then, I suppose. On the plane." We didn't shake hands.

I took the elevator upstairs, carefully checking the hallways for maids and service carts, and made it safely to bed, the alarm set for 11:15 P.M. I was dreaming about fingerprints, packages, and Loretta Diaz, and when the ringing awakened me, I was just about to invite her to dinner. The clock at bedside said 10:45 P.M., Eddie Chun was on the phone, and I was hungry.

"Boss, can you come down to Green's room?" was all he said. The urgency in his voice wiped away the lingering cobwebs of sleep and I was out the door in less than three minutes.

"I did like you said with the luggage. Put the name tag on Green's bag, locked the rest of ours in the room across the hall, and then we all went to dinner," Eddie outlined. "Then I went through the bags again when we came back and I found this," he said, holding up a flat, clear plastic bag filled with a white powder and carefully sealed with tape.

"Just this one?"

He lifted one corner of the lining against a side wall of the Samsonite and pointed to four identical bags, still nestled together like rabbits in a crowded hutch.

I lifted the one he had been holding and guessed its weight. A pound, a little more or less, the powder surprisingly heavy. Which meant five pounds, roughly two kilograms of white powder in plastic. I had a hunch the stuff wasn't powdered sugar or coffee creamer.

"Where's Green?"

"Next door with Horace," Eddie indicated with his chin.

"Get them in here," I said and Eddie opened the connecting door and called them in.

"Either of you seen this? Eddie tell you about it?" The blank looks on both were answer enough.

"OK, Eddie. Tell me exactly what you did this evening."

"Well, we ate, and then like you suggested, we all took a little walk along the esplanade and went down to the Pizza Hut, three or four blocks away." I had not recommended the Pizza Hut although the walk was my idea.

"And then?"

"We had a pizza."

"You had a gourmet meal in one of Hong Kong's finest restaurants and thirty minutes later, you walked three blocks and ate a pizza?" I asked incredulously, the plastic bags forgotten for the moment.

Sheepishly, Eddie explained, "Green hadn't had a good pizza in a long time and he," pointing to Horace, "loves pizza, so we had a pizza. That's all we had though. One big one, with pepperonis and mushrooms."

"All right, forget the pizza. Then what happened?"

"We walked back, came up to the rooms, and then I checked the bags again, like you said to do."

Green was looking on, confused. I asked him, "Before you went to dinner, you packed everything?"

He nodded yes.

"You didn't see these bags in the suitcase?"

"Of course not," he answered angrily. "The suitcase was empty. It was brand new."

Ignoring the anger, just collecting the facts, I asked, "When you came back from the walk, you and Carmichael went next door while Eddie came in here to check the suitcase, right?"

"That's right. Yes, he told me to stay next door while he checked the room."

"Let's clarify all of this now. Eddie, you checked the rooms and luggage before you went out to dinner?'

"Right."

I continued. "This room is registered to Green?"

Again, right.

"This suitcase has a tag with Green's name on it. You put it there," directing my question to Eddie once more. Right. "Empty before dinner, containing strange merchandise after dinner, and none of us put it there." Right. "And unless we do something to get rid of it, we could face serious trouble, like jail." Emphatically, right. The question was, how much time did we have? Bath's Rolex was ticking. Clever, really, I was his alibi, as the merchandise had arrived while he and I were together in the bar. Which also meant that he was my alibi, so maybe we had a little longer than I thought. But it was a gamble.

Carmichael, who had spent the trip in the relative comforts of civilization, the only intrigue being how to work the basketball down to the low post, remained mystified while Ken Green and Eddie understood all too well what the problem was. He became involved when I asked, "Horace, the second Samsonite is exactly like this one?"

"Yes, that's what you wanted, wasn't it? Two identical suitcases."

"Where is it?"

"Across the hall in the other room. The one registered to Bill Laimbeer. He's not really here, is he? I'd like to meet him."

Eddie answered for me, looking at Carmichael in disbelief as he said, "He hasn't checked in yet. When he does, I'll try to set up an introduction."

We repacked Green's belongings into the second Samsonite, took the name tag from bag number one and put it on bag number two, and hauled the black Louis Vuitton from its safe haven in Laimbeer's room. "Eddie, take a pair of rubber gloves from my medical bag, you still have my medical bag I hope, put them on and wipe these plastic bags clean. NO fingerprints. Then stuff them inside this bag, here, hiding them under the lining on the bottom. See how it can be pulled loose, right there."

"All five of the bags," he asked.

"All five, Eddie. We don't want any of them around, that's the whole point."

By then, it was almost midnight so I called Harry Kee. He was a good listener, every now and then making a comment such as, "Repeat that" or "Are you sure that's what you want?" or "what time do you want them to be there?" and then, with the slightest hesitation in his voice, "Yes, I can arrange it. It will be difficult but certainly not impossible. Nothing is impossible." All at a fraction of the previously agreed upon price.

In fact, he was relieved at not being required to supply the heroin. "I have it if you need it," he said, "but it will be no problem to send it back where it came from. Don't worry about the rest, I can take care of it. Just repeat that one last item again." I did and he chuckled. "Now won't that be a surprise?"

"I hope so," I told him and hung up. Once off the phone, I warned the other three, "Keep only the clothing you're going to wear in the morning, plus your shaving stuff. Pack everything else. Someone will be here in fifteen minutes to pick up the luggage."

Eddie looked at his watch and I cold see him thinking. Luggage to the airport eight hours before check-in? I nodded, yes, Eddie, right now. "All of it, ours and the Louis Vuitton."

Actually, it wasn't going to Kai Tak, only to Harry Kee's establishment on Nathan Road. I extracted forty crisp hundreds from the envelope deposited in my pocket by Lionel, using my unprotected fingers as fingerprints on the envelope no longer mattered. I took a larger manila envelope from my carry-on, inserted the remaining currency, addressed it, added a brief note, which said, "Lionel, thanks for the emergency loan. Didn't need it all. Check for $4,000 to follow. Dinner on me in Macao. Mike," and sealed it. Called the front desk, tipped the bellhop $20 to take the envelope down for the concierge to post with the morning mail. Minutes later, two additional bellhops arrived with a luggage rack and carted everything away to a back elevator, $40. They carried away with them an envelope with twenty hundreds intended for Harry Kee. The money would reach him. These were his men. The twenty leftover hundreds I tucked inside my wallet, just-in-case money.

The General was at lunch, and he recognized at once that none of this was going to work quite right unless he did his part, too. "This is a dangerous game you're playing, Mike," he warned. Spare me, I thought. I was probably the only character in this whole damn drama that wasn't playing a game.

Choosing my words carefully, I said, "General, I know what you've been able to do from back there. You've been pulling strings. You have to pull one more."

Speaking just as carefully, he replied, "I don't know what you mean, Mike. This has been your show!"

A lie, but if it was my show, I intended to give one more order. "Make the call, General. Make it now! If you want Ken to come home and if you ever expect to sit in the United States Senate, do it."

I thought we had lost the connection. That maybe the line had gone dead, but no, he was only thinking. Quietly, he made the deal. "I can make a call," I heard him say. He didn't say to whom, he didn't have to. All he had to do was make it.

Then he was gone – the line dead. I sighed. There was nothing to do right now except sleep and see what happened in the morning. Except that I couldn't fall asleep. Eddie, Carmichael, and Green were all locked up tight in Laimbeer's room, Eddie to stay awake until four, Carmichael to replace him on sentry duty at that time, and all of us to meet for breakfast at seven. I should have asked the General about Kendra, but I hadn't. I feared Diaz's evasiveness was a forecast for bad news and I didn't want to hear it. I wanted to see Kendra, tell her that I missed her, and hold her hand once more. I fell asleep, somewhere around five, having watched four episodes of Bonanza dubbed in Chinese. I had no idea what was going on with Little Joe and Hoss, being totally preoccupied with all that could go wrong after daylight.

What happened was, nothing went wrong. Call it excellent planning or call it luck, or fate, but the next morning while Green, whose appetite was increasing exponentially day by day, polished off a plate of eggs, hash browns, and bacon with biscuits, and Carmichael was demolishing fruit and oatmeal, Eddie walked through the lobby accompanied by one of the Harry Kee bellhops from the night before and flashed me a thumbs up sign indicating that all was well. Twenty minutes later, he joined us at the front entrance where a puzzled doorman was placing my medical bag and one small carry-on into the cavernous Mercedes trunk. Nothing else to do, I told him and tipped him $20. We had watched Bath, Canby, and four other Pan Unionists leave five minutes earlier, the trunk of their limousine bulging with bags. I had no idea what they had tipped but it should have been much more.

"Magellan?" I asked.

"Hasn't left yet," Eddie answered, "but I saw him talking to the bell captain so he's ready to leave. Probably be right behind us."

A skycap with an empty cart met us at the west entrance to the terminal. He, too, appeared surprised at the paucity of our possessions, but carefully placed them aboard and wheeled his way through the door, the four of us following. I wasn't surprised to find Inspector Fong matching us stride for stride when we were less than fifty feet inside the terminal. "Doctor Osten, how nice it is to see you once again," he said, all sincerity and tourist friendly.

I greeted him as an old friend, "Inspector, how very nice to see you again as well. I was afraid we might be going to miss you this trip. Another short visit, as you no doubt know. Rush, rush all the time."

Still smiling pleasantly, he said, "I can understand that. We have the same problem here in Hong Kong. Work, work. Never enough time to catch up. I'm sure you must be happy to be traveling with a man who is returning home after so many years. I take it this is your Mr. Green who is traveling on temporary papers assembled by your embassy in Bangkok?" He was looking at Ken, waiting for confirmation. I introduced them as we continued walking towards the check-in counter.

But now the Inspector was steering us to one side and he was joined by two of his men, clearly indicating that he wanted us to join him in an office straight ahead. "I must check Mr. Green's papers," he explained.

I protested. It would not have been good form not to. "Inspector, his papers are all in order, as you know from his arrival yesterday. Why do you need to bother again?"

"No bother, Doctor," he said blandly, "just a formality."

Kidding no one, most of all himself. The almost empty luggage cart bothered him. "You seem to be traveling very light," he observed. "Is this all of your luggage?"

I threw back my head as if that was highly amusing and said, "Good heavens no, Inspector. It would be nice to travel that lightly but unfortunately, it's not possible. We sent everything ahead. It should be at check-in by now." If Harry Kee ran an on-time delivery service.

Carmichael and a constable went to fetch it while we went inside the nearest room, the inspector fumbling indifferently with Green's papers, and waited. In a matter of minutes, the cart was back, our luggage piled atop and the Inspector viewed it carefully and removed the obviously new Samsonite. "You don't mind if I examine the luggage?" he asked, knowing perfectly well that it didn't matter if we cared or not.

Still, I managed to look offended. "Is something wrong, Inspector? This is not normally done, is it? I mean, you don't normally prowl through the dirty laundry of visitors leaving Hong Kong, or do you?"

"Not normally," he admitted, "but this isn't to be a normal day, I'm afraid. We've been asked to exercise a little extra vigilance today, but as usual, they don't tell us why." I bet. "So you don't mind if I look, then, do you?"

My cheerful and ready acquiescence seemed to surprise him. "Not at all, Inspector. We're early for the flight so do what you have to do."

They were thorough in their work and it didn't take long. They paid extra attention to the Samsonite, even removing the lining from the sides and bottom, scrutinizing every pocket, examining every inch. They found nothing.

I registered another protest, stronger this time. "Really, Inspector, this is extraordinary. I've never seen anything like this. Look at the damage your men are doing to Mr. Green's suitcase. Are they deliberately ruining it?"

Both of his constables were looking at him as I spoke, hands at their sides, their meaning clear. "Nothing here. What now?"

Fong was not quite ready to admit defeat. "Does Mr. Green have additional luggage?"

"Inspector, you are looking at Mr. Green's luggage. What is left of it. All of his worldly possessions are now strewn across the table in front of you. He has just come back from captivity and everything he has was purchased right here in Hong Kong less than 24 hours ago."

"Including the suitcase?" he asked.

"Yes, that, too. As a matter of fact, Horace, show him the receipt." And Horace produced a Visa card receipt, showing the purchase of one Samsonite two suiter, model 44, dated one day earlier. "Mr. Carmichael put it on his card," I explained. "Mr. Green still has no card of his own, as you can imagine."

Fong examined the slip of paper, noted something on his pad, and handed it back. "Thank you for making that available to me," he apologized. "The clothing, as you said, it all appears to be new."

"It is," I assured him. "Do you need receipts for that as well?" and I started fumbling in my pockets as if on the search for more Visa charges.

I was hoping to leave Harry Kee's business out of this and was relieved when Fong waved me off, saying, "No, that won't be necessary." He paused and finally decided, "I'm truly sorry for any inconvenience this may have caused you. I hope all of you have a safe journey home. And Mr. Green, I hope your return to America is an especially happy one." Strangely enough, I think he was sincere.

Of course, we left without revealing that Carmichael had purchased a second Samsonite, for cash, a mile further down Nathan Road the previous afternoon. Right now, most likely still contaminated by traces of heroin, it was in the possession of a seller of fake Rolex wristwatches and Gucci handbags, plying his trade in a Kowloon back alley, a place where Hong Kong police seldom ventured. I hoped.

The phlegmatic skycap reloaded our luggage onto the cart and we resumed our interrupted march to the check-in counter, a path that led us directly in front of another doorway which suddenly opened to reveal a dozen or more men, some in the uniform of a constable and others dressed in dark blue business suits. What caught my eye was the black Louis Vuitton bag in the firm grasp of a uniformed Hong Kong policeman and the set of handcuffs snugged around the wrists of a man wearing a sparkling Movado wrist-watch on his left arm. He was well dressed, his hair slicked back, and he appeared to be uttering a vocal protest. His words, however, were having little effect upon the stony faced officers that seemed bent on hustling him to the nearest exit, the one where the police car with the revolving red and blue lights waited.

Fong, having finished with us, now joined the group just inside the office door, leaving four confused Pan Unionists standing outside. Canby was off to one side with a matron. Disbrow, limping slightly, walked towards her, but was restrained by a constable. Before we lost sight of this interesting tableau, one man, the one talking to Fong, slowly turned and looked in our direction. He had an overcoat carefully folded over his arm, he was wearing a hat, and he was not Chinese. His features looked familiar and I wondered where I had seen him before. He avoided making eye contact with me, looked directly at Ken Green, and from the corner of my eye, I saw Green looking back. They nodded to one another simultaneously, in recognition.

Moments later, in the general confusion of checking in, Green sidled up to me and said, "Did you see the man with the handcuffs?" I nodded. "That was Towel. Or Bath, as you call him. What do you suppose they wanted him for?" Ken Green. Mr. Innocent.

Eddie responded, having overheard. "Jeez. He must have done something wrong. Maybe even broke a law." Mr. Chun, the cynic.

There were a number of empty seats in first class. Six of them, corresponding to the number of Pan Unionists we had seen standing around in confusion at Kai Tak; five with their hands in their pockets, and one with his hands in handcuffs. A seventh, Magellan, didn't seem surprised to find Bath and the others absent. Quite the contrary, he walked aboard with hardly a care in the world, took his seat in the rear of the cabin, accepted a complimentary drink, downed it in a single gulp, and went to sleep. Or seemed to, at least, thus avoiding conversation although I knew of no one wanting to speak to the Explorer, so the sleep act may have been unneeded.

I sat at the very front with Ken Green, one more opportunity to see if his story would come unglued.

Armed with the x-ray and pathology reports from Diaz, I went to the heart of the matter without any delay, not even waiting until after beverage service. "Ken," I began, "the man you refer to as Lee Duc Than is really Ho Phan Van. You've mentioned him, he spent time at the University, and you claim he is dead. He isn't. He's in the hospital bed in Bangkok." Why weren't any of these men in the right bed, I wondered? "So the man you say rescued you from a prison camp and who was supposed to be a North Vietnamese official is someone else. You must have known that."

He didn't challenge me, merely asking, "How can you be sure of that?"

"Look, I kept records. Still have them. They show that almost twenty-five years ago, I treated a student with a persistent cough and I sent him to the Health Service for a chest x-ray. At that time, the radiologist reported the films as being normal and when I looked at them, I saw nothing unusual either. But there was something there that we both missed and recently, another radiologist looked at the old films, pointed out what he saw, and we made new films at Yellow Garden. They've been compared, the old and the new, and the man definitely has sarcoidosis. He had it twenty-five years ago, an early case, and he has it now, progressive and much worse. But sarcoidosis is a relatively rare disease and it's unlikely that I saw two Vietnamese students with the same condition in a matter of a couple of weeks. The man I saw then is the same man now. His name is Ho Phan Van."

He didn't deny the possibility even then, asking instead, "Is it catching?"

What a strange question! "No, it almost certainly isn't catching, although we're not certain of the cause. Many investigators," I was beginning to sound like a professor now, "think that there is some defect in the modulation of the immune response after exposure to an antigen. That sets off a number of reactions leading to tissue fibrosis, probably related in some unknown manner to interleukins as well as to T and B cell activity, all of which stimulates the production of chemotactic and colony-stimulating factors, which recruit monocytes, the monocytes becoming the building blocks for granulomas which are the hallmark of the disease." I doubted that he understood all of that. I only understood part of it myself. "It's mainly a respiratory disease," I told him, moving to an area he could more readily understand, "although other organs can become involved. It occurs in anywhere from 1 in 10,000 to 1 in 2,500 Americans equally divided between men and women, and is about three times as prevalent in African-Americans as it is among whites. Obviously, Vietnamese can have it, too."

"And you found it confined to his lungs?" he questioned. He was frowning and now I was almost certain he hadn't followed everything I had told him, but he surprised me by rightly recognizing that the main problem was in the lungs. I went on, hoping to clarify the illness but concerned that I would only confuse him even more.

"Mostly. He may have some cardiac involvement because of an occasional irregular heart beat and his kidneys may be damaged, according to early changes in the urine. But primarily, it's the lungs. There are a couple of changes in the blood studies so I still worry about liver damage. We'll have to follow those. As you know, he was weak and short of breath at Yellow Garden, but most of that may have been from malnutrition and dehydration. That should improve quickly, already had improved by the time we reached Bangkok, and can only get better now that he's under appropriate care."

"How do you treat it?"

"Like I said," still the professor, "with intravenous fluids and antibiotics, vitamins, and a good diet, of course. Because of the compromised lung function, we'll be using prednisone, starting with a fairly heavy dose and tapering it over a year or more, depending upon his response. Ho Phan Van should respond fairly well and be able to get up and about in fairly short order. He's not that old; he's just rundown."

He was speaking so softly that I almost missed what he said, but what it sounded like was, "Ho Phan Van is dead."

I wondered how he could possibly have learned that, seeing the patient was still alive, in the hospital, when we left Bangkok one day earlier. Huy Thacht! Had he gotten past AcChan's security? I started to protest when I realized he wasn't finished.

"He died five years ago, maybe longer, in the reeducation camp where they imprisoned him. He never would admit the error of his ways. Lee Duc Than pleaded with him, begged him to make a token admission of guilt, so he could be moved and ultimately freed. He refused, sent Lee Duc Than away, telling him that he wanted nothing to do with a man, or a people, that had betrayed their own. It was when Ho Phan Van died that Lee Duc Than decided to flee and to take me with him. Even in death, Lee Duc Than was proud of his friend. He told me, 'He won the battle of the heart and he was right. I betrayed my own people. Out of fear. Not out of righteousness or conviction, but because of fear.' Lee Duc Than felt that by leaving Vietnam, he was helping Ho Phan Van win a small victory."

It was a nice try, another interesting spin, but there was the little matter of records, all of which said I had never seen Lee Duc Than and that Ho Phan Van wasn't dead, that the dead man must have been someone else, if indeed anyone had died at all. Musical chairs and musical beds and no record of Lee Duc Than. I told Green exactly that.

"You always come back to your records, Mike, as if they are some kind of Bible."

"They are my Bible, Ken, that's why we keep them. And mine say I never saw your benefactor."

He stared me straight in the eyes and said, "Your records are wrong. But it wasn't your fault."

"Wrong? You want to explain?" I challenged.

"When Lee Duc Than had a cough that wouldn't go away, he called your office and told them he had to see the doctor. He was asked what health insurance he had. None, he told them. How would he pay, they asked? How much, he wanted to know, and they quoted a figure he knew he couldn't meet. He wasn't enrolled in the University at the time so couldn't go to the health service, had no job, so money was always short. He couldn't even speak good English at the time so he asked Ho Phan Van what to do. His friend said, I'll go with you, I have health insurance from a part time job and maybe they'll let me pay. Someone in your office did better than that, they just wrote down Ho Phan Van's name on the records, sent the bill to his health insurance company, you saw Lee Duc Than and never knew it. That's all there was to it. Ho Phan Van was never a patient of yours. Lee Duc Than was."

It was possible that the ghost of my ex-office manager had just reentered my life. It was exactly the kind of switch Clark Wherrington might have pulled. Lee Duc Than had offered to have fingerprints settle the matter of identity. It looked like a better idea now than it had earlier. And dental records. We could check those, too, to look for a gold tooth.

Well now, if Ho Phan Van was dead, and I had to consider that possibility in light of this new story, and Co Phan was in Chiang Mai while Lee Duc Than was in Bangkok, then who was in Seattle? The name Truang Van Dang, former South Vietnamese secret police official turned North Vietnamese defector, instantly came to mind. How nice to think that he might be living in style in our Pacific Northwest. Even a life of poverty would be much too good for him.

And suddenly, as if tired of sarcoidosis and Ho Phan Van, Ken Green, for the first time, showed the proper depth of sibling concern for the desperate plight of his twin sister. "What happened to Kendra? How did she find out she was ill?"

Another brief lecture. "Fatigue, initially. Tired, short of breath, usually late in the day, then she noticed that her gums were bleeding after she brushed her teeth. Her dentist found nothing wrong with her teeth and she went to her physician. He did a blood count, found anemia which can be caused by many things, especially in women. Eight months earlier, though, all blood studies had been normal at an annual checkup, and one test followed another until a hematologist, a blood doctor, made a diagnosis of myelodysplastic syndrome. All too often, that goes on to become an acute leukemia and that's where we are now."

"How often is all too often?"

He winced when I told him the truth. "At least thirty to forty percent of the time."

"A transfusion could save her?" he asked, apparently understanding the gravity of the situation, maybe for the first time.

"Not a transfusion, Ken. A bone marrow transplant. Actually, that's something of a misnomer because although they do remove bone marrow cells from the donor, they actually transfuse them into the recipient's veins in just about the same way they give a transfusion. What we've been hoping is that your blood type is a close enough match so that you can be the donor. Take some cells from you, drip them into Kendra, and stand back. You make new ones, she uses the ones you loaned and if lucky, she makes new ones, too."

"And then they get better," he asked hopefully.

I hated to give him another 40% estimate, it sounded so dismal, so I hedged, "A lot of them get better. A lot of them. Let's just hope that your blood is a match so we can get it done." Why hadn't Diaz given me the results that must have been in her file folder? "I'll be calling the hematologist as soon as we land in California and he should be able to tell us what we have to know."

I was asleep, dreaming of sunswept beaches and soft music, alone, when I came awake, trembling, cold sweat on my face. My hands, moments before desperately holding onto Kendra's, were locked tightly onto the armrests of the spacious seats. Blood had been unable to find its way into the fingers and I was afraid I had lost both hands, they were so numb. While I was waiting for the tingling to disappear and the color to return, the 747 encountered severe turbulence and the huge plane was tossed about, a matchstick swept along by the frenzied spring thaw, and I feared that a storm drain might be somewhere ahead where we would be lost. I was comforted when Eddie peered down at me and asked, "You all right, Boss? I thought I heard you say something."

The plane passed through the turbulence, of course, just as my emotional turbulence faded, and I walked the length of the plane to clear my mind. I collected a diet drink on the way past the galley and returned to my seat. "Ken, I wouldn't say anything right now about Bath being at Yellow Garden. In fact, I wouldn't mention Yellow Garden at all. The press will be waiting in Los Angeles and they'll have a million questions. Wait until you get home and see the General before answering. Tell them you're too tired right now. I'll verify that you're weak, need rest, shouldn't answer questions for a while." Actually, in his present state, it was the truth. "Talk to the General or his representatives before you make any statements. That would be the best course."

"I'm not a traitor, Mike. You're making it sound like I have something to hide. I didn't sell out my country."

I explained what I considered to be a fundamental aspect of life. "Ken, we all have something to hide. All of us. Often we don't know what it is. But it's out there. Just keep quiet for now. Don't talk about Bath and Fantus. Don't mention the name Yellow Garden. Don't bring it up. All of that is a can of worms." Well, that was about all I could do. Hell, I couldn't put a gag on him. Chun and Carmichael were no problem, Chun because he was naturally taciturn. Carmichael, on the other hand, knew nothing. Can't be any safer than that. Well, almost nothing. I knew he wouldn't be going around town talking about shopping trips in Hong Kong. If anything, he would look for Magic Johnson instead. Me, I had absolutely nothing to say. Unless they wanted to talk about Osten-Burrows. Then, ladies and gentlemen of the press, turn on your tape recorders.

When we deplaned, they were waiting at last. The press. Newspaper reporters, cameramen, radio reporters with microphones forming a thicket of electronic underbrush, everyone and everything trying to get at Ken Green. They ran alongside, shouting questions as Green, who despite my warnings of what lay ahead, still seemed dazed by the din and confusion all around. I noted with satisfaction, though, that even as he was ushered through customs as efficiently as visiting royalty or a reigning movie star, he said nothing. Minutes later, he was escorted to a waiting limousine, shielded by a cordon of uniformed deputies, a dark suited man with wrap around sunglasses on either side. Escorted by three police motorcycles, blue lights flashing, the limousine pulled smoothly away from the terminal. First it had been AcChan's men, then Harry Kee's, and now the General's, all providing escort for the returning Ken Green. Sooner or later, he would have to walk alone, on his own. But not yet. Too much at stake.

With their primary prey safely away, several enterprising reporters were looking around for someone to interview to justify the lunch time expense account at one of the terminal's many bars. Who better than to find someone who had crossed the Pacific with the returning Ken Green? They looked at me, turned away, at Chun and looked elsewhere, and finally one of them fastened his gaze onto Carmichael and headed directly for him. "Aren't you –," he began.

"Yeah man, that's me. Horace Carmichael." He had done it again, shifting effortlessly into his famous 'aw shucks' routine. "You probably recognize me from when I was playing college and pro hoops. Man, them were the days." It always worked on interviewers who had forgotten who he was and was just as effective on those who had never known who he was. The baffled reporter, a political analyst, was one of the latter, and he clicked off his recorder and strode away, still looking for the bar.

"Man," Horace laughed, watching the sight of the retreating back, "we might as well be anonymous."

"Horace," said Eddie, "this may come as news to you, but we *are* anonymous."

But even anonymous people can use the phone, if you have a calling card. I took mine and went to find the Northwest lounge where I could put it to use.

# 20

I didn't see either the General or Ken Green again until after the funeral, eleven days later. I never again saw Kendra alive. My last memory of her was a lingering good-bye kiss as I left her at the hospital, my fresh bouquet of flowers still visible behind her shoulder, a splash of color in a white vase. That kiss, that one kiss, was the final kiss. The end. When had that been, a mere three weeks earlier?

I had begun to suspect the worst in Hong Kong when Loretta Diaz avoided eye contact when talking about Ken's blood type. Suspicion hardened when the General danced around the issue during the phone call from Los Angeles and then became a certainty when I heard Bertinoldi's, "She's critical," delivered in a detached and impersonal manner that means there is no hope. Even then, with him anxious to pull away and "return to his patients," I was compelled to ask, "Did we get a match? Ken Green's blood type? Was it a match?"

"No, it wasn't a match. We wouldn't have been able to use his marrow even if it hadn't been too late." He made it sound like it was my fault. Perhaps sensing that, he added, "Don't feel too badly about it. You tried." Then hung up.

Of course it wasn't my fault. Genetics, genes, chromosomes, they were at fault. I hadn't given the Green's their blood types. That was decided at conception by others, sheer chance. Genetic roulette. When I put down the phone, I was desolated. I sat in the huge international terminal with tears streaming down my face, a grown man with nothing better to do. Scores of weary travelers caught up in their own personal happiness or tragedies, glanced at me and quickly turned away, not wanting to be involved.

Except for Eddie. He came over, took the phone from me, hung it up, and put a hand on my shoulder. He didn't say anything. He didn't have to. He was there. Kendra died a day later, never regained consciousness after lapsing into a coma, and I was advised it was best if I remembered her as she had been, not as she was then.

At the funeral, I had little opportunity to talk to the General. He was surrounded by political and military power brokers, forming a protective ring around one of America's brightest new stars. Jordan had announced his candidacy and received almost universal acclaim from all sides. Everyone agreed that with his record, a rediscovered son at his side, and coping bravely with personal tragedy, as he was, he was unbeatable. There would be no opposition in the primaries and he was a shoo-in for the fall election. He was, in a word, the next United States Senator from his state.

At the funeral home, I shook his hand, uttered the usual condolences, was ready to move on when he surprised me by turning to the men on either side of him and saying, "Will you excuse me for a moment," and then, touching my arm lightly, led me into a heavily paneled anteroom off to one side and closed the door. He briefly embraced me and stepped back, the two of us looking at one another uncertainly for a moment. "Mike, thank you for bringing Ken back. Now that his mother and Kendra have left us, he's all I have. He looks well, don't you think?"

I agreed, searching for the words that I knew had to be said. I hesitated, wondered if this was the time or place, and as he turned away to return to the casket once more, said, "Jordan, you used me."

He stopped, one hand on the brass knob, and slowly turned to face me, his face expressionless, his eyes hard. "I'm not certain I know what you mean, Mike, about being used."

"The lies and deceptions, Jordan, a long string of them, from the very beginning. Nothing but lies."

He removed his hand from the doorknob and stepped closer to me. "Lies and deceptions? What kind of lies and deceptions are you referring to?"

"Let's start with the biggest lie of all. The lie that Ken sent a handwritten note asking for help. Asking for me. You and your experts confirmed the note as being in his handwriting. That's a lie. He never wrote any note. Not a word."

"Mike, I showed you the note. You saw it. Kendra saw it."

"Damn you, Jordan! Leave her out of it. It was either a forgery or an outright fake. I didn't know what his handwriting looked like and she never had a chance to examine it because she was ill. Anyone who saw it just assumed that you wouldn't lie and that his handwriting might have changed in fifteen years. They took your word for it and you lied!"

"Why are you saying this, Mike? Why now?"

"Because your son himself denies he ever was in Vientiane. He denies ever having written anything to you or anyone else. So it was a lie."

He was standing erect, rigidly erect, taut, but under control. He had been under stress before, had always controlled it, had risen high in his profession without snapping, and was aiming even higher now. I had become a threat to those ambitions.

"But an even greater lie was this. You've known for some time that Ken was alive. That he wasn't dead. Yet you waited until now to mount an aggressive effort to bring him back home. Why? To bolster your campaign for the Senate? To use him, like you've used me?"

He hadn't expected this. The fake note, maybe, but not this. His face had been drained of blood and he trembled slightly, but recovered quickly to say, "Mike, I'll deny all of this, you know that, and I suspect you'll have a hard time proving any of your accusations." The implication was clear, Ken would keep quiet. "But yes, I've suspected that Ken was alive for a couple of years now. A rumor here and there, a suggestion and a brief report or two, but we had no proof. That's why we needed you. You could prove it was Ken, you would be able to recognize him and treat him if he needed medical care. In that sense, you were used, but it was in a good cause. And I was sincere in my thanks a moment ago. You did a good job. I needed you once more, like I did before, and you came through. I knew you would."

He was still using me. That good cause he was talking about, that was his cause.

I stopped him again as he reached for the knob by saying, "It was Broward, wasn't it?"

He took a deep breath but didn't turn. I didn't think he would respond at all but he finally did. "Broward? My old top sergeant? What on earth would he have to do with any of this?" He left the door open and I followed him out.

Burial was up the Hudson, near Nyack, on a bluff overlooking the river. Kendra was laid to rest alongside her mother, beside a huge oak, whose foliage would shelter them on hot summer days, protect them from winter's cold wind. We watched somberly under the leafless giant as the priest spoke his words and sprinkled holy water over the casket. Mourners drifted away to waiting automobiles in a timeless scene that Norman Rockwell could have captured so well but to my knowledge, had chosen to avoid.

Everyone who was anyone had come. The rich and powerful, the politicians and ward heelers that Jordan was soon to know all too well, townsfolk who had known the Green's in pre-military days, men who had served under the General in numerous campaigns, and the curious with nothing better to do. And of course, Eddie, Horace, Marge, Burrows, Howsam, and me. Plus hordes of reporters and commentators who recognized a good story when they saw it or made up their own if they didn't. This, of course, was a story with a capital S.

Ken Green intercepted me on the way to our cars. We stood to one side as the others went on. "I didn't have a chance to talk to you last night," he said. "I owe you a great deal of gratitude for saving my life. I doubt if I ever would have left Yellow Garden alive if you hadn't come."

I didn't believe that. The General would have found another way, although Ken may not know it now. I wanted to tell him that he didn't owe me a thing. I had felt the same way years earlier when I credited his father with saving my life and look what it had led to. Too many entanglements, a sense of unfulfilled obligation. A debt that can never be paid off. Something that never ends.

I didn't tell him that, of course. I just said, "Repay me by making the best possible use of your life that you can. You've lost too many years already so I know you have a lot of catching up to do. Dedicate it to Kendra. She missed you."

"She may have missed me, Mike, but she loved you. At first I thought it was just a kid's crush on an older man. Only it didn't end and she continued to feel the same way, right up until the end. She spent the last few days of her life writing you this note. We found it on her bedside table after she died." He handed me a pale blue envelope, her light floral scent still present. She'd written and I hadn't even sent a card.

He handed me something else. A small package, velvet box inside, golden draw strings guarding the top. I opened it and found three stones inside; a blue sapphire flashing its brilliance despite the wintry day; a blood red ruby, speaking of infinite love; a sea green emerald, bold enough to dazzle one and all. All three were huge, priceless. Well, everything has a price, even love and loyalty, but the value of these stones could not be measured in dollars.

"They're for you," he told me. "From Yellow Garden. This is what I did there. I found stones like these. I wanted you to see. I want you to believe."

They were almost too beautiful to contemplate. I offered them back to him but he drew his hand away. "Ken, I can't take these. They must be worth a small fortune."

"They're yours. I brought one home for Kendra. She's gone and I want you to have it." He saw the question in my eyes and answered, "The other two? My grubstake I guess. What I was going to use to pay the bills while I looked for work. I don't need them. Jordan has other plans for me."

"Where did these come from, Ken? We're not at Yellow Garden now and Huy Thacht didn't send them as a present."

He laughed, the first laugh I'd seen from him in a long while. "In my pocket. They came back with me all the way. Don't you remember, everyone was so busy looking at suitcases that they never bothered to check our pockets. At least mine. They're pocket change, you could say."

He might have been joking, but then again maybe not. They were exceptional stones, I decided, took one more look at them, pulled the draw strings tight and put the bag in my pocket. I was almost to my car when he called, "That ruby. Have that made into a ring for your JoElle. She may deal in gems but she's never going to own a finer stone than that one. Call her, tell her what you're doing, and then do it." He drove away, and as they passed a row of parked limousines from another funeral, I caught a brief glimpse of the driver. Not enough to be certain, but he bore an amazingly resemblance to McLemore. McLemore the son, not the father. Later, I wondered how Ken had known of JoElle. Had I talked about her without meaning to?

Montgomery was standing by alongside my rented Crown Victoria, everyone else having departed. "Thanks for waiting, Montgomery," I greeted him. His face was as frozen as that of the sculpted angel on the nearby headstone. "I didn't wish to bother the General at a time like this but there is some information that I want him to have. I am sure he can pass it on to the proper authorities." Montgomery may have been angry at me for confronting his employer the night before but he would see that my information did indeed reach his ears. "There is a man living in Seattle who calls himself Co Phan. He isn't. The real Co Phan is in Chiang Mai, much too ill to travel. The man in Seattle is most likely Truang Van Dang, a former South Vietnamese double agent who spent time at the University as a student, served in the Hanoi secret police or intelligence service, and who now has taken up residence in our country. It should be checked out. Do you have that? Got the name spelled correctly?"

Of course he had it, every word and the correct spelling as well. The loyal retainer would see that the information was properly and promptly relayed. What happened after that depended upon a lot of things such as who really was in Seattle, and if it happened to be Truang Van Dang, what was he doing there? As I'd learned long ago, things are not always what they seem to be. So I did what had to be done. Now let the professionals take over.

"Yes, sir, I have it all. And before you leave, I have a request to pass on from the General."

"A request? Of me?"

"Yes, sir. The General would like you to be a member of his campaign committee, for the primary and general election, both. He would very much like you to join him in his effort to renew the faith of the American people in the electoral process. He said to tell you."

He stood waiting for a response. I gave him one, leaving the door slightly ajar. "Would you tell the General for me that because I have been away for so long, and because our busy season is upon us, I really don't have the time to devote to outside activities. Possibly after Labor Day, for the general election (shouldn't that be for the General's election, I wondered?), I could join and help out. If he would still like me to be there at that time, that is." Let him wait and wonder, just a little.

"I'm sure the General would appreciate that, sir. I understand him not to be worried about the primary election. I believe he is all but unopposed. He may need some help in the fall." For a moment, I expected him to salute and I tensed to return it, but he thrust out his hand, shook mine perfunctorily but firmly, and strode away. Put a fitted red tunic and bearskin shako on him and he could join the Buckingham palace guard.

Before leaving New York, Burrows and I swung by Clozyme Towers at the request of CEO Frederick Bernard. Without a preamble, before we had touched our salad in the executive dining room, he blurted, "I've dismissed Bradley. The man was a disaster. A fraud. Here we are on the verge of a major new drug discovery, TA 97-C, and the man didn't have a clue how to get approval for advanced clinical studies, couldn't assemble the data, had no idea what to do next. We could leap to the front ranks of this industry with one major drug and we were stuck with a clown in research. He left us, all of us including the stockholders, reeling in dismay at his incompetence. He made the company look foolish. He made me look foolish. He had to go." Of course, the greatest sin of all. Making the boss look like a fool.

He hadn't mentioned a replacement. Burrows and I sampled our Boston lettuce with mushrooms and tiny bits of carrot laced with raspberry vinaigrette and waited. "What I would like to do is this," he continued. "I like your people. I like your Tony Howsam and Arlie Vicelio. Both first class." We weren't going to let them go. He sensed that if he were to offer them money, we would offer more.

He sensed that we were saying, "You want them, you take us all."

And that's what he did. Maybe he could have lured one away. They had no contracts with us, something I insisted upon, something Burrows continued to fight, but on this issue, we were united. Before we left the office ninety minutes later, after a light dessert of vanilla ice cream and fresh strawberries, we had agreed upon a contract that called for us to take over all product development, clinical research, and marketing for Clozyme, the work to be done in New York, London, Singapore, and in our own facilities at University City, new facilities to be built upon land just down the road from our parking lot, property Burrows had been stockpiling for just the right move. This was that move.

Everett was exultant as we walked outside. "In five years, Osten, we'll own this company. As a matter of fact, we'll practically own it once he signs the contract." I couldn't deny that. As an afterthought, now that the deal was all but done, he threw me a worried look and asked, "You can do this, can't you?" I noticed the 'you.' His contribution was on the yellow pad he and Bernard had used to draw up the deal. Mine was to be the work. He didn't bother to wait for an answer as he hurried into a cab. He had done his part. As far as he was concerned, it was done. It was almost time for golf. Now it was my problem.

As we snailed through traffic on our way to LaGuardia, I told him, "In answer to your question," he looked at me as if to say what question, "Yes. We can do it." I was a Gemini. Go for it.

We were almost to the airport when he asked, "How did you get along with Eddie Chun? Give you any trouble?"

"No trouble at all, but you've lost a night security guard."

"What do you mean? He quit?"

"No, I've promoted him. He's now my administrative assistant and in the fall, he goes back to graduate school. He hopes to become a scientist. Maybe even a doctor."

Burrows eyebrows shot up to the top of his forehead. "Graduate school? I didn't know he'd ever been to college! How does one go from being a security guard to being a doctor?"

"He liked carrying a doctor's bag. It kind of grew on him."

Everett flew back to the office; I went to Washington to see the good people at Pan Union. The building didn't look any different. The same stairway leading to the front door, the same giant chiseled X in the corner limestone, the same slightly disheveled Canby, looking worse for wear after her trip to the Far East, behind the same desk. Hard to believe she had been in

Hong Kong and Bangkok a little more than two weeks earlier, serving chicken and whisky to the Pan Unionists, their ranks depleted now by death, desertion, and detainment, although I was certain new recruits were already undergoing orientation not too far away. She looked at my card, it still read Osten-Burrows Inc., and turned it over as if expecting to find a hidden message on the back side. "Who did you wish to see, Mr. Osten?" she inquired. On the blotter in front of her, I could see my name written in for a 1:30 appointment. It was now exactly 1:29 P.M. It was clear she had a memory defect or needed new bifocals.

"It's Doctor Osten," I reminded her.

"We have no one by that name here – oh, you're Doctor Osten. I see. I remember. You've been here before."

"Yes, I have. If you check your book, you'll see that I have an appointment with your new chief executive. He made it. He called me. As a matter of fact, if I'm not mistaken, you were the one who placed the call, yesterday."

"Oh, well, in that case, I'll see if I can find where he is today. There have been a lot of changes around here recently." She wandered off down the hall, peering into each open doorway as she passed, and I half expected her to start calling "Where are you" as she disappeared around a corner.

The Terpning painting was still in place, but it had been moved to allow room for two small bronze plaques, one on each side. The first read: In Memory of Alexander C. Fantus who died in the service of his country, December 28, 1986. The second read: In Memory of Leonard T. Dirkens who died in the service of his country, December 29, 1986. I looked in vain for a third and saw none.

Canby ambled back, handed me my card, saying, "You may want this." And sat down.

I went down the hallway without instructions and easily found the Explorer in Bath's old office. Where else? The nameplate read Fredric C. Magellan, Director (Acting). No k. The name ending abruptly, just a c. Unlike Bath, though, he stood and extended his hand. Unlike Bath, also, he was wearing a modestly priced wristwatch, better than mine which was still keeping perfect time despite the rigors of the jungle, but Spartan simplicity compared to his predecessor. Unlike Bath, he was smiling; seemed happy to be there, possibly happy to be alive as well.

"You've moved up in the world, Fred," I observed, sitting in the only chair. It didn't appear as if we were anticipating company. Even the cameras overhead didn't appear to be working but their silence didn't mean they hadn't acquired new ones and hidden them better.

He waved off his promotion, if that's what it was, modestly saying, "It's only temporary, but I hope to have it made permanent soon. Maybe the end of the month when the board meets. Meanwhile, Mike, I'm glad you could come. I know how hard this funeral thing has been on you and the Greens. Terrible thing to have your son come home and a daughter die, almost at one and the same time. The General must be devastated." I didn't confirm or deny any of his suppositions. "Of course, he still plans on making a run for the Senate, doesn't he?" he asked, and it occurred to me that here was another man who stood to profit once the General was in office. He had, after all, been involved in the rescue of Ken Green. That could score points for any appearances he might make before committees where the General had a vote.

I remained noncommittal, answering, "I'm sure whatever Green decides will be reported immediately in the newspapers. It usually is." Much more interesting to me was what had happened to Bath. That hadn't been in the newspapers. I asked.

Magellan gave me a lingering look before responding. He leaned back in his chair and clasped his hands behind his head, then recycled himself and reached down to push a call button, summoning, I guessed, Canby. "Would you like something to drink? Tea, coffee, a soft drink?" Another tradition broken. No more hard stuff. Nothing, I told him, but he ordered coffee for himself and we waited as the slow moving Canby took the order and stumbled off to fill it. The woman had a problem. Maybe she'd picked up a virus overseas.

"I suppose, Osten, that you saw what I saw. The Hong Kong police leading Bath away in handcuffs. A strange turn of events. Very strange. A shock to all of us and to you as well, I'm sure." He didn't sound that sure. "You have no idea what happened to him, then?" he asked, as if disappointed.

"Not really. I did see him in handcuffs, a horrible sight to see an American being treated like that in a friendly country, and I was afraid it wasn't because he spit on the sidewalk or anything like that, but just what it was I still don't know. I'm in the dark."

"In the dark, yes. Well, to the best of our knowledge at this time, Mr. Bath has been accused of smuggling."

I tried not to overdo the surprise. "Smuggling! Surely you're joking. Bath! Head of Pan Union whatever —"

"Trade Association," he prompted, as if the full name was more important than smuggling.

"Head of the Trade Association, as you say, smuggling. Smuggling what? A rare stone or piece of art. Purloined jade, perhaps, an ivory figurine? Something for the fireplace mantle?"

"No, none of that. Worse. He denies it, of course, but they say it was heroin. Quite a lot of it, as a matter of fact, much more than for his own personal use. A kilogram, they tell us, worth a lot of money."

One kilo. There should have been two! So, had Harry Kee's bellhop done a bit of skimming, or Harry himself, or a constable? Certainly not the inspector. It was so hard to know who you could trust these days.

I acted surprised. "Heroin! Incredible! Who would ever have thought it possible?"

The Explorer smirked. "Don't overdo it now. You must have expected something like this. After all, young Green must have told you he saw Bath at Yellow Garden on more than one occasion."

Another one in on the secret. How? He hadn't been in the room when Green was identifying photos of Bath and Fantus.

"We've suspected something like that for a long while now, back here at Pan Union." I almost finished the sentence for him by adding Trade Association but managed to stop just in time. "Both Fantus and Bath have been the subject of rumors, you know, about smuggling. At first we thought it was gems, there's a lot of that going on, you know," which reminded me of the velvet bag in my pocket, "but it appears that it became drugs, even if it hadn't always been drugs. Nevertheless, it is out of character for Bath to have made a blunder like this. He went in and out of Hong Kong dozens of times and he knew the procedures and risks that drug smuggling entails. I don't understand how he could have made a mistake of that magnitude."

"Everybody gets careless," I remarked piously.

"Not Bath. Not really. He didn't make mistakes like that."

I just shrugged. "It seems as if he did. Do you have any idea what will happen to him now?" In short, how soon will he be a problem for any of us? I'm sure Magellan wanted to know the answer to that question as much as I did. He would like to remove the Acting designation from the nameplate. I didn't think it would ever happen.

"Drug laws are quite severe in Hong Kong and I understand the crown court is pressing for early prosecution, using him as some form of example that no one is above the law. He faces anywhere from fifteen to twenty years in prison but Bath is fighting it by claiming diplomatic immunity. Hong Kong has dismissed the idea saying that they find no evidence to support his claim."

"Couldn't you help him there? Back up his assertion? I always thought Pan Union was a State Department by-product." He didn't correct the name, he challenged my assumption.

"Not at all. We are what we say we are. A Trade Association, a group designed to foster world trade and although from time to time we work closely with governments, ours and others, we are an independent agency relying upon contributions and membership dues for our financial support." He looked at me smugly, as if to say how about that for a mission statement, one we worked up within the past 24 hours and one that I've already memorized to perfection. He was ready for radio talk shows and Sunday morning television. It was all about deniability, always had been, and right now, they had hung Bath out to dry. It was obvious he would be retained for a mite longer by the crown colony.

"What about Naroogian?" I quizzed.

Magellan was surprised. "What about him?"

"I didn't see a plaque out there on the wall in his memory."

"I haven't seen his body. Did you see his body or do have solid information as to what became of him?"

"No," I admitted.

"Well, without a body we can order no plaque, that's policy," explained the new leader.

"And Fantus?"

"He's dead. His plaque is out there on the wall."

"I saw it, but doesn't it seem a little odd that in one breath you tell me that Bath was dirty but that his smuggling partner has been honored with a plaque on the wall?" His silence seemed to indicate that he didn't think it odd at all. "Who killed him and why?"

"Open to speculation," said Magellan. "My own theory is that Huy Thacht was the one. Probably mad as hell that we got past his men and burned out the store. If he was working with Bath and Fantus, as we suspect, he probably went to have it out with them. Simple, Bath wasn't around, Fantus was, and he got himself killed. The plaque, it's a nice touch, don't you think?" A version very close to the one AcChan had offered. Could even be correct. But where did McLemore, the younger, and Broward come in, if they did at all?

"What about me, Fred? Why haul me into this thing. Ken Green sent no letter. You know that. No one asked for me. You know that, too."

"Not true, Osten. Lee Duc Than did ask for you. At least that's what Chamburon claimed when he called me in Uzbekistan. That part is true. He said he had a man by the name of Lee Duc Than who was sick and that you had treated him long ago and he needed you now. Crazy thing but when I discussed it with our board, they said, one of them said, let's get Osten involved. He's a good man, knows the young Green, and as long as someone is asking for him, send him."

I let that pass for the moment. "So Chamburon is calling you, saying he represented Lee Duc Than. He didn't. He had a man by the name of Co Phan as a client. Why are they using Lee Duc Than, why Ken Green, why me? None of that makes sense."

"It does, Mike. Really does. Since you and I left Chiang Mai we've had people interrogating Co Phan –," He saw the anger on my face and accurately interpreted what it was all about. "Not rubber hose guys, Mike. Just gentle questions, asked with patience and consideration for his condition. He's doing fine and the questioning hasn't bothered him at all. Seems to enjoy it, if anything. Glad to have people around. And this is what he told us. He was a nobody. An obscure professor, a teacher, nothing more. But he knew Lee Duc Than, knew that he was an important man, that he had defected to the north, and most importantly, that Lee Duc Than knew you, had met Jordan Green through you, and now had struck up a friendship with the imprisoned younger Green. If he cried for help as Co Phan, who would listen? If Lee Duc Than called for help, someone might respond. And of course, that's exactly what happened. Problem was, Huy Thacht picked up rumors of a Lee Duc Than in Chiang Mai, didn't like it because he knew it might call attention in his direction, and he finally allowed his father and Green to go to the city. I'm surprised he didn't just send some thugs in to eliminate the problem, but maybe he was distracted or something and we know what happened then."

"Not exactly. How do you account for the tears Lee Duc Than shed when he saw Co Phan in bed? They may have known one another but they weren't close friends."

"Yes, I know. Maybe, though, he had expected to find his old friend Ho Phan Van instead," Magellan offered, hopefully.

"I don't think so. Ken Green tells me that Ho Phan Van died in a reeducation camp while Lee Duc Than was still in North Vietnam. His death, in fact, may have been one of the reasons he left and went to Laos."

"Well," Magellan tried another tack, "maybe he had been hoping to see Truang Van Dang, another old comrade of his from the north. Tears of disappointment when he didn't find him?"

"He cries because he doesn't find Truang Van Dang? A defector and known Vietnamese intelligence officer who has dropped out of sight. That doesn't worry you? It should."

He said quietly, as he made a note on his yellow pad, "It does. A little."

Magellan didn't have to work on making a friend of the General. He already had a pipeline to him, one that ran both ways. The clue? I had just told the General about knowing that Ken had never written any note, what was it, three hours ago. Magellan had received a call while I was in the air.

"So the General has been kept up to date on everything while we were in Thailand and Laos, then, as usual," I said, as if I knew.

Puzzled, not knowing what I knew or what the General may have told me in the past few hours, Magellan said, "Well, the General has always been privy to secrets. He's on our board, I'm sure you know that. Some say he makes the major decisions while others believe it is another. A man we seldom, if ever, see."

"Well, there are secrets that some of us never are able to unravel. They," the unspecified they of conspiracy themes, "don't trust us enough to keep us informed." Magellan was nodding. "By the way, how is Disbrow? His leg OK?"

"Oh, he's fine. Happy to be back in one piece. He's applied for leave and I think we'll terminate him as unfit. He wasn't of much help when the pressure was on, you know."

I knew. I could also remember others who weren't, like the man who stood on a knoll flipping useless switches on useless equipment, although instead of termination, it had earned him a promotion.

"Dirkens? You figure Naroogian shot him in the back to protect Bath after he heard Green tell me about the illegal visits?"

He looked worried. "You're implying that Naroogian was an accomplice of the other two?"

"Was he?"

"We figure Dirkens was killed by a stray bullet," he said, firmly, case closed.

"Not Naroogian, despite the angle of the shot, his nearness to the scene and his disinclination to leave when we did?"

"A stray bullet. Official finding." No further discussion. So where was Naroogian, the man without a plaque?

"Well," I told him. "I should be going. Burrows wants me to ask about the bill. When can he expect payment?"

"Worried, is he? Tell him not to. I've signed off on it and sent it to the paymaster. Full amount, plus the extras he tacked on. The man seems to find extras everywhere. Even charged us for three suitcases. Three, not one, but three. Two Samsonites and a Louis Vuitton. For Green, I suppose. I understand you bought a lot of clothing for him in Hong Kong. But three suitcases full? We're lucky he didn't send the bill for suits, shirts, and whatever. But three suitcases, that's a lot. The Louis Vuitton, by the way. Nice piece of luggage. Bath's favorite. Expensive, but nice."

"I guess he did have good taste," I conceded. "I suppose that's why he needed to visit Yellow Garden from time to time. For extra change. It must cost a lot for expensive wristwatches and to support three names."

The Explorer frowned. "What do you mean?"

"Well, he used three. Drove people crazy. Never knew whether to call him Bath, Towel or Towle, or something else. Why didn't he just go by John Smith and let it go at that?"

Magellan clasped his hand and leaned forward like he was going to tell me something he wouldn't want repeated, and here it was, "That name bit, it bugged me. It was nothing but an affectation. His name was Bath. Really was. All that other stuff, just window dressing. He loved to pretend he was big time. Like in espionage, you know? Codes, secret words, drop boxes, stuff like that. Ridiculous."

"Well, like I said, I have to be going. I'll keep in touch, Fred."

He stopped me half way out of the office. "Mike, if you call, don't use the old nickname. You know – Explorer. I never liked it. And don't use my real name if you really want to get through on the first try."

"If I don't use your name, Fred, what do I call you?"

"Canby will answer, at least for a while. She seems to have come unglued on this last trip, too, so I may have to replace her. Don't know where her real loyalties lie anyway, you know, she was with Bath a long time. But if she's still here, don't ask for me by name, just ask for TopOp. She'll know that's the key word and put the call straight through into my inner office." He didn't recognize the irony.

"I'll remember that," I assured him soberly. "You know, Fred, it's all right if I still call you Fred in person isn't it, you know we were awfully lucky that Broward made contact with Huy Thacht in Yellow Garden. Working undercover like that is dangerous but once he ran into Ken Green and was able to get word to the General, and once AcChan was brought into the picture with the Blue Stars, well, things all worked out pretty well."

He smiled. Someone to confide in. "Sure, we were lucky. Broward and AcChan have been tracking Huy Thacht for years. Special drug unit, international support. Once Broward was able to talk to Green and convince him to stay on at Yellow Garden until help came, then it was a matter of figuring out who to send."

"Why not the army?"

"Whose? There is no effective force in Laos that isn't riddled with corruption. The Thais aren't going to cross the border and create an international incident. So AcChan was selected. But he didn't have enough men. We miscalculated."

"Who miscalculated? I thought Pan Union was a voluntary trade association. How could you miscalculate?"

"Well, not us exactly," he hurriedly corrected himself. "The board or something, the ones who make decisions."

"Right, TopOp. Well, it's really time to go."

"You know, Mike, I'm surprised the General told you all about Broward and what went on behind the scenes. That's out of character for him. He usually plays it close to the vest."

"He didn't tell me, Fred." He was standing in shock. Had the same look on his face as he had while hiding behind the tree, expecting snipers to be lining their sights on his exposed posterior. "You just did."

I knew then, no one needed to tell me, that Magellan was destined to remain the Acting Director of Pan Union whatever. He wouldn't need a new name plate.

I flew back to Detroit and went in to the office, ready for anything, early the next morning. Marge was overjoyed to see me at last, immediately set down the sports page, and gave me a small welcoming kiss. The Pistons won, she informed me, Laimbeer had 15, points I assumed, and she ushered me proudly into my newly, she told me, redecorated office. The paint looked fine, smelled fresh, but what I really wanted to see wasn't anywhere in sight. I couldn't find it. There was no in-basket; there was no out-basket; there was no basket at all.

"Marge," I pleaded, "the basket?"

"That's what you'll find so exciting," she said, flushed with excitement, pointing to a light gray object perched on the corner of my new gray desk. Yes, a new desk, a new chair, and – a new computer! *New* computer? I had never owned an old computer! "Everett wanted everyone to have computers," she explained. "He's so happy we're growing so rapidly that he says it's time to go modern. He did the same in his office."

"Yes, Marge. Growth is good. Modern is good. But no in-basket is bad. I look forward to emptying my in-basket after a trip."

"No longer a problem. Not with computers. We've computerized everything. Even Clovis." That I had to see.

But for now, oh, God. Everything I needed to know was hidden inside a gray box with a blank face.

I stood for a full minute contemplating what modern looked like. Then looked at my Benrus. It was almost nine o'clock in the evening in Bangkok. I shrugged in surrender. "OK, Marge. I've got to make a phone call and when I'm done, I want you to come in here and show me how to turn this thing on."

I closed the door after her and sat down, picked up the new phone, even that was new, and dialed the international access code 011 followed by 66 and then 2, tapped in JoElle's number, and after the third ring, heard her melodic voice on the other end of the line, half a world away, but she was right beside me as I said, "Hello, it's me."

# News Release

OBC International
Media Contact: Charles Heath
New York, N.Y. February 28, 1997

OBC International, a major pharmaceutical firm, today reported earnings per share increased 21 percent in 1996 to $3.36 from $2.65, with all three of its divisions posting a record year in operating income and revenues. Net income rose to $241 million on worldwide sales in excess of $3 billion.

"The 1996 economy was challenging but due to the redeployment of numerous resources and the efficiency of new facilities, and most of all, the continuing excellence of thousands of talented employees, we exceeded our EPS goal for the fourth consecutive year," said Dr. Mikhail Osten, Chairman and Chief Executive Officer. "We expect 1997 to be even more productive and we intend to meet the goals we have established for ourselves: to discover and introduce new therapeutic agents in the never ending struggle against disease and to increase shareholder value."

In separate action taken today at the annual board meeting of OBC International, a company formed with the merger of Osten-Burrows and Clozyme Pharmaceuticals five years ago, Dr. Osten was reelected Chairman and CEO while Dr. Anthony C. Howsam, general manager of pharmaceutical operations, was elevated to the new position of President. In another change, it was announced that Dr. Edmund Chun would direct the newly opened research laboratory in Scottsdale, Arizona.

Both Dr. Howsam and Dr. Chun played prominent roles in the discovery of the ATFNine anticancer drug, development of which was begun almost ten years ago when Dr. Howsam brought specimens of a rare plant back from Malaysia. That one product now accounts for a third of all OBC sales. Dr. Chun, meanwhile, is credited with the discovery of a potent new antifungal antibiotic being introduced to the market this month.

The election of a new board of directors was completed when Kenneth Green of New York was named to fill the position left vacant following the death of Everett Burrows, one of the cofounders of OBC. The new research facility to be headed by Dr. Chun was named the Everett M. Burrows Research Center in his honor and a chair at the University was endowed in his name.

Immediately following the meeting, Dr. Osten and his wife, the former JoElle Montparnier, were to leave for Bangkok to dedicate a new Institute for International Trade funded by GemElle, the renowned precious stone firm still owned and managed by Mrs. Osten.

# Epilogue

Jordan Green won election to the United States Senate and easily captured a second term six years later. There are rumors that he is considering stepping down and that his son, Kenneth Green, a former Vietnam war prisoner who was released after fifteen years of captivity, is being urged to become a candidate.

An American with a murky past, variously described as Armand Bath, or Roger Towel (possibly spelled Towle) is still being held in a Hong Kong prison after a conviction on heroin smuggling charges. His fate now that China has taken control of Hong Kong is uncertain.

Somchai never joined Ken Green in the United States. She is believed to have returned to northern Thailand.

Lee Duc Than is alive and is under continuing medical care in Bangkok. He lives in an expensive high rise apartment with a magnificent view of Lumphini Park.

Co Phan was released from the hospital in Chiang Mai and has disappeared.

A man called Truang Van Dang was questioned and released by federal agents in Seattle, but has since dropped from sight.

Loretta Diaz married Tony Howsam. They have three children, two boys and a beautiful little girl. Mrs. Howsam teaches at the University.

Eddie Chun returned to college and earned a Ph.D. in microbiology and analytical chemistry. He now has his own parking spot close to the door of the main building but, of course, will be moving to Scottsdale where he will have the first parking spot nearest the door.

Horace Carmichael runs the central clinical research laboratory for OBC. He also coaches and plays on the company basketball team. Marge goes to watch the team whenever the Pistons aren't playing

Fred Magellan continues to serve as the Acting Director of the Pan Union Trade Association in Washington. He attended the opening of the Institute for International Trade in Bangkok as an official delegate.

Avram Naroogian has not been heard from since last seen at Yellow Garden, ten years ago. His wife lived for a time in a small apartment in Silver Spring, Maryland. She has since moved into a much more expensive unit at the infamous Watergate.

At Yellow Garden, a Thai-Laotian consortium headed by AcChan

571

Sumkhavit, a well known Southeast Asian entrepreneur, has begun construction of a $500 million (US) resort and golf complex, a process made easier now that the airfield has been improved and enlarged, made possible only after the area had been cleared of a notorious guerrilla band headed by a self styled warlord, Huy Thacht.

Huy Thacht is rumored to visit Bangkok often and to have moved his base of operations to a site near Fang, on the border with Myanmar. Neither rumor can be confirmed.

Marge retired. Grant Hill has replaced Bill Laimbeer in her pantheon of heroes. Before she left, she did teach me how to turn on, and later to use, the computer. If it hadn't taken so long, she might have retired sooner, but she didn't mind. It took her that long to properly train Clovis as her replacement and I have to admit, despite my misgivings, that has turned out pretty well.

# About the Author

Born in Norway, Michigan, Dr. Van Gasse attended the University of Michigan where he earned his Bachelor's and Medical degrees, returning later to acquire a Master's degree in Public Health. He has worked in the pharmaceutical industry, served in the army, and was a member of the United States Committee to the World Health Organization. He currently resides and practices medicine in Ann Arbor, Michigan with his wife, Kathryn. They have three sons and six grandchildren. He is also the author of *What Am I Allergic To?*, *Fathers and Sons*, and *Night's Soft Folds*.

To order or for more information, contact:
IMS Corporation
P.O. Box 1322
Ann Arbor, Michigan 48106